For Helen
remembering 1947
and her spirited encouragement
ever since

THE *GREAT PLAINS STATES* OF AMERICA

People, Politics, and Power in the Nine Great Plains States

NEAL R. PEIRCE

W · W · NORTON & COMPANY · INC ·
NEW YORK

 Published simultaneously in Canada by George J. McLeod Limited, Toronto. Printed in the United States of America.

Library of Congress Cataloging in Publication Data
Peirce, Neal R
The Great Plains States of America.
Bibliography: p.
1. Great Plains. I. Title.
F595.2.P44 917.8 72-13928
ISBN 0-393-05349-0

2 3 4 5 6 7 8 9 0

THE
GREAT PLAINS STATES
OF AMERICA

By Neal R. Peirce

THE MEGASTATES OF AMERICA

THE PACIFIC STATES OF AMERICA

THE MOUNTAIN STATES OF AMERICA

THE GREAT PLAINS STATES OF AMERICA

THE PEOPLE'S PRESIDENT

CONTENTS

FOREWORD

THIS BOOK IS A BOOK ABOUT the Great Plains States, part of a series covering the story of each major geographic region and all of the 50 states of America in our time. The objective is simply to let Americans (and foreigners too) know something of the profound diversity of peoples and life styles and geographic habitat and political behavior that make this the most fascinating nation on earth.

Only one project like this has been attempted before, and it inspired these books: John Gunther's *Inside U.S.A.*, researched during World War II and published in 1947. Gunther was the first man in U.S. history to visit each of the states and then to give a good and true account of the American condition as he found it. But his book is a quarter of a century old; it was written before the fantastic economic and population growth of the postwar era, growth that has transformed the face of this land and altered the life of its people and lifted us to heights of glory and depths of national despair beyond our wildest past dreams. Before he died, I consulted John Gunther about a new book. He recognized the need for such a work, and he gave me, as he put it, his "good luck signal."

But what was to be a single book became several, simply because I found America today too vast, too complex to fit into a single volume. A first book, *The Megastates of America*, treated America's 10 most heavily populated states. The series of eight regional volumes, completing the exploration of all the states in our time, began with publication of *The Mountain States of America* and *The Pacific States of America*. This is the third regional volume, and will be followed by books viewing separately people, politics, and power in the states of the Deep South, Border South, Mid-Atlantic, New England, and Great Lakes.

A word about method. Like Gunther, I traveled to each state of the Union. I talked with about 1,000 men and women—governors, Senators, Representatives, mayors, state and local officials, editors and reporters, business and labor leaders, public opinion analysts, clergymen, university presidents and professors, representatives of the Indian, black, and Spanish-speaking communities—and just plain people. Some of the people I talked with were famous, others obscure, almost all helpful.

I went by plane, then rented cars, made a personal inspection of almost every great city and most of the important geographic areas, and must have walked several hundred miles in the process too, insanely lugging a briefcase full of notes and tape recorder into the unlikeliest places. Usually I got names of suggested interviewees from my newspaper friends and other contacts in new states and cities and then sent letters ahead saying I would like to see the people. From the initial interviews, reference to still more interesting people invariably ensued. Rare were the interviews that didn't turn out to be fascinating in their own way; the best ones were dinner appointments, when the good talk might stretch into the late evening hours.

Altogether, the travel to 50 states took a year and a half, starting in 1969; then came more than three years of writing, all too often made up of 15-hour working days. The writing was complicated by the need to review hundreds of books and thousands of articles and newspaper clippings I had assembled over time. And then each manuscript, after it had been read and commented upon by experts on the state (often senior political reporters), had to be revised to include last-minute developments, and still once more given a final polish and updating in the galley stage.

Amid the confusion I tried to keep my eye on the enduring, vital questions about each state and its great cities:

What sets it (the state or city) apart from the rest of America?

What is its essential character?

What kind of place is it to live in?

What does it look like, how clean or polluted is it, what are the interesting communities?

Who holds the power?

Which are the great corporations, unions, universities, and newspapers, and what role do they play in their state?

Which are the major ethnic groups, and what is their influence?

How did the politics evolve to where they are today, and what is the outlook for the 1970s?

How creatively have the governments and power structures served the people?

Who are the great leaders of today—and perhaps tomorrow?

A word of caution: many books about the present-day American condition are preoccupied with illustrating fundamental sickness in our society, while others are paeans of praise. These books are neither. They state many of the deep-seated problems, from perils to the environment to the abuse of power by selfish groups. But the account of the state civilizations also includes hundreds of instances of greatness, of noble and disinterested public service. I have viewed my primary job as descriptive, to show the multitudinous strands of life in our times, admitting their frequently contradictory directions, and tying them together analytically only where the evidence is clear.

The ultimate "verdict" on the states and cities must rest with the reader himself.

For whom, then, is this chronicle of our times written? I mean the individual chapters to be of interest to people who live in the various states, to help them see their home area in a national context. I write for businessmen, students, and tourists planning to visit or move into a state, and who are interested in what makes it tick—the kind of things no guidebook will tell them. I write for politicians planning national campaigns, for academicians, for all those curious about the American condition as we enter the last decades of the 20th century.

From the start, I knew it was presumptuous for any one person to try to encompass such a broad canvass. But a unity of view, to make true comparisons between states, is essential. And since no one else had tried the task for a quarter of a century, I decided to try—keeping in mind the same goal Gunther set for *Inside U.S.A.*—a book whose "central spine and substance is an effort—in all diffidence—to show this most fabulous and least known of countries, the United States of America, to itself."

THE GREAT PLAINS STATES

A REGIONAL VIEW

WEST OF THE MISSISSIPPI and east of the Rockies lie the nine states of the Great Plains that constitute the very heart of the American continent. The northern outposts are Minnesota and North Dakota, running some 700 miles along the Canadian border; proceeding southward on the Mississippi River tier, one comes to farm-rich Iowa and variegated Missouri; on the western tier are lonelier lands of the Dakotas, Nebraska, and Kansas, then Oklahoma, and finally the great anchor of Texas.

The Lone Star State does include another kind of climatic belt—the moist, low plain along the Gulf of Mexico, the scene of one of America's most spectacularly growing cities, Houston, with the vibrant Dallas-Fort Worth concentrate not far distant. But geographically, most of Texas lies within the regions of Prairie and High Plains typical of all of the nine-state region, and in fact it was an illustrious Texas historian, Walter Prescott Webb, who wrote *The Great Plains*, a classic definition of this great region of America.

What characterizes the Great Plains States in our time? First, there is dwindling population as the countryside and little towns empty out—a movement offset by the growth of major cities. But here the process of urbanization, which is occurring all over the world, is different because so many people have moved out of the region altogether, and almost all of the great cities lie on the periphery of the region, not at its heart. Secondly, this classic breadbasket region continues as a major source of food for the nation, even while diversified industries intrude in more than a few locations. But there are fewer independent farmers than at any time in this century, and their future is clouded by the rapid rise of big "agribusiness" and corporate farms. Third, the Great Plains States have been rather dormant intellectually over the postwar period. For the most part, they have practiced a careful and conservative politics, regardless of party label. But now one sees flashes of what might be called a new "people's politics" (most apparent in Minnesota, but on other Great Plains States as well), a kind of harkening back to the Populist movement of yesteryear, and perhaps a foretaste of broad national trends in the 1970s.

The Sea of Grass and the 98th Meridian

One cannot write of the Great Plains without feeling the hand of a very recent, often poignant history. It was little more than a century ago that the first homesteaders ventured into this land. What they found was grass—a seemingly boundless sea of grass, tall in the more humid eastern section called the Prairie Plains, shorter in the arid High Plains further to the west. The land was at times as level as any land on earth, then rolling, but never mountainous. Only an occasional stand of trees along a stream bottom, often cottonwood or burr oak, broke the rhythm of the grass with its broad variety of wildflowers.

The homesteaders also came upon a natural environment of startling extremes. This was a land of fiercely cold winters and furnace-like summers, of relentless winds, blizzard, tornado, thunderstorm, and prairie fire, of vast skies and celestial pyrotechnics, a region of infinite spaces that almost dared man to tame it. The Plains Indians had instinctively known better; they lived nomadic lives in delicate balance with the countless millions of buffalo and prairie dogs who had held the land as their own from time immemorial. The Indians had even done the prairie a regular favor, oddly enough, by setting fire to it. Prairie fires are efficient ways of killing off weeds and forest seedlings, while they do little to harm the deep-seated perennials.

As European man emerged from the familiar forests of the East onto the spacious Great Plains, he passed over what Walter Prescott Webb has described as "an institutional *fault* (comparable to a geologic fault)" of profound significance:

> Practically every institution that was carried across it was either broken or remade or else greatly altered. The ways of travel, the weapons, the methods of tilling the soil, the plows and other agricultural implements, and even the laws themselves were modified. . . . In the new region—level, timberless, and semi-arid—the people were thrown by Mother Necessity into the clutch of new circumstances. Their plight has been stated this way: east of the Mississippi civilization stood on three legs—land, water and timber; west of the Mississippi not one but two of these legs were withdrawn,—water and timber,—and civilization was left on one leg—land.

As the settlers crossed the line, however, they only saw the prairie—a challenge for their plows—and thought little of the difficulties that awaited them. And in the somewhat more humid and benign Prairie Plain nearer the Mississippi, they were able to establish an agriculture of corn and livestock that endures to this day and in fact has prospered magnificently in the affluent meat-consuming economy of the years since World War II. The abundant outpouring from the farms here is interrupted occasionally by dry spells, though the droughts have not been quite so severe as those farther to the west.

The most severe aridity occurs on the High Plains west of the 98th Meridian—a line of demarcation which one can trace from a northerly point some 50 miles west of the North Dakota-Minnesota border straight south to Texas. The High Plains extend westward to the foothills of the Rockies. Within this massive climatic belt, the settlers found that in years of drought the prairie they had upturned, thus destroying the deep grass roots that had formerly given it stability, could be transformed into a storm of dust that darkened the midday sun. Many indeed fled in terror during the worst droughts. Only in the last generation has man learned—not perfectly, but in substantial measure—to conserve this soil, increase its yield in wheat and other grains by a myriad of technological advances, and preserve the precious rainfall for his own advantage. With pumping of underground waters, a veritable vegetable bowl has developed in parts of the High Plains so arid in their natural state that explorers called them the Great American Desert. This is not only the great breadbasket of America but also the storehouse for much of the world's grain. It is a land dotted with towering grain elevators, those cathedrals of the plains whose bountiful load has become the prime headache of a nation's farm-policy makers.

But still the specter of drought lingers on, and John R. Borchert, a distinguished professor of geography at the University of Minnesota, suggests "the time may well be near when the next widespread drought will plague the region." The historical record shows there have been four periods of extensive drought in the Great Plains. Two of these, made far worse by an unusually high occurrence of cyclonic storms, occurred in the late 1880s and early 1890s and in the 1930s—the latter the era of the now celebrated Dust Bowl, when farmers deserted the Great Plains in staggering numbers. The two other droughts, times of great aridity but less devastating winds, took place in the 1910s and again in the 1950s. Borchert observes:

> The great droughts in the Grassland have occurred rhythmically, and they are related to physical changes in the circulation of air and delivery of moisture. . . .
>
> Intervals between central years of the major droughts of record have averaged slightly more than 20 years: The duration of each major dry period has averaged about a decade. Hence it is likely that the next widespread deterioration of summer rainfall will center on the mid-1970s, just before the drought-breaking rains begin.
>
> If the geographic pattern of the next drought resembles that of the 1930s and late 1880s-early 1890s, it will affect virtually all of the Great Plains and spread extensively through the Midwest. And it is likely to be accompanied by more severe wind erosion than the region experienced in the 1950s. If it resembles the droughts of the 1910s and 1950s, it will be most severe in the central and southern Plains and bring less wind and erosion risk.

Any future drought is likely to carry the same catastrophic consequences—summertime rainfall off as much as 50 percent, streams down to a fraction of their normal runoff, agricultural output vastly reduced. Federal farm programs will be there to help the farmers, more than ever before. Eventually, as in the past, there will be recovery. But as for the virgin prairie, it is practically a thing of the past. There is much native prairie grass land in use, but much of it grows on land originally broken by the plow—"go-back land," as it is known in the local vernacular. Some of the few patches of essentially untouched prairie are in the cemeteries of the early settlers, which often stand a foot higher than the surrounding tilled land—mute testimony to the erosion-resistant characteristics of the mat of grass of the native prairie, in contrast to what happens when man plows the land, and the wind and water do their work, and the soil built up over millennia of prairie growth and decay is lost forever.

The Missouri and the Mississippi

Away, away, I'm bound away
Across the wide Missouri.

While drought is the most fearsome threat on the Great Plains, flooding from her great rivers has historically held a firm second place as a threat to peaceable life there. No development of the postwar years has had more significance for the people of the Plains than the massive strides taken to tame the mighty, at once life-giving and destructive Missouri River. The Missouri is the most important waterway of the region, gathering in the Montana Rockies, flowing through the heart of the Dakotas, dividing Nebraska from Iowa, and then slicing Missouri in two parts before it empties into the Mississippi near St. Louis. Longest river in the United States, the Missouri is notorious for her springtime floods and the constant wastage of Plains soil she causes—a river "too thick to drink, too thin to plow," the natives of her banks were long fond of saying. Before it was finally "tamed," the springtime Missouri might be a raging torrent, overflooding its banks and cutting new channels; in a dry summer she might degenerate to a trickle of her normal self, the channel blocked by sandbars. Men used to make the effort to navigate her waters all the way from St. Louis to Fort Benton, in northern Montana, but "Old Misery" resisted their efforts and more than 250 steamboats were wrecked between 1819 and 1897.*

For years an acrimonious debate raged in Congress about the idea of a Missouri Valley Authority patterned on the TVA. No such authority was ever formed, but in 1944 Congress approved the so-called Pick-Sloan plan to

* One of the wrecked boats, the stern-wheeler *Bertrand*, which went down 20 miles north of Omaha in Nebraska Territory in 1865, was excavated from a dried-up portion of the channel in 1968. Some 140 tons of cargo was recovered, including—according to Gordon Young of the *National Geographic*—fur hats, French champagne, canned oysters and peaches, bolts of silk, and 780 *gallons* of a suspiciously high alcohol-content potion called Dr. J. Hostetter's Celebrated Stomach Bitters.

control the great river with six major upstream dams plus countless smaller dams on the river's tributaries and 1,500 miles of levees and flood walls. The concept was to harness the river for a multiplicity of uses, ranging from flood control and conservation to irrigation, electric power generation, navigation, and recreation. Development proceeded at a snail's pace for several years as private and public power interests clashed, conservationists debated with flood-control engineers, and the railways tried to avert threatened competition from new barge lines. In 1951, however, "Big Muddy" churned up the most disastrous floods of modern times, displacing thousands and inundating Omaha and Kansas City, the damage so great that President Truman was led to declare it a national calamity. Flood control work moved forward rapidly after that.

Now the dams have been largely completed, including all the larges ones. Huge reservoirs have been created upstream—Fort Peck behind the dam of the same name in Montana, massive Lake Sakakawea behind the Garrison Dam in North Dakota, Lakes Oahe and Francis Case behind the Oahe and Fort Randall Dams in South Dakota, and others. The upstream dams have no locks, so that boats and barges can move no farther upstream than Sioux City, Iowa. But from there, the navigable channel now extends 735 miles to St. Louis, and the river carries several million tons of commercial freight each year—more grain, in fact, than all the railways serving the Great Plains. The navigation is much safer than in earlier times because the farthest downstream main-stem dam, at Cavins Point north of Sioux City, stores enough springtime water so that there is an adequate flow through all months of the year.

The damming of the Missouri exacted a price, including the submersion, for all time, of several villages and many farms which the Indians had held for centuries and also the permanent loss under water of many important archeological sites. The benefits have included hydroelectric power to light up prairie homes, vast new recreation areas, and several big irrigation projects (although irrigation has been made available for only a fraction of the territory which the overenthusiastic Corps of Engineers had earlier predicted).

The changes on the Mississippi River have not been as dramatic since World War II, but conservationists have been up in arms in recent years over the Engineers' proposal to deepen the river channel from its present nine-foot depth to 12 feet along the 853-mile stretch from Cairo, Illinois, to Minneapolis-St. Paul. The Engineers say the deeper channel would make it possible for cheaper barge traffic to keep pace with the population and industrial growth between St. Louis and the Twin Cities. The reply of opponents is that the river would be turned into a "big, dirty ditch," and that there would be a great deal of dumping of the sand from dredging onto riverside wetlands, thus endangering wildlife. Conservationists also argue that locks and dams on rivers—like those built on the upper Mississippi in the 1930s or on the Missouri more recently—become catch basins for the fantastic loads of sand and silt washed downstream by the rivers. The result, inevitably, is to raise the river level, thus exacerbating flood dangers in future years.

Even at their best, dams and levees cannot obviate all flood dangers. The Missouri and the Mississippi and their many tributaries still pose mortal danger to Midwestern cities when the snows of winter melt and come cascading down the channels. The damage may not be as great as it would have been a generation before, but it is still awesome. Later in the year, the people of this region will live with an eye ever watchful of the sky, knowing, as playwright William Inge has written, that it may "destroy a season's crops in a few hours, by hail or blizzard or relentlessly burning sun that can desiccate the land like an Old Testament curse." Thus Plainsmen are reminded again and again that this chunk of the continent they have taken as their own is the subject of violent, elemental forces of nature, a place where man is still guest, never master.

The Plains Economy and the Population Plight

Although agriculture was the first occupation of Plainsmen, manufacturing now accounts for twice as much income in the nine-state region. More than a third of the area's value added by manufacturing is in Texas alone, but even in the more farm-oriented states of the upper Great Plains, there are only three—Iowa and the two Dakotas—where farm products still rival industrial products in value each year. The manufacturing has a broad base, from petrochemicals in Texas to advanced electronics in Minnesota and aerospace in Texas, Kansas, and Missouri. But a significant share of the value added by manufacturing actually represents processing of food, part of the great "agribusiness" complex of the American West. And outside of Texas, the Great Plains have failed, with the exception of a few dynamic centers like the metropolises of Missouri and Minnesota's Twin Cities, to share in the dynamic growth of the modern-day American economy. These states have not, for instance, shown a growth in the affluent $15,000-a-year and up income segment of the population comparable to the East and West Coasts.

The region's decline began when the Great Depression and the droughts of the 1930s struck it with such severity, causing thousands to flee. When World War II came, defense contracts flowed to the coasts and hundreds of thousands more Plains people left their home states to work in distant war plants, never to return. The region's economy was temporarily buoyed by record wartime food production, but when peace came it was the coasts, not the Great Plains, which had the manpower and the physical plants to move into an advanced technological economy. The Plains were left behind—in jobs, scientific skills, population, federal school and urban grants, and in wealth. The problem was most acute in the western tier of Plains States (the Dakotas, Nebraska, and Kansas), but it affected the easterly tier as well. Only Texas proved immune to the decline, and in fact moved successfully from an agrarian to a robust industrial, urbanized economy. The population figures since 1930 tell much of the story:

State	*1930*	*1950*	*1970*	*% Change 1930–1970*
Missouri	3,629,367	3,954,653	4,676,501	+29%
Iowa	2,470,939	2,621,073	2,824,376	+14
Minnesota	2,563,953	2,982,483	3,804,971	+48
North Dakota	680,854	619,636	617,761	− 9
South Dakota	692,849	652,740	665,507	− 4
Nebraska	1,377,963	1,325,510	1,483,493	+ 8
Kansas	1,880,999	1,905,299	2,246,578	+19
Oklahoma	2,396,040	2,233,351	2,559,229	+ 7
Texas	5,824,715	7,711,194	11,196,730	+92
Regional total	21,517,679	24,005,939	30,075,146	+40
Percentage of U.S. population	17.5	15.9	14.8	

Excluding Texas, the regional population increase in the 40-year period was 20 percent, compared to 65 percent in the United States as a whole. The net migration figures, again excluding Texas, indicate that the region lost no less than three million people between 1940 and 1970—1,386,000 in the 1940s, 978,000 in the 1950s, and 636,000 in the 1960s. (The entire regional population would have dropped if natural increase—the excess of births over deaths—had not exceeded the net outmigration.) Texas, by contrast, actually experienced a net inmigration of more than a quarter million people between 1940 and 1970.

Yet even in Texas, the population increases were virtually all in metropolitan areas, and in the 1960s a tenth of all the counties in America that lost population were in Texas. In all, 600 of the 950 counties of the Great Plains States declined in population during the decade. The downturn was general across the region but most pronounced in the High Plains of wheat farming and ranching west of the 98th Meridian. All the way from the Canadian border into Texas, this belt has extremely light population, is devoid of a single large city, and cannot boast a single important university. (It is also extremely conservative in its politics, and there have been several years when the entire strip, including the westernmost congressional districts of the Dakotas, Nebraska, Kansas, Oklahoma, and the Texas Panhandle, have been represented by some of the most rigidly conservative men in Congress.)

Thus we come to the essential malady of the Great Plains: the flight from the land and the decline—sometimes total depopulation—of its little towns. As writer Dale Wittner observed in 1971:

> Across the table-flat plains, from North Dakota to Texas, the lights are going out. Small towns are shriveling and dying, farmhouses stand abandoned and stark, sun-bleached mementos of an era lost in a sea of prairie grass. The rural life anchored on little farmers' towns, which only 50 years ago dominated the American heartland, has come quietly to the edge of extinction.

It was just such little towns and their surrounding farmlands that first set the character of the white man's civilization on the Great Plains. Walter Prescott Webb wrote in 1930:

> As yet the Great Plains have produced but few cities, and fewer that do not lie along the timber line. Minneapolis, Chicago, St. Louis, Kansas City, Fort Worth,

and San Antonio mark the line that separates the East from the West. These cities owe much of their growth to the fact that they receive tribute from the Plains. Plains wheat made Minneapolis and St. Paul; Plains cattle helped to make Chicago, St. Louis, Kansas City, and Fort Worth. These were the railheads and distributing centers for the Great Plains.

Today the economic role of almost all these cities has shifted radically, with agriculture and supplying the towns of the Plains only one of their many interests. As an example, the meat slaughtering and packing industries have so decentralized that the stockyards have completely disappeared in two of their great cities of yesteryear, Fort Worth and Chicago. Widely scattered regional trade centers (easily reached by automobile), college towns, and a variety of small and large cities more interested in finance and manufacturing than agriculture—these seem to be the places to which more and more people will be migrating across the Great Plains region. In time, profound changes in the regional character are likely to ensue.

Yet no one with a sense of American history and culture can view the fading away of the small towns with equanimity. For here, in a way, the essence of so much that is American, and of the self-reliant Protestant ethic, once thrived. One's mind goes back to elm-lined Main Streets with their neat clapboard houses, to the little schoolhouses and county fairs and Methodist church suppers, to towns that were totally attuned to the vagaries of the weather because their livelihood was the land, to cattle drives and steamboats round the bend. The population figures prove it—these were the places so many Americans of the great coastal and Great Lakes cities "came from." But what happens to a national consciousness when men and women's childhood memories encompass nothing more than a series of nomad-like sojourns in faceless suburban subdivisions from Long Island to the California "Southland"? George McGovern, who grew up in the little South Dakota city of Mitchell, touched on the problem in an interview for *Life* in 1972:

> In the war for the first time I met people—big-city boys, ones who had moved around a lot—who did not have any sense of belonging to a particular place. I still love to go back to Mitchell and wander up and down those streets. It just kind of reassures me again that there is a place that I know thoroughly, where the roots are deep.
>
> There are the big old cottonwood trees, the big American elms, the little roadways in and out of town that have always been there—without much work ever done on them—the parks. There are not lots of high schools; there's one. There aren't a lot of libraries; there's the Carnegie Library. Each one of the stores always had its personality—Mr. Becker, who ran a clothing store—and the three movie theaters—each had a distinct character. At one drugstore you got malted milks; you went to another for sodas. Everything had a place, a specific definition.
>
> I think that makes it easier to find one's own place in the world. When people talk about the small-town sense of community, the role of the family, relationship with neighbors, fellowship of the church, school spirit—I had all those things, and they meant a great deal to me in providing guidelines, a foundation, a personal security.

McGovern saw a connection between that background and his goal—which, despite his own defeat for the Presidency, may be a leitmotiv of Amer-

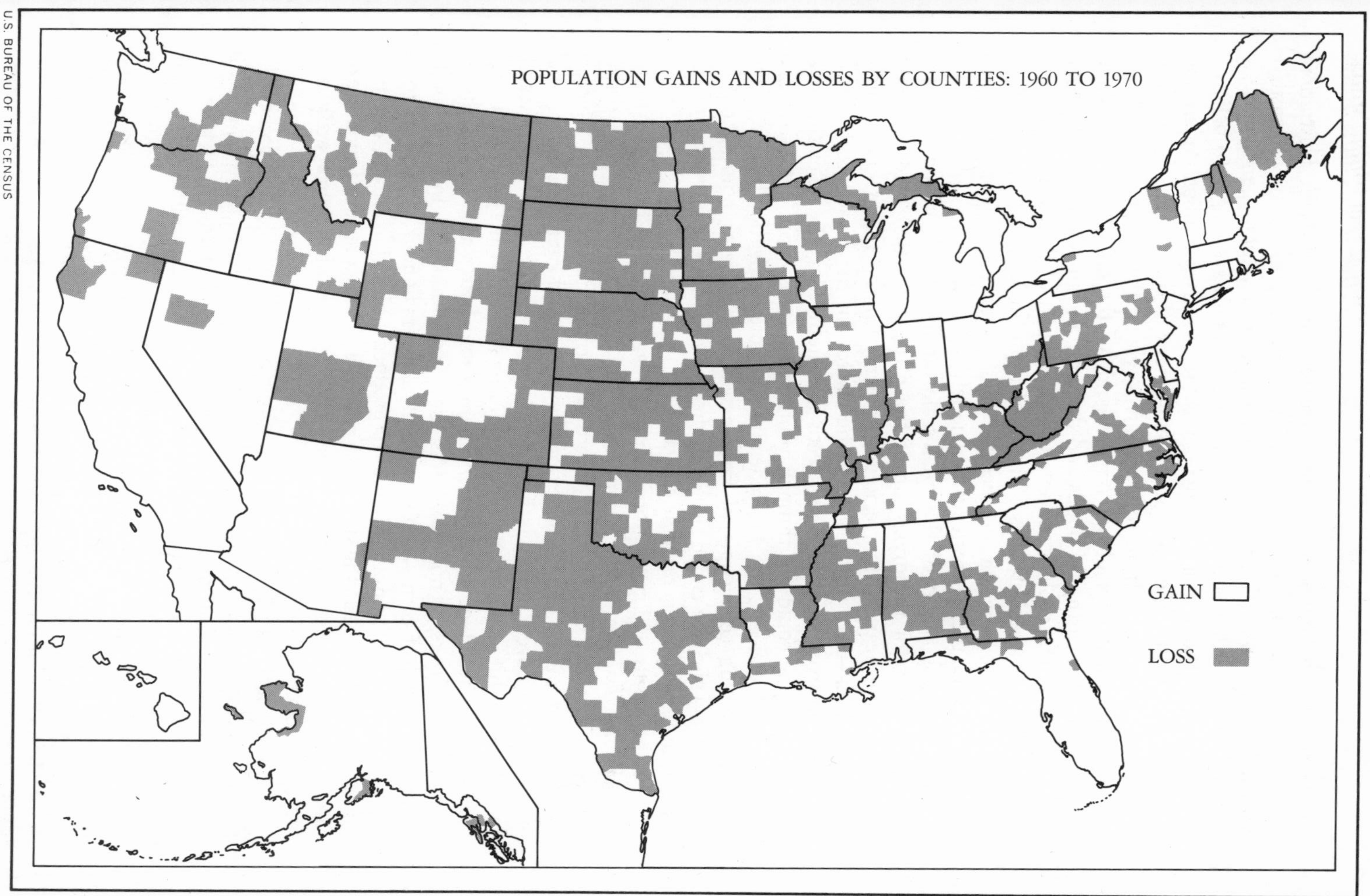

U.S. BUREAU OF THE CENSUS

ican politics in the 1970s—"to bring a greater sensitivity to the frustrations and anxieties of people, so that the government becomes a more sensitive instrument. In a sense, I guess these are small-town values—neighborliness, responsibility for others—extensions of what I was always taught to believe."

Along with the loss of "belongingness" for so many million Americans, one must view with some concern the movement of such a great segment of the national population from the rural areas, where they automatically learn and appreciate their dependency on the land, to the crowded metropolitan centers, where the earth and floods and drought, and man's tie to nature,, all seem so distant. The ecology movement may fill part of the gap, but more in a theoretical than a real-life sense. The flight from the land, the demographers tell us, is about to taper off, not because rural America offers people a good living but because there is scarcely anyone left to flee now.

The unhappy plight of the small-scale family farmer, whose declining fortunes account for the drying up of the little towns that used to supply him, lies at the heart of the regional problem. All the things one thought might help him—the substitution of the tractor for the horse, great reapers and threshing machines, improved seeds and herbicides, the splendid vocational training he could get through youth farm clubs, adult extension, and the land-grant colleges, the big federally sponsored irrigation projects, and even the seeming cornucopia of farm assistance programs pouring out of Washington—all have ended up being the nemesis, not the salvation, of the smaller farmer lacking acreage or capital.

In the words of Lauren Soth, editorial page editor of the Des Moines *Register and Tribune* and a leading expert on farm problems, "The consequences of the massive drive for improved farming techniques in America have been profound. The efficiency of labor, land and capital in agricultural production improved slowly at first, but the cumulative effects of research and education hit with smashing power during World War II and have continued." As a result of advanced mechanization, better seed strains, herbicides, and fertilizers, it now takes less than five minutes of man's labor to produce a bushel of corn—a job that took a full man-*hour* of work in 1940. Now it takes just six minutes of labor to produce a bushel of wheat, where 40 minutes were required at the start of World War II. As a result of such breakthroughs, Soth notes, "agriculture has been plagued by overcapacity and surplus production."

The big-scale family farming operations have been able to weather the storm by heavy capital investment, borrowing, and reliance on federal farm subsidy programs. But millions of smaller, marginal farmers, lacking the sophistication or size of operation to utilize fully the new technology, to capitalize massive machinery or irrigation systems, or to get the most out of the farm aids handed down from Washington, have been forced to distress sales of their properties. During the Eisenhower administration of the 1950s, the number of farms in the country declined by 20 percent. In the 1960s, under Kennedy and Johnson, the figure declined 33 percent. And in the first three years of the Nixon administration, another drop of 10 percent was noted. The nation now has only 2.7 million farms, compared to 6.4 million in 1940, and may well have less than two million by 1980. The number of Americans living on farms, 85 percent of the country's population in 1800, was down to 23 percent in 1940—and less than 5 percent by the early 1970s. And 2,000 farmers a week are still selling out. As they leave, the small towns that used to supply them are weakened more and more.

It was probably inevitable that the number of viable farms in the country would sink dramatically in the face of industrialization, mechanization of the farm, scientific and marketing breakthroughs. But to those who say the entire loss was "inevitable," others reply that the policies of the federal government itself bear part of the guilt. Across America, *The Wall Street Journal* noted in 1971, "enormous corporate farms, consisting of thousands of acres of the best land and backed by enormous amounts of capital, have replaced farmers with a few hundred acres of land, no capital and plenty of debt." Big irrigation projects favor large farms the most, and the lion's share of federal subsidies go to large farming operations. (In 1970, for instance, 23 big farm operations got more than $500,000 each in subsidies, while a million low-income farmers got an average of only $400 each.) Federal tax laws favor the corporation or investor who puts his dollars into farm operations for a tax write-off over the man who actually farms for a living.

Many farmers regard the big "agribusiness" corporations, who benefit so much from federal policy, as their real enemy—although in terms of actual land holding, the corporate farm is more a phenomenon of Florida and the Southwestern states, which have traditions of baronial land ownership, than it is of the Midwest, where livestock raising and fattening is still done predominantly on family farms. Nick Kotz, an Iowan writing for the Washington *Post*, observed

> For the farmer, agribusiness means all the other elements in the food supply chain that are highly organized and represent big business: the national retail food chains, the giant national food processors, and the conglomerate companies that perform an interrelated series of functions in the food system. The farmer has seen these other segments of the food supply system consolidate their economic power while he—even as his numbers have dwindled by the millions—remains unorganized and relatively powerless in the marketplace.

It was the dispute over agribusiness and its role that caused the substantial delay, in 1971, of Senate confirmation of President Nixon's appointment of Dr. Earl Butz to be Secretary of Agriculture. Butz had served on the board of four agribusiness corporations, including Ralston-Purina and Stokely-Van Camp. The small farm-agribusiness debate seems likely to continue, in various forms, for years to come. As Kotz notes, the difficult task of saving the family farmer will take more "than just another farm program." Somehow, farmers will have to find a way to bargain collectively like labor unions, to get the financial backing to form co-ops that can face the big farm interests on equal terms, and to persuade the federal government to apply the antitrust laws against agribusiness corporations that try to monopolize various crop sources. Federal tax policies will have to be altered, the federal government's enormous food-purchasing power will have to be turned around to benefit the family farmer, and there will have to be an end to what Kotz calls "the cozy triangular arrangement in which government and land grant colleges serve agribusiness and neglect other rural interests."

Politically, such fundamental shifts in policy sound nearly impossible. But change may be in the offing in the 1970s, the political clout of big agribusiness notwithstanding. Already, some Congressmen from the Plains have offered bills to curb corporate farms. There is at least the possibility that the farmers and small town merchants may launch a ballot-box revolt against present federal policies—a kind of modern-day Populist uprising that the Democratic and Republican parties would ignore at their peril. Across the Plains, such a revolt might be joined by business and civic leaders who have already observed what a stagnant economy means for their region: a lack of decent jobs, the forced departure of one's children as they reach working age, the oppressive tax burden of educating young people who will lead their adult lives in another part of the nation, and a general lack of economic and cultural opportunity.

Moreover, increasingly serious national attention is likely to be turned to the anomaly of overcrowded cities (where many dispossessed farmers, among others, now flee) and deserted rural states that have become the economic backwater of modern America. With sound planning, the underpopulated Great Plains States might eventually play as great a role in the solution of population imbalances as they now play in exacerbating the problem. Senator Harold Hughes of Iowa, who was governor of his state for six years in the 1960s, suggested in an interview:

> It may be important for some states to remain unglutted and unoverpopulated and having a moderate growth that is well planned and decently laid out, so that they remain the garden of the future. . . . There is some Providence in this, that we have been slow. We're part of the whole United States, and our time is coming. . . .
>
> Our region is in a uniquely beautiful position. We have the two major rivers of America (the Mississippi and the Missouri); we can preserve them from becoming gutters and sewers. We have the finest land in America, and we have a great deal of natural beauty—lakes and timber and open spaces—beginning with the Great Lakes and going out to the Plains and the Rocky Mountains. We don't have the massive cities that are deteriorating and rotting with ghettos. Now with good planning in recreation, conservation, culture, highway planning—the whole works —we actually should never get into this fix that the East and West coasts have gotten into, with rioting, millions of people living with rats and this type of thing. We can avoid all that. In a few years, with right decisions and right planning, our region is going to start to grow tremendously. We're on the beginning of what I think is going to be the golden era of development of our part of the country.

There are some Plainsmen, of course, who abjure all planning and are anxious to prevent any economic development that might disturb their private hunting and fishing reserves or bring black people in its wake. Hughes actually believes that a light infusion of blacks into the Plains might ease national race tensions—a development that would cause, at least initially, consternation and fervent opposition in the small towns and cities of the region.

But in the long run, the decision on the speed and complexion of population growth is not likely to remain exclusively with the people who now inhabit these states. It was federal policy that diverted population away from the Plains in the war and postwar years; likewise it may be government pressures or incentives that will one day play the key role in population redistribution to the lonely prairies.

Great Plains Politics

In the national mind, the Plains States have an image of standard, conservative Republicanism in the northern grouping, and standard, conservative Democratic politics in the southern grouping of Missouri, Oklahoma, and Texas. The states of Nebraska and Kansas, for instance, are in the running for "most Republican" in the nation, and Texas is clearly the most Democratic, and the most conservative, megastate in the Union. In the close Presidential elections of recent years, the upper Great Plains States—with the exception of Minnesota—have almost always gone Republican. Oklahoma has moved into the Republican camp in Presidential elections, and Missouri and Texas are closely contested territory.

Whether Republican or Democratic, the state legislatures of the region are all conservative in complexion—Minnesota, again, being the exception, by virtue of its heavily Scandinavian, intellectual, and liberal farmer-labor politics. Appropriate to the ingrained political habits of the states, there are conservative Republican legislatures in the northern Great Plains, conservative Democratic legislatures (chosen by the legendary "brass collar Democrats") in the southern belt. Generally speaking, the same pattern applies to elections to the U.S. House as well, though Democrats have been making more breakthroughs in the upper Great Plains, Republicans in the southern Great Plains, in recent years. As a result of the 1972 elections, the congressional delegation from the region had 43 Democrats to 22 Republicans—the Democratic edge based almost entirely on the Democrats' big 20–4 lead in Texas. The 18 U.S. Senate seats were balanced eight for the Republicans, 10 for the Democrats. And a number of Republican reversals in the politically risky area of governorship elections had produced a regional figure of seven Democratic governors and only two Republicans (in Iowa and Missouri).

Many of the Democrats who win across the Great Plains are just as conservative as their Republican counterparts (or more so). But significant Democratic strength also springs from a tradition of radical agrarianism—the fight against the railroad barons, grain magnates, and tight-money bankers—which dates back to the Populist era at the turn of the century. Another part of the tradition is the strength the Democrats gained among farmers as a result of New Deal farm programs; even to this day in the upper Great Plains States, for instance, one may find the actual farmer precincts going Democratic, even if the towns and small cities vote more heavily Republican than any other bloc in America. Thomas E. Dewey learned about the farm backlash, to his sorrow, in the 1948 Presidential election (losing to Missouri's Harry S Truman), and several Democratic politicians of the Plains got their start by attacking Ezra Taft Benson, Eisenhower's Secretary of Agriculture, in the 1950s.

Both the Populist and New Deal traditions helped make it possible for men like George McGovern of South Dakota, Hubert Humphrey and Eugene McCarthy of Minnesota, Quentin Burdick of North Dakota, and Harold Hughes of Iowa to win election to the United States Senate in the postwar era. Once there, several of these men became national leaders, exercising an influence in the urban-oriented national Democratic party far out of proportion to their home-state electoral bases. Humphrey became Vice President under Lyndon Johnson and his party's Presidential candidate in 1968; George McGovern's band of youthful idealists seized the Democratic nomination for their candidate in 1972, though his defeat in the general election was as overwhelming as that of another Plainsman—Alf Landon of Kansas—a generation earlier.

One change in the Plains States and general Midwestern frame of mind is clear for all to see: the disappearance of the isolationism and separatism of the 1920s and '30s. World War II, the Korean and Vietnam wars all made it clear to the people of this region that they are inextricably bound up with the world at large. They know that their own exports—in farm machinery, livestock, feed grains, and now especially wheat in view of the new trade frontiers being opened with the Societ Union and China—depend on a sound foreign policy. American military policy is also important to the region, as antiballistic missile sites are located on the upper Plains. The typical Midwestern Senator today—be he conservative Republican or liberal Democrat—would far prefer a seat on the Foreign Relations Committee to the prize committee assignment of decades past, the Agriculture Committee.

But what, then, do the Great Plains States stand for in America today? Are they *simply* a backwater, a largely forgotten region in the swirling currents of the late 20th century? I think not, and I would submit these words by Alf Landon in evidence:

> From the time of the first settlers, the Great Plains States developed a strong and compassionate people out of the hardships and suffering of the destructive blizzards—"northers" that swept over the region with white clouds of blinding snow and ice—and southern winds that brought the black blizzards of dust storms.
>
> The people of the Plains are realistic about the nation's domestic and international affairs. They view both with intense interest and with anxiety, for they know that—although stubborn resistance to change can lead to catastrophe—change often has unforeseen ramifications.
>
> What Americans must find in our time is a way to square their diversification, and the freedom upon which it is based, with the older sense of identity and stability. Perhaps the contemporary Great Plains States offer the answer in their freer acceptance of people as they are and as they are capable of becoming—a surviving characteristic of mutual helpfulness, willingness to accept change, not for change's sake but on its merits.

MISSOURI

MICROCOSM U.S.A.

One of the most sensitive descriptions by an American writer of his home state was produced by Irving Dilliard when he was editorial page editor of the St. Louis *Post-Dispatch* several years ago:

> Missouri is more than the heartland. The heart is also the whole. Missouri is all America in one place. It is the 48 states of the Union joined together, superimposed on one another, fused into a composite of many outlooks and moods and experiences and ways of thinking and speaking and doing things.
>
> Missouri is the abolitionist North with its belief in equal rights for all men and women. It is the plantation South with its old ideas of a leisure society. It is the industrial East, busy, noisy, mechanical, commercial. It is the grazing West, miles on miles of pasture and prize livestock in every direction.
>
> In May, Missouri is Virginia and billowing apple orchards pink-white for blossomtime. In late June, it is the beginning of the Great Plains and waving, golden-ripe wheat of Kansas, Nebraska and Dakotas. In August, Missouri is Illinois' blazing cornland prairie. It is rocky New England farmlands, bright with larkspur and hollyhocks along rail fences. It is sun-baked mine fields of Oklahoma, New Mexico and Arizona. It is broad patches of cotton and beet pickers with their bulging bags from Alabama, Mississippi and Louisiana. . . .

In 20 years, Missouri has changed; for one thing, the mechanical cotton picker has driven the black field hand onto the jobless rolls, or into the big city, or both. The "abolitionist North" no longer seems so tolerant, the Southerner's ideas of a leisure society are a bit frayed, and Missouri has received a good dose of the suburbs and every kind of urban ill. Harry Truman and the Missouri gang have long since vacated the White House, aerospace has helped Missouri fight off obsolescence, and on the banks of the Mississippi at St. Louis has risen a magnificent Arch that so perfectly symbolizes the better hopes and vision of a technological age that it may well be remembered and admired by archeologists of some future age when the rest of what we write is dust. Missouri today is perhaps less typical of the whole U.S.A. than it was when Dilliard wrote, because it has no people-packed "suncoasts." But aside from that, it is still about the best microcosm there is of our country.

Part of the reason lies in Missouri's unique geographic position. William Seward, Secretary of State in the cabinets of Abraham Lincoln and Andrew Johnson, grasped the potentialities when he said in an address in St. Louis during the 1860s:

> I see here one state that is capable of assuming the great trust of being the middle man, the mediator, the common center between the Pacific and the Atlantic—a state of vast extent, of unsurpassed fertility, of commercial facilities that are given to no other railroad state of the continent, a state . . . through which is the only thoroughfare to the Golden Gate of the Pacific. It is your interest to bind to Missouri the young states of the Pacific of this continent, while they are yet green and tender, and hold them fast to you. When you have done this and secured the Pacific states firmly, you will have bound the Atlantic to the Pacific Coast, and have guaranteed an empire . . . over the entire continent of North America.

In our time, one may dismiss those romantic ideas of empire but still recognize the unique role of a state whose borders are abutted by such wildly contradicting ecologies and cultures as those of Nebraska and Tennessee, Kansas and Kentucky, Illinois and Oklahoma, Iowa and Arkansas. The state in the midst of those eight is bound to be something of a potpourri of America.

Then there are the two great cities—St. Louis, last metropolis of the East, and Kansas City, the first of the West—the two set on Missouri's longitudinal extremes, making her, as Seward envisioned, a real connecting point between the American East and West.

And to the equation one must add Missouri's two great arteries of water, providing her with 1,937 miles of navigable waterway and access to the entire heartland and the Gulf of Mexico. From the northwest comes the muddy, turbulent Missouri River, now finishing its course over a thousand miles of prairie as it cuts eastward through Missouri toward St. Louis in its inexorable surge to the Mississippi. From the north comes the "Father of Waters" itself (ironically with less water flow than the Missouri it absorbs), forming Missouri's eastern border before it dips into the Deep South.

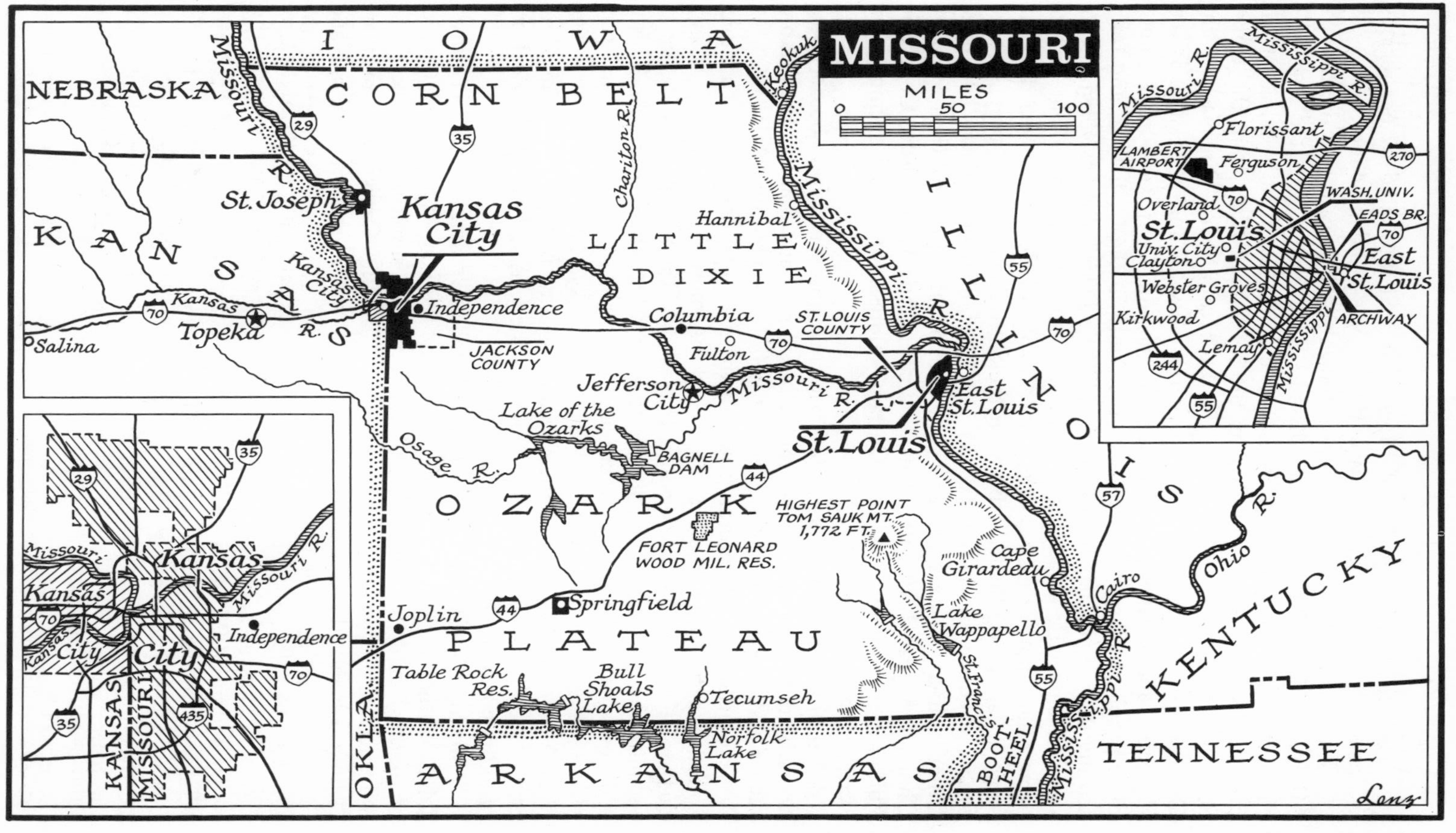
MISSOURI
MILES
0
50
100
IOWA
NEBRASKA
CORN BELT
KANSAS
ILLINOIS
KENTUCKY
TENNESSEE
ARKANSAS
OKLA.
LITTLE DIXIE
OZARK PLATEAU
Kansas City
St. Joseph
Topeka
Salina
Independence
JACKSON COUNTY
Columbia
Fulton
Hannibal
Keokuk
Jefferson City
ST. LOUIS COUNTY
St. Louis
East St. Louis
Lake of the Ozarks
BAGNELL DAM
HIGHEST POINT TOM SAUK MT. 1,772 FT.
FORT LEONARD WOOD MIL. RES.
Springfield
Joplin
Table Rock Res.
Bull Shoals Lake
Tecumseh
Norfolk Lake
Cape Girardeau
Lake Wappapello
Cairo
BOOT-HEEL
Missouri R.
Mississippi R.
Chariton R.
Kansas R.
Osage R.
St. Francis
Ohio R.
Florissant
LAMBERT AIRPORT
Ferguson
Overland
WASH. UNIV.
EADS BR.
Univ. City
Clayton
Webster Groves
Kirkwood
Lemay
ARCHWAY
Kansas City
Lenz

The microcosmic quality of Missouri is well illustrated by her regions, clear cut in geology, in the ancestry of their people—and in politics.

Rich farm land not unlike that of neighboring Iowa covers the third of Missouri which lies north of the Missouri River; this is glaciated land with thick, rich soil, ideal for field crops, cattle feeding, and hogs. Some of the first settlers of Missouri, traveling up the Mississippi River from the Upper South—Kentucky, Tennessee, and the back country of Virginia and the Carolinas—settled in counties between the Missouri and Mississippi Rivers in central and northeastern Missouri. Slaveholding was widespread among these people, they sympathized with the South in the Civil War, and for a century their region has been known as "Little Dixie" and has voted as constantly Democratic as any part of the old Deep South one might care to name. One county of Little Dixie, Pike, actually invaded Iowa under the Confederate flag during the War Between the States; another, Callaway, seceded from the Union and established its own "Kingdom of Callaway" to resist Union militia. Callaway got a new measure of fame in 1946 when Winston Churchill appeared with President Truman at tiny Westminster College in Fulton to give his famous "Iron Curtain" address, the official opening, as it were, of the Cold War.

North and northwest of Little Dixie are a number of Iowa border counties settled by sturdy yeomen from Ohio, Iowa, and Kansas. Predictably, these counties have been among the most solidly Republican of Missouri.

Proceeding to the territory south of the river, one finds poorer, bumpier land; the agricultural result is more chickens, more dairying, less beef production. The most famous region is that of the Ozark Mountains (better to say hills, though, since the highest is only 1,772 feet above sea level). This is a picturesque and in places remote land of 10,000 natural springs, first peopled by the suspicious backwooders of Kentucky, eastern Tennessee, and West Virginia. They scorned the slaveholding ways of their fellow Southerners in Little Dixie, sided with the Union in the war, and developed a culture of hillbilly ballads and rich mountain lore.

Most of the Ozarks vote Republican and have done so for a century.* John Gunther uncharitably called this region "the Poor White Trash Citadel of America" and the people thereof "undeveloped, suspicious and inert"; he did quote another authority, however, who said the Ozarks woodsmen are "simply a highland race that loves solitude and scorns comfort, literature and luxury." There are still few places in America as isolated as parts of the Ozarks; when the police were pursuing Pretty Boy Floyd, he would disappear into a hillbilly area known as the Boston Mountains-Cookson Hills section of far southwest Missouri and northwest Oklahoma, the area of his birth, where the mountain people would hide him effectively for months at a time. Poverty sometimes reaches extremes in the Ozarks, one of America's most deprived areas. In 1959, per capita income there was $1,233, even lower than the better known Appalachian region. One survey in the mid-1960s found

* The further west in the Ozarks one goes, the more Republican; actually there are some eastern Ozark counties the Democrats can normally count on.

that 44 percent of the Ozarks people had family incomes of less than $3,000 a year, and that in more than half the households the family head was 55 years of age or older.

For several decades, "civilization" has intruded into parts of the Ozarks through scenery-despoiling billboards and cheap curio and trinket shops ringing spots like the 100-mile-long Lake of the Ozarks, a man-made creation of the New Deal era, and the Bagnell Dam. The 1960s brought a rash of more expensive resorts to exploit the scenery-boating-fishing-horseback-riding potential of this area, bringing in hundreds of thousands of dollars of new tourist income each year. The National Governors Conference even came to the Lake of the Ozarks in 1970. Yet in the backwoods, the old customs and dialects and folklore linger on. "The nasal sing-song drawl of an Ozark square dance caller," one St. Louis paper recently reported, "may occasionally still be heard in Ozark hill communities above the sound of a fiddle, a mouth organ and a mandolin that provide the dancing music." On rare occasions, prospective Ozark brides still continue the ancient backwoods custom of washing their faces with dew at sunup on May 1—once considered a sign that a girl would marry the man she loved most. Sometimes, when towns celebrate centennial festivals, woodsmen will fire off an anvil with black powder just as their forefathers did for all manner of great days before the blacksmith shop disappeared down the corridor of time.

In several counties of east central Missouri, south of the river, early German settlement was heavy. Freedom-loving Germans at the time of the Civil War, led by Carl Schurz, were said to have saved Missouri for the Union, and in some of the rural counties they settled, a German Republican vote persisted for generations. Even today, vestiges of the German language may be heard in towns like Hermann. (Germans in beer-drinking St. Louis, by contrast, turned Democratic when Franklin D. Roosevelt backed repeal of Prohibition.) Another ethnic island, not yet obliterated by time, may be found in old French settlements like St. Genevieve and Old Mines in southeastern Missouri, where one can still detect a Creole dialect derived from 18th-century France, gently melded with English and Spanish and even Indian words.

Finally, we must mention the seven counties of the Missouri "Bootheel" which digs in between Tennessee and Arkansas on the state's southeastern extremity. These counties are dead ringers for the old South—on flat delta cotton-growing land, with high percentages of blacks and solid South Democratic voting habits. The Bootheel was actually a wheat-growing area and North-oriented until 1924, when the boll weevil ruined the cotton crop in adjoining Southern states and encouraged the invasion of black belt cotton growers, who brought thousands of Negro sharecroppers with them. To this day, blacks are trucked from one precinct to the next to cast multiple votes at election time. But the mechanical picker has replaced the black man in the fields, and soybeans are crowding out cotton.

Not regions in the broad geographic sense, but nevertheless vital factors in the microcosm of Missouri, are its two great cities and their environs.

Between them, the metropolitan areas of St. Louis and Kansas City account for 57 percent of the 4,676,501 people living in Missouri. They reflect almost every urban problem and prospect known across America. We will have more to say of them later.

The "Show Me" State and Its Contributions to the U.S.A.

"I come from a state that raises corn and cotton and cockleburs and Democrats," a now forgotten Congressman, William Vandiver, declared in 1889. "Frothy eloquence neither convinces nor satisfies me. I am from Missouri. You have got to show me." Today the Random House dictionary even includes a definition of the phrase "from Missouri." It means: "Unwilling to accept without proof, skeptical."

That peppery, independent spirit, not entirely foreign to the ornery mules who helped make Missouri famous, has surfaced again and again in Missouri history, recent decades not excepted. One thinks most fondly back to 1948 and that grinning, delighted face of a President Harry S Truman on his way back to Washington after thwarting every prognosticator to defeat Thomas E. Dewey, displaying for photographers an early edition of Colonel McCormick's Chicago *Tribune* with the ill-considered headline "Dewey Elected President." Of the momentous decisions, foreign and domestic, which Truman as President made to set the nation on its course in the postwar years, no recital is required here. At the simple memorial services for Truman at the Washington Cathedral, shortly after his death at Christmastime 1972, Dean Francis B. Sayre evoked the Truman background in a simpler America and offered a prayer for Missouri, "the land he loved." "There were no wrinkles in his honesty," Sayre said; he was a man "earthy, plain, of sturdy soul and tempered true."

Of all the Missourians Truman brought into public life, none served longer and with more distinction than his "good counselor," St. Louisan Clark M. Clifford, an immensely influential man in formulating American foreign and defense policy in the postwar years. The first major public post Clifford ever accepted was as Secretary of Defense under Lyndon Johnson in 1968; he was viewed as an embodiment of the military-industrial establishment, and most people expected his role to be fairly ceremonial in the waning year of an unpopular Presidency. But, as it turned out, it was Clifford who exerted the crucial pressure to get Johnson to announce an end to the bombing of North Vietnam and take the first steps toward disengagement from a war that was sapping national strength and unity. Again, a healthy dose of Missouri skepticism, in this case about the accepted war credo of the administration, was good medicine for a nation.

Missouri has made her mark in Congress ever since the immortal Thomas H. Benton represented her in the Senate during her first 30 years of statehood, from 1820 to 1850. Benton went to Congress as a Southerner, became a spokesman of the Western frontier people, and finally lost his seat when his stalwart stand against slavery destroyed his base of support at home. In 1837 a journalist described him as a statesman "above the attraction of office," who always went "fearlessly forward" as an activist making public opinion, not a broker politician balancing the demands of various interest groups.

An especially vigorous group has served Missouri in Washington in the years following World War II, many the embodiment of the inquisitive "show me" spirit. Stuart Symington, born of an aristocratic Maryland family, moved to Missouri early in his adult life and made his mark as an industrialist with a special touch in labor relations. Like Clark Clifford, he was to undergo a remarkable transformation in his attitude toward the Vietnam war and America's global role. First known nationally as a persistent advocate of strong U.S. defenses, he quit as Truman's Secretary of the Air Force because of military budget cuts, then went to the Senate, where he fought for bigger bombers in the 1950s and still bigger ones in the 1960s. Symington's influence was immense as senior member of both the Senate Armed Services and Foreign Relations Committees. But sometime between 1966 and 1967 he was transformed from Vietnam hawk to Vietnam dove and likewise became an eloquent opponent of high defense budgets, warning that the country had already wasted some $23 billion on missile systems deployed and then abandoned. Of spiraling defense commitments in the multimegaton age, Symington warned: "If we do not stop this, we are headed for nuclear war." Symington believes that his antiwar stand in Missouri, said to have been one of the most "hawkish" of states, almost cost him his Senate seat in 1970. Journalist Flora Lewis wrote of him the following year: "Stuart Symington's mental odyssey has been a national journey, a part of the country's passage through fears and convictions to new questions and new demands." A smaller man would surely have stumbled along the way.

A lesser but distinct contribution was made by Missouri's Senator Thomas Hennings, who as Senate Rules Committee chairman fought for basic reform in the country's campaign finance disclosure laws. (A political liberal with real depth, Hennings was an alcoholic. Harry McPherson has described him as "a walking tragedy, or perhaps high-grade Tennessee Williams.")

Thomas F. Eagleton, first elected to the Senate in 1968, four years later had the unhappy distinction of being the first Vice Presidential candidate of an American political party who was forced to resign his place on a national ticket. Selected by George McGovern to be his running mate, Eagleton did not tell McGovern that he had been hospitalized on three occasions in the early 1960s for nervous exhaustion and fatigue and had undergone electric shock treatment for depression on two occasions. When McGovern learned of the episodes, he first said he had made "an irrevocable decision" to keep Eagleton on the ticket and was "1,000 percent" behind the Missouri Senator. But some party professionals passed the word to McGovern that it would be a fatal error to keep Eagleton on the ticket, and several of the country's major newspapers—including the New York *Times*, Washington *Post*, Baltimore *Sun*, and Los Angeles *Times*—urged editorially that Eagleton withdraw. Finally, McGovern asked Eagleton to resign from the ticket, and Eagleton complied—amid furious protest by Democratic leaders in Missouri. (In the general election, McGovern and his replacement running mate, Sargent Shriver, won only 37 percent of the Missouri vote. But little of the blame could be assigned to Eagleton, who did not sulk or go into seclusion after being dropped from the ticket, but rather campaigned wholeheartedly for McGovern. His personal popularity—in Missouri, and around the country, where he had been little known previously—was remarkably high.)

Eagleton, the grandson of a poor immigrant laborer from Ireland's County Cork, was originally picked by McGovern with an eye to his Roman Catholic religion and residency in St. Louis, a big city. But Eagleton also offered, as one reporter noted, "intense social conscience, revved-up personal drive, and a first-rate extroverted wit." At 27, he had been elected Missouri's youngest prosecutor, at 31 the youngest attorney general in the state's history, and at 35 (in 1964) the youngest lieutenant governor. During his first years in the Senate, he built an almost spotless record by standard "liberal" definitions (over 90 percent correct in the eyes of Americans for Democratic Action, for instance). He joined the ranks of Senators fighting to end U.S. involvement in the war in Vietnam and took a major hand in several floor fights to reduce defense spending. He also became chairman of the Senate District Committee and in 1971 helped obtain the largest federal payment in history for Washington, D.C.

In the House of Representatives, Richard Bolling from Kansas City, an antimachine man and independent thinker, was groomed for House leadership by Sam Rayburn but lost favor with that body through his frontal assaults on its antediluvian rules and procedures. Bolling served with distinction on the Joint Economic Committee and brought a liberal voice to the powerful House Rules Committee.

St. Louis has sent two exceptionally able representatives to the House. Leonor Kretzer Sullivan, first elected in 1952, by the early 1970s held the longevity record among women in the House. As the chairman of a House subcommittee on consumer affairs, she displayed tenaciousness and skill appropriate to her German background in fighting for years to win acceptance of the food stamp program for the poor, which she authored, and also truth-in-lending legislation that she introduced and guided to passage. In 1971 she was the only woman in Congress to vote against an equal rights amendment, explaining: "There are differences between male and female roles in our society and I hope there always are." Mrs. Sullivan's power in Congress was enhanced in 1973, when she became chairman of the House Merchant Marine and Fisheries Committee. She was expected to reflect St. Louis interests by placing emphasis on river shipping and safety standards on inland waterways. One interesting piece of legislation Mrs. Sullivan had previously brought to passage exempted the last of the sternwheel passenger riverboats from deep-sea safety rules. Unless the bill had passed, the *Delta Queen*, which still operated as an overnight cruise boat on the Ohio and Mississippi Rivers, would have been forced into retirement.

Republican U.S. Rep. Thomas B. Curtis of St. Louis, who served 18 years in the House until he gave up his seat for a close but losing Senate race in 1968, was second-ranking Republican on the Ways and Means Committee and served ably on the Joint Economic Committee. Curtis combined a generally conservative voting record with strong fights for civil rights legislation, fair trade, adequate minority staffing on congressional committees, and improvements in House leadership and procedures. There have been few more conscientious and hard-working legislators in Congress in recent decades. Now his House seat is held by Democrat James Symington, son of the famous Stuart.*

For sheer Missouri orneriness, no Missouri Congressman of recent decades has matched Clarence Cannon, a House member from Little Dixie for 42 years before his death in 1964. Cannon was chairman of the House Appropriations Committee for 19 years. In 1962 he and another octogenarian, Senate Appropriations Committee Chairman Carl Hayden of Arizona, got in an imbroglio over whether appropriations conference committees should sit on the House or Senate side of the Capitol. The money bills to finance the government of the United States were held up for three months until the two old men could resolve their impasse. Sam Rayburn, who ought to have known, called Cannon a "stubborn" and "bullheaded" man.

The old Missouri independence showed up in a somehow more appealing form in the person of William L. Hungate, who succeeded to Cannon's seat in the House. Assigned to the House District of Columbia Committee, he rose to be chairman of its judiciary subcommittee but became increasingly disgusted with its mediocre staff and the continual kowtowing to special interest lobbyists who had close ties to South Carolina's John L. McMillan, chairman of the overall District Committee. After a 1971 incident concerning consumer and banking legislation, in which lobbyists for small loan companies played an especially egregious role, Hungate resigned in anger from the committee. Capitol Hill observers could not recall an earlier instance in which a subcommittee chairman had quit in protest over his committee's practices.

Where does Missouri's independent "show me" spirit and cussed streak come from? The roots of the people are a factor: a major share of the modern Missouri bloodstream descends from the Southerners who came before the Civil War, and they were not a conforming lot but rather independent backwoodsmen or restless younger sons of plantation owners seeking *lebensraum*. And in this century, Missouri experienced relatively little of the southern and eastern European migration stream that prompted Anglo-Saxons to forget their differences and make common cause in other states.

Finally, consider the legacy of the War Between the States. The con-

* James Symington, 41 when he first won the seat, had formerly served as Chief of Protocol in the State Department and deputy director of the Food for Peace Program. He is also an accomplished folk guitarist and might well run to succeed his father in 1976, should the Senator decide to retire that year.

flict tore Missouri cruelly asunder. Some 30,000 of her youth fought in gray uniform, about 109,000 in blue. Exactly 1,160, or 11 percent of the engagements of the war, took place on Missouri soil. And the conflict was not just formal and military, but internal too; the passions of the war set family against family, neighbor against neighbor, county against county. There were murders, bushwhacking, and general guerrilla warfare. When the war was ended, the enemy had not retreated to some distant other region of America but was still immediate: if not at one's own supper table, then over the hill in the next county. In rural Missouri, with its more static population, the enmities of the war would eclipse every other political issue and influence elections for more than 100 years. In that atmosphere of suspicion and latent hostility, no easy consensus of a people could emerge; rather questioning, conflict, and perversity marked their character.

A state as diverse and complex as Missouri, though, lends itself to no neat analysis. Any character portrait has to be leavened with the list of great national leaders, from Benton to Truman, Clifford, and Symington, whom we have already mentioned, plus this heterogeneous group of renowned Americans who first saw the light of day or lived out their lives in Missouri: Samuel Clemens, the novelist; Thomas Hart Benton, whose great, controversial murals of heartland life still grace the state capital; Jesse James, the notorious bandit; John J. Pershing and Omar N. Bradley of military fame; T. S. Eliot, the poet who scorned both his native St. Louis and America for a life abroad; Joseph Pulitzer, one of the greatest newspapermen America has ever known; George Washington Carver, renowned as an agricultural scientist; Dale Carnegie, the success lecturer; Ginger Rogers and Betty Grable of the silver screen; Tom Pendergast, the political boss *sui generis;* Sally Rand, the fan dancer; Casey Stengel of baseball fame and Drs. William H. Masters and Virginia E. Johnson, the medical sex crusaders (*Human Sexual Response*) from St. Louis, who were married in 1971.

Or, to return to Irving Dilliard again, Missouri is all these things:

> It is the channel catfish and small mouth black bass, the mallard, the squirrel and the rabbit. It is the red flash of the cardinal and the hoarse call of the crow. It is Jack in his pulpit and lace along the road for Queen Anne. It is the corn-cob pipe, square dance and quilting bee; the county fair, potluck supper, school picnic and moonlight boatride. It is old Arrow Rock Tavern, Louis Sullivan's pioneer skyscraper, and the fiery race between the *Natchez* and the *Robert E. Lee*. It is machine politics in the cities and tent revivals in the hills. It is Frankie and Johnny, the St. Louis Blues and the Missouri Waltz.

The "Low-Tax, Low-Service" State

The excellence that has sometimes distinguished members of Missouri's congressional delegation is rarely reflected in the capitol at Jefferson City. In fact, Missouri has traditionally had a low-tax, low-service state government, despite significant budget increases in recent years. Among the 50 states, Missouri ranks 42nd in tax effort (the percentage which state and local taxes represent of total personal income). Its expenditures per capita for welfare (despite major poverty pockets in the cities and the Ozarks) is only 35th, its expenditure per capita for highways 40th, for local schools 34th.

Apparently Missourians are relatively unconcerned about the poor showing their state makes in terms of people services. Indeed, history records that Missouri missed the Populist sweep of the late 19th century altogether, largely because the Democratic party of Missouri came out for free silver (while staying conservative on other subjects). Until the Republicans scored a breakthrough, electing their first governor in many years in the 1972 elections, all of Missouri's postwar chief executives had been Democrats who placed somewhere between moderate and conservative on an ideological scale. Missouri has never had a liberal Democratic experience in state government.

The basic reason for conservatism in the Missouri government is the superior political skill of rural and small-city legislators and politicians. The familiar seedbeds of governors are Little Dixie and the Bootheel, hardly ever the urban areas. There is sporadic talk about St. Louis and Kansas City getting together behind a gubernatorial candidate, but the continuing jealousy between the two cities mitigates against coalition.

"Missourians seem to find it impossible to get a creditable legislature," *Fortune* reported in 1945, and the situation has not changed appreciably since. The Citizens Conference on State Legislatures, which incidentally has its headquarters in the state at Kansas City, in 1971 ranked the Missouri legislature only 35th among the 50 of the nation in terms of its ability to act in a "functional, accountable, informed, independent, representative" manner.* Malapportionment, especially egregious in the lower house, was corrected under court orders in the mid-1960s, but legislators from the conservative rural areas—men accomplished in the wily arts of legislative infighting—still outmaneuver, quite consistently, the rather mediocre delegations sent by St. Louis and Kansas City. Cries of the cities for help are unheeded or half loaves are given; little effective action is taken to stimulate economic development in the declining rural and small-city areas. Melodramatic power plays between various factions occupy a great deal of the legislators' attention.

"Jefferson City," one of Missouri's most respected citizens told me, "is still a playground for politicians with a business-as-usual attitude." A shining example was provided in 1969, when the rural-based president of the state senate, Earl Blackwell, turned on the governor and blocked a desperately needed tax increase. The only way Blackwell's power was broken was purely personal: it was discovered that he had married for a second time, but no divorce from the first Mrs. Blackwell could be discovered. The fiscal crisis of the state government reached such proportions that the legislators in 1970 finally raised the corporate income tax from 2 to 5 percent and the graduated tax on individual incomes from a 1-to-4-percent scale to a 1.5-to-6-

* The commission acknowledged that Missouri had taken a major step forward through passage, in 1970, of a constitutional amendment authorizing annual legislative sessions and automatic legislative review of gubernatorial vetoes. But specific reforms were still needed, the Commission said, in regard to reduction of the size of the house (with 163 members, the seventh largest state legislative body in the country), reduction of the unwieldy number of committees, regulation of lobbyists, and more effective conflict-of-interest rules.

percent scale. That was enough to launch Blackwell on a campaign for the governorship in 1972, running on a simple antitax platform. He was defeated in the primary, however.

Two glaring examples of Missouri's problems are its university and penal system. The University of Missouri has some very adequate faculties and is famous for its school of journalism, first in the United States.* Nevertheless, the university's overall quality falls far short of the mark set by Illinois, Michigan, or other Midwestern states. "Missouri has always felt it would like to have a state university as long as it didn't cost too much money," I was told. Faculty salaries have consistently ranked near the bottom of public universities in the Midwest. Now the university is facing formidable obstacles in trying to control from its central campus in rural Columbia the new branches it has established in St. Louis and Kansas City. In an effort to overcome political obstacles to the university's growth, its president in 1971 proposed that most of the advanced graduate programs be transferred to the St. Louis and Kansas City campuses, a suggestion that prompted the Columbia *Missourian*, daily paper of the journalism school, to editorialize that the transfer would "answer the hungry cries of the young urban campuses of this university with no better advice than to cannibalize their own mother." In addition to the University of Missouri, the state also has several rather mediocre four-year state colleges and a promising new group of community colleges emphasizing technical and vocational education. Overall, the state ranks only 39th in per capita state expenditures for higher education. Facilities are crowded and the capital budget has dwindled to the vanishing point. In 1971, the level of frustration among the public colleges and universities reached such a high point that they seriously considered launching their own initiative petition to get the voters to approve new building funds.

As for the penal system, Missouri newspapers long complained of deplorable conditions at the century-old state prison at Jefferson City, a structure with damp, rat-infested cells and little real rehabilitation effort. A major reform effort was made between 1965 and early 1972, when Fred Wilkinson, one of the nation's top penologists formerly in a high position with the federal prison system, served as Missouri's director of corrections. Wilkinson ended segregation in the state penitentiary, opened an "honor building" for cooperative convicts, and won their confidence and respect. But the legislature never gave Wilkinson the money he wanted for a true rehabilitation program, replacing the antiquated penitentiary at Jefferson City with a new maximum security prison, or building an intensive care facility for juveniles.

No state legislature, of course, is totally immune to its times, and Missouri vastly increased its expenditures for government services during the 1950s and 1960s—though not at a rate comparable to most of America's medium- and large-sized states. A large measure of the credit for the increases that were made went to Governor Warren E. Hearnes, a young (mid-forties)

* Since 1959, the journalism school has sponsored a freedom of information center, which has been described as "the world's largest clearinghouse for information on the public's right to know." The center responds to some 2,000 queries from all over the United States, each year.

native of rural southeastern Missouri and a West Point graduate who turned out to be a superb politician with a sixth sense of what the people would accept or reject at any given moment. By nature, Hearnes is conservative on social and fiscal issues. Once in office, however, he saw the need for more expenditures and persuaded the legislature to increase the Missouri budget more than any other governor had done in its history. His major achievement was in increased state aid to local schools, which rose 161 percent during his eight years in office. But Fred Lindecke of the St. Louis *Post-Dispatch* reported early in 1972:

> Missouri tax increases have channeled millions of dollars in extra state aid to local school districts in recent years, while at the same time other state services have deteriorated or struggled to stay even. Such programs as welfare and mental health, unable to match the school lobby in flexing political muscle, have had to take a comparative back seat in the fight for a greater share of state funds. . . .
>
> In welfare, for instance, the state is giving mothers with dependent children only 48 percent of what is deemed necessary for them to live decently. . . . For the aged it is 77 percent, for the blind 79 percent and for the disabled 68 percent. . . .
>
> The mental health program has improved vastly since the snake pit conditions of the 1950s, with patients tied to beds and sleeping naked on the floor. . . . But in the last year and a half, the division [of mental health] lost 400 professional level employees—psychiatrists, doctors, nurses and technicians—because of money problems. . . .
>
> Arthur O. Hamm, president of the Missouri State, County and Municipal Employees Union, said his union represented about 6,000 employees in state mental hospitals, penal institutions and other agencies. "Some of them still work at full-time jobs for less than $4,000 a year, which is below most poverty standards. Some receive state welfare checks at the same time they are working at a full-time job for the state," Hamm said.

In addition to increased school aid, Hearnes also made such important innovations as a network of regional clinics for the mentally retarded and a state-financed council on the arts (first in the nation after New York State's). But he bulked at giving the major cities all the help they asked for.

Politics and Power

Among the more powerful lobbies operating regularly in Jefferson City are the Missouri Farmers Association and the AFL-CIO (both quite conservative on state issues); the Missouri Bus and Truck Association (another evidence of the awesome power of truckers in the U.S.A. today); and the Teamsters. At least once a year, a big cart covered with a canvas sheet cruises down the legislative hallways; underneath are cases of Cutty Sark, Budweiser, or whatever, all the Teamsters' munificence for thirsty lawmakers. Then some legislators will phone the press room and graciously give away a bottle or two to the reporters; if you have ever wondered about reporters' cynicism, recall incidents such as this. Or another Missouri phenomenon: not far across the Mississippi River in Illinois there are two racetracks where 70 percent of the cars parked will have Missouri license tags. Legalized racing, which would bring important money into the state treasury, is opposed by Missouri rural and church groups. For years, some reporters suspected that southern Illinois racing interests were paying off Missouri legislature members to keep racing out of the state.* And then there are lobbies like the Roadside Business Association, responsible, according to the St. Louis *Post-Dispatch*, for "Missouri's reign as the undisputed billboard king of the United States."

Aside from the governor, the most powerful men in Missouri today are said to include the following: August A. Busch, Jr., of Anheuser-Busch, the famous St. Louis brewers; Harold Gibbons, president of the Missouri-Kansas Council of Teamsters; James Kemper, who heads the largest bank in Kansas City (the Commerce Trust Company); Donald Hall of Hallmark Cards (the firm which is redeveloping a huge swath of land in downtown Kansas City); James McDonnell of McDonnell-Douglas, the St. Louis aerospace manufacturers; and Sidney Salomon, Jr., owner of the St. Louis Blues professional hockey team. Salomon is also an immensely successful man in real estate, insurance, and investments; he served for a period as Democratic National Committeeman for Missouri and was once a national fund raiser for John F. Kennedy.

Until a few years ago, the true power in Missouri's state government was said to be held by the so-called "Establishment," consisting of old-line Democratic leaders centered around the Central Missouri Trust Company in Jefferson City. That bank held and controlled most of the state's funds at considerable profit to itself. The Establishment regularly dictated the choice of Democratic candidates for Governor, working in concert with key leaders in the Bootheel, St. Louis, and Kansas City. But in 1964 Hearnes upset the applecart by challenging and defeating the Establishment's chosen gubernatorial candidate. As the David who had slain the Establishment Goliath, Hearnes entered office with phenomenal power and even got through a constitutional amendment letting him run for a second consecutive term. The "Establishment" seemed dead. But to anyone who would take a close look, it was apparent that the state treasurer, an independently elected official, was still in the corner of the Central Missouri Trust Company and placed a major share of the state's liquid cash reserves in that bank.

One reason the Republicans could position themselves for a major breakthrough in Missouri state government in the 1970s was a plethora of nickel-and-dime scandals among the ruling Democrats. In 1970, for instance, Jack Flach of the St. Louis *Globe-Democrat* broke the story of how William Robinson, the state treasurer, had accepted a gift of $2,500 from a small bank which subsequently received substantial deposits of state funds. Robinson was indicted—the first time a Missouri state official had ever been indicted. He claimed that the $2,500 was a "campaign contribution" and thus won acquittal, but the aroma of scandal lingered on.

* Eventually, the corrupt element faded in the legislature, and in 1971 the legislators actually authorized a popular vote on a constitutional amendment to legalize parimutuel betting at Missouri racetracks. But just at that time, the big scandal about sale of racetrack stock to politicians was breaking in Illinois. The news may have been a vital factor in popular rejection of the amendment.

Missouri voters in 1968 retired a man who symbolized the old-line, Establishment-oriented, politics-as-usual school in the Missouri Democratic party, U.S. Senator Edward V. Long. Long was 60 years old, a small-town lawyer and banker by profession who had held numerous Missouri political jobs over more than 30 years and voted an unexceptional liberal line in the Senate. His downfall came when *Life* magazine charged that he had misused a Senate investigating committee he headed "first as an instrument for trying to keep [Teamsters Union President] Jimmy Hoffa out of prison; subsequently for trying to get Hoffa's conviction reversed." *Life* said Long had received $48,000 in legal fees from Morris Shenker, a Missouri lawyer who was chief counsel for Hoffa. Long did not deny receiving the fees; "some people," he told the Senate, "apparently value my legal advice and are willing to pay for it." But he denied any wrongdoing or indirect receipt of money from Hoffa, and the Senate Ethics Committee cleared him—an action that prompted *Life* to cry "whitewash."

The voters apparently agreed with *Life*, and in the Democratic primary they nominated in Long's place the energetic young liberal, lieutenant governor Thomas F. Eagleton. The winning edge for Eagleton came from suburban St. Louis County, flexing its muscles for new politics over the old politics of the rural countryside. Explaining his vote for Eagleton, one voter said he was "young and honest, and a real leader, which is more than we've got now."

Youth and honesty were themes that the Republicans, too, used in their revival of the late 1960s and early 1970s. The first glimmering came in 1968, when the GOP was able to elect its first candidate for a statewide office in 22 years. The winner by 80,000 votes in the contest for state attorney general was 32-year-old John C. Danforth, a Ralston Purina heir, lawyer, and ordained Episcopal priest. Danforth had some highly unconventional backing for a Republican candidate, including the Robert F. Kennedy Club of St. Louis, Americans for Democratic Action, and many youthful supporters of the 1968 McCarthy for President effort. He campaigned for law and order but with a balance of social justice, suggesting steps to modernize the state's penal system and improve police, parole, and probation practices.

Two years later, Danforth ran for the U.S. Senate, challenging no less a figure than Stuart Symington. Danforth ran an extremely sophisticated (and expensive) campaign, heavy on staff, research, and television. His final TV blitz was rumored to have cost as much as $1 million (financed largely, it appeared, out of the family fortune). James M. Perry of the *National Observer*, observing the campaign, reported that Danforth's speeches reflected the unique combination of a legal and theological background: "sermons, but each point nicely structured and footnoted, like a lawyer's. . . . I can't remember when I last saw a candidate mesmerize an audience. When Danforth speaks, everyone is absolutely silent. They actually listen. Danforth can make points while dropping his voice almost to a whisper." Danforth was able to inspire hundreds of students to work for him, and he spoke frequently of the campaign as one between "the old and the new," but he never found an issue (except, perhaps, Symington's age of 69 years) that could really hurt the incumbent. When the votes were counted, Symington emerged the winner by a margin of 36,928 votes (51.0 percent)—the closest election of the senior Senator's career.

Danforth's close loss left him still a rising and potent factor in Missouri politics, and he would have been the Republicans' logical candidate for the governorship in 1972—an option that was impossible, however, because he could not meet the 10 years residency requirement of the Missouri constitution. Instead, Danforth chose to run for another term as attorney general, and won by an overwhelming majority.

A second GOP star emerged soon after Danforth: Christopher S. ("Kit") Bond, an intelligent and ambitious young man, endowed with family wealth (A.P. Green Refractory), a graduate of Princeton University and the University of Virginia Law School. Bond was elected state auditor in 1970 and proceeded to investigate state and county offices that had not been audited in years. In 1972, when Danforth could not run for governor, Bond stepped into the breach and ran a vigorous campaign, assailing the Democrats for running Missouri government with minimum efficiency and maximum patronage. The "spoils" system, Bond said, had to go, and he campaigned for a strong civil service, a state code of ethics, controls on lobbyists, for penal reform and more women in state government. Bond also urged equalized spending among well-to-do and poorer school districts, state aid for day care centers, and more spending on mass transit. He opposed a Constitutional amendment to outlaw school busing.

Bond's campaign got a boost when it was revealed that his Democratic opponent, Edward L. Dowd, an ex-FBI agent who was campaigning as a "law and order" candidate, had received campaign funds from the violence- and scandal-tainted Steamfitters Union of St. Louis. When the votes were counted, Bond was ahead by almost 190,000 votes. President Nixon's 447,000-vote plurality in Missouri the same day may have helped Bond and the Republican candidate for lieutenant governor, who was also victorious. But the GOP lost two other statewide races at stake, and elected only one out of 10 Congressmen from the state. The legislature and county courthouses remained strongly Democratic.

At 33, Bond was the nation's youngest governor when he took office. Despite his Phi Beta Kappa key, he is probably not the intellectual that Danforth is. But if an engaging personality, a mild Missouri twang, and a progressive reformer's instincts are the right credentials for political success in the 1970s, Bond's political future may be just as bright.

President Nixon's landslide in Missouri in 1972 seemed like a big exception in a state traditionally considered Democratic. But in fact, except for the unusual Lyndon Johnson margin of 1964, the state has not given a big margin to a Democratic Presidential candidate since its own Harry Truman in 1948. Eisenhower carried Missouri in 1952, Stevenson in 1956, Kennedy in 1960, and Nixon in 1968—but all by margins of less than 30,000 votes and less than 51 percent of the two-party vote. The general pattern is for St.

Louis City and Kansas City to go heavily Democratic, St. Louis County to be fairly even, Little Dixie and the Bootheel to go Democratic, and for the Republicans to do well in most other rural and small city areas—with their highest vote, of course, in the Ozarks. Missouri Republicans are perennially feuding over ideology and, when their party controls the Presidency, patronage.

A final note on Missouri politics: it seems largely devoid of racism. The state moved quickly to comply with the Supreme Court's decree of an end to racially segregated schools. Despite an active Wallace movement, the Alabaman garnered only 11.4 percent of the vote for President in 1968. All of this was a far cry from the 1930s and 1940s, when official Missouri went to sometimes ridiculous lengths to stop Negroes from registering at its universities.

Country vs. City and the Missouri Economy

A great gulf is apparent between the people of the large cities and all the rest of Missouri, as though they lived in different worlds. Spiritually, this may be true; economically it is not. Missouri is unique in having two federal reserve banks, one in St. Louis, the other in Kansas City; along with the great commercial banks of those cities, they watch and foster a variegated and highly interdependent economy. But Missouri's growth—measured by such yardsticks as increases in income, per capita income, and the number of jobs added—has fallen somewhat short of national averages. In population, Missouri ranked fifth in the United States in 1900, ninth in 1940, and 13th in 1970.

Led by aerospace and automobiles, manufacturing dominates the Missouri economy with an output approaching $6 billion a year. St. Louis is the aerospace fountainhead through McDonnell-Douglas, but there are four other important aerospace plants in southwestern Missouri. The total for transportation employment—combining aerospace, automobile and truck assembly, and railroad cars—has been the most dynamic element of the postwar years, up from 19,000 jobs in 1947 to 72,500 in 1971. Such gains have offset losses in recent times in such industries as shoe manufacturing, food processing, and apparel manufacturing—although all still employ thousands of Missourians. Among the goods manufactured in the state are beer, chemicals, metal products, milled grain, charcoal, and even corn cob pipes (not to mention moonshine whiskey). Several important minerals are mined, including lead from one of the world's greatest deposits west and south of St. Louis. Missouri woodlands yield an annual timber harvest with a retail value of some $500 million. Just under a third of Missouri's nonfarm labor force is unionized, the eighth highest level of unionization among the states.

Agriculture is the state's second largest income producer with an annual output of about $1.5 billion, eighth largest in the United States. Although thousands of acres of farmland succumb to suburban and industrial encroachments each year, new lands are put under cultivation and close to three-quarters of Missouri's land area is still in farms. Over 70 percent of the farm cash income comes from livestock; Missouri's hog production is fourth in the country, her beef production sixth, her turkey production fourth. Field crops range from corn and soybeans to winter wheat, apples and peaches, alfalfa and popcorn. Soybeans, the wonder crop of the postwar era, account for almost $200 million in annual sales. Cotton, a mighty factor when the Bootheel was first drained and cultivated, now accounts for only $31 million. The number of farms, 266,000 in 1920, shrank to 142,000 by 1970, and farm employment dropped 34 percent (down to 147,800) in the decade of the 1960s alone. Negroes, the faithful field workers of yesteryear, have largely been forced off the land: they own only 196 of the 86,503 full-time producing farms. But corporate farming has also made little headway; only 546 farms are in that category. As one newspaper writer observed in 1971: "Horses, coal-oil lamps and outdoor privies have all but disappeared from the Missouri rural scene, but at least one thing remains the same. Farming is still largely a family venture."

The third largest factor in the state's economy (some $800 million annually) is tourism; each year over two million out-of-staters visit the Ozarks, the state parks scattered across Missouri, and her great cities.

One reason for the distant feeling, at least on the part of city people toward their country cousins, may be the location of the state capital in smallish (32,407) Jefferson City, arbitrarily located halfway between the two metropolitan centers on the Missouri River. The location is so undesirable that a law had to be passed *requiring* state officials to live there.

The largest of the second-rank cities is Springfield (population 120,-096), situated southwesterly in the midst of the Ozarks. Despite its growing population and a sophisticated central pedestrian plaza and walkways installed by enterprising local businessmen, Springfield has maintained its informal, personal character, and every Friday night the Ozark farmers can be seen arriving in overalls to do their weekly shopping. Springfield is a dairy center, the site of Kraft Food Company's biggest cheese plant, and has diversified industry (Zenith Corporation and the Lily Tulip Paper Company, for instance).

The third largest city in Missouri is Independence (population 111,662), a town twice made famous: first by the great Western trails of the mid-19th century, secondly by Harry Truman. The Santa Fe Trail, starting in the 1830s, began its westward trek from Independence; so did the Oregon Trail, some 2,000 miles long (twice the length of the Santa Fe), over incredibly rough terrain, for years the principal conduit of trade and settlers into the huge Northwestern frontier. Today, Independence is actually a suburb of Kansas City, though Truman always insisted the relationship was the other way around. Finished with his job as Chief Executive, Harry Truman retreated into the comfortable big Victorian house with gables and jigsaw work and several porches that had been Mrs. Truman's family home, wrote his memoirs, presided over construction of the Truman Presidential Library, and made scarcely a ripple in national life again.

Close behind Independence on the population chart is St. Joseph

(72,691 souls), a Missouri River town north of Kansas City that was the start of the California Trail in the past century and also the eastern terminus of the Pony Express run in 1860 and 1861. Today St. Joseph lives primarily off its stockyards and grain trade and enjoys a small share of national attention as the home town of Walter Cronkite, the place to which Cronkite sometimes repairs to gauge the national mood and see what Middle America thinks of television newscasters.

Among other Missouri cities is Columbia (58,804), which exists and prospers almost entirely from the University of Missouri and other colleges; Joplin (39,256), once famed as America's richest and wildest lead and zinc mining camp and now a quieter place of diversified industries; and St. Charles (31,834), which scored an amazing 50 percent population growth in the 1960s as a result of its strategic location on the new Interstate Route 70. In St. Charles, a 19th-century atmosphere has been recreated in an historical district that was transformed from near-slum conditions to a variety of new restaurants and antique and specialty shops, including the restored first capitol of the state of Missouri.

Some hundred miles north of St. Louis lies the almost legendary town of Hannibal, which was home for Samuel Clemens during his boyhood and setting for many incidents from *Huckleberry Finn* and other Mark Twain novels. In many ways, Hannibal is as it has always been, as Twain wrote: "a white town drowsing in the sunshine of a summer's morning . . . [beside] the majestic, the magnificent Mississippi, rolling its mile-wide tide along, shining in the sun." A writer for *Fortune* spent several days in Hannibal and found almost the perfect prototype of the small city bypassed by the currents of the times.*

For half a century, close to 20,000 people have lived in Hannibal; by the 1960s the flight of young people to big cities for jobs was so severe that the town actually suffered a net loss of some 1,400. A run-of-the-mill central shopping district is being eclipsed by the modern bane of almost every small-town merchant, the outlying shopping center (in Hannibal, appropriately named for Huck Finn). The great Hannibal industries of yesteryear have all closed up shop and left town—railroads, sawmills, breweries, shoe factories. A small food-processing plant, a college yearbook printer, and a cement plant, none with a payroll of much more than 200, are the principal employers today. The whole town suffers from low incomes and a quarter of the households live on less than $3,000 a year.

Hannibalians have a justified feeling of being buffeted about by exterior forces they cannot control or understand. The town's retailing is dominated by chain stores and franchise operators. The decision to close down or move out Hannibal factories is made in faraway executive offices or even by cold-hearted conglomerates. And the strange outer world to which their children must escape for decent jobs seems to be filled—if the television is to be believed—with problems of crime, disorder, racial discord, immorality, disrespect for God and country. Hannibal lies in "Little Dixie" and has voted

* Harold B. Meyers, "How They See It in Hannibal, Mo.," *Fortune*, December 1969.

Democratic since the Civil War, but its democracy is not that of the big cities, the black, or the dispossessed. The Vietnam war received firm support, though four Hannibal boys lost their lives in it. Hannibal schools were desegregated right after the Supreme Court's 1954 decision, but Negroes were held to menial jobs and kept at the outer fringes of the town's political and social life.

The essential quandary of Hannibal—and I would apply the same to thousands of other small cities and towns across America—is how, on the one hand, to remain an oasis of quiet and decency in a turbulent, sometimes degenerate world (as Hannibalians would put it, "a real good place to raise kids") while also creating a healthy economic base to stop the town from dying. But economic change means sailing into uncharted waters—perhaps trade union disputes, boycotts, or militant racism. Thus the dilemma, since Hannibal above all yearns for the cry of "mark twain!"—safe water ahead.

So much for small-town Missouri. Now we move to her two great metropolises, the other worlds within the same state borders.

The New Spirit of St. Louis

"I have found a situation where I intend establishing a settlement, which in the future, shall become one of the most beautiful cities in the world." These first words about St. Louis were written by the French fur trader Pierre Laclède in 1763. Two hundred and five years later, with completion of the city's great and delicate Arch of shimmering stainless steel, towering 630 feet at the spot along the Mississippi where Laclède had decided on a settlement, the Frenchman's prophecy at last seemed to have a chance of fulfillment.

St. Louis, one adds quickly in candor, is still not exactly a swinging town; her German ancestry, plus wealth and maturity, have often led to complacency. Frightfully confined in 19th-century borders, she has lost her economic heart to her suburbs. In 1971, in a report on derelict housing in seven large cities, the National Urban League and the Center for Community Change stated that St. Louis was "farther down the road toward total abandonment of the central city than any other city in our sample and probably than any city in the country." This writer would suggest that Newark and Detroit are in still worse shape, but early in 1972 *The Wall Street Journal* stated flatly that St. Louis "is dying of blight." Essentially, the city's postwar story is one of steady population and economic decline, but rises and falls in her spirit: depression up to the mid-1950s, a period of revival and hope under a courageous professor-mayor from the mid-1950s to the mid-1960s, and the decline into the slough of decay and despair in which she finds herself today.

However uncertain St. Louis's future may appear in the 1970s, the glory of the late Eero Saarinen's achievement in the Gateway Arch is not to be gainsaid. Even the most callous observer, standing at ground zero below the Arch and looking upward to see its flanks brushed diagonally by the sun and then following with the eye as the clear, cutting lines of the great arms soar upward to a delicate, perfect juncture at an apex so far above, must be awed by what has been wrought. And then as one moves through the city streets, both in the vast areas cleared by urban renewal and among the decaying tenements, there is always the glance toward the levee and the Arch, and suddenly each part of the urban scene is enhanced or in some measure redeemed by its lordly neighbor. (My architect friend, Stuart Knoop, takes a different view. To him, the Arch is "an enormous *tour de force* leading to and from nothing.")

The Arch symbolizes St. Louis, the gateway, the central point on the Mississippi from which trapper, explorer, sodbuster, and railroader launched their adventures into the virgin West. In its first century and a half, St. Louis was first a great port of call for the steamers,* then a great railhead and manufacturing center (everything from shoes to beer). In the 1860s, James Eads made engineering history by building his graceful triple-span steel arch bridge across the turbulent waters of the Mississippi at St. Louis, a job the experts had said couldn't be done. (The bridge still stands, near the Arch.) After the Louisiana Purchase Exposition of 1904, however, St. Louis seemed to lose its grandeur. Prohibition forced the great brewing industry to close down. Corruption afflicted the city government, and the land along the river which Laclède had first sighted became a grimy, smoky no man's land of decaying warehouses and tenements, many deserted.

It was in 1933, in the depths of the Great Depression, that the first flicker of renewal appeared. The proposal was made to tear out a great chunk of land on the water's edge as a memorial to Thomas Jefferson and the Louisiana Purchase of the central heartland which he had consummated. President Roosevelt in 1935 established by executive order the "Jefferson National Expansion Memorial National Historic Site" and with joint local-federal financing the first building demolition started four years later.

With the advent of World War II, development ground to a halt. Then for years there was total deadlock because the federal government refused to finance further demolition until the unsightly elevated railroad tracks along the river had been removed.

Enter now the central figure of St. Louis' postwar history, Raymond R. Tucker. Readers of Gunther's *Inside U.S.A.* may recall Tucker as the professor of chemical engineering at Washington University who helped pioneer the civic ordinances which began a clean-up of St. Louis' smoke-clogged air by restricting use of furnaces burning the sludgy bituminous coal of the great southern Illinois fields. One day in 1953 Tucker received a call—"out of the

* By the 1860s, St. Louis had a larger river shipping capacity than any port on the Mississippi. According to one account: "Double-decked, tall-stacked, curlicue-bedizened, white-painted packet boats, the favorites of the Currier and Ives engravers, were changing St. Louis from a wilderness settlement into a city dreaming of national and world importance. They made possible the sensational boom of the 1840s and 1850s, checked only temporarily by the Civil War." The boats, it must be remembered, carried not only goods but people. "For all their finery, the boats brought land-hungry settlers and traders in such numbers that their cabin floors were frequently carpeted with sleepers. Often, a missionary held a prayer meeting at one end of a boat's deck, while a gambler with ruffled shirt, gaudy vest, Paris boots, and easy manners, plied his trade at the other. The boat would stop at a landing, a handful of people would go ashore, and soon another settlement would rise in the wilderness."

blue," as he described it—from civic-business leader Sidney Salomon, asking him to run for mayor. Tucker bucked the old-line Democratic organization and won. And one of the major achievements of Tucker's first years in office was to get agreement on suppressing the tracks, so that the memorial plans could proceed.

In the meantime Eero Saarinen had won the competition for the memorial design. Saarinen would later relate to Tucker how he got the idea for the Archway. He had been concerned to find a true gateway symbol; one day he was holding a chain between his hands and saw its form as an inverted catenary. Saarinen's inspiration was simply to flip the form over and build it. Of course the implementation would prove to be one of the great engineering feats of the century. (Sadly, Saarinen died in 1961 at the age of 51, never to behold the realization of his greatest conception.)

St. Louis: The Tucker Years

The conditions in St. Louis which Tucker discovered on taking office were little less than appalling. As he recalled them in a 1969 interview: "The city government had a $4 million deficit. We had a late report that 50 percent of the housing in the city was blighted or close to it. There had been no capital improvements in years. We needed lighting and new streets, our hospitals were in a sad state of repair, we needed more parks and playgrounds. Not a single major expressway came through the city of St. Louis."

With magnificent energy, Tucker went to work to turn St. Louis around. To solve the city's recurring financial crises, he lobbied successfully with the state legislature to make permanent a .5 percent payroll tax (now 1 percent), chargeable to residents and commuters alike. The tax was then approved by the voters, by a 6–1 margin. Then Tucker went to all of the city's business and leading civic groups and asked them for their ideas on what needed to be done to give St. Louis a new birth. Starting with grass roots citizens meetings, a list of $250 million worth of projects emerged; the shopping list was then scaled down to $110 million and incorporated in 23 separate bond issues which the people approved overwhelmingly (their approval due in no small part to their own participation in formulating the list of projects). With this money work could begin on the massive Mill Creek Valley urban renewal project in the heart of the city, recreation centers, lighting, hospital improvements and one brand new hospital, and a new workhouse to replace an old dark hole of Calcutta on the south side of town. The long-standing impasse on highways was broken and a number of major freeways built.

Important backing for Tucker's proposals came from a businessmen's group known as Civic Progress, patterned after the Allegheny Conference in Pittsburgh. Still very much alive today, Civic Progress consists of the chief executive officers of the large locally domiciled companies—McDonnell-Douglas, Monsanto, Emerson Electric, Interco, Brown Shoe, Anheuser-

Busch, Ralston-Purina, and the like—plus the heads of Washington and St. Louis universities and the mayor of St. Louis and supervisor of St. Louis County. All are of sufficient rank to commit their companies or organizations to new policies. A president of Civic Progress in the late '60s and early '70s, for instance, was Frederic M. Peirce, chairman of the board of the General American Life Insurance Company of St. Louis, chairman of the Federal Reserve Board in St. Louis, and a trustee of Washington University. Civic Progress has no staff and develops no new projects on its own; its function rather is to provide backing, where it sees a need, for the ideas of government and other private groups. The group gave its complete backing to Tucker's first bond issues to start the rehabilitation of downtown St. Louis, the earnings tax, the stadium that was built near the Archway, and a $90 million water pollution bond issue. In the late 1960s, Civic Progress decided that civil rights was the key issue and sparked a local NAB (National Alliance of Businessmen) employment effort for blacks, with James McDonnell as regional NAB chairman and Peirce as metropolitan St. Louis chairman. Civic Progress also set up "BYU"—Business, YMCA, and the Urban League—a privately financed training facility for the hard-core unemployed.

When I interviewed Peirce at the turn of the decade, he was taking a lead through the Chamber of Commerce in efforts to get mass transit for St. Louis. The proposal was for a seven-corridor system of 86 miles, with five lines in St. Louis and surrounding St. Louis County, and a connection to two lines serving East St. Louis and other communities on the Illinois side of the Mississippi. The system would cost about $1.4 billion, with two-thirds of the cost paid by the federal government and the remainder raised by local bond issues. Local officials were warning that without mass transit, St. Louis's crushing peak-hour traffic could expand from the present three or four hours a day to 16 hours a day by 1990, and double-decking of expressways might be necessary. If studies made by the East-West Gateway Coordinating Council were correct, the proposed rapid transit system could be a tremendous boon for the entire St. Louis area. The value of land, mainly near transit stations, would rise by $635 million, commuters would save $81 million in time and expenses by 1990, and the system would create 143,000 jobs between 1973 and 1990, including 6,400 construction jobs over 10 years of construction. One official said the system would mean adding the employment equivalent of two McDonnell-Douglas Corporations to the area economy. Scenting the immense possibilities for investment and jobs, local financial institutions and labor unions lined up enthusiastically behind the project. Another interested party was the St. Louis Car Division of General Steel Industries, one of the nation's largest makers of rail cars.

Following his initial election in 1953, Tucker stayed on as mayor for 12 years. He died in 1970, but the fruits of his endeavors literally dominate the St. Louis skyline today. Ironically, Tucker could never get the city Democratic organization to support him; the greatest plurality he amassed in any primary election was less than 1,500 votes. But today it is difficult to find a St. Louis leader who does not recall Tucker with reverence and affection.

Under Tucker, some 40 blocks of the immediate Archway area were cleared and are now filled with new office buildings, apartments, and an interesting circular-design hotel. The new stadium is not far distant.

Close to the Arch, however, are some delightful remembrances of St. Louis's past. Along the levee, between the Arch and the river, several restored steamboats are moored, housing restaurants and theatre, a kind of throwback to the pre-railroad era when the levee was lined with majestic sternwheelers, sidewheelers, and excursion boats that discharged their passengers onto the cobblestoned streets of the old riverfront. Immediately to its west, the Arch frames the old domed Courthouse of Greek Revival architecture, where slaves once stood on the auction block and Dred Scott's lawyers in 1857 pleaded for his freedom.

To the north of the Arch, in the so-called "Laclède's Landing" area, are several blocks of narrow, steep streets of rundown old brick buildings, some with exquisite iron frontings, the last remnant of the riverfront of yesteryear. A typical urban renewal plan to level the area and substitute standard high-rises was approved by the city government, but in 1969 it reversed itself and adopted a substitute that will preserve the character of the Landing by keeping about half the existing structures while adding two 24-story towers. There will be plazas and courtyards, shops and theatres, a place of human scale and value.

The entire Archway area is but a fraction of the 12 square miles—a fifth of its total land area—which St. Louis has bulldozed or completely rehabil itated. The massive 465-acre Mill Creek Valley project, in a post civil war residential district that had become a desperate Negro slum, lies 20 blocks west of the Arch; before demolition the attractions of Mill Creek included 5,000 outhouses, almost universally substandard conditions, high crime and disease rates—a place where children were often bitten by rats or burned to death. But, as was typical of the massive projects in the first wave of urban renewal (New Haven and Washington's Southwest were others), the demolition of vast inner-city stretches was not followed by rapid reconstruction but by a generation of weeds. The planners had simply failed to get firm commitments on who would build on the vacated territory. When suggestions were made that a major national developer like Zeckendorf (then in his heyday) be invited in to implement a comprehensive rebuilding plan, St. Louis real estate interests objected and got parcels of the project for themselves.

What has been wrought in Mill Creek is a classic failure in city design. Despite its "Valley" title, Mill Creek lies principally on heights directly west of center city; in fact it is on the city's major east-west geographic axis, with magnificent views (smog permitting) toward the Archway. But consider what St. Louis's axis is, and might have been. Starting from the Archway on the Mississippi, the axis proceeds westward on Market Street to the old Courthouse and a central Mall, the new stadium, a federal building, the curiously domed 19th-century City Hall, the municipal court and post office, and the ornate and once great Union Station. With the major banks and stores nearby, this area is the very heart of St. Louis's life. But then, abruptly, Market Street swings southward; if one continued straight westward, he would run smack up against an expressway; unordered Mill Creek is on the other side. As Philadelphia planner Edmund Bacon is reported to have said, what begins with a bang peters out in a whimper of confusion.

All too much of Mill Creek is filled with helter-skelter apartments and low-rise industrial buildings of an undistinguished sort, and on what should be the great axis marching westward one finds a Holiday Inn, three used car lots, Al's Radiator Shop, and similar enhancements. The irony is that a few miles farther westward, once Mill Creek is passed, one comes on St. Louis University and then lovely Forest Park (site of the 1904 Exposition, the Municipal Opera, McDonnell Planetarium, City Museum, and Zoo), beyond that Washington University, and a few miles farther out the towering high-rises of a new suburban metropolis, Clayton, of which we will say more later. Mill Creek could have been a vital connecting link for all of St. Louis and a distinguished contribution to a great city's architecture. But instead it stands—no matter how urgent the demolition of the old slums may have been—as a monument to Negro removal and mediocre planning.

On 11 of Mill Creek's 465 acres, however, a residential community of distinction was built by New York developer James H. Scheuer (who later became a Congressman from the Bronx). This 656-unit complex, Laclede Town, consists of pastel-toned, stage-set-like town houses designed by an imaginative Washington architect, Chloethiel Woodard Smith. (The design is almost identical to Capitol Park, the largest single development in Washington's Southwest, also begun by Scheuer and designed by Mrs. Smith.) Laclede Town's houses were built for moderate income families ($7,250 to $11,500 a year income) under limited profit provisions of the Federal Housing Act; from the start successful racial integration (70 percent white, 30 percent black) was achieved, a rarity for St. Louis or other inner cities. Laclede Town offers an intermingling of small grocery stores, laundromat, outdoor cafe, and pub among the residences (a great victory for Scheuer and Mrs. Smith over the FHA bureaucrats). Partly because of that Jane Jacobs type of mix, there has been real conviviality and neighborhood spirit among the residents, who were described by one writer as "a microcosm of the total city, a confluence of race, age and class unique to downtown U.S.A."

St. Louis also has a number of other large urban renewal projects, both residential and industrial, scattered north and south along the waterfront and inland all the way to the city's western border. Many stress rehabilitation rather than the bulldozer technique; none involved so much demolition as Mill Creek Valley. St. Louis has hundreds of blocks of 19th-century houses and shops that are finally being rehabilitated; one group has purchased over 300 century-old homes and is redoing them. There is hope that in the traditionally German working-class neighborhood around the Soulard Market, the St. Louis farmers' market that has been in operation since the 1700s, a new community with some of the oldentimes flavor can be created.

St. Louis: The Nightmare Now

Despite the myriad initiatives of the Tucker years, the St. Louis of today is in desperate straits. Of America's 25 largest cities, its population decline was the most rapid in the 1960s—19 percent (from 750,026 down to 607,718). In that decade alone, 183,000 more people left the city than moved in. The federal government rates 29 percent of the city's total housing stock as "poor" and another 40 percent as "fair" but below standard. Business confidence in the inner city has eroded alarmingly. When I visited St. Louis to do interviews for this book, I spent several nights as a guest at the delightful old University Club at Grand and Washington Boulevards, enjoying the mellow 18th-century decor and high-ceilinged Williamsburg dining room. But early in 1972 that prestigious club, well described by the *Post-Dispatch* as "a showcase of St. Louis's professional talent," announced it would abandon its downtown site and decamp for the suburbs—following the flight of its membership.

Even the gleaming Arch can be part of a very disturbing experience in St. Louis today. It is possible to ride one of the eerie half-train, half-elevator capsules that creep up inside the legs of the Archway to the top, where one can peer out through narrow slit windows to the terrain below. To the east, directly below, there is the silt-laden Mississippi, and just beyond it the industrial nothingsville called East St. Louis. To the west, there is the sprinkling of fine new and old civic buildings—but then the vast expanses of uninspired urban terrain. And everywhere there is a thick pall of foul air. Ray Tucker may have cleaned up the sooty black air of the coal-burning age, but the factories and automobiles of the intervening years have totally undone his work.

As one departs the few blocks close to the Archway and the rebuilding it sparked, one often finds himself following long, dreary streets of marginal businesses. The slums of St. Louis are of the grimmest kind: countless deserted and boarded-up buildings (the highest percentage of any American city), trash in the streets, rotting wood and brick structures of uncertain to ancient vintage.

The most frightening site of all, however, is less than 20 years old: the Pruitt-Igoe public housing project, built in 1954, which by general consensus of the nation's urbanologists, is the most monumental failure of public housing ever constructed in America. Fifty-five acres of dilapidated old shotgun frame houses were demolished to make way for this mammoth project, a ghastly series of 33 characterless, forbidding high-rises. The original idea, as with most public housing, had been to provide temporary shelter for upwardly mobile whites and some blacks. In the first years after Pruitt-Igoe's construction in 1954, an income balance was maintained with only about

10 percent of the tenants on any form of welfare. But in the late 1950s, urged on by a hard-pressed welfare department, the housing authority began to admit more welfare recipients and many recent emigrés from deepest Dixie. Eventually, Pruitt-Igoe became all black and, in the words of the *Globe-Democrat*, "a terrified city within a worried city, a matriarchal society of too many unwed or deserted mothers and uncontrollable children, a community on the dole with an estimated two-thirds receiving some sort of welfare assistance, most surviving on ADC handouts."

Around 1970, federal and local housing authorities decided that Pruitt-Igoe was such a disaster that it would either have to be demolished entirely or the top stories chopped off all the buildings to create an entirely new environment. To anyone who had visited the project, the decision came as no surprise. I had been struck first by the acres and acres of broken windows —more than half in many buildings. Streets between the high rises were covered with old glass and tin cans. Not a minimum of maintenance seemed to be taking place (although millions were poured into a vain effort at rehabilitation in the late 1960s). Inside hallways or corridors, one was assailed by the stench of mixed garbage, urine, and assorted debris. Lights were often broken and the elevators vandalized. Gangs, narcotics pushers, and robbers frequented the corridors and stairwells, making them a place of terror for other tenants. (And indeed the real tragedy of such a place lay in the quiet desperation of its law-abiding, decent tenants, who found themselves the object of violent assault and victims of the brutalized welfare concentration camp they lived in.)

Pruitt-Igoe's woes were exacerbated by the cheap corner-cutting of the designers and federal overseers at the time of its construction. There were no balconies or breezeways; steampipes were uncovered and frequently burned children; and, perhaps most appalling of all, each building had but a single elevator, which stopped only every third floor, meaning that tenants had to risk being assaulted in stairwells each time they came or went. Some, in terror, tried never to leave their apartments. In 1969 alone, police reported 10 murders, 14 rapes and 129 assaults in the project, and vandalism was running at $1,700 a day. Ironically, Pruitt-Igoe received a national design award the year it was built, and its praises were sung in national architectural magazines. It seems only fair to record that it was the St. Louis firm of Hellmuth, Obata & Kassenbaum which did the basic design, assisted by such national greats as Minoru Yamasaki. But it was the federal government, Tucker told me, that insisted on many of the cost-cutting steps in construction that would lead to such misery later.

Pruitt-Igoe was originally designed for 10,000 people; eventually 12,000 to 20,000 people crowded in. But as the terror quotient mounted and the physical deterioration advanced, the people began to flee. Early in 1972, the housing authority brought in demolition experts who demolished a pair of the 12-story buildings on the theory that reduced density might improve living conditions in Pruitt-Igoe. But no provision was ever made for clearing the rubble, and the problem was compounded later in 1972 when the St.

Louis Housing Authority, its general operating funds at the exhaustion point, voted to close down *all* public housing in the city sometime in 1973. That disaster was avoided by a stopgap federal subsidy of $3.7 million, temporarily averting eviction of St. Louis's 25,000 public housing tenants. The housing authority was faced by bankruptcy for three major reasons: escalating maintenance costs, the refusal of the city of St. Louis to provide even the most minimal services without charge, and the decreased rent income that had resulted from a 1969 public housing rent strike in the city. At the end of that strike, the authority agreed to limit rents—which had in some cases been as high as 70 percent of tenants' income—to one-quarter of their income. The federal government then inaugurated a subsidy program for local authorities like the one in St. Louis, but it was proving to be too little, too late.

Before that final stage, I talked with Father John Shocklee, the engaging Irish pastor of St. Bridgit's Roman Catholic Church, immediately adjacent to Pruitt-Igoe. He accused the city of St. Louis of making the project a scapegoat, pointing to the tenants' bad behavior when the real evil lay with the city and its own callous indifference. The project, Shocklee pointed out, was set in the midst of an already existent slum so that it would not impinge on middle-class residential areas. Not a single store was allowed in the project, though its population was many times that of small towns with a full array of services.

I asked Father Shocklee how the church could operate effectively in this desperate setting. "We're the wrong color and on someone else's turf and know it," he replied. His parish stayed fairly well aloof from the internal politicking of the anti-poverty warriors and other local black organizations, though it did work in close accord with neighboring Protestant parishes. The tenants did accept help in educational and self-help projects, Shocklee said. and the church's sacramental role continued. "But I can't really improve this place," he added. "My job is to help people to get out."

Father Shocklee said the church and its personnel were rarely molested, despite the high crime rate of the neighborhood. But the church was tightly barred, and while I spoke to Shocklee, someone outside shattered the window of my rented car in an unsuccessful theft attempt. "Now you're getting an appreciation of the place," Shocklee said. He noted that on the nearby corner, where 12,000 cars pass by each day, young hoodlums push a pedestrian button and then rob motorists of their watches and handbags.

Most of the area around Pruitt-Igoe consists of long, dreary blocks of decrepit brick row houses, badly in need of renovation. But there are some signs of hope. Directly across the street from the project's high-rises, the Brown Shoe Company showed great courage in 1969 by building a new plant with jobs for 200 local people. The company had fled the city for the suburbs some 16 years earlier.

And just a few blocks distant, a public housing project of a totally different character may be found. It is Carr Square, several blocks of neat two- and three-story row houses behind carefully tended lawns, a pleasant neighborhood with nothing wrong with it that a little paint couldn't fix up. The basic lesson, which one learns in city after city: high-rise public housing is an invitation to disaster; low-rise has a real chance of success.

No simple formulas, however, are likely to save St. Louis. The path of blight, which took a northwesterly path as whites fled to suburbia with an assist of the federal interstate highway program and GI and Federal Housing Administration mortgage insurance, now threatens to invade the hitherto largely white and relatively stable southern parts of the city. In 1971 it was reported that speculators had bought up pieces of slum property, insured them for several times their worth, and then hired "torchmen" to burn them down. Proposals for subsidized housing are stubbornly resisted in white sections of the city, not to mention the suburbs. *The Wall Street Journal* has noted that once St. Louis's business-financial community completed Mill Creek, it let its interest in the city wane. Most existing housing is 60 to 80 years old, and no major new low-income housing has been started since the 1950s. Only a few new ideas were in the air in the early 1970s: a potential $37 million downtown low- to middle-income housing project, which received $2 million in seed money from Ralston Purina Company; the idea of two Washington University professors for a major "new-town-in-town" project to be funded by the federal government; and the concept of Danforth Foundation planners for a regional development organization as a privately capitalized public utility. But behind it all there was the gnawing fear that St. Louis might already have reached the point of no return.

St. Louis: Politics and Institutions of a Great City

St. Louis was Republican until the New Deal, then moved Democratic because of the Depression and President Roosevelt's support for repeal of Prohibition. For years the city had a typical big-city boss in the late Thomas Callanan; in 1952, however, Callanan opposed Stuart Symington and lost even his own post as sheriff. Since then power has been split, generally among the Democrats holding the multiplicity of elected citywide offices (ranging from the treasurer, who has 79 political appointees under him, to the collector of revenue, the license collector, the circuit attorney, the coroner—some 12 in all). Against this array of petty chiefs, who are said to collect a "lug" (one percent of salary) from all their workers for political expenditures, the mayor has only 18 appointees and whatever moral authority he can muster. Tucker's achievements in office are thus all the more remarkable.

Most of the citywide officeholders, many veterans of a quarter century in the same post, have been long on patronage details and short on hard work. Hopes have risen in recent years, however, for more competent and progressive government simply because some savvy young organization Democrats are winning these jobs. One of them is Treasurer Paul M. Berra, an alert man in his forties who doubles as Democratic city chairman. Berra was earlier in the state legislature and has a full grasp of both state and city government. He defends the system that elected him but seems genuinely concerned about integrity and efficiency in government and recognizes full well that the days of big "delivered" vote blocs are over. "It used to be possible to predict the vote in your ward down to a very close percentage," he told me. "Now voters are much more educated, influenced by television and the like. . . . To run for office now, you have to have proper credentials, some newspaper or TV support, some general popular appeal. It's not enough to have the wards for you. This is for the good, since it gives the organization incentive to look for younger, presentable candidates." Berra backs the patronage system because it gives people a stake in their jobs. But the low salaries mean that patronage jobs attract mostly women today, and often jobs go begging.

Despite its dwindling vote base (down from 303,650 in 1960 to 183,526 in 1972), the city still produces a strong Democratic vote edge in most elections. In 1960, for instance, John Kennedy carried the city by 100,988 votes, and in 1968 Hubert Humphrey had an 84,798-vote plurality there. (In 1972, by contrast, McGovern won by only 44,038 votes in the city.)

Like so many cities its size, St. Louis faces overwhelming fiscal problems. The public schools are an example: in the 15 years up to 1969, tax revenue in the city went down 15 percent while school enrollment increased by 26,000. The result: obsolete buildings, teachers leaving the city in droves for better paying jobs and work conditions. Mayor Alfonso J. Cervantes, Tucker's successor and a scrappy liberal, reported in 1969 that the elevators at the city hospitals were breaking down frequently but couldn't be replaced because of finances; that there was only enough money to resurface the city streets every 50 years; that the city had 820 vacant and vandalized buildings, a menace for children who play in them and a haven for rapists; and finally that the fire department needed 108 men, 54 to fill vacancies, but didn't have the money to hire them.

The problems of running the city are not simplified by the presence of a substantial Mafia pocket in St. Louis, which has many connections into organized labor, the city government, and the ruling Democratic party. *Life* magazine once alleged, without conclusive evidence, that Mayor Cervantes has extensive personal ties to the Mafia. Early in 1972, Cervantes' close friend and choice as head of the St. Louis Commission on Crime and Law Enforcement, attorney Morris Shenker, resigned that post in the wake of complaints by some Justice Department officials. They were reportedly upset by Shenker's alleged ties to the underworld through business dealings and as an attorney for criminal elements, and were alarmed at the prospect of Shenker handling part of a $20 million federal grant to fight crime in St. Louis. Cervantes is a gregarious, energetic politician; his administration has lacked the class of Ray Tucker's, but he has tried to be a supersalesman for St. Louis and has refused to become pessimistic about its chances for survival. He is frequently at odds with the powers in Jefferson City, which he claims have made St. Louis a stepchild. One local reporter described Cervantes to me as "the thickest-skinned politician I've ever seen, impervious to furiously negative newspaper editorials, a man of many talents but limited knowledge, and a great love for handshaking. If Tucker was the statesman, Cervantes is the politician, always at home with the boys in the back room."

St. Louis's more positive contributions to the U.S.A. include a fine symphony orchestra and of course the St. Louis Cardinals baseball team (four times world champions since 1944). Two good newspapers, the illustrious *Post-Dispatch* founded by Joseph Pulitzer and the industrious *Globe-Democrat,* grace the city scene. The *Post-Dispatch* still offers the finest international coverage of any inland American newspaper and does a creditable job on local and state affairs, though it has frequently been scooped by the *Globe-Democrat* on local scandals. The *Globe-Democrat,* owned by the Newhouse chain, is the more conservative of the two papers. The public affairs programming of the city's television stations, on the other hand, leaves much to be desired, even though the *Post-Dispatch* owns the local NBC station and the *Globe-Democrat* the ABC outlet. The stations have failed, for instance, to mine the potential for documentaries on such issues as the St. Louis Mafia, corrupt unions, and the spoils system in city government.

St. Louis University, an excellent Jesuit institution, and especially Washington University, have grown in stature in the postwar years. Washington University provided a home for the Masters' inventive and daring Sex Research Project (now more conservatively titled the Reproductive Biology Research Foundation), and is also the home base of one of the nation's leading ecologists, Dr. Barry Commoner. It was with major aid from Washington University that St. Louis in 1966 established the first detoxification and emergency care center in the United States for persons found drunk in public. Instead of jailing drunks, the St. Louis police automatically bring them in for medical attention and rehabilitation counseling; the process relieves the courts and jails of common inebriates, cuts down on repeat offenses, and saves hundreds of thousands of dollars each year in penal system expenditures.*

St. Louis's economy has grown, albeit behind the national pace, since World War II. The area's traditional top products were beer and shoes. "But we would have had a grim scene," a *Post-Dispatch* editor told me, "if we hadn't had Monsanto, the fantastic growth of McDonnell-Douglas, and our continuing role as a major auto assembler." (GM, Ford, and Chrysler all assemble in St. Louis, making it second only to Detroit in the auto industry.) In 1971 *St. Louis Commerce* could boast that "from canoes to carburetors, from freight cars to brake fluid, this area turns out more transportation equipment and components then any other place on earth." The product list also includes trucks, rapid transit and subway cars, aircraft, space vehicles, railway cars, towboats, and barges—in total value of some $3 billion a year, accounting for 61,000 jobs. The chemical industry, led by Monsanto, Ameri-

* Detoxification centers are beginning to spread in the U.S.A., and ought to. Almost half the arrests in the country are related to drunkenness and cost governments a total of at least $100 million. In St. Louis, ex-patients of the Detoxification Center have shown remarkable results in abstinence levels and ability to return to gainful employment, thus reducing the need for future arrests.

can Zinc, and Mallinckrodt, produces goods worth some $1 billion each year in the St. Louis area, providing jobs for 25,000. By contrast, the old-time leaders seem small indeed: the beverage industry, with 8,000 employees, and shoes—hard-hit by foreign competition—with only 6,700 jobs in 1970 (compared to 50,000 before World War II). Among the industries now much larger than beer and shoes are machinery, metal products, printing, and food processing.

If space permitted, much could be written of Monsanto's research "campus" and global activities directed from its suburban headquarters outside St. Louis. Started as a three-man plant producing saccharin in 1901, Monsanto has grown to a $2-billion-a-year firm. More than a quarter of its sales are abroad, making the firm one of the world's largest diversified manufacturers and a truly multinational company. Monsanto's profit margins of recent years, however, have failed to match those of its two larger competitors, Du Pont and Dow Chemical, and there have been a number of executive shakeups that culminated in 1972 when the firm, for the first time in its 71-year history, went outside its own ranks to hire a new president and chief operating officer—John W. Hanley, formerly of Procter & Gamble. A year before, Monsanto had scrapped an unwieldy organization of nine operating divisions, replacing them with a group of four largely autonomous, worldwide operating companies: commercial products, industrial chemicals, polymers and petrochemicals, and textiles. Some of Monsanto's top officers, like Edwin J. Putzell, Jr., the firm's secretary, general counsel, and vice president, wield immense influence, both through their own company and as advisers in national policy making. Putzell was reportedly once offered the directorship of the Central Intelligence Agency. (The role of men like Putzell in national life usually goes undetected by the Eastern and national press. Another St. Louis businessman, Samuel Krupnick, is known locally as a leading merchandising and advertising executive—but few people realize that he is influential in national Jewish affairs and has been an adviser to Presidents, even dispatched by them on international missions.)

An amazing industrial success story surrounds James S. ("Old Mac") McDonnell, the Arkansas-bred Scotsman who began his aviation firm with two employees in 40-by-40 quarters at Lambert Field in 1939 and by 1967 had absorbed once mighty Douglas Aircraft of California. Making space capsules, fighter planes, and commercial jets (including the new DC-10 trijet), McDonnell-Douglas has a payroll of 35,000 in the St. Louis area alone. Sales of $2.1 billion made it the country's 45th largest industrial corporation in 1971—a year when the company, through various tax loopholes, avoided paying any federal corporate income tax at all on its net profit of $144 million. A gigantic new world headquarters building was scheduled for completion in St. Louis County in 1973.

St. Louis's role as a transportation center cannot be ignored, and has a lot to do with its crucial location—on the Mississippi, at the juncture point of three interstate highways, 30 miles from the center of population of the U.S. (in nearby Illinois), and equidistant between the Canadian border and the Gulf of Mexico. The city has historically been the hub of upriver transportation on the Mississippi, and barge traffic has been booming in the postwar era so that—in the words of one observer—"the Mississippi looks more like a busy freeway than the slow-moving Old Man River of the past." Just in the past decade, the volume of cargo has more than doubled on the busy stretch between St. Louis and Cairo, Illinois, the juncture point with the Ohio. River transportation is a major reason that St. Louis has advanced to the ranks of the top ten metropolitan areas producing manufactures for foreign markets.

St. Louis is also the second largest trucking center of the United States, with 200 common carriers, and reminds the visitor that it is also the second largest railroad center of America, with 16 trunk line railroads. The latter boast, however, has an element of pathos. Recall these words from Gunther's *Inside U.S.A.*:

> For the romance of the railroads, St. Louis is the first city in the nation, and its Union Station has the largest traffic in the world. The sleek trains are lined up like race horses in adjoining stalls—the Pennsylvania's Spirit of St. Louis and the New York Central's Knickerbocker to New York, the Baltimore & Ohio's Diplomat to Washington, and all the streamliners: The Rebel (Mobile & Ohio) to New Orleans, the Ann Rutledge (Alton) to Chicago, the Burlington Zephyrs to the Twin Cities, the Colorado Eagle (Missouri Pacific) to Denver, the Green Diamond (Illinois Central) to Chicago, and several to Texas and points south and west.

Today the cavernous Union Station is a desolate no man's land, down to a paltry eight arrivals and departures from a one-time peak of 143 each day. There have been suggestions, however, to rebuild the huge train shed behind the station into a four-level structure that could tie together all modes of passenger transportation: air, rail, bus, automobile, and eventually rapid transit. The station's "headhouse," which has been proclaimed a National Historic Landmark, would be revamped to hold a large shopping mall, restaurants, and offices. One of the interesting questions is what airports might be served. St. Louis's own Lambert Field will probably be retained for short-haul flights of less than 500 miles, but there has been heated debate about whether a new and necessary regional airport should be in Missouri or at the most discussed location, several miles south of East St. Louis on the Illinois side of the river.

Black: The Coming Majority in St. Louis

St. Louis is a polyglot of German, Irish, Yankee, Negro, Italian, and Pole with some ethnic fortresses still easy to identify—the southside "Dutch" (Germans) in aging, blue-collar neighborhoods where the young people move out and the old folks stay on to vote against bond issues but for Democrats; the insensitively labeled concentration of Italians south of Forest Park on "Dago Hill"; Cass Avenue, where the Poles congregate; the Irish so-called "Kerry Patch" area; Ozark hillbillies on the near south side; wealthier and Republican-voting Yankee stock in Saint Louis Hills on the far southeast side; and then, most important of all for St. Louis's present and future, the big black population belt north of the Archway-Clayton axis.

The black population of St. Louis has reached 41 percent, up from 29 percent in 1960, and is headed toward a majority. During the 1960s, the white population of the city declined by 32 percent while the black population rose by 36 percent. All of the ingredients of conflagration are present: heavy influxes of ill-prepared blacks from the Deep South, substandard housing, an unemployment rate twice that of whites, one of the biggest income gaps between whites and blacks in the entire country, poor schools, bureaucratically snarled welfare at rates almost impossible to live on. Yet despite these problems, there has been no major racial disturbance in St. Louis. "We'd like to delve into the reasons," one newspaperman told me, "but we're afraid to cover the subject for fear black militants would say, there's the white establishment bragging, and then do something radical to prove us wrong."

The peculiarities of the St. Louis political system may offer a clue. There is a big board of aldermen (28 members), each alderman with a single ward, to which he is close; there have been Negro aldermen for many decades, and by 1970 eight were black. The aldermen have tremendous power and patronage influence; in their own wards they control an old-style organization firmly entrenched at the grass roots through job favors, Christmas baskets, and helping people over the hump with late rent. The result of all this is that St. Louis blacks do feel they have some recourse through the political system. Militants find it hard to get a strong following in the black community, and traditional Negro groups—the Urban League, NAACP and black businessmen—have failed to provide unified strong leadership outside the political structure.

Like all major cities, St. Louis has witnessed a hardening in race relations in recent years. But again, the situation is not altogether discouraging. Under a project called "Block Partnership," groups of comfortable white suburbanites, usually connected with a church, team up with the residents of individual inner-city blocks to help them clear up and paint up their neighborhoods, install locks, or start day care centers; the dangers of paternalism seem to have been overcome and some real trusts and friendships created.

St. Louis blacks did produce a new thing in 1968 by electing one of their number, 37-year-old William L. Clay, to Congress under a new districting bill. Clay got his political start as a labor union (Steamfitters) official and St. Louis alderman. His initial reputation was as a militant, serving 112 days in prison for participating in a 1963 demonstration to get black tellers at a local bank. By the time Clay went to Congress, he was considered a shade less militant than in his CORE days, but still a very articulate man. When the Black Caucus was formed in the U.S. House, Clay quickly became one of its driving forces. He is the most outspoken politician in the U.S. for establishing facilities at prisons so that men may have their wives with them.

"It is inhuman treatment to divorce a man from normal sexual relationships; with wives at the prisons, we could greatly reduce homosexuality and attacks," he argues.

The election of Clay from the heavily black north side does not necessarily mean that blacks are on the verge of an early takeover of St. Louis City Hall; even with the huge numbers of Negroes moving into St. Louis in the 1960s, the percentage which blacks represented of the total voters registered remained under one-third, apparently because of apathy among the new black residents. So far, there have not been enough registration and get-out-the-vote efforts among Negro voters to change this picture significantly in the 1970s.

St. Louis: A Unique Teamster Boss and the Weird Saga of the Steamfitters

One of the most remarkable men in organized labor in the country today is Harold J. Gibbons, president of the powerful St. Louis-based Teamsters Local 688, president of the Missouri-Kansas Council of Teamsters, and a vice-president of the national union. The latter post is one that came to him after he had managed James R. Hoffa's successful campaign for the Teamster presidency in 1957. Son of a coal miner from Archibald Patch, Pennsylvania, graduate of the University of Wisconsin, member of the Socialist Party for several years in the 1930s, and a man known as a hellraiser and agitator in his early union organizing days, Gibbons was once despised and scorned by the St. Louis business establishment. In 1958 hearings before the McClellan committee's Senate investigation of labor racketeering, Gibbons was subjected to brutal cross-questioning over his organizing tactics by Senator Robert F. Kennedy and by McClellan, who called him a man who "encouraged and condoned violence."

Gibbons, however, was able to justify or cover most of the tactics he had employed and emerged largely unscathed from the Senate hearings. In the 1960s, as Local 688 grew in power, Gibbons found himself drawn into the business leaders' decision-making apparatus of St. Louis to such a degree that he commented, "I'm getting suspicious of myself; the doors are so wide open to me now." Among Local 688's undertakings were construction of a health and education camp for Teamsters in a rural setting outside the city, a full medical service for Teamsters (financed by employer payments of 3½ percent of payroll), and construction of two handsome high-rise apartments for limited income persons through federal mortgage guarantees.

Still a tough, hard-rock union organizer, Gibbons is now regarded as an unusually perceptive urban affairs scholar and effective fighter for civil rights in the city of St. Louis. On his desk one can see copies of *Daedalus, Foreign Affairs,* and books on environmental control, politics, and urban planning. Gibbons' predilection for social issues, which led to an eventual falling out with Hoffa (and an end to his hopes of succeeding Hoffa), also equipped him well to participate with the United Auto Workers on local political and social projects. Now a gray-haired man in his early sixties, surviving on some four hours sleep a night as he travels across his region and the country, Gibbons symbolizes the amazing transformation of advanced elements in American labor leadership in a time when the old battles over "socialism" versus "capitalism" have yielded to far more complex social change.

Another St. Louis labor story, of quite a different stripe, must be told: that of the Pipefitters Local No. 562, more familiarly known as the Steamfitters. Wracked by the death of several of its leaders, including the bloody murder of one early in 1972, Local No. 562 today faces an uncertain future at best. But between 1947 and the late 1960s, according to its own head, this remarkable organization of less than 5,000 members dispensed $18 million in cold cash to political candidates and causes. The money was gathered in a very simple way: by assessing members a dollar *a day* for the union's "flower fund"—officially the Voluntary Political, Educational, Legislative, Charity and Defense Fund. No other U.S. union, as far as I can learn, has ever dunned its members so heavily. But the Steamfitters members could easily afford the tab, since they are one of the highest paid unions in the entire United States—receiving $7.77 an hour in 1968, with contract increases to $10.37 an hour in 1973, plus double pay for overtime on construction jobs. Members' annual salaries range from a rock bottom of $15,000 a year to more than $50,000. (With a strong nudge from the federal government, the Steamfitters finally enrolled their first Negro journeyman in the late '60s.)

Heavy gifts from the Steamfitters went not only to Democratic candidates in St. Louis municipal elections but to influential statewide figures including Warren E. Hearnes and Edward V. Long and, on the national scene, to President Johnson's reelection campaign in 1964 and Hubert Humphrey in 1968.

The longtime head of the Steamfitters was one Lawrence L. Callanan. Larry Callanan's colorful career included a 1927 conviction for armed robbery and a 1954 conviction on charges of extorting $28,000 from a construction company. When Callanan went to prison in the '50s, his assistant business manager, John L. (Doc) Lawler ran the union in his stead. Lawler also served as the St. Louis Democratic chairman. After serving half his 12-year sentence for extortion, Callanan received a pardon from President Johnson in 1964. Shortly after this, the Steamfitters' "flower fund" made campaign gifts totaling $50,000 to Mr. Johnson's reelection campaign. The joint counsel in the effort to get Callanan returned to active control of Local 562 after his initial parole on the extortion term were Morris Shenker, the Teamster lawyer whose fees to Sen. Edward Long sparked the *Life* campaign that led to Long's defeat, and Paul Porter of the powerful Washington law firm of Arnold and Porter from which Abe Fortas was appointed to the Supreme Court by Lyndon Johnson. Paul Porter was treasurer of the 1964 Friends of LBJ to which the Steamfitters channeled half their $50,000 for the LBJ reelection effort.

Thus the reader will not be entirely surprised to learn that the Justice Department leadership under the Johnson administration was very unhappy when aggressive government attorneys began an investigation in 1967 of the Steamfitters and their political activities. By the spring of 1968, a large body of evidence had been accumulated to show that the Steamfitters in 1964 and 1965 had made contributions of about $150,000 to federal campaigns through the "voluntary fund," which in fact was not so voluntary and was a creature of the union. (Direct union gifts to federal campaigns are a violation of the Corrupt Practices Act.) But political pressure kept blocking indictments; it was not until enterprising reporters for the St. Louis *Globe-Democrat* and *The Wall Street Journal* wrote incriminating exposés of the foot-dragging by high-ranking Justice Department officials that the administration finally permitted the indictments to be filed. (Two *Globe-Democrat* reporters received a Pulitzer Prize for their stories.) The Steamfitters, Callanan, Lawler, and another official of the union were all charged with conspiring to make illegal political contributions. Four months later a federal jury convicted them, and a one-year prison sentence was imposed.

That summer of 1968, the Steamfitters had their last big political fling in an all-out effort to keep their favorite Senator, Edward V. Long, in office. By some accounts, fully a third to a half of Long's primary campaign fund was supplied by the Teamsters. By the end of that year, it was clear that Steamfitters backing could be a kiss of death (as it had apparently been for Senator Long), and that Larry Callanan would never again make mayors and governors and Senators and influence Presidents of the United States. But no one could have predicted the weird chain of events that would take place in 1971–72.

Aging and in poor health for some years, Callanan died of natural causes in May 1971. Edward J. Steska, regarded by his contemporaries in the labor movement as a bright and honest leader, succeeded to Callanan's post as the Steamfitters' chief. Steska was primarily a bread-and-butter unionist, and he left the management of the union's political interests to "Doc" Lawler. Then, in January 1972, Lawler died of a heart attack. Soon Steska was in a bitter struggle for control with a group of former convicts whom Callanan had brought into the union. A fearless man, Steska began to lift the union cards of hoodlum-connected union members who frequently spent their time drinking and gambling on the job and "could not even thread a pipe." (The result of such practices is to escalate the price of construction jobs by millions of dollars, undermining the regional economy and general welfare.) In the process of his crackdown, Steska must have stepped on the toes of the Syrian and Italian gangs that had infiltrated the union. Less than a month after he had taken over from Lawler, Steska was found dead in his office, five bullet holes in his body.

St. Louis County: Suburban Outcast that Outgrew Its Parent

The city of St. Louis is actually a half-moon-shaped enclave of 61 square miles crowded up against the Mississippi River; to its north, west, and south lie the vast suburban reaches of St. Louis County, an entirely separate governmental jurisdiction. Up to 1876, the city was part of the county, but the city chafed under the inefficient administration of its country cousins. The conservative Dutchmen who ran St. Louis asked for and got a divorce.

At the time, the separation seemed eminently sensible; there were 310,000 people in the city to only 40,000 in the remainder of the county, and the city could see no reason to pay high taxes to a county government that gave them little in return. Today, of course, the tables are turned. From a largely pastoral setting with some 240,000 people in 1940, St. Louis County mushroomed by 1970 into a thickly settled suburban concentration of 951,-352. St. Louis city, by contrast, slipped in population from 816,048 people in 1940 to 622,236 in 1970. And while those remaining in the city fret over problems of race, crime, short budgets, and paralyzed government, St. Louis County enjoys one of the most efficient governments in the United States and is happy to run its affairs on a modest annual budget of some $32 million. The city's woes are made all the worse by the flight of industry to the county; in 16 years the number of jobs in the county has increased five times while those in the city declined by 20 percent. More than half the jobs of the St. Louis metropolitan area are now outside the city.

Under the circumstances, a remarriage would make eminent sense, especially for the city. The wealth of the suburbs is precisely what the city needs to solve its problems. But the last merger proposals, in 1959 and 1962, were overwhelmingly rejected by the voters. Direct unification seems even less probable now, since countyites would tremble at the thought of taking on the city problems which they fled to suburbia to avoid in the first place, while blacks in the city would quickly detect a plot to dilute their mounting electoral strength. The more likely course is that bodies like the area's East-West Gateway Council (which St. Louis County, interestingly, took the lead in founding) will gain increasing authority to deal with problems of obvious area-wide scope like air and water pollution and possibly even police protection. Such devices, however, fail to attack the central problem: the concentration of problems in one jurisdiction (the city), the wealth to solve them in another (the county). In the 1960s the county seat, Clayton, even stole the march on St. Louis city in what is supposed to be center city's major strength: high-rise office buildings, progenitors of a heavy tax base. For several years, there was much more big office construction in Clayton than in St. Louis. What was once a drowsy county seat with a ramshackle courthouse now pridefully calls itself "the new executive city" and "the second downtown." In 1971, the city of St. Louis was happy to hear that one of America's great corporations, General Dynamics, would move its headquarters there from New York City. The company explained that "St. Louis is well located, offers excellent facilities at reasonable cost and provides major living advantages for our people." A few months later, it turned out that St. Louis had nothing to cheer about: where General Dynamics headquarters really went was to Clayton.

This is not to suggest that St. Louis County is an uninterrupted Garden of Eden. It has some superb residential communities but also a number of early postwar subdivisions built so sloppily that they will soon be slums. The county also has a balkanized political structure of 95 separate municipalities or, counting special school and fire districts, 160 separate taxing jurisdictions. Some of the little towns are little more than tax dodges; 65 have no parks, 10 have no police department. The county government has the almost impossible job of filling the chinks of unmet services and trying to coordinate the whole.

County government, however, has reformed itself fundamentally in the past several years and recently obtained home-rule powers that will permit it to override the decisions of self-minded towns within it. Up to 1950, the county labored under the same kind of troika—three "judges" who combine executive and legislative functions—that most rural American counties still have. In that year, a new charter with an elected single supervisor was substituted, together with an elected council. But the charter left intact the system of electing about a dozen other officials directly, ranging from the recorder of deeds to the highway engineer. The attitudes of the county's semirural days carried on fairly well intact: the courthouse was a cesspool of politics, county administration grossly inefficient.

To clean up the mess, the county's voters in 1962 chose as county supervisor a 41-year-old Jewish banker and former Republican state legislator, Lawrence K. Roos. Roos is a calm man with a face that has been likened to "a patrician Bert Lahr," but he started a whirlwind of activity in the Clayton courthouse. One of the toughest conflict-of-interest laws in U.S. local government was adopted. A master zoning ordinace set forth a pattern of physical development for the county for years ahead. Bond issues for capital improvements, rejected by the people for several years previously because of their distrust of the old county government, were passed; they financed new roads, parks, and public buildings, a new juvenile center, and a $20 million governmental center at Clayton. Recommendations of a "little Hoover commission" appointed by Roos led to automation of numerous county record-keeping functions, saving hundreds of thousands of dollars each year. An air pollution control ordinance, with some of the stiffest regulations in the country, was adopted. In 1968 a new county charter abolished direct election of the miscellaneous department heads who had operated independently of the supervisor. Finally, the 1969 legislature authorized and the state's voters subsequently approved a county home-rule amendment which will permit the county government to rearrange governmental units within the county, even against their will.

Before his election, Roos claims, St. Louis County was undefined in people's minds despite its fast-growing population and economic weight. "Now," he says, "we've brought county government to the same position and prestige as the government of St. Louis City." Across the country, Roos suggests, county government is suddenly evolving as one of the better vehicles of coordination over vast metropolitan jurisdictions.

Roos was reelected overwhelmingly in 1966 and 1970, and the county became increasingly Republican in its voting patterns. But, like true suburbia, it knows how to split its ticket, even against a favorite son. In 1968 Roos ran for governor against the popular Warren Hearnes. Not only did Roos lose the state by a wide margin, but he lost St. Louis County as well.

Despite its proximity to the concentrated Negro population bloc of the city, St. Louis County is still practically all white. Less than 5 percent of the county's population is Negro, and most of that is in one area that itself adjoins the city ghetto. Hearings before the U.S. Civil Rights Commission revealed a vicious circle of government and business practices that abet segregation and exclusion of Negroes, including a rapid deterioration in government services in an area that begins to turn black, refusal of insurance companies to grant policies in integrated or black neighborhoods, efforts by real estate dealers to keep blacks from white communities and whites from buying in integrated or black sections, and foot-dragging on equal employment practices by the leading employer, McDonnell-Douglas. Of the aerospace firm's 33,000 St. Louis employees in one recent year, only 2,500 were black, including none of its salesmen or foremen and only 41 of its approximately 5,000 officials and managers. Housing discrimination in the suburban areas near the McDonnell-Douglas plant prevents many Negroes from working there, it was reported. In a decade, less than 1 percent of the 84,000 home purchasers assisted by federal mortgage insurance in St. Louis County were Negro. To most people in St. Louis County, subsidized housing means integrated housing, and in Roos's words, his constituents have a "deep, almost hysterical resistance" to subsidized housing.

Just how hysterical that resistance can be was illustrated in 1970 in the improbably named town of Black Jack—an old farming community where large blackjack oaks once grew some 20 miles north of St. Louis, filled in recent years by subdivisions in the $30,000–$35,000 range. The St. Louis Inter-Religious Center for Urban Affairs had been looking for a site to build subsidized housing for people just above the poverty line but still not wealthy enough to buy standard suburban housing, and just before December 1969 purchased 11.9 acres of a former bean field in Black Jack. Word of the proposed integrated project for 210 family apartment units caused consternation in Black Jack, and the outraged local citizenry quickly petitioned the St. Louis County Council for permission to incorporate so that they could control their own zoning. As *Newsweek* later reported, "After hundreds of tight-lipped Black Jack housewives picketed the county courthouse, carrying American flags and flanked by their children, the council granted the incorporation request. Thereupon Black Jack hastily formed a zoning board and promptly banned all multifamily housing—including the proposed project."

Black Jack's zoning posed a major policy decision for the Nixon Administration: what to do about racially motivated zoning in the exclusionary suburbs? Attorney General John Mitchell reportedly favored a cautious approach, while Housing and Urban Development Secretary George Romney wanted a strong response to open up the suburbs. Romney finally won out, and in June 1971 the Justice Department sued Black Jack, charging that its zoning action would deprive the prospective residents of the low-income housing project of their right to fair housing under the Civil Rights Act of 1968. It was the first separate suit of its nature ever filed by the federal government. Its final resolution could go far to determine a vital policy question of the 1970s: how far can predominantly white suburban communities go to zone out the blacks of the center cities? As one of the attorneys in the case said, "The outcome of the Black Jack case could prove to suburban housing what the landmark 1954 case of Brown vs. Board of Education was to school integration."

"Ev'rythin's Up to Date in Kansas City"

St. Louis and Kansas City are in the same state, both happen to be situated on rivers, and both have poor satellite cities across the water (East St. Louis, Illinois, and Kansas City, Kansas). But the essential similarity stops there.

Where St. Louis is cosmopolitan and perhaps even haughty with her Archway and cultural adornments, Kansas City conveys an infectious Midwestern warmth and pretends to be little more than the overgrown cowtown she is. Where St. Louis is Germanic and settled and often pessimistic about her future, Kansas City is more nativist American, more open and free-spirted, and expects a better tomorrow. Where St. Louis looks East and South, Kansas City looks West. Where St. Louis is the home town of many great corporations, Kansas City is principally a branch town. Where St. Louis is hemmed in to the same 60 square miles of land she lived in 85 years ago, Kansas City has steadily annexed neighboring territory, including a number of fairly affluent suburbs, until it is now 316 square miles in size. As a result, while St. Louis city's population is declining, Kansas City's is growing—now 507,087, up from 399,178 in 1940. The Kansas City metropolitan area has 849,409 people within Missouri and another 246,474 in the state of Kansas. Where St. Louis on occasion feels overwhelmed by its race problems, Kansas City thinks it can deal with them.*

Both cities have Democratic hearts, but Republicanism in St. Louis's suburbs sometimes cancels out the solid Democratic vote the organization produces in center city. In the Kansas City area, on the other hand, there is only one large Republican suburb which might dilute the city's Democratic strength, but it is safely tucked away across the state line in Kansas, Finally, where occasional scandals and old-time politics still carry the day in St. Louis, Kansas City has so effectively reformed herself since the days of Pendergast that her politics seem a bit pedestrian—or, as one group of Kansas Citians told me, as if the good church folks took over in 1940 and everything has been quiet ever since.

It has been 30 years since the obese body of Tom Pendergast was lowered into its grave, but the memory of this most venal of American political

* Kansas City's Negro population, now 22 percent, has risen only moderately over the past two decades. But despite its superior overall race relations record in the past few years, Kansas City experienced one serious racial outbreak, in which six Negroes were shot to death, in 1968.

bosses lingers on. During his heyday, Kansas City was one of the nation's safest gangster hangouts, a city with a hoodlum reputation second only to Chicago's. Underworld killings were climaxed by the famous Union Station massacre of 1933, when four officers and gangster Frank Nash were murdered. A red light district a dozen blocks in size flourished, protected and collected from by the police under Pendergast's control. Gambling joints ran wide open, narcotics were easily available. Everyone paid protection money to the machine, and even the cop on the beat had to contribute 10 percent of his salary to the local ward or precinct "club." Pendergast had a "legitimate" business, too—cement. Massive government buildings, still standing, were built with Pendergast cement, and Kansas Citians still remind one that Brush Creek, winding for several miles through the city, is literally paved with the stuff.

Pendergast was rising in power in Kansas City from the first decade of the century on, but it was 1932 before he became statewide boss as well. The governor's veto of a congressional redistricting bill forced all of Missouri's congressmen to run at large that year. Since Pendergast could turn in astronomical margins for his hand-picked candidates in Kansas City, leading Democrats from across the state paid homage to the king. He exacted a price—making them all agree to support his candidates for other state offices. In the Democratic primary, the Pendergast candidates scored an almost clean sweep and Pendergast then controlled statewide primaries for the rest of the decade. Whenever he lacked enough honest votes, he could conjure up as many as 60,000 "ghost" ballots; there were several election-day murders of poll workers for reform candidates.

When rural voters showed signs of losing confidence in the Kansas City machine, Pendergast won them back by supporting a friendly small-town war veteran, Harry S Truman, for county judge. Truman apparently never shared in the machine's spoils, but he did help give it a respectable "front." During the mid-1930s, while Truman served in Washington as a U.S. Senator, Pendergast tapped vast new sources of patronage through the New Deal's public works projects in Missouri.

Defenses of Pendergast have been few and far between, so I will relate this one told me by a prominent Missouri lawyer.

> When Pendergast was at his prime, he had Kansas City in his hip pocket, worked well with Swampeast [the Bootheel] and Little Dixie, and even had Republican business support. Times were rough economically and Kansas City and Chicago were in a battle to the death for the cattle market—which both have lost since. The cattle came to market in trainloads. The question was, would ranchers ship to Kansas City or Chicago? If they went to Kansas City under Pendergast, they were paid promptly. Kansas City was wide open with gambling, prostitution, even restaurants with nude waitresses. Cattlemen knew that no matter how drunk they got, they'd never be robbed. If you were a cattleman, you could safely lie down in the gutter and go to sleep with $5,000 in your pocket and wake up the next morning and it would still be there. Business people thus supported Pendergast. He was absolutely a man of his word.

In the late '30s, things began to turn sour for Pendergast. A governor he had helped elect turned against him and cut off his state patronage. A federal income tax investigation revealed that Pendergast had concealed a $750,000 payoff in an insurance scandal. Tried and convicted of tax evasion, Pendergast served 15 months in Leavenworth and died shortly after being paroled.

The indignation of an aroused citizenry finally ousted the Pendergast machine. The Kansas City newspapers had checked out the voting lists and found thousands of ghost voters on the rolls, leading to federal convictions of 280 of the party faithful for vote fraud. Preparing for the 1940 city elections, a group of Kansas City housewives organized a woman's crusade to clean house. Backed enthusiastically by the Kansas City *Star*, a reform party, the Citizens Association, then elected its own council and mayor in April 1940. The new mayor, John B. Gage, installed as city manager L.P. Cookingham of Saginaw, Michigan, who instituted an honest, efficient government, laid plans for a highly successful Kansas City highway system, and sparked the city's big annexation effort. Slowly, Kansas City lost this gangster reputation, though there were rather embarrassing incidents like the 1950 murder of political-hoodlum Charles Binaggio and his bodyguard. On the wall above the corpses was a large photograph of Harry Truman, then President of the United States. Truman must have been horrified to see who was using his portrait for wall decor and/or political effect.

For three decades, the Citizens Association—basically nonpartisan, but with a strong admixture of efficient Republican business types—remained the dominant force in Kansas City government. It was temporarily displaced by the old-line Democratic factions between 1959 and 1963, an event that resulted in Cookingham's ouster, but the governmental chaos that resulted helped the Citizens elect one of their chief stars of all time, Ilus Davis, as mayor in 1963. A cool, reserved man with a steel-trap mind, completely selfless in his approach to government, the very antithesis of the traditional big-city politician, Davis provided superb leadership for the city until his retirement in 1971. The man elected to succeed him was Dr. Charles B. Wheeler, Jr., a pathologist and lawyer who actually beat the Citizens Association candidate to win the mayoralty. But Wheeler is also an antithesis, in a different way, of old-time politics: a maverick and reformer by temperament, more of a talker than a manager, and an appealing man who has managed, among other things, to save the Kansas City Philharmonic from threatened extinction. The city manager's office continues to wield wide-ranging powers. Civil service, instead of patronage, controls jobs in city government. Kansas City does have a typical big city's fiscal headaches, intensified by refusal of the voters to approve sufficiently increased sales or property taxes to keep city services operating at satisfactory levels. But in terms of structure rather than policies, about the most serious criticism I heard of Kansas City government today is that the nonpartisan technicians in charge lack good access to Jefferson City, simply because the name of the game is politics, and they lack partisan connections.

But when the Pendergast machine was thrown out of City Hall, the voters did not go across the street and throw his organization out of the Jackson County courthouse. The county government stagnated for a quarter century, with no new hospitals, no juvenile home or other needed facilities. Scandals of the old style reappeared not infrequently; in 1946, for instance, the door was blown off a safe at the courthouse and election records being used in a vote-fraud prosecution were stolen. Numerous murders of politicians and gangsters racked the city, and in 1952 the county sheriff was not a little embarrassed when nine men broke out of the jail on the 12th floor of the courthouse, their escape from the supposedly escape-proof prison abetted by an acetylene torch left carelessly behind the bars.

Pendergast's nephew and heir apparent, Jim, tried to hold the old organization together, but it was evident he lacked Uncle Tom's skills. The old-line machine actually broke up into a number of feudal baronies, each faction controlling a number of wards and parceling out patronage to the faithful. But eventually even this comfortable agreement began to teeter. Blacks began to object to having white bosses control their precincts. And the once mighty north side "delivery wards," largely Italian areas that turned in astronomical majorities for the machine, were bled of population through highway construction and urban renewal. In 1964 the factions tried to get together on a purge of Congressman Richard Bolling, a man too liberal and fiercely independent for their taste, but Bolling mounted a model grass-roots and media campaign and whipped them with two-thirds of the primary vote.

Change finally came to county government in the 1960s when one Charles E. Curry, elected presiding judge (administrative officer) of the county, turned out to be a skilled reformer. A "Committee for County Progress" was formed and in 1964 elected one of its candidates (Dr. Charles Wheeler, now Kansas City's mayor) to the office of coroner. This followed scandals involving kickbacks to morticians. In the 1966 election, Curry's Committee for County Progress decided to apply some professional modern political techniques to an old-line county. It hired Matt Reese, a professional campaign organizer who had worked with the Kennedys, to survey voter attitudes and help formulate strategy. Almost the entire reform slate, which had promised to do away with all patronage, was elected. Among the winning candidates was a Negro circuit court clerk candidate, the first black man to win countywide office.

The reformers won again in 1968, and though they fell to quarreling among themselves thereafter, and even though Governor Hearnes seemed to undercut them by hiring several old-line Democratic machine men, it did seem that a permanent change had been made. One development of vital importance was the approval by the voters, in 1970, of home rule and a new charter form of government for Jackson County. Curry, who was retiring as presiding judge that year, made effective use of Reese-style methods to get up the large number of signatures needed to put the charter proposal on the ballot, even risking a substantial sum of his own money. Then, in three weeks just before the election, Curry raised $100,000 for the pro-charter campaign. Thus it was that charter government, which had gone down to defeat in campaigns 10 and 20 years before, was approved—a splendid legacy of the Curry-reform years. As a result, Jackson County now has a single strong executive in place of the old judge troika, and a 15-member county legislature, and it is no longer required to go to Jefferson City for permission to make changes, minor and major, in its own form of operation.

Strangers are apt to think of Kansas City as being a flat place, like the Kansas in its name; actually it is a quite attractive town of trees and rolling (and some very steep) hills, its principal buildings on high land a few blocks from the Missouri River. A lot of the downtown is dominated by fortresslike 1930s skyscrapers including the 500-foot City Hall and the county courthouse, built of Pendergast cement. But there is a lot of modern construction as well, including a massive new federal building for which Representative Bolling claims credit.

One of Kansas City's most stolid old buildings is the Hotel Muehlebach, glowingly described by John Gunther. During his Presidency, Harry Truman made the Muehlebach a kind of mid-America White House, and on the 11th floor one will still find a piano he used to play. Yet the New York *Times* reported, in some sadness, early in 1972:

> Ten Presidents have slept in the 57-year old Hotel Muehlebach, each reassured of his importance and dignity by its hand-rubbed oak paneling, its burnished marble floors and gleaming brass fittings.
>
> But the last time Richard Nixon was in town, he checked into the Holiday Inn, a brand new plate glass and plastic palace topped by a spinning restaurant, au formica. . . .
>
> Hard times are now besetting the Muehlebach, where the paneling has begun to fade, the marble is showing grime, the brass is dull with tarnish and the occupancy rate is down to 60 percent, the traditional break-even point.*

Kansas City has slums, but they lack the grimness of St. Louis and many Eastern cities. Urban renewal has proceeded at a steady rate and with some outstanding results. In one formerly blighted area near the center city is the handsomest residential community for moderate-income blacks I have seen anywhere in the United States. Known as Parade Homes, it consists of 510 town houses on 50 acres, built in garden style with meticulous landscaping and maintenance. Reynolds Aluminum was the original sponsor and builder, and infused colors directly into the metal sidings of the houses. The project is a cooperative; one makes a $125 down payment and then pays $60 a month for a two-bedroom unit or $76 a month for a three-bedroom unit. Lawrence K. Parker, the resident manager, embodies all the standard middle-class values of neatness and propriety which whites expect from Negroes; he assured me that he did a thorough credit and "social" check on each appli-

* The *Times* noted that old hostelries like the Muehlebach are losing customers all over America, slipping into shoddiness, some even closing, because of their location in economically sick downtown areas. In 1948, the year Truman beat Thomas E. Dewey, there were 30,000 hotels and 26,000 motels in the country; in 1972 there were 21,000 hotels and 43,500 motels. "Every 30 hours," the paper reported, "somewhere in downtown America, an old hotel closes. Every 30 hours, somewhere in suburban America, a new motel opens."

cant to live at Parade Homes and that "we put up with no foolisness whatsoever" from tenants. "My philosophy," he said, "is to take your home and make it so beautiful and attractive the white suburbanite will wish he lived where you do. This place is to be an example of how well a Negro community can exist and maintain itself." (There are a handful of whites in the project, mostly through intermarriages; my reaction was that moderate-income whites of Kansas City had missed one of the nation's best housing offers.)

Among the other creditable urban renewal projects of Kansas City are Hospital Hill, with a number of excellently designed new medical facilities in a parklike setting, and nearby, the ambitious new $200 million "Crown Center" being built by Hallmark Cards (which has its headquarters in the city). Crown Center will eventually cover 85 acres and include over a million feet of office space, 2,400 apartment units, and three hotels. The architect-planner, Edward Larrabee Barnes of New York, has been told by Hallmark that it is in no great hurry to recoup its investment; the early prognostication was that some extremely distinguished design—and new vitality for center-city—would result. Among other features, there will be a network of pedestrian bridges that will enable Crown Center's residents and guests to move between hotels, apartment buildings, and offices without encountering automobiles; as a focal point of the network of walkways, there will be an 80,000-square-foot bridge scheduled to contain a pavilion of restaurants, shops, and theatres. Kansas Citians were happy to see the first section of Crown Center start in the late 1960s, since the location was directly atop a scraggly, weed-ridden ridge opposite Union Station, called Signboard Hill for its unsightly billboards.

Hospital Hill and Crown Center are some 10 blocks south of center city; about 20 blocks farther south is a remarkable complex of public and private facilities which includes the renowned William Rockhill Nelson Gallery of Art, the Kansas City Art Institute and Museum, the Midwest Research Institute, and Country Club Plaza, the first totally planned shopping center in the United States (1923). Would that subsequent shopping centers had matched Country Club Plaza's quality; it is built in Spanish style architecture, has subdued signs and design control throughout, and includes a delightful outdoor cafe. One can criticize the Spanish motif as scarcely indigenous to Kansas City, but the overall effect is pleasant, which is about all I have ever learned to demand of shopping centers. This section of Kansas City and adjoining parts of Johnson County, Kansas, also contain some of the country's most tasteful residential sections.

Kansas Citians differ sharply on the quality of their cultural life. The boosters point to some of the fine museums, repertory theatre, lyric theatre, and art institute, saying few cities can equal the quality. Others report a reserve or tentativeness among Kansas City people in regard to the fine arts and say there is a failure to relate to the region in cultural activities.

Kansas City still has its stockyards, but they play a subsidiary role in the city's economy today. Mayor Davis told me that almost all major branches of American industry are represented in Kansas City except shipbuilding and tobacco processing. The larger employers include Ford, TWA, Western Electric, Hallmark, GM, and Armco Steel. Kansas City competes with St. Louis to be the second largest U.S. auto assembly city outside of Detroit. The city is regional headquarters for many federal offices, which employ 23,000 people, so that the feds are the largest single employer. Over the postwar years, Kansas City's economy has grown at about the national pace —and much faster than the rest of the Midwest.

That growth seems likely to continue. One reason is that the city is a major financial capital for industry and agriculture in the six-state Missouri-Kansas-Oklahoma-Iowa-Nebraska-Arkansas region; it is among the top five cities in the country in the amount of activity with respondent banks; check clearings were below $25 billion in 1960, are now over $50 billion. (This may mark a change in the area's traditional shortage of risk capital, which has precluded it from "taking off" like a Dallas, Houston, or Denver.) A second force behind present-day growth is the new Kansas City International Airport, opened in 1972. The new airport location, about 16 miles northwest of downtown, is over 5,000 acres, one of the continent's largest; it includes TWA's international overhaul facilities and is attracting new airport-related industries. Over 7,900 persons work at the new airport complex, a figure expected to double within a decade. The new airport, in fact, is designed to handle up to 10 million passengers a year by 1980, if necessary. It shares the innovative "gate-arrival" system of the new Dallas-Fort Worth airport, in which a single terminal building is replaced by a series of C-shaped terminals with interior parking to allow a passenger to park as close as 75 feet from the plane he is planning to take. L. P. Cookingham masterminded the new airport planning by arranging purchase of the land in the early 1950s, mainly as a way to keep TWA's overhaul base near Kansas City. He never dreamed that one of the country's largest airports would eventually be built there—an event of immense importance in our time, when an airport, as one financial writer put it, "has the economic importance of a canal or a transcontinental railroad link in the 19th century." The Kansas City government has invested more than a quarter of a billion dollars in the new facility.

Important economic power in Kansas City appears to lie in loose coalition of business leaders, many of them owners and operators of large business, organized into the Civic Council. (The Civic Council concerns itself chiefly with civic projects and lobbying for the area's interests in the state legislature.) The heart of the power structure—where money is involved—is certainly the grouping of a few major banking families.

The city has strong, cohesive black leadership, more effective in winning its goals than its St. Louis counterparts. (Things were not always that way; Kansas City used to discriminate more severely than any other Northern city, and there were many years when the YMCA and Fred Harvey's were the only places a white man could go to lunch with a Negro in downtown Kansas City.) The construction trade unions are a power to be reckoned with; in 1970, for instance, they closed down all construction projects for 196 days in a strike aimed at achieving sky-high, grossly inflationary wage increases. (Some Kansas City economic leaders predicted that it would take years to recover from the strike, which prompted three big corporations to cut back on their construction plans in the city.) Amazingly the United Auto Workers, sparkplugs of socially oriented labor activity in many cities, are tied to the remnants of the Pendergast machine and are of little influence. Following through from the days when they helped dump Pendergast, women remain unusually active in politics and city affairs. Jews are important in business but have only recently been accepted into major clubs like the University and Kansas City Clubs.

On the local scene, the Kansas City *Star* continues to play a significant and fairly conservative role. But its reputation as a great crusading newspaper has vanished almost entirely, and it is little read or referred to outside its immediate region. The decline of the *Star* came in two stages: first, when founder William Rockhill Nelson turned it over to its employees; and second, when the powerful and colorful editor of many years, Roy Roberts, passed away. Despite the split ownership, Roberts had a big chunk of stock and could dominate by his personality as well. The paper had fire, glamour, and class while he lived, and did not hesitate to throw its political weight around. Now, however, six executives have substantially equal shares of stock and paper has all the problems that come when newsmen are worried about profits and advertisers' feelings. Nonetheless the *Star* has fought assiduously over the years for reforms like charter government for Jackson County.

Kansas City's Innovative Foundations

The Kansas City story would be incomplete without mention of one of its most vital institutions, cumbersomely titled The Kansas City Association of Trusts and Foundations. Homer C. Wadsworth, chief of this remarkable organization since its formation in 1949, coordinates a group of family trusts but with a new wrinkle in the foundation field: federating their interests instead of pooling them. On the surface, the difference may not sound significant, but it is. A normal community trust simply puts the resources of lots of small grantors into one large pot, with the distribution generally supervised by bankers and others. Some community trusts, such as Chicago's —with 150 funds worth some $60 million in all—are vital factors in their communities; however, they have a tendency to become appendages of community chests, helping YMCAs and similar "safe" causes.

The Kansas City system, on the other hand, leaves the foundations technically independent; Wadsworth's association, for instance, is purely advisory to its member trusts; they must agree only to pay a share of the association's administrative costs, to receive requests for aid through the association, and to get the association's recommendation on each application. They then make grants under their own names. The trusts thus retain their independence, get staff assistance they might otherwise not afford, and, most important for the community at large, are more likely to put their money into truly inventive and promising projects.

An early decision in Kansas City, Wadsworth relates, was "that we didn't have the money to bail out people's leaky boats, like a community chest deficit. We decided to look at the points where the community was in trouble and then seek fresh ways to meet problems."

In 1949, for instance, Kansas City had mental patients packed into the basements of its general city hospitals and faced a general crisis in psychiatric care. Wadsworth's association therefore founded the Greater Kansas City Mental Health Foundation, which in turn told the city of Kansas City that it would assume complete responsibility for providing mental care services to people admitted to the city's own hospital system, on a cost basis, with the understanding that the new organization could provide teaching, research, and clinical services, aiming at reform of mental care facilities for the metropolitan area population on the Missouri side. The city agreed, and the Mental Health Foundation took charge. One of the first decisions was to scrap two segregated mental health hospitals then planned in favor of a combined (and cheaper) one with Hill-Burton federal aid and local money.

Two decades later, the Greater Kansas City Mental Health Foundation was still providing training and other services, though the clinical services for all of western Missouri had been taken over by a state-operated mental health center—one of three such centers, covering all of the state, which the legislature set up at the association's urging. Thousands of patients were receiving rapid care at the district centers instead of being sent to the rural state mental hospitals to vegetate for the rest of their lives. The association's annual grant to the mental health foundation was only $25,000 to $50,000 a year—simply seed money to generate over $5 million a year from numerous government sources. Washington soon learned that any request from the foundation was thoroughly prepared and thought out and deserved serious attention. The result was to multiply federal funds flowing in.

After the success in psychiatry, Wadsworth assisted in forming another organization to take over the city hospitals in a similar fashion. The result has been the creation of a full medical complex and a medical school. The new organization, the Kansas City General Hospital and Medical Center, Inc., currently operates under a $7 million a year contract with the city to run the hospitals; in fact, the city's money has been doubled by integrating medical care and teaching and research with the care of patients. Outstanding medical personnel were attracted and federal assistance requested for new hospital construction; grants were obtained for a children's hospital and dental center. By 1980, some $150 million worth of new facilities are expected on Hospital Hill. And the goal, as Wadsworth's group sees it, is not only to create a medical school and training ground for doctors, nurses, and technicians, but a base hospital through which a system for delivery of medical care to the entire population can be developed.

A third project of the Kansas City Association has been its Institute for

Community Studies, a kind of community chaplain for the Kansas City area. The institute is a social and cultural research agency, staffed by competent young social scientists, available to the community at large and providing the kind of relevant and needed social science research that universities ought to provide but often do not. In fact, it was the first attempt in the United States to form a nonuniversity group for action research. Many research projects have been in the field of educational reorganization, public affairs (especially problem areas of local government), social services (such as studies of effectiveness of poverty programs), health, hospitals, and geriatrics. Institute studies have been extremely helpful to city government, with the quick availability of trained researchers an invaluable resource.

The Kansas City Association's system of seed money, careful research, and expert management was bound to appeal to family trusts in other cities, and did; now similar associations of trusts are operating in Cleveland, Milwaukee, St. Louis, Boston, and the state of New Hampshire. Thus Tom Pendergast's Kansas City leads in one of the most innovative and promising philanthropic experiments of our times.

IOWA

AGRISTATE EXTRAORDINARY

"It was the funniest damn thing you ever saw," Roswell Garst recalls of the day in 1959 that a visiting Soviet Premier Nikita S. Khrushchev descended on his farm near Coon Rapids, Iowa, to learn something of American agriculture. The Russian leader was accompanied by a veritable army of American and Russian diplomats, translators, assorted officials, national television crewmen, commentators, reporters, photographers, and security men—perhaps the biggest "international" event ever to take place on a farm. "Khrushchev came for symbolic reasons, to show the Russian people his interest in agriculture," Garst told me. "He was a real man. He knew how to laugh and yell. So we laughed and yelled back and forth for three or four hours. I enjoyed him, frankly."

Roswell Garst is a hearty man himself, hale and still strong as a horse in his mid-seventies, encumbered only by a voice box he has to use as a result of an operation to remove a throat cancer. Garst could hardly be called a typical Iowa farmer. His holdings cover thousands of acres of land; he breeds and raises some 2,500 head of beef cattle each year but abjures that other famous Iowa commodity, hogs. He and his family own a highly successful hybrid corn seed business that distributes more than a million bushels each year through the entire corn belt; what's more, the Garst Store, founded by his father in 1869, is the leading retailer of Coon Rapids, and his family runs the local bank as well. Garst is also atypical as a loyal Democrat in Republican Iowa.

Roswell Garst's true distinction is as an agricultural pioneer and unequaled enthusiast for American farming—its past and present. And farming is what Iowa, the great American agristate, is all about. In recent decades, a pervasive technological revolution, boosting farm yields beyond the dreams of earlier decades, has taken place. To produce more than enough food for the nation (if we only knew how to distribute it properly), less than 5 percent of the American people now live on farms, a fifth of the percentage at the start of World War II. Coon Rapids' most famous citizen is a master at explaining how all this came to be:

> I'll tell you a pretty good story. We have quite positive proof that horse breeding was an honorable profession for 2,500 years—since the days of Alexander the Great. We did a helluva job of breeding horses of every kind. Then came two unique individuals: John D. Rockefeller, who was good at taking oil out of the ground and making gasoline, and Henry Ford, who was good at making an internal combustion engine for power on an assembly line. In 40 years, those two men and their associates completely destroyed the effectiveness of 2,500 years of accumulated knowledge on how to breed a horse. What we farmers did was leave our budget for power where it was and between 1930 and 1945 we reduced the number of horses by 25 million. And we bought tractors that equipped us with many times as much power as we had before. That's why we don't need so many farmers.
>
> Here's another pretty good story. There was a great Roman named Pliny the Elder. He lived at the same time as Christ. He wrote that crops that follow legumes yield more. So we studied legumes for 2,000 years and had a wide variety of them. But we finally discovered that crops that follow legumes did better because legumes fed nitrogen into the soil. So then a German scientist perfected a method to capture nitrogen from the air around us, so now we can buy nitrogen for one-tenth the cost of raising legumes. Crop rotation is practically a thing of the past.
>
> Mrs. Garst and I were married in 1922. Up to 1930, and discovery of hybrid corn, our average corn yield was 26 bushels an acre. In the following 15 years we changed to hybrids of corn and the yield went up to 39 bushels an acre—a 50 percent increase. Mechanization—being able to plant the corn in better patterns and at the right times—helped with that too. By 1955 the yield increase seemed to be leveling off. But since then we've learned use of nitrogen fertilizers,* plus insecticides and herbicides, to get a yield of 78 bushels an acre—twice as much as in 1955. Since 1930, we've had a three-times increase in yield. If you add together all our savings, then you find the bushel of corn it took 30 minutes of man time to produce in 1930 takes three minutes today.
>
> We've learned some other things too. In 1930 the average hog went to market at nine or ten months because we lacked protein for rapid growth. Now with soybeans we can market a hog in five or six months. Or take hens. In 1930 the average hen laid 75 eggs in a year. Now she lays nearly 240 eggs a year. Why? The main reason again is soybeans, providing ample proteins for our chickens.

The Corn Belt Today

If there was to be such an explosion of agricultural abundance anywhere on the American continent, it is not surprising that it occurred in Iowa.

* In 1970–71, work was completed on an 1,800-mile pipeline carrying anhydrous ammonia, used for fertilizer because of its high nitrogen content, from the Gulf of Mexico through Louisiana and Arkansas into Missouri, Iowa, and Nebraska. The pungent-smelling ammonia is derived from natural gas. It was estimated that the transportation breakthrough of the fertilizer would facilitate a 12 percent increase in the corn acreage of Iowa alone.

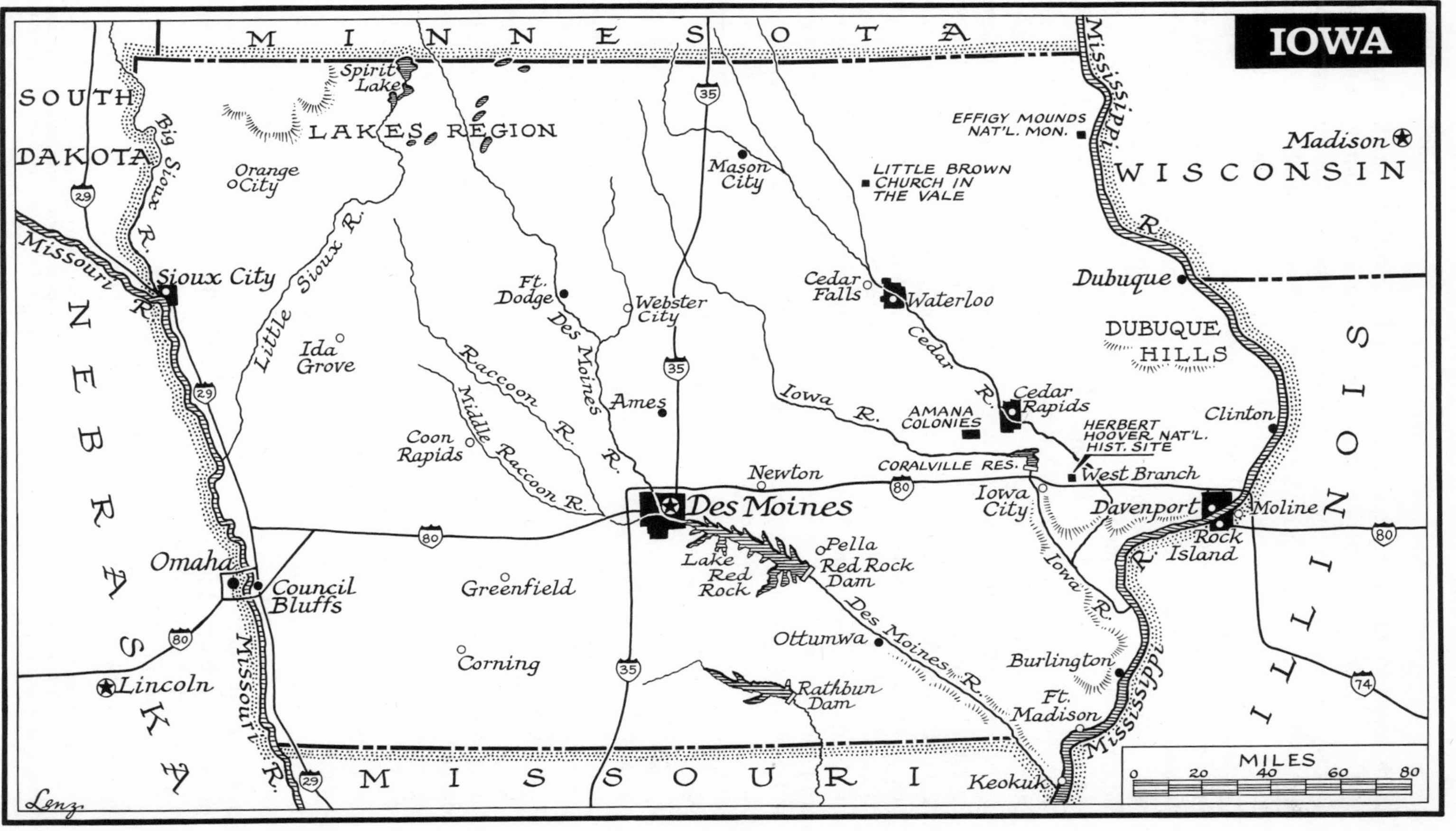

IOWA
MINNESOTA
SOUTH DAKOTA
WISCONSIN
ILLINOIS
NEBRASKA
MISSOURI
Madison
Spirit Lake
LAKES REGION
Orange City
Big Sioux R.
Missouri R.
Sioux City
Little Sioux R.
Ida Grove
Ft. Dodge
Des Moines R.
Webster City
Mason City
LITTLE BROWN CHURCH IN THE VALE
EFFIGY MOUNDS NAT'L. MON.
Mississippi R.
Dubuque
DUBUQUE HILLS
Cedar Falls
Waterloo
Cedar R.
Cedar Rapids
Iowa R.
AMANA COLONIES
HERBERT HOOVER NAT'L. HIST. SITE
West Branch
Clinton
Raccoon R.
Middle Raccoon R.
Coon Rapids
Ames
Newton
CORALVILLE RES.
Iowa City
Davenport
Moline
Rock Island
Des Moines
Pella
Red Rock Dam
Lake Red Rock
Omaha
Council Bluffs
Greenfield
Corning
Lincoln
Ottumwa
Rathbun Dam
Burlington
Ft. Madison
Keokuk
Mississippi
35
29
80
74
MILES
0 20 40 60 80
Lenz

With only 1.6 percent of the land area of the United States, Iowa has 25 percent of its Grade A topsoil, a legacy of four glacial sweeps across her surface, the last only 10,000 years ago. A native of rockier places, Robert Frost, once said of the rich Iowa earth that developed like a thick blanket on the glacial drift: "It looks good enough to eat without putting it through vegetables."

Iowa is the very heart of the Corn Belt which stretches from Nebraska and South Dakota clear through to central Ohio, but only one other state, Illinois, comes close to Iowa's production (some 900 million bushels a year).* Together with soybeans, alfalfa, and other grains, the crop income of the state's farmers is about $1 billion out of $3.8 billion annual farm receipts—a figure second only to California. The corn is fed through those convenient creatures, cattle, hogs, and sheep, to create a $2.8 billion-a-year industry in Iowa; no other state has such a high livestock income. Iowa remains the banner state of the Union for hog production—about 21 million a year, eight times the human population of the state. She is also the second largest cattle state of America, with about 7.4 million head, lagging only behind Texas. Traditionally, calves were bought from Western ranches and then fattened in the Corn Belt for eventual marketing. Now, however, the West and Southwest have moved rapidly to fattening of their own feeder cattle until they are ready for market. (The burgeoning population of the West and Southwest provides a ready market for their increased production of beef, and those regions, though much more arid than the Corn Belt, can produce the crops with which to feed the cattle through irrigation and increased pumping of underground water. In 1971, as noted in the Texas chapter, that state for the first time surpassed Iowa in the number of cattle it was fattening in feedlots.) With fewer Western-bred calves available, the Corn Belt has been obliged to become more self-sufficient, producing more and more of its own feeder calves. Iowa's number of brood cows, for instance, has tripled in recent years. Despite the shifts in calving-feeding patterns, no cattle region is suffering or is likely to soon, because Americans are eating more pounds of meat each year (more than 110 pounds a year per person now). From a 1968 production of 36 million beef cows, the figure is expected to rise to 50 million by 1980.

In addition to its amazing corn-hog-cattle production, Iowa in recent years has ranked sixth among all states in milk cows, third in chickens and turkeys, and eighth in sheep. The wonder of it all, as Roswell Garst puts it, is that all of this should have happened in the scant century since his father and others put the first teams of oxen to work plowing up the virgin grasslands. In those days, there were millions of prairie chickens and wild ducks on this lonely rolling prairie called Iowa. "Dad said you could just sit in the buggy and shoot 'em."

But the unmolested prairie must also have been a lonely place, belittling man with its immensity; this is surely one of the places on earth where man's

* "The Corn Belt," according to J. Russell Smith (quoted by John Gunther), "is a gift of the gods—the rain god, the sun god, the ice god, and the gods of geology." More scientifically, it is land with at least these attributes: a mean summer temperature of at least 70 degrees, frequent summer showers, and a growing season of 140 or more days.

transformation of the natural landscape was an improvement.* There are few more beautiful sights in America than Iowa's farmlands in early autumn, the glistening fields of eight- and ten-foot-high hybrid corn, delicately tasseled, billowing in the wind over softly undulating hills, the patches of dark green sorghums, the beef cattle and pigs in corral or pasture, occasional clumps of trees, the farm houses bright white or red on ordered grounds often abundant with flowers, the neat silos, a place where every inch of ground seems to radiate fertility. Some 95 percent of the land area of this Iowa is under cultivation, and the people who till it benefit immensely; no state has a higher rural standard of living.

But this is not a static farm economy. Hear Roswell Garst speak of the future:

> We've about hit the limit in the amount of corn we can raise on an acre, at least for a while. But that doesn't mean we can't continue to increase our livestock production feeding from that same acreage. A corn field is half grain and it is half stalks, leaves, and junk. The same is true of grain sorghums used for feeding cattle. So we grind up the corn cobs, stalks, and leaves for feed—they are a cellulose that is good nourishment. But they need a protein supplement. We know that urea, a nitrogen product rich in proteins, is potentially as unlimited in supply as the air and the water and the natural gas from which it is made. So we give our cattle urea in molasses as a supplement to their diet of ground stalks, leaves, and cobs. Only a few farmers do this now. But in time more will, and the price of beef is sure to fall eventually.

Garst was already feeding his cattle urea in molasses when Khrushchev visited his farm. The pictures of that day show gooey muzzles dripping with the stuff, and Garst admits that the result was often a sticky mess, covered with flies. Since then, Garst and his farmer sons have found a solution: they still "serve" the molasses, but they have constructed wood lattice frames that float on top of the molasses trough, with openings just wide enough for a steer to get his tongue through. The sandpapery tongues eventually wear out the lattices, but the basic problem is solved.

"And now we're discovering," Garst says, "how damned little we knew about cattle breeding. We used to hesitate cross-breeding beef breeds and dairy breeds, for fear of getting mongrels. Now we're trying all sorts of new cross-breeding, and the calves grow much faster, and in a few years we'll be able to market 1,000 pounds of steer at one year instead of 18 months of age."

Iowa has some 140,000 farms (half the number of three decades ago) now averaging about 240 acres, but there are vast differences between types. Almost universally, the successful, industrious farmer will reject crop farming alone for a combined crop and livestock operation. His fields are frozen from Thanksgiving to April, and he can use that time to good advantage tending the cattle he has pastured in summer, fattening a hog litter that came in the fall, or tending a cow herd and raising beef calves. The land he

* My friend Drake Mabry of the Des Moines *Tribune* reminds me that there is considerable land in southern Iowa that is far from prairie land—a setting, he points out, similar to Ozark country, with patches of timber spotted with pasture, and more livestock raising than grain farming. "It's quite picturesque," he says, "like a Grant Wood oil."

farms, frequently exceeding $100,000 in value, is not his only great investment; he must also borrow up to $15,000 to $30,000 a year to buy livestock herds and apply the necessary chemicals to his land (at a cost of up to $35 an acre). All of this requires keen business judgment, a knowledge of machinery, moment for maximum gain—and luck. But if the farmer can clear perhaps $2,500 after farm and family expenses each year, then after 40 years he will have an estate of $100,000.

What makes a man devote his life, though, to a job that takes up to 70 hours a week—11 hours six days a week and four on Sunday? Thirty-four-year-old farmer Robert Lewis of Orchard, Iowa (population 129) explained it this way to a reporter for a business magazine, *Forbes*, in 1969:

> I'm 50 paces from my work. I can be with my family any time of the day. You know, particularly in these days of easy travel, it's great for children to grow up on a farm. . . . We are two hours from a major ball field. We have the camping bug and manage to get in a Saturday overnight some weekends. If we can camp, I don't get in my game of golf at the country club, but I enjoy both.
>
> I love the land, and it's a family way of life. And you know, when we go to a football game, we don't even have to lock the door.

The marginal farmer is of another breed—the kind, one banker told me, "who doesn't work in the winter and plays pinochle at the pool hall." He may have inherited his land, know it will be worth a small fortune whenever he decides to leave it and retire, and decide to avoid the seven-day-a-week routine of caring for cattle and hogs so that he can travel for weekends like everyone else. Or if he owns just a small chunk of land, he may—as 40 percent of the people living on Iowa farms do—get his principal income from a factory job or some other nonfarm occupation, depending on mechanized equipment to let him farm one or two hundred acres on weekends and evenings.

Cattle and Pollution

When Iowa's cattle are ready for marketing, they no longer take a long trip to faraway stockyards. A network of packing houses has spread into every rural area. I heard some predictions that within a decade Iowa will raise, slaughter, cut, freeze, price, package, put on an airplane, and fly its meat products to all the major cities of the country. (Today it is more generally whole sides of beef that are shipped.)

Some 40,000 farms in Iowa now feed cattle till they are ready for market, but the vast commercial feedlots, more familiar in the mountain and High Plains states, are making inroads. State Commerce Commissioner Morris Van Nostrand, in 1969 when he was a principal owner of the big Oakland Feeding Corporation in Western Iowa, took me on a guided tour of the feedlot where 11,000 cattle might be in residence at any time. In a feedlot of this type the cattle, mostly owned by investors, come in weighing 550 to 850 pounds, are kept for four to six months, and then are sent to the packing house when they have reached 975 to 1,150 pounds.

"A feedlot is a beef factory," Van Nostrand explained. "We take a range animal and convert it into a marketable beef product through a quick, efficient job of fattening." But the scene is a far cry from the placid pastureland nearby. The cattle are in vast dirt pens, each holding some 150 head, without a blade of grass in sight. At the head of each pen there is a long, concrete trough where one can see an unbroken line of brown, black, and white heads munching away on corn, hay, cobs, or molasses, shaking off swarms of flies, the baleful eyes following each visitor who passes.

The south end of each animal is as likely as not to be eliminating its wastes, and therewith starts the great problem of all feedlots: pollution. The wastes flow into a big lagoon, where they are supposed to settle gradually. But at Oakland, a lingering subsurface frost the previous spring had caused tons of topsoil to wash into the holding pond; then continued rains made it impossible to get the pond dry for dredging, and an auxiliary lagoon was also nearly full. The major lagoon was a big stinking, swilling, bubbling sight with you-know-what floating on top. Local farmers were up in arms lest there be a break in the auxiliary lagoon that would wash down over their lands. The irony, Van Nostrand said, was that the feedlot had won a 1967 Izaak Walton League Cleaner Streams Award for its control facilities—which had simply proven to be inadequate. A measure of the problem of such a feedlot is the fact that a steer excretes each day a cubic foot of liquid and solid wastes—about the same as 18 to 20 human beings. Thus the Oakland feedlot has the same sewage problem as a city of close to 200,000 people.

The biggest feedlot in the U.S.A., near Greeley, Colorado, has 100,000 head of cattle; its waste problem is much greater than that of the entire Denver metropolitan area with 1.2 million people. Often the problem is compounded by the presence of slaughterhouses in the vicinities of feedlots, pumping paunch manures, blood, and grease into the same polluted streams. Randall S. Jessee, regional director of public affairs for the Environmental Protection Agency, says that at least until recently, animal waste was the most acute pollution problem of the Missouri Basin: water collected in lagoons, he said, until a big rain came, and then it moved in a huge sludge down the river, killing fish and presenting horrible results. The wastes can cause the amount of dissolved oxygen in the water to drop rapidly, while the levels of ammonia, nitrates, phosphates, and bacteria increase alarmingly. Now, Jessee says, there has been impressive improvement in the lagoons and other treatment facilities, especially by the larger feedlots that have presented the bulk of the problem. Many operators are also learning to scrap their lots and use the fertilizer on the fields.

The issue of secondary treatment, both from cattle production and city sewage systems, threw the usually equable state of Iowa into an imbroglio with the federal government in the late 1960s. Under the Federal Water Quality Act of 1965, all states submitted to the Interior Department proposals and deadlines for improving the quality of their waters. Of all the 50, only Iowa's response was so widely at variance with announced federal standards that federal hearings were called. Scientists presented reams of evidence to show that the Mississippi and Missouri Rivers, which bracket Iowa, are filthy with chemicals, intestinal bacteria, and slaughterhouse waste including "grease balls as big as oranges," thus impairing the recreational uses of the rivers, killing millions of fish and dirtying the water supplies of downstream states. Finally the dispute was resolved by a compromise between the Iowa and federal authorities.

Town and Country in "Agristate"; the Farm Groups

The picture of Iowa as one vast breadbasket, the agristate *par excellence,* is both true and false. It is true because about three-quarters of the state's people survive economically on industries related to agriculture—either farming itself, or small town economies geared to the surrounding farmlands, or food processing, or making tractors and other machines of the fields. Scratch an Iowa factory worker and one is almost sure to find the son or grandson of a farmer. No state is so consciously aware of its tie to the land, which has always been and remains its greatest resource.

But the breadbasket image is false because the young people are fleeing the land, and because the daily life of the vast majority of Iowans is remote from farm chores, crops, and livestock. Especially since World War II, Iowa has developed a diversified industrial base to balance agriculture. While farm income has increased 50 percent in two decades, industrial production has gone up threefold. A sampling of Iowa's biggest industries shows a remarkable mixture of agribusiness, branch factories for big national firms, and Iowa-born industries that have run successfully for many years with no farm ties at all. This list was provided by the Iowa Development Commission: Amana, Bendix, Collins Radio, Du Pont, Firestone, Fisher Governor, General Electric, International Paper, John Deere, Link-Belt, Massey-Ferguson, Maytag, National Gypsum, Oliver, Procter & Gamble, Quaker Oats, Rockwell Standard, Sinclair, Sylvania, Union Carbide, U.S. Gypsum, Weyerhaeuser, Zenith.

A review of the major cities is perhaps the best explanation of why the life style of modern Iowa veers farther and farther away from the pastoral. To Des Moines (population 200,587—metropolitan area 286,101), the state capital and largest city, we will return later; here it is sufficient to note that it is a major insurance, banking, and printing center and is advanced industrially with Firestone and Armstrong rubber plants, plus factories of John Deere and Massey-Ferguson. Cedar Rapids (population 110,642), halfway from Des Moines to the Illinois line, is growing rapidly with Collins Radio (now a subsidiary of North American Rockwell), Quaker Oats (where the wheat is shot from guns), Penick & Ford, Wilson Packing, and road machinery firms. Nearby Waterloo (75,533) harbors the world's biggest tractor plant (John Deere, over 5,000 workers), plus Rath Packing, the huge hog slaughterers. On the Mississippi River (Iowa's eastern border) is Davenport (98,469), which is incidentally a center of red-hot right-wingism in Iowa. The Davenport metro area is a major farm machinery center and also has a big aluminum plant and aircraft instrument manufacturing. Several miles to the north, Dubuque (62,309), situated on bluffs of Iowa's "little Switzerland" overlooking the river, is big in packing, tractors, and fertilizer. On the Missouri River, which flows along the western border, are Sioux City (85,-925), a boisterous town famed for its stockyards, and opposite Omaha, Nebraska, the Iowa town of Council Bluffs (60,348), a railroad, flower, and playground equipment town.

Even smaller cities than these may harbor important manufacturing enterprises. Clinton (34,719) is home, for instance, for plants of Du Pont, Allied Structural Steel, the Climax Engine Company, and Hawkeye Chemical Company. Fort Madison (13,996) is home of Schaeffer Pen. Newton (15,619) has been the locale of Maytag Washers ever since the first motor-driven washing machine was produced there in 1911. The bucolic setting of the Amana colonies is also the manufacturing point for Amana refrigeration equipment. And in the little town of Forest City (3,841), there are now two dozen millionaires—owners of stock in the Winnebago Company, a firm manufacturing trailers and campers which local businessman John K. Hanson started in the 1950s. By 1972, Winnebago was doing $133 million worth of business a year and its stock had a market value of more than $1 billion. Hanson, who owned a furniture store and ran the local mortuary before he started Winnebago, owned 50 percent of the stock. But some 1,000 other people in Forest City owned a piece of it too.

A not untypical mix of farm and industrial concerns can be found in a small city like Webster City (population 8,488), situated 65 miles north of Des Moines in the flat, rich-soiled farmlands of north central Iowa. Webster City's most famous sons are the author MacKinlay Kantor, on whose suggestion I paid a visit there, and reporter Clark Mollenhoff.

The visitor to Webster City finds an urban enough place, with one or two multistoried buildings set among several blocks of low brick retail outlets. There are several schools (drawing from a wide area), close-in residential sections of decades-old vintage but good quality, and an unpainted railroad station with grass growing on the platform. The town's first reason for being was as a farm supply point and county seat, and the rural tone remains. Yet Webster City's growth and apparent economic health are due instead to about a dozen industries, far and away the largest of which is the Franklin Manufacturing Company, a private label washing machine company that employs 900. Not a few of Webster City's factory workers still live on farms.

The business leadership group of Webster City is a combination of businessmen and farmers; both can be found on school boards, civic associations, or among church elders. "We have few really rich or really poor people," insurance man Carlton W. Crosley, one of Kantor's friends, related. "Our country club will welcome a foreman from a local factory or a better-off farmer. If our social lines were once rigid, they are no more." The race problems of Webster City are summed up in its Negro population figure: zero. Industry drives up wages some, "but we have less tension than the major cities." As for the politics, Webster City is in rock-ribbed Republican territory "because we're basically conservative people. We're against things being too militant. We're against too rapid change." Appropriately, the town boasts in a big sign: "Webster City—Main Street—U.S.A." Its Congressman in Washington is the conservative gadfly, H. R. Gross.

Despite its relative prosperity today, Webster City has reason to worry about its more prosperous neighbor, Fort Dodge (31,263), a city with a shopping mall and more diversified shops which is already cutting into Webster City's retail base. There is also a real possibility that Fort Dodge, only 21 miles distant, might one day usurp Webster City's role as a county seat in a regional amalgamation. Iowa has 99 counties, laid out a century ago so that a man could ride with horse and buggy to the county seat to pay his taxes in a day, and then get home by sundown. Wasteful and inefficient, the system cries for consolidation into a few jumbo counties or administrative units. (To get rational county consolidation in Iowa and other states, a federal official told me, "we are going to have to develop a program of 'municipal euthanasia.' ")

One of Iowa's most prosperous little cities is Ames, along Interstate 35 north of Des Moines (and south of Webster City). Ames's population jumped by 12,502 during the 1960s, to a total of 39,505, largely on the basis of growth at Iowa State University. The "cow college town" image of past years is fast fading as new retail outlets and factories open and the local residents take home $57 million a year in salaries from various jobs at the university. The student body is a rather conservative one, so normal "town-grown" conflicts are muted, and the university also keeps itself popular by paying voluntarily a percentage of local fire protection and sewage treatment costs.

While there is economic health on Iowa farms and its cities of any substantial size, a sickness almost unto death afflicts many small towns, the little hamlets which first sprang up as supply points for surrounding farmlands but are now skipped by the remaining farmers who speed on good roads to larger retailing and supply centers. Especially poignant scenes can be witnessed in southwestern Iowa if one deserts the monstrous interstates to travel the older country roads past struggling little villages, half their stores and houses boarded up. One of these is Brayton, Iowa (population 151), a depressed little hamlet with decaying sidewalks, dilapidated houses, and abandoned automobiles along the road. All that is left is a struggling feed store ("Gooch's Feeds"), a bar, a cafe, two gas stations and an auto repair shop, a lumber and coal company, a small food market, and a bravely white painted little town hall. In front of an abandoned house near Brayton's center corner, its rotted wooden steps boarded up to keep out intruders, the visitor sees this forbidding sign:

NO. PARKING.
IN FRONT.
ED. JUHL.

In most of Iowa's counties, the county seats have survived fairly well—at the expense of the smaller villages. Roswell Garst's Coon Rapids (population 1,381), also in southwest Iowa, is not a county seat but is holding on and even growing moderately because of the Garsts' $1 million-a-year seed corn business.* The main street is a scruffy affair with autos parked down its center, but there are no boarded-up stores. Several feed stores and a wide variety of retail outlets prosper in varying degrees, and there is an ultramodern round bank building, the Garst-founded Iowa Savings Bank, presided over by Garst's nephew, John Chrystal. Chrystal, like his illustrious uncle, is untypical in that he is an active Democrat in rock-ribbed Republican small-town Iowa; Chrystal was an active political supporter of Democratic Governor (and later Senator) Harold Hughes, who appointed him to the board of regents of the state university system. He also served a period as state banking superintendent, and in 1968 he supported Robert Kennedy for President. But to survive as a banker in Coon Rapids, Chrystal cannot give too much time to politics; the first order of business has to be understanding every minute detail of the business of his chief borrowers, the farmers of the area. That skill he has, clear down to reciting the seasonal prices of calves, sows, feeds, and fertilizers.

Lest anyone think Coon Rapids is in an impossibly remote area, let it be recorded that the day I visited there, Chrystal and his brothers were planning a whale feast! They had all gone whale hunting at Hudson Bay with Eskimo guides and brought back the meat for a banquet to which scores of friends were invited. One hears stories about remote Iowa farms with swimming pools, or farmers making trips to exotic distant places. (The Iowa Farm Bureau, for instance, regularly offers its members charter flight tours to the Caribbean, Hawaii, South America, the Orient, Australia, and around the world.) One can still find, if one looks, the legendary Iowa farmer coming into town with his bib overalls and manure on his boots; but if he has anything special planned these days, the farmer may well be wearing an Ivy League suit—or flares. And he may well have locked up the old homestead before he leaves for town; the last several years have brought a wave of hard-to-control pilferage of equipment and livestock on Iowa farms, and the day when Iowans could boast of their unlocked front doors may be fading. (Still, the overall crime rate is one of the lowest in the country.)

One American image holds true: the placid streets of quiet little Iowa

* Coon Rapids is a mild example of unique small town names; one travel guide suggests the following to illustrate the humor in rural Iowa nomenclature: Bonaparte, Correctionville, Cylinder, Defiance, Diagonal, Early, Fertile, Gravity, Hardy, Lost Nation, Manly, Morning Sun, Mystic, Plain View, Rembrandt, Spillville, Steamboat Rock, Strawberry Point, What Cheer, and Zwingle.

towns with their houses of neat white clapboard, surrounded by carefully tended lawns, shaded by towering elms (that is, wherever Dutch Elm disease has not yet worked its ravages). It is a world with its own special social strata (in Coon Rapids the Methodists are top dogs), the kind of bedrock America where, until recent incidents of school protests over the firing of popular teachers or coaches, people could scarcely conceive of kids refusing to conform or openly bucking their parents. It is a place where gossip of neighbor about neighbor often runs rampant, and each man's life is to some degree an open book. But it retains unique flavor and warmth, a cordiality our cities lost long ago.

There is also the Iowa world of carefree marching bands, the setting for Meredith Willson's *Music Man*; if one is in Cedar Falls or Algona or Clarinda or Mason City or a score of other Iowa towns on the right day of the year, he will hear the spirit poured forth in band concerts unparalleled elsewhere in America. The essential rural flavor of Iowa is also reflected in such events as springtime tulip festivals at Pella and Orange City,* the famed Iowa State Fair each August (where prizes are awarded to 4-H winners and the handsomest pigs as the bands blare day and night), rodeos at Sidney and Fort Madison, and the Midwest Old Settlers & Threshers Reunion at Mt. Pleasant late each summer. But Des Moines and Davenport have symphonies they are proud of, and in the late 1960s a new concert hall of bold exterior design and careful acoustic effect was opened at the Iowa State University campus at Ames, with none less than the New York Philharmonic, under the direction of Seiji Ozawa, playing the opening night.

And lest anyone believes that Iowa is a cultural wasteland, he should be reminded of the University of Iowa Writing Workshop at Iowa City, widely regarded as the best in America. The poet Paul Engle, a native Iowan, began the workshop more than 30 years ago, and, as B. Drummond Ayres of *The New York Times* has reported from Iowa City, "sooner or later most of the established and aspiring writers in America make a pilgrimage here . . . to lecture and learn, to argue and discuss. . . . Like hybrid corn, good writing thrives here." Its faculty has included Robert Penn Warren, Philip Roth, Marvin Bell, William Price Fox, and Vance Bourjaily, its graduates Flannery O'Connor, Richard Kim, William Stafford, and W. D. Snodgrass. When Vance Bourjaily, the novelist and drama critic, was asked why it had all happened in Iowa City, he replied: "Well . . . Iowa City because there's just a certain pleasantness of life here."

Some 40 miles south of Coon Rapids in western Iowa is the picturesque county seat town of Greenfield (population 2,212). At the center of the old town square is an old red brick courthouse, surrounded by ancient trees; around the square one will find canvas-shaded shops like Wiig's 5c to $1.00

*** Some 85,000 people a year visit Pella and Orange City at tuliptime, and the scene, replete with windmills, native costumes, and wooden shoes, may be more Dutch than Holland. In fact, the Ambassador to the United States from the Netherlands, Baron Rijnhard Bernhard van Lyden, believes there may be more wooden shoes in Orange City than in modern Holland.**

Store, Yount Wallpaper, Bob and Ellen's Laundry, Don Carlos Loan & Title, and the Eagle Rock Cafe. The latter, I gathered, was in special honor of the fictional town of Eagle Rock, the locale of Norman Lear's movie *Cold Turkey*, which was being filmed—with a thousand Greenfielders as extras—in 1969. The story revolved about a prize of $25 million offered to Eagle Rock if it could stop smoking for 30 days; the cynical tobacco company that made the offer was confident it would never have to pay up and even bombed Eagle Rock with cigarettes to be sure. Catching the spirit, Greenfielders did try to stop smoking for a month. *Cold Turkey* star Dick Van Dyke lent moral assistance as the townspeople threw their cigarettes in a huge bonfire. The Adair County *Free Press*, edited by Edwin Sidey (brother of *Life* magazine's prominent commentator on the Presidency, Hugh Sidey), ran a survey and found about three-quarters of the smokers really had stopped. (Philip Morris, however, later did a survey that "proved" quite the opposite.) Seeking out Edwin Sidey to inquire about this story on a Sunday afternoon, I found him with his son at the local airport watching gliders being borne aloft by World War II biplane trainers. Small-town America, one quickly learns, is not without its own amusements.

Not far from Greenfield in the rolling cornfields of southwest Iowa is the little county seat of Corning, which has yet another claim to fame: it is the national headquarters of the National Farmers Organization (NFO), youngest and most militant of all farm groups in the U.S.A. The NFO actually got its start in Iowa in 1955 when a group of farmers became angry about the low prices—then 10 cents a pound—which they were being paid for hogs. Soon there were protest meetings all over southwest Iowa, and then the movement became national. NFO's approach is simple: because the farmer is the only unorganized man in the highly organized economy of the nation, he is at the mercy of the buyers who set the prices for his goods. Unless this exploitation can be broken, the family farm is doomed. Therefore farmers must organize by boycotting production of selected commodities, or withholding commodities from the market, until a vacuum occurs in the normal supplies and buyers are forced to bid up the price.

In NFO's early days, its members sometimes resorted to roughshod tactics to prevent the goods of noncooperating farmers from going on the market in their target areas. Today the organization is matured and stabilized with more peaceful tactics, though it still resorts to theatrical milk dumping. NFO's chief problem, always, is to get enough farmers organized to be a truly effective market force; its success here is spotty. But the idea of farmers organizing for their own economic self-interest in the marketplace is being recognized; when I asked Iowa's Senator Hughes about the NFO's boycott techniques, he replied, "Has any other underpaid, underfed group in the country ever achieved anything by any other tactic? How did labor get organized? The railroads go on strike and they don't ask anybody. If all these sophisticated forces use the same tactics, why should the farmer be criticized?"

Another staunch defender of the NFO is editor Paul Gauthier of the Adams County *Free Press* in Corning, a skilled journalist who was General Patton's briefing officer in World War II but deliberately chose to spend his life editing the same small-town weekly his family had owned for generations. The NFO, Gauthier maintains, has developed outstanding leaders and is the most effective farm group in the country today. The NFO started with a one-room office on a back street in Corning (population 2,095); 15 years later it had a jerrybuilt set of offices covering a half block in the town, employed some 200 people, and was Corning's biggest industry. (Other distinctions of Corning are the high percentage of high school graduates—80 to 85 percent—who go on to advanced education; the fact that it was the site of the first public housing in Iowa; the decision of the Presbyterians to tear down their church and use the Roman Catholic parish hall for services; and a successful County Home that draws old folks and buoys the town population figure even while young folks leave in droves and nearby small towns waste away.)

Iowa's largest farm organization is the Farm Bureau, which boasts of 110,000 family memberships and a highly developed buying, lobbying, and insurance operation that makes it a major force in the state's life. By general consensus, the Farm Bureau is the most potent influence in the legislature, active on policy issues affecting education, highways, property, and income taxes. The major rebuff the Bureau suffered in recent years was on reapportionment, when the voters emphatically rejected its stand for rural overrepresentation in a statewide referendum. The vote suggested there might be validity to the charge that many Farm Bureau members join simply for fringe benefits like insurance, or maybe small town businessmen join for fear of being boycotted if they do not.

In reply to criticism of the Farm Bureau's emphasis on its businesses like insurance, Iowa Farm Bureau president Merrill Anderson replies that when the Bureau started with casualty insurance for farmers, the regular insurance firms disdained the farmer's business. (About 70 percent of the Iowa Farm Bureau members now have insurance policies with the Bureau.) The Bureau likewise got into the farm supply business—through cooperative buying of gasoline, fertilizer, and other supplies—at the request of its members. Whatever the reasons, the Farm Bureau is a big business in Iowa today. Its positions in favor of reduced price supports and taking more farm land out of production run directly contrary to NFO policy, and the two lose no love on each other. Fittingly, the Farm Bureau is located not in a tiny rural spot like Corning but in a comfortable downtown Des Moines office building. But its power was reduced by the legislative reapportionment following the 1970 Census, since 74 of Iowa's 99 counties, all in rural areas, lost population during the 1960s.

An often underestimated force in a farmer's life is the cooperative movement, especially in electric power supplying. "If a farmer had to make a choice between the Farm Bureau and his cooperative," Senator Hughes believes, "he'd probably go the political route of his cooperative."

Politics and Harold Hughes

Iowa is by instinct and normal voting pattern Republican, a clear reflection of the Protestant hard-work ethic of its countless county seats and little towns. History helps explain why: though the state was first peopled by Southerners, coming by way of Kentucky and Missouri, they were followed in the 1840s by settlers from New England, northern New York, and the northern sections of Ohio, Indiana, and Illinois, a more numerous Yankee Protestant element that is still dominant. The state also received many Germans (some Protestant, others Catholic), and a number of Scandinavians and Dutch and Czechs—but never enough to upset the Yankee dominance. Although James B. Weaver, the Populist candidate for the Presidency, came from Des Moines, Iowa never had the strong Populist impulses of the cash grain and heavily Scandinavian Plains States like Minnesota and the Dakotas. The towns have rarely deviated from straight Republicanism, although the farm areas have veered occasionally to the Democrats for more than a generation now, both in state and federal elections. The farmers' most celebrated rebellion was in 1948, when they helped reelect Harry Truman because of their fear that Thomas Dewey and the Republicans might take away their federal farm programs.

The larger cities, by contrast, tend to have more Roman Catholics and certainly vote more Democratic than most rural areas. If one draws a pie shape on the Iowa map, the western anchor set at Des Moines and with separate lines going to the northeast and southeast corners, only 35 to 40 percent of the state's geographic area is included. But the triangle contains the vast majority of Iowa's major cities—Des Moines, Cedar Rapids, Davenport, Dubuque, Waterloo, Clinton, Ottumwa, Fort Madison, and the like, most of which are growing at the expense of the towns and farmlands. If one puts a couple of jogs on the lines of the triangle, the principal state universities are included as well. This triangle is where the principal liberal and Democratic voting strength of Iowa is located. It is also the area of population growth, while the rest of the state declines. Its growth explains why Iowa is becoming increasingly marginal in its politics, relegating to the status of historical oddity the statement of a great turn-of-the-century Republican Senator, Jonathan Dolliver: "When Iowa goes Democratic, Hell will go Methodist."

Iowa had been staunchly Republican from the late 1850s to modern times, electing only two Democratic governors in the span of 98 years ending in 1956. Only in exceptional years (1912, 1932, 1936, 1948) had the Democrats won for President. Most congressional delegations had been Republican, although Guy Gillette, who looked like an actors' studio choice for Senator, was elected to the Senate on the Democratic ticket in 1936 and three times subsequently, finally losing out in 1954. Another Democratic winner was Hershel C. Loveless, who won the governorship in 1956 and 1958;

in 1958, with the farmers up in arms over Ezra Taft Benson's farm policies, Democrats also took half the U.S. House seats.

But Republican normalcy seemed to reappear in 1960 as Loveless lost a race for the Senate, Nixon swept Iowa, and control of the House delegation went back to the GOP. With the Benson irritant removed, a Republican decade seemed in the offing.

All those prognostications failed to take account, however, of a tall, black-haired man with a rumpled suit and Indian-looking face, a blunt ex-truck driver absolutely determined he would become governor of Iowa in 1962. The man was Harold E. Hughes, native of little Ida Grove, Iowa, the product of a Fundamentalist home and a sometime Methodist lay preacher. Until the age of 32, less than a decade before, Hughes had been an apparently hopeless alcoholic, reeling off weekend after weekend on long drinking sprees. Then, in the mid-1950s, he had suddenly stopped. "If I hadn't quit," he said years later, "I'd either be dead or a bum by now."

Hughes had been a Democrat only five years and had occupied but a single government post (state commerce commissioner) when he entered the 1962 governor race. (He had tried for his party's 1960 governor nomination but lost that year.) What Hughes did bring to statewide politics was a rare combination of deeply held convictions and exceptional natural intelligence that would make him within a few short years one of the most charismatic, effective reformers the Plains States have produced in this generation.

But why Harold Hughes, in rockribbed Republican Iowa, in 1962? Students of politics are hard put to fathom the strange interrelationships of men and events which will popularize an issue or a personality at some particular moment of time. One part of the equation for Hughes was the ongoing Iowa debate about whether liquor could be served legally by the drink, in bars and restaurants. Many Democratic candidates before Hughes had talked about liquor by the drink but had been generally ignored. But when Hughes seized on the issue in 1962, it sparked, perhaps by the very bluntness and forthrightness with which he attacked it.

Hughes' principal argument was that it was hypocritical to forbid liquor by the drink when key clubs, veterans, and fraternal clubs were selling liquor in almost every county of the state. "I told the people I'd close it up or I'd legalize it, that if the country club set wanted to drink every night of the week, then the laboring man was entitled to it too." Reporters on the campaign trail began to notice that even in dry areas there was a lot of sentiment to change the liquor law. Part of Hughes' strength was the unpopularity of the Republican governor at the time, Norman Erbe. But something deeper was taking place; as reporters Nick Kotz and James Risser of the Des Moines *Register* wrote some years later:

> On the surface, it seemed ironic that reformed drunk Hughes was speaking out boldly in favor of legalized liquor-by-the-drink in Biblebelt, dry, conservative Iowa. In reality, he was igniting a revolution in Iowa politics. The state was in the throes of a transition from a rural to an urban economy and urban mores, and was without

any political leadership. . . . Hughes tapped a latent Iowa majority who desired a more progressive state image (they were tired of jokes about the little old lady from Dubuque and about key clubs) and who wanted more of their political leaders than cautious mediocrity. . . . The real surprise is that so few politicians, reporters, or business leaders really understood what was happening in the state.

But the election returns proved the point: Hughes was elected governor with 41,944 votes to spare (52.6 percent).

Once elected, Hughes could have pursued a "safe" moderate-to-conservative course in the style of his more cautious fellow Democrats, Morrison of Nebraska or Docking of Kansas. But if Hughes had ever harbored such thoughts, they were put to rest by his inaugural address before the Republican-controlled legislature. "It is sometimes said that the knack of skillful government is to hang back, to do as little as possible, and make no mistakes," Hughes noted. "I hope there is another way—for between you and me, this prospect does not invite my soul."

Hughes then proceeded to press for numerous reforms of a fundamental nature, appealing where he thought necessary over the legislators' heads and directly to the people. Liquor by the drink was indeed approved after a stormy legislative debate, a major victory for the governor. Another Hughes triumph came when the voters rejected by a three-to-one margin a proposal from the legislature to leave the rural areas in perpetual control of one house (the so-called "little federal" system). Hughes had campaigned for a straight population-based apportionment instead, and the vote seemed to indicate that Iowans were willing to make an even greater break with the old small-town order of things.

In retrospect, Hughes downgrades the importance of both the liquor and apportionment battles. "Liquor by the drink was probably the least important thing I did, even if it is the most remembered," he told me. As for reapportionment, he finds its results "disappointing" because the legislators still tend to be semi-retirees or lawyers who can afford to spend several months in Des Moines with minimal pay and facilities. The result, Hughes believes, is that "the legislature is not a clear response to the people of the state." (As Hughes was finishing his last year as governor in 1968, however, the legislature and people approved five amendments to the state constitution to modernize legislative operations, including annual, unlimited sessions. In 1971 the Citizens Council on State Legislatures reported that the amendments helped create a momentum for improvement so fundamental that the Iowa legislature ranked sixth in the entire Union, and first among small states, on a scale of its capacity to act in "a functional, accountable, informed, independent and representative manner." In particular, the Council praised Iowa's legislature for its limited number of comittees in both houses with parallel jurisdictions, the open access which the press and public have to the work of the legislature, single-member districts that focus the relationship between legislators and their constituents, and effective conflict-of-interest statutes.)

Hughes believes that the more important achievements of his years as governor lie in the areas of penal reform, mental health, education, and industrial development. He fought successfully to eliminate capital punishment ("to erase the moral stigma of public hangings"), to establish a pre-release farm for prisoners before their reinfusion into society, to obtain Iowa's first public defender and its first alcoholic treatment facility, and to improve law enforcement training. Efforts in the mental health field included Iowa's first facilities specifically for the treatment of the criminally insane. Substantially more assistance for the state universities was authorized and the state's share of expenses for local schools went from 11 to 39 percent. State taxes rose sharply to finance the increase in the state budget from $200 million to $500 million annually during the Hughes regime (earning him a reputation as a big spender), but reform measures such as reduced taxes for the elderly and a withholding system to catch tax-dodgers and accelerate payments were instituted. An intensive industrial promotion effort included "Sell Iowa" trips to major U.S. cities and countries abroad * and the establishment of 15 regional vocational-technical schools to train workers for the rurally located light industries the state was trying to attract. The merit system for state employees was expanded and a state planning office established. The state's public utilities were brought under more effective control, and interest payments were required on previously idle state funds in Iowa banks. On the latter two issues, Kotz and Risser wrote later, Hughes and his chief aide, Park Rinard, "put together a new populist coalition of city men and farmer legislators who had their own dislike of the small-town bankers, merchants, and private utilities who so often had squeezed them hard."

Iowa has but 1.5 percent black population, but there are pockets of dismal Negro slums in Des Moines, Cedar Rapids, and Waterloo, mini-ghettos which most Iowans—including Hughes—were largely oblivious of until disturbances began. A riot in Waterloo obliged Hughes to call in troops, and he walked the streets of the state's ghettos in an attempt to quiet tensions. "I was shocked by what I saw," Hughes said after his first trips to the ghettos. "I couldn't believe the venom I found. I'd go home nights and couldn't sleep and felt like I couldn't face the world the next morning." Hughes has assailed some Iowa audiences as hypocrites for ignoring or scorning the blacks, Indians, or other poor. He expanded the state civil rights commission and supported a state open-housing law as governor.

Hughes' peak in Iowa politics came when he first sought reelection as governor in 1964. The voters accorded him a stupendous plurality of 429,479 votes (68.0 percent), substantially ahead of even the showing which President Johnson made against Barry Goldwater in Iowa. The same election swept the Democrats to control of all but one of Iowa's seven U.S. House seats and gave them both houses of the state legislature for the first time in 30 years. In 1966 Hughes won a third and final term as governor, albeit by a lesser plurality (99,741 votes). It was shortly after that election, in

* Foreign trade missions are more important for Iowa than one might think, since 10 percent of its farm goods are sold abroad, including a number of the animal glands scorned in America but popular in Europe for various delicacies. Foreign trade is one reason the state has rejected the isolationism of earlier decades.

which Democratic candidates, virtually abandoned by President Johnson, lost badly across the country, that Hughes broke with his old friend, LBJ, and candidly told reporters how much confidence Johnson had lost among the nation's Democratic governors. He also began to disassociate himself from the Johnson administration's Vietnam policy, which he had previously supported. (By 1970, Hughes' transformation on the war issue was complete. War, he said, "is useless as a political instrument. I hate war, all war. Humanity is at stake.")

During the spring and summer of 1968, as the Democrats went through the agony of preparing and conducting their Chicago convention, Hughes first emerged as a national figure. He had been preparing to endorse Kennedy just before the Los Angeles assassination, took charge of an *ad hoc* party rules reform group which made a number of influential proposals, and ended up placing Senator Eugene McCarthy's name in nomination for the Presidency.

In Iowa, however, Hughes was running for a vacated U.S. Senate seat and discovered that the accumulated antagonism of several years in the governorship, the higher taxes and ballooned state budget, had cost him much support. To make things worse, Hughes insisted on running his whole campaign on his opposition to the Vietnam war and on the Negro problem —neither especially popular issues in Iowa. His budget was substantially less than that of his Republican opponent, state Senator David M. Stanley. Finally Hughes won, but by a slim margin of 6,415 votes (50.2 percent).

In the Senate, Hughes was soon drawing attention as chairman of a special subcommittee on alcoholism and narcotics. Some accused him of being practically a one-issue Senator with his constant attention to "the problem," but in a column on Hughes, a Washington *Post* writer noted it was also true that "Washington has trouble with politicians who have passion. They upset the pace." (One sidelight is that Hughes has become a quiet but very effective father confessor for high-ranking Democrats of many states who had alcohol problems to contend with. When I interviewed Hughes, he told me that one of these was former Governor Phillip Hoff of Vermont; later Hoff publicly acknowledged the help Hughes had given him in conquering his problem with alcohol.)

Hughes' hearings also produced a broad range of interesting new testimony on drug problems, leading him to remark: "Why, instead of following sane and professional recommendations, do we continue a [drug control] system that busts up kids' lives, makes treatment of addiction impossible, and overpunishes the nameless, wretched addict or pusher, while channeling easy profits into the hands of the underworld?" On another occasion, Hughes said, "How the hell can Father sit in his chair at night sipping his third martini and yell at Johnny about the evils of pot?"

Although South Dakota's George McGovern was chosen over Hughes to head the Democratic party's official reform commission after the 1968 election, Hughes served as vice chairman, devoted long hours and days to the task, and left his imprint in the unprecedented requirements for party democracy that emerged. (According to the commission's counsel, Eli Segal, Hughes was "the most outspoken advocate of the prohibition of rigged caucuses, proxy voting, unit rules, closed slatemaking, excessive fees for becoming a party delegate, and the automatic designation of certain public officials as delegates.") Many Democratic reformers were drawn to Hughes through this work, and became part of the *ad hoc* group that supported Hughes' tentative but never announced Presidential candidacy, which flowered through late 1970 and into the spring of 1971. (Hughes' financial support, however, came heavily from Iowa businessmen, many with a Republican background, who had become loyal to him when he was governor. One of these was Watson Powell, Jr., president of the Des Moines chamber of commerce and chairman of the American Republic Insurance Company.)

Reporters who watched Hughes during his Presidential explorations soon noted his unusual attributes. There was, for instance, Hughes' combination of a rough-hewn truck driver and idealistic reformer, thus potentially combining blue-collar and intellectual support—a natural answer, some thought, to the Republicans' Spiro Agnew. But there was more to Hughes than that. As David S. Broder wrote:

> His assets are a magnificent, deep bass voice, controlled in volume and flexible in tone, that may well be the best voice in American politics today; a commanding physical presence, and a face whose strength is the visible record of past travail. . . . He simply will not be confined to the polite generalities of politics but insists on raising questions of ethics in highly individual terms. . . . He has spoken so powerfully of life and reconciliation that audiences of hard-bitten politicians have been reduced to tears.

The reporters were also intrigued by Hughes' openly expressed religious faith, at once mystic and evangelistic. When Paul R. Wieck pressed Hughes on reports that he had consulted astrologists or psychics, Hughes denied it (though he has not denied an interest in the occult and extrasensory perception, or the possibility of speaking with his dead brother through a medium). Pressed by Wieck on the issue of his concept of God, Hughes replied:

> If I could adequately describe God, he'd be unworthy of consideration. God is a very personal thing. . . . I believe the prophets spoke truth to all. . . . I accept Jesus Christ as the incarnate word of God. . . . God is omnipresent, omniscient, the spiritual presence of all things. . . . I'm impressed with his concern for man.

On another occasion, Hughes spoke of "a longing in the hearts of men to love each other" and of the necessity "to measure men by the persistence of their spirit and their soul" rather than by the standards of power and money.

Perhaps those thoughts and forces in a man were inconsistent with the cold-blooded calculations expected of a Presidential candidate; perhaps the practicalities of a clash with a man who shared his views so completely, George McGovern, helped to deter Hughes from an open candidacy. In any event, in July 1971 Hughes announced he would not run for the nomination. His given reasons; his failure to attract sufficiently broad support, and his conviction that his undeclared candidacy was preventing him from dealing with the problems he believed were "eating the heart out of this country"—drug abuse, crime, and the decay of the cities.

Was Hughes the Democratic Senator an aberration in Republican Iowa? Most people assumed so until 1972, when a dark horse Democratic contender suddenly won the state's other U.S. Senate seat, ousting two-term incumbent Jack Miller, the ranking Republican on the Senate Agriculture Committee. The surprise winner was Dick Clark, 43, whose previous claims to fame had been restricted to a staff role in Robert Kennedy's 1968 Presidential campaign and service as a campaign manager and staff aide to U.S. Rep. John Culver of Iowa. How did Clark, who ran a shoestring campaign against a well-financed incumbent, pull his upset? First, like Florida's Senator Lawton Chiles and Illinois' Governor Dan Walker, he walked from one end of Iowa to the other (some 1,300 miles in all) to meet the people and gain visibility. Secondly, he struck the voters as a much warmer personality than Miller. And third, he made much of Miller's effort to exempt from retroactive taxes a Bahamas investor group represented in Washington by lobbyist Thomas Corcoran, the one-time New Deal whiz kid. The voters seemed to accept Clark's assertion that Miller was too close to big business interests—and to dismiss as irrelevant Miller charges that Clark, like George McGovern, was "soft" on social issues like amnesty for Vietnam draft evaders and "decriminalization" of marijuana usage. In the same election, Iowa voters also pared down Republican control of both houses of their legislature—even while Nixon was sweeping Iowa with 59 percent of the vote and Governor Ray was winning reelection in a landslide vote of comparable dimensions.

Hoover, Wallace—and H. R. Gross

Iowa remembers with fondness two great and totally different leaders it gave to America in decades past: Herbert Hoover and Henry Wallace. Hoover so reviled in the 1930s as the supposed architect of Depression during his White House years returned to a position of national eminence and honor in the postwar years through his distinguished work on reorganization of the Executive Branch under Presidents Truman and Eisenhower. (The term "Hoover Commission" has become common parlance among American government leaders determined to clean up organizational tangles in their cities or states.) Past his 90th birthday, in 1964, Hoover was laid to rest under the soil of the place of his birth, West Branch, Iowa, where his Presidential library is located.

Henry Wallace, born a few miles from Greenfield in 1888, is honored by Iowans for his development of several strains of hybrid corn, that incredible boon to the Iowa farmer. The Pioneer Hybrid Corn Company he founded still prospers in Des Moines today, a global business still researching, producing, and selling hybrid corns as well as chickens, cattle, sorghums and alfalfa. Other Americans remember the sad story of how Wallace was dropped from the Democratic ticket for reelection as Vice President in 1944, of how he mistook Soviet intentions in the immediate postwar era and was cruelly used by the left-leaning Progressive party as its Presidential candidate in 1948. Many forget that Wallace subsequently split with his Progressive backers over U.S. entry into the Korean war, which he favored, and that he shifted to deep distrust of Soviet aims. One of the fascinating conjectures of modern American history is how Wallace might have handled the problems of the immediate postwar era if he had actually been retained as Vice President and had succeeded Roosevelt as Chief Executive in 1945.

Until the emergence of Harold Hughes, no Iowa politician of the past quarter century seemed even to have the potential of a Hoover or Wallace. Sen. Bourke B. Hickenlooper was a conservative and man of the corporations but also a forthright man who grew in office; he was ranking Republican on the Foreign Relations Committee before his retirement in 1968. No great lights have appeared in the congressional delegation, in part because of the political gyrations which have cost it all significant House seniority. Fitting the state's industrialization-population pattern, the most inflexible, uncompromising conservatives represent rural areas of western and central Iowa.* The southwestern area congressman, William Scherle, favored U.S. withdrawal from the UN after the ouster of Nationalist China and seating of Red China. The congressional district which includes Des Moines almost invariably elects a Democrat, and the representatives from the two more urbanized eastern districts along the Mississippi are liberal Democrats or moderate Republicans. One of these, Democrat John Culver, was a college roommate and later aide to Senator Edward M. Kennedy, dubious credentials for success in Iowa politics; still, even when Vice President Agnew spoke for his opponent in 1970, Culver won with 60 percent of the vote. In 1972, Culver refrained from challenging Senator Jack Miller because he thought the race was hopeless—only, to his chagrin, to see his former aide, Dick Clark, win the seat.

The other eastern Iowa Congressman until his defeat in 1972, liberal Republican Fred Schwengel, made his mark in Congress as that body's most adept Lincoln scholar.

Iowa's most conspicuous Congressman for the last two decades has been H. R. Gross, a cantankerous man of diminutive stature and booming voice who wages an unrelenting, personal war against bloated federal budgets, junketing of his colleagues, and hanky-panky in high places.† He can be seen any day Congress is in session wandering at random about the House floor, hands in pockets, an ashen look of anger on his heavy-lidded face, ready to press time-consuming quorum calls and force his colleagues to consider if not heed his puritanical counsels. ("When they start shoving me around," Gross says, "then I ram one right down their throats with a

* Western Iowa has not always been so conservative. George Mills points out that the northwestern counties were the area where the Farm Holiday movement was spectacularly violent during the Depression of the 1930s, "where rampaging farmers pulled a judge off the bench and left him with a rope burn around his neck for refusing to pledge that he would not sign mortgage foreclosures." One county in the region—Palo Alto, near the Minnesota border—still refuses to conform to western Iowa's standard conservatism; in fact, it remains one of America's classic bellwether counties, having voted for the Presidential winner for as long as anyone now living can remember.

† Gross's definition of the improper is not universally shared. One of his targets was President Johnson's aide, the Rev. Bill Moyers, who incurred the Grossian wrath for dancing the frug in the White House.

quorum call.") The bright side of Gross is that his caustic remarks often enliven dull House debates, and that he performs a positive service in forcing legislators pushing their favorite bills to be well prepared for debate; through his questioning, he pins down the meaning of ambiguous legislation. (He must be the only member of Congress who reads the entire contents of *every* piece of legislation that comes to the floor.) A widely held view is that of Massachusetts' Silvio O. Conte, a liberal Republican: "I think Gross performs a hell of a great service for the Congress." Many Iowans remember Gross as the voice of doom on Des Moines radio station WHO in his newscasting days (before he went to Congress in 1948). The man who introduced Gross and did his commercials was—yes, Ronald Reagan. Oddly enough, Gross, the Iowa Gothic champion of olden values, may have been one of the first "media candidates" of American history; Iowa political experts believe that it was only his fame as a broadcaster that enabled him to upset a well entrenched incumbent to win his first congressional race in the 1948 Republican primary.

Back in his 16-county district in north central Iowa, Gross restrains the wild tactics displayed on the House floor. His wife—"Mom"—will come along to campaign with Gross. At a church coffee, with everyone gathered around to hear him, he'll be like just one of the folks, giving the impression that he's with them against big government, trying to save them the injustice of seeing their tax money spent on frills and silly programs. Gross and Hughes have but one trait in common: both are utterly blunt and straightfoward.

Some other Iowans who have distinguished themselves in national life include these: physicist James A. Van Allen of radiation belt fame; journalist-columnist Marquis Childs; the Pulitizer Prize-winning cartoonist Jay ("Ding") Darling; novelist MacKinlay Kantor; Presidential adviser (under F.D.R.) Harry L. Hopkins; painter Grant Wood of "American Gothic" fame; musical director and composer Meredith Willson; circus king Charles Ringling; evangelist Billy Sunday; and "Buffalo Bill" Cody. George Washington Carver, born in slavery in neighboring Missouri, was the first Negro student at Iowa State University. Two Iowans of a very nonconformist bent who have made an impact in national life in recent years are Sam Brown, youthful organizer of the 1968 Presidential campaign of Eugene McCarthy, and Nicholas Johnson, the first member of the Federal Communications Commission to challenge the profit-first practices of the commercial networks and radio-television stations that lease the nation's airwaves.

Problems of State Government, Population, and the Aged

Harold Hughes left Iowa's state government exalted (in terms of new services) but exhausted (in terms of finance). The big tax increases in 1965 and 1967 stirred a rebellion among the taxpayers, who were likely to take little solace in being told their tax effort established Iowa as one of the more responsive state governments.

The man who succeeded Hughes as governor was Robert Ray, a thoughtful, low-keyed man whose gentle demeanor belies unusual inner toughness and resistance to caving in to pressures. Ray is a genuine liberal on race matters and social issues in general, but also a pragmatic individual.* "When I became governor," he told me, "the cupboard was bare and the departments and agencies wanted a 50 percent increase." Urging more taxes and increased budgets right after the Hughes years would probably have been politically suicidal, or useless, or both; Ray therefore opposed new taxes during his first term and strove to hold the line on the budget. The predictable result was that localities were obliged to increase their taxes so sharply for schools and other local services that people began to cry out to the state government for relief from the onerous local property tax. The climate was then right for creation of a legislative tax-study commission, which recommended a general state tax increase.

In his second term, starting in 1971, Ray switched to support of new taxes, urging that they be progressive in nature—largely through an increase in the corporate and personal income taxes. (The conservatives would have preferred increasing the more regressive sales tax.) Ray won that battle, with corporate and income taxes both increased by about a third. The legislature also enacted a temporary freeze on property taxes for schools and approved Ray's "foundation plan" for school aid, which has the effect of equalizing per-pupil expenditures in the various school districts through a steadily rising state aid guarantee figure. While school financing is sure to remain a major headache for years to come, the new legislation should help to maintain Iowa's traditional record of first-rate school education. Up to this point in time, the success of Iowa schools has been reflected in one of the nation's lowest illiteracy rates, a low high-school dropout figure, and a low rate of military service rejections of Iowa youth.

The financing of higher education is another knotty problem of Iowa state government, and Ray was not successful in preventing slashes in the budget for the state-supported institutions. Iowa has had reason, over its history, to be proud of its universities. Iowa State University at Ames, first land grant college in the U.S. and still a major agricultural and scientific center, is a leading institution in nuclear fission research. The University of Iowa at Iowa City is a strong liberal arts college with schools of law, medicine, and business; in recent years it has gained notice for its space research conducted under James Van Allen. But while the state's population has re-

* Ray had distinguished himself as the Iowa Republican chairman, winning appointment as chairman of the national Republican state chairmen's association. In 1964 he had tried to stem the lemming-like rush of the heartland GOP to Goldwater by backing William Scranton and withholding 10 of the state's 24 convention votes from the Arizonan. Only Minnesota and North Dakota among the Plains States showed comparable resistance to Goldwaterism. At the 1972 Republican Convention, Iowa was also one of the few states west of the Mississippi with substantial moderate-to-liberal strength on its delegation. Ray, who can take credit for much of this, has never been popular with the conservative wing of the Iowa GOP, which would like to retire him to private life. But through his third-term victory in 1972, all the wins (including election of a lieutenant governor, Arthur Neu, who shares his moderate politics) were on Ray's side.

mained static, the universities have mushroomed; together with the new community colleges (20 of which were authorized by the legislature in one fell swoop in 1965), the financial burden is heavy. Over most of the post-war era, Iowa college administrators seemed to believe that federal money for university facilities and research was somehow tainted, so that the state failed to receive its share of aid from Washington. Yet Iowa graduates more Ph.D's per capita than any other state, and outlays per student at the major state institutions of higher learning went from $350 to $2,300 per student year in the period from 1947 to 1967. At last count Iowa ranked 18th among the states in its tax effort, related to population, for higher education.

The financial problems of Iowa state government may be alleviated to a degree by cost-cutting reorganization measures effected by Ray. And as a result of a constitutional amendment approved by the voters in 1972, the increasingly troublesome system of two-year terms for the governor and other top officials are replaced by four-year terms. Under Ray's leadership, the legislature has enacted a number of progressive laws, including a unified court system, a statewide building code, a new state department of environmental quality, and one of the country's first statewide ombudsman's posts.

One problem for which few solutions are in sight, however, is the demand of the cities for direct aid from the state, or new taxing authority, to solve their budget crises. For years the rural legislators, antagonistic to the cities, turned a deaf ear to all cries for help. The glimmering of change appeared in 1971, however, when at least local school districts were allowed to levy a surtax on the state income tax of their residents. Increasing state help with school expenses may reduce the kind of overburden on the local property tax that led to instances like the 1969 strike of firemen against the hard-pressed Des Moines City government.

Ultimately, the movement toward more responsive state government will depend on the state's economic health. In 1970 the Census takers found 2,824,376 people in Iowa (exactly halfway down the ranking list of the 50 states' populations). But Iowa has failed to grow at a rate equaling the national average in any decade of this century. During the 1950s, a very modest 5.2 percent population increase (up to 2,757,537 souls) was registered in Iowa, but by the time Hughes took office in 1963, only West Virginia was losing population more rapidly. "We were going downhill rapidly," Hughes told me in an interview. For one thing, there was the flight of 2,000 to 6,000 people from Iowa farms each year, many then unable to find other jobs within the state. Another reason was the lack of sophisticated, high-paying jobs within the state. The result was an hour-glass population figure, heavy at the top (Iowa trails only Florida in its share of population 65 or over), thin in the middle (because of the outward flights of working-age people), and close to the national average at the bottom (the young, staying around long enough to be educated at Iowa's expense). But about two years after Hughes took office, the population decline was halted, and by 1970 Iowa's population had risen a total of 66,839 (2.4 percent) over 1960. Nevertheless, there was a net outmigration of 183,000 people from the state during the decade, the slight general population rise attributable only to the excess of births over deaths. (Actually the overall growth rate would have been somewhat higher if the birth control pill had not come into vogue during the decade; in the words of my friend George Mills, who for decades was the chief political reporter for the Des Moines *Register*, "the Soaring Sixties turned out to be the Contraceptive Sixties." And Iowa could take a little comfort in the fact that the number of people leaving it for other states actually declined 20 percent from the 1950s to the 1960s.)

If Iowa is indeed turning the corner economically, important credit should go to Hughes' industrial recruitment effort, which brought in a substantial number of new jobs, mixed between well paying positions in the standard manufacturing industries and some low-paying, needle-type operations, especially in the rural areas.* An essential Hughes contribution was to make the investment of public funds needed in areas like education, recreation, and culture, so that an appropriate business climate could develop. During the 1960s, the per capita income in Iowa rose 86 percent, an increase greater than the national average income growth, even though the absolute national dollar figure remained a few hundred dollars higher. But major work remains for Iowa in this decade if it is to develop a rationalized "systems approach" to new development in industry, highways, schools, water quality control, and natural resources, along the lines of the Kansas effort.

One positive thing one can say of Iowa's population profile is that the people are well dispersed geographically, with no huge metropolitan centers. (Even the Des Moines metropolitan area accounts for just 10 percent of the Iowa population.) As Hughes points out, dispersal makes it possible to hold down social problems.

But the problem of the state's more than 350,000 elderly people is especially pathetic; most frequently in rural areas, the old folks are often left in total desolation as their children and grandchildren migrate to more prosperous locales. Forced to fend for themselves, the aged of Iowa, like those across the country, must cope with pensions that fail to keep pace with inflation, inadequate housing, spotty medical care. The Medicare program for the elderly probably is the greatest social welfare innovation of the postwar years, but even it cannot create physicians and facilities where they are lacking. The 1970 Census found that 28 percent of Iowans over 65 were living below the poverty line, with the situation the most grave in rural areas. Reporter Veryl Sanderson of the Des Moines *Register* related this story of a single aging man in Des Moines:

> Ray Goff is an island, 73 years old, drifting aimlessly in a sea of humanity which has chosen to ignore him and others like him.
>
> Goff's world is framed by the window sill of his $45-a-month apartment. He sees farther with his weak eyes than his failing legs will carry him.

* As an example of new rural-type development, the people of Leon, a depressed little town in southern Iowa, raised $100,000 and simply gave it to a Chicago lingerie firm that was interested in a location with a better labor climate than the big city. The employees are mostly women, paid just over the minimum wage, their meager earnings helping their families to stick it out on marginal farms. The successful operation in Leon prompted the same firm to start a cutting factory some 50 miles away, and then a shipping location not far distant.

For as many as 12 hours a day his world rotates around a wooden, straight-backed chair in front of the window.

His view takes in two taverns, a hardware store, a paint store, a garage, parking lot, Locust Street and (far in the distance) Third Street traffic east of the Veterans' Auditorium and—ironically—the towering shape of a modern, yet-uncompleted retirement home.

His only companion is a mongrel dog, Jumbo, who is just as hungry for affection as his master. . . .

He receives $168 a month: a $90 Social Security check and a $78 World War I pension. The average pensioner in the Des Moines area receives $100 a month or less. . . .

"I'm most generally broke every payday," Goff says. "The man at the restaurant trusts me when I run out of money until payday. I skimp on the meals. My breakfast costs $1.03 and I don't usually eat dinner. I go out again for supper, but sometimes I only have a roll and a cup of coffee.

"Then there's Jumbo. He has to eat too. He's my only companion and I have to take care of him. If I have to buy any clothes, I go broke." . . .

Goff's daily routine. "I get up around 9 a.m. I fix Jumbo something to eat and then get something to eat myself. . . . I take him for a short walk, because I can't walk too good anymore. Then, I come home and sit right down in this chair in front of the window.

"When it starts getting dark, I take Jumbo for another walk. . . . I come back here, sit at the window, and go to bed about 8 p.m."

Goff has lived this existence since his wife died two years ago. "After she died, cooking for myself just didn't seem worth the bother. If I get lonesome, I talk to the dog and to myself."

Goff has five daughters, none of whom live in Iowa.

His living quarters are two ancient, large rooms, illuminated by two bare light bulbs in each room hanging starkly down from the high ceilings. However, Goff mostly sits in the dark until he goes to bed.

Sitting in his chair, petting Jumbo, Goff reminisces, "I lived on a farm near Blockton, Iowa, with my step-dad and mother. I went to a country school, but only through the second grade. I was nine years old then. I rolled up a pair of overalls and a shirt and went up the road. I've been on my own ever since. . . .

"Every week or two, a neighbor will talk to me. If I get real lonesome, I go for a walk. Sometimes, people on the street talk to me, but not very often. . . .

"Nobody checks to see if I'm okay. If I got sick, dog here might let out a war-whoop, and somebody might find me that way. . . ."

Des Moines: Multifaceted Capital

It was hot that August afternoon in Des Moines, blisteringly hot. The waitress saw me sweltering. "Never mind," she said, "this is the kind of weather that's good for corn."

Thus John Gunther reported on Agristate's capital some 25 years ago, suggesting that, like the rest of Iowa, Des Moines' real preoccupation is with the soil. Even now, one hears from some that Des Moines is "a kind of county seat at the state level." Its chief business is state government, bringing the rest of Iowa to its doorstep, and the factory and office workers of Des Moines are likely to have dads and moms back in the small towns or on the farm.

But Des Moines for many decades has also been an important printing, banking, and especially insurance center; it has even been labeled the "Hartford of the West, although its insurance holdings (substantial firms like the century-old Equitable Life of Iowa, Bankers Life, Central Life, etc.) pale in comparison to Hartford or Los Angeles. In modern times Des Moines has acquired significant amounts of manufacturing. And with 6 percent Negroes in its population of 200,587, it faces race problems like every other American city.

Surprisingly, Des Moines ranks high among U.S. cities in per capita income, with some amazing concentrations of wealth. But the money was first accumulated by men who specialized in minimizing their risks in banking and insurance, not in maximizing income. As a result, the city has actually suffered from a shortage of risk capital, in contrast to a city like Minneapolis which has spawned so many new products and ideas. The principal manufacturing plants are owned by outsiders, not Des Moines interests, and its downtown fails to reflect the national postwar office building boom. In the mid-1960s, city leaders feared that offices and major retailers would all filter to the suburbs. A strange turning point was reached when a single store, J.C. Penney Co., was prevailed upon—after considerable persuasion by downtown business groups—to build a new outlet in center city instead of in the suburbs as it had planned. Somehow this single decision by a less than elegant chain retailer restored confidence in the future of downtown. Now some of the casualty firms, which one might have expected to start much earlier on their own initiative to rebuild their home city, are beginning to invest a small fraction of their billions in downtown construction.

Des Moines operates under a city manager form of government with a popularly elected mayor and council; up to 1967 its management had been under the control of an older group of men not much interested in innovation. Then a charter revision was approved under which some councilmen would be elected by districts, giving its own representation to the poor east side of town which had previously been eclipsed by the wealthier west side. This preceded the election in 1967 of a much younger group of city leaders led by a 33-year-old mayoralty candidate named Thomas Urban. Urban defeated a 72-year-old opponent to win the office by a margin of about 700 votes out of 40,000 cast. An articulate, fast-talking Harvard graduate, Urban defied any outsider's preconception of what a mayor of Des Moines, Iowa, would be like. He and his young allies, constituting a bare majority on the city council, tried a number of interesting new programs, including the first joint sensitivity training sessions for white establishment and black leaders ever officially sponsored by an American city.

Other innovative programs included a project with potential school dropouts, letting them work half a day on a real job while continuing with regular schooling the other half day. "We found," Urban said, "that the kids learn more in four hours than they used to in eight." A "drop-in" school system was established for youngsters who had already left school, boys and girls for whom the system had otherwise "snapped closed." The "drop-in" school, located in center city, had a completely informal curriculum—and good attendance. The council passed an extraordinarily effective open-housing ordinance, providing that if a person refused to sell to a minority buyer, he could be confronted within 24 hours with an injunction preventing him from selling to anyone else.

Urban was generally regarded as a liberal, but he tried to avoid the tag. "I've tried to involve the people who feel left out on the right and the left in real problems," he told me in an interview. "I put very conservative-type Birch people on our finance committee and tried to make openings on the other side for spokesmen of disadvantaged groups often excluded from the political process. When dealing with a city, you don't have time for ideology. You have concrete problems to solve—and the question is, "What is the solution?"

For unexplained "personal reasons," Urban declined to run for reelection in 1971. A young insurance executive named Richard Olson, liberal-to-moderate in political ideology, replaced him as mayor, and the liberals lost their effective control of the city council. In 1972 the city found itself immersed in disputes about expanding the federal model cities area from predominantly black to several white areas.

Des Moines thinks of itself as a rather cosmopolitan and tolerant city, allowing Jews, for instance, to join its best clubs, a step which the leading country clubs in Omaha have yet to take. Its community fund effort is one of the most successful in the country. Special pride is taken in the $700,000 Des Moines Art Center, designed by Eliel Saarinen and opened in 1948; this museum has acquired a number of major works and ranks close to the top galleries of the country.

Des Moines suffers, however, from severe problems—those of its aged (referred to earlier), race discord, and fundamental issues of poverty and hunger within its borders. In this great city of a great agristate, a reporter for the *National Observer*, Mark Arnold, discovered people digging in the dump for food and infants dying for lack of milk. A 26-year-old mother of two small children, whose husband was unable to find work, told him:

> We mooch same's other folks, I guess. One thing we always got is milk 'cuz my ma keeps a goat. We don't always eat the same thing all the time either. One day I'll fix macaroni for lunch, the next day spaghetti, or potatoes so we get a little variety too. . . . I had a steak once, about three months ago. A boy friend of my husband's was servin' it and invited us over. Imagine that, me going 26 years without tastin' steak. I took one little bitty bite and said, "Boy, it sure was worth waitin' for."

A Great Newspaper and Other Powers

Highly significant voices for moderation and reason in Iowa have for decades been the illustrious Des Moines *Register* and *Tribune*, part of the Cowles family publishing chain which includes the Minneapolis papers. The morning *Register* enjoys a unique position among American newspapers in that it is truly a state rather than a city newspaper; on Sunday, when its circulation is nearly 500,000 (reaching two out of three Iowa households), less than 20 percent of the copies are actually delivered in Des Moines. Sunday *Register* delivery, in fact, is available to any farm or home in any of Iowa's 99 counties.*

What a newspaper tells a state about itself, through the type of interpretive, deep news coverage which the *Register* attempts to deliver, has a lot to do with what a state becomes—its essential character, its mirror to itself. Moreover, a list of the causes championed editorially by the *Register* goes far to explain why Iowa is not strictly the conservative rural bastion many outsiders see it to be. The paper has been strongly internationalist since before World War I; it spoke out for American entry into the League of Nations and, a generation later, the United Nations. For decades, it has been a strong voice for civil rights, improved race relations, and academic freedom. It has been for maintaining farm income through government programs, for legislative reapportionment, for liquor by the drink (though it refused, until 1971, to take liquor advertising itself). Publisher-editor Kenneth MacDonald describes the paper's policy as "partisanly independent"; in 1960 it backed Nixon, in 1964 Johnson, in 1968 Humphrey, though half-heartedly. In 1972, the paper was severely critical of President Nixon on issues like Vietnam, the Watergate affair, and secret campaign contributions—but endorsed his reelection anyway. Endorsements have gone to Governor Ray in his races and to Democratic Senators Hughes and Clark. Not a small part of the *Register*'s enlivening influence has come through aggressive investigatory reporting, a business on which reporters like Clark Mollenhoff and Nick Kotz (who later moved on to the Washington *Post*) have built national reputations.

Despite its statewide circulation, the *Register* disclaims any desire to replace local newspapers outside the Des Moines area; the theory is simply that the reader needs a journal with statewide focus to supplement his local paper. Anyone who has traveled extensively in America will be aware of the paltry quality of most medium- and small-city newspapers, a cultural and informational wasteland to rival the worst of what television has to offer. Iowa has several of that stripe, but there are bright exceptions, the chief of which is the Cedar Rapids *Gazette*, a journal of outstanding quality which has taken a leading role in the rejuvenation of its part of Iowa. (Cedar Rapids is perhaps the physically most attractive city of Iowa, has the state's best television station, and enjoys the liberalizing influence of Iowa University in nearby Iowa City.) Other Iowa newspapers of note are the Waterloo *Courier* and Council Bluffs *Nonpareil*, both of which are extremely conservative, articulate papers, the Davenport *Times-Democrat*, the Burlington *Hawk-Eye*, and the Mason City *Globe*. High on the mediocrity scale are the Sioux City and Dubuque papers.

The Des Moines *Register*'s principal crusade of recent years has been against the big truckers, which it alleges have never paid their fair share of

* The afternoon *Tribune*, published weekdays only, has a smaller circulation, largely confined to Des Moines and the immediately adjacent counties.

highway costs and maintain lobbies reminiscent of the railroads in their heydays of the late 1800s and early 1900s. The *Register* carries more news on trucking than practically any other U.S. paper and backed Governor Ray in his effort to get an increase in truck license fees. Harold Hughes, who got his business start through trucking, disparages the *Register*'s activities in this field.

A final word on power in Iowa. By general consensus, the Farm Bureau has demonstrated the most durable and pervasive influence. Even its antagonists ruefully admit its power with state legislators is still great. Senator Hughes identifies the Farm Bureau as "the major factor in the status quo image of the state." On issues like reapportionment, the Bureau has found an able rival in the Iowa League of Municipalities, a group also known for its influence on constructive legislation—despite its failure, to date, to win general state aid for the cities.

Labor unions have traditionally been weak in Iowa and an insignificant factor in legislative battles. (Iowa is a right-to-work state). But the United Auto Workers, headed by a burly diamond-in-the-rough named Soapy (actually Edris) Owens, have made phenomenal advances in the past few years —up from 11,000 Iowa members in 1957 to over 30,000 today. The backbone of UAW's membership is in firms making farm implements—John Deere, J. I. Case, Oliver Corp., and Massey-Ferguson. Owens, who comes out of the UAW local at Maytag in Newton, is a strong liberal in Detroit-UAW mode and is trying to build his union into a politically conscious political arm in the state. His problem is that the great bulk of his members come from farm backgrounds; it is foreign enough to their background to join a union, not to mention becoming liberal political activists. Owens takes a strong stand for civil rights, but only two or three of his locals have any blacks, and he might be hard-put to get backing for his rights stand if he put the question to a vote of the membership. Nevertheless, the growth of a strong UAW in Iowa may have interesting long-term effects.

MINNESOTA

THE SUCCESSFUL SOCIETY

"MINNESOTA is a state spectacularly varied, proud and handsome, with a progressive political tradition," John Gunther reported in *Inside U.S.A.* The intervening quarter century has done little to tarnish the bright image of the North Star State. Its leaders, in fact, have played an increasingly prominent role in national life, far out of proportion to the state's modest 2 percent of the national population. Its political structure remains open, issue-oriented, responsible. Its state government has been a leader in services for people, even though citizens and corporations alike have had to pay a high tax bill for those services. Few states exceed Minnesota in the quality and extent of the education offered its citizens; none appears to provide health care of comparable quality. Economic growth has been strong and steady, encompassing the brainpower industries of the electronic era along with traditional farming, milling, and mining. And Minnesota maintains a clear focus of economic and cultural leadership in her Twin Cities, towns whose great industries have resisted the siren call of the national conglomerates.

Minnesota is a state in which its people can take justifiable pride and, despite a number of shortcomings which we will not ignore, as good a model as one can find in these United States of the successful society.

But why successful? The visitor to Minnesota hears many reasons, but none is so convincing as perhaps the simplest: these people appear to have control of their own destiny. No single industrial cabal, no bank group, no patronage-hungry courthouse crowd controls Minnesota. Ask Minnesotans who "runs" their state, and you get a blank stare in response. The special interest groups are there lobbying in the legislature: railroads, private power companies, labor and business groups, for instance. But none is consistently successful, and the crucial decisions of a public nature are made through the political process with few invisible powers lurking behind the throne. The political parties, constituted by an especially democratic process from local precinct caucuses on up, wield the significant power—and through them, the people.

"People's politics," of course, can lead to excesses, since a determined faction can on occasion pack the precinct caucuses and in turn a party's state convention. This occurred in 1972 when extreme liberals, most identified with the Presidential candidacy of George McGovern, took control of the state Democratic-Farmer-Labor convention and forced through platform planks endorsing the legalization and open sale of marijuana, full rights (including marriage) of homosexuals, and full amnesty for both draft evaders and military deserters. The positions were clearly unrepresentative of the broad mass of Minnesota Democrats, and the party's chief officeholders quickly sought to disassociate themselves from the platform.

But usually the system works well, and as a general rule one cannot find another state in which party platforms and campaign promises are taken more seriously. An example was provided by the pledge of Democratic candidate Wendell R. Anderson, in the 1970 gubernatorial campaign, to work for property tax equalization and a much greater state share of school financing. After Anderson had been elected, he pressed the legislature—which was under control of the opposition party—to pass the tax and school finance reforms. The issue was hotly debated through the regular legislative session and two special sessions in 1971, culminating in passage of a program to increase the state's share of school costs from 43 to 65 percent with a guarantee of $750 per child. The school financing reform was part of a revamping of the entire fiscal relationship between the state and its localities so sweeping that the national Advisory Committee on Intergovernmental Relations later hailed it as "The Minnesota Miracle." While receiving substantial new state money both for schools and other functions, the local government units were also limited to budget increases of 6 percent a year—the goal being to achieve property tax reductions averaging 15 to 20 percent for each property owner in the state. This was the same year that courts across the country, starting with the landmark *Seranno* decision in California, began to invalidate the local property tax as the chief source of school financing. An October 1971 decision by a federal judge in Minnesota required the same change in the tax system. But in Minnesota, the court action was almost an afterthought; the essential point is that in this state the issue had already been handled in its most appropriate forum, the political-legislative system, not the courts.

Another, more "quiet" revolution has also been taking place in Minnesota. Quite rapidly, the policy-setting boards in state and local government, traditionally dominated by professionals of one type or another, have been "cleaned out" through replacement of the professional members by dedicated and interested lay citizens who are more concerned with the breadth and quality of services delivered than with special professional prerogatives. The examples are myriad. The members of the new Twin Cities Metropolitan Council, one of the most advanced regional government bodies in the country, come directly out of the citizenry, a sharp contrast to most metro government boards in America, which are filled with elected officials (a kind of "professional") defending their own domains. The Higher Education Coordinating Commission, which divides up federal money flowing into the state, was made up until 1971 of college presidents who sidestepped controversial issues; now, by decision of the legislature, the commission has a genuine citizen membership and may not include anyone with a vested interest in one of the public or private colleges. Citizens have replaced industry representatives on the Water Pollution Board, and are setting priorities for the new health maintenance organizations. The state has its second highway commissioner who is not an engineer. Consumer representatives are moving onto the state licensing and standards boards for barbers, watchmakers, plumbers, electricians, and the like. Minnesota is finding a reservoir of citizens able to assume these key policy-making roles in the society—leaving the implementation of programs, of course, to the professionals under their direction.

In 1971 Minnesota launched the nation's first statewide press council to receive complaints from citizens who feel they have been unfairly treated by the newspapers; the 18 members are divided equally between nonjournalists and representatives of the state's daily and weekly press. In a remarkable departure from their normally self-protective ways, most of the state's newspapers have agreed to publish reports of council grievance hearings and recommendations for corrections or retractions. The founders of the press council, including the innovative head of the Minnesota Newspaper Association, Robert Shaw, hope that at least in their state, some of the "crisis of confidence" facing the American press may be overcome when citizens know they have recourse if the newspapers treat them unfairly.

The openness of Minnesota public life, the willingness of leaders to try new ideas, and the state's demonstrated capacity to handle money and programs well and honestly, bring dividends of many kinds. For instance, Minnesota's reputation has enabled it to become in recent times a kind of R & D (research and development) grant center for new programs of the federal government and foundations.

In sum, Minnesota is a deceptively simple example of how a democratic society should be run. A responsive political system lies at the root of this success story, and our search into Minnesota's unique character must begin with that system and how it came to be what it is today.

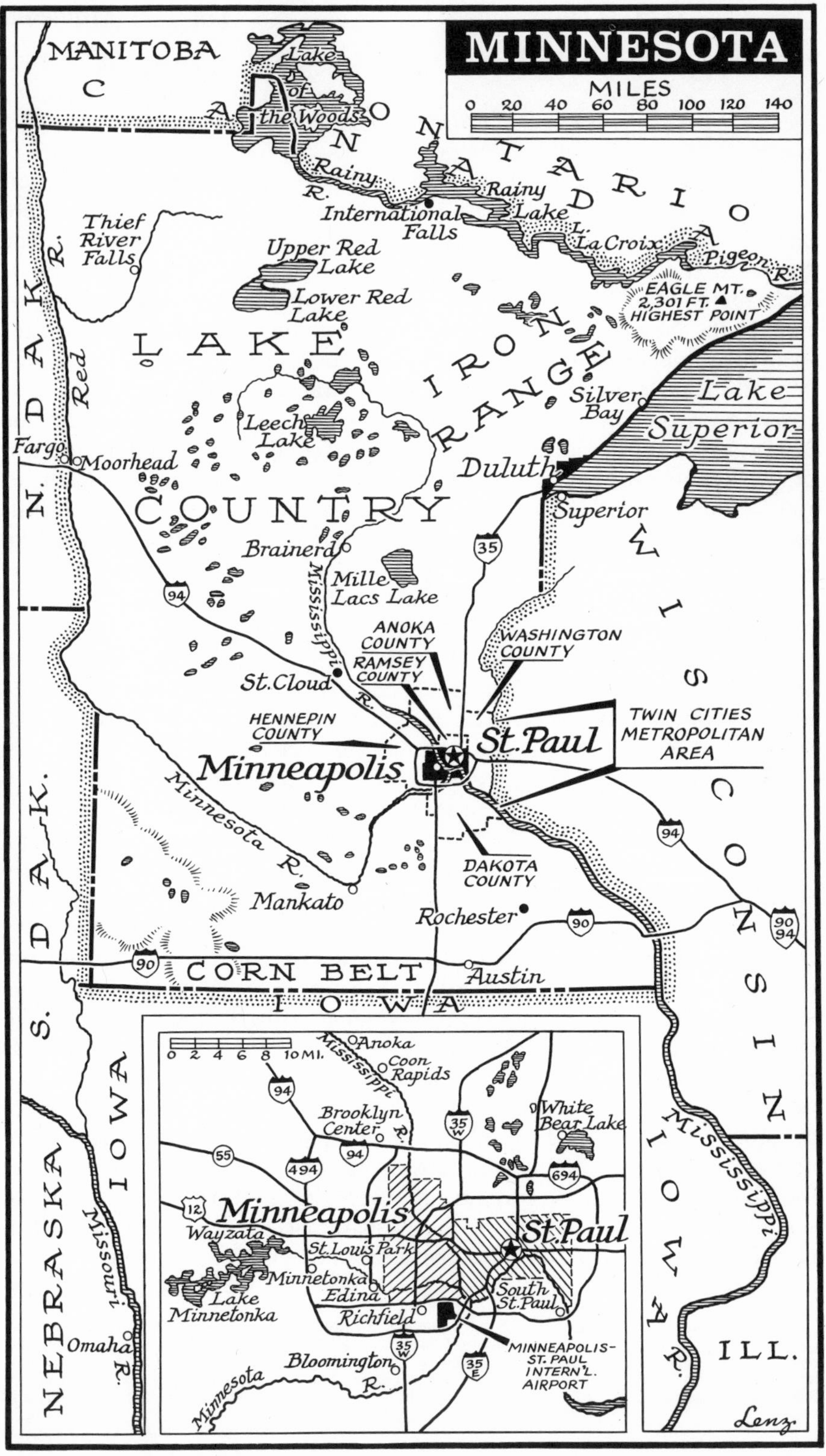
MINNESOTA
MILES
0 20 40 60 80 100 120 140
MANITOBA
CANADA
ONTARIO
Lake of the Woods
Rainy R.
International Falls
Rainy Lake
L. La Croix
Pigeon R.
EAGLE MT. 2,301 FT. HIGHEST POINT
Thief River Falls
Red R.
Upper Red Lake
Lower Red Lake
LAKE COUNTRY
IRON RANGE
Silver Bay
Lake Superior
Leech Lake
Fargo
Moorhead
Duluth
Superior
Brainerd
Mille Lacs Lake
Mississippi R.
ANOKA COUNTY
RAMSEY COUNTY
WASHINGTON COUNTY
St. Cloud
HENNEPIN COUNTY
St. Paul
TWIN CITIES METROPOLITAN AREA
Minneapolis
Minnesota R.
DAKOTA COUNTY
Mankato
Rochester
Austin
CORN BELT
IOWA
N. DAK.
S. DAK.
WISCONSIN
NEBRASKA
IOWA
Missouri R.
Omaha
ILL.
Mississippi R.
35
94
90
90 94
0 2 4 6 8 10 MI.
Anoka
Coon Rapids
Brooklyn Center
White Bear Lake
55
494
694
12
35 W
35 E
Minneapolis
St. Paul
Wayzata
St. Louis Park
Minnetonka
Edina
Lake Minnetonka
Richfield
South St. Paul
MINNEAPOLIS-ST. PAUL INTERN'L. AIRPORT
Bloomington
Minnesota R.
Lenz

Ethnic Roots and Early Politics

From the first years, Minnesota's dominant ethnic strain was northern (American Yankee, Scandinavian, German) and her leading religions Protestant. Achieving statehood in 1858, Minnesota was the first state to offer troops to the Union side; later her sons fought with special gallantry at Gettysburg. Republicanism became the natural order of the day; until the advent of the New Deal, Minnesota never once voted for a Democratic Presidential candidate, and Republicans won 30 of 35 elections for governor.

Minnesota's Republicanism, however, was remarkably progressive. In the wake of the Civil War, a massive inflow of literate, liberal Swedes and Norwegians naturally allied themselves with the Yankee Protestant element of the Republican party that was opposed to slavery, liquor, and Catholicism.* Numerically, the combination of Yankees and Scandinavians had little difficulty outvoting the remnants of the Democratic party, which looked for support to German Catholics, the Irish, and, after 1890, East European immigrants brought in to man the forestry and mining industries of the north.

Most importantly, the Republicans found ways to bend government to meet the needs and problems of laborers and particularly the Scandinavian wheat farmers, who were often caught in a price squeeze and blamed their plight on warehouse and commission merchants and the railroads. Every decade or two, discontented farmers and laborers would respond to a new movement designed to help them—the Grangers and the People's Anti-Monopoly party in the 1870s, the Farmers Alliance in the 1880s and '90s, the Progressives in the early 1900s. In the 1880s, the Republicans enacted a state-enforced system of grading and inspection; in the 1870s and '80s, they regulated railroad, freight, and elevator charges; in the early 1900s the Republicans enacted the nation's first mandatory statewide primary law and prosecuted the Northern Securities Company, a giant scheme to monopolize control of the railroads engineered by Pierpont Morgan, Edwin H. Harriman, and other financial interests. In 1895 a child labor law was passed, in 1913 a workmen's compensation act. This responsiveness of an established political party helped create the attitude that the regular political process can be used to gain ends for people. One result was that Minnesota abjured the initiative and referendum and other Populist-era devices used by people to check governments they did not trust; this left responsibility squarely in the hands of the regularly elected legislature, and Minnesota's is still one of the most powerful and sensitive to public demand in the country today.

* The Yankees conceded power to the Scandinavians when the population shift dictated a change. Up to 1893, every Minnesota governor was a Yankee—names like Sibley, Ramsey, Swift, Davis, Pillsbury, Merriam. Then the first Scandinavian, Knute Nelson, was elected. Since 1899 all Minnesota governors, regardless of party, have had Scandinavian names. The list includes surnames like Eberhart, Burnquist, Christianson, Olson, Petersen, Stassen, Thye, Youngdahl, Andersen, Rolvaag, LeVander, and Anderson.

The long-dominant Republicans, however, made a serious mistake in 1918. Three years before, the Non-Partisan League had been organized in neighboring North Dakota. NPLism soon infected the Scandinavian wheat growers of western Minnesota, who were attracted to its socialistic platform, which included establishment of state-owned packing plants, elevators, and flour mills in an effort to relieve the farmer of gouging by the middleman. The NPL entered a full slate of candidates in the 1918 Republican primary, but the Republican governor of the moment, fearing a Soviet-style revolution, responded by setting up a Commission of Public Safety which labeled the NPL'ers as traitors and broke up their meetings with strong-arm tactics. The NPL faction lost in the Republican primary and again, under the label of Farmer-Labor party, in the general election. But a major change in Minnesota politics, shifting thousands of Scandinavians and like-minded progressives out of the Republican party and into the new Farmer-Labor party, had been effected. The Republicans were left a primarily nativist party; political scientist James Fenton has prepared maps showing an almost exact correspondence between the Protestant, non-Scandinavian counties and the highest Republican vote in the state in recent times.

The new Farmer-Labor party, heavily Scandinavian in complexion, elected two U.S. Senators but remained a minority faction until 1930. Then, in the depths of the Depression, Floyd B. Olson was actually elected governor on the Farmer-Labor ticket. Olson disdained liberalism and ran on a platform which called for abolition of capitalism and state ownership of banks, mines, utilities, transportation, and packing plants. But once elected, Olson tended to push for New Dealish rather than socialistic programs; remaining in office until his death in 1936, he won approval of conservation, old-age pensions, and expanded welfare programs. Olson was succeeded in 1937 by another Farmer-Labor candidate, Elmer Benson. Benson proved to be inept and was accused of corruption and pro-Communism, and in 1938 the Farmer-Laborites were ousted from power. But the interlude of third-partyism had put the regular parties on notice that they could well be outflanked unless they showed enough flexibility to accommodate desperate voices within their state. The lesson has apparently been well learned.

The Parties of Harold E. Stassen and Hubert H. Humphrey

We come now to the men who must be considered the fathers of modern Minnesota politics: Harold E. Stassen and Hubert H. Humphrey.

Stassen is remembered today by most Americans as the quixotic, perennially unsuccessful candidate for President of the United States, governor of Pennsylvania, or mayor of Philadelphia; his downfall, born of overweening ambition, must be considered a poignant personal-political tragedy. But in Minnesota this big, sandy-haired, hard-thinking man of just 31 years was a godsend for his Republican party—and state government—when he ran for and won the governorship in 1938. Few men in American politics have demonstrated a comparable faculty for arousing dedication and instilling belief in the system among his followers; many of the "Boy Scouts" of Stassen's first campaign have gone on to positions of important leadership, not the least of whom is Chief Justice Warren Burger of the United States Supreme Court.

In office, Stassen not only cleaned up the mess left by the Benson regime (sending several officials to prison) but also instituted a number of reforms the effect of which is still felt today. Perhaps the most important of these was a comprehensive civil service law; this fundamental reform has transformed the nature of Minnesota politics, making it a highly honorable profession in which citizens participate as willingly as in a united fund drive or PTA; there simply are no "bosses," and virtually no one goes into Minnestoa politics out of a patronage motive. By taking politics out of the back room and engaging thousands in political activity, from women to college students, Stassen made the governmental process in Minnesota a superior instrument of the people's will.

Stassen and his moderate-liberal Republican successors in the governorship held sway for 16 years (1939–55) and made significant advances in welfare, conservation, and mental health.* They also fashioned the Republican party of their state into a vehicle of moderation which was influenced by the business world but by no stretch of the imagination controlled by it. In the late 1960s, for example, Republican Governor Harold LeVander (another Stassen worker of the early years) would win office with substantial conservative support but nevertheless fight vigorously for stiffer state standards to control radioactive emissions from nuclear power plants than those favored by the Atomic Energy Commission—much to the offense of the influential Northern States Power Company and its business friends. (This particular effort to impose state environmental standards more stringent than the federal was struck down in 1972, however, by the U.S. Supreme Court, which ruled that the Atomic Energy Commission is the sole arbiter of regulations affecting nuclear power generation.)

While Republicans prospered during the Stassen era, the Farmer-Labor party and the Democrats split the opposition vote. In 1944, however, a young political science professor at Macalester College named Hubert H. Humphrey took the lead in persuading the Democrats and the Farmer-Laborites to merge, arguing that as long as they stayed divided, the Republicans would be assured of victory. Largely through Humphrey's efforts, a formal alliance took place and the new combined Democratic-Farmer-Labor party fielded

* Stassen burst onto the national scene as keynoter and then floor manager for Wendell Willkie at the 1940 Republican National Convention. He left Minnesota for war duty in 1943, then served on the U.S. delegation to the San Francisco conference which founded the United Nations in 1945. His really serious bid for the Presidency was in 1948; he was victorious in several primaries and might well have won the Republican nomination had he not "lost" a radio debate to Thomas E. Dewey in Oregon. Stassen then moved to Pennsylvania to become president of the University of Pennsylvania for five years; under President Eisenhower, he was foreign aid chief and then a special Presidential assistant on disarmament, a position in which he tried to advance his passion for world peace but ran afoul of John Foster Dulles and had to resign in 1958. Then came successful years as a Philadelphia lawyer but the ignominious defeats for governor of Pennsylvania (1958), mayor of Philadelphia (1959) and President (1964 and 1968).

candidates in the 1944 elections. This merger meant joining in a single party the urban German, Irish, and Polish Catholics who had been the mainstay of the old Democratic party with the rural Scandinavian Lutherans whose support had been the backbone of the Farmer-Labor party. But it also meant trying to combine some conservative middle-class Democrats with a number of left-wing elements of the Farmer-Labor party. An open battle for control of the amalgamated party was climaxed in 1948 when less radical, anti-Communist elements led by Humphrey won control of the DFL state convention and then swamped its opponents in the primary.* The Humphrey-led victory over the left wing was a boon to his political fortunes and those of his allies, who could present themselves as political moderates between the more conservative Republicans and the left-wing farmer-laborites, socialists, and Communists. That same year, Truman swept Minnesota with a plurality exceeding 200,000 votes. Humphrey, with two successful terms as mayor of Minneapolis behind him, ran several thousand votes ahead of Truman to win election to the U.S. Senate.

In the succeeding years, the DFL offered a series of "stars" for public office. Interestingly, all had either been students or faculty associates of Humphrey at the University of Minnesota or came from similar academic backgrounds. There is scarcely a parallel in American history of a group of men from the halls of academe moving as a group into such positions of power. Orville Freeman, a former student of Humphrey's and then DFL chairman, became governor from 1955 to 1961 and then served as Secretary of Agriculture during the entire Kennedy-Johnson period in Washington. Eugene McCarthy, a Representative from 1949 to 1959 and then Senator until 1971, was a former professor; so were Arthur Naftalin, mayor of Minneapolis for eight years, and John Blatnik, U.S. Representative from Minnesota's northwest corner (the Iron Range country). The father of the DFL's able Minneapolis Congressman, Donald M. Fraser, was dean of the University of Minnesota Law School. Few more illustrious groups of men have ever led a state party simultaneously, the phenomenon all the more remarkable because the election day troops who sustained the intellectual coalition were the minions of labor and the frugal farmers of the western wheatfields.

With the passage of time, the "star" system began to fade. The first reversal came in 1960 when Orville Freeman was defeated in what has been described as "that classic gubernatorial Waterloo, the try for a fourth term"; the winner was a self-made industrialist and political liberal, Republican Elmer L. Andersen. In 1962, with the gubernatorial term extended to four years, the DFL nominated not a star but a party war horse and pleasant old-shoe type, Karl Rolvaag, for governor. Rolvaag emerged the winner by 91 votes, but only after a recount that stretched out over several months. In office, Rolvaag proved to be an indecisive, weak administrator, and in

* The left-wing faction, led by former Farmer-Labor Governor Benson, had actually hoped to nominate Henry Wallace as the DFL candidate for President in Minnesota, thus denying President Truman a place on the ballot—just as the Dixiecrats succeeded in doing for Strom Thurmond in several Southern states.

1966 he was challenged by the vigorous young DFL lieutenant governor, A. M. Sandy Keith. The DFL then proceeded to destroy its long-nurtured unity by engaging in a bloody endorsement fight at its state convention, with Keith emerging the victor only after 20 ballots; in the ensuing primary, Rolvaag capitalized on a wave of public sympathy over his unceremonious dumping and won the nomination. Republican Harold LeVander beat Rolvaag in the general election, however.

Humphrey's election as Vice President in 1964 had elevated the DFL's founder and superstar to the heights of national prestige, but then came 1968 with McCarthy's challenge to President Johnson, and then to Humphrey, over the Vietnam war issue. McCarthy forces (their major strength centered, ironically, in the university community) actually wrested control of the DFL apparatus from the Humphrey regulars in three congressional districts. The Humphrey forces went on to the tumultuous Democratic National Convention in Chicago with the lion's share of Minnesota's votes in their control, and that autumn the Humphrey-Muskie ticket won Minnesota with ease. But McCarthy, one of the great DFL stars of earlier years, had been mortally wounded in his native Minnesota and did not even seek reelection in 1970. He probably would have lost had he tried.

Humphrey returned to the state arena to win overwhelmingly for the U.S. Senate in 1970. As their gubernatorial candidate, the Democrats picked a man distinctly not part of the early Humphrey-intellectual grouping: Wendell Anderson, 37 years of age, a former state legislator from the blue-collar east side of St. Paul, who had first won fame as a University of Minnesota and Olympic hockey star. Anderson won his party's primary with the support of organized labor, and some observers expected he might give the party much less innovative leadership than the old DFL stars. But he proved the skeptics wrong with his bold tax reform and school-financing program, written with the help of the university-based intellectuals.

With Humphrey heading the ticket, the Democrats scored an impressive victory in Minnesota in 1970. Not only did Humphrey win with a 220,231-vote plurality (57.8 percent), but Anderson won with 116,141 votes to spare and the Democrats took the lieutenant governorship and attorney general's office. They also made strong gains in the state house and barely missed winning control of the state senate, which the DFL faction had never been able to capture. Most observers credited the DFL resurgence to Humphrey's coattails, but in fact Humphrey helped the entire DFL ticket in another, very important way. The campaign consulting firm of Valentine, Sherman & Associates, headed by Norman Sherman, Humphrey's former press secretary, and Jack Valentine, a political scientist, was brought in to provide a comprehensive package of research, technical assistance, and financing for the entire DFL ticket.

The keystone of the Valentine-Sherman effort was the computer. All of the 1.1 million telephone subscribers in the state were put on magnetic computer tape, and local volunteers then phoned each household to determine party preferences, registration status, the number of children and old people, union membership, and the like. With this data added to the tape, the computer than began to churn out thousands of "personalized" letters with specific appeals to different kinds of voters. The letters asked support not only for Humphrey but for the other DFL statewide candidates and the specific DFL-endorsed candidates in each legislative district. The technique of informing Democratic and independent voters about the identity of DFL candidates was an immense breakthrough in Minnesota, where no party designations whatever had appeared on general election ballots for the legislature since 1913. The result had been that many Republican conservatives, capitalizing on name recognition and playing down their party, had been able to win, even in strong DFL districts—an advantage akin to the one which Republicans had enjoyed in California before that state's complex cross-filing law was repealed by a Democratic-controlled legislature in 1959.

In addition to their new emphasis on direct mail, the DFL strategists also used the computer-produced precinct lists for door-to-door canvassing to get out the Democratic vote on election day. As Alan Otten later reported in *The Wall Street Journal*, the Minnesota effort had major national implications:

> The Democrats seem finally to be recognizing the computer as a tool potentially far more valuable for them than the Republicans. The reasons for this are simple. There are more Democrats than Republicans, but Democrats don't usually register and vote as readily. Generally poorer and less educated, they aren't as motivated, or as self-starting. . . .
>
> Democrats also tend to be far more diverse—ethnically, racially, economically. Anything that helps target appeals to different groups more precisely is also likely to help Democrats more.

The final payoff of the DFL's new strategy came in 1972, when the party swept to control of both houses of the legislaure for the first time in its history. Over three elections, the party had gained no less than 48 legislative seats.

The DFL remains a hyphenated party, and its real organizational strength is provided by labor in the urban areas and the Farmers Union in the countryside. Although the university-based intellectuals provide "stars" and new issues, they can be an extremely divisive element. After their 1968 victories in the Twin Cities area in winning some convention delegates for McCarthy, they controlled some of the local party organizations and began a systematic purge of party officials who failed to agree with them on virtually all elements of DFL policy. As a result, they deeply offended both the labor and farm elements. The laborites rallied in 1970 and ousted most of the McCarthy element, which was eloquent on the war issue but lacked the skill or muscle to win elections without union backing. The farm group also developed strong new leadership to resist the ideological means test being imposed by the McCarthyites.

The unions count for so much politically because Minnesota is unique among the Plains States in having an exceptionally virile labor movement.

The labor strength was born of a landmark 1934 truckers' strike in Minneapolis which broke the back of an employers' coalition that had used strikebreakers and brute force in an effort to stop unionization. After the strike, in which four persons were killed in street fighting, organized labor was a factor to reckon with in Minnesota. Union strength is now centered in the Teamsters, the iron ore miners organized by the Steelworkers in the north, packing house workers in southern Minnesota, and monster industries like Honeywell, 3M, and Univac. The degree of unionization ranks high among the states, though some of the major firms, including Control Data and IBM, are not unionized. The quality of union leaders is superior; many, in fact, serve in the state legislature and one, Joseph E. Karth, represents St. Paul in Congress.

The modern-day Minnesota successors of Harold Stassen, on the other hand, have gone a diametrically opposite route. The Minnesota Republican party is one of the best financed, professional political organizations in the entire United States. Its annual budget usually exceeds $1 million, and it employs a full-time professional staff of about 35 which uses the advanced techniques of the business world: computers, polls, in-depth research, sophisticated public relations including sustained communications with membership, a network of field men, rental cars, and expense accounts. The party's "Neighbor to Neighbor" annual fund-raising drive for small contributions brings in some $400,000 from more than 60,000 persons each year and is recognized as the nation's most outstanding effort to broaden the base of political financing. The Minnesota GOP can recruit a promising candidate for an office and launch him with a firm financial base; thus assured of support, the candidate can be more independent of big business and other special interests.

To do its leg work, the GOP depends on a wide group of competent, educated, able, young managerial-oriented businessmen and attorneys. An effective college and Young Republican organization works in close liaison with the adult leaders, but perhaps the most unique element of the Minnesota Republican party is the role it assigns to women. This goes back to the days of Stassen, who elevated women to the same status as men in party work. Each party organ has equal cochairmen, a man and a woman, not the structure of a male chairman and female vice chairman familiar elsewhere. Among other activities, women are the backbone of the grass-roots fund-raising program. What makes this activity all the more amazing is that it takes place without the lure of patronage for anyone involved. (The DFL assigns women the same role in official party organization, but their general activity level in the DFL does not appear to be as high.)

Starting in 1959, three exceptionally able Republican state chairmen—the late Ed Viehman, Robert Forsythe, and George Thiss—built the Minnesota GOP to its preeminent position. A major initial success came in 1962, when a group of skillful young state legislators centered in Minneapolis and its suburbs were elected with party backing. Until their 1970 reversals, the so-called Conservatives (actually Republicans) controlled two-thirds of the legislature. The party held the governorship, five of Minnesota's eight U.S. House seats, the Minneapolis city council, and the board of growing, prosperous Hennepin County.

Despite periodic counterattacks by the party's more conservative and rurally oriented factions, the GOP leadership has remained consistently moderate. In fact, the Minnesota Republican party may well be the most liberal west of the Alleghenies. In 1964 the Goldwater forces (with special strength among 3M officials in St. Paul) made a bid for control of the national convention delegation. But Forsythe and other moderate leaders banded behind former U.S. Rep. Walter H. Judd as a nominal favorite son and narrowly carried the day at the state convention. (At San Francisco, the delegation split, 18 for Judd, 8 for Goldwater.) In 1968 Minnesota was the only Midwestern state to give a majority of its Republican National Convention votes to Nelson Rockefeller over Richard Nixon. In 1968 the Minnesota delegation to the Republican convention was the only one in its region to cast a strong majority vote for the liberal-backed delegate apportionment plan for future conventions.

In the face of their recent reversals at home, the Minnesota Republicans have been considering ways that they might revamp the party's approach, broadening the GOP's base of support and correcting the image of organizational genius almost wholly lacking in the human touch. By 1972, the Republicans' centrist wing was laying plans to retire many of the conservative rural legislators they felt were holding their party back. A respected Minnesota civic leader without partisan ties told me, "The Republicans over the last few years have done much more solid work on governmental reorganization and basic revisions of Minnesota's programs and policies than they're given credit for."

Minnesota ranks high in citizen participation in elections; in 1968, for instance, 76 percent of the voting age citizenry turned out to vote for President, the second highest rating among the states. In 1972 the Minnesota turnout was down to 66 percent—but the national average, in a year of voter apathy, had declined to only 55 percent. Today, while St. Paul and Minneapolis are normally Democratic, they fail to produce the cushion of heavy Democratic margins that Wisconsin Democrats can count on from Milwaukee or Illinois Democrats from Chicago. The Iron Range country of Northeast Minnesota, with its heavy Finnish and East European population and history of labor-management tensions, has long been a Democratic bastion and remains one today. But both the Iron Range and the Scandinavian wheat-growing counties the Democrats once counted on are static or declining in population. The Republicans have always done well in the rich corn-hog country which adjoins Iowa in the southern part of the state and now are garnering an increasing vote from the Twin Cities suburbs. But the Republicans will not do well unless they cut significantly into the independent and even the DFL vote. Despite all the Republicans' organizing efforts, the hearts of far more Minnesotans have been won over to the DFL in the postwar era, as the following survey of basic party loyalty (from the excellent Minnesota Poll, published in the Minneapolis *Tribune*) clearly indicates:

	1944	*1972*	*Change*
Democratic-Farmer-Laborites	30%	43%	+13%
Republicans	32	23	− 9
Independents, Minor Parties	38	34	− 4

Minnesota, indeed, was the one state of its region that author Kevin Phillips despairingly had to cross off his list of *The Emerging Republican Majority:*

> It is safe to say that the large, progressive Swedish, Norwegian and Finnish population is one of the principal reasons why Minnesota is the most liberal and Democratic-minded of the farm states. . . . Minnesota should be a frequent dissenter from the otherwise solid farm-state participation in the evolving Republican coalition.

In 1972 President Nixon eked out a 52 percent victory in Minnesota—his smallest percentage in any of the 49 states he carried.

The Economy: Adaptive, Diversified

Minnesota was hard hit by the Depression and had every reason to become an economic backwater in the post-World War II era, suffering the same fate as the neighboring Dakotas or Michigan's Upper Peninsula. Set far to the north, the state is off the principal, national trade routes. And by midcentury, Minnesota had depleted her natural resources to a staggering degree. Her virgin stands of timber had been raped in the previous century, with regrowth (especially in quality timbers) quite slow. The iron ore deposits of the Mesabi Range, American steelmakers' principal source of supply for half a century, were fast approaching the point of exhaustion. Wheat, the great crop of Minnesota's early years, had become a glut on world markets, and the soil was often exhausted in any event. Milling was moving eastward, closer to the point of consumption, endangering the state's once mighty milling industry. (It costs more to ship flour than grain, so that with completion of the St. Lawrence Seaway, it became cheaper to send the grain by barge to Buffalo, which is now the real milling capital of the U.S.—one of the few examples, incidentally, of an American industry moving from west to east.)

Yet instead of declining, the Minnesota economy moved forward with vigor. For natural resources or key geographic location, the state substituted intelligence-devouring industries: Honeywell, manufacturers of computers, thermostats, and aerospace components *; Minnesota Mining & Manufacturing, which had started with the world's worst sandpaper but then developed Scotch Tape, photo duplicating equipment, and a myriad of related prod-

* In 1970 Honeywell demonstrated its vigor by buying out General Electric's faltering computer operation—and then adding smartly to its gross and profits.

ucts; Control Data, a spin-off of Univac in the electronics field. From giants like these a plethora of smaller science-oriented industries developed. Much of the scientific talent came out of the University of Minnesota, and the state became one of the top ten in the country in the number of scientists in its labor force.

At the same time, the traditional industries began to adapt to changing economic conditions. With iron ore deposits exhausted, Minnesota scientists found a way to convert low-grade ore-bearing rock (known as taconite) into high-grade concentrates. The great milling companies (General Mills, Pillsbury, Cargill, Peavey, International Milling, etc.) kept their home offices in the Twin Cities, but several of them diversified into other consumer foods and even totally unrelated products. General Mills, for instance, either produces itself or has acquired companies that make candy bars, meat snacks, bubble gum, potato chips, specialty chemicals, "Monopoly" and other games and toys, paints, and even jewelry. It is also experimenting with spinning the fibres of soybeans or peanuts into substances which can be colored, flavored, and textured into a high-protein food that looks, feels, and tastes like bacon, chicken, or ham. ("Why not try the meat analogues?" a General Mills official asks. "We say soybeans are no more synthetic than a hog.")

Considering its geographic isolation and relatively small population, Minnesota is the home of a phenomenal number of major industries. Some 30 companies listed on the New York Stock Exchange have their headquarters in Minnesota (chiefly in the Twin Cities). Those listed in the *Fortune* directory of the 500 largest industrial corporations include three with assets of more than $1 billion—Honeywell, 3M, and Control Data—plus General Mills, Hormel, Pillsbury, Archer Daniels Midland, Land O'Lakes Creameries, Green Giant, Hoerner-Waldorf, and Farmers Union Central Exchange. Among the most important firms present in the state but owned outside are IBM and Univac. The Northwestern National and Minnesota Mutual insurance firms rank among the 50 largest life underwriters in the country, and the state is home for two of the 50 largest transportation companies: Northwest Airlines and the Burlington Northern (result of the 1970 merger of the Great Northern, the Northern Pacific, and the Chicago, Burlington & Quincy Railroads into a system which extends from Minneapolis-St. Paul and Chicago to Seattle and Portland, with ties also to St. Louis, Denver, Dallas, and Galveston). Minneapolis is headquarters of one of the country's most aggressive retailers, Dayton's—or, as the company is officially known since it took over Hudson's in Detroit, Dayton Hudson Corp. In three generations Dayton's has moved from a small dry goods retailing operation in Minneapolis to absolute dominance of the department store business in the Twin Cities and ownership of department, book, jewelry, and discount stores throughout Minnesota and in such far-flung locations as Boston, Kansas City, San Francisco, and Philadelphia.

Investors Diversified Services of Minneapolis, of which Richard Nixon was a director for five years in the 1960s, is one of the world's largest mutual fund conglomerates. Two huge bank holding companies with headquarters in the Twin Cities (Northwest Bank Corporation and First Bank Systems) control most of the banks in Minnesota and North Dakota, a substantial share of those in South Dakota, and even the largest bank in Des Moines, Iowa. (The bank holdings have frequently led to charges of economic exploitation by Minnesota, especially in North Dakota, a state also dependent on Minnesota to handle its grain crop.) In 1970 the presidents of both the American Bankers' Association and the Investment Bankers' Association of America were Minnesotans.

There are plentiful theories to explain this vigorous economic base in Minnesota, ranging from the ethnic mix of the people and the Yankees' early bent for advanced education to the benefits of having the population, business, and intellectual power of the state concentrated in the single Twin Cities area. A relevant factor was Minnesota's historic economic base in small units—farmers and small businesses—without a single dominant industrial interest, and with extremely little out-of-state ownership. Pride in maintaining that local ownership was certainly a factor in the postwar era—the determination of local leadership to "keep Minnesota green" by preventing the control of Minnesota corporations from drifting into the hands of other states and cities. (There are men in Minneapolis trust companies, one hears, who make their living figuring out ways to keep companies under local ownership so that Minneapolis won't become a branch-office town like Omaha or Des Moines.) Many members of the great old families who started the Twin Cities on the road to economic success are still actively engaged in their company firms, although virtually all have gone to professional management: the Bell family of General Mills, the Pillsburys of Pillsbury, Sweatts of Honeywell, Heffelfingers of Peavey, McKnight of 3M, MacMillan of Cargill, Bean and Ritz of International Milling, and of course those savvy Johnny-come-latelies, the Daytons of Dayton Hudson.

The result of all this, in the words of Wheelock Whitney, a Twin Cities civic leader and Republican gubernatorial aspirant, is that "when we want to do something like getting the Tyrone Guthrie Theatre here, or to boost our United Fund, or any project for civic improvement and betterment, we don't have to wire back to some home office to see what a company is willing to do. The money and the resources and the people are here."

Among Twin Cities leaders, one senses a deep orientation to change—and a determination not to be engulfed by that change, but rather to make it work constructively. This same quality certainly was a part of their companies' rapid adaptation to an altered national economic situation in the postwar era, a shift which many other Midwestern cities, still mired in a pre-electronic industrial base, have yet to make. The leaders of the prestigious national and international firms in Minneapolis and St. Paul live on the edge of "two worlds"—the small-scale 19th-century America that begins with the Great Plains, but also the sophisticated Eastern world of high finance and complex organization. By moving in both worlds, they maintain a human, unpretentious quality (many still answer their own phones) even while adapting their economy to professional management and organization.

Part of the Twin Cities' economic stature comes from the fact that they are a great regional capital, the only significant metropolis in the Upper Midwest territory of the Ninth Federal Reserve District (headquarters in Minneapolis) which stretches from the copper mines and timberlands of northern Michigan westward for 1,500 miles through woods and prairies and High Plains to the copper mines and timberlands of western Montana—one of the loneliest and surely the coldest stretch of territory in the continental United States. (Straight west from Minneapolis, in fact, there is no city of its size until one reaches Seattle, Washington.) Of the Upper Midwest's entire population growth in the past several decades, nine-tenths has taken place in the Twin Cities metropolis alone. The farm population and mining employment of the region are declining and the entire economy is in a painful transition from a resources-extractive-exploitive economy to a high-value manufacturing and service-oriented economy. The business leaders of the Twin Cities, working since 1957 through the privately sponsored Upper Midwest Research & Development Council with headquarters in Minneapolis, has been looking for ways to make the transition a rapid and successful one and to pull together the economic and planning activities of the metropolis with its vast semirural hinterland.*

Across most of the Upper Midwest, hamlets and convenience centers have been losing farm trade and services to more diversified and widely spaced shopping centers, and young adults and families have been migrating in great numbers to the larger centers of trade and employment—places like Mankato, Rochester, and St. Cloud in Minnesota, Rapid City and Sioux Falls in South Dakota, Grand Forks and Dickinson in North Dakota, and Missoula and Bozeman in Montana. One of these cities, St. Cloud (1970 population 39,691), was the focal point of a 1971 study, *Micropolis in Transition,* prepared by Dr. Edward L. Henry and his colleagues at St. John's University, a small Roman Catholic institution near St. Cloud. Successful "microcities" like St. Cloud, according to the study, are enjoying continuing expansion of light, diversified industry, often have a college or junior college that enlivens the local cultural scene and creates employment, and are generally situated close enough to a large city to enjoy its economic and intellectual stimulation—but far enough away so that the big city does not compete for the trade of nearby villages. St. Cloud, which gained 17 percent in population during the 1960s, has a thriving new industrial park, a state college with 10,000 students, a large medical center, and according to its boosters, "one of the best school systems in the state." According to Daniel

* With the possible exception of the New England Council, the Upper Midwest Research and Development Council represents the most advanced privately sponsored attempt trying to focus on *regional* problems and policies within the United States. Regional efforts of this type are only in their infancy, perhaps no further advanced than metropolitan area planning was in the 1950s. As national priorities shift to population redistribution in the 1970s, we are likely to hear more of them.

One of the observations of the Upper Midwest Council's research staff, which this writer also observed across the Plains States, is the movement of many small city families to find homes in the nearby countryside, picking lake shores or wooded hillsides or former farmhouses for their homes, even if it requires commuting up to 25 or 35 miles to work.

Donahue, a young Bostonian who heads the local poverty program and was interviewed by reporter Seth S. King, "There is still a sense of community here. It's a place where you can know people, a lot of them by their first names." Banker Jerry Kigin observed: "I'd say that $10,000 a year would be a good, comfortable salary for a family in St. Cloud. So maybe it can be good here in a little city. Maybe we shouldn't try to grow any bigger. But then if we did not, we'd lose our kids and there'd be nothing new for the area."

Manufacturing replaced farming as the major source of Minnesota's income about two decades ago, and the state now ranks 20th among the 50 in the value of her annual industrial output. "Agribusiness," however, remains an important industry; actual farm employment plus food processing, marketing, and supply industries for the farm account for almost 30 percent of the jobs in Minnesota. Wheat, once virtually the only crop grown in the state, slipped behind corn during the 1930s, and Minnesota ranks only 17th among the 50 in wheat production, most of it concentrated in the Red River Valley along the North Dakota border. The big crop is corn and, through it, livestock. The rich farmlands along the Iowa border are the premium corn-growing land and also heavy in soybeans and vegetables. Two-thirds of the state's agricultural income actually comes from livestock; among the 50 states, Minnesota is fifth in hogs, 10th in cattle. Minnesota also ranks second only to Wisconsin in number of milk cows and second only to California in her turkey production. (The town of Worthington in southwest Minnesota is the self-proclaimed "turkey capital of the world.") Other important crops are oats (first in the U.S.A.), rye, alfalfa, and sugar beets. Overall, Minnesota's farm output approaches $2 billion a year and ranks fifth in the nation. Scandinavians have a great predilection for co-ops, and Minnesota's farm cooperatives, active in everything from wheat to gasoline, gross about $1 billion a year. The Farmers Union Central Exchange at St. Paul does a $150 million business annually and ranks among the top 500 U.S. corporations.

While the southern part of Minnesota is prairie and prime farmland, the less fertile northern reaches, remote and often wild, are studded with hills, forests, and many of the 10,000 lakes (actually more than 14,000) for which the state is famed. The tourist trade in this "land of sky blue waters" draws some five million out-of-state visitors each year and is a major source of income (some $750 million annually), even though the quality of many Minnesota resorts is declining as they age. One of the northwest Minnesota lakes, Itasca, is the headwater of the Mississippi River. Minnesota fishing has gone down some in quality, but the state still sells more fishing licenses than any other. She also has deer herds totaling some 800,000 head and sells the most deer stamps for hunting of any state. In winter an abundance of mink, beaver, muskrat and raccoon makes trapping a $1.5 million business for some 12,000 licensed trappers. And there are well over 100,000 snowmobiles registered in Minnesota, ready to pollute with noise and smoke the once inviolate quiet of the blue, arctic northern winter.*

Minnesota's winters, incidentally, have a well-earned reputation for ferocity, and weather may be the state's most serious drawback (though also a boon to wintertime sports). In the winter of 1970, it was 34 degrees *below* zero one day in Minneapolis. The average minimum temperature in the northern half of the state is under zero in January. Average annual snowfall ranges from 20 inches in the southeast corner to 70 inches in the extreme northwest. Yet summer may bring intense heat waves and even tornados; in most of Minnesota the average July maximum is between 80 and 90 degrees.

The steel with which America won two world wars and built her 20th-century industrial machine was produced principally from iron ores from the massive Iron Ranges near Duluth on Lake Superior. But in the immediate postwar years, as the mines became depleted of high-grade ores, the region faced a possible economic catastrophe. For decades, experiments had been going on to convert low-grade taconite into high-grade ore, but it was only in the nick of time in the 1950s that the process was sufficiently developed to be economically feasible; now all but a small fraction of Minnesota's ore production is in the form of concentrated pellets made from taconite, ready for the blast furnace. Much of the processing is done by the Reserve Mining Company of Silver Bay. Minnesota continues to provide well over half the nation's iron ore supply at an annual income to itself of more than half a billion dollars, although the highly automated taconite plants do not employ as many men as the industry once required.

One reason the steel companies were willing to make the investment in taconite processing was a state constitutional amendment, backed by the Republicans but at first blocked by the DFL, to guarantee taxation at a rate no higher than that of other Minnesota industries for a quarter of a century. (The Republicans pushed for the amendment while the DFL unwisely argued against it at first, charging a sop to big steel. With jobs in the offing, the Republican argument carried the day.)

Not long after Reserve Mining began its taconite operation in 1955, some biologists and conservationists became concerned about the 67,000 tons of taconite tailings—the tiny grains of rock left after magnets have plucked the flakes of iron ore from the crushed taconite—which the plant has dumped each day into Lake Superior. Superior holds one-twelfth of the world's fresh water and is the cleanest of the Great Lakes, thousands of years behind the others in natural aging. The tailings, equal in magnitude to a pile the

* The American snowmobile phenomenon is one of sometimes frightening proportions. Since production of the first of these agile, tracked vehicles in 1959, their population has zoomed to about two million. They delight sportsmen and are said to be a great antidote to wintertime cabin fever in the 19-state Northern Snow Belt. But the noise of the 30-horsepower machines sometimes exceeds the 85 decibel level at which human ears can be injured, and according to the National Wildlife Federation, they are a grave hazard to animals, who lose strength and weight in wintertime. "They are easily routed and killed by shock," the Federation asserts. Many localities have put restrictions on the hours and terrain for snowmobile use. But except for barring snowmobiles from downtown, the little city of Thief River Falls, Minnesota (population 8,618), has refused to do so. It is home of Arctic Enterprises, the country's largest producer of snowmobiles and a godsend to the otherwise stagnant local economy.

size of a football field half a mile high each year, are greater than the total volume of other sediments carried into the lake's waters by its tributaries. Company officials at first asserted that the rock particles would drop into Superior's 900-foot deep Great Trough, which is five miles offshore from the plant. Some may indeed have sunken into the Great Trough, but not many years after the plant opened, residents noticed a gray-greenish cast to the lake water where it had once been possible to look down 20 feet and see trout swimming. It became apparent that the lighter particles were going into solution, thus creating the "green waters."

As the country's environmental consciousness rose in the late 1960s and early 1970s, Reserve Mining came under increased pressure to stop the offshore dumping and switch to disposal of the tailings inland, perhaps in some of the huge pits dug for iron ore over the past century. Major credit for the public pressure goes to a Washington, D.C. housewife, Mrs. Verna Mize, who had grown up on Lake Superior. In an amazing demonstration of woman- and citizen-power, she gathered thousands of petition signatures, badgered and cajoled officials, and helped to precipitate a wave of state and federal action against the offshore dumping. Under the Nixon Administration, there were strong counterpressures, in both the White House and the Commerce Department (Reserve Mining's two owners, Republic and Armco Steel Corporations, are an important part of Republican fund-raising activities in Ohio, and the company complained that inland dumping would cost as much as $200 million). But the Environmental Protection Agency won the political battle, and in 1972 the federal government sued Reserve Mining to schedule a timetable for the end of all its pollution of Lake Superior.

With completion of the St. Lawrence Seaway, the city of Duluth (third largest in Minnesota with 100,578 people) became the westernmost port of the Atlantic Ocean. But the great shipments from which it makes its living—iron ore and grain—are mostly destined for other Great Lakes ports. Perched on hills that are almost as steep as San Francisco's and overlooking a beautiful natural harbor, Duluth has one of the most attractive settings of American port cities. Some of the homes of the city, many straight out of the 1910s and '20s, tend to be amazingly well maintained. But Superior Street, the main artery which runs for a mile parallel to the water front, has been depressed for years, and rebuilding of the central core did not begin until the late 1960s. A local bond issue was floated for a top-grade convention center, which may draw more tourists to the city's cool, pleasant shores in summertime. Set in the quiet, sylvan pines-and-lakes setting of Minnesota's northland, Duluth has long been a pass-through city for tourists on their way to the woods.

Duluth's chief problem has been economic dominance by a few old families with great wealth, a wealth they have refused to invest in their own city. Dependence on the iron industry has been almost complete; in earlier years other industries were resisted for fear of creating wage competition for the steel firms. The lack of economic diversification has spelled trouble, especially in the postwar years as iron employment, despite taconite's development, fell off sharply. The result has been generally depressed conditions in Duluth and the entire Iron Range district, and difficult times for the descendants of the hardy Finns, Swedes, Italians, and Slavs who first peopled this distant ore-rich land.

Power and Progress in the Amazing Twin Cities

The 1970 Census found that 1,813,647 of Minnesota's 3,804,971 people were congregated in the metropolitan area of Minneapolis and St. Paul, the Siamese but by no means identical twins from whose borders virtually every facet of Minnesota life is guided. The metropolitan area population now ranks 15th in the country and grew by 22 percent in the 1960s alone. Virtually all its postwar population growth has been concentrated in the suburban towns, which now represent 55 percent of the area population. But almost everything of note in modern Minnesota is concentrated in the Twin Cities orbit: the state capital, the state university, the state fair, all trade and finance, the great newspapers and cultural facilities, sports, and transportation—a center as important to Minnesota, one might say, as Paris is to France.

St. Paul (population 309,980) the smaller and more easterly of the two big cities, grew steeply up and down the Mississippi River bluffs and early became a great port and railroading city. She is still a major port, grain terminal, and stockyards city, big in publishing and insurance, and headquarters of the now-merged Great Northern and Northern Pacific Railways. St. Paul's population is heavily German-Irish Catholic, her outlook on the world careful and conservative. The dominant business voice in the city—if it cared to use its power—would be 3M, one of the great modern U.S. corporations. Up to now, 3M has contributed little to the community, though the Bush Foundation, with a couple million dollars out of the 3M fortune, could play a vital role in the next years. The rich old families of St. Paul—the Hills, Ordways, O'Shaughnessys, and Weyerhausers—have exerted little influence in the postwar era; many of them had seen their fortunes in rails and timber decline in the Depression and apparently decided in the future they would invest in "sure things" and let St. Paul, already in decay, go its own way.

By the late 1950s, St. Paul was a dreary, crumbling city, 56 of its 87 downtown buildings of pre-1900 vintage. The man who lit the first spark of renewal was not a member of the old aristocracy but the self-made young president of St. Paul's First National Bank, Philip Nason. Nason persuaded Dayton's, the highly successful Minneapolis department store, to open a branch in St. Paul, thus beginning the long process of regeneration in a once illustrious American city. Later the Hilton Hotel group agreed to build a large hotel in the city, and in the late 1960s agreement was finally reached on a $13 million Civic Center development bond issue. (A prime mover in the latter undertaking was Harold J. Cummings, the 73-year-old board chairman emeritus of the Minnesota Mutual Life Insurance Company.)

St. Paul's pride and joy is its compact but excellent Capitol Center urban renewal project; it lagged several years behind the major developments in Minneapolis but had more design consciousness and control. The project is anchored at one end by the domed State Capitol of white Georgian marble and to the south by the Roman Catholic Cathedral of St. Paul. (The juxtaposition recalls a comment of author Meridel LaSueur, quoted by David Butwin: "My father used to say that only in St. Paul could you come to the horizon and see the three controllers of the city's destiny—the Cathedral, the First National Bank, and the Capitol. St. Paul is frank about itself; there is no secrecy.") Between the Cathedral and Capitol, slumlike buildings have been cleaned out but good structures preserved. Several blocks of new downtown St. Paul buildings include second-story level pedestrian skyways, reserved as public easements just like regular sidewalks. The pedestrian skyway device, also being pursued in Minneapolis, both separates pedestrians from traffic and counters the trend to suburban shopping by providing quick and comfortable access to shops—a not unimportant attraction in Minnesota's hostile climatic belt.

The central precinct of power in St. Paul is still the doughty, high-ceilinged Minnesota Club, where the movers and shakers assemble each Saturday for a kind of ritualistic cocktail luncheon. Many of the city's men of wealth still occupy mansions on the hills overlooking the workers in the valley, but the combination of interstate highways and urban renewal has demolished practically all of the city's slums.

Among the powers to be reckoned with in St. Paul are the labor unions (St. Paul is a strong DFL town) and the Catholic Church. Precisely 46 percent of St. Paul's families have a labor union member; likewise 46 percent are Roman Catholic. What the archbishop thinks or says still carries weight, and over the years the church has had a strong religious and moral impact on the city. In 1969, however, I found the foundations of established Catholicism shaking in the wake of the resignation and then marriage of the city's popular auxiliary bishop and former president of the local College of St. Thomas, the Most Rev. James P. Shannon. Shannon's marriage to a divorcee led to automatic excommunication. He had been one of the church's most articulate and progressive leaders but found himself in basic disagreement with Rome on birth and population control and felt that the First Vatican Council had been compromised by Pope Paul VI. Of the ultimate impact of such happenings on an establishment church city like St. Paul, no one can speak with much certainty.

The DFL appeared to strengthen its hold on St. Paul in 1972, when the voters ousted an independent incumbent mayor in favor of 38-year-old attorney Lawrence D. Cohen, a longtime participant in DFL activities. A few years earlier, Cohen had been one of the founders of MECCA (the Minnesota Environmental Control Citizens' Association), which proved its mettle as one of the nation's best environmental groups through its work on water pollution and nuclear power plants.

In contrast to St. Paul, Minneapolis (population 434,400) is a flat prairie town that got her start as a miller of the West's wheat; she is larger, more sophisticated and cultured, a more important banking and finance center, and generally more Scandinavian in her population—though she also has many Germans. In an era when Americans are searching for ways to beautify their old cities or add a human dimension to new ones, they might well look at Minneapolis' 153 landscaped parks and 22 treelined lakes, many restricted against the use of motor boats. Even if the parklands are a bit threadbare now, they still stand as a monument to foresight of past decades, especially that of the late Theodore Wirth, the park commissioner for several decades early in the century. (In our time, a major test for the entire metropolitan area is whether it can do as good a job of park acquisition in its suburban reaches as Wirth did for Minneapolis 50 to 60 years ago.)

Minneapolis was badly frightened in the 1950s by the opening of Dayton's high-quality Southdale shopping center in the southwest suburbs and the decision of both General Mills and Prudential to build office complexes outside the downtown area. The chief response was the 17-block Gateway Center redevelopment project between the heart of the city and the Mississippi River, including the excellent Yamasaki-designed home office of the Northwestern National Life Insurance Company. Now a 56-story building by Investors Diversified Services, a skyscraper of a scale which will put Minneapolis in a league with other big U.S. cities, is being constructed. Many Gateway blocks stood vacant for years, however, and the project lacks the clear focus of St. Paul's Capitol Center undertaking. One outstanding project in Minneapolis was the $3.5 million Mall, transforming eight blocks of Nicollet Avenue, a key downtown shopping street, into a landscaped promenade. The city also has a largely successful public housing program for the elderly, though there is still an acute shortage of adequate housing for the poor or low-income families. (Minneapolis has some apartment buildings but is still primarily a city of single-family dwellings—and an exceptionally high degree of home ownership by tenants.)

The business leadership of Minneapolis tends to be more urbane, tolerant, consciously liberal on race issues and moderately Republican than its counterpart in St. Paul. In 1964, for instance, St. Paul was a hotbed of Goldwaterism (especially among 3M executives) while in Minneapolis there was strong opposition to Goldwater's nomination and many of the normally Republican leaders ended up voting for President Johnson, egged on by the once unshakably Republican Minneapolis *Tribune*.

With a Negro population of only 19,005 (just over 4 percent), Minneapolis would seem to be the last city in the U.S.A. where race tensions would become acute. But there were small riots in the summers of 1966 and 1967, prompting business leaders to set up an Urban Coalition in the city and the city council to authorize a human relations commission. Some fascinating insights into the power structure of the city were revealed in the furor that followed the appointment to the new commission of a 29-year-old black militant, Ronald Edwards. Mayor Arthur Naftalin had met Edwards at a meeting on the near north side the day after a night of vandalism in summer 1966, and he felt that the young man would be an able spokesman for "the boys on Plymouth Avenue." What Naftalin did not know when he appointed Edwards (and 14 others) was that Edwards had a police record of four misdemeanors in earlier years. But the Republican president of the city council, Daniel Cohen, found out about it and blew the whistle on the mayor, saying he would oppose a man with a criminal record. A majority of the city council sided with Cohen, and there ensued a three-month battle in which some of the city's most powerful business and civic leaders tried to press the council to confirm Edwards. Among these were Raymond Plank, president of the Apache Corporation and a civil rights leader; John Cowles, Jr., president of the Minneapolis Star and Tribune Company; and Stephen Keating, president of Honeywell, Inc. Naftalin submitted the name a second time, and it was again rejected. Finally, on a third submission, approval came and Edwards told the *Star* "Man, before this thing started, you couldn't have made me believe that white cats like Plank, Cowles, and Keating would have come out and supported me. When Cohen first hollered on me, I figured, 'Here we go—they're going to put me out to the wolves.' I was surprised when that didn't happen."

The Edwards case also brought forth an interesting admission from the *Star*—that while the nomination was being debated, news reports made it look like a struggle principally between the black community and some city councilmen. There was no coverage, the *Star* acknowledged in a later series on the affair, of the crucial roles of the businessmen, many prominent religious leaders in the city, president David Roe of the State AFL-CIO, or the newly founded Minneapolis Urban Coalition. Among other business leaders who took an active role in resolving the affair, the *Star* named board chairman Donald Dayton of the Dayton Corporation and his vice president, Wayne Thompson, executive vice president Dean McNeal of the Pillsbury Company, president Judson Bemis of the Bemis Company, Inc., president Earl Ewald of Northern State Power Company, vice president Paul Parker of General Mills, president F. Van Konynenburg of Midwest-Television Inc., and Wheelock Whitney, chief executive officer of Dain, Kalman and Quail, Inc.—an excellent cross-section of the city's business power elite.

An example of Minneapolis businessmen's creative response to problems of the black underprivileged is Control Data Corporation's northside manufacturing plant for computer components and wiring systems, set up in the late 1960s when the company encountered severe labor shortages in the suburban areas where it has most of its plants. Welfare mothers, ex-convicts, and high school dropouts were among the labor force recruited and then exposed to an extensive training program—including counseling, sensitivity training sessions on race relations, day care facilities, intensive on-the-job instruction, medical and legal aid assistance. Control Data found its average cost per trainee about $2,500, well below the national average of $3,000 in federal jobs programs, and similar plants were set up in St. Paul, Washington, D.C., and the impoverished Appalachian community of Campton, Kentucky.

The city of Minneapolis has had three unusual mayors in the postwar period—Hubert Humphrey, Arthur Naftalin, and Charles S. Stenvig. All three have been obliged to rule by little more than moral authority, since the careful Scandinavians who wrote state laws, which were collected as the "city charter" back in the 1920s, were suspicious of the bossism they saw in other cities and gave almost all the power to the city council. The city is administered by department heads who are appointed by the council and report to it, not the mayor. Although they were Democrats, Humphrey and Naftalin had the most cordial and successful relationships with the city's business leadership when they were in office. Humphrey also succeeded in closing down gambling houses and brothels, reorganizing city law enforcement functions, and obtaining passage of the first municipal fair employment practices law in the country.

The city's mayor through most of the 1960s was Arthur Naftalin, a self-styled "ultraliberal intellectual" who had served as executive secretary to Mayor Humphrey two decades before. Naftalin vigorously protected Minneapolis' urban renewal efforts, started the city's widely acclaimed Urban Coalition, got millions of dollars for health care, job training, poverty programs, urban renewal, and education, and was the first leader of the city to begin real dialogue with the black community. A university professor and a soft-spoken, intense man, Naftalin lacked some of the glamor of mayors like a Lindsay in New York or Stokes in Cleveland, and he failed to use the tact he could have with the city council. Some critics said he was badly out of touch with the typical people of his own city, listening instead to members of the business and university community élite (a large proportion of whom no longer lived in the city at all) and failing to understand the concerns of middle-class people about the new black militancy. But he did understand the fiscal and management problems of city government, and helped start the moves toward eventual metropolitan government for the Twin Cities.

In 1969, after eight years in office, Naftalin retired voluntarily. "I can abide opposition from those opposed to me," he said, "but when I'm no longer appreciated by natural allies, then what's the use? The job of mayor is too demanding, too frustrating, too unrewarding."

Charles Stenvig, the man who succeeded Naftalin, was a totally different kind of man. A Methodist of Norwegian stock, he became a policeman and rose through the ranks to be a burglary squad detective and head of the Police Federation. He jumped into the mayor's race as the candidate of the oft-neglected garden variety of lower-income white city dweller. "People are sick and tired of politicians and intellectuals. They want an average workingman from the community to represent them, and that's me," Stenvig declared. He also assailed "the Gold Coast people" who he said were running the city. Practically the only plank in Stenvig's platform was a promise not to "appease hoodlums," referring to the black militants who had demonstrated in 1966 and 1967 and hippies who staged protests in downtown Minneapolis.

Richard M. Scammon and Ben J. Wattenberg later selected the 1969 mayoralty election as a key example of the "social issue" in American politics, pointing out that the original candidate of the DFL, Gerard Hegstrom, "was perceived by the voters as being a candidate of the 'university liberals.' His campaign was run largely by McCarthy types of the New Politics." Hegstrom ran third in the primary. In the runoff, Stenvig defeated the Republican endorsee, Dan Cohen, who had the endorsement of everyone from Eugene McCarthy to Richard Nixon, with an amazing 62 percent of the vote. Why did it happen? Primarily because there was no regular Democratic candidate left in the field after Hegstrom's defeat. In Minneapolis, where the DFL vote is basically a labor vote, the Republican starts out as the last choice. Therefore Stenvig, as a political independent, was preferable to most voters.

As he assumed office, Stenvig announced: "God's gonna be my chief adviser and it won't cost the city a penny." After that, in the opinion of most impartial observers, the quality of his appointments declined precipitously. In fact, Stenvig did very little in office, though he claimed credit for influencing the city council to hold down the budget and new taxes. Although he did not create the "police state" some of his adversaries feared, he continued to preach the gospel of law and order, and there were increased charges of police brutality against blacks. The middle-class white citizenry obviously felt more secure. When Stenvig ran for reelection in 1971, his opponent was W. Harris Davis, a Negro civic leader and president of the Urban Coalition of Minneapolis. This time Stenvig won with 72 percent of the vote—adding extra support, it appeared, from organized labor and from the elderly, who represent more and more of the Minneapolis population as young people move to the suburbs.

My friend Bernie Shellum, political correspondent for the Minneapolis *Tribune*, suggests that the standard analyses of Stenvig miss one salient point:

> While he is simplistic, uninformed and in many ways contrary to other politicians who have made it in Minneapolis, Stenvig from the beginning has tapped the same kind of political sentiment that [Minneapolis Congressman] Don Fraser has. He talks to people, not at them. He listens. His manner is low-key. He has never been a demagogue. He doesn't look or sound like a politician.
>
> And when he first ran for mayor, he was quite well known in Minneapolis. For years, as a part of his personal life and in his role as police federation president, he had been going around to neighborhood meetings, talking to people about their problems. In talking to them about safety, in parks or on the way to school or in their own homes, Stenvig had touched people's lives in a way that Art Naftalin never did.

It is worth noting that regular liberal Democrats have continued to win Minneapolis by big margins since Stenvig appeared on the scene, and that Stenvig has been unable to persuade the voters to endorse the conservatives he campaigned to elect to the city council.

Few inland cities can match the Twin Cities as a fountainhead of culture; they not only have an excellent symphony orchestra, but the distinguished Tyrone Guthrie Theatre (which moved into one of the outstanding modern theater buildings of the nation in 1963), some 50 or 60 community theaters, the Walker Art Center (described by one critic as "this country's most vigorous outpost of in-art"), and the Minneapolis Institute of Arts. The University of Minnesota has been a major contributor to the cultural development of the region. The Guthrie Theatre with its now famed repertory company was brought to Minneapolis through the efforts of John Cowles, Jr., helped not a little by Ford Foundation support. On the musical front, there is not only the Symphony but the Center Opera of Minnesota, considered one of the most progressive ensembles in the country. One survey by the Minneapolis *Tribune* showed that attendance at major cultural events in Minnesota was greater than that of major league baseball and football combined—even though the big league sports, as we shall see, are immensely popular.

No small measure of credit for Minnesota's moderate-to-liberal political climate and internationalist point of view in the postwar era must go to the Cowles family's *Tribune* and *Star*. The Cowleses, who had moved into the Minneapolis newspaper scene from their Des Moines, Iowa, base in 1935, brought quality journalism: substantial and balanced coverage of news from the local to the international level, the Minnesota Poll of public opinion (perhaps the best newspaper operation of its kind in the United States), searching examination of education issues, a science-reading series and world affairs program. Editorial stands of the papers included staunch internationalism (offsetting traditional Scandinavian and German isolationism), support for substantial high school and university budgets, opposition to the demagoguery of the era of Senator Joseph McCarthy, freedom of speech and civil rights. In 1972 the *Tribune* was one of the few major dailies in the U.S. to support George McGovern for the Presidency.

In recent years, some resentment was reported in Minneapolis about the power and the civil rights-style liberalism of the *Star* and *Tribune*, one factor, many thought, in Stenvig's election as mayor. The papers' call for charter reform to give the mayor of Minneapolis more power was thrice rejected by the voters of the city. On a professional level, the papers were sometimes criticized for a much smaller "news hole" than they could afford and very episodic coverage—doing one story or another in depth but lacking continuity on a wide range of stories. Reporters for the papers, concerned about the problem, began to pressure management for a greater role in policy-making decisions. Until the late 1960s, the papers remained under the active direction of John Cowles, Sr., who had been their guiding spirit during their formative years under his family's ownership. He was able to drive circulation up to half a million daily and over 600,000 on Sundays. He was succeeded by John Cowles, Jr., who gave the editors of the papers increased autonomy and in 1972 brought in Charles W. Bailey, a highly regarded professional who had been Washington bureau chief, to be editor of the *Tribune* in Minneapolis. The *Star* and *Tribune* also have a major share of ownership of radio station WCCO (one of the most influential local stations in the country), 22 percent ownership of the large New York publishing firm, Harper & Row, and complete ownership of *Harper's Magazine*. In the Plains States region, the Cowles voice is also strong through ownership of the Des Moines *Register* and *Tribune*.*

While the *Tribune* and *Star* circulate heavily throughout western and northern Minnesota, the St. Paul newspapers—the *Pioneer Press* and *Dispatch*, flagships of the Ridder chain—have more circulation and influence in western Wisconsin. The St. Paul papers tend to be more consistently Republican in their politics and less serious in their national and international coverage than their Minneapolis counterparts; a local civic leader suggested to me that the Ridders are more interested in sports than ideological subjects. Both St. Paul papers have improved appreciably over the past several years and editorial page editor William Sumner turns out material equal to the best the Minneapolis *Star's* writers can produce. Outside the Twin Cities area, the Minnesota paper of the most distinction is the Rochester *Post-Bulletin*.

A fierce rivalry once distinguished relations between the Twin Cities, but it has faded—partly because the suburbs, whose people play such a prominent role in area business and are the chief patrons of sporting and cultural events, have little interest in the old competition. The days are now long past when provincial St. Paul business moguls boasted that their stores had no branches in Minneapolis, or when both cities had baseball teams in the American Association and intercity rivalry reached the point of fisticuffs on the fields and in the stands. Sports, indeed, were an important factor in getting the Twin Cities together; it became clear to business leaders that as long as Minneapolis and St. Paul went their lone ways, they would be classified as the 27th and 43rd largest markets in the country and be forever doomed to Triple-A baseball, never a major league team. But when they finally did get together, they were the 15th largest market in the U.S.A., and so the American League Minnesota Twins were organized and played

* Separate corporately from these holdings are those of Cowles Communications, Inc., headed by Gardner ("Mike") Cowles, the man who founded *Look* magazine and was long a major force in American journalism and behind-the-scenes national political power-brokering. In the 1960s, Cowles Communications entered a heady era of acquisitions, reaching a zenith in 1966 in numbers of newspapers and other properties and in earnings (about $4 million on a gross of $150 million). But one reversal after another hit Cowles Communications in the late 1960s and early 1970s, forcing it to divest itself of many properties, including the San Juan *Star* (founded by Cowles in 1959), Suffolk *Sun* (another Cowles creation, born in 1966, dead in 1969), *Family Circle* magazine, newspapers in Florida, a book company, Cowles *Comprehensive Encyclopedia*, and a Memphis television station. In 1971, as its losses mounted and postal rate increases promised even more red ink, Cowles was obliged to kill the flagship publication of his group, *Look*.

What had gone wrong? *Business Week* commented that the situation was "the classic one of a chairman calling the shots to a chorus of acquiescence from a tier of high-salaried, long-time executives. . . . Cowles showed a penchant for investing huge sums of money in ventures that lost huge sums of money, and for squeezing marginally profitable operations dry to turn failures into successes." But the wolf was not at the door. Cowles still had three television and four radio stations and some smaller businesses. At 68 years of age, he remained as president of the Minneapolis *Star* and *Tribune*, where he began in journalism in 1925. And by virtue of one of his major divestments, he had become owner of 2.6 million shares of *New York Times* stock and was a director of the *Times*.

their first season in 1961. The stadium, appropriately, is on neutral ground —in suburban Bloomington.

Wheelock Whitney, a leader of the businessmen's group which brought in the Twins, argues that big league sports are a vital part of a city's image, and that only by acquiring the Twins (and later the Minnesota Vikings in football and North Stars in hockey) could the Twin Cities area achieve the general national prominence it needed if its industries were to compete effectively with other parts of the country for top scientists and management. "You can have the best symphony orchestra or theater, but that's not in the newspapers elsewhere," Whitney says. "With our teams, now we're in the major league class of town." Sports boxoffices have also bolstered the economy by drawing in spectators from the rest of Minnesota, Iowa, the Dakotas, Wisconsin, and even down from Manitoba and Ontario.

Twin Cities unity is now being achieved on many fronts. The decision of the Dayton retailers to move into St. Paul has gone far to break down the insularity between the two towns. More and more trade union negotiations are taking place on a merged basis. The Guthrie Theatre has played part of its seasons in St. Paul. The St. Paul Arts & Sciences Center has come to Minneapolis. The Minneapolis Symphony changed its name to the Minnesota Symphony. On the religious front, the Archdiocese of St. Paul renamed itself the Archdiocese of St. Paul and Minneapolis. The auto ride from one city to the other, which used to be an excruciating 45 minutes at busy times of the day, has been cut to 15 minutes with an interstate road opened in 1969. The joint Minneapolis-St. Paul International Airport is one of the handsomest in the United States.

Since its establishment in 1967, the Twin Cities Metropolitan Council has also provided one of the country's most interesting examples of an areawide government with limited but very specific powers. It all got started through the inelegant subject of sewage. With the tremendous growth of single-family homes around the city in the postwar era, there were often no central water or sewer systems to tie into, so that people sank their own wells and dug their own septic systems. By 1959 almost 400,000 persons were using such systems. That year, a suburban housewife phoned the state health department to report that a glass of water she'd just drawn from her tap "has a head on it, like beer." Checks revealed that half the wells were recirculating soapsuds and other sewage from the septic tanks.

Municipalities moved rapidly to construct their own central water supplies, but it proved impossible for them to lay out a central sewer system without a central authority to decide between all the competing plans. Four successive legislatures failed in an effort to set up a sanitary control district, but finally in 1967 the legislature did vote to set up the new Metropolitan Council, covering seven counties (an area of some 3,000 square miles). The council, with a staff of more than 100 and an annual budget of $2.8 million, is financed by a state-authorized levy on all taxable property within its area. The rate, originally five cents on each $100 of assessed valuation, was later moved up to seven cents. The council has already shown an ability to move decisively on area-wide problems such as the sewers, solid waste disposal, parks and open space, and a transportation-highway program. It has the authority to review the development plans of the 300-odd governmental units within its jurisdiction, matching those plans to its own long-range plans for the orderly physical and economic development of the Twin Cities region. All applications by local governments for federal grants and loans go through the council's hands, and the federal government is unlikely to approve any project the council opposes. Already the council has been able to bar a new airport near a wildlife refuge, to modify state highway building plans, and to require that new shopping centers be limited in number and be real people-centers with offices and apartments as well as the shining new shopping malls. Such use of power for the interests of the whole region, one observer has noted, "could mean the difference between chaos and orderly development during the rest of this century." The council's muscle-flexing has also generated the first political opposition, with pressure from some suburbanites to strip it of its powers.

The council's representation is unique in that the 14 councilmen are from equal population districts; the legislature narrowly voted down a system of popular election, but that feature will probably be substituted in the next few years (for now the governor appoints the members).

A corollary reform of immense importance in the Twin Cities region is a law, passed by the legislature in 1971, which provides that 40 percent of the tax yield from new commercial and industrial buildings of all types constructed from that year onward be pooled for redistribution to the various municipalities and school districts of the area, on the basis of population and need. The law, which was first proposed by the influential Citizens League * and supported by the Metropolitan Council, will go far to correct the fiscal imbalance of the region—the familiar phenomenon of fat tax yields in areas with the least acute problems, while the most troubled areas suffer along with the slimmest yields. Every community will benefit from future business growth, no matter where it occurs in the region. As Paul Gilje of the Citizens League points out, "Some of the valuation of a new shopping center in Minnetonka Village or a new industrial park in Eagan Township or a new skyscraper in Minneapolis will be made part of the tax base of all communities in the metropolitan area." This will reduce the inequalities of the urban development game "winner-take-all." Localities will no longer be so tempted to resort to "fiscal zoning" to encourage new plants and shopping areas within their borders and discourage low- and medium-income housing that allegedly doesn't "pay its way." There should be an environmental payoff, too, because municipalities will no longer feel so impelled to allow development on marginal land (like floodplains) just to build an adequate local tax base, and they may feel freer to designate more land for open-

* The Citizens League prefers to focus attention on the activities of its volunteer members, but the fact is that its executive director, Ted Kolderie, is one of the most brilliant young civic leaders in the country today.

space uses. But these benefits may not be fully appreciated until the set-aside is increased to much more than the initial 40 percent. That will be a challenge for the unique coalition that pushed the law to passage—legislators from the center cities and less affluent suburbs against the more prosperous suburbs.

The postwar exodus to the suburbs in the Twin Cities area differed from that in many other cities in that it could not be blamed on racism. There were simply not enough Negroes in the cities to account for the shift. The reason was simpler: the core cities were full, and people wanted grass and trees. Federal housing policies also played a role; a Polish priest in one of Minneapolis' old ethnic neighborhoods, noticing how few baptisms he had been called on to perform over a period of several years, made a survey to discover why. He found that the Federal Housing Administration was demanding such high down payments on purchase or renovation of homes in the older sections that young people found it much less expensive to move to the suburbs, where they could get a new home for a down payment of just a few hundred dollars. Again, the federal government contributes to a problem it must later spend millions of dollars to rectify.

Whatever the reasons, the Twin Cities suburban flight meant what it meant everywhere else in the U.S.A.: a depletion of the wealthy, the educated, and the most talented population segments, leaving the blue-collar workers and older families to man the decaying houses of the center city. The blue-collar remnants, in turn, became frightened by the black militancy and student demonstrations of the 1960s and were likely candidates for the Stenvig Crusade. If the suburbs had also voted in his first election, Stenvig would most likely have been defeated. As Mayor Naftalin lamented about the exodus of the élite, "You haven't left me anyone to work with."

As for the suburbs—136 of them in all—they have formed a new world, at once a reflection of and quite independent of their Twin Cities parents. In earlier decades, workingmen's homes were centered in the northern and eastern parts of Minneapolis and St. Paul, while higher class homes gravitated to the west and south. Now, Ted Kolderie points out,

> The Twin Cities suburbs are divided basically by a line from the northwest through downtown Minneapolis, through downtown St. Paul, and southeast toward Chicago. To the north and east of this line incomes, valuations, and public services are almost uniformly lower than in the higher-value subdivisions and commercial-industrial areas in the rolling country to the south and west. . . .
>
> [The postwar] dispersal of offices, stores, and industry into the suburbs largely followed, and reinforced, the residential pattern, the shopping centers orienting to the high-income neighborhoods, industry centers orienting to the high-income neighborhoods, industry relocating around the new freeways and the airport to the south, and offices gravitating toward both, creating a new kind of suburb—psychologically independent of the rest of the area, aggressively working to build a tax base, increasingly a wealthy and influential rival to the center cities. Bloomington (directly south of Minneapolis) is the prototype, a rural township in 1953 and today, with 81,970 residents, the fouth largest city in the state—in large measure (ironically) as a result of state, metropolitan, and central city investments in the stadium, new international airport, and two freeways.

Closing out our Twin Cities story, it should be noted that St. Paul's suburban push has been of somewhat less magnitude than Minneapolis', perhaps because more of her conservative Irish and Germans were content to stay in the old city. About two-thirds of the region's postwar suburban growth has been on the Minneapolis side, and Minneapolis is said to have completed its "third tier" of suburbs and to have begun on a fourth. Minneapolis' élite, of course, have long sought watering places well removed from the city proper; one of these is Wayzata on Lake Minnetonka, a resort of beauty and renown. One of the more interesting Minneapolis suburbs, closer in, is Edina, filled with salaried executives and professionals. Edina had 44,046 people in 1970, compared to a mere 9,744 just 20 years before. Despite all the newcomers, it remains one of the highest per capita income communities of America.

State Government: High Tax, High Service

Minnesota is a high-tax, high-service state. She has the highest corporate tax in the nation (11.33 percent in 1970) * and one of the heftiest income taxes (on a sharply graduated schedule that reaches 11.7 percent, for instance, on an income of $40,000). There is a 4 percent sales tax plus substantial luxury taxes. Her county and city property levies are some of the highest in the U.S.A., although there is a "circuit breaker" system that protects the very lowest income households from property tax overload situations. Only six other states tax a greater bite of citizens' income in combined state and local taxes.

For this substantial tax effort, Minnesotans get a lot in return. The state's educational effort is a uniquely serious one, and she is a leader in mental health. The absence of a patronage system means that little of the citizens' tax money is siphoned off for political satraps along the line. The state government appears to function with substantial efficiency. And in the policy area, there has not been a really conservative governor of Minnesota since the 1920s. It all smacks of the kind of watchful progressivism that a Yankee-Scandinavian society would like to call its own.

A new measure of rationality and fairness was added to the fiscal system of the state in 1971—the "Minnesota Miracle" referred to earlier in this chapter. Taxes that year were raised in the aggregate by about 23 percent but with substantial benefits, ranging from indirect state control of property tax assessments (which must now be made at realistic market values) to elimination of business personal property taxes and broadened income tax credits for property taxes paid by renters and the low-income elderly. As the Advisory Committee on Intergovernmental Relations commented:

> State and local fiscal fortunes are now tied together in unprecedented fashion. The job of setting the aggregate level of taxation and the relative mix of different

*** Since state taxes can be deducted from the federal, however, the effective corporate tax rate is only 3.2 percent, or a maximum of 5.8 percent on personal income.**

taxes will rest chiefly with the state legislature not, as in the past, on the uncoordinated actions of state and local policymakers. Local governments in future years will devote less time and energy to raising revenue and will shift their focus increasingly to how best to use the revenue which the legislature makes available to them. . . .

By assuming a dominant role in state-local fiscal policymaking, . . . the Minnesota lawmakers and governor intended to reduce the fiscal disparities among school districts, strengthen the general fiscal position of cities and counties, and ease the burden of property taxes on home owners and business firms. In the process, they made Minnesota a model for other states to follow.

In the wake of their takeover of both the senate and house in the 1972 elections, the Democrats prepared legislation to have candidates for the legislature run in the future under party labels. The reform would be an important one, because if Minnesota state government has had a serious fault, it has been in the officially nonpartisan system of elections. As in Nebraska, the nonpartisan system removes the element of party discipline, making every man his own party and opening the way for log-rolling and influence by special interest groups. One of the most avid defenders of the nonpartisan legislature, for instance, was state Sen. Gordon Rosenmeier of Little Falls, a brilliant trial lawyer and spokesman of rural, conservative interests who on occasion represented private firms before regulatory agencies. For many years the railroads' lobbyist was known as the 68th senator (there are officially 67), and many former legislators, including a former speaker of the house, work for the railroads. A tax law expert who also happened to be a Honeywell lobbyist was observed sitting in on closed sessions of the house taxation committee to mark up revenue legislation in the 1960s.

In 1972 a reform-minded Conservative, house majority leader Ernest Lindstrom, blew the whistle on a cozy relationship between a core group of powerful Conservative house leaders, including the house speaker, and a group of lobbyists for some of Minnesota's biggest corporations and industries. The business interests, functioning as the "Good Government Committee," included the state Railroads Association, 3M, Dayton Hudson Corporation, Northern States Power Company, Honeywell, Northwestern Bell Telephone Company, and the banking, liquor, beer, and iron mining industries. They had been raising campaign money jointly with the Conservative core group, reportedly exacting promises from candidates who got contributions that they would support the Good Government Committee's candidate for speaker of the house. The core group then advised the speaker in the sensitive matter of selecting the chairmen and membership of legislative committees. Lindstrom was successful in forcing the resignation of a political aide to the Conservative caucus who had doubled as chief fund raiser for the Good Government Committee.

Overall, however, the feeling of Minnesota legislators that they have one of the "cleanest" systems in the nation is probably well founded. Often the "public" lobbies—the Minnesota Education Association, defending teachers' interests, or departments of state government—exert more effective influence at the state capitol than the power companies, truckers, railroads, and influential lobbies like the Minnesota Association of Commerce and Industry, the Minnesota AFL-CIO, and the state's chapters of the Farm Bureau and Farmers Union. The Minnesota League of Women Voters is especially outspoken and often quite effective.

In the past decade, there has been an incursion of vital, capable "Young Turks" who have taken long strides to make the Minnesota legislature more relevant. A crucial factor in this shift has been reapportionment effected in stages from 1959 to 1965, which added to suburban influence while cutting down the voice of small towns and farms areas. Another factor was the program of the Minnesota Republican party, started in 1962, to recruit legislative candidates who would accept party support and vote in accordance with the party platform once elected. The program was spectacularly successful, and there now is a substantial group of younger party-oriented members on the Republican side, the bulk of them from the Twin Cities area but some from smaller towns and rural areas as well. As for the Liberals, they now call themselves the DFL faction instead. The younger members have been far less responsive to the railroads, timber industry, and other special interests and in fact were the spearhead in winning approval for the Twin Cities Metropolitan Council—over the bitter opposition of the entrenched Conservative faction that included some committee chairmen who had held their offices for 30 years or more. In the early 1970s, many of the old guard legislative leaders retired voluntarily or were defeated at the polls.

In 1971 the Citizens Conference on State Legislatures ranked Minnesota 10th in the nation in its ability "to perform in a functional, accountable, informed, independent, and representative manner." The outstanding feature, the conference said, was the Minnesota legislature's "general openness and accessibility of its processes and activities." Among the weaknesses noted were the constitutional limit on sessions (120 days in every biennium), limited staff and information services for members, and an excessively high number of legislators (134 in the house, 67 in the senate, the latter the largest in the country). Reforms on several of these fronts were under debate by 1972, however, and the newly elected Democratic legislators—following the mandate of the platform on which they were elected—promised important reforms like making rules committee sessions open to the public and guaranteeing minority representation on committees.

Despite its more urban orientation, Minnesota's "new look" legislature has not ignored rural Minnesota. In 1969 it passed a comprehensive regional planning act that acknowledges the decline of the small towns but tries to involve them in coordinated planning in each of 11 regions covering the state outside of the Minneapolis-St. Paul area. Part of the process is inevitably painful: fear of the selection of towns to be regional "capitals," in effect downgrading their competition. The hopeful feature for the smaller towns is that they will be involved in regional planning for land use, transportation, pollution control, and other matters which affect their destiny.

Minnesota's small town-farm culture is similar to that of Iowa and the Dakotas, discussed elsewhere in this book. And I will skip a sentimental return to Sauk Centre, Sinclair Lewis' birthplace and the Site of *Main Street.** Small-town Minnesota animosity toward the Twin Cities is not as great as one might expect, even in the days of deep concern in rural places about "law and order" and the fabric of urban society. As for the farmers, Congressman Albert Quie, a highly regarded Republican from the politically moderate, nativist Republican territory of southeastern Minnesota, believes they are amazingly aware of national and even world issues, and that with their substantial farm exports—including the search for new soybean markets abroad—isolationism is a thing of the past.

Education: Good Schools, a Great University

Minnesota is highly committed to education, as her tax and school spending statistics quickly demonstrate. Until recently, the entire state income tax was earmarked for schools. A high proportion of the state budget goes for education; Minnesota's overall educational tax effort—as related to income of the people—is fifth highest in the country. The state ranks only 20th in per capita income and 19th in population, but she has the fourth largest university system in the United States.

On the elementary and secondary level, an advanced state foundation program went far toward equalizing the school dollars available between rich and poor counties—even before the fundamental equalization program and increase of state aid to 65 percent that was enacted in 1971. Minnesota's high school dropout rate is the lowest in the country, and the percentage of her young men who fail Selective Service mental tests is but a quarter of the national average. In short, Minnesota has invested heavily to build a highly literate population.†

The University of Minnesota is a great national institution with especially distinguished faculties in political science (seedbed of the Humphreys and Naftalins, *et al.*), engineering and physics, mining, agriculture, medicine, and dentistry. Perhaps its weakest field is business. Without the research activities of the University, Minnesota might never have benefited from the discovery of an economic way to convert taconite to high-grade ore (thus saving the Iron Range), or enjoyed its electronic boom of the postwar era, or prospered in agriculture through the development of rust-resistant wheat, corn hybrids, or northern-growing fruits. Minnesota is one of the few states where the land grant institution and state university were deliberately combined, and the only one where the combined institutions were located

* Other famous literary figures from Minnesota have included F. Scott Fitzgerald and Ole Edvart Rolvaag, father of the DFL governor of the 1960s, Karl Rolvaag. The elder Rolvaag's *Giants in the Earth* was one of the most powerful novels ever written about pioneer life on the Plains. Minnesota is also the native state of Charles A. Lindbergh and the NATO commander of the postwar era, General Lauris Norstad.

† During the 1960s, Minnesota's school districts went through the familiar crisis of consolidation, shrinking from more than 1,000 to 430 in number. But many a small town resisted the process ferociously, fearing a disruption of the local economy and political culture, an increase in taxes, or the prospect of having its children exposed to the big, sophisticated world before it is necessary. There are still a few rural one-room schools in Minnesota, protected by a tenacious group known as "Friends of the Local School."

in the principal population center of the state. The central campus at Minneapolis-St. Paul has about 53,000 of the system's 60,000 students and plays a vital role in the life of the capital cities. (By contrast, the University of Wisconsin has had to come as a virtual stranger from Milwaukee, the University of Illinois into Chicago, etc.).

The university has one of the nation's outstanding medical schools, a place where Dr. Owen Wangensteen supervised some of the first breakthroughs in open-heart surgery in the 1950s.* Competition in earlier decades with the Mayo Clinic at Rochester may account in part for the university medical school's excellence; now the two cooperate through the Mayo Graduate School (largest graduate medical center in the U.S.), which is affiliated with the university. The Mayo Clinic remains an outstanding example of what it pioneered: the group practice of medicine with specialists working together. The other great national clinics—Lahey in Boston, Ochsner in New Orleans, and, in mental health, Menninger in Topeka—are all modeled on it. Some 200,000 people come annually from all parts of the nation and abroad to seek out the services of the Mayo Clinic's 440 full-time staff physicians. To its credit, the clinic (fortuitously set in a prosperous town) has never turned away a patient because he or she could not afford its services. The Mayo and University traditions together go far to explain why some studies have ranked Minnesota first among the states in health and welfare services.

Malcolm Moos, the political scientist and onetime speech writer for President Eisenhower, became University of Minnesota president in the late 1960s.† He has made some excellent administrative appointments and maintained tolerably good relationships with the legislature despite some grumbling that he was too soft on militant black students who staged a temporary takeover of administrative buildings. Comparatively speaking, Minnesota has had little student turmoil; its problems have been but a fraction of those, for instance, at the University of Wisconsin. Wise administration and the tolerant political tone of Minnesota both seemed to play a role in this. A perhaps significant sign of the times came in 1969 when the university

* Another especially distinguished member of the university faculty is Dr. Walter Heller, who was chairman of the Council of Economic Advisers under President Kennedy and Johnson and the first proponent of federal tax sharing with the states. Others of note have included the physicist Alfred O. Nier, the historian David Nobb, and the poet Allen Tate.

† Moos deserves a special niche in postwar American history as a principal architect of President Eisenhower's Farewell Address in January 1961, in which the President warned his countrymen: "We must guard against the acquisition of unwarranted influence, whether sought or unsought, by the military-industrial complex." Moos has acknowledged that "people thought it incongruous for Ike to be saying something like that," but insists that Eisenhower on a number of later occasions "expressed pride in the speech and its importance as a warning."

Not as well remembered is another warning Eisenhower raised in his address: "The prospect of domination of the nation's scholars by federal employment, project allocations and the power of money is ever present—and is gravely to be regarded." Moos's own University of Minnesota in 1966 ranked 16th among American universities in federal research grants of various types, the dollar total just under $36 million for a single year. But what is given can also be taken away, and the Carnegie Commission on Higher Education reported in 1971 that federal cutbacks had begun to affect the University of Minnesota in several areas, "and because of the decline in the economy, administrators see little chance of improving gifts and endowments. . . . Withdrawal of federal funds for local projects aggravates the local need for state tax resources. . . . The public is losing confidence in higher education." Nevertheless, in the face of its financing problems, the university in 1972 opened two new medical schools—one at the Mayo Clinic, and another in Duluth.

recognized as a legitimate student organization a group known as "Fight Repression of Erotic Expression," or FREE—a band of homosexuals organized under the motto "Gay is Good." The university noted that "recognition" does not indicate "approval," but its relations with its Republican-controlled board of regents were not improved. In 1971 the former head of FREE, Jack Baker, an avowed homosexual, was elected president of the university's student government body.

The university was also the spawning ground of the proposal to build somewhere on the sparsely peopled plains of western or northern Minnesota the first truly "Experimental City" of American history. As conceived in 1966 by Dr. Athelstan Spilhaus, then dean of the university's Institute of Technology, the city would differ fundamentally from the nation's new towns (mostly real estate developments close to metropolitan centers on the coasts) in that it would be virtually self-contained and employ radically new methods of technology and social planning for its 250,000 people.*

The new metropolis would be an "instant city" (to be completed within 10 years of an early 1970s starting date); unencumbered with old street, utility, and housing patterns, it could put many essential services (free mass transit, waste disposal, power generation, and the like) underground, leaving overground streets free for pedestrians. Spilhaus, a remarkably prodigious and enthusiastic inventor of things and ideas, insists that the city would be planned for an optimum population size. When it reaches that capacity, he insists, no more growth would be permitted, "just as machines are not overloaded when they reach capacity." Socially, the goal would be "an open society in an open city" in the hope of demonstrating that people of differing races, education levels, income, and skills can productively and compatibly inhabit the same city with maximum social mobility. To prevent uncontrolled suburban conglomerations nearby and enhance the physical environment, a broad swatch of encircling territory—many times the acreage of the Experimental City itself—would be preserved as open country and parks. There would be ample provision for modern man's increased leisure time and educational opportunities to cover his entire life span. A national data information center might be Experimental City's chief source of income, drawing a number of firms oriented to research and technological innovation.

There were many skeptics who doubted whether all this would come to pass, but Experimental City did receive early financial support from many of Minnesota's scientifically advanced business élite, from their corporations, foundations, the state and federal governments. Oriented to continuing innovation and experimentation, the city might provide a model for future new metropolises as national policy moves to conscious redistribution of swollen populations. But the planners were sailing into difficult, uncharted waters; no blueprint had ever been drawn for building a city *de novo* on such a scale.

* The Experimental City should not be confused with Jonathan, a "new town" similar to Virginia's Reston and Maryland's Columbia, now being constructed in a rural setting 20 miles southwest of Minneapolis.

While the university enjoys its illustrious national reputation, some of the most interesting innovation of recent years has come in the six state colleges, outgrowths of the old normal schools for training teachers. The college system board, in a quandary to find a new chancellor, called in for advice a political scientist from private Macalester College, G. Theodore Mitau. When Mitau received a telephone call later the same evening asking him to consider the chancellorship himself, he thought it was a joke. But the offer was serious and, after negotiations, accepted.

Mitau had come to the United States as an immigrant from Germany, penniless and without education, in the late 1930s. A short, nervous man of incredible energy, Mitau worked his way through Macalester and then joined its faculty, later writing a well received book on Minnesota politics. As state college chancellor, he shook up the old bureaucracy, forced out some of the less competent presidents of the individual colleges, and then sought ways to push out the walls of the lecture hall to create more student contact with the real world, acting on the assumption that modern college students were becoming uneasy with traditional classroom experiences under professors in safe tenure positions. College students now intern for a half year in major corporations, hospitals, newspapers, and government. Among other programs, an association was set up with St. Paul's excellent Arts and Science Center so that students could work with real professionals. Musicians and artists from the center also visit state colleges in all parts of Minnesota. Faced with rising construction costs and a need for substantial new facilities, Mitau began to experiment with a "systems" method of less expensive modular construction to create flexible and rearrangeable buildings that might be adapted to new curricula. If evidence were needed of the openness of Minnesota society, Mitau's career seemed to prove the point.

Minnesota also has a network of 17 junior colleges which had been locally supported—and underfed—until the state took over their financing in 1967. The state is working toward an association of the junior colleges with its advanced group of area vocational schools, which teach everything from aerodynamics to cosmetology. Competition with the increasingly popular junior colleges for state funds has actually begun to hamper the growth of the University of Minnesota.

Yet another innovation in higher education began in Minnesota early in 1972 when a news report out of St. Paul read: "Minnesota Metropolitan State College opened here today with no campus, no classes, no semesters, no classrooms, no grades, no required courses, no library, no student organizations, no tenured faculty, and no teen-age students." Minnesota Metropolitan's major goal was to attract adults who want to resume their education and win degrees—an extension, in a way, of the high school equivalency tests that made it possible for many World War II veterans to earn degrees. According to Minnesota Metropolitan's president, Dr. David E. Sweet, "the community will be our campus. We will use schools, factories, laboratories, churches, libraries, stores, museums, auditoriums, streets, and parks, wherever we can find them in the [Twin Cities] metropolitan area and wherever they will help meet people's educational needs." Each student has an adviser with whom he draws up a contract stipulating his educational goals and suggesting how he should attain them and be evaluated. Thus programming can be designed especially for each student's needs, and the college can be run without the costly (and sometimes irrelevant) physical plants and administrative structures of traditional universities. Parallels to Minnesota Metropolitan are springing up in other parts of the nation, including New York's new nonresidential Empire State College and an analogous program at the University of Oklahoma.

Not to be overlooked are the many excellent private colleges in Minnesota; of these the acknowledged leaders are Macalester, Carleton, and St. Olaf. Macalester has the third highest number of merit scholars in the U.S. and pioneered with the first coeducational dorms in the country and recruitment of a substantial black enrollment—with a whole host of accompanying problems. It welcomed Hubert Humphrey as a visiting professor of political science after his defeat for the Presidency in 1968.

Minnesota's Role in the Nation

Man for man, it would be hard to name a state which has contributed as many men of stature and depth to national political life in the postwar era as Minnesota. Hubert Humphrey and Eugene McCarthy have been the superstars of the constellation, Humphrey by dint of decades of creative legislative activity and his years in the Vice Presidency, McCarthy by his single act of daring in challenging President Johnson and then transforming the course of the 1968 Presidential election year and United States policy on Vietnam. Given a different twist of events in 1948, Harold Stassen might have been elected President; likewise Humphrey's spunky 1968 campaign against overwhelming odds will long be remembered. Two of the nine Justices of the U.S. Supreme Court are now Minnesotans: Chief Justice Warren Burger and Associate Justice Harry Blackmun.

A host of lesser luminaries also require mention. On the DFL side, the politically famous Minneapolis law firm of Larson, Loevinger, Lindquist, Freeman and Fraser produced over the years a governor, United States Secretary of Agriculture, member of the Federal Communications Commission, federal judge, U.S. Representative, and U.S. Senator. Orville Freeman, governor and Agriculture Secretary, may be remembered in the future as the first high-ranking official to argue for a national policy of population redistribution to maintain the viability of the great cities and reinvigorate the countryside (a plea to which his chief, Lyndon Johnson, lent a deaf ear). Walter F. Mondale also made his start with the firm; later he became Minnesota attorney general and, in 1964, United States Senator. Mondale made his mark fighting for civil rights and a variety of consumer-oriented causes, first as state attorney general, and later as Senator. Hard work rather than flamboyancy has been Mondale's trademark; I heard him described as "a hard-working, intelligent man who stays home, does his homework, and sleeps with his wife." He does not shy away from issues with little political payoff (like the plight of migrant farm workers) or real political risk (a defense of busing as a way to achieve integration in the public schools). He also fought for legal services for the poor, was the chief author of a comprehensive child development bill vetoed by President Nixon, and led the Senate fight to cut naval carrier funds and to kill the space shuttle program. In many states, that liberal a record could endanger an incumbent Senator's reelection chances. But Mondale, in an interview with David Broder, dismissed "that stuff about a liberal being undefeatable in Minnesota." Mondale did say there was a progressive climate in the state, and that Minnesotans did not "mind my being concerned about black children, or poor people, or migrants or Eskimos or Indians, as long as I'm still concerned about our own problems. I make sure," Mondale added, "that they know I'm their Senator. I'm back here 20 or 25 times a year. We run a strong service operation—I learned that from Humphrey."

Running for reelection in 1972 (he won in a walkaway), Mondale jokingly commented, "Minnesotans are used to their people running for President. We usually have two or three in there." Hubert Humphrey, in fact, was publicly pumping Mondale as a 1976 Presidential candidate on election night 1972, even in the midst of George McGovern's big defeat. Privately, however, Mondale has expressed grave apprehensions about leaping from a statewide electoral base into Presidential politics, where he might feel obliged to trim his sails and compromise on issues like school busing. And he lacks Humphrey's exuberance for political battle.

Congressman Donald M. Fraser, from the same law firm as Freeman and Mondale, is a quiet man of intensely humanitarian instincts who has used his position on the House Foreign Affairs Committee to press for an end to the Vietnam war; he is also a strong defender of the United Nations and proponent of civil rights. He succeeded George McGovern as head of the Democratic party's reform committee in 1971. John Blatnik, Democratic Congressman from the Iron Range for more than a quarter century, was once described as a man "whose gentle manner is merely the moss on a block of granite"; he ably defended the interests of his depressed district through his chairmanship of the Public Works Roads and Waterways Subcommittee, a post with enormous power over federal construction projects. In 1971 he became chairman of the full Public Works Committee. Blatnik also contributed beyond parochial interests, coauthoring the basic national water pollution control legislation with Senator Muskie of Maine.

On the Republican side, three Congressmen have left a distinct mark: Albert H. Quie, ranking minority member of the House Education and Labor Committee and a man of moderate to liberal political persuasion who became one of his party's most prominent spokesmen on education and poverty bills; Walter H. Judd, a onetime medical missionary in China who was a staunch cold war warrior and anti-Communist voice in Congress until Fraser defeated him in 1962; and Clark MacGregor, a member of the House

Judiciary Committee who labored hard for the civil rights bills of the 1960s and a constitutional amendment to give the people a direct vote for President. MacGregor ran for the Senate against Humphrey in 1970 and was defeated, but a grateful President Nixon made him chief liaison officer with the Congress, and later director of his reelection campaign. MacGregor's successor in the suburban Hennepin County area congressional seat was Bill Frenzel, who had been an outstanding member of the "Young Turk" legislative faction that surfaced in 1962.

No recital is required here of how the two old Minnesota Senate colleagues, Humphrey and McCarthy, became estranged over Vietnam policy and the 1968 Democratic nomination. For both men, the story had tragic implications. For Humphrey, by nature a truly happy warrior for his liberal causes, the election was tragic because at his moment of greatest opportunity he remained loyal to a domineering President and was unable to see the implications of the great moral issue of the year, the Vietnam war. For McCarthy, always the distant loner, the episode had its measure of pathos because, once having made his moral point about the war, he seemed incapable, even if he had cared to, of capitalizing on the outpouring of support in his behalf and thus making a really serious bid for the nomination. McCarthy, the more inscrutable of the two, has been explained to me as a brilliant but fundamentally mystic person, wonderfully witty and personable when he cares to be and without a touch of demagoguery, but also a lazy man, incapable of working well with staff, arrogant in the extreme, and even cruel on occasion. Only a moral issue really motivates such a man, making him perfectly willing to tear down a party to improve it; once that divinely appointed work is done, there is a vast disinterest in other issues or the day-to-day drudgery of practical politics. When he obliquely offered himself for the 1972 Democratic Presidential nomination, Austin Wehrwein of the Minneapolis *Star* noted that McCarthy's step had slowed, "his ennui barely if ever concealed," and that his position could be summed up in lines from a poem he wrote in 1968, "Lament to an Aging Politician"—

> My metaphors grow cold and old . . .
> I have left Act I, for involution
> and Act II. There mired in complexity
> I cannot write Act III.

The words turned out to be prophetic; McCarthy fared badly in the 1972 primaries he entered and ended up endorsing McGovern for the nomination.

Hubert Humphrey is presently remembered as the man who could not resist the opportunity to try for the Presidency again in 1972, even when his brand of traditional big government liberalism was passing out of style. When Humphrey debated McGovern in the California primary, discrediting McGovern's welfare proposals and saying that McGovern defense policies would make the U.S. a "second-rate power," he destroyed the South Dakotan's credibility for the later general election campaign more effectively than a Republican would ever have been able to do. Though Humphrey campaigned as a good soldier for McGovern that autumn, the damage could never be repaired. It is doubtful, of course, whether McGovern could have defeated President Nixon in any event, but the same was probably also true of Humphrey—and he had had his chance against a much less formidable Richard Nixon in 1968.

In retrospect, it is sad that Humphrey, after his return to the Senate in 1971, did not devote his full energies in his golden final years in public life doing what he is so superb at—legislating. That opportunity may still come to him, perhaps as a successor to Mike Mansfield as Senate Democratic Leader. But whether it does or not, Humphrey's greatest contribution to the country may have been made in his first Senate career, when he not only guided the landmark Civil Rights Act of 1964 to passage but was the father of such monumental legislative enactments as "Medicare" for the aged under Social Security, the Peace Corps, the Arms Control and Disarmament Agency, many parts of the National Defense Education Act, "Food for Peace," and the Wilderness Act. In the light of such accomplishments, Minnesota's role in the history of postwar America seems assured a shining place.

NORTH DAKOTA

STILL THE LONE PRAIRIE

NEAR THE LITTLE TOWN OF RUGBY, some 45 miles from the Canadian border in the north central part of North Dakota, a stone cairn marks the geographic center of the North American continent. From Rugby, one would have to travel some 1,500 miles to reach the Gulf of Mexico or, turning northward, a similar distance to the Arctic Archipelago, or similarly 1500 miles to the Atlantic or Pacific. North Dakota seems—and is—far from everywhere.

And in truth, for hundreds of miles from this central point of the continent, the prairie lands of America—so vast, untreed, and unpeopled that the first explorers called them the Great American Desert—stretch relentlessly to distant horizons. Predictably, the people who inhabit such vast and lonely lands are a sturdy, tenacious lot, honest, thrifty, proud. These days there are fewer of them. Between 1960 and 1970, the population dropped by 14,685 to 617,761. In fact, the state population is now 96,093 less than it was in 1930; there has not been a Census since 1910 in which North Dakota's growth equaled or surpassed the national average.

Especially in North Dakota, the Plains people have been anything but dull conformists. North Dakota has been celebrated as one of the most radical states of the Union; the record shows she has rebelled against manipulation by outside interests ever since the Populists revolted against absentee ownership in the 1890s and the Nonpartisan League arose to fight the grain merchants and railroads early in the century. To this date, North Dakota has the only state-owned bank in the United States, but her leaders still chafe under the ownership of most of the larger banks in the state by massive Minneapolis-based bank holding companies. North Dakota's most famed politician, gravel-voiced governor and later Senator William ("Wild Bill") Langer, was at once a warmhearted prairie Populist and a man of picaresque ethics who flirted with the edges of the law but was never convicted. It was North Dakota's Senator Gerald P. Nye who roused national attention with a sharply critical investigation of the munitions makers in the early 1930s; in 1936 it was North Dakota's Congressman William Lemke whom Father Coughlin was backing in an agrarian-isolationist campaign for the Presidency. One observer concludes that while North Dakota may be the most agricultural state of the Union, it is "about as sedate as a thrusting pitchfork."

A few other facts to set the North Dakota stage: With its cool, sunny climate, North Dakota is classic small-grain country, producing a hard, flinty high-protein grain ideal for making bread; in all the U.S.A., North Dakota ranks second only to Kansas in overall wheat production; it is actually first in durum wheat, in barley, rye, flaxseed, and sunflower seed. Vast wheat farms make average farm acreage—close to 1,000 acres—several times the national average. Agricultural income in 1970 was $693 million. Farm cooperatives are nowhere so strong as in North Dakota, and it is the banner state for the liberal-inclined National Farmers' Union. To supplement farm income, oil from the Williston Basin near the Montana border has grown in importance since its discovery in the early 1950s. Annual production is in the neighborhood of $70 million. Beneath the state's western reaches lie 28,000 square miles of lignite coal deposits, one of the nation's richest energy stores. Most of the region has, in fact, already been leased for coal production, and three mine-mouth power plants—the harbingers of an estimated 10 to 15 in the next few years—have already been opened. They are plugged into a major power grid and ship most of their electricity out of state. Increased concern has been evidenced, however, about the threat to the natural landscape posed by widespread strip mining, and whether North Dakota's reclamation laws are tough enough.

Not counting grain elevators, North Dakota has just one skyscraper: its striking 19-story Capitol building at Bismarck, built after a humdrum domed predecessor fortuitously burned some 40 years ago. North Dakota also boasts one of the largest man-made lakes in the world (Lake Sakakawea, behind the Garrison Dam), the only state-owned grain mill and elevator in America, and the longest road in America without a curve, some 110 miles long.

Regions and People

To think of North Dakota as one vast, undifferentiated prairie would be a mistake; in fact, there are at least three distinct geographical regions to the state. Along the Minnesota border to the East lies the relatively humid Red River Valley, an ancient lake bed that is underlain with deep humus that produces rich chernozem soils and in turn wheat, potatoes, oats, barley,

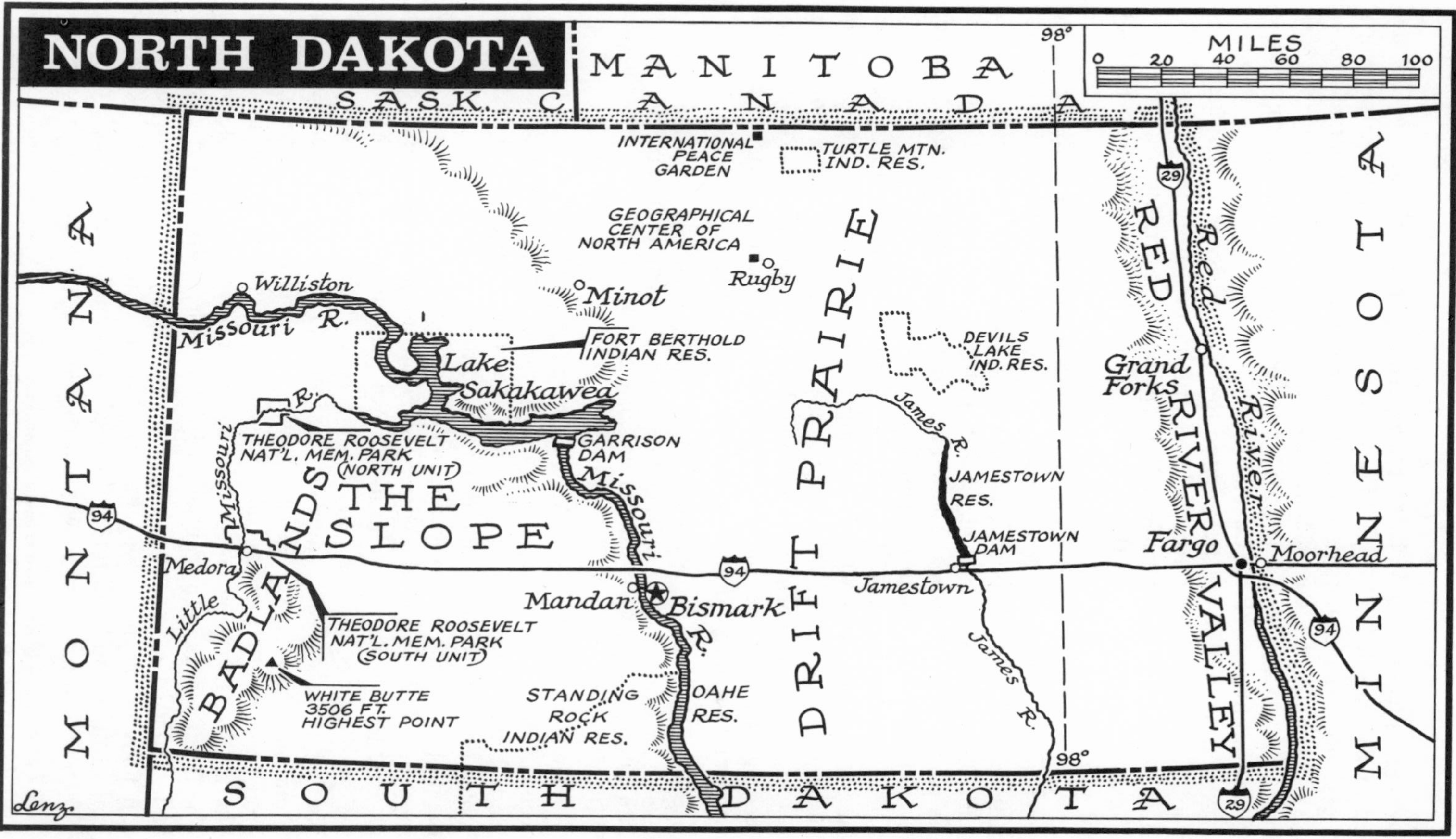

NORTH DAKOTA
MANITOBA
SASK.
CANADA
98°
MILES
0 20 40 60 80 100
MONTANA
MINNESOTA
SOUTH DAKOTA
INTERNATIONAL PEACE GARDEN
TURTLE MTN. IND. RES.
GEOGRAPHICAL CENTER OF NORTH AMERICA
Rugby
Minot
Williston
Missouri R.
FORT BERTHOLD INDIAN RES.
Lake Sakakawea
DEVILS LAKE IND. RES.
Grand Forks
RED RIVER VALLEY
Red River
29
James R.
GARRISON DAM
THEODORE ROOSEVELT NAT'L. MEM. PARK (NORTH UNIT)
JAMESTOWN RES.
JAMESTOWN DAM
Missouri
THE SLOPE
DRIFT PRAIRIE
94
Medora
BADLANDS
Fargo
Moorhead
Jamestown
Mandan
Bismark
Little Missouri
R.
THEODORE ROOSEVELT NAT'L. MEM. PARK (SOUTH UNIT)
WHITE BUTTE 3506 FT. HIGHEST POINT
STANDING ROCK INDIAN RES.
OAHE RES.
Lenz

flax, corn, soybeans, sugar beets, sunflowers, legumes—the farm variety the rest of the state longs to have. Fargo (1970 population 53,365), the state's largest city, a regional trade center (also for neighboring Minnesota counties) and home of some of North Dakota's few industries, lies in the Valley.* So does Grand Forks (39,008), number two city in the state and home of the University of North Dakota.

West of the Valley, stretching to the Missouri River at the state's midpoint, lie thousands of square miles of drift prairie, softly undulating fields, much dryer and largely treeless. Here, in late summer, one can see fields of golden wheat as far as the eye can reach; in July there are also fields of colorful blue flax.

Still farther west and running to the Montana border is the high, dry ranchland known as the Slope, a semiarid belt of short grasses, buffalo berries, deep valleys, and flat-topped, steep buttes and hills. Here wheat farming gradually gives way to land fit for little but grazing. The rainfall is very low, the population very sparce. The most dramatic landscape is in the Badlands region in the state's southwest corner.

Astride the Missouri River, at the border between the drift prairie and the Slope, lie the state's third- and fourth-ranking cities, the state capital of Bismarck (34,703) and Minot (32,290) some hundred miles northward. Traversing the continent with his now legendary dog Charley, John Steinbeck was struck by the change of worlds on the Missouri River between Bismarck and the neighboring town of Mandan (11,093):

> On the Bismarck side it is the Eastern landscape, Eastern grass, with the look and smell of Eastern America. Across the Missouri on the Mandan side, it is pure West, with brown grass and water scorings and small outcrops. The two sides of the river might as well be a thousand miles apart.

There are few points in America where geography defines not only the economy but also the character of the people so vividly. Elwyn B. Robinson, North Dakota's distinguished historian, notes that the people of the Red River Valley are relatively reserved, conservative, formal. As one moves westward, the people became more friendly, more liberal, increasingly informal. Finally, the North Dakotans of the western Slope are an often hard-drinking, poker-playing, free-and-easy lot who like to call their ministers and dignitaries by their first names and dress in Western style clothes. The railroads settled North Dakota, and depending on one's view of national characteristics, the ethnic mix may be said to match the geographic. The Northern Pacific brought in mostly Germans and Russians; they settled mostly in southern North Dakota, leaving an isolationist, conservative, and Republican legacy. The Great Northern, by contrast, went across the northern part of the state and recruited mostly Scandinavians to ride westward on its lines; today one still finds liberal and strong Farmers Union territory in cities like Grand Forks, Minot, and Williston, and indeed across most of the northern counties. The Scandinavian heritage was mostly Norwegian, with some Swedes and

* Fargo is distinguished by one of the lowest crime rates among all cities in America. As a state, North Dakota has the lowest murder rate of any in the Union.

Danes. Finally, one must add in numbers of Ukrainians, Bohemians, and Finns, found mostly in the west.

Little will be said here of cities, since they count for comparatively little in North Dakota life except as government and trade centers. Bismarck is considered the state's most attractive town, with a high degree of home ownership and no seedier back-of-the-tracks section like those in Grand Forks and Fargo. The central business districts of the cities are uniformly dreary and more reminiscent of the U.S.A. of the 1940s than the U.S.A. of the '70s.

Man and the Elements

North Dakota is a young state; she received her first settlers just over a century ago and in 1870 numbered less than 2,500 souls. Then, during the 1870s, as the Northern Pacific Railroad was extended across the territory, land speculators ("boomers") and homesteaders flooded in. No other state received so many of its settlers directly from the old country; Bismarck received its name in a promotional bid by the railroad to attract settlers from Germany. One-way tickets were offered from "Bremen to Bismarck." (The Northern Pacific, which was the largest landowner in the state because of congressional generosity, then sold land to the flood of immigrants.) By 1920 half the people of North Dakota were bilingual, speaking some old world language in addition to English. (Even in 1970, the Census found that 15 percent of North Dakota's people listed German as their native tongue—the highest percentage of any state.)

The great attraction for settlers, of course, was the vast, virgin prairie, which soon yielded to the plow and began to produce magnificent crops of wheat. By 1880 the state had 37,000 people, by 1890 (a year after statehood was achieved) 191,000. Scarcely any of them lived in towns; the wealth and attraction lay in the land.

But it was not an entirely hospitable land to which the settlers came. Precariously set in the heart of the great central plains, without mountains or trees to break the fast-moving winds of the central continent, North Dakotans found themselves exposed to cruelly cold winters and searingly hot summers. North Dakota in fact still holds the Western Hemisphere record for absolute range of temperature in the same year. It happened in 1936, when it was 60 degrees below zero at Parshall on February 15 and 121 degrees above at Steele on July 6. The *average* temperature in January in North Dakota is a chill seven degrees! CBS news commentator Eric Sevareid has written of his childhood home at Velva, N.D.:

> It was a trial of the human spirit just to live there, and a triumph of faith and fortitude for those who stayed on through the terrible blasting of the summer winds, the merciless suns, through the frozen darkness of the winters when the deathly mourn of the coyote seemed at times to be the only signal of life.

In more recent years, as schools have consolidated for efficiency, some North Dakotans have expressed the fear that busloads of children—who in some remote areas must travel so far that they leave home in the midwinter morning darkness and return after sundown—could be frozen to death in a blizzard.

An Air Force man who suffered through a tour of duty at Minot published a book of cartoons on North Dakota entitled *June, July, August and Winter*. North Dakotans are not universally happy about the kind of image all this conveys; there has even been a serious movement in the state to take the frigid word "North" out of the state name and simply call it "Dakota."

Governor William L. Guy told me his state had been unfairly maligned as a Siberian wasteland; several states, he said, actually have more snowfall each year; not long ago a ski resort near Bismarck went broke because of inadequate snow. (Weather charts show that the annual snowfall is at least half again as great in neighboring Minnesota, Wisconsin, and Michigan, and even more in northern New York and New England.) As for hot summers, Guy protested, North Dakota's are not nearly so unbearable as those in Kansas and Nebraska. (Again, the weather maps show average top temperatures in summertime 10 degrees cooler in North Dakota than in some of its Plains States neighbors to the south.)

Some North Dakota partisans have gone so far as to make a virtue out of the state's weather—with special emphasis on the many days of sunshine. The North Dakota air, prospective settlers were told in an 1887 territorial publication, was "dry, pure, and full of invigoration." A North Dakota anthropologist wrote that Ojibway Indians who moved from their earlier woodland home to the open Northern prairies acquired "an optimism and swagger" he thought might reflect "the dazzling sunlight, the blue sky and waving 'sea of grass' of the Plains."

Inevitably, Theodore Roosevelt found North Dakota—where he went in 1884 as a young Easterner to regain his health—the test of a man's mettle he liked. In his years as President, he took time to recall:

> We worked [on the cattle ranch] under the scorching midsummer sun, when the wide plains shimmered and wavered in the heat. . . . In the soft springtime the stars were glorious in our eyes each night before we fell asleep; and in the winter we rode through blinding blizzards. . . . Ours was the glory of work and the joy of living.

And healthful the climate must still be; North Dakotans boast of their clean air and water and tell the visitor their life expectancy is 10 years greater than in Los Angeles.

North Dakota's dazzling skies exact a price, though: arid land below. Aridity, as we have noted, becomes an increasing problem as one travels from east to west in the state. Before the white man came, the thick matting of grasses and their roots on the open prairie retained a measure of moisture and protected the soil from the winds. But the first generations of farmers lacked foresight; they failed to diversify their crops, concentrating on the single great moneymaker: wheat. And in their haste to make a profit from the soil, they overworked it. In the 1930s, nature brought both severe drought and high winds. By 1936, no crops could be grown except in the Red

River Valley. Dust storms obscured the sun; banks failed; mortgages were foreclosed; in the last five years of the 1930s, some 86,000 persons fled North Dakota.

Forty years later, long since recovered from the trauma of the "dirty '30s," North Dakota is still a basically agricultural state—indeed, no other state depends so much on agriculture and so little on industry, none has so high a percentage of its people living on farms and little villages. Crop rotation, irrigation, and conservation have made the land viable again and protected against drought as best as man can. Great new reservoirs on the Missouri River promise a bright future in agriculture. Except among the Indians, there is little poverty in North Dakota today. The state's problems lie in other areas: the constant loss of her young people to the industrialized states, a chronic inability to attract industry. Across the state, once prosperous little farm supply towns are in a grim struggle for survival; some have even died. The problem is that as the number of farms contract and supplies are purchased from afar or in regional shopping centers, the little towns have little more reason for being. As more and more people leave, economic survival and the quality of life become harsher for those who remain—often only elderly and retired people. In the winter of 1971, reporter Douglas Kneeland of the New York *Times* reported on a trip to one little North Dakota town:

> Lincoln Valley is two and a half miles of gravel road from Highway 14, an island of pleasant trees, houses and church steeples on a sea of snow-covered farmland that stretches from horizon to horizon. But there are no tracks in the shallow snow on the road leading into it. Once there, the main street is eerily silent in the flat light of the afternoon winter sun.
>
> A small black dog, probably from a neighboring farm, patters cautiously away. A snowmobile has left its marks along the main street.
>
> The stores are weathered and empty, their broken windows gaping into nothingness. The remains of a bar, two groceries, rusted gas pumps. A score of houses, vacant, boarded. . . .

Clark Robinson's Farm and the Garrison Dam

One of North Dakota's most prosperous farmers is Clark Robinson, a vigorous man in his mid-fifties who was president of the state Farm Bureau during the late 1960s. Robinson and his brother Dave, a Republican state senator, farm 4,500 flat, rich acres of farmland at Riverdale, some 60 miles north of Bismark. The Robinson farm is bigger and richer than most in North Dakota, but the family story is not untypical.

John J. Robinson, their grandfather, came to McLean County in 1884 and homesteaded on the standard allotment of 160 acres. Good fortune was with the Robinsons to start with; they drilled a well and got good drinking water. By the time John Robinson died in 1902, the farm had grown to 1,280 acres. In the early days of the farm, half the acreage was range land too tough to plough. So the family started early with cattle—as it turned out, a blessing during leaner years that would follow.

Clark and Dave's father held on during the depression, including some years when there were scarcely any crops at all, and later turned over the farm to his two sons, both of whom had graduated from college. Today they live in two large, substantial farmhouses surrounded by a neat white picket fence, close by picturesque red-shingled farm buildings, one dating back to 1904. Each year they raise 1,500 to 1,800 acres of grains—wheat, flax, and rye, as well as barley and oats to feed to their cattle. Between 400 and 500 acres are kept in tame grass for early spring grazing of the up to 1,000 steers the brothers buy for fattening and sale each year.

Mechanization has come in a big way to the Robinson farm: the brothers own $40,000 worth of tractors and a huge combine with a separator and thrasher; even more equipment would be needed if Dave didn't have a natural mechanical aptitude which makes it possible to adapt machinery for multiple purposes. Electricity, of course, plays a major role in the Robinson's farming operations; Clark Robinson says that the annual bill from the local rural electric cooperative is more than his dad's entire income in the depression years. Long hours and sometimes a frantic rush to feed the cattle on schedule mark the Robinsons' days on the farm, but with mechanization and electrification, the two of them can successfully run a farm that once required eight hired hands.

The growth of farms like the Robinsons' has of course been accompanied by a steady drop in the number of farms in North Dakota; in 1932 there were 80,000 farms in the state; by 1970 fewer than 46,000, the attrition striking evidence of a grim sort of economic survival of the fittest. At the same time, the value of cropland has spiraled upward: the value per acre near the Robinson farm was $15 around World War I, $33 in 1937, $66 in 1959, but close to $150 by the late 1960s. The value of the Robinson's farm today would be several hundred thousand dollars; across the entire state, according to the 1969 Census of Agriculture, the value of farms averaged $87,222 (compared to $58,450 only five years before). The average age of the state's farmers is strikingly high, 49 years.

If they had their way, the Robinsons would like to incorporate their farm for the tax advantages that might accrue. But a suspicious North Dakota citizenry, fearful of the destruction of small towns, schools, and churches by monstrous corporate farms, has rejected corporate farming at the polls. Actually, the Robinsons themselves would remain family farmers, even if incorporated. Clark Robinson says he doesn't believe a large corporation can compete with the family farmer in raising crops or ranching, for the very simple reason that a corporation can't find good enough people to manage the land properly, to handle intricate and costly farm machinery, to understand the delicate problems of crop timing, moisture of the land and the crop, or in a bad year, be able to call on the whole family to pitch in without a paycheck until times get better.

Part of the Robinsons' prosperity, of course, stems from the price stability given wheat by federal price supports and crop diversion payments.

REA power rates are another form of federal assistance. And in the coming years, Robinson and the other farmers of the Dakotas will benefit immeasurably from the vast irrigation potential of the Missouri River. In one of the huge water conservation-flood control-irrigation-power projects of modern times, the Army Engineers have dammed the great Missouri all the way from Wolf Point, Montana, to the South Dakota-Nebraska border; in fact, the entire river valley is flooded for all that distance except for a 70-mile stretch in North Dakota.

Robinson drove me to the headwall of the gigantic Garrison Dam, just two miles from his home. Looking north, one can see the starting point from which the river backs up some 200 miles from this huge earthen dam, 210 feet high and over two miles long, creating a vast (though as yet largely undeveloped) recreation area through broad, arid lands at the heart of the continent. (It is somewhat incongruous, though, to an eye accustomed to the intimate relationship of nature-made waterline and shoreline, to see deep blue waters lapping up against the parched grass dunes of the High Plains.) Robinson and his fellow farmers are ecstatic about the irrigation potential that will result in the next few years. Up to now, North Dakota has been confined by its climate and aridity to little more than one crop—wheat, which is a surplus commodity on national and world markets. With the quarter million acres of land that can be irrigated from the Garrison project, they can raise corn and, with that corn, fatten livestock. As the tastes of an affluent nation shift from grains to beef, North Dakota can build a far more balanced and prosperous agricultural economy.

Even those like Robinson who may benefit the most directly speak wistfully, though, of the price of the great dam: the flooding of some 300,000 acres of choice river bottom land in North Dakota, the loss of many homes, and the death of the three towns (even though some brand new ones were built to replace them). One can imagine the furor the conservationists might have raised if the destruction of such rich bottom lands, with their beautiful natural stands of cottonwood, had been proposed in the late 1960s rather than the more callous era of the 1940s when the dams were authorized. And sadly, much of the flooded land was part of the Fort Berthold Indian Reservation, which lies along both sides of the river.

A heartrending account of the high-handed way in which Congress and the Army Corps of Engineers mistreated the Indians is related by Arthur E. Morgan, the first chairman of the Tennessee Valley Authority, in his book, *Dams and Other Disasters*. For centuries, the fertile river bottom land, protected from the subzero winter winds of the prairie, had provided a hospitable place for the Indians' homes, their garden crops and grass, water and shelter for their cattle. An 1851 treaty had guaranteed the land to them in perpetuity. Yet when their land was seized, and they were forced onto the barren, high prairie, the government callously refused their request for a modest amount of electricity from the dam to pump water for their cattle and homes, to pasture their cattle along the margin of the reservoir, or to use the soon-to-be inundated timber for building houses and fences.

Some of the Indian leaders were ordered to Washington to sign, unwillingly, the agreement to take their land. A photo still exists showing the officials gathered around the desk of Interior Secretary J. A. Krug for the signing; in it one sees George Gillette, chairman of the Fort Berthold Indian Tribal Business Council, openly weeping.

The Co-ops and the Farm Groups

North Dakota is one of the most rural of American states,* and there is no state in which farm organizations are so important. In a reversal of form from most states, the North Dakota Farmers Union (with 32,000 members) is actually bigger and more powerful than the Farm Bureau (with 14,000 members). Sometimes the two groups agree on tax policies specially affecting farmers. But on the big issues—farm price supports, corporate farming, reapportionment, training of their young—they split sharply.

The heart of Farmers Union strength in North Dakota is the vigorous structure of farmers cooperatives—for grain, oil and gas, transportation, lumber, sometimes even hardwares and groceries—active in every county of the state. The co-ops are in major part a legacy of the New Deal; the Farmers Union started in North Dakota in the 1920s but got its real forward thrust in the 1930s when it could use Farm Security Administration loans to build co-ops. Today at least half of the grain marketed in North Dakota moves through co-op elevators, and the co-ops are a major force in every other area of a farmer's life. Many of the co-ops have a Farmers Union dues check-off procedure; a substantial portion of that money goes to the Farmers Union youth educational program.

The Farm Bureau, on the other hand, requires $15 in cash dues payment from its members each year. Generally, the Bureau attracts the operators of larger, more prosperous farms—men who agree with its long-term objectives of ending federal farm acreage controls and support payments so that the market can decide prices. The Farmers Union takes a precisely opposite view, demanding a controlled market with price supports to save the small family farm. And many of the Union's co-op operations are aimed at maintaining the viability of economically weak rural towns to service small farm operators.

On the legislative reapportionment issue of the 1960s, the Farm Bureau fought hard to maintain special rural advantages while the Farmers Union was willing to shift to one-man, one-vote. Thanks to the Supreme Court, the Union position prevailed. But it was a referendum vote of the state's people which overwhelmingly rejected a corporate farming bill supported by the Bureau and opposed by the Union.

In politics, the Bureau is predictably Republican-oriented, though it leaves it to its members to take their own initiatives in elections. The

* In 1970, 55.7 percent of the state's people lived in remote places or towns of less than 2,500 people; the national figure for this category was only 26.5 percent.

Union is avowedly Democratic and works hard to elect Democratic candidates. In North Dakota, cities and especially the towns tend to vote the most Republican, while the farm precincts are the heart of Democratic strength.

Perhaps the most revealing difference between the two farm groups lies in the kind of educational programs they have designed for their young people. The Farm Bureau each year brings up to 250 junior and senior high school students together for a three-day series of lectures and seminars about Americanism and the dangers of socialism and communism. The students must be from the upper third of their classes; each must pay $35 for the sessions. Lecturers are often from right-wing universities; the man who heads the program, former FBI agent Cleon Skousen, is friendly to the John Birch Society and has tangled with the state's senior Republican Senator, Milton Young, over that issue.

The Farmers Union youth program begins with seven- and eight-year-old children and involves over 6,000 juveniles a year, 580 of them through attendance at camps. The program starts with courses that stress nature, the relationships of people, the worth of the individual. Older children are instructed in the workings of cooperatives, on the United Nations, on conservation and water resources. Farmers Union leaders complain that there is significant racial intolerance among the Plains and mountain states people; thus understanding of other races is stressed and programs have been begun to send North Dakota children to view the urban problems of Denver and bring black, white and Mexican children from poverty areas of Denver to spend several days on North Dakota farms.*

Though still dominant today, the North Dakota Farmers Union faces the problem of a diminishing membership base. In 1956 there were 58,000 farmers in North Dakota, of whom 44,000 belonged to the Union; by 1970 there were only 46,000 farmers and 36,000 Union members. Yet another danger to Farmers Union membership comes from the militant National Farm Organization (NFO), which has had spurts of intense activity in the state.

The Economy: How to Diversify?

As most of America moves from its industrial age into a postindustrial era, North Dakota is still struggling to develop the rudiments of the simplest industrial plant. Only a quarter of the state's new wealth added each year comes from nonagricultural sources, and North Dakota stands 48th on the list of 50 states in the value added by manufacturing.

The price North Dakotans have to pay for an undiversified economy is

* North Dakotans have considered themselves far removed from the race problems of the metropolitan states. The 1970 Census found only 18,726 non-Caucasians in the state; of these, 14,369 were Indians, 2,494 Negroes, and a scattering Oriental and other races. When the state's National Guard was instructed by Washington to integrate during the 1960s, it could find only one qualified black, and he didn't care to join. However, a number of blacks serve at the Air Force bases at Grand Forks and Minot. There are also several Negroes at the University of North Dakota at Grand Forks; they formed their own Black Students Union and protested alleged racism on the part of the local police.

high indeed. No state outside the South has such a low per capita personal income (only 76 percent of the national average). What's more, North Dakota is one of a handful of states in which per capita income is not only alarmingly low but is growing more slowly than the national average. Each year, the state falls further and further behind.*

The narrow economic base, in turn, means that North Dakota has to tax itself more heavily, in terms of a percentage of the people's income, just to maintain basic state services. Some charts put the state's per capita taxation at the highest level in America. State services inevitably suffer: for instance, North Dakota ranks a very respectable seventh among the states in the percentage of the people's income which goes for education, but it can only pay its elementary school teachers $6,740 a year—a sad 47th place among the states.

And then, because of a shortage of nonfarm jobs—at least any at a decent rate of pay—high numbers of young people begin to leave the state once they have completed school or college. Of the 121,365 young people between nine and 18 years of age in North Dakota in 1960, only 88,580 (32,785 less) were still there in 1970. Most who left were in search of better jobs. Since 1940 the state has had a net *out*migration of 316,000 people—more than half the total of those living in the state today. The outmigration percentage for the 1960s, 14.9 percent, was the greatest of any state. The excess of births over deaths helped to even the tables some, but nevertheless, North Dakota managed to be one of only three states (along with South Dakota and West Virginia) that had fewer people in 1970 than they did in 1960. The state lost one of its two Congressmen in the automatic reapportionment following the 1970 Census, cutting exactly in half its voice in the national House. At home, there are fewer and fewer people in the working-age years to pay the taxes and provide productivity for growth.

Since the early 1950s, earnest efforts have been made to introduce new elements into the North Dakota economy. But not much has been accomplished. To attract new industry or tourists, for instance, an attractive environment and accessibility are key factors. But North Dakota must labor under the burden of its drought and blizzard image; moreover, the simple fact is that North Dakota lies far, far away from the nation's major markets and population centers.

This is not to say that state leaders have not done what they could to encourage new industries and tourism. North Dakota offers municipal industrial development bonds and a five-year forgiveness on real property and corporate income for some new industries. Governor Guy strove during the '60s to reduce the state's high power rates through the building of three cooperative power plants on the Missouri River, all funded with REA money;

* Part of the state's problem lies in the economically deadening effect of federal payments to farmers for not producing wheat. Millions of dollars in federal land retirement payments go to North Dakota farmers each year, but the one-shot subsidies are no substitute for a healthy economy in which money constantly recirculates as farmers purchase farm machinery and equipment, fertilizers, oil products, tires, seeds, and insecticides from local merchants.

by the end of the decade Basin Electric, the key co-op power company, was pumping power to co-ops and municipal systems in an eight-state area. In the early 1970s, Basin Electric was planning a huge addition to its lignite-fueled electric power plant (though not without complaints from environmental protection groups).

But all in all, the amount of new industry in the state has been small. The most pathetic industrial development bulletin I saw anywhere came out of the North Dakota Business and Industrial Development Department; in the month I read it the bulletin was reduced to headlining a small addition to a chisel plow factory, the fact that a man in Stanton was building glass boats as a hobby in his garage, a new machinery plant which would employ 10 people in Wahpeton, the expanding pumpkin and sunflower seed industry in Fargo, and home manufacture of apiary aids by a retired beekeeper. Guy attributes part of the small industrial pickings to lack of knowledge on the part of prospective industries, which may conclude incorrectly that the state lacks recreation facilities or an adequate supply of skilled labor. There have been a few successes. Borden's came into the Red River Valley to make flaked and powdered potatoes; within a few years it had closed all its other potato processing plants in favor of its North Dakota plant. A highly successful jewel-bearing plant is operated by Bulova Watch on one of the Indian reservations. And for several years, all of the Greyhound buses in the U.S. have been assembled at the little town of Pembina, N.D., near the Canadian border.

A second approach to North Dakota development has been taken by members of its congressional delegation, especially the senior U.S. Senator, Milton R. Young. They have pressured to get the state included in some of the military-industrial contracts of recent years, and indeed North Dakota's northern location made it an ideal place for the SAC bases which went to Grand Forks and Minot. Not far from the same cities, an impressive number of Minuteman missile installations later went in; at the start of the 1970s the controversial antiballistic missile (ABM) followed on the northernmost edge of the 90-mile-long Minuteman field that starts at Grand Forks. (The Strategic Arms Limitations Talks with the Soviet Union resulted, in 1972, in U.S. agreement to drop all but two of its ABM facilities—the one in North Dakota, and the other—which may never be built—around Washington, D.C. The massive seven-foot walls of the monstrous ABM command post loom over the prairie close to the Canadian border, relics of a barely averted general escalation of the arms race.)

Tourism provided another hope for North Dakota development, and with the encouragement of Guy and others, tourists were bringing more than $100 million a year into the state by the start of the 1970s. North Dakota lacks woods and lake resorts that can hold tourists for a week or two, but it can provide attractions with a special flavor of the Old West. Lest the reader be at a loss to name any, I will list some here: the western Badlands, an area of roughly sculptured hills in subtle hues; the Theodore Roosevelt National Memorial Park, filled with buffalo herds and prairie dogs; on the Canadian border, the joint North Dakota-Manitoba sponsored International Peace Garden; near Washburn, the place where Lewis and Clark encamped for the winter of 1804–1805 on their trek to the Pacific Northwest; on the Standing Rock Indian Reservation, the burial place of Sitting Bull; and, last but not least, in Strasburg, the birthplace of that king of "champagne music" and famous North Dakota native, Lawrence Welk.

Some North Dakotans are a bit leery of the tourist influx, fearing competition for their favorite camping areas or fishing spots. (One native was even quoted as suggesting that the tourists would be more accommodating if they could just mail the money in.) But generally the state has approved of efforts like Guy's to call a 1961 conference of governors at Minot which set up the five-state Old West Trail program, or North Dakota's later participation in the first international tourist loop, including North Dakota, Minnesota, Manitoba, and Saskatchewan.

In raw dollars, North Dakota has not invested much in tourist promotion. But one of its private citizens, Bismarck businessman Harold Schafer, helped to make up for that by investing more than $1 million restoring the old cowtown of Medora near the Badlands and T. R. Park. Founded by a French adventurer named Marquis de Mores as what he hoped would be the keystone of a vast meatpacking empire, Medora was christened by cracking a champagne bottle over a tent peg in 1883. But de Mores met a violent end at age 38 after his financial schemes had gone sour, and Medora won its real claim to fame as headquarters for Teddy Roosevelt and his Roughriders.

Both T. R. and de Mores would surely appreciate the man who has restored their old hunting grounds. Harold Schafer, raised on a North Dakota farm, started life as a traveling salesman and store clerk; then in 1942 he started the Gold Seal Wax Company, which he has since built into a $25 million-a-year business with several smart acquisitions along the line (Snowy Bleach and Mr. Bubble). But Schafer is pure outdoorsman and seems a bit ill at ease penned in his office. At his invitation, I drove with Schafer to see his Blackburn Buffalo Ranch near Bismarck; the man's love for the wild Dakotan landscape, for his stately buffalo (over 200 head) and his herd of swift, graceful elk, was contagious.

Gold Seal has offices in New York, Chicago, Los Angeles, Houston, and Atlanta. But Schafer prefers Bismarck, and the headquarters stay there. (Sadly, all of Gold Seal's production facilities are outside of North Dakota, but it is the largest privately owned firm directed from the state.) Just before I interviewed Schafer, he was voted one of the world's best-dressed men, on a list with Nixon, Reagan, and Prince Rainier of Monaco. (A tip from his shrewd Chicago tailor was reportedly at the base of his selection.) When told the news of his election, the local press dutifully reported, Schafer had just come in from herding buffalo on his ranch and was wearing thermal underwear, a dirty Medora shirt, and cowboy pants.

Politics: From NPL to Normalcy

What made North Dakota politics so erratic and radical for so many decades was the Nonpartisan League, a farm revolt of 1915 born out of the yeomen's conviction that they were being victimized by big city money, by the railroads, and by grain combines. A legendary incident occurred that year when a group of farmers went to the state capitol to protest their lot, only to be told by a big-town legislator named Treadwell Twichell to "go home and slop the hogs." The NPL philosophy was well summed up in the movement's chant: "Put a lawyer, a miller, and a banker in the barrel and roll it down a hill, and you'll always have an S.O.B. on top."

Two years after its founding, the NPL controlled all major state offices in North Dakota and promptly enacted one of the most socialistic programs in American history. A state-owned bank was begun; the state began its own mill and elevator; a state workmen's compensation bureau was inaugurated; the state established a fire and tornado fund and even went into hail insurance.

The League's heyday ran to 1921, but in that year three of its main officeholders, including the governor of the moment, were recalled by the people. The NPL would never again exert such complete control, but it did remain a potent force through World War II, sending men like Langer and Nye to the Senate and Lemke and Usher Burdick to the House. The League's founder was a Lincolnesque spellbinder named A. C. Townley, but chief leader and spokesman from the early '30s on was William Langer, who skillfully combined straight Populism with a stiff isolationist streak that appealed mightily to the German elements in North Dakota. (Even World War II failed to cure Bill Langer of his isolationism; he was one of two Senators against U.S. entry into the United Nations and later voted against the Marshall Plan and the North Atlantic Treaty.)

From its birth until the 1950s, the NPL operated as a splinter group within the Republican party—apparently, as John Gunther learned, because the Democrats were as rare as ocelots. But in the wake of World War II, a group of young veterans, many with ties to the Farmers Union, decided they would rather have the liberal NPL tied to a party with liberal national ties—the Democrats. A six-year fight by the Democrats and the Farmers Union to take over the NPL ended in total victory in 1956, helped not a little bit by the unpopularity of the Eisenhower-Benson farm policies of that era. But the victory that made the NPL part of the Democratic party also meant the death of the NPL as a separate force in North Dakota politics. Some NPL Old Guarders stood pat with the Republican party; those who switched to the Democrats soon forgot about their special NPL identity.

The shift of the NPL has made North Dakota politics a lot duller but probably more responsible. For the first time, the state now has a viable two-party system; the Republicans are the normal majority, but strong Democratic candidates can sometimes overcome the odds against them. Governor Guy, elected to two two-year terms and two four-year terms in the 1960s, proved the potential for Democratic breakthroughs; so did his successor, former Congressman and state house speaker Arthur Link, one of the liberal NPLers who switched to the Democratic party in 1956. Governor Link's agrarian liberalism comes naturally, since he was one of six children born to a family of immigrant homesteaders who settled on a ranch in far western North Dakota early in the century. He has spent almost his entire life on that family ranch, now expanded to 5,000 acres. The issue of corporate farms helped Link win election, he said the state would be opened to an invasion of corporate agribusiness if his Republican opponent won and succeeded in repealing the ban against corporations running farms and ranches. Another former NPLer is Quentin N. Burdick, whose election to the U.S. Senate in 1970 signaled real strength in the new Democratic party. Fittingly, Burdick filled the seat vacated by Bill Langer's death in 1959, though he lacks the old man's fervor.

Nor did the NPL shift make the Republican party hopelessly conservative. The state's senior U.S. Senator, Republican Milton Young, was never an NPL man, but he combined his conservative Senate votes with a liberal twist on farm legislation and in the early 1960s had the courage to denounce the Birch Society, which was making inroads in normal Republican circles in North Dakota. Sensing farmers' aversion to Nixon administration farm policies, Young broke with his party to oppose the confirmation of Dr. Earl Butz, a man closely identified with corporate agribusiness, as Secretary of Agriculture in 1971. The Republicans' most promising up-and-coming younger leader is a moderate, U.S. Rep. Mark Andrews, a contemporary of former Governor Guy; by chance both own farms in the same county.

Though dead and gone, the Nonpartisan League has left an indelible mark on North Dakota. Its socialistic programs continue to this day. The state bank, which protected thousands of farmers from ruin in depression days, now has assets of $130 million and turns in an annual profit of up to $3 million for the state treasury. Just as importantly, the bank helps make capital available in a capital-short state. The state-owned mill and elevator, after losing money for its first 20 years, turned the corner during World War II and has channeled some $8 million in profits into the state's general fund in the past quarter century. The mill in its first years led the way in paying a premium price for North Dakota's high-protein hard spring wheats, leading to a shift in grain marketing that has added uncounted millions to the income of North Dakota farmers over five decades. Except for the hail insurance program, which was dropped during the 1960s, all the NPL's "socialistic" schemes remain in successful operation. The last effort to drop a major NPL program came in 1959, when a Republican state senator had the temerity to suggest that the state mill might be sold. Not only was his suggestion overwhelmingly rejected by the legislature, but a pot of flowers wrapped in black crepe was placed on the senator's desk by his opponents.

A few fiery NPL types remain; the most prominent is a Republican, Bismarck auto dealer Robert McCarney, a pink-shirted, cigar-chomping, rough-spoken maverick who learned his politics as Bill Langer's chauffeur 30 years ago. McCarney is as true a political godson as Langer has in the state, fighting a rough and tumble (and some say unprincipled) battle against taxes, for the little people, against government extravagance. When the legislature approved a major tax increase bill proposed by Guy, McCarney got a repealer on the ballot and saw it approved by the people, seven to one. But the regular Republicans wanted none of him; they defeated him in a gubernatorial primary in 1964; four years later he won the nomination but was undercut by Republican professionals in the general election, even though some friends like Harold Schafer gave him major financial backing.* (McCarney says the GOP professionals approached him and asked for a right to hire and fire in his administration; "I told them to go to hell.") In 1970 McCarney ran for Congress and won the Republican nomination by the startling margin of *one vote* out of 34,763 cast; again the establishment forces worked against him, and he lost the general election by 528 votes. McCarney's political Waterloo came in 1972, when he got less than a third of the votes in the GOP gubernatorial primary, losing to 36-year-old lieutenant governor Richard Larsen, a professor of economics at the University of North Dakota. (Larsen's professorial image also failed to spark with the voters, and he lost the general election to Democrat Arthur Link—even though Richard Nixon was sweeping the state the same day with 63 percent of the vote.)

Two years before, in 1970, all the old NPLers, Democrat and Republican alike, united to turn back a high-powered, high-financed campaign against one of their own, Senator Quentin Burdick. Congressman Thomas Kleppe, a conservative who had built up a small personal fortune as a one-time associate of Harold Schafer in Gold Seal Wax, decided to challenge Burdick. When President Nixon asked Kleppe what he needed, Kleppe replied: "A professional campaign manager, a professional media man, and substantial financing from outside the state." And not only were those things delivered but President Nixon himself made two flying trips into the state to campaign for Kleppe, and even sent his daughter Tricia, Vice President Agnew, and Interior Secretary Walter Hickel to help in the effort to unseat the liberal-voting Burdick. "Kleppe's entire campaign," the Washington *Post* reported, "was, in fact, financed and directed from Washington, D.C., by a team of professionals assembled by the White House."

With support from Republican national headquarters, business, and medical groups, Kleppe spent a total of about $300,000, compared to Burdick's expenditures of some $150,000. (Like Kleppe's, Burdick's campaign was financed primarily from out of state, in Burdick's case from contributions by Democratic, labor and antiwar groups, and the liberal National Committee

* McCarney so offended the modern-day Republican establishment that the Fargo *Forum*, North Dakota's largest paper, broke with decades of loyalty to GOP candidates to endorse Guy for reelection over McCarney. All of North Dakota's major papers—the *Forum*, the Bismarck *Tribune*, the Grand Forks *Herald*, the Minot *Daily News*—are Republican oriented; the small but striving *Morning Pioneer*, published in Mandan, is the only Democratic daily. The papers are of slightly above average quality for a state North Dakota's size.

for an Effective Congress.) The result was a scarcely believable $2.37 expenditure for each of the 190,000 North Dakotans who voted, a campaign the likes of which the state had never seen before.

The *cause célèbre* of the campaign was a Republican newspaper ad and television blitz concentrated on school prayer, riots, and antiwar protests. At least by implication, the ads seemed to question Burdick's dedication to God, country, and domestic tranquillity. But they backfired drastically; North Dakotans had known Burdick and his family for as long as most could be remembered, they resented the attacks on his honor, and their Populist blood boiled when the Democrats suggested the GOP was trying to buy their vote with a slick and expensive campaign of innuendo. A familiar figure in a rumpled suit, Burdick toured the state playing the Populist theme, talking about the Nixon farm policies, high interest rates and grocery bills, and farm closings and business foreclosures. He ended up carrying all but three of the state's 53 counties and winning reelection with a solid 61.3 percent of the vote.

The man-to-man familiarity and closeness of North Dakota society underscored by the Burdick campaign is illustrated in another way, through the state's voter registration system. The fact is that since 1951, voters have simply not been required to register in advance to vote on election day. They simply go to the polls, give their name, age, and residence, and unless challenged (a fairly rare occurrence) just take a ballot and mark it. No other state has such a liberal system, and North Dakotans are quite happy with it.

Power and Policies in State Government

Given the peculiarities of its geographic and economic position, North Dakota deserves credit for remarkably progressive and able small-state administration in recent years. Democrat William L. Guy was governor from 1961 through 1972, facing not only the problems of limited gubernatorial powers under the North Dakota constitution but also a consistently Republican legislature. Many of Guy's programs were thwarted, but many did pass, evidence that partisanship took at least some holidays. The state's biennial budget rose from $75 million to $283 million during the 1960s.

Guy's greatest contribution appears to have been a modernization of state government, making it far more efficient and economical. Most of his appointments to state office were excellent. And he was a great ambassador for North Dakota, surprising strangers disdainful of his remote state with a sophisticated, facts-first approach to problems. In 1966 Guy was chosen chairman of the National Governors Conference for a year.

A few specifics on the state's achievements in the '60s may be in order. The tax system was reformed and rates increased. Area mental health clinics were established; major advances were made in building nursing homes for the elderly; the state penitentiary population was reduced almost

50 percent by revised probation and parole techniques. North Dakotans believed they had the nation's best highway system; in fact, they were a leader in interstate highway completion. With consolidations, the number of school districts dropped rapidly; regional administrations (a bypassing of antiquated county governments) were set up to handle welfare, parole services, and health; tourism and public power-generating facilities were pushed.

Guy believes the "most significant development" of his years in office was the start of a comprehensive water resource plan for the Red River and its tributaries, including irrigation, municipal and industrial power, recreation, and wildlife preservation. This basin-wide planning was adopted in conjunction with Minnesota and South Dakota; Guy failed, however, in an effort to get the same type of planning started for all 10 states in the Missouri River Basin.*

The North Dakota constitution limits the legislature to a single session of 60 days each two years, with each legislator paid just $5 a day. An organizational shambles and highly mediocre membership should be the result, but for some reason North Dakota seems to have one of the best organized and ably manned legislatures among the smaller states. Knowing they have just 60 days to do all their work, the legislators assemble early, agree on assignment of all bills, on all committee membership, before the official session even starts. In the next years the legislature plans to move into complete retrieval of statutes and bill drafting by computer. Close observers of the legislature report that the quality of legislators has improved remarkably in the postwar years. Still to be accomplished, though, are a number of reforms—from annual sessions to adequate office space for legislators—to improve general legislative operations.

No single lobby group seems able to dictate to the legislature; the most important pressure groups, I was told, are probably the amalgamated education groups—the North Dakota Education Association, parent-teachers groups, school boards, the Department of Public Instruction. The lion's share of the state budget goes for education, from elementary to higher. Other powerful influences in Bismarck are the Farmers Union and Farm Bureau (though they often cancel each other out), the strongly conservative and Republican North Dakota Stockmen's Association, and the Association of Rural Cooperatives.

Every state government has its successes and failures, and North Dakota is no exception. In 1968 the federal government praised North Dakota for being one of the first in the nation to eliminate or screen the auto junkyards along all 4,000 miles of its primary road system. But just a year later, a budget-conscious state legislature refused to appropriate enough money to inspect North Dakota's intrastate slaughterhouses under stiff requirements of the national Wholesome Meat Act of 1967. The result: North Dakota became the first state in the nation to have the federal government take over inspection of all its meat-slaughtering and meat-processing plants.

* The federal government in 1972 finally established a Missouri Basin Regional Commission, one of several around the country modeled on the Appalachian Regional Commission. But there was doubt whether it would ever receive sufficient funding to make a substantial impact.

Another negative note was added to the state experience in 1972, when the voters rejected, by a 3–2 margin, a proposed new constitution that was designed to increase flexibility in state government operations and update procedures in the executive, judicial, and legislative branches. Hammered out by 98 delegates over months of deliberations and committee meetings, the new document would have been 8,000 words long, compared to the 25,000-word, 1889-vintage constitution still in effect. The new document contained a right-to-work provision, which evoked opposition from the AFL-CIO and some of its liberal allies, and at the same time the John Birch Society and other conservatives were opposed. A separate proposal, to create a unicameral legislature, went down to defeat by better than 2–1 margin.

Perhaps the brightest note in North Dakota public life is a very new one: the experimental—and to date very successful—effort to introduce informal school classrooms dedicated to individual learning, diversity, self-motivation, and creativity. Pressed for more and more assistance by the state's school districts, the legislature in 1965 ordered a complete study of North Dakota's primary education system. Some of the findings were chilling indeed: revelation that 59 percent of the state's elementary teachers lacked a bachelor's degree, and that only 22 percent of the five-year-olds were enrolled in kindergarten. But the report included one highly innovative idea: that the University of North Dakota establish "an autonomous new school of behavioral science" leading to introduction of the informal classroom mode being used in England's infant schools and a few school districts around the U.S. In response, the university then established, in 1968, its New School for Behavioral Studies in Education and recruited an imaginative and skilled native of Michigan, Dr. Vito Perrone, to be its dean.

From the very start, the New School broke fresh ground. Instead of separating teacher education from the liberal arts, it recruited faculty members with diverse academic backgrounds in the humanities, social sciences, natural sciences, and education. Students included both undergraduates and experienced teachers. According to Perrone,

> The New School has operated on the assumption it must become a model of the kind of environment it is promoting. Believing that teachers teach essentially as they have been taught, faculty members are continually seeking ways to personalize and individualize the university level program. . . . We want our teachers to be self-starters, persons who take major responsibility in their classrooms for planning and implementing learning, able to infuse a spirit of inquiry and a capacity for discovery among elementary school children.

At first it appeared the New School might become a point of intense political controversey; indeed the state John Birch Society assailed it, and some traditional school administrators expressed their hostility. But as New School graduates began to filter into the classrooms of the state, Perrone traveled extensively explaining the new approach to faculties and parent groups, and the opposition subsided. New School techniques were made an issue in 1971 school board elections in Bismarck, with opponents suggesting a lack of discipline and such dire goings-on as kids taking off their clothes and touching each other in the classrooms. But the incumbent school board, identified with the New School approach, was easily reelected.

By 1971, well over 10 percent of the state's 74,000 elementary school children were being taught by New School graduates in informal classroom settings. Maximum improvisation has been the key: instead of making children sit still for a prescribed series of lessons, each pupil is allowed for much of each school day to do what he likes: reading, playing word or numbers games with other children, drawing, observing small animals, manipulating puzzles and small machines and tape recorders and record players. Many parents were at first concerned that their children would only "play" and fail to learn basic skills in the "three r's." But informal classroom pupils were found to do at least as well as other students in standardized tests. More importantly, parents found their children developing more inquiring minds, learning more to think for themselves, continuing their learning process with projects and activities out of school—and complaining lustily when forced to miss a day of school. Attendance rose sharply, and discipline problems abated sharply.

One reason the New School's experiment was working was the peculiar North Dakota setting; as Fargo's school superintendent, Kenneth Underwood, told a *Wall Street Journal* reporter, "Our classes are relatively small, and, compared to much of the rest of the country, we just don't have any financial or social problems here. There's no social strife, and we don't have to negotiate with unions for every minute of our teachers' time." Even at that, there was still some opposition from professional educators, and years of work ahead until all teachers would accept the informal classroom idea. Nevertheless, most observers felt it fair when Charles Silberman, in his best-selling *Crisis in the Classroom,* singled out North Dakota as having "easily the most exciting teacher education program" in the country. The state's informal classrooms, he wrote, "are in many ways more exciting, and certainly more innovative, than anything one can find in the Scarsdales, Winnetkas, Shaker Heights and Palo Altos of the United States."

Why a North Dakota?

Eric Sevareid remembers thinking, "Why are we here on the cold flat top of our country?" when as a boy he traced on a map "the meaningless rectangle of Dakota." Situated on the lone prairie hundreds of miles from any major American city, North Dakotans have long tended to feel like country cousins to the American mainstream.

Bigness is certainly the best single word to describe North Dakota; in *An American Notebook* Philip Hamburger repeats these comments of a Bismarck resident: "We look out over all the space and figure, it's too big for us, it's too wide, there's too much of it, and we get gloomy. Your North Dakota man can get good and gloomy." An English visitor, Brian Goodey, commented on the lack of the familiar landmarks or weathered buildings to which an individual can somehow relate. "In North Dakota," he writes, "the towns are new, the view at the end of the main street often reveals the flat plain doorstep, people are still alive who can remember pioneer settlement, and man seems scarcely to have scratched the surface. Often one feels like a camper rather than a resident in this environment."

In political terms, not a little of the North Dakotan's gloominess—and tendency to radical politics—has stemmed from the exploitation of his state by Minneapolis and St. Paul. "The Twin Cities take our raw materials, our capital, and our young people," a North Dakotan complained to a Minneapolis salesman some years ago. "And what do they send back? Nothing." But in sum North Dakota seems today less like an economic colony of Minneapolis than it once was. New laws and regulations, plus their own state-owned mill, make North Dakota wheat farmers less dependent on the vagaries of price setting by the Twin Cities' milling syndicates. In addition to the state bank, more indigenous private banks are springing up in North Dakota, to loosen, at least to some degree, the grip of the Twin Cities holding companies. The heavy hand of out-of-state ownership continues—the vast majority of stores in downtown Bismarck, for instance, are parts of national chains; the railroads, most insurance firms, and all brokerage houses are also in out-of-state hands. North Dakota is left somewhat at the mercy of decisions made outside its borders; in 1972, for instance, its economy was set back by an estimated $5 million when pilots of the primary east-west air carrier, Twin Cities-based Northwest Airlines, went on strike for three months. But deliberately unfair exploitation of North Dakota seems to be declining and, with that change, radical politics as well.

The isolation of North Dakotans grows smaller too. Interstate highways shrink distances from town to town; rural electricity, followed by radio and television, transform life on the farm. The second, third, and fourth generation families abjure the rigid conservatism of the first immigrants.

Just as important, the North Dakotan's dependence on the elements, his fear of drought and flood and blizzard, recede in some measure as he learns better to conserve the soil and as modern science brings him well heated homes, massive flood control and irrigation projects, and that marvelous heatable or coolable wheeled capsule, the automobile.

Still the question arises, though, why a North Dakota? Is a population base of three-tenths of one percent of the national total, spread across 70,665 square miles, an adequate base for a modern state with all the services it is called on to perform? We have already reviewed the excruciating economic pains North Dakota suffers as it tries to pay for all the educational and governmental services of modern America without an adequate industrial base. Merger with a neighbor or neighbors could be one solution, but a very unlikely one because the states would lose most of their representation in the U.S. Senate.

A step is being taken toward unifying functions, however; since the early 1960s, four states of the old Dakota Territory—North and South Dakota, Montana, and Wyoming—have had a joint legislative conference; now they are talking of actual pooling of resources to deal with their problems in law enforcement, prisons and penal rehabilitation, facilities for the criminally insane, or other areas where there could be substantial savings by avoiding duplicative capital and administrative expenditures.

Savings like that certainly make sense, but one can ask if there might not be an early limit to fruitful cooperation between these sparsely populated Plains and mountain states; in a sense they might just compound their problems, since they all share a common problem: the lack of a strong central city with its wealth, industry and creativity. Without affiliation with a major metropolis, they may all remain backwaters.

North Dakota, at least, might solve some of its worst problems by merging with its progressive neighbor to the East, Minnesota. The Twin Cities, as we noted before, have long treated North Dakota as a kind of economic colony. It might be well to formalize the relationship so that some tax dollars could start flowing from the prosperous Twin Cities into the hard-pressed Dakotan prairies.

No matter what North Dakota's fate in years to come, one can hope that its independent, questioning, open spirit will remain. Except for Minnesota, no other state of the Plains has tried to be so responsive to the needs of its people.

And before the nation looks disdainfully at North Dakota with its problems, it might remember that this icebox state on the Canadian border has contributed a remarkable number of industrious, clear-headed workers and leaders to the rest of the nation. I found them everywhere on my travels for these books, and each was impressive in his own way.

Being governor of North Dakota, William Guy told me, is a little like the job of PT boat commander: he has to do everything for himself. No one writes a speech for him, his press releases are his own to compose, no security guard is on duty, and he answers his own phone at home. Sometimes it even rings at odd hours. To help even the score for those cruel jokes that make North Dakota their brunt, I reprint Guy's version of a call he received at 2 A.M. one morning:

Caller: "Governor, this is not a crank call. Is there a North Dakota?"
Guy: "Where are you calling from?"
Caller: "Florida."
Guy: "What state is that in?"

SOUTH DAKOTA

STATE OF RELUCTANT CHANGE

In the language of the Sioux, "Dakota" can be translated roughly as "league of friends." North and South Dakota are set neatly on top of one another and share a common border some 360 miles long. Most Americans think of them as a bloc. If Republican Senators had not been greedily intent on adding four instead of two Senators of their party to the Union in the 1880s, the Dakota Territory would probably have been admitted as one state, not two.

But separately the states were admitted, and not only do they view the world differently, but they have little indeed to do with each other. As John Gunther summarized the situation 25 years ago:

> Nothing is more remarkable in the United States than the difference between the Dakotas. North Dakota is one of the most radical states of the Union, and South Dakota one of the most conservative. . . . South thinks North is inhabited mostly by Bolsheviks; North thinks that South is a preserve for all people to the right of Hoover. South looks down across the river to Iowa and southward to Nebraska; it never looks North at all, if it can help it. . . .
>
> Extraordinary as it is to tell, travel between the two states is difficult in the extreme. When I was there no bus or air lines connected them at all. . . . In a manner of speaking railways do exist, but you will not thank me for the suggestion.

Not much has happened in the succeeding years to unite the two neighbors, though there are now air connections (cut back, ironically, from jets to prop planes in 1969 because of low traffic and high state taxes). Still years ahead is the first interstate highway connection between the two; even when it comes, it will be so far to the east that it might as well be in Minnesota instead.

There are continuing similarities between the Dakotas. Each is still so young, comparatively, that the sweat and blood of the frontier heritage is not yet dry. Except for West Virginia, they have the highest percentage of people living in small villages and farms among all the states. The agrarian mentality still dominates, because almost three-quarters of the people either live on farms or grew up there. The 1970 Census found that 21.5 percent of the South Dakota population and 20.9 percent of North Dakota's still worked on farms—compared to a scant 3.1 percent national average. (No other states came close to those percentages; even in Iowa, for instance, the farm worker figure is now down to 12.5 percent.) Both of the Dakotas experienced an overall population drop of just over 2 percent during the 1960s, and both had a net outmigration rate of about 90,000 during the decade. They are also fairly close in population: South Dakota had 666,257 people in the 1970 Census, compared to North Dakota's 617,761.

The Dakotas also have a geographic similarity: fertile and humid river valleys to the east (Red River in North Dakota, James and Big Sioux rivers in South Dakota); then steadily increasing aridity on vast butte-dotted plains and marginal ranchlands that reach to western borders, uninterrupted except for the central flow of the Missouri River. But the agriculture is different—South Dakota produces a lot more corn and livestock and substantially less wheat.

Corn, in fact, was this writer's first vivid impression of South Dakota. As a boy of 13, I made a first automobile trip across the U.S.A. with my father; for mile after mile we drove across what seemed like endless South Dakota cornfields, only to arrive late in the day at Mitchell, which has the distinction of being the site of the World's Only Corn Palace (and, as I would learn years later, the home town of George McGovern). There in the midst of an unspectacular little plains city rose the turrets and spired domes of a whimsical palace built to honor corn, its pennants waving in the breeze. The puffed-up Oriental architecture could hardly have been more incongruous, but the corn theme fitted its environs perfectly.

But corn is not the only thing that distinguishes South Dakota from her northern neighbor. South Dakota also has a packing industry, great deposits of gold, a prospering tourist industry, and miles of timber-covered mountains—all lacking in North Dakota. And, since statehood, the states have taken quite different political paths.

People and Places

South Dakota's population base has been described as a kind of rural cosmopolitanism, with substantial numbers of Anglo-Saxons, Norwegians,

Germans, Swedes, Russo-Germans, Danes, Czechs, and Dutch. As in North Dakota, the greatest influx came in the several decades beginning with the 1880s, and the state has yet to match the population peak of 692,849 which the census-takers recorded in 1930. There has been a tremendous outflow of young people in their productive years, balanced only in part by natural increase due to the excess of births over deaths. One young woman told me that of her 50 cousins, only five were still living in South Dakota; many would like to return but simply can't find satisfactory jobs. California apparently gets the lion's share of South Dakota's emigrants, followed by cities like Minneapolis, Chicago, and Denver.

The mass departure of youth adds a sad note to the real effort the state is making in higher education; enrollment in the seven state-supported colleges and universities has tripled to approximately 20,000 since the late 1940s, and South Dakota today ranks a very respectable 15th in the United States in her per capita expenditures for higher education. Yet some 60 to 70 percent of the state's college graduates leave South Dakota to find their first jobs. The countervailing population trends—such as some settlement of wealthy Eastern retirees in the Black Hills—are insubstantial in comparison.

The gross population figures also obscure the major population trends within South Dakota: a continued flight from the land and the small villages, a modest growth of the medium-sized towns, and continued population domination of the eastern quarter of the state in cities like Sioux Falls (the state's largest with 72,488 people), Aberdeen (26,476), Huron (14, 299), Brookings (13,717), Watertown (13,388), Mitchell (13,425), and Yankton (11,919). Sioux Falls is a major trade, insurance, and industrial center and is generally considered the state's most attractive city. Most of the colleges (the University of South Dakota at Vermillion preeminent among them) are also east of the Missouri River, as is the best farmland.

West of the river there is little but great expanses of bleak plains and grazing land with few inhabitants; as one easterner told me disparagingly, "West of the river we have a lot of ranchers living like feudal lords." The west does have its tourist attractions in the Bad Lands and Black Hills; it also has most of the Indian reservations of the state, and Rapid City.

Second largest in the state, Rapid City more than tripled its population between 1940 and 1970 (to 43,836), profiting from tourism and a heavy influx of military installations. Then, during the night of June 9, 1972, Rapid City was dealt a staggering blow as once-in-a-century weather conditions dumped 10 inches of rain on the Black Hills, and walls of water swept through the city. "Rapid Creek, normally clear and placid, sounded like a freight train passing in the night," reporter Jerry Mashek of the Rapid City *Journal* recalled. "It must have been 150 feet wide." Explosions and fire erupted as power lines collapsed and propane gas tanks ruptured. Streets were ripped up, 1,000 homes were destroyed, cars were swept away in the waters, and landslides sent mud cascading down the hills. The total damage was estimated at $100 million; more appalling, over 200 people were known

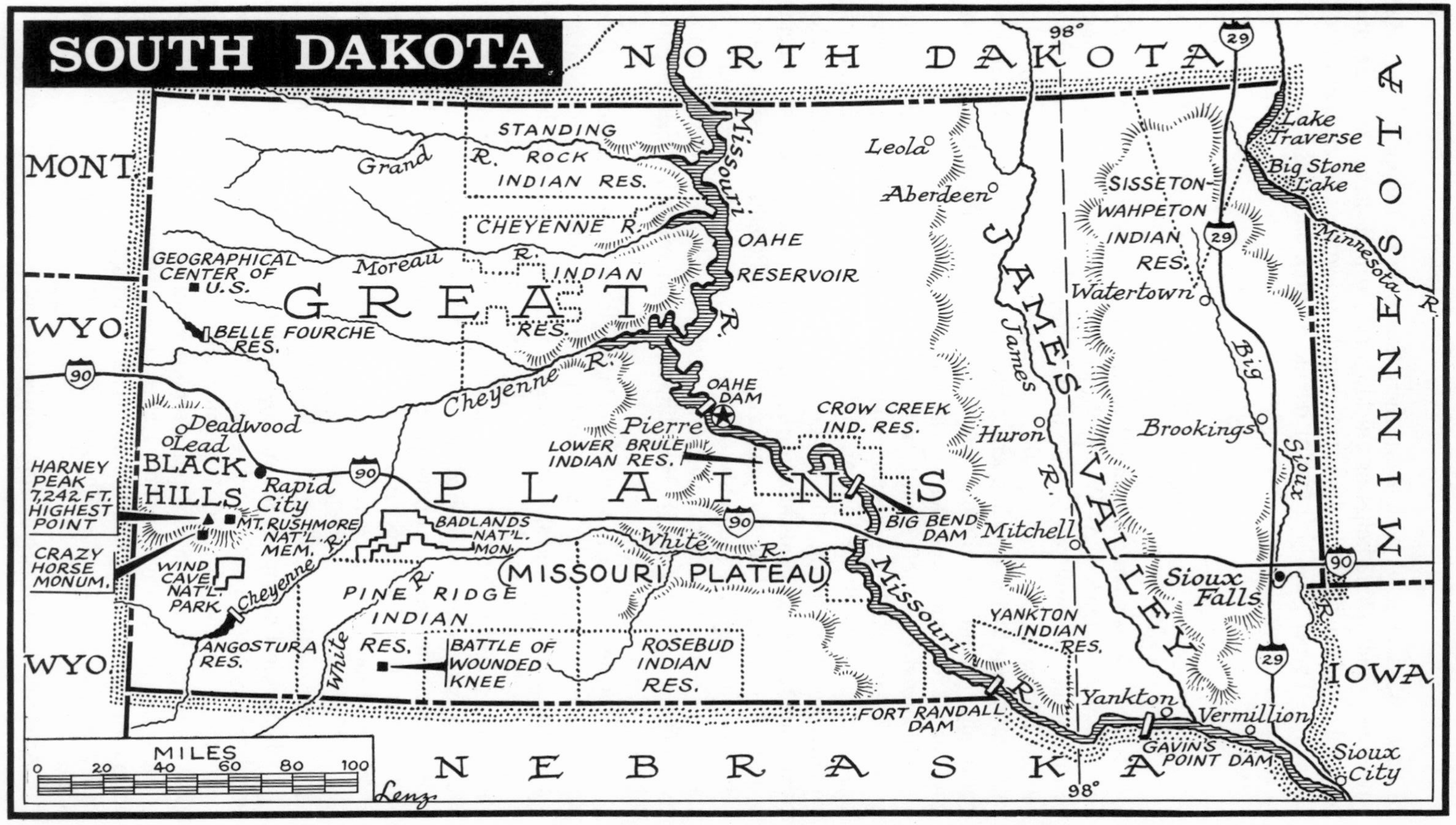
SOUTH DAKOTA
NORTH DAKOTA
MINNESOTA
IOWA
NEBRASKA
MONT.
WYO.
WYO.
98°
98°
29
29
29
90
90
90
90
Lake Traverse
Big Stone Lake
Minnesota R.
SISSETON-WAHPETON INDIAN RES.
Watertown
Big
Sioux
R.
Brookings
Sioux Falls
Leola
Aberdeen
JAMES VALLEY
James
R.
Huron
Mitchell
YANKTON INDIAN RES.
Yankton
Vermillion
Sioux City
GAVIN'S POINT DAM
FORT RANDALL DAM
Missouri
R.
STANDING ROCK INDIAN RES.
Grand
R.
CHEYENNE R. INDIAN RES.
Moreau
R.
OAHE RESERVOIR
Missouri
R.
GREAT
PLAINS
OAHE DAM
Pierre
CROW CREEK IND. RES.
LOWER BRULE INDIAN RES.
BIG BEND DAM
Cheyenne
R.
GEOGRAPHICAL CENTER OF U.S.
BELLE FOURCHE RES.
Deadwood
Lead
BLACK HILLS
Rapid City
HARNEY PEAK 7,242 FT. HIGHEST POINT
CRAZY HORSE MONUM.
MT. RUSHMORE NAT'L. MEM.
WIND CAVE NAT'L. PARK
Cheyenne
R.
ANGOSTURA RES.
BADLANDS NAT'L. MON.
White
R.
MISSOURI PLATEAU
PINE RIDGE INDIAN RES.
R.
White
BATTLE OF WOUNDED KNEE
ROSEBUD INDIAN RES.
MILES
0 20 40 60 80 100
Lenz

to have lost their lives, with more than that number simply missing. But government and private help was quickly provided in generous measure, and under the leadership of the city's sincere and hardworking 29-year-old mayor, Donald V. Barnett, the long task of rebuilding from one of the worst floods in American history began.

The Political Tides

South Dakota's radical political experience came during the 1890s, the first decade of statehood. As Walter Prescott Webb later described the state of that decade, the isolated farmers of the lonely Plains, "far from markets, burned by drought, beaten by hail, withered by hot winds, frozen by blizzards, eaten out by the grasshoppers, exploited by capitalists, and cozened by politicians," found that through radical politics they could at least get some government recognition of their special needs.

Organized into the Populist party, the farmers demanded railroad and grain elevator regulation to stop manipulation by outside interests, free silver to loosen the hold of the bankers, and initiative and referendum as a curb on government. In fusion with the Democrats, the Populists actually elected their man to the governorship in 1896 and 1898. The protest movements splintered in 1900, but, in the years that followed, Populists working in concert with the national Progressive movement were able to seize control of the South Dakota Republican party and push through measures such as a direct primary, railway controls, and limitations on campaign spending and lobbying.

The key figure of early South Dakota politics was a self-described "Theodore Roosevelt Republican" and careful reformer, Peter Norbeck. Norbeck was elected to the governorship in 1916 after a campaign in which he attacked as socialistic the left-wing Nonpartisan League, which was making its successful bid for power in North Dakota at the same time. But Norbeck was no sooner in office than he pushed successfully for adoption of several NPL-type reforms, including workmen's compensation, child labor legislation, and state-sponsored enterprises including a rural credit system, hail insurance, a coal mine, and a cement plant (the latter still in operation at Rapid City). Norbeck's way of dealing with NPL demands was simple and pragmatic: "When the water gets too high, let a little of it over the dam."

Thus radical control of the state government was averted and the NPL failed to become the lasting force it was in North Dakota. During the Depression, several of the socialistic-type programs enacted during the Norbeck years actually failed or at least put a serious strain on the state treasury. The result was a conservative reaction against new government programs which continued into the years since World War II, giving South Dakota, for most that period, one of the most Republican and most conservative governments in the nation.

After four years as governor, Norbeck went on to the United States

Senate, where he worked closely with the leading Progressives of the era, including Nebraska's George Norris and California's Hiram Johnson. Norbeck became a recognized leader in conservation matters and was chairman of the Senate Banking and Finance Committee when it conducted its investigation into the stock market and banking and insurance industries just before the advent of the New Deal.* Since Norbeck's death in 1936, South Dakota has sent no progressive Republican to Congress.

Charts of party strength in South Dakota show a pattern of normal Republican dominance, broken by a few short eras of Democratic breakthroughs—in the early New Deal days, in the late 1950s, and a wave that started in the late 1960s. Overall, Republicans have won close to 90 percent of all statewide partisan elections since statehood was achieved. The state has voted Republican in 17 of 21 Presidential elections, including 1972, when its own George McGovern was the Democratic nominee. In 20 popular elections to the U.S. Senate, the Republicans have won 14 times, the Democrats only six times. Until the Democrats captured the governorship in 1970, the GOP had held it for all but two years since 1937.

A recognized expert on South Dakota politics, Prof. Alan Clem of the University of South Dakota, concludes that since the New Deal, his state "has been something of an economic and political backwater," and that while most national leaders in both parties have adopted "a positive and optimistic attitude about the potentialities of all kinds of governmental actions, in South Dakota voters and candidates alike, for the most part, have been marching to a different drummer."

Where continuing Democratic strength is to be found in the state, its base is usually among the farmers—especially those of Scandinavian background, a direct throwback to the agrarian protests of the turn of the century. The same streak of farm unrest surfaced again in the 1950s with bitter rural protest against the Eisenhower-Benson farm policies, the issue that started George McGovern on his way to national prominence. The Farmers Union (stronger than the Farm Bureau in South Dakota) is a major support for the Democrats; so are the rural co-ops and rural electrification interests. Union members and Catholics and Indians tend to be Democrats; all, however, are distinct minorities in South Dakota.

Indeed, the natural Republican majority is apparent from a listing of groups normally Republican in their voting: people who live in towns and cities,† older people in general, the Farm Bureau, the Chamber of Commerce, lawyers, bankers, realtors, private utility executives, and, in general, people of "Wasp" and German-Russian background. The power structure of South Dakota and the Republican party are often so closely entwined as to be virtually indistinguishable. Major power lies in the two great Minneapolis bank

* Norbeck's investigations subsequently provided the basis for federal regulation in such legislation as the Securities Act of 1933 and the Securities and Exchange Act of 1934.

† The state's two big cities, Sioux Falls and Rapid City, are almost always in the Republican column, as are most other towns; the only cities of any size that normally vote Democratic are Mitchell (McGovern's home town), Aberdeen, and Watertown. Rapid City, traditionally Republican, switched to heavy Democratic pluralities in the 1970 election. But cities are not the key to South Dakota politics; less than a third of the people live in cities of more than 10,000 people.

holding companies, which control a substantial percentage of South Dakota bank deposits; in groups like the South Dakota Wheat Growers Association and the ultraconservative South Dakota Stockgrowers Association; in private utilities like Northern States Power; and in the gold mining interests represented by the Homestake Mine.

A vital source of Republican strength has been the reported willingness of banks and utilities to make arrangements for their employees to participate in Republican campaigns; moreover many utility and bank men serve in the legislature, where the real governmental power lies in South Dakota. The highway department, which dispenses over a third of the state budget, is so powerful that it has been nicknamed the fourth branch of government. The governor—almost invariably a Republican, until 1970—appoints the highway director and commissioners, officers with ample political instincts. The point was not lost on highway contractors and sand and gravel suppliers; they ended up contributing generously to Republican campaigns. The Democrats lacked a comparable financial base.

Karl Mundt: A South Dakotan Symbol

If Peter Norbeck symbolized South Dakota's early politics, Karl E. Mundt embodied its dominant strains in the era following World War II. The Mundt era has only recently drawn to a close—Mundt did not file for reelection in 1972, as a result of a disabling stroke he suffered in November 1969 which left him temporarily speechless and kept him away from his seat in the Senate to the end of his term.

A short, gregarious figure who got his start as a speech teacher, Mundt had the home state reputation of a man who "never gave a bad speech." He was first noted nationally, a decade after he had arrived in Congress, when he presided over the 1948 House Un-American Activities Committee hearings which uncovered the "pumpkin papers" and led to the conviction of Alger Hiss. The same year, Mundt sponsored (with Richard M. Nixon, then a California Congressman) the Mundt-Nixon bill to require registration of Communist-front organizations and their officers.

Subsequently elected to the Senate, Mundt in 1954 presided somewhat uneasily over the widely publicized Army-McCarthy hearings. In 1957 he voted against Senate censure of McCarthy, saying, "Joe is one of the best friends I have in the Senate."

After the McCarthy hearings, Mundt's name slipped out of national notice except on occasions when he proposed bills like a 1959 measure to create a "Freedom Academy" to train cold war warriors or to shift the electoral college to a district system which would increase the voice of small, conservative states in Presidential elections. Mundt usually voted a conservative line on domestic affairs, but he did back farm subsidy bills, voted for the civil rights acts, and backed legislation for international cooperation. He eventually became the ranking Republican on the Government Operations Committee and second-ranking on Foreign Relations and Appropriations—the latter a position from which he could bargain for federal funding for dams, irrigation projects, and military bases for his home state.

At home, Mundt was honored with election to an unprecedented (for South Dakota) four terms in the Senate, usually by wide election day margins. One source of his strength was press support; the leading Sioux Falls *Argus-Leader* was invariably in his corner with full news coverage and warm editorial support. Occasionally right-wing extremists obliged Mundt by attacking him; a John Birch-type candidate even opposed him in the 1966 GOP primary, giving Mundt the image of the reasonable man between extremes.

On the stump, Mundt's chief stock-in-trade was an assault on godless, atheistic Communism and its evils. To South Dakotans, he seemed to represent a kind of folk wisdom and solid patriotism. I found several prominent Republicans in the state who were at a loss to name what Mundt had actually accomplished in Congress. But they liked his image. A typical reasoning came from a successful Aberdeen businessman and Republican contributor: "Karl was always a clean, upright citizen. He was friendly to the Midwest farmer. He had a good, conservative philosophy and opposed the New Deal and Fair Deal spending programs. Basically, he thought right."

A legacy of a slightly different order was left by Republican Francis Case, who represented South Dakota in the U.S. House from 1937 to 1951 and then in the U.S. Senate until his death in 1962. A fitting epitaph for Case has been offered by Harry McPherson, who was a Senate aide to Lyndon Johnson during the 1950s:

> Somewhere in every public school room in America, there is a little boy who throws and throws his hand up before the teacher before the child she has called upon has had a chance to think of the answer. He knows the answer at once; his soul cries out for the chance to give it, perhaps because he needs to be praised, or because he must hear the orderly "click" when the right answer fits into the question. He is oblivious to the scorn of his fellow students: the information is the thing.
>
> Francis Case was that little boy grown up, pale, square, and deadly dull. His revelation that a gas lobbyist may have tried to bribe him hit the Senate like a truck loaded with wheat from the hard plains of South Dakota. . . .
>
> When he died, this little man, so tidy and severe, left a monument which archaeologists a millennium from now may find to be proof of our productive genius, or madness, or both—the Interstate Highway System.

George McGovern and the New Democrats

The inevitable question about South Dakota politics is how a state long symbolized by men like Karl E. Mundt and Francis Case could also send George S. McGovern—and now several of his followers—to the United States Congress. In philosophy, background, and natural constituency, the McGovern group is the antithesis of its Republican predecessors and colleagues.

Part of the answer, of course, lies in South Dakota's history of agrarian protest. McGovern is a defender of the family farm, of high price supports, of increased bargaining power for farmers, of rural electrification and liberal farm credit. The issue on which he first won a seat in Congress in 1956, and then reelection two years later, was opposition to the farm policies of Ezra Taft Benson under the Eisenhower Administration. After an unsuccessful attempt to defeat Mundt for the Senate in 1960, he served as director of President Kennedy's "Food for Peace" program, returning to South Dakota for a successful 1962 Senate race as a man with real interest and abilities in distributing America's farm surplus abroad. He defeated a colorless Republican opponent with only 597 votes to spare.

In the Senate, McGovern's major field activity broadened from agriculture to include foreign affairs. "A desire to make some contribution to world peace," he declared, was the "single strongest motivation" in his public career. McGovern became one of the most outspoken critics of the Vietnam war and urged cutting billions of dollars from the defense budget on the grounds that America already had a strategic "overkill" capacity and could better spend its wealth for education, job training, health, urban programs, conservation, and agriculture. McGovern's "peace" appeal found some real response in South Dakota, where he had been an active Methodist and was able to mobilize important support among church people. In addition, a rejection of unnecessary foreign commitments was part of the traditional Populist-isolationist movement in the Plains States. South Dakotans remind one that a McGovern predecessor of decades ago, Senator Richard Pettigrew, opposed the Spanish-American War and saw his law office in Sioux Falls painted yellow by irate locals when he opposed the draft in World War I.

But McGovern's soft-spoken ways and roots in a sparsely populated prairie state did not suggest credentials for a national Democratic leader, and most of his party—not to mention the rest of the country—were astonished when McGovern announced shortly before the Democratic National Convention of 1968 that he would be a stand-in candidate for the delegates who had favored Senator Robert F. Kennedy for the nomination. It was too late to mount a serious campaign, but McGovern did impress many delegates with his grasp of national issues. When he was asked why he did not defer to Minnesota's Eugene McCarthy, the principal antiwar candidate of 1968, McGovern replied that he differed with McCarthy in his concept of the Presidency. McCarthy, he said, had a "passive view of the office"; but he, McGovern, believed the President should play "a stronger and more active and vigorous role," especially in dealing with domestic problems. In the actual convention balloting for President, McGovern received a total of 146 votes; he emerged from the convention with new national stature.

That fall, while Republicans swept the Presidential and gubernatorial vote in South Dakota, McGovern was reelected with a handsome 38,010-vote plurality. Again, he benefited from weak Republican opposition (former Governor Archie Gubbrud, an honest, well-meaning farmer who had been one of the most humdrum state chief executives of the 1960s). The Republicans had hoped McGovern's association with the chaotic and violence-plagued Chicago convention would harm his reelection chances; in fact the television exposure he got in his short Presidential campaign seemed to help him at home, perhaps from natural home-state pride in a local boy making his mark in the nation at large.

McGovern's reelection campaign was also remarkable in that he made no apologies for his strong antiwar views or votes for liberal domestic programs. Instead, McGovern seemed to be telling the people of his rural, Republican home state that they must form a sort of grand alliance with the urban society of modern America, despite all its problems and disruptions. The appeal was partly pragmatic: farmers and ranchers, McGovern said, could not get help they want from Washington without support from the more powerful urban states. McGovern indirectly reminded South Dakotans of the many federal aids already channeled to rural areas in the form of farm subsidies, irrigation and conservation districts, and agricultural research. Finally, he suggested there was a moral and civic duty to help urban America: "Let us not pretend we ought not to be concerned with the problems of the big cities," he said. "We are all Americans. Our hearts ought to be big enough to embrace all mankind, but we can at least be big enough to embrace all America." It was an extraordinary appeal to make to rural South Dakota, many of whose people were repelled by the violence and upheaval of the great cities they could see on their television sets. Was the McGovern campaign a harbinger of a new era in the state's politics, a softening of the traditional suspicion of the great cities, new openness to the attitudes of youth? Or was McGovern's success more a reflection of old-time Populism, isolationism, and pride in a home-state celebrity? No one in South Dakota was quite sure.

It was clear that hard organizational work counted for a substantial part of McGovern's success. When McGovern forsook the security of his political science professorship at Dakota Wesleyan College in Mitchell in 1953 to become executive secretary of the state Democratic party, that organization was little more than a shell. It had won scarcely any elections since a brief interlude in New Deal days, and many of its officials were patronage hunters like the old "Post Office Republicans" in the South; indeed there were rumors that a number of South Dakota Democrats landed postmasterships for themselves by contributing some $2,000 to $3,000 to the party. When he took on the job, McGovern recalled in a magazine interview years later, "almost everybody thought I was crazy. Bradley Young, the leading Democrat in Mitchell, told me, 'George, you're a good man, but it's hopeless. Forget it.' " At that time, McGovern recalled, many people were even afraid to admit publicly that they were Democrats. But he went to work to build the party almost single-handed, and the Democrats began steady gains, spurred on at first by Benson's unpopularity in the state. In 1958 they even elected a governor for a single two-year term while McGovern won reelection to Congress over former Governor Joe Foss, one of the most popular Republicans of the postwar years. Then the Catholic issue of the 1960 campaign dealt the Democrats a serious reversal, from which they slowly recouped during the 1960s.

Half an hour before he would fall before an assassin's bullet in Los Angeles, Robert Kennedy was on the telephone congratulating Sioux Falls stockman Bill Dougherty, his manager in the South Dakota Presidential primary, on the clear-cut victory of a Kennedy delegate slate in that state. Eclipsed almost totally by the California primary the same day and Kennedy's subsequent death, the South Dakota primary of 1968 marked a turning point in the state's Democratic party. The Kennedy slate defeated rival slates pledged to South Dakota native Hubert Humphrey as well as McCarthy, putting the party machinery into the hands of young, activist liberals. That same Kennedy organization, plus a healthy infusion of liberal out-of-state money, helped McGovern win reelection the following fall by such a substantial margin.

Bill Dougherty, the man who managed the 1968 Kennedy slate victory and McGovern's 1968 Senate campaign, and then went on to win election as lieutenant governor himself in 1970, is a fascinating composite of the strains in American politics. A prairie native, he has spent most of his adult days buying and selling cattle in the Sioux Falls stockyards; with his lean figure, Western blue jeans, cowboy hat, and boots, he looks as if he would be more at home in a Marlboro cigarette ad than working closely with the sophisticated Kennedy clan of the old East. But it takes just a few minutes with Dougherty to see his affinity for the Kennedys; here is a clear-eyed, fast thinking, totally articulate, idealistic man with his own political contacts from coast to coast. At 36, he became the youngest member of the Democratic National Committee and had a major post in McGovern's Presidential campaign.

When I first interviewed Dougherty in 1969, I was amazed by his confidence that the South Dakota Democratic party of the 1970s could become consistently competitive with the GOP, building a coalition of farmers, college people, intellectual suburbanites, and labor and cutting down the Republican edge in the cities. The breakdown in South Dakota's insularity through television and travel was leading in that direction, Dougherty argued; he said his own attitudes on race were altered greatly by travel with Bobby Kennedy to the ghettos of the great cities and subsequently by the nine-hour ride on Bobby's funeral train from New York to Washington, watching impoverished blacks and others who lined the train platforms in 100-degree heat to honor their fallen hero. Urban self-help corporations like the agricultural service boards in rural America might help, Dougherty suggested.

By the time of the 1970 elections, it appeared indeed that a Democratic rebirth might be occurring in South Dakota. Farmers' discontent with their costs and low price supports, some local Republican scandals, and the energy of the new breed Democrats all added up to election of Democrat Richard F. Kneip as governor, Bill Dougherty as lieutenant governor, and Democrats—for the first time since New Deal days—to both of the state's seats in the U.S. House.

Two months later, in January 1971, George McGovern became the first avowed candidate for the 1972 Democratic Presidential nomination. He had acquitted himself well in 1968 and then taken on the chairmanship of the party reform commission that wrote rules opening up the party conventions to minority groups and women—a development many thought presaged a fundamental transformation of American party politics. McGovern's early opposition to the Vietnam war seemed to be receiving the vindication of time. He seemed to represent a kind of unique moral rectitude in a time of national disillusionment. Young people flocked to his banner, and his grass-roots organization was the envy of many of his competitors. The organization helped carry him, in fact, to victory in many of the 1972 Presidential primaries, and finally to a first-ballot nomination at the Democratic National Convention in Miami Beach.

The convention, time would show, was the high-water mark of the McGovern campaign; from there on it all would be downhill, into the trough of one of the most crushing defeats ever suffered by the Presidential candidate of a major party.

The seeds of disaster, it was later apparent, had already been planted by the time of Miami Beach. The son of a fire-and-brimstone preacher, McGovern viewed the world in stark terms of good and evil, in which he—out of a lifetime of self-perceived dedication to service of fellow man—regarded himself as the champion of the good, dead set on saving America from "the old rhetoric, the unmet promise, the image makers, the practitioners of the expedient." The moralistic approach had stood McGovern in good stead in the early primary season, as he built his narrow but faithful constituency. But he had almost lost the California primary when Hubert Humphrey pinned him down on his $1,000-grant-to-every-citizen program, and McGovern admitted he had no idea how much it would cost. Then there was McGovern's unrealistic faith that Senator Edward Kennedy would run on the ticket with him for Vice President, the lack of planning for a second choice, the sudden selection of Thomas Eagleton (imposed on the convention, in defiance of the spirit of the very reform rules McGovern had wittten), the Eagleton health fiasco, and McGovern's ill-starred promise to stand behind the Missourian "1,000 percent."

McGovern would later say, time and again, that Eagleton's removal from the ticket was necessary to prevent mental health from becoming the central issue of the fall campaign. But the people saw it differently: the White Knight of truth had been guilty of duplicity and expediency, both weak-kneed and cruel at the same time. Instead of a duplicitous Richard Nixon, George McGovern himself became the issue of the campaign, and in most Americans' judgment, he simply lacked the capacity to govern. Every issue McGovern then could raise—corruption in government, the Watergate affair, suspicious wheat sales to Russia, and of course the familiar Vietnam issue—would be viewed as secondary to the issue of McGovern's own consistency and competence. And while McGovern spoke of his campaign as a Biblical struggle between light and darkness, he discredited himself by his own actions as he assiduously courted Lyndon Johnson and Richard Daley and other tainted old powers of the Democratic party, thus offending many of his own early supporters and political independents.

In American politics, of course, the losers often have a consolation prize—seeing the issues they raised borrowed and popularized by the next and more skilled political leaders. John Kennedy seized on Adlai Stevenson's idealism, for instance, and Richard Nixon owed much to Barry Goldwater, especially Goldwater's trailblazing of the "law and order" issue. McGovern popularized issues, even in losing: not only the moral bankruptcy of the Vietnam war, but also the evils of political espionage and sabotage and corruption condoned in high places, tax codes favoring the rich, and bloated defense spending. Would McGovern be like that other prairie populist, William Jennings Bryan, who thrice lost the Presidency but set the agenda of public issues for a generation? Only time would tell.

Back in South Dakota in November 1972, home state loyalty was not enough to save McGovern from losing to Nixon by some 10 percentage points. But for McGovern's Democratic colleagues, it was a bright day. Richard Kneip and Richard Dougherty easily won reelection as governor and lieutenant governor, and the Democrats swept most of the other constitutional offices up for election. James Abourezk, a personable and hard-working freshman Congressman whose immigrant Lebanese father had once been a back-peddler on the Rosebud Indian Reservation, took Karl Mundt's Senate seat from the Republicans. Except for Dougherty, Abourezk is more closely associated with McGovern than any other South Dakota politician, and his proposed Family Farm Act, designed to curb the growth of agribusiness conglomerates, echoes McGovern's own agrarian populism. The election also saw the Democrats retain one of the U.S. House seats they had captured in 1970. And for the first time since 1936, the Democrats dislodged the Republicans from control of both houses of the South Dakota legislature. By contrast, when George McGovern took over leadership of the state Democratic party in the early 1950s, there had been only 11 Democrats in the entire 119-member legislature.

Prosperous Agriculture, Great Dams

More than 90 percent of South Dakota's land surface is in farmland, and agriculture—now a billion-dollar-a-year business—dominates the economy, sustaining both the farms and the cities. The combination of vast grazing lands in the western part of the state and heavy on-farm feeding of corn and other grains in the eastern sections makes South Dakota primarily a livestock-producing state. Almost eight out of every 10 dollars in farm income are derived from livestock, in sharp contrast to North Dakota, where wheat and other grains represent 60 percent. South Dakota is second only to North Dakota in spring wheat, however, and produces more rye than any other state.

South Dakota farmers get about $90 million a year in government farm subsidies, but all the federal programs backed by the Farmers Union and Plains States politicians have failed to stop the inexorable trend to bigger and bigger farms and a general eclipse of the small family farmer. In 1930 South Dakota had 83,000 farms, today about 45,000; the average farm size has risen from 439 to about 1,000 acres. Driving through the state, I saw many vacant farm buildings. The defenders of this trend to bigness claim it was economically inevitable; in the early days, they say, land was cheap and many farmers of marginal ability tried to till it; today a farmer has to use a wide range of skills to survive. Farming has become big business; a viable farm unit, for instance, will have a worth in machinery, buildings, and land of $200,000 or more. (Indeed, the investment is so huge that there are scarcely any farmers who didn't inherit their first land and most of their machinery.)

The prosperity of today's mechanized agriculture makes it hard to believe that there are men still tilling the South Dakota soil who remember starting out with four or five horses and a mule hitched up to a plow, or that drought and depression so devastated this land in the decade preceding World War II that 40 percent of the people were driven onto government relief rolls.

The nationwide economic recovery of World War II years coincided with a cycle of relatively heavy rainfall in the Plains, and South Dakota has not since experienced a serious depression. As in North Dakota, the damming of the Missouri River plays a vital role in a state's agricultural economy; South Dakota's equivalent of the Garrison diversion project is the Oahe irrigation project, which will one day irrigate some half a million acres of central and eastern South Dakota. An initial stage to irrigate 190,000 acres, authorized by Congress in 1968, will increase farm income more than $30 million a year through greater and more reliable production of feed, forage, and livestock. (The Bureau of Reclamation expects to spend $249 million on the Oahe project by the time it is completed, but Congress did not appropriate more than planning funds up to 1972.) Eventually South Dakota expects to increase its agricultural activity by a third over late 1960s levels, serving as one of the nation's great cattle and hog and lamb feeding areas. It now ranks eighth in the U.S. in cattle (4.5 million), fourth in hogs (two million), and fifth in sheep (over one million).

This is not to say that life for a South Dakota farmer has become soft. Much of the irrigation activity is still in the future, and he still lives with the great danger of droughts which seem to come every five or six years and dry out everything that grows. Complementing the hot summers are fierce winters with heavy snows; it takes a tough man still to survive in this environment.

Nevertheless, life has improved measurably since the 1930s, and the future is even brighter. A start has been made on erasing the prairie's age-old scourge of aridity, by the addition of vast areas of new water surface through artificial water impoundment. The benefits from South Dakota's great Oahe Dam, completed in the late 1950s as the largest rolled-earth dam in the world, are worth considering. The danger of floods has been vastly curtailed (and the region indeed suffered some vicious floods in the early 1950s). Irrigation for vast areas is being developed. New water recreation areas have made fishermen of many farmers. And Oahe can generate more than half a million kilowatts of power. The dam's costs are also worth considering, however: originally estimated by its builders, the Army Corps of Engineers, to cost $73 million, it ended up costing $347 million—a cost overrun of 375 percent, a record overrun in large dam projects in the United States.

In common with other Plains States, South Dakota is fattening and slaughtering much more of its own beef today, rather than shipping to Iowa or points farther east for final feeding and butchering. The next stage, already begun, involves complete processing of beef into various cuts, all prepackaged before they leave for distant markets.

Across the Plains, the meat-packing firms are rapidly shifting from old multistory buildings to efficient one-story units for rapid killing, dissection with air knives, and shipping. In Sioux Falls, however, one can still visit the traditional high-storied plant of John Morrell & Co., oldest meat-packing firm in the world. Each hour 130 cattle, 200 sheep, and 660 hogs are processed on the firm's dressing room floor; the actual slaughtering is as humane as any but a vegetarian could ask, with the animals knocked unconscious by electronic prods or air hammers to the skull before being hung up to have their blood vessels cut. The carcasses of the small white lambs, the plump hogs, and massive steers then proceed on conveyor belts to be skinned and dissected by rapid, deft knife work with the efficiency of a Detroit auto production line. It's all quite hygienic and impersonal, though one can get a bit of a start from a row of beady-eyed hog heads staring up glassily from a conveyor belt.

A Little Industry and Something for the Tourists

Industrialization has proceeded at a snail's pace in South Dakota, and only five other states have a lower level of manufacturing. What industrial income there is (about $175 million a year) comes chiefly from food processing, electronic products, tool making, printing, and publishing. And it is highly localized; some 60 percent of the industrial employment is located in a single city, Sioux Falls. Job growth in the 1960s ranked a rather mediocre 38th among the states.

South Dakota's remoteness from major markets probably precludes any heavy industry within her borders; the key acquisitions of recent years have tended to be in light goods like electronic components. Nor is South Dakota likely to become a center for advanced space-age technology; Aberdeen rejoiced over a new Controlled Data plant, only to find that its 400 employees would almost all be women in rather menial assembly-type jobs. With the exodus from the farm, the state has plenty of willing but untrained workers; ironically it exports the bulk of its college graduates, so that when an employer needs sophisticated workers, he may have to look outside to find them. When Raven Industries, the Sioux Falls parachute firm, wanted engineers in the 1960s, it felt obliged to advertise out of state. Raven's ads in the Los Angeles papers read: "Are you tired of the rat race? Would you like to return to the Midwest?" The appeal brought in several good engineers.

Richard Bowen, the perceptive young president of the University of South Dakota, suggests that the prairie states have so little industry today because the population rush into them came just before and at the turn of the century, when agriculture was beginning to lose its dominance; depopulation, in fact, began before economic stability could be achieved. Another factor was that the railroad went ahead of most civilization in the prairie states; indeed many prairie towns sprang up as way-stations on a railroad line. With railroad service from the East, there was no need to start indigenous industries to serve agriculture and the farm population. The seeds of local industry were never planted as they had been in more easterly Midwest states like Illinois and Indiana.

Keeping organized labor in its place is apparently one of the ways in which South Dakota hopes to attract new industry. There is no state department of labor, right-to-work is written in the state constitution, and there are also restrictions on picketing. One result: the state's workers earn less than the national average; per capita income is 19 percent below the U.S. average. A promotional pamphlet of the South Dakota Industrial Development Expansion Agency declares:

> South Dakota residents are, for the most part, of Northern European origin, physically rugged and mentally alert. They possess a healthy attitude toward their jobs and are ready to deliver a full day's work for a day's pay. Work stoppages in South Dakota are practically nil. . . . Only 9.5 percent of all non-agricultural employees are enrolled in unions, compared with a national average of 29.5 percent. All of these facts indicate that South Dakota labor understands the problems and goals of management.

Two final elements must be fed into the South Dakota economic equation. For 20 years the state had led the U.S. in gold production, thanks to the vast output of the century-old Homestake Gold Mine at Lead in the Black Hills, largest in the country. Homestake has long been a major political power in South Dakota, renowned for its ability to shape tax laws to its own liking. Except for benefiting its owners and paying local taxes, Homestake makes two contributions to South Dakota: it employs some 1,800 men, and each day it pumps 75 pounds of deadly poisonous cyanide, used in leaching out its gold, into an unfortunate local stream (Whitewood Creek). Before the cyanide began, Homestake used an even more frightening leaching agent: mercury. Local officials never saw fit to ban the pollution, but the Federal Environmental Protection Agency proved less tolerant and told Homestake to install an adequate water purification system.

South Dakota grosses millions each year ($250 million at latest count) from tourism, an industry boosted by one of the most aggressive and successful tourist promotion efforts in the country, run by the state highway department. One great attraction is the barren wasteland known as the Bad Lands in the southwest, aptly called by General Custer "a part of hell with the fires burnt out." The Bad Lands' 2,000 miles of water- and wind-eroded buttes, pinnacles, and fluted ridges also lie close to the kinder pine forests of the

Black Hills on the Wyoming border. The Black Hills are the site of a renowned Passion Play, held at an amphitheater in Spearfish each summer. What they are best known for, however, is Mt. Rushmore, the mountain on which sculptor Gutzon Borglum carved 60-foot-high heads of Washington, Jefferson, Lincoln, and Theodore Roosevelt. The busts, viewed by a million and a half people each year, are proportionate to men 465 feet tall.

Only a few miles away a modern-day sculptor named Korczak Ziolkowski is trying to outdo Borglum with a statue of Crazy Horse and his horse which will be a stupendous 641 feet long and 563 feet high when (and if) it is finally hacked out of a mountainside. Ziolkowski, who was born more than 60 years ago in Boston and worked on the Mount Rushmore project back in the 1930s, got his inspiration in 1939 when a Sioux, Chief Henry Standing Bear, wrote asking him to "caress a mountain so that the white man will know that the red man had great heroes too." Ziolkowski got his start after World War II, buying his South Dakota mountain from which he has already chipped and blasted away 3 million tons of rock (eight times what Borglum chiseled off Mount Rushmore). A great, bearded, barrel-chested man of immense energy, he lives with his family of five boys and five girls at the base of the monument. Completion of the project is at least a decade away; then with more than 35 years and $10 million invested, the finished product will be there for the ages to see: Crazy Horse, astride a galloping pony, pointing southward to the hills and valleys and free-flowing streams he knew and loved.

Not far from the Black Hills is the little cowtown of Wall (population 629), home of the Wall Drug Store, a thriving establishment (now the world's largest drug store) that survived the Depression by advertising free ice water, later mounted a global sign advertising campaign and today draws more than a million visitors a year. Of another South Dakotan man-made invention for the benefit of tourists, the Corn Palace at Mitchell, we have spoken already.

South Dakota still prides itself on being the pheasant-hunting capital of the world; I happened to arrive in the state on the opening day of the season and found practically every South Dakotan alive with excitement about the pheasants he hoped to bag. But the truth is that pheasant hunting has encountered some bad years. In the peak year of 1945, there were at least 40 million pheasant in South Dakota, and the happy hunters chalked up a record slaughter of 7.5 million birds; natives recall the ring-necks were everywhere and that many people went out to shoot some at lunchtime on successive days. Increased land under cultivation, the use of pesticides, and some killer storms had almost decimated the population by the mid-1960s, however; one year there were only two million birds alive in the entire state, by 1969 still only 3.3 million. The state was working furiously to replenish the supply.

Out-of-staters are permitted to buy (at a premium price) pheasant-hunting licenses, but South Dakota's love of visitors has its limits. After World II, when authorities noted outsiders buying up many choice hunting grounds in the state, all non-South Dakotans were barred from hunting for duck and goose. The prohibition lasted for 20 years but was finally eliminated by virtue of a Pennsylvania Congressman's temper. He was John P. Saylor, ranking Republican on the House Interior Committee, which had to decide whether to authorize the multimillion-dollar Oahe irrigation project. Visiting the state to review the Oahe project, Saylor told his hosts he would like to go duck hunting. The embarrassed reply was that as a non-South Dakotan, he could not. Saylor, a big, gruff man, exploded, pointing out that the Oahe project would create vast new reclamation and hunting areas and that he flatly would not vote federal dollars to develop South Dakota's water resources if out-of-state people were excluded from hunting. Oahe was subsequently authorized, in fact, with a prohibition against funding until South Dakota removed its restrictions. The legislators in Pierre grumbled about unwarranted Eastern dictation, but the Oahe development was so important that they finally went ahead and bowed to Saylor's will.

Pierre, State Government, and the Problems of Ruralism

No American capital is as much disdained by the people of its state as Pierre (pronounced "Peer"), a drab prairie town of 9,699 souls settled between mustard-colored buttes along the Missouri River valley. Centrality is apparently Pierre's main virtue; if you take an official South Dakota map and fold it so that the eastern and western borders are lined up evenly, the center crease will barely miss Pierre.

A family town where the streets are rolled up early each evening, Pierre has an outmoded business district, a few new motels, a main street that runs gracelessly directly into the river, an undistinguished capitol building, and little traffic except for cowboy-booted ranchers and legislators who congregate each winter. Before modern comforts came to the farm, it used to be said that many farmers ran for the legislature just to get away from the cold and monotony of home for three months in the warm capital at Pierre.

The city's location has something to say about the character of state government. As political scientist Alan Clem reports:

> The capital was originally placed in Pierre because western interests were not willing to see it located any farther east. Between the James River 80 miles to the east and the Black Hills 140 miles to the west, South Dakota is principally arid, sparsely-populated rangeland. It is in the middle of this vast sea of grass that the nerves of state government are collected. These nerves are thickly insulated by the vastness of the prairie from popular pressures, and as a result the response of state government to many needs and wishes has often been relatively slow. It is natural to associate the isolation of Pierre from the bulk of the state's population with the state's isolation and resultant sense of withdrawal and disassociation from the nation as a whole. . . . State and local programs and budgets reflect yesterday's and today's problems, seldom tomorrow's.

Up to 1972, the state government structure showed a confusing mishmash of 164 boards and commissions, all appointed by the governor; a surfeit of popularly elected statewide officials; a constitutional debt limit at a scarcely credible $100,000; no income tax; initiative and referendum laws which circumscribe the ability or willingness of governors and legislators to strike out in new directions; and continued control of the legislature by rural and small-town interests. South Dakota ranks 47th among the 50 states in per capita state tax revenue; one reason is that support of the schools is left almost entirely to the localities. Some important change, however, was promised by the voters' 1972 approval of a massive reorganization plan for state government, including a limit of 25 on the number of departments. The governor's term was extended from two to four years, and he was given power to reorganize the state government by executive order, subject only to veto by both houses of the legislature.

Up to 1970, South Dakota's only governor of the post-World II era with an especially imaginative view of the state's potential was Republican Joe Foss, a legendary hero of the Pacific Theater in World War II who was governor four years before losing a race for Congress against McGovern in 1958.* Frank Farrar, elected governor in 1968, was initially billed as a strong personality but soon became bogged down in a fight over state regulation of the popular rural electric cooperatives. Charges by a 1970 primary opponent that he had used public office to become a millionaire softened Farrar up for a successful challenge by Democrat Richard S. Kneip, who ran a low-keyed campaign, emphasizing "honesty in government" and won by 23,260 votes. Kneip proved less vigorous than Farrar in recruiting new industries for South Dakota, but he did press for the much-needed executive reorganization and seemed to have a chance of eventually winning tax reform (including an income tax) for the state. In Kneip's first year in office, the Republican-controlled legislature approved the first workmen's compensation law in South Dakota history.

In 1968 the voters had already indicated a willingness to break with the familiar past by approving a public school reorganization plan to compel consolidation of tiny village and country schools into big districts centered around the larger towns. When the vote was taken, South Dakota still had more than a thousand isolated schools with only one teacher. Of the 212 high schools in the state, only 58 had more than 200 students. Clearly, consolidations were required if the students were to have access to specialized courses, sophisticated laboratory equipment, and adequate library facilities.

A proposal for consolidation, however, tears at the very heart of rural life. Often a school maintains a small town's base as a trade center; there are intense loyalties to local basketball and football teams; loss of its school may mean death for a small town. The situation is even more acute in the western range country, where a consolidation may mean a family will have to leave its lands to live in town for the winter or send children to board with friends. The big ranchers of the western reaches also had some special tax advantages to lose by consolidation.

* After that defeat, Foss did a creditable job as commissioner of the American Football League in its formulative years and became known nationally for his hunting and sports programs broadcast on television.

Despite such financial and emotional obstacles, however, the consolidation plan was approved. But the people's ambivalence was reflected in the close vote: passage was by 1,705 votes out of almost 240,000 cast.

The fear of change which South Dakotans indicated through most of the years after World Warr II seemed to have two roots: the people's rural, isolated prairie existence, and the remembrance of the 1930s. In this state which has just finished burying its pioneers, the virtues still are sturdy self-reliance and individualism. One oldtimer told me, speaking of his childhood: "When I was on the farm with my folks, we always had chickens in the yard, a cow we could kill, beans we could harvest, or at least a jackrabbit or a pheasant or a grouse we could shoot on the prairie. So we took care of ourselves, or any neighbor in trouble." That frame of mind is poor preparation for the changes of the modern world, though, either at home or afar. Especially in the small towns, there is a suspicion of "fancy" schools or any "frills" in government and deep resentment of taxation that saps a man's livelihood. The comments of these hardy survivors of the prairie about big-city people on welfare are scarcely printable; they cannot conceive of people being unable to solve their own problems through hard work or of being alienated from their local government.

For decades, in fact, South Dakota was controlled by the generation of the 1930s: extremely cautious, frightened, with a built-in inferiority complex. Some local seer is reported to have said: "The philosophy of South Dakota is that there might be a drought next summer." The result is the state's continued bar against a debt of more than $100,000 and stiff rural opposition to any kind of change. The era of fear and doubt is passing, of course, as witnessed by the recent reorganization votes and victories of men like McGovern, Kneip, and Dougherty. But the transition into a new age is difficult.

The Unhappy Plight of the Sioux

One out of every 25 South Dakotans is a Sioux Indian living on or registered with one of the five reservations that cover hundreds of thousands of acres from the Missouri River valley westward, the greatest concentration of Indians in any Great Plains state today. There is no more tragic aspect of South Dakota's life.

Once a resourceful, proud, nomadic people who could send 10,000 warriors into battle, the Sioux were forced onto reservations and had to become ranchers and farmers on barely arable land. A Messiah craze appeared among the Sioux in 1890, when one of their number reported a vision in which he had seen the buffalo restored and the white man evicted. Before the resultant disturbances were ended, the great Sioux chief, Sitting Bull, had been killed and several hundred Sioux men, women, and children intercepted by U.S. Cavalry and brutally slain at a creek called Wounded Knee. The Sioux still remember that massacre with intense bitterness; nor have the succeeding years been kind to them.

Except for those on the payroll of the Bureau of Indian Affairs or some other government agency, or a lucky few who have succeeded as ranchers, the Indians on the reservations are destitute; in winter months, when neither the tourist trade nor farm helper jobs are available, the unemployment rate is a staggering 50 percent. A third still live in log cabins; for many home is a tarpaper shack, a rusted trailer, or just a tent, the dwellings so small inside that the yard becomes a kind of attic for every waste, from discarded furniture to junked cars. Yet to assimilate into the white world seems equally impossible for most Sioux; many go for a while to cities but then return to the reservation, where mounting frustrations lead to alcoholism and high crime and suicide rates. As one reporter put it after a visit to the Pine Ridge Reservation: "The 70 years of occupation have debased and beaten down what is Indian, but the people have not been converted into white men."

The decade of the 1960s saw the beginning of a real effort by tribal councils to develop more pride among the Sioux in their own institutions, to start small industries and obtain more federal aid of various types. Most successful were the Rosebud Reservation Sioux, who appealed for and got the largest concentrated housing program on any Indian reservation in the nation. But even that promising start, initiated with the help of a talented Roman Catholic priest on the reservation, ran into difficulties with vandalism during construction and getting water and sewage to isolated housing units; the problems seemed to be a ghastly kind of fulfillment of the callous remark I heard from a white businessman in the state: "Give an Indian a house and by the next spring he'll have the partitions out for kindling wood."

If cash investment by the federal government could be called the solution to the Indians' problems, the future should look much brighter just now. On the Pine Ridge Reservation, according to one study, the BIA spends about $8,000 a year per Indian family to increase the people's self-sufficiency. If one wonders where all the money goes, another statistic elucidates: there is reportedly one BIA officer for each Indian family on the reservation. The Indians' own annual income is around $1,910. Things are a bit different on the Rosebud Reservation, where federal spending has almost doubled since 1965, to about $4 million a year. The tribal council controls about 40 percent of this money. So there is more self-control but, at the same time, a rise in political conflict among the Indian politicians, each battling for control of some part of the pie.

The crux of the Indian problem in South Dakota seems to lie in employment. There are few enough jobs for white men in the barren, empty prairie lands where the reservations are located; any jobs which do appear are likely to pay the Indian, with his limited education, little more than the minimum wage—and with that, he can scarcely support his family.

Congressman Ben Reifel, the only Indian to serve in the House or Senate in the postwar years, was actually a native of the Rosebud Reservation, where he was born of a full Sioux woman and her German-American husband in 1906. Reifel distinguished himself by receiving a doctor of public administration degree from Harvard University; after several years of work for the

Bureau of Indian Affairs, he captured South Dakota's eastern congressional district in 1960. A Republican and moderate conservative, Reifel had no difficulty in winning reelection to five terms. A quiet man, he made few headlines and certainly failed to use his unique status as the sole Indian in Congress to develop and win approval of bold programs that would really change the condition of his people. But he did work behind the scenes on the Appropriations Committee and especially its Interior Subcommittee, of which he became the ranking Republican member, to gain better funding for Indian-related projects. Reifel retired voluntarily in 1970.

Leola, South Dakota

If I really wanted to get an idea of South Dakota, friends in Senator Mundt's office told me, I must visit a small town. They recommended Leola (population 787), a farm village and local trade center some 30 miles northwest of Aberdeen, close to the North Dakota border. So I went to see for myself. A bright green water tower proclaimed Leola from afar; the town itself was a brief succession of tree-shaded streets lined with cleanly white frame houses, a place of grain elevators and a few middling sorts of stores, of railroad tracks covered with grass, of leaves being raked on a sleepy autumn afternoon with the prairie to be glimpsed at the end of almost every street.

Leola is luckier than many towns: it not only has not lost its school but now provides schooling services for a wide area where there used to be nine rural schools. So some 500 children attend the schools in Leola today, and school politics and financing are a principal source of local concern and debate. Indeed, Leola was unlucky enough to find two cells of the John Birch Society, a fairly rare commodity in South Dakota, spring up in its midst; the local Birchers (mostly farmers) fight for lower school expenditures at every turn, for reduced taxes, against any hint of sex education in the schools. Clark Schemp, the competent school superintendent, was horrified to discover one Bircher on his school board, two on his teaching staff, and one as president of the PTA. Schemp fought off most of their onslaughts but gained no love of his adversaries in the process; the Birchers, he told me, are a devious and "dirty bunch of back-stabbing characters."

Opposition to the Birchers made no liberal of Superintendent Schemp, however. He was deeply upset by what he saw as a national breakdown in morals, represented by movie stars bearing illegitimate children and *O Calcutta!* drawing big crowds in New York. Every year, he complained, four or five girls in Leola's high school of 170 youngsters become pregnant and must withdraw from school, an evidence of the moral breakdown reaching the town. Drugs haven't made it to Leola yet, he said, but they're in Aberdeen, and he recalled the distressing case of McGovern's daughter being apprehended on a pot charge (which was later dropped on a technicality). Karl Mundt, not George McGovern, is the kind of man Clark Schemp likes to have represent him in Washington. Leola agrees, casting a vote as high as 80 percent Republican in many elections. The county it lies in, McPherson, is one of those in north-central South Dakota which political analysts like Sam Lubell have pointed to as bastions of Republicanism with strong German and Russian ethnic roots.

Like all of South Dakota, Leola is a great producer and educator of children who end up leaving their birthplace. Some 60 percent of Leola's high school graduates go on to college; of that number, hardly any return to make their careers in Leola. So education becomes a one-way ticket for youth to escape—doubtless one reason that many South Dakotans opposed school consolidations and spending a lot of money to give their children sophisticated educations they can only use in distant places. Of the two daughters in the house across the street, Schemp told me, one had gone to Pacific Lutheran College in Washington state and even studied a year in Germany before settling down in Columbus, Ohio; the other had gone off to be a TWA hostess.

After I had written the first draft of these pages, I was startled to pick up a copy of the New York *Times* and read a story about Lodi, California, a town 34 miles south of Sacramento in the rich farmland of the northern San Joaquin Valley. Reporter Douglas Kneeland wrote:

> Everyone in Lodi isn't from the Dakotas. It only seems that way. As it did, for instance, to Leon Leberman when he moved here seven years ago from Leola, S.D.
>
> "When I first came out here, when I naturally didn't know anybody except my sister that I'd known before," the wavy-haired, 28-year old Mr. Leberman said, . . . "One Sunday I was sitting in church and I counted 21 people from St. Paul's Lutheran Church in Leola that were now in St. Peter's Lutheran here. There was an old Sunday school teacher of mine and her husband and various people I had known—some farmers and others.
>
> "Here you are, 1,600 miles from home and you run into them,'" he went on, shaking his head in disbelief. . . . "Out of our family of eight, there are four of us right here in Lodi. And, of course, I have several uncles and cousins here. I only have one sister who lives back there."

Aside from economic opportunity, Lodi offers another inducement: a mean winter temperature of 44 degrees and, at worst, some fog and drizzle instead of the long months of bitter cold and snow.

Actually, as a school center and county seat, Leola is not losing population at nearly the rate of many towns of its size or smaller. Many retired farmers move into town to replace the young people who leave, and the biggest source of employment is actually government: courthouse personnel, the post office, Department of Agriculture soil conservation officers, and even the Federal Housing Administration. But retailing and medical services have deteriorated seriously, partly because the larger city of Aberdeen is little more than half an hour away by auto. All the auto and farm implement dealers (there used to be several of each) have disappeared. A few years ago there were four grocery stores; now there is just one. Add the local co-op ("Leola Equity Exchange"), a single clothing store, two grain elevators, two small restaurants, and the local bank, and you have Leola's commerce almost in sum.

Leola also has a "drug store," but the store has no pharmacist in attendance; prescriptions are phoned to another town 35 miles away and driven in daily. Leola's community hospital, in which it had taken so much pride, had to close in 1966; now if you're sick at night, I was told, "they'll load you in an ambulance and take you to Aberdeen." The rights and wrongs of the end of rural medical care are difficult to unravel; a real plus for the area is that Aberdeen now has two large hospitals, many specialists, and a level of medical care Leola alone never could have hoped for.

To complete the Leola inventory, only a few items must be added: a Masonic temple; a Legion hall (the Legion actually runs the local bar, a booming business among the town's dominant Russo-Germans); many churches; and, at the side of town, a charming wooded park with a duck pond and picnic tables, a place local teenagers find most delectable for beer-busts or summer evening necking.

NEBRASKA

"A PLACE TO COME FROM OR A PLACE TO DIE"?

In July of 1961 a dinner was held in McCook, Nebraska, to honor the hundredth anniversary of the birth of George Norris, Nebraska's great progressive Senator who had been the driving force behind such reforms as the direct election of U.S. Senators and his state's unicameral legislature. The invited speaker was Theodore C. Sorensen, a native Nebraskan then seated in the cockpit of national power and influence as special counsel to President John Kennedy.* Focusing his remarks on the quality of education in Nebraska, Sorensen offered some exceedingly sharp comments. George Norris, Sorenson said,

> knew the value of a good public education. He had to struggle to achieve it. He endured hardship to teach it. He defied his [Republican] party to praise Al Smith's support of it. . . .
>
> But here in Norris' own state—where the pioneers once vowed that every child should go to the common school, where the proportion of high school graduates has ranked high and illiteracy low among all states of the Union—education is no longer a primary concern.
>
> Budgets are cut. Federal aid is opposed. Teachers and faculties are harassed and underpaid.
>
> And one result is a steady exodus of young people from this state, seeking, as their ancestors sought, a better life for their children—until this state, already containing a higher proportion of old people than California, Florida, or almost all other states, is left behind, old, outmoded, a place to come from or a place to die.

* Kennedy once said: "I've hired more people from Nebraska than voted for me." But Sorensen, for one, had not lived in Nebraska since his youth.

"A place to come from or a place to die?" An angry howl of protest arose, especially from Nebraska Republicans, who demanded that Democrats make public apologies for Sorensen's remarks. The cold statistics, however, suggest that Sorensen's formulation of the problem, however impolitic, had some basis in fact. In the 40 years from 1930 to 1970, the U.S.A. gained 65 percent in population but Nebraska only 8 percent.* Since 1940, 326,000 more people have left Nebraska than have moved into it. With Florida and Iowa, Nebraska was one of the three states with the highest percentage of its people 65 or older; few states had a smaller portion of their people in the productive age groups.

As for the specific problem of education which Sorensen cited, Nebraska waited until 1967 to begin a modern program of general state aid to local schools—except for New Hampshire, the last of the 50 states to do so. It has more school districts (some 2,300) and one-room schoolhouses than any other state; its comparative tax effort to support schools is one of the most anemic in the nation, and it pays its public school teachers (especially in rural areas) far below the national average.

The Nebraska state government occasionally surprises one by taking what seems to be a bold and innovative step—for example, its approval in 1971 of a state ombudsman, following Hawaii's trailblazing action. But as a rule, Nebraska government in our times has lagged consistently behind its sister states in making changes necessary to meet the new conditions of mid- and late-20th-century America. Counting the school districts, there are still a grossly inefficient 4,500 governmental units in the state. In an era when bond financing of capital expenditures is considered an essential of government. Nebraska still labors under an 1875 constitution which forbids the government to issue bonds for more than $100,000 except for the express purpose of "repelling invasion or suppressing insurrection"—a provision which raises the dark specter of invasions by predatory neighbors like South Dakota and Iowa. (One result of the state bond limitation has been that local subdivisions have piled up fairly heavy debts; also the state university and colleges, possibly in violation of the state constitution, issued $50 million worth of bonds for facilities before the process was "legalized" by constitutional amendment. Voters made a break with past tradition in 1968 by specifically authorizing limited state obligation bonds for highways.) Before World War II, Nebraska advertised itself to businesses considering migration as a "white spot" on the U.S. map, with no sales tax, no income tax, and no bonded debt; it was not until the mid-1960s that any type of broad-based tax was passed. For years, Nebraska had the lowest per capita state tax in the United States, and in 1970 still ranked only 47th. Levels of state public expenditures remain exceptionally low.

For 30 years now, Nebraska has also turned a negative face to the outside world; instead of a George Norris or William Jennings Bryan, Nebraska has

* Nebraska's actual population count in 1930 was 1,377,963; in 1970 it was 1,483,493. A few urban areas have accounted for whatever growth has taken place; 76 of 93 Nebraska counties, for instance, have yet to match the vote turnout they produced in 1934.

offered the nation such immortals as Kenneth S. Wherry, Hugh A. Butler, Roman L. Hruska, and Carl T. Curtis.

We must start, though, with a glimpse of the giants of yesteryear. Three times the Presidential nominee of his party, Bryan was the friend of farmers plagued by drought, depression and creditors; his free-silver banner united the Democrats and Populists. (Of him the poet Vachel Lindsay would write: He was "Nebraska's 'shout of joy' . . . a gigantic troubadour, speaking like a siege gun, smashing Plymouth Rock with his boulders from the West. . . .")

And for 40 years until his ultimate defeat in 1942, Nebraska voters sent to Washington one of the most gifted legislators of all time, William George Norris. Norris led the successful fight against the autocratic rule of House Speaker Joe Cannon (a battle which would win him a place in John Kennedy's *Profiles in Courage*.) He fought for direct election of Senators, fathered the Tennessee Valley Authority, wrote the Lame Duck amendment to the federal Constitution, and showed the courage of his convictions by voting against the nation's entry into World War I. Norris said the accomplishment he most wanted to be remembered for was the Rural Electrification Administration he authored; his reason was that electricity to the farm would free women of the slavery of farm work. And of Nebraska, Norris said, "I am a part of its soil, and its soil is part of me."

By 1942, though, Nebraskans had had enough of the spunky old fighter in his baggy black suit and limp old bow tie; in place of the 81-year-old Norris they elected Kenneth Wherry, a bombastic, pugnacious ultraconservative and bitter opponent of the Democrats' "socialistic welfare state." Wherry led right-wing Republicans who opposed the Marshall Plan and North Atlantic Treaty and was for three years actually Senate minority leader, taking his cue from Policy Committee Chairman Robert A. Taft of Ohio.

A more courtly but equally conservative figure was Hugh Butler, a true pioneer (he came to Nebraska as a boy in a covered wagon) who decades later became a U.S. Senator, fighting all increased government debt, voting a straight isolationist line, and acting as spokesman for the railroads, the cattle blocs, and the grain trade, in which he had a personal financial interest. Butler built an amazingly efficient political organization of 40,000 people—especially businessmen—who were intensely loyal to him. He died in 1954.

The two Republicans who currently represent Nebraska in the Senate, Roman Hruska and Carl Curtis, have national reputations as run-of-the-mill no-sayers to every new idea. Many an observer of Capital Hill smiled with quiet satisfaction in 1972 when columnist Jack Anderson had the temerity to go into Lincoln and tell an audience of Nebraskans that Hruska and Curtis were "dolts" and "the two worst members of the United States Senate." Curtis is a scrupulously honest man and efficient "service Senator" on small matters, but his pudgy, owl-faced appearance might be his undoing in a state where cosmetic politics are more important. He occasionally seizes on a worthwhile cause, like better staffing for the minority on congressional committees. But he was last noticed by most Americans when he fought early and hard to make Barry Goldwater the 1964 Presidential nominee. His peak years seem

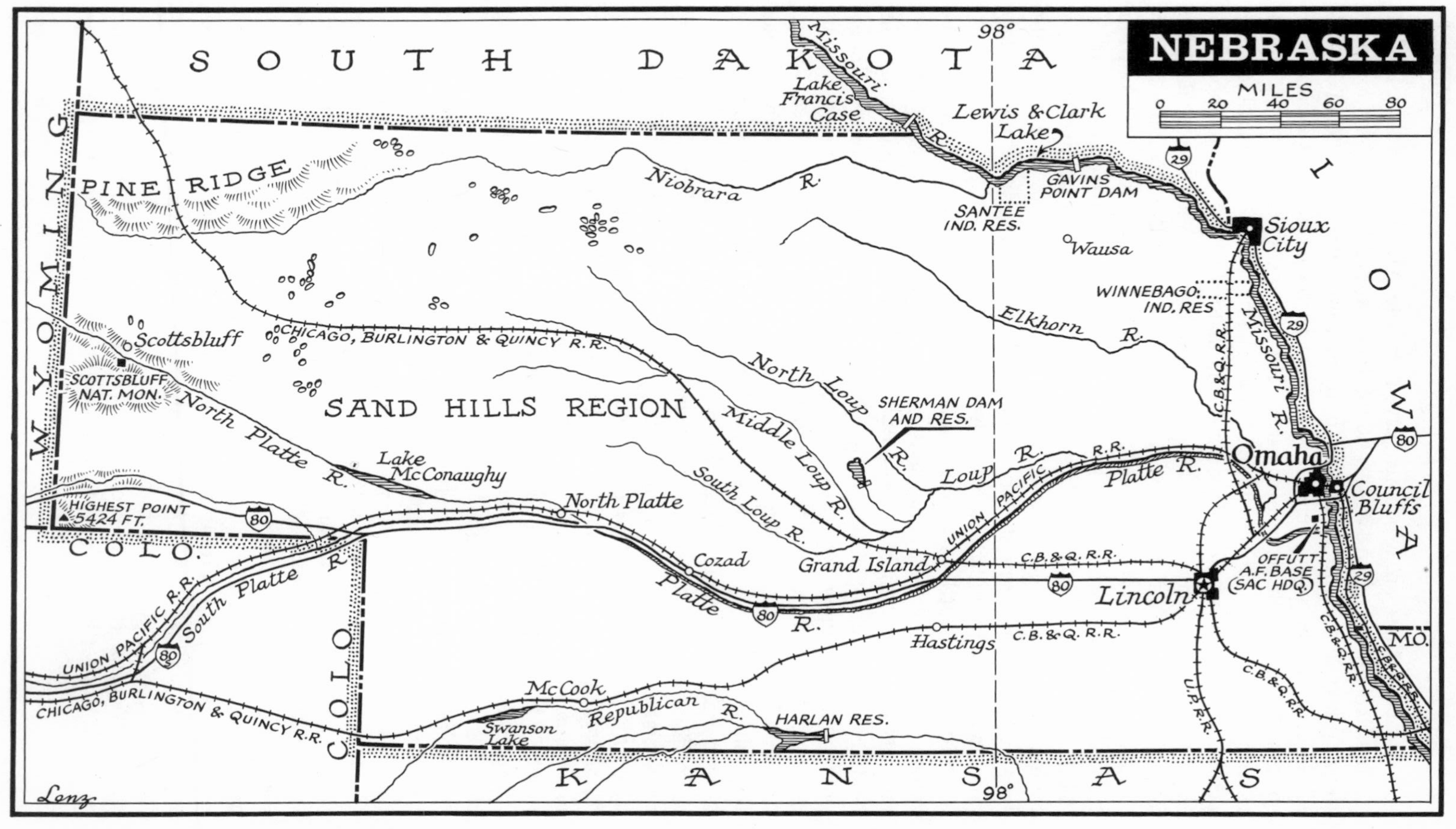
NEBRASKA
MILES
0 20 40 60 80
SOUTH DAKOTA
IOWA
MO.
KANSAS
COLO.
WYOMING
98°
Missouri
Lake Francis Case
Lewis & Clark Lake
GAVINS POINT DAM
SANTEE IND. RES.
Sioux City
Wausa
WINNEBAGO IND. RES
Niobrara R.
Elkhorn R.
Missouri R.
PINE RIDGE
Scottsbluff
SCOTTSBLUFF NAT. MON.
CHICAGO, BURLINGTON & QUINCY R.R.
SAND HILLS REGION
North Platte R.
North Loup R.
Middle Loup R.
South Loup R.
Loup R.
SHERMAN DAM AND RES.
Lake McConaughy
North Platte
HIGHEST POINT 5424 FT.
Cozad
Grand Island
UNION PACIFIC R.R.
Platte R.
Omaha
Council Bluffs
OFFUTT A.F. BASE (SAC HDQ.)
Lincoln
C.B.&Q. R.R.
Hastings
South Platte R.
UNION PACIFIC R.R.
CHICAGO, BURLINGTON & QUINCY R.R.
McCook
Republican R.
Swanson Lake
HARLAN RES.
U.P. R.R.
29
80
Lenz

to have been those in which he served on the McClellan Labor Rackets Committee and was active in the Bobby Baker and Billy Sol Estes investigations. When he ran for reelection in 1972, Curtis typically offered a "profile in courage" by voting against a 20 percent Social Security increase, despite Nebraska's high share of oldsters. His opponent was Nebraska's most colorful maverick of modern times, state senator Terry "the Terrible" Carpenter, a perennial party switcher and candidate who is still remembered as the man who nominated a fictitious "Joe Smith" for Vice President at the 1956 Republican National Convention, as a protest to the unanimous acceptance of Richard Nixon. (Carpenter is a veteran member of Nebraska's unicameral legislature, where the Lincoln *Journal* characterized his record as "almost as erratic as his party allegiance, ranging from constructive legislation to unmitigated mischief-making.") Curtis was favored to beat Carpenter by a big margin but squeaked through with a fairly threadbare 5 percentage point margin in the midst of a Nixon landslide.

Hruska has a little-publicized moderate side, springing from his Transylvanian, Unitarian background, and has on occasion sponsored progressive criminal justice reform legislation. But his demeanor and public stands—including outspoken opposition to gun controls—have given him quite the opposite image. Syrup-voiced and unctuous in debate, he seems forever hung up on some musty point of Senate procedure. He hoped to succeed Everett McKinley Dirksen as the Republican Senate Leader but was rebuffed by his Republican colleagues. A noted opponent of violence and pornography, Hruska was deeply embarrassed in his 1970 reelection campaign when his opponents revealed he was the half-owner, secretary, and director of a group of Nebraska drive-ins and theaters that purveyed skin flicks and the likes of *The Blood Drinker* and *Girl on a Chain Gang*. His opponent, former Governor Morrison, said: "Can Roman Hruska sermonize against loose sex and low morals while displaying filthy situations upon the public scene for money?" Hruska's sanctimonious reply was to (1) disclaim any role in active management of the theater chain, yet also (2) claim credit for the fact that the chain actually ran no films with an X-rating.

If history takes note of Hruska, it will probably be for his role as the first Senator ever to advocate a quota for "mediocre" men on the Supreme Court. It came during the 1970 debate on President Nixon's nomination of G. Harrold Carswell to the high court. Hruska, who became Carswell's most vocal advocate, was asked on a television interview about charges that Carswell's record was "mediocre." Hruska replied: "There are a lot of mediocre judges and people and lawyers. They are entitled to a little representation, aren't they? We can't have all Brandeises, Frankfurters, and Cardozos." The remark was a crucial turning point in the Senate fight over the nomination, giving wavering Senators a perfect excuse to oppose the President's nominee. It also succeeded in making Hruska and his "mediocrity" theme the laughingstock of Washington—and even in less sophisticated Nebraska. This blooper, as well as a bitter Republican intraparty fight in Nebraska that year, may have had as much to do with Hruska's unusually narrow 1970 winning vote (53 percent) as the celebrated movie chain case.

The Conservative Image, Public Power, and the Unicameral

One Nebraska newspaperman startled me by suggesting that his state was "the Mississippi of the North"; as proof he pointed to a predilection for minimal government, a fear of outside influences, and insularity common to both states. There is little difference (except on an occasional civil rights vote), he suggested, between Mississippi's Sen. James Eastland and the two unflinching conservatives Nebraska sends to the United States Senate, Hruska and Curtis; all three, he said, vote alike on economic and social issues and were "hawks" on the Vietnam war. With an equally conservative U.S. House delegation, my newspaper friend said, Nebraska must be considered an essential state for the coalition of Southern Democrats and conservative Republicans in Congress.* Senator Curtis himself has described his home state as "the most conservative in the Union."

But what then of the two great Nebraska reforms instituted with Senator Norris's backing—the unicameral nonpartisan legislature and public power? Don't these refute the conservative Nebraska image? On closer examination one learns that they really do not.

The unicameral legislature was proposed in the early 1930s when Nebraska was in the grip of drought and depression. Its frugal citizens had just finished paying for the construction of their magnificent skyscraper Capitol in Lincoln on a pay-as-you-go basis over 10 years, and the unicameral appealed mightily as a way to cut down on state government expenses; as John N. Norton, the man who worked the longest for unicameral, declared, it would "save time, talk, and money." Senator Norris's strong personal campaign for unicameral helped; so did the fact that on the same day in 1934 that unicameral was up for a vote of the people, they also had to decide on legalizing parimutuel betting and beer drinking. Proponents of the measures adopted a "vote for all three" slogan, and all three won, unicameral by a vote of 286,086 to 193,152.

Nor has the unicameral legislature thwarted the special interests as Norris hoped it would. ("I congratulate you," Norris said in an address to the first session of the unicameral in 1937. "Every professional lobbyist, every professional politician, and every representative of greed and monopoly is hoping and praying that your work will be a failure.") The most significant element of the system is not its unicameralism, but the fact that the 49 "senators" are elected on a nonpartisan basis. Thus there are no party leaders to set

* His analysis was made, however, before the 1970 elections, when Nebraska elected two more moderate and vigorous House members—Republicans John Y. McCollister, an Omaha businessman, and Charles Thone, a Lincoln attorney and protegé of Hruska. McCollister is considered the heir apparent to Curtis, and Thone a not unlikely successor when Hruska retires.

priorities and put a quiet kibosh on bad bills; in effect each man is his own party, and logrolling is rampant.

Under the old bicameral-partisan system, 15 to 35 percent of the bills introduced might be passed in any particular year; under unicameral, two-thirds of the measures proposed are regularly passed, and the governor is reluctant to veto even the bad ones for fear of offending individual senators. A minor example, from the 1969 session: a bill to require *licensing* of landscape gardeners. The lobbies work smoothly: for instance, the education lobby can count on 30-plus votes for any measure it advocates, the truckers 13 votes, labor eight votes. The Farm Bureau gets its way on about two out of every three bills affecting its interests. The unicameral nonpartisan system, one lobbyist has said, "is beautiful—you only have to buy 25 votes."

The relationship between lobbyists and senators is a close and warm one, according to a survey made in 1967 by University of Nebraska political scientist Bernard D. Kolasa. Many ex-legislators become lobbyists, and lobbyists frequently run for and win seats in the legislature. Legislators depend heavily on lobbyists for information and research and welcome their presence in the legislative halls. And in a complete reversal of what Norris had hoped for, two-thirds of the lobbyists said they liked the nonpartisan system and would not want to substitute a conventional partisan legislature. (The political parties disagree: both have adopted platform planks calling for a partisan system. But to date they have not pushed hard enough to get the change made.)

One must recognize several positive features of Nebraska's unicameral system, even though they all seem more procedural than substantive: bills cannot be stalled by petty bickering between two chambers, for instance; committee work is not duplicated; almost all bills introduced get a public hearing. An interesting experiment would be for some state to try a *partisan*, unicameral legislature.

Public power, the second Nebraska reform pointed to as evidence of progressive spirit, has been going strong since the 1930s and indeed has given Nebraska some of the lowest power rates in the nation. No one now suggests going back to private power. But the fact is that public power evolved not because of distrust of the private power interests or a desire for cheap power for all the people. Rather, the drought-plagued farmers sitting in the legislature at the depth of the depression voted for public power so that they could get the federal government to finance irrigation for their fields; the vehicle that would accomplish that goal—large reservoirs that would also have hydroelectric generating capacity—was in many ways incidental.

Thus neither the unicameral nonpartisan legislature nor public power appear to qualify Nebraska as a specially progressive state. Conservative rule —usually Republican, occasionally Democratic—has been the dominant theme of Nebraska politics for many decades. Since 1940 there has been a steady chain of GOP Presidential victories, broken only by the Goldwater debacle of 1964. Nebraska's performance in the 1968 and 1972 Presidential elections, when she gave Richard Nixon 59.8 and 70.3 percent of her vote—16.4 and 9.5 percentage points, respectively, above his national scores—was not a bad measure of her basic political outlook. Republicans have held the governorship for all but eight of the past 30 years; when Nebraskans did elect Democratic governors, it turned out that a major part of their appeal was a conservatism that exceeded even that of their Republican election opponents.

But all we have said to this point of Nebraska's conservatism and resistance to change is only prelude to a new episode, starting in the mid-1960s, when Nebraska would move into a period of rapid change and adjustment to the modern world. Ironically, the man to spark the new change was not a Democrat of Ted Sorensen's stripe but a Republican who defeated Sorenson's own brother to win the governorship in 1966.

Of Timid Government, a Man Named Morrison, Taxes and Tiemann

By the early 1960s, some of the harsh realities of budget balancing in postwar America were pressing in on Nebraska. The cost of every phase of government was rising, inflation posed special problems, it was clear that state aid to education would have to be instituted to prevent disaster at the local school level. Except for nuisance taxes (cigarettes, liquor, etc.) and one of the country's highest gasoline taxes, Nebraska government survived up to the mid-1960s on one tax alone, the property tax—the tax which responds most slowly of all to inflation. Every expert said Nebraska had no alternative: she must either move to a sales tax, or an income tax, or both.

But the thrifty Nebraskans resisted, as they have resisted every expansion of government since their state began. Consider the tortuous process by which Nebraska got a state government at all. In 1864 Congress decided it was time to consider admitting Nebraska to the Union and actually passed an enabling act. A constitutional convention was called in Omaha. But the convention, as soon as it had completed its organization, voted to "adjourn sine die, without forming a constitution." The reason? History records that the delegates simply wanted to avoid the expense of having a state government.

Two years later, in 1866, the territorial legislature had a change of heart and did draft a constitution. In order to forestall objections to the increased expense, the document provided for the barest framework of government, the fewest possible officers, the lowest salaries, and the most meager functions. After a heated campaign, the people approved it. The vote: 3,938 in favor: 3,838 opposed. Such was the mandate by which Nebraska first decided to take on the responsibilities of self-government and statehood.

The situation was not altogether different in the 1960s. In the governor's chair sat the hulking form of Democrat Frank B. Morrison, a big bear of a man with a unique "plain folks" rapport with the voters. A fiscal conservative described by some critics as "a Copperhead Democrat of the Grover Cleveland stripe," Morrison was a great fence-straddler and had a predisposition to appointing study committees to blunt the edge of any issue. Even when he considered taking a strong hand, Morrison was discouraged by the Republican hold on the technically nonpartisan legislature.*

At the same time, even while the state's budget crisis boiled to a head, Morrison was torn between his knowledge that the state needed new taxes as desperately as the voters wanted to resist them. In his successful 1964 election campaign, Morrison did bring himself to say that he would not veto a broad-based tax if the legislature passed one. But his heart was not in it.

Then, to everyone's amazement, the legislature in 1965 did indeed vote an income tax, the first in Nebraska's history. It would completely replace the state property tax. Morrison was suddenly where he desired passionately not to be: on the spot. He first said he would veto the legislation because of a technical flaw; then protax senators and the lieutenant governor of the moment, liberal Democrat Philip C. Sorensen, brother of Ted, physically held the bill back from the governor until they could pass other legislation to perfect the flaw and deprive Morrison of his veto excuse. Morrison let the tax bill become law without his signature; then he signed a referendum petition to repeal it.

The following election would not have just one tax question on the ballot, however. Spokesmen for well-heeled political conservatives had organized the campaign to invalidate the new income tax; now farmers, who bore the brunt of the existing property tax, drummed up an initiative for a constitutional amendment to bar the state from taxing property. The result was predictable: Nebraskans voted for both propositions, repealing the new income tax law and forbidding the state property tax forevermore. Nebraska was left with no general tax law at all, and it was up to the next legislature to untangle the mess.

On the same day in November 1966 that the voters said no to both taxes, they also elected a new Governor. He was a man few of them had even heard of two years before: Norbert T. Tiemann, a 42-year-old banker from the little farm town of Wausa (population 724) in northeast Nebraska. The Tiemann story is worth telling, for it shows that things may not be what they seem, even in the quietest and most conservative of states.

"Nobby" Tieman grew up in dust bowl days in a little Nebraska town where his father, a Lutheran minister, often ended up making no more than five dollars a week. After service in the Pacific in World War II, he returned to finish up at the University of Nebraska, tried his hand as a county agent, even played semipro baseball for a time, and then traveled around the United

* Morrison had little appetite for partisan politics anyway. He failed to bring any appreciable amount of bright, young Democrats into state politics while he was governor; in fact, many of his appointments to judgeships and state posts were Republicans. The condition of the Democratic party after Morrison left office was such that the following joke was circulating in the state: The suggestion is made to a politician that he ought to "capture the Democratic party." His reply: "That would be like kidnapping a corpse."

Oddly enough, Morrison showed up in 1972 as campaign chairman for George McGovern in the Nebraska Presidential primary. This oddity was explicable only when one knew that McGovern had come to Nebraska to help Morrison raise funds to run against Roman Hruska for the Senate two years earlier. Two of McGovern's most skillful young political operatives, Gene Pokorny and Lou Lamberty, had worked in Morrison's campaign and developed the advertising campaign which drew attention to the rather liberated films being shown in Hruska's movie-house chain.

States as head of industry relations for the National Livestock and Meat Board. In 1954 the death of his father-in-law left the only bank in Wausa without executive leadership; Tiemann was offered and accepted the presidency on the agreement he could buy controlling interest.

Bank examiners were soon shaking their heads over the Tiemann tactics. Throwing overboard typical bankers' conservatism, he called in farmers to ask why they didn't want to borrow more money. Tiemann had noted that the local farmers were simply raising grain and shipping it out, leaving them idle in winter; the economy was declining and young people were leaving town. So Tiemann offered to finance up to 100 percent of the cost of livestock for feeding; "we actually begged farmers to take money to buy cattle." The tactic worked: soon the Wausa bank had over 80 percent of its deposits out on loan, compared to a Nebraska bank average of 43 percent (causing no little consternation in state banking circles). Within a decade, millions in new income had poured into Wausa, its main street was prospering again, and the average age of the farmers had dropped from 55 to 44 years, well below state and national averages.

Tiemann eventually became president of the Nebraska Bankers Association, getting limited statewide exposure, and in 1965 began thinking of running for governor. He was troubled in large part by Nebraska's economic shortcomings, just as he had been by Wausa's; some research demonstrated not only the state's miserable performance in state aid to education but also that it ranked 47th among the 50 states in research grants and 50th in defense and aerospace research—even though Senator Curtis sat on the Senate Space Committee.

Tiemann's soundings among Republican professionals about a 1966 governorship race were discouraging; most of the pros were preparing to and later did support Val Peterson, a governor of the first postwar decade and former ambassador to Denmark. But Tiemann put together his own organization, mostly young people without earlier political experience. Then he spent $50,000 of his own money on a blitz campaign to get his name known in the state; by the time Peterson finally announced, Tiemann had made his 100th speech. Tiemann brought to the campaign not only tenacity, but other attractive political attributes: he was tall (six feet, three inches), masculine, confident, aggressive, handsome, and could make sense on issues to almost any audience he encountered. In an amazing upset, he defeated Peterson in the primary with 15,000 votes to spare.

The Republican primary hurdle behind him, Tiemann's toughest job was done. Governor Morrison was running for the U.S. Senate, and the Democratic gubernatorial nominee—Lt. Gov. Philip Sorensen—was a prominent liberal in a basically conservative, Republican state. Tiemann won 61.5 percent of the vote, a plurality of over 112,000.

Tiemann appealed to the Nebraska temperament in his campaign with a conservative overlay of talk about introducing business efficiency and principles into state government. Sorensen's forthright stand for a combined sales-income tax permitted Tiemann, with political safety, to say he would back a broadened state tax if the voters rejected both taxes pending in the referendum.

Few Nebraskans, however, really expected radical change under this small-town banker. Thus the astonishment was all the greater when, within a few months of taking office, Tiemann had done the hitherto impossible: won passage of a sales-income tax package from the legislature. An entirely new financial base for the Nebraska state government was created as the state property tax passed into history. On the scale of tax effort—per capita state *and* local taxes in relation to personal income—the state rose from a rank of about 40th in the United States to 27th within the first two years of Tiemann's adminisration.

Using a sometimes heavy hand, Tiemann and the young men of his administration got a lot of other changes through the legislature as well. A proposal allowing limited bonding for highways was passed on to the voters for approval in 1968, the first break in Nebraska's archaic $100,000 limit on bonded indebtedness. State aid to local school districts, dropped at the turn of the century, was reinstated. Major increases were also made in the higher education budget. Reforms in the mental health and retardation fields, including decentralization of treatment facilities, were begun. A little Hoover Commission was established by executive order. A new state department of economic development was established. And an extraordinarily broad open-housing bill, pushed vigorously by Tiemann, was approved in 1969. For Nebraska, it was an amazing performance.*

Tiemann's performance did not please all Nebraskans; some of the most vigorous dissenters were in his own party, and his refusal to declare for Nixon cost him a seat on the state's delegation to the 1968 Republican National Convention. In the 1969 legislature Tiemann got a taste of old Cornhusker conservatism when the lawmakers, riding a wave of so-called "law and order" sentiment, passed a constitutionally dubious self-defense measure to free citizens of all legal jeopardy for taking any action necessary to protect themselves or their property against theft or assault. Tiemann called it a "shoot-your-neighbor bill" and "vigilante law enforcement" and vetoed it; the legislature promptly overrode him. (In a bicameral legislature, incidentally, such a bill might well have been waylaid before original passage. Several persons attempted to invoke the new law as a murder defense, but it was declared unconstitutional by the Nebraska supreme court.)

A remarkable testament to Tiemann came from a former staff member of Governor Morrison with whom I spoke in 1969. "Tiemann," he said, "has been an exceptional and courageous governor and good for the state of Nebraska. If he's defeated next time, it will be because he did the right things."

His words proved to be strangely prophetic. In the 1970 primary, Tie-

* This account is not intended to downgrade some major breakthroughs in Nebraska government before Tiemann took office; the 1965 legislature session, for instance, voted a modernized system of central budgeting, accounting, and payrolling for the state government, considered far more advanced than most states. In a sense, Nebraska was so far behind in many fields that when it did move, it could avoid the mistakes of others and go to model-type systems. Its income and sales taxes, for instance, are models in coverage and in their cheap cost of administration.

mann was challenged by an archconservative state senator from Omaha and wealthy businessman, Clifton Batchelder—the man who had authored the unlimited self-defense bill passed over Tiemann's veto. The main issue, though, was state spending: Batchelder pointed out it had risen some 25 percent, to $355 million a year, under Tiemann, and that the tax per person had almost doubted, from $87 to $150. Batchelder's message to obsessively thrifty Nebraska: cut back both expenditures and taxes. Tiemann replied that the increased government had "put Nebraska on the go," and pointed to more money spent on schools, roads and medical facilities. In 1968–69, Tiemann said, per capita income in the state had grown 12.5 percent, the most of any state in a single year in the 1960s.

Tiemann won the primary—but by a bare 8,000 votes, softening him up for the general election, when he faced J. James Exon, a seller of office equipment from Lincoln and a man philosophically well to the right of Tiemann. Exon attacked Tiemann for "taking Nebraska down the road to blank check spending" and promised to hold the line on the sales-income tax rates. It was just what Nebraskans wanted to hear. A measure of arrogance and aloofness in Tiemann's personality also contrasted unfavorably with Exon's more folksy manner. Democrat Exon ended up winning by a 46,558 margin vote and Tiemann's political career seemed at an end—too early, too disturbing, too brash, it seemed, for rigidly conservative Nebraska.

In office, Exon deferred to the legislature more often than Tiemann had, fought to keep welfare costs down,* and stressed rural development programs. He did not attempt to repeal the sales or income taxes, but he did try—albeit unsuccessfully—to have the 2.5 percent sales tax on food repealed. The 1972 legislature session attempted a sudden leap to sound financing by passing a bill under which the state would have paid two-thirds of all local school costs (about $160 million a year, instead of the existing $35 million aid figure). The measure would also have limited local property taxes. But it involved an increase in the state sales and income taxes, and Exon vetoed it. Exon might best be characterized as a caretaker governor—but one popular with the "little man."

Nebraskan Land and Water, "Agribusiness," and the Economy

Still unmatched for their history, folklore, customs, and fascinating miscellanea about the states are the 1930s-vintage individual state volumes prepared by the Federal Writers' Project of the Works Progress Administration.

* Nebraska ranks only 44th in the U.S. in per capita expenditures for welfare. The state for several years refused to raise benefits for dependent children in relation to rising living costs, as required by 1967 federal legislation. For this reason, a complete cutoff in federal assistance payments was threatened during Exon's first months in office. Exon and conservative forces in the legislature agreed to the legislation Washington wanted to see pass but were then taken aback when the legislature also appropriated money for increased welfare benefits by such a wide margin (over two-thirds) that it was not subject to a governor's veto. Later, Exon effectively undid this generous action by administratively reducing benefits to dependent children on welfare.

The volumes do, of course, suffer from the dated nature of much information: the reader of *Nebraska—A Guide to the Cornhusker State* would do well to recheck the report that Omaha is served by 10 railroads, that exactly 12 passenger and mail planes land at the airport each day, that the taxi fare starts at 10 cents, and that three streetcar tokens cost 25 cents.

The WPA volumes were a make-work project, and the solo writer of a volume like this one may be excused a moment of envy when he reads that more than a hundred writers and researchers were called into federal service for two years to write the Nebraska chapter alone. But, like many of the state books, the Nebraska chapter—as Alfred Kazin has written of the whole series —"resulted in an extraordinary contemporary epic." * Consider these lines from the volume, by Addison E. Sheldon, then superintendent of the Nebraska Historical Society:

> Some of us in Nebraska know what it is to have made the first wagon track across an unbroken sea of grass into a new land, with no guide but the sun, the distant hilltops, and our own resolution.

And for a quick grasp of the state's face and character—perhaps because it has really changed so little—these paragraphs would be hard to improve on:

> The traveler crossing Nebraska gets an impression of broad fields, deep skies, wind, and sunlight; clouds racing over prairie swells; herds of cattle grazing on the sandhills; red barns and white farmhouses surrounded by fields of tasseling corn and ripening wheat; windmills and wire fences; and men and women who take their living from the soil.
>
> Statehood came in 1867, and many of the old inhabitants can remember the land before it was touched by the ploughshare. Corn grows on slopes where buffalo once grazed. Tractors pull plows and harrows over land where the war whoops of Sioux and Pawnee once echoed. . . . Graves mark the routes of the great overland trails.
>
> Here the Middle West merges with the West. The farms and small towns in the eastern half suggest the rich, more densely populated country of Iowa and Illinois. The cities have much of the fast tempo and businesslike ways that prevail in the larger cities of the Midwest. But, in western Nebraska, fields give way to the great cattle ranches of the Sandhill area, life is more leisurely and manners are more relaxed. Something of the Old West still survives—a cowboy riding hard against the sky, a herd of white faces coming down from the hills to water, bawling calves at branding time. . . .

Set astride the 98th Meridian like its Plains neighbors, the Dakotas to the North and Kansas to the South, Nebraska has the familiar pattern of a moist east and a semiarid west. The 60-mile wettest strip on its east, separated from Iowa by the Missouri River, is where Nebraska grows most of its corn and feeds most of its cattle and hogs; then there is a transitional strip until one reaches the arid, short-grass country of the west, devoted to wheat and grazing. Coursing from west to east across Nebraska and joining the Missouri near Omaha is the Platte River, its valley a fertile, irrigated strip in which corn, sugar beets, potatoes, or beans can be grown even in the driest

* The volumes are presently being updated and reissued by Hastings House, and the whole story of the Federal Writers' Project has been told by Jerre Mangione in a new book, *The Dream and the Deal* (Little, Brown, 1972).

regions. In all America, Nebraska ranks sixth in farm income (over $2 billion a year); her cattle herds, from which 3.5 million marketings are made yearly, are so extensive that only three states rank higher; she is sixth in hogs, fourth in winter wheat and rye, fifth in corn and alfalfa. More than three-quarters of her farm income comes from livestock.

"Agribusiness," indeed, is what Nebraska chiefly lives on; some 14 million acres are under cultivation in addition to the great ranches, some as large as 120,000 acres, where one to two million Angus and Herefords graze over the Sandhills. Nebraska's interior ranchers and farmers are some of the most brilliant business operators in the state, observing the latest scientific and technological applications to increase yields, livestock poundage, and profits. In the manner in which they accept large risks of borrowing short-term capital, they are polished gamblers. Their business acumen, in fact, puts them light-years ahead of their small-town cousins in business.

Nebraska's thick rug of alluvial soil is her most significant asset. Agriculture supports, directly or indirectly, about 85 percent of the population. The state's natural resources (chiefly oil in the southwest corner) are meager indeed. There are scarcely any scenic attractions to draw visitors, though many come to participate in the excellent game hunting. Some have suggested that if it had not been for Nebraska's central continental position, the chief factor in the Union Pacific's decision to put its first transcontinental line through her rolling prairies, the state might have remained "the abode of perpetual desolation" it was described as in an Army Engineers' report of 1820.

Next to land, water is doubtless Nebraska's most important asset. Most of the water is underground, but it is a fantastic resource: an estimated 547 trillion gallons, or enough to cover the entire state to a depth of 34 feet if pumped up. Some of this water has already been tapped for irrigation purposes; together with the water gathered by dams for flood control, power generation, and irrigation, it should (with proper management) assure an adequate supply for the state's agricultural and industrial growth well into the 21st century. Some 2,500,000 acres of Nebraskan farmland are now irrigated —third highest among the states. Floods are still a great menace to some parts of Nebraska, but less so as the Missouri Valley and Republican River dam systems are completed and other flood control projects along the Platte come to fruition.

Nebraska factory jobs, chiefly related to agriculture, have been growing and in the late 1960s outstripped actual farm employment for the first time. Value added by manufacturing exceeds $1 billion a year. Some of the new factories have been in fields like electronic component assembly and garment production, providing low-income employment in which women fill most of the jobs. Others in variegated fields, including everything from church furniture to playground equipment, have been godsends for the little farm communities in which they have settled. For example, the town of Cozad, on the Platte River in western Nebraska, attracted a shock absorber plant of the Monroe Auto Equipment Company. It provided 835 jobs, the weekly payroll totaling $70,000. As a result, Cozad grew in population from 3,184 to 4,219 during the 1960s, a rise of 32.5 percent while most of the towns in its part of the state were in rapid decline. Without the factory, according to W. E. Young, president of a local bank, "We'd have just shriveled up and blown away."

Yet, on a broad scale, Nebraska has been unsuccessful in attracting the quality and quantity of industries to hold its rural and small-city population. Governor Tiemann acknowledged that many businessmen he met on industrial recruitment tours were likely to comment, "Oh, Nebraska is one of the states we always fly over." The state's economic liabilities seem as formidable as they are legion: a lack of risk capital and refusal of the small-town bankers, who represent a potent political force, to loan out a very high percentage of their deposits; long distances to any major markets; a lack of any comprehensive scientific and research base to attract sophisticated industries; absence of a diverse cultural or social environment that could draw or keep young executives and scientists. Some believe that the right-to-work laws of states like Nebraska may scare off some new businesses, since they may fear having to repeat the fights over basic union status that they settled long ago in the industrial Midwest and East.* Employers are attracted by tax breaks communities are able to give them, by the cheerful and positive attitude of workers, and their willingness to work for substantially less than workers demand and get in the heavily industrialized Eastern and Great Lakes states. But if cheap and willing labor were an all-answer cure in attracting industry, Nebraska would have done a lot better before now.

Strategic Air Command headquarters, the place from which the command would go forth if the United States were to launch an airborne nuclear attack, is located at Offutt Air Force Base, south of Omaha. There are some 32,000 servicemen and their dependents in Nebraska, and they account for no small part of the state's economy, spending more than $100 million each year, principally in the Omaha area. Early in the 1960s, the Lincoln Air Force Base was closed down as part of the phase-out of the B-45 bomber; some city fathers foresaw economic ruin with the shutdown and fought tooth-and-nail to stop it; actually, the town survived the closing quite successfully.

The Character Born of Adversity

Westward-bound prairie schooners were making their way across Nebraska on the Oregon and Mormon Trails years before the Civil War. But

* Nebraska got a dose of militant unionism in 1969–70 when the Amalgamated Meat Cutters and Butcher Workmen of North America (AFL-CIO) went on strike against the Iowa Beef Packers of Dakota City, demanding a "master butcher" salary of $3.53 an hour for all their workers after the company automated its production line. (Journeymen butchers earn about a dollar less.) In one of the bitterest U.S. labor disputes since the 11-year dispute against the Kohler Co. of Wisconsin in the early postwar years, Iowa Beef hired guards and police dogs, built a four-foot-deep split trench around its 150-acre facility, and then began to hire Mexican-Americans from Texas and California to break the strike, constructing a complete "company town" within the factory compound to house them. The strike was marked by 56 bombings, more than 200 tire slashings, and more than 20 shootings including one fatality. After seven months, the union settled for only 20 cents an hour more than the company had first offered, without equal pay for the journeymen butchers. Iowa Beef would have liked to squeeze out the union altogether, but at least it held labor costs low enough so that it could continue to earn profits far above industry averages from its highly automated production lines.

earnest settlement of the future state of Nebraska did not begin until the 1860s with passage of the Homestead Act of 1862 and the construction of the Union Pacific across her prairies. Two great strains of settlement appeared: veterans of the Grand Army of the Republic, and hardy settlers from abroad —chiefly Germany, but also great numbers from Scandinavia and Czech lands. The Yankee settlers tended to dominate the public life of the young state and set its early priority on education. The other immigrants, many of them plain folk who had hurried through the coastal cities to find their place on the free prairie, were thrifty, religious, conservative. Many communities were so isolated that they carried on Old World languages and customs for decades.

Yankee or European, though, all learned in short order how arduous life could be in a sod hut on the short-grass prairie, a kind of life immortalized by Willa Cather, a Red Cloud, Nebraska, girl, in novels like *O Pioneers!*, *My Antonia*, and *A Lost Lady*. The story of the early cattlemen and the Indians was captured vividly by a Nebraskan novelist, Mari Sandoz, of *Old Jules* fame. The 1870s brought infestations of grasshoppers that stripped Midwestern fields bare; whole herds of cattle were frozen to death in the blizzard and sleet storms of the 1880–81 winter; many a settler family gave up the fight and headed back east in its prairie schooner.

The World War I boom was followed by farm depression; most thought recovery had come by 1929, with corn at 67 cents a bushel and wheat at a dollar. Three years later, corn was down to 13 cents, wheat to 27 cents, hogs down from $8.20 to $2.30 in the worst farm disaster of American history. And the drought which struck in 1930 stayed for a decade; the soil dried up, and remorseless winds blew it away, creating darkness at midday. In 1934 there were 10 consecutive days of heat above 100 degrees, killing many cattle. The grasshoppers returned; hundreds of banks failed; nearly 100,000 Nebraskans were on relief. Pathetic photographs still record scenes like a farmer from Arcadia, Nebraska, burned out by the drought, starting back to Indiana with his horse and an ox pulling a wagon with all his earthly belongings.

Since the disaster of the 1930s, when millions of acres of farmland topsoil were blown away, an extensive program of soil erosion control has been undertaken; the methods include terracing, strip cropping, contouring, crop rotation, and the like. But the weather can still strike with sudden terror and elemental violence; in 1949 one of the worst blizzards on record swept the western two-thirds of the state; in May of 1953 the little town of Hebron was virtually leveled by a tornado; other possibilities are hail, cloudbursts, violent thunderstorms, and floods; yet it is only fair to say that one of the continent's most beautiful sights is a prairie sunset stretching across a limitless horizon with its hues of violent red and purple advancing into night.

Many think that Nebraska weather—or having endured it—is the reason that Nebraska (1) leads all states in the percentage of its young men who pass the full complement of mental and physical tests given by the Selective Service, and (2) can boast a remarkable health record, including the next to the lowest infant mortality rate in the U.S.A., and an exceptional resistance rate to virtually all the classic modern diseases. A stretch of Nebraska prairie south of the Platte River, in fact, is the most healthful place in the entire United States; if you live there you have a statistically demonstrable better chance than other Americans of escaping heart disease, a stroke, or even lung cancer. The whole Great Plains area tends to be the most healthful in America, but Nebraska more than any other. And the phenomenon is not entirely rural; in Lincoln, for instance, the rate of fatal coronaries in the adult white male population is only half that of the placid city of Augusta, Georgia.

Holiday magazine sent a reporter out to Nebraska's health belt to try to discover a reason; she came back quite baffled, reporting Nebraskans work as long as anyone else, that "the diet alone would drive any self-respecting cardiologist mad," that a goodly number of people smoke cigarettes, that they get about as much physical exercise as other Americans. The best answer to the riddle I have found was in a dry report by a Nebraska political scientist, Dr. James Maynard: "Life in Nebraska was extremely rugged, both physically and emotionally, up to the 1950s and the parental stock . . . have met and survived some of the most basic laws of nature."

In other words, a sheer rule of survival of the fittest has been at work; those who made it through drought, plague, blizzard, and storm without quitting are the Nebraskans of today. The weak bodies have left; the rugged individualists, or their children, are the remnant. If there is validity in this, then, some observations about the Nebraskan character are easier to understand.

By general consensus, the Nebraskan's characteristics are sturdy independence, personal strength, essential caution, a common sense approach. The state was settled, one native pointed out to me, by boomers, people with great expectations. The agricultural depressions, he said, scared out the optimists and builders and retained the conservators—those who buy property and hold it (an especially favorite German trait). Combine that with a dash of embittered agrarianism springing from the old feeling of exploitation by Eastern bankers and outside milling interests, add the fact that Nebraskans have inbred and received few outside population infusions for two generations, and the components of the Nebraskan personality begin to emerge. Economically this means: don't overextend yourself, keep taxes down, be cautious. Politically it means: I've always done for myself, so should other folks; government should stay away from giveaways; or, as a slogan printed on the taxicabs in Lincoln proclaims: "Beat Poverty the American Way—Go to Work." Socially it means: enjoy the company of people like you, whose parents may well have known your parents; avoid flashiness and drugs and hippies; join clubs like the Elks and Moose and Odd Fellows for socializing and good works; but don't worry if blacks and Mexicans are somehow excluded. This reporter's impressions mesh closely with those of a New York *Times* reporter dispatched to Grand Island, Nebraska, to gauge the mood of the people: "The people," he said, "work hard, pay their bills, go to church, spank their children when they think they deserve it, live longer than most Americans, love football and generally believe their way of life is better than any other."

It is correct that no discussion of the Cornhusker personality would be complete without mentioning football. The sport is almost an obsession in Nebraska; the stadium of the "Big Red" at the University in Lincoln has 68,000 seats, more than Yankee Stadium (and is being expanded!); every football game—against such top competition as Oklahoma, Minnesota, and Southern California—has been sold out for years. Football has played a central role in Nebraska life for decades—in fact, ever since the 1920s, when the Cornhuskers turned out to be the only team able to vanquish Knute Rockne and his Four Horsemen. As *Life* has noted, "football has been the Nebraska idiom, the bright thread of pride that could lighten even the burdens of drought and Depression. Football Sundays are red-and-white sabbaths: Omaha lawyers and ranchers from Chadron recite a shared litany of the team's past glories. School boys and farm wives know every word to *Dear Old Nebraska U.*" The ecstasy was never greater than in January 1972, when the Cornhuskers beat Alabama in the Orange Bowl, their second straight national championship and 32nd game without a loss in over three years.

Nebraskans also love rodeos, their annual cornhusking contest, and the state fair at Lincoln—one of America's great agricultural shows. They would have one remember that their state was not only the home of Norris and Bryan, but also of Dean Roscoe Pound of the Harvard Law School, General John Joseph Pershing, General Alfred M. Gruenther, the Reverend Edward Joseph Flanagan (founder of Boys Town at Omaha), and Loren Eiseley (an outstanding American humanist-naturalist-essayist).

Also born in Nebraska was Susette La Flesche (Bright Eyes), an Omaha Indian artist who became a prominent publicist for her race before her death in 1903. Bright Eyes' talents could be used today. Her Omaha Tribe has made great efforts to improve itself, but many of its people still live in old, collapsing huts and houses with no fuel save for corn cobs; many burn to death in the winters. Grinding poverty and deprivation is likewise to be found on the Winnebago Indian Reservation in northeast Nebraska, but options are limited for a Winnebago Indian who tries to drink his sorrows away; signs can still be found in the local taverns reading "No Indians Allowed."

In 1972 one of the most celebrated modern-day cases of brutalization of an Indian occurred in the little northwest Nebraska town of Gordon. Late one Saturday night, in one of Gordon's poorly lit alleys, several white men abducted 51-year-old Raymond Yellow Thunder, an Oglala Sioux from the reservation in nearby South Dakota. They hauled Yellow Thunder around in the trunk of their car and then stripped him of his trousers and underwear and shoved him onto the dance floor of an American Legion hall. Apparently as a result of his manhandling, Yellow Thunder died several days later from a cerebral hemorrhage, touching off massive demonstrations among Indians. (One result of the incident was that the Oglala Sioux tribe, the nation's third largest with 12,000 members, decided to affiliate with the militant American Indian Movement.) Under pressure from the Indians, local authorities indicted and convicted two Gordon brothers of manslaughter and false imprisonment in the case.

The white man's cold indifference toward Indians is not unique to Nebraska, but it is fair to note that for all the hardy virtues of Cornhuskers, some elements seem less developed in their societal personality. One thinks especially of compassion, generosity, tolerance. Perhaps, as the cruel depression years recede further into history, nature and the times will provide fertile ground for such values as well.

Railroads and the Cities

The essential settlement of Nebraska was accomplished by the railroads; they got the land, laid the lines, and then brought the people to till it. Millions of dollars, in fact, flowed to the railroads in profits from sale of lands the government had given them as inducements to build during the 1860s and 1870s. In the early years, free railroad passes for legislators were a major source of corruption. Two railroads dominated Nebraska's development. The Union Pacific went west from Omaha, its tracks running north of the Platte River and carrying the voice of the Omaha *World-Herald* west toward the Sandhills. The Burlington's tracks were laid south of the river, with Lincoln the principal city and carrying that city's newspapers hundreds of miles west and south. Thus the Platte became Nebraska's most important dividing line. For years, the UP was to control one U.S. Senator, the Burlington the other.

Today, the automobile has freed Nebraska from its dependence on the rails; it is along the right-of-way of the state's sole superhighway, Interstate 80, that Nebraska's modern growth takes place. (The road crosses the Missouri into Nebraska from Council Bluffs, Iowa, connecting Omaha, Lincoln, Grand Island, and North Platte before it heads toward Wyoming and Colorado.) The Platte no longer separates Nebraska as it once did; a more relevant break is between the eastern third of the state, which has Omaha and Lincoln and 70 percent of the people, and the western two-thirds, light on people and heavy on distrust of the cities. There are actually seven counties, all in the Sandhill district in west central Nebraska, with total populations of less than 1,000 people. With a population of 31,269, Grand Island is the largest city west of Lincoln. But it is only 88 miles from Lincoln, and from Grand Island it is another 302 miles to the Wyoming border. In the entire western third of the state, there is no city larger than Scottsbluff (population 14,507).

Omaha, according to the 1970 Census, has 347,328 people, with 79,601 more in its suburbs, a huge metropolis by Plains standards; as some of its partisans proudly point out, it is the biggest city between Chicago and Denver (on an east-west axis) and between Minneapolis and Kansas City (on a north-south axis). If most of Nebraska is static, Omaha is dynamic in comparison; John Gunther found it "one of the most masculine cities in America . . . full of dust, guts, noise and pith," an apt description of a great cattle market and meat-packing center.

The packing plants have fallen on evil days, largely because of their glaring obsolescence; Armour, Cudahy, and Swift have all closed down, costing the city up to 5,000 jobs; many smaller packers, however, are still operating thanks to the city's foresight in floating $6 million in bonds for a treatment plant to handle the packing house waste the federal government said could no longer be pumped into the Missouri River. Some of the most promising new industrial development in Nebraska, including Western Electric, AT&T, and Fruehauf Corp. plants employing some 10,000, have moved into Omaha; the insurance industry flourishes, and the population is rising steadily.

A city of mixed old and new, high-rise and squat industrial, Omaha sits on a wide bend of the Missouri River. In the 1960s, taken aback by corruption in its city government that led to indictment of two city councilmen and a mayor for bribery, Omaha chose as mayor a nonpolitical business type and energetic Dane of generally conservative persuasions, A. V. Sorensen. Sorensen's election began a rebirth for Omaha, but it started in a strange way: he sold City Hall. Actually it was an antiquated 75-year-old building long overdue for replacement. The site was then used by the Woodmen of the World Life Insurance Company to build a handsome $40 million skyscraper, downtown Omaha's first significant building in decades. By the late 1960s, Omaha was in a real business boom.

No Nebraska city is as Catholic or as Democratic as Omaha; the explanation lies with the Irish hired to build the railroad and the Poles and Czechs later imported for the back-breaking physical work in the stockyards. These folk tend to be conservative, as Democrats go, and though the city has a 20,000 Democratic registration edge (in contrast to a GOP statewide margin of 52,000), it rarely votes for candidates other than conservative Republicans for national and state office. In the 1972 Presidential primary, Hubert Humphrey easily defeated George McGovern in Omaha while almost all the rest of Nebraska was going for McGovern. The apparent reasons: heavy AFL-CIO backing for Humphrey, and the heavily Catholic and ethnic complexion of the city. The official Catholic diocese newspaper in Omaha attacked McGovern for his alleged stands on abortion and the legalization of marijuana, obviously hurting his candidacy there.

Some 35,000 Negroes live in Omaha, remnants of the early Union Pacific and stockyard payrolls. Hemmed in by railroad tracks and industry in a rigid ghetto on Omaha's north side, the blacks face the same problems of unemployment, poor housing, and spotty education evident in other big cities. Because of their small numbers, they tended to be invisible until tempers reached a flash point and three days of street riots broke out in 1966. Omaha, which had always insisted it had no race problem, was as taken aback as a parent who discovers his 17-year-old is smoking pot. Mayor Sorensen determined the best answer was to use private money to hire several rebellious young blacks with prison records as "keepers of the peace." A few years later he recalled how "the city council and people gave me hell, but I thought we had to put out the fire first." Youth and employment programs were then instituted, but for three more summers Omaha would "blow" ahead of almost any other American city, and disorders would result in several young blacks being killed by police. And a policeman was killed by a bomb when investigating a phony call about a woman screaming for help.

By the time he retired as mayor in 1969, Sorensen was complaining about polarization of the races or, in his own words, "the inability of black and white communities to stop throwing rocks at each other." He acknowledged that the riots had served to focus attention "on the indignities and needs and frustration and poverty of the black citizen," but said the riots had become counterproductive. In fact, Sorensen, like many whites, was losing patience and had a harsh remedy in mind: "We have just 20 black militants raising hell and actively promoting antagonism to the white community in Omaha. Throw 'em in jail and we'd have peace," Sorensen said.

Mayor Sorensen, just retired from office in 1969, had some of the most candid words I heard anywhere about how modern cities can get help:

> After all is said and done, it takes a mayor who can make love to [the federal bureaucrats], so that they'll really want to write the checks to help you. The governors won't help—they're held down by rural legislators. Senators won't really help—they're preoccupied with national issues. Congressmen are a dime a dozen and don't swing any real weight. So it comes back to the mayor and what he can accomplish on his own.

No one can visit Nebraska without being told of "Ak-Sar-Ben" (Nebraska spelled backwards), a combined civic organization–livestock show operation–Mardi Gras substitute–something-for-everyone-in-the-family type of operation. As its main source of income, this nonprofit, tax-exempt organization runs the Ak-Sar-Ben Race Track for parimutuel betting. Every fall it conducts a coronation carnival complete with king and queen in medieval costumes. Eighteen princesses from Omaha are presented, as well as 18 countesses from neighboring towns (usually described in the press as being of "sturdy Swedish stock.") The king is likely to be one of Nebraska's most powerful men. University of Nebraska Chancellor Clifford M. Hardin was Ak-Sar-Ben king when President Nixon selected him to be Secretary of Agriculture; there was actually some muttering around Omaha that Hardin had permitted himself to be diverted by the cabinet job during his reigning year at Ak-Sar-Ben. Other Ak-Sar-Ben kings have included Peter Kiewit, head of Peter Kiewit Sons' Company, an international construction firm that builds anything from skyscrapers to airfields. Kiewit is a man of immense wealth whose holdings include the pervasively influential Omaha *World-Herald*; he sits on the board of powerful banks and utilities and could well be one of the mightiest behind-the-scenes powers of American state politics if he so chose; actually he is relatively apolitical.

The board of Ak-Sar-Ben—likely to be the sons or grandsons of major local business founders, plus the regional managers of large national firms operating in the city—is likely to include most of Omaha's basic power structure. Acknowledged powers include the heads of the Omaha National Bank board, the Northern Natural Gas Company, the Union Pacific Railroad, and Northwest Bell Telephone. A trend toward political moderation and civic enlightenment, including regular off-the-record dialogue sessions with local black leaders, has been reported among these men in recent years.

The Omaha *World-Herald*, Nebraska's most powerful tone setter, has a huge outstate circulation in addition to its metro area coverage; for most of the postwar years it was a bastion of conservative, insular thinking, offering strong support to men like Butler, Wherry, Curtis, Hruska, and Goldwater. Kiewit outbid newspaper magnate Samuel Newhouse to get control of the *World-Herald* when it was on the selling block in the early 1960s; a heady price of some $40 million had to be paid, however, lest, as some Omaha traditionalists feared, the paper fall into the hands of an out-of-state Jew. In 1964, after praising Goldwater for months, the paper suddenly fell silent on a Presidential preference; later it was rumored (though denied by sources close to the paper) that President Johnson, on a visit to the state, had reminded Kiewit which side his defense contract bread was buttered on.

Even its severest critics were ready to say by the early 1970s that the *World-Herald* had become somewhat more moderate, less antifederal, more pro-civil rights. Many states would envy the comprehensiveness of its news coverage. Two interesting sidelights about the *World-Herald:* it actually has morning and evening editions but never changes its name; almost all its columnists are right of center, but in a "sunrise edition" for Omaha distribution alone, several liberal columnists appear who are not seen in the outside editions for the conservative little towns and farmlands.

Sixty miles to the west of Omaha lies Lincoln, a nice, clean, green, churchy, Protestant-dominated town once lambasted by Willa Cather and other authors for its insularity and smugness. Lincoln has been growing (1970 population 149,518); it lives off the state government, the University of Nebraska, insurance, grain storage, and marketing. Its distinctive landmark is the white shaft of the state capitol, rising 437 feet above the plains and nicknamed, inevitably, "the penis of the prairies." Registration books show a nominal Republican edge, but with its university influence, Lincoln is the most liberal voting community in Nebraska. In the 1972 Democratic Presidential primary, George McGovern won his biggest Nebraska majorities in Lincoln. Two years before, while Exon's antitax and antispending campaign was carrying most areas of Nebraska, he lost badly in Lincoln. As the authors of *The Almanac of American Politics* later wrote, "State employees and academics are not fond of politicians who are eager to cut the budget." The Lincoln *Journal*, a liberal Republican sheet with strong-minded editorial leadership, is second in state circulation to the Omaha *World-Herald*.

The University of Nebraska, 29th largest in the U.S.A. with a total enrollment of 32,000, exercises an awesome influence in the state. There is now a large University branch at Omaha as well as the principal campus at Lincoln. More than a third of the university's budget is for agricultural instruction, research, and extension work, which goes a long way to explaining its popularity with the legislature. Successful football teams and clever political footwork by the chancellor also help.

In January 1971, President Nixon chose the University of Nebraska as the place to deliver a remarkable "hands across the generation-gap" appeal. His address, marking a sharp turn away from the heavy-handed partisanship and antiyouth theme which Republicans had pursued in the 1970 midterm elections, included announcement of a merging of the Peace Corps and VISTA into an expanded volunteer agency to increase the opportunites for public service for American youth. "The destiny of this nation is not divided into yours and ours—it is one destiny," the President said. "I believe one of America's most priceless assets is the idealism which motivates the young people of America. . . . Let us together seek out those ways by which the commitment and the compassion of one generation can be linked to the will and the experience of another, so that together we can better serve America [and] mankind." The occasion was combined, of course, with huzzahs for the unbeaten Nebraska football team, and cynics could say Nixon had picked perhaps the safest campus in America to make his appeal. But in conservative Nebraska, the state which gave Nixon has largest vote shares in both the 1960 and 1968 Presidential elections, it marked a vital turn of policy.

The university has long been a fountainhead of much of Nebraska's literary activity, music, theatre, and art. Painters and sculptors, I heard, prefer the Lincoln milieu to Omaha's, but the difference is being eased by the university's Omaha branch. It is worth recording, in fact, that tough old Omaha fosters a wide range of cultural activities, including a resident symphony orchestra, the Joslyn Art Museum (ostentatiously housed but holding some distinguished works), some new galleries which show work of some prominent young Omaha artists, a community playhouse and ballet society. Midwestern artists, one learns, are more careful, less faddish and experimental than their contemporaries on the coasts; working in a less frenetic atmosphere, they have time to carry out their ideas well.

KANSAS

THE ECLIPSED STATE

"WHEN ANYTHING is going to happen in this country, it happens first in Kansas," William Allen White, fabled editor of the Emporia *Gazette*, once wrote. Kansas, he said, is "hardly a state" but "a kind of prophecy."

On went the list of Kansas firsts: scene of the fiery abolitionist crusades of the 1850s, birthplace of the prohibitionist movement in America, seedbed of the Populist party and embittered agrarian dissent, early and strong adherent of Bull Moose Progressivism.

White wrote between the world wars. Today Kansas is scarcely the place where things happen "first." Indeed, nowhere on the American continent can the eclipse of a region or state as a vital force—a focal point of creative change or exemplar of national life—be felt so strongly and poignantly as in Kansas.

If the Plains States have become an economic and political backwater in the postwar years (a case not difficult to document), then the slide into obscurity is all the more tragic for Kansas, simply because she stood for so much and gave so much to the nation in her earlier years.

In those early decades, for instance, her list of great personalities reflected crucial national movements in each generation:

- John Brown, compelled by some burning inner imperative to free the black slave, drawn from the East to wage a war of cruel retribution against proslave border ruffians who had mistreated his five Kansas emigrant sons. Later executed after his abortive attack on Harper's Ferry, Brown's name and deed would be immortalized by the folksong, "John Brown's body lies a-mouldering in the grave, but his soul goes marching on."

- Sockless Jerry Simpson of Medicine Lodge, Kansas, magnetic Populist leader, champion of the oppressed prairie farmer, enemy of Wall Street and all special privilege, three-term Congressman of the 1890s who said on his deathbed: "Populism will never die—it is a cumulative imagination which shall come again and again." (And who will dispute him?)
- Mary Elizabeth Lease, Populist propagandist who stumped the state telling farmers that "money power" was conspiring to ruin them, a woman best remembered for her incendiary counsel: "Kansas had better stop raising corn and start raising hell."
- Arthur Capper, governor and later U.S. Senator from Kansas, a battler for social reform who fought the unfair practices of natural gas companies, helped write the Volstead Act to enforce Prohibition, and became a leading member of the powerful farm block that dominated Congress in the late 1920s and early 1930s.
- Charles Curtis, part Kansas Indian, longtime U.S. Senator, a serious but losing candidate for the 1928 Republican Presidential nomination; instead he became Herbert Hoover's running mate, sharing in the sweeping victory of 1928 and the ignominious defeat of 1932.
- Alfred M. Landon, resourceful Depression years governor of his state, always for the "little fellow" against the big economic interests, nominated by the Republican party for the Presidency in 1936, winning only Vermont and Maine while Franklin D. Roosevelt swept the rest of the nation (including Kansas).
- William Allen White, whose sharply honed editorials reflected so accurately the depth and tone and spirit of the small-town Kansas he lived in that, through him, Kansas seemed real (and important) to the nation at large.

The Peopling of Kansas

It was only 14 years before William Allen White's birth in 1868 that the Kansas-Nebraska bill repealed the Missouri Compromise and opened the way for proslavers and free staters to fight it out for possession of the new land. In the "Bleeding Kansas" of 1854–57 was held the dress rehearsal for the Civil War; the state's admittance to the Union as a free state in 1861 marked an historic victory for a determined contingent of New England Abolitionists whose fierce piety would dominate Kansas culture for years to come.

As White described the peopling of Kansas:

> We still have in our veins the blood of the New England settlers who came in with the immigrant societies in the fifties and filled the first three eastern tiers of counties. Following the first settlers in the fifties came the young soldiers of the Civil War and their wives seeking free homesteads. They were Union soldiers. They came from the North. They pushed the Yankee blood westward in one great im-

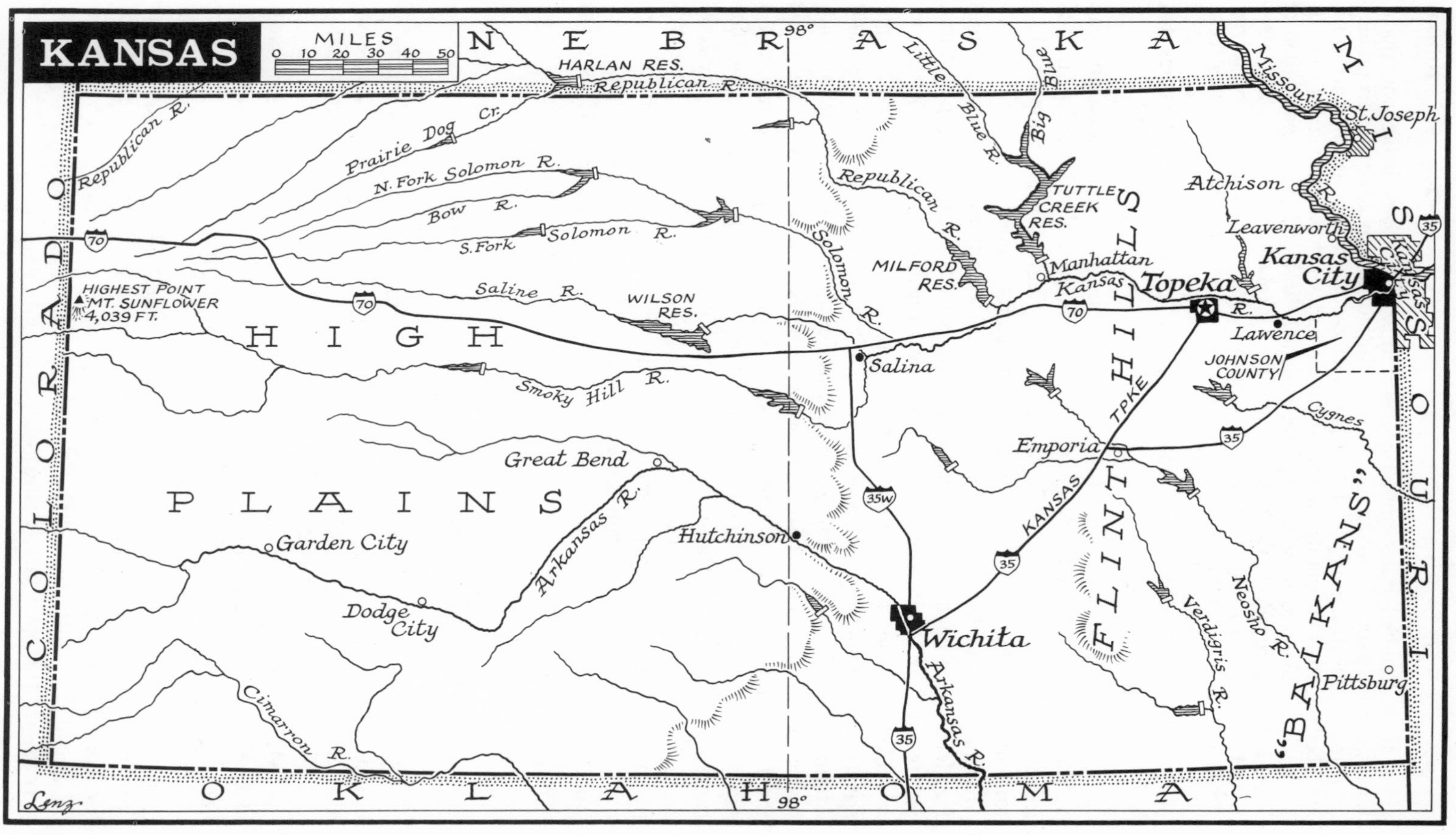
KANSAS
MILES
0 10 20 30 40 50
NEBRASKA
COLORADO
OKLAHOMA
MISSOURI
98°
HIGH PLAINS
FLINT HILLS
"BALKANS"
HARLAN RES.
Republican R.
Prairie Dog Cr.
N. Fork Solomon R.
Bow R.
S. Fork Solomon R.
Saline R.
WILSON RES.
HIGHEST POINT
MT. SUNFLOWER
4,039 FT.
Smoky Hill R.
Great Bend
Garden City
Dodge City
Arkansas R.
Cimarron R.
Hutchinson
Salina
Solomon R.
MILFORD RES.
Little Blue R.
Big Blue
TUTTLE CREEK RES.
Manhattan
Kansas R.
Topeka
Lawrence
JOHNSON COUNTY
Atchison
Leavenworth
Kansas City
Missouri R.
St. Joseph
Emporia
KANSAS TPKE
Cygnes
Wichita
Verdigris R.
Neosho R.
Pittsburg
70
35
35W
Lenz

pulse, three hundred miles from the Missouri border. Then being puritanical, Kansas in 1880 adopted prohibition. More than that, Kansas advertised its prohibition, and in advertising its prohibitory law erected a barrier against the beer drinking, liberty loving immigrants from northern Europe which Kansas needed so badly to enrich her blood as these people have enriched the blood of the population of Minnesota, Wisconsin, Iowa, Nebraska and the Dakotas. So when it came to settling the western part of the state, the semi-arid plains, one of the few foreign strains that came were the Mennonites who came into central Kansas, being teetotalers, and occupied the wheat lands there. With them came turkey red wheat. And up the hill charged a second wave of Kansans in the late nineties to settle lands that had been abandoned by early pioneers.

As colorful as it is, some caveats must be entered to White's analysis. While influential, New Englanders were never numerically dominant; indeed in 1860 there were only 4,208 Kansans of New England birth compared to a total of 78,539 born in other states, the four states immediately to the east—Missouri, Illinois, Indiana, and Ohio—most important among them. Francis H. Heller, vice chancellor for academic affairs of the University of Kansas, points out that White passed too lightly over the history prior to statehood. It took three tries to produce a state constituion, largely because the proslavery and antislavery forces were so evenly matched. "Leavenworth and Atchison," Heller notes, "are to this day as Southern in atmosphere and outlook as if the Mason and Dixon line were at the Nebraska border." And while the Union veterans played a major role in Kansas history, there was also a significant influx of Confederate veterans. Out of Georgia and Arkansas, they came up the valleys of the Arkansas (always pronounced ArKANsas by Kansans), the Neosho and the Marais des Cygnes—and Democratic strength persists to this day along their routes. The legacy of the postwar Confederate migration explains in part the conservative cast of modern Kansas Democrats. And, as we will note later, the diversity of foreign ethnic strains in Kansas was much greater than White's words would lead one to expect.

William Allen White: A Remembrance

As time goes on, White appears more and more as the pivotal figure of Kansas history, the man in whom her strange juices of protest and conservatism, ruralism and wise worldliness, all seemed to have been concentrated—and whose death diminished his home state.

Most of White's childhood was actually spent in the little frontier town of El Dorado, Kansas, some 60 miles from Emporia; visits by Indians, shootings, lynchings, cowboys, open gambling, and wide-open saloons were all part of life in the town. As a boy, White also witnessed the worst of the natural disasters of the frontier. Prairie fires often endangered the settlement. One year the town was completely destroyed by a tornado. Terrible droughts, and then infestations of millions of grasshoppers, came in the 1870s. Throughout his boyhood, White could watch thousands of "mover" wagons carrying settlers toward the open prairie lands of western Kansas.

White's childhood and early professional years also witnessed some of Kansas' historic reforms: state regulation of the freight and passenger rates of the rapacious railroads, an eight-hour labor law, compulsory education, outlawing of child labor, control of oil and gas companies, "blue sky" legislation to control investment companies, banking regulation, and pioneering in women's suffrage.

At the age of 27 White purchased the Emporia *Gazette*; just a year later he wrote the editorial that would make him famous, "What's the Matter With Kansas?" As White saw it then, Kansas' trouble was a surfeit of free silver, Democrats, and hell-raising Populists; under their domination, he said, Kansas had become "poorer and ornerier and meaner than a spavined, distempered mule." In time, though, White decided that what Kansas suffered from was not too much radicalism but too much conservatism. He freely acknowledged his error in condemning the radicals of the 1890s. "The rumps of the seedy farmers sticking out of the courthouse windows, as the Farmers' Alliance met, cast the shadow of a great twilight," White wrote. "Being what I was, a child of the governing class, I was blinded by my birthright."

The first decades of the century would see White become a confidant and publicist of President Theodore Roosevelt and the Progressive movement, bolting his own Republican party to help Roosevelt's Bull Moose effort of 1912. As a reporter he attended the Paris Peace Conference of 1918, then backed American entrance into the League of Nations. When the Ku Klux Klan reared its head in the Kansas of the 20s, White set out to fight it, even by running for governor on an anti-Klan platform.* He helped launch Herbert Hoover's and later Alf Landon's Presidential campaigns; while remaining true to the GOP at election time throughout the 1930s, he did support many New Deal laws to tame monopoly capitalism. Just before World War II, he was an active opponent of isolationism. The Republican party had no more influential and tenacious spokesman for moderation, liberalism, internationalism, and adaptation to changing times.

And yet it was White's special human qualities which gave him the power he had. As the St. Louis *Post-Dispatch* commented on his death, "There was a wonderful kindliness and neighborliness about White, typical of American wilderness days when men in trouble or in want had to lean upon one another." In 1921, White's daughter Mary, only 17, died after a horseback riding accident, and the editorial White wrote for the *Gazette*, picked up and reprinted throughout the land, established his national role as a sensitive interpreter of life. After commenting on Mary White's simple life, her pure, intense, girlish enthusiasms, her fight to get a restroom for the Negro girls at her high school, her father concluded his commentary:

> For her pallbearers only her friends were chosen: her Latin teacher, W.L. Holtz; her High School principal, Rice Brown; her doctor, Frank Foncannon; her friend, W.W. Finney; her pal at the Gazette office, Walter Hughes; and her

* Alf Landon recalls: "In 1924, when I spent a night with the William Allen Whites, as I frequently did in those days, he said: 'I think both the nominees of the Democrat and Republican parties belong to the Klan. I think it's time we count noses. I'm thinking of running for governor on an independent ticket.' I said: 'Go to it. I'll be for you.' He laughed the Klan out of Kansas—and the country generally, I think, also—as a result of that campaign."

brother Bill. It would have made her happy to know that her friend, Charley O'Brien, the traffic cop, had been transferred from Sixth and Commercial to the corner near the church to direct her friends who came to bid her good-bye.

A rift in the clouds in a gray day threw a shaft of sunlight upon her coffin as her nervous, energetic little body sank to its last sleep. But the soul of her, the glowing, gorgeous, fervent soul of her, surely was flaming in eager joy upon some other dawn.

Increasing steadily in influence in Kansas and the nation at large, White lived on for two more decades. Reaching 70 years of age in 1938, he would comment: "I've lived a swell life." Six years later a Chicago *Sun* reporter would end his report of White's own funeral: "In the cemetery, in the dying sun, under the dead trees, William Allen White was only a tired editor gone home to greet his little girl."

Kansas in the Shadows

By the sheer force of his personality and writing, White had kept Kansas' name alive—if no longer as a driving political force, at least as an exemplar of the best of American life—to 1944, the year of his death. Since his passing, Kansas seems to have slipped into the shadows. Occasionally a Kansan name appears in newspaper headlines across the country—Alf Landon making a pronouncement on national policy, or Senator Robert Dole speaking out for the Republican cause. Student unrest at the University of Kansas has received some national notice. But as a general rule, people or events in Kansas are rarely of enough importance to be reported outside the state's borders. Kansas seems to have become an extraordinarily unextraordinary place, unnoticed by most Americans.

Kansans—quite understandably—may take exception to my analysis. After reading an early draft of this chapter, Francis Heller of the University of Kansas wrote: "I think you have very accurately perceived the stagnant mood of the public scene in Kansas today. *I wish you were wrong.*" Perhaps, Heller suggested, Kansas ought to be declared "a national monument, the best source of quality human talent—most of it for export." During the last 20 years, he pointed out, the University of Kansas alone has produced more Rhodes Scholars than any other public university in the country. Today those scholars are "scattered from Boston to Australia." Perhaps, Heller concluded, "Kansas is not the eclipsed state but the exporting state. Somehow, that sounds less depressing."

When one speaks of famous Kansan exports, the name of Dwight David Eisenhower must head the list. Eisenhower spent his boyhood in Abilene, that little Kansas city that had once been the great receiving station for the massive cattle drives from Texas. His military career removed him from the Kansas scene, though he did come back for rather frequent visits. But in Eisenhower's selection for the Republican Presidential nomination in 1952 an important role was played by three Kansans: Roy Roberts, famed editor of the Kansas City *Star*; former Senator and Republican National Committeeman Harry Darby; and Senator Frank Carlson. This Kansas group was instrumental in recruiting Eisenhower to run as a Republican for President that year, and subsequently Roberts was among those who conceived the brilliant strategy—which was probably crucial in the General's nomination—of demanding openly approved rules in an open convention and challenging the rigged Southern delegations for Senator Robert A. Taft. Later, Eisenhower would choose Abilene as the place for his Presidential Library and final resting place, to which he came in 1969. But he had lived so many places, and been away from Kansas so many decades, that no one thought of him primarily as a Kansas President. There was no "Kansas gang" in the White House when he was President, and it will be recalled that Eisenhower chose Gettysburg, Pennsylvania, rather than Abilene, as his home for the last two decades of his life.

Since an aging Arthur Capper stepped down in 1948, Kansas has sent few powerful leaders to Congress. Senator Frank Carlson, whose public service spanned 40 years, was a cautious, hard-working man of conservative-to-moderate views whose high moral standards embodied the best of Kansas' New England heritage, even though his own parents had emigrated from Sweden. Carlson's Senate colleague for many of the postwar years, fellow Republican Andrew F. Schoeppel, was a conservative oil and gas lawyer from Wichita who opposed Eisenhower's foreign aid programs.

Republican Senator James B. Pearson, who succeeded Schoeppel in 1962, is a moderate conservative in the Eisenhower-Carlson tradition. Many of his votes are on the conservative side, but he has fought to reform Senate cloture rules so that filibusters can be broken more easily, and he bucked his own party to oppose the ABM system and voted only with expressed reluctance for some key Nixon appointees, including Clement Haynsworth and G. Harrold Carswell as Justices of the Supreme Court, and Earl W. Butz as Secretary of Agriculture. Robert Dole, who took over Carlson's old seat in 1969, is a tough, ambitious partisan who has single-handedly fought his way up in national politics. He overcame serious wounds he suffered in World War II to become first a state legislator, then a member of the U.S. House for eight years, a Senator, and in 1971, also chairman of the Republican National Committee. Dole attracted little attention during his years in the House, but in the Senate he became a highly articulate, self-appointed defender of the Nixon Administration, flying to the defense of "his President" on issue after issue and showing remarkable skill in debate with his Senate elders.* His selection as Republican National Chairman was initially opposed by moderates like Senate Minority Leader Hugh Scott. Dole served creditably enough as Republican

* Dole's most remarkable coup was in 1970 Senate debate over an amendment to limit American military involvement in Cambodia. Foreign Relations Committee Chairman William J. Fulbright and other war opponents were hoping to curb the Nixon administration by offering an amendment to repeal the Gulf of Tonkin Resolution. Dole upstaged them by offering the repealer himself, pointing out that the administration had said it did not need to rely on the authorization any longer. The Dole amendment passed overwhelmingly, over the querulous opposition of Fulbright, who said his committee's prerogatives had been ignored. Dole also twitted Democratic Presidential hopefuls by suggesting that the Senate set aside a "Presidential hour" for four groups: "First, those Senators who think they are President; second, those Senators who think they should have been President; third, those Senators who think they want to be President; and fourth, for those Senators willing to settle for being Vice President."

Chairman, traveling far and wide for various GOP candidates but playing little role in President Nixon's 1972 reelection campaign, which was run by the separate Committee for the Reelection of the President. He clashed occasionally with Nixon's inner coterie, and was relieved of his chairmanship (sooner than he had wanted) in January 1973.

Dole was reported in some home-state difficulty in the early 1970s, critics charging him with being too "partisan" and "flippant." (Dole's "sharp words and sarcasm," Topeka *Capital-Journal* observed in 1971, represent "an approach that seems to alienate Kansas voters." Some of them were also objecting to Dole on purely personal grounds after he obtained, in 1971, an emergency divorce from his wife of 23 years, the former Phyllis Holden. She had been an occupational therapist who helped to nurse Dole back to health after his wartime wounds and then wrote his notes and exam answers for him so that he could get through college and law school despite his paralyzed right arm. After it was finalized, Mrs. Dole told reporters she had not really wanted the divorce at all.) There was some chance Dole might have difficulty winning reelection in 1974 against a respected moderate like the state's sole Democratic Congressman, William R. Roy, who was building a reputation for his work on health care issues after upsetting a Republican incumbent in 1970.

The Kansas Democrats' most important breakthrough in recent years has been in the governorship. George Docking, a conservative Democrat, was elected in 1956 and 1958, and his equally conservative son, Robert, won election to four terms, starting in 1966—a record unequaled in the state's history. Robert Docking won by holding onto traditional Democratic strongholds in the cities and within organized labor while being sufficiently conservative to sap off some of the normally Republican vote in the rural areas. In 1972, Docking won his fourth term with 63 percent of the vote—the same day Kansans were showing their ticket-splitting adeptness by giving President Nixon 68 percent of their vote, Senator Pearson 72 percent, and Congressman Roy 61 percent. Docking is another possible opponent for Dole in 1974.

With few exceptions, obscurity has been the fate of Kansas' U.S. House delegation, 100 percent Republican in all but five of the 14 postwar Congresses.* Like the Senators, the House members have had the disadvantage of being Republicans in an era when the Democrats controlled Congress.

Few states, in fact, are as consistently Republican as Kansas. The average Republican vote for secretary of state—an essentially anonymous position which the political scientists often pick to gauge a state's basic politics—has been about 58 percent since 1896. Republicans have had overwhelming margins in most Kansas legislatures. Except for 1964, the GOP has won every Presidential election since 1940. Many Kansas Democratic politicians have been in the game for the federal patronage benefits, with little interest in winning locally.

Despite Kansas' general national eclipse of recent decades, a special niche in the hearts of his countrymen has been carved out in his twilight years by

* Kansas had six U.S. House seats until the 1960 Census reapportionment, which reduced it to five. One Kansas Congressman who did have important national influence was Clifford Hope, chairman of the House Agriculture Committee in 1947–48 and 1953–54.

Alf M. Landon. Unfairly characterized by Democrats and many in the media as a colorless, standpat Midwesterner during and after his disastrous race against F.D.R. in 1936, Landon did in fact initiate the long process of reshaping the Republican party from its Depression-era neanderthalism into a broadened vehicle that could deal in rational terms with the emerging phenomena of big government, conservation, farm relief, and social security.

One of the most delightful experiences in interviewing for this book was to spend several hours with Landon on a late summer afternoon talking on the front porch of the spacious Georgian home he built at Topeka after his defeat for the Presidency. (The house is so large that one observer suggested that since Landon could not get a lease on the White House, he had built one of his own.) Landon, at 85, has not lost an iota of his gusto for life or keen perception of national and international issues. He is intensely proud that even decades after his defeat for the Presidency, he has frequently spoken out, and frequently is heeded, on causes close to his heart—control of nuclear weapons, free trade, restraints on secret foreign military commitments, normalization of relationships with China and Russia, and the little oil producers (of which he is one) against the big companies. Landon feels his major contribution of postwar years was to goad the Kennedy Administration toward a strong free-trade position in the landmark Trade Agreements Act of 1963, and then rounding up Midwestern votes for the bill in Congress. Though his own power in Kansas politics was largely eclipsed by 1948, Landon never abandoned his interest in the Grand Old Party, doing what he could to encourage candidates of a moderate-liberal-pragmatic stripe across the country.

Landon's personal contacts and interests are scarcely those of the typical partisan. He recalls with warmth, for instance, his longtime association with the late Norman Thomas, who ran several times for President on the Socialist ticket. Landon first met Thomas in 1933 and, a year or two later, found himself in an interesting position when Thomas went to Topeka to give an address. "The committee in charge," Landon recalls, "called me a night or two before and frankly said they had not found anyone who was willing to introduce him. Would I? I said I would be honored to, and did." Years later, Landon and Thomas shared the same platform before the Sane Nuclear Policy Meeting in 1960 in New York. Landon recalls saying, as early as 1940, that "before we got through with the changes ahead of us in America, we would be glad to settle for the 'Christian Socialism of Norman Thomas.' "

In 1972 the Los Angeles *Times* wrote that Landon "now lives in retirement." A protesting letter to the editor was soon dispatched from Topeka, in which Landon sought to dispel the "retirement" notion by citing his schedule for "a normal day":

> Yesterday morning, I started in as usual at 6 o'clock. After reading the morning papers, I squeezed in a short horseback ride, getting back by 10:30 to visit, at his request, with the Republican nominee for governor for an hour and a half about his coming campaign.
>
> Had lunch with the manager of my three radio stations. (He remarked, "They don't know that you're liable to call at any time of the night about a mispronounced well-known name in our state news.") Spent the afternoon on letters.

Home at 4 o'clock. After a short nap, I worked on reviewing galley proofs for Neal Peirce on his coming book, "The Great Plains States." Listened to the 5:30 news. Read the evening papers—editorial columns of one or two others—that I get daily, the letter from Research Institute, Kiplinger Letter, Broadcasting magazine and the Oil & Gas Journal. Talked to my farm boss (oil) on my Greenwood County properties. Finished up by reading some of Bill Lawrence's great book and then listened to the last part of the Cardinals baseball game broadcast.

ALF M. LANDON
Topeka, Kan.

Economy of Abundance: From Dust Bowl to Vegetable Bowl

The strange irony of modern Kansas is that while its national role has diminished, the life of its people has improved immeasurably since the dust-bowl and Depression days of the 1930s. In those lean years the dust storms howled so unremittingly across the High Plains that many lost their faith in the land; indeed thousands fled the state. The situation was worst in the High Plains of western Kansas, but serious enough in the Flint Hills region of center state (an area of rolling hills with heavy grass cover) and in traditionally more moist and fertile eastern Kansas. But today, even on the High Plains, an agriculture of abundance has emerged through irrigation, soil conservation, and new techniques. This blooming of the desert, combined with advanced food processing, has made "agribusiness" an economic force which probably has a gross impact of $6 billion on the Kansas economy each year. A moderately growing population base of over two million has also been sustained since the Second World War by small industrial plants and the thousands of jobs generated by the aircraft assembly industry in Wichita.

Thus in its century-plus history, Kansas has never had it so good. In part, this may explain the diminution of its national role. Kansans are no longer poor and hungry and inventive and rebelling; instead they have forgotten all about raising hell and are concentrating on "corn" instead. Full stomachs generate complacency and materialistic values. This judgment, for instance, was made by a native Kansan, the novelist-biographer Kenneth Davis:

> In most of the key areas of Kansas I've known, the economic man has become dominant almost to the point of excluding values and interests that differ from his. There is a tacit assumption among our ruling elite that the proper major aim of all education, scientific research and cultural activity is the increase of profits. Education is defined as vocational and professional training; scientific research is the development of new, more profitable products and processes.

To the reader we will leave the decision of what is most important to a people—creativity and renown, or simple well-being. Kansas has opted for the latter, but as we have seen, there is at least one Plains State (Minnesota) which appears to have both.

Kansans began their climb from the trough of agricultural depression through an act of God: the moist weather which the 1940s brought in the wake of the arid '30s. But many other factors played a role. In 1935 Landon had reported to F.D.R. on the state's brutal dust storms and persuaded an Assistant Secretary of Agriculture to come from Washington and drive with him to the Colorado line and back, "when, at times, we couldn't see the road a few feet ahead of the car radiator." As a result, Roosevelt—at Landon's suggestion—initiated a program of federal engineering counsel for farmers building ponds on their property; the result is that Kansas is now dotted with good farmponds which have added much to the water resources of the state.

In 1951 the Kansas River, which flows into the Missouri at Kansas City, went on a veritable rampage, inundating a million and a half acres, driving 100,000 from their homes, killing 28, and causing close to a billion dollars in damage in Kansas and Missouri. Pressed by Roy Roberts, Harry Darby, and others, the Eisenhower Administration began long-overdue flood prevention work including 17 big reservoirs which assured Kansas, for the first time in its history, an adequate water supply. (Some believe that the reservoirs and farmponds may be causing a change in the dry climate, with more annual rainfall because of evaporation.)

A second major project, this one with no federal funds involved, came on the parched High Plains near the Colorado border, territory where rainfall is a scant 10 to 18 inches a year. It was found that subterranean water could be pumped up from depths of 200 to 600 feet for irrigation. Perhaps the largest private irrigation system in the world has resulted. To date, the greatest dividend of this western plains irrigation has been in vast crops of corn, milo, and sorghums, enabling plainsmen to feed their own cattle in feed lots that hold as many as 30,000 head.

Now a second great return is appearing: crops of fresh vegetables—cucumbers, tomatoes, carrots, beans, even lettuce and cantaloupes—in the very heart of the dustbowl. In the 14 counties of southwestern Kansas alone, some 5,000 wells have been dug by farmers at an average cost of $20,000, and there are thousands more in the surrounding High Plains sections of Colorado, Texas, Oklahoma, and Nebraska. Millions of dollars of vegetable crops, picked by giant mechanical harvesters, are already being realized, and Kansans think that as the population crush develops in California's rich Central Valley, displacing farm lands there, demand will increase for vegetables from the Plains.

To be sure, the ferocity of High Plains weather still brings hazards; hail and disease, for instance, have been known to wipe out hundreds of acres of sweet corn or cantaloupes. But Plains farmers long ago learned to live with the whims of midcontinental weather; a man of the soil in those parts has to have a touch of the gambler in him, hoping for bonanza crops but ready to face reversals. Even drought-resistant wheat, the traditional crop of the Plains, remains chancy in modern times; the agricultural agent in Grant County, Kansas, told an Eastern reporter about wheat crops in the 1960s: "We've missed seven in a row. It was froze out two years, the drought got it two years, the aphids two years, and the grasshoppers one." Many farmers find themselves facing a kind of perpetual debt; as one wheat farmer from the endless stretches around Salina said: "You borrow more and more but you make less and less and so you go deeper and deeper into debt." The cost of farm supplies escalates continually, while prices are often in the doldrums; the value of farmland has risen in most years, but real estate taxes go up much more rapidly. The average age of farmers has increased to more than 51 years, as fewer and fewer young men choose farming as a career.

Some plainsmen fear that just as overuse and neglect of the land once set the stage for the great dust storms of drought years, so the underground water supply used for feed grains and vegetables may one day be exhausted. In southwest Kansas, for instance, continued digging of new wells and exhaustion of the water table could lead to aridity in some 40 to 45 years. By then, the plainsmen hope, they will be getting Mississippi River water, diverted from hundreds of miles away; this story we will discuss in the Texas chapter.

Kansas is still the number one wheat state of America; she produces half again as much wheat as North Dakota, her closest competitor.* Wheat is the predominant crop in the short-grass country of central through west Kansas; eastern Kansas has more conventional farming and is the westernmost extension of the corn belt. Farms are still much bigger in the west than the east of Kansas, but average acreage of all types has risen to almost 600 acres. Kansas now produces eight times the farm products it did in 1930 with less than half the work force. Electrification, running water, late model cars, color television, sometimes even Caribbean or Mexican holidays are now the lot of the Kansas farmer—a totally different world from the 1930s.

In raw dollar terms, it is not wheat but livestock that leads the modern Kansas economy. Consider, for instance, these figures from a typical year in the late 1960s. Cattle sales were $597 million, pig sales $101 million, and the income from meat packing and processing $521 million, for a livestock-related total of about $1.2 billion—a country mile ahead of the $325 million realized from wheat sales and $334 million from grain mill products manufacturing. In a single decade, livestock production had increased sixfold, and Kansans except that trend to continue. The state ranked seventh in the U.S.A. in the value of its farm products sold ($1.8 billion in 1969).

All the official farm statistics of established governments, however, ignore a major Kansas crop of intense interest to a certain segment of the American population: the *Cannabis sativa* plant, better known as marijuana. It flourishes across the Plains States, but nowhere in such profusion as Kansas.† *Cannabis sativa* was once planted intentionally by farmers, who sold its strong fibers to rope manufacturers. But that market has long since vanished, and for years the 8–10-feet-tall stalks were little more than an obnoxious, bothersome weed, clogging untilled spaces along fences, railroads and river beds. Farmers dubbed it "loco weed" for the giddy effect it had on farm animals. Agencies like the Kansas Department of Agriculture's Noxious Weed Division encouraged the use of every known exterminant, from fire to chem-

* Kansas grows winter wheat, a tough variety planted in the fall, dormant in the winter, and then hardy enough to withstand furnace-like summertime temperatures well over 100 degrees before harvesting. North Dakota, with a cooler climate and shorter growing season, is the leading area for spring wheat, which is harvested the same year it is planted.

† A New York *Times* survey also indicated marijuana crops in such diverse places as Oregon, Texas (allegedly on the state capitol grounds at Austin) and Vermont, where the Champlain Valley reportedly produced "marijuana almost as good as that of most of the Mexican varieties." Midwestern marijuana is said to be of fairly mediocre quality.

icals, to kill the plant, but it persisted—still some 50,000 acres strong in Kansas alone.

Such was the condition when the weed became the opiate of the young in the 1960s, and even at such supposedly staid places as the University of Kansas at Lawrence, students foraged into the countryside to gather the long-scorned marijuana, carry it back to dormitories, garages, or other secret hiding places, and let it dry upside down so that the potent sap would dry in the leaves for later smoking pleasure. Spoiling the fun, narcotics agents and other officials arrested almost 200 Kansas marijuana harvesters in 1969 alone.

Not all of Kansas' wealth comes from its fields. In sharp contrast to its industry-poor neighbors to the north, this state has shared since World War II in one of the U.S.A.'s great growth industries: aerospace. Some half a billion dollars a year are realized in aircraft sales; Cessna, Beach, Gates, Learjet, and Boeing are all in Wichita, where 60 percent of the nation's private airplanes are produced. The value of manufactured goods, including a big share in food processing, is about $2 billion a year. A lot of Kansan income is also realized from military installations including two posts that date back to the Indian wars of the 19th century—Fort Riley, the home of the 24th Infantry Division, and Fort Leavenworth, which houses the Command and General Staff College, the world's largest tactical school for advanced military training. The Department of Defense spends almost $600 million in Kansas each year.

Kansas has major oil fields, but they have been under constant extraction since 1902 and many are becoming exhausted. Natural gas, of which there are vast Kansas deposits, advanced tremendously in the postwar years; no other state, for instance, produces as much helium. In recent years, the state has ranked fifth in U.S. oil and gas production with an income of over $400 million annually. But a member of the Kansas congressional delegation, who himself votes to maintain the special tax advantages of the oil industry, told me that Kansans overestimate the importance of oil in their state's economy.

Despite its popular image—"a flat, endless, almost treeless expanse of land"—Kansas does have some 1.5 million acres of woodlands, especially in the moist eastern third of the state. The trees, found principally in narrow belts along the river valleys and as windbreaks planted by frugal farmers around their prairie outposts, are mostly hardwood and yield a harvest of several million dollars a year. On the dollar scale, of course, such harvesting is overshadowed even by as obscure an industry as the mining of salt.

Really significant income comes from tourism—$525 million a year, by latest estimates, even though the "sights" to see are relatively few. (They include the Eisenhower Center at Abilene, Dodge City of Old West fame, the Agricultural Hall of Fame near Kansas City, the Wichita Art Museum, and recreational lands around federal reservoirs and lakes.) A lot of the tourist dollars are dropped by travelers on their way to or from Kansas' western neighbor, Colorado; as they race across the west Kansas prairies, a few even pause for a look at Holcomb, the town made famous by Truman Capote's *In Cold Blood.* And if the tourists will take time to look carefully as they drive across the Flint Hills region of eastern Kansas, they will catch a glimpse of what the native prairie was like before men tilled most of it for fields of corn and wheat. This area contains what is probably the largest area of essentially untouched prairie anywhere on the continent, with rolling hills and flats and broad vistas, the original tall bluestem grass, the magnificent wildflowers blooming from spring into the autumn.

Economically, Kansas' Achilles heel has been its southeast corner, known as the "Kansas Balkans" because of its variegated east European ethnic base, divisive (and sometimes radical) politics, and a history of labor discord. Coal, lead, and zinc strip mining in this region have all declined precipitously, though the area is now making a concerted and often successful effort to get its hands on any new kind of industry, from campers to toys.*

A major Kansas concern has been to find new kinds of jobs to balance agriculture and employ the thousands leaving farms. The lion's share of existing Kansas industry is in a lopsided triangle that stretches from Kansas City west to Topeka and Salina, then southwesterly to Wichita and back to Kansas City again. Outside those areas, there is only a scattering of small industry, not enough to stem a population decline in the rural counties.

In the 1960s, Kansas put together its first really serious industrial research and promotion program. Local industrial development corporations were begun in many communities, issuing industrial development bonds and offering development assistance for new firms. The number of new nonfarm jobs began a marked increase.

State legislators, however, insisted that the Kansas Department of Economic Development eschew the helter-skelter, industry-at-any-price factory hunting techniques popular in many states. Basic questions should be answered first, they said: Why should Kansas seek new industry—to create jobs for its own people, or to draw population from the outside, or to widen local tax bases? What was happening to the state's water supply, and would it be sufficient for new industries and new towns? Would there be enough tax base, without a serious strain on state or local resources, to provide highways, new schools, and other public services in areas selected by industries? The questioning was not intended to be hostile, but to force state government to set priorities and then encourage industries which would match Kansan needs and not harm the Kansan environment. In effect, it was a careful systems approach to economic development, aided in part by federal funds. The overall results would not be apparent until well into the 1970s.

Developments of the '50s and '60s indicated that there are limits to what a state can do to guide its own economic development. Though still the nation's foremost flour-milling state, Kansas lost many mills to the South because of more favorable train and water freight rates in that region. All of official Kansas' efforts, including major research work by Kansas State University

* The Balkans city of Pittsburg (population 20,171) plays an important, little known part in American life: it is the home of "Pittsburg Personal Census Service Branch," where the U.S. Census Bureau keeps more than a billion Census listings—one for every household and its inhabitants in the eight Census counts from 1900 through 1970. Just by giving the name of the head of household, the Census year and state, a person can obtain a certificate attesting to his age at the time of the Census, his place of birth, race, and sometimes even his occupation—legal proof, often unobtainable elsewhere, for inheritance and insurance claims, passports, Social Security and Medicare benefits, and naturalization.

couldn't stem the trend. Yet, totally unexpected by state leaders, a great boom in mobile home production developed around Newton (near Wichita).

State Government, Prisons, Newspapers, and Power

Kansas state government, actually controlled by Populist governors for a period in the turbulent '90s, has settled down to complete typicality in modern times. Take any measure of government policy and performance—from taxation to services, highways to education—and Kansas will rank about midway in the 50 states. For obscure reasons, however, Kansas seems to need more people to govern it; the state ranks among the top three in the proportion of state and local government employees to the total population.

Perhaps the oustanding governor from the 1940s onward was John A. Anderson, Jr. (1961–65), a thoughtful moderate who was incidentally one of the few political allies of Alf Landon to head Kansas government in the postwar era. Anderson began major strides in reform of the state prison system; under his administration a board of probation and parole was set up to cut down on the prison population, and a prisoner reception-diagnostic center was established in cooperation with the famed Menninger Clinic at Topeka. A sweeping program to reduce school districts (from 1,290 to only 325) went through under Anderson. He laid the groundwork for a full program of state aid to local education, a program carried through by his successor, fellow Republican William H. Avery (1965–67). But Avery was obliged to put through a substantial tax increase to finance school aid; the backlash from the taxes enabled a conservative Democrat, Robert Docking, to defeat Avery in 1966.

Neither Avery nor Docking followed through on Anderson's prison reform program. Among the casualties was a medium security facility that Anderson had planned from which inmates would have been permitted to hold daytime jobs. Years of penal neglect culminated in 1969 with a full-scale riot at the Kansas State Penitentiary at Lansing, an 11-acre compound dating from the years immediately following the Civil War. The inmates, never provided adequate rehabilitational services, had formed their own "inmate power structure," often enforced by terror, murder, and homosexual gang rape. A new penal director, appointed by Docking, ordered a crackdown; within the long tiers of 5-by-12-foot cells immense quantities of drugs and weapons—including knives, clubs, and a loaded pistol—were discovered. Confiscation of the drugs and weapons triggered the riot in which inmates took control of the cell blocks for several days, held at bay only by occasional tear-gas and rifle fire from the control towers. Finally, shot-gun carrying highway patrolmen could come in and restore a semblance of order. To protest that, convicts began a wave of arson and escape attempts and many mutilated themselves by such techniques as cutting their Achilles tendon, hoping to force a federal investigation of prison conditions.

In 1971 a report of continued shocking conditions in the Kansas prisons was made by the Kansas Association of Mental Health. The lengthy, documented report, made in consultation with Drs. Karl Menninger and Robert Settle of the Menninger Clinic, aroused public opinion so much that the state legislature agreed, in its 1972 session, to make the funds available for the medium security prison that Governor Anderson had proposed almost a decade before.

John Anderson was close to the Nelson Rockefeller–William Scranton wing of his party and, in 1964, while serving a term as chairman of the National Governors Conference, actually called a meeting at his hotel suite during the annual Governors Conference in Cleveland to try to coalesce the anti-Goldwater forces. Rockefeller, Scranton, George Romney, Ohio Governor James Rhodes, and even General Eisenhower were all present. But Eisenhower was persuaded by his old Treasury Secretary, George Humphrey, not to oppose Goldwater, so that a contemplated move to mobilize the moderates behind Scranton never got off the ground.

Anderson the politician has, in fact, been a frustrated man for many years now. The Nixon Administration considered him too liberal, and offered him no federal post. And when he tried a comeback in the 1972 Republican gubernatorial primary, he received only 30 percent of the vote. But Anderson was able to make an important contribution by his chairmanship of the Citizens Conference on State Legislatures, a public service group set up with assistance from foundations, including Ford and Carnegie, to encourage work in the 50 states on modernization and revitalization of the state law-making bodies. "Our country," Anderson told me, "had changed radically in 30 years, but the legislatures were still meeting only 30 or 60 days every two years, with no decent pay for legislators and no place for them to do their work. So the country has simply abandoned its dependence on legislatures to get things done. The demand moved to Washington, along with receptiveness to needs." The Citizens Conference pushed for annual sessions, higher legislative salaries, adequate professional staffs, and decent working conditions for legislators across the country; by the early 1970s solid success was apparent in many states.

Robert Docking's years in the governorship, starting in 1967, have left Kansas in poor financial health in relation to state services, universities, and aid for local schools. One critic, liberal Republican state representative Donn J. Everett, charges that Docking and the Republican-controlled legislature have cut state agency budgets "to a point where they can't operate." (Everett's lonely counsel: the state should reverse course and shoulder the primary burden for raising taxes, returning large blocs of money to the hard-pressed local governments.) Docking deserves credit for seeing the deficiency in atomized county government and ordering, in 1971, the creation of 11 official state development regions to focus planning and development in their areas and coordinate local plans with programs of the federal and state governments.

On questions like "law and order," Docking took a conservative line. Starting in 1971, he had company on the issue from the first Kansas Democratic attorney general since 1895, Vern Miller. Miller made his fame as a law-and-order-or-else sheriff of Wichita, where the police he headed clashed frequently with local blacks. After his election, Ray Morgan reported in the Kansas City *Star*, Miller spent his time "banging around the state leading raiding parties against anything he deemed needs cleaning up." Miller is considered a potential future gubernatorial candidate.

In 1933, under Governor Landon, Kansas had become the first state to establish a full-time legislative council, a group which commanded increasing respect over the years. In 1971 it was replaced by a new legislative coordinating council with control over both legislative research and legislative studies done between sessions. Kansas still pays its legislators well below the annual average, however. The typical Kansan legislator is not hard to envision; he was described to me as a stand-patter, likely to be a deacon of his church and a pillar of his community, perhaps an attorney or bank president or owner of the biggest business in his little town. He doesn't want to spend more money for schools or on metropolitan area improvements. He's rather content, in fact, to let his state and community be the same way it was when he was born and reared. He is an accurate reflection of the tone and temper of small-town Kansas—and his counterpart is to be found in every legislature from Maine to Alaska.

The small-town denizens, however, are no longer as overwhelming a force as they once were in the Kansas legislature. For decades, in spite of the clear mandate of the state constitution, Kansas legislators refused to reapportion themselves, so that by 1961 Kansas senate districts varied between 16,083 and 343,231 in population and house districts between 2,069 and 68,646. Then came court-forced reapportionment, triggered in Kansas by a courageous publisher in the William Allen White tradition, John P. Harris of the Hutchinson *News*. For years Harris and his editor, John McCormally, had been demanding editorially that the legislature reapportion itself to reflect population changes. In 1961 they decided that editorials were not enough. Harris and the *News* went to court, and in 1963 the Kansas supreme court ordered the first meaningful reapportionment of the century in the state senate. Most of the *News* circulation area is rural, and a howl of protest arose from local politicians, advertisers, and subscribers alike. But Harris stuck to his guns and in 1965, in the wake of a Supreme Court ruling, he filed another suit challenging the validity of the state constitutional provision guaranteeing each county, no matter how small, a seat in the state house. The state supreme court ruled in his favor, and in the next election equally apportioned house districts also went into effect.

Reapportionment was not the only unpopular stand editor Harris took in the years before his death in the late 1960s. He also fought for birth control, legalized abortion, and the sale of liquor by the drink. He was an important supporter of the successful 1948 referendum to expunge prohibition, a Kansas institution long honored in law and scorned in fact, from the state constitution. The proposition even carried in Carrie Nation's home town.*

* Serving liquor by the glass is still illegal in Kansas (except in private clubs), a decision last reaffirmed by the voters in a 1970 referendum.

Kansas' political history is inextricably bound up with its newspapers. For decades, no influence could rival that of the Kansas City *Star*, edited and printed in Missouri but carried wherever the rails went, and farther, into Kansas. (John Gunther had this to say about Kansas City, Missouri, home of the *Star*: "This great and extraordinary city, while not the capital of its own state, is in effect the capital of another, a situation without parallel in the country.") The *Star*'s editor until his death in 1967, 300-pound Roy Roberts, actually lived on the Kansas side and was a dominant (some said dictatorial) personality. Working under him, the *Star*'s Kansas correspondent, Lacy Haynes, was said to be the real kingmaker of Kansas politics. For decades, there was not a Kansas governor or Senator who had not risen to power with the blessing of the *Star*. Today that is no longer true; in fact, the last Kansas governor the *Star* really "made" was Edward F. Arn in the early 1950s. No paper now published or distributed in Kansas has either the distinction or influence of papers like the old *Star* under Roberts, White's Emporia *Gazette*, Harris's Hutchinson *News*, or Ed Howe's Atchison *Globe*.

Real power in Kansas today, close observers of the legislature relate, are the banks, the power companies, pipeline companies, and still to a substantial degree, the railroads. Among the farm groups, only the Farm Bureau can exert substantial influence, but even it triumphs only when its stands coincide with those of the economic interests named above.

Kansas' traditional liberalism, rooted in its New England heritage, is by no means dominant but does reappear from time to time. In the first postwar years, there was an enthusiastic UNESCO movement headed by Milton Eisenhower; Kansas State University reported that its United Nations Conference was a highly successful extension activity. In the late 1960s, a major part of the push for Biafran relief started in Kansas. Kansas's peculiar dedication to education is reflected in high enrollments (compared to overall population) at Kansas University (Lawrence), Kansas State University (the land grant institution at Manhattan), Wichita State University, three state colleges, and 24 community colleges. The state's tax effort for higher education was for many years above the national average. Kansas also has many private colleges, often church supported. On the elementary and secondary school level, only Colorado among the neighboring states spends more per pupil or per capita than Kansas.

People and Places

Who lives in this state, most aptly described by William Allen White as a "parallelogram with one corner nibbled off by the Missouri River"? The ethnic strains are principally these: early settlers from New England and the heartland states; Negroes, many descended from former slave families who came into Kansas soon after the Civil War; Italians and Yugoslavs, who came to mine the Kansas Balkans early in this century; Mexicans, brought to work on the railroads some 70 years ago; and Mennonites, who came from the steppes of Russia in the 1870s and brought with them that magnificent strain, Turkey red hard winter wheat. Modern historic research, by Professor J. Neale Carman of the University of Kansas and others, has shown that the aggregate of German, Czech, Swedish, and Russian immigration was much more important in Kansas' development than many people believe. In 1895 there were numerous townships, scattered across the Kansas map, in which a high proportion—sometimes even a majority—of the people had a native language other than English.

Kansas has the lowest birth rate of any state and one of the highest percentages of retirees; the net migration figure (which excludes births and deaths) shows a population drain of 287,000 since 1940, almost half the outflow in the 1960s alone. The total population rose by 14.3 percent in the 1950s but only 3.1 percent in the 1960s, producing a 1970 Census total of 2,246,578.

Kansas' only serious metropolis is Wichita, a big, sprawling town (population 276,554—metro area 389,352), which busily produces jet parts and general aviation craft, processes grain and livestock, mills flour, and even refines some oil. Wichita was once an important point on the Chisholm Trail over which Texas longhorns were driven north to the railheads of Kansas, and its stockyards still process well over one million head of cattle a year. Today the city has little color; most other Kansans think of it as a mediocre town with little class and a lot of right-wing extremist activity. The city is headquarters of the Kansas Right to Work Committee, which was primarily spawned from executive ranks of Boeing and the Coleman Company (makers of camping equipment and Wichita's largest nonaerospace manufacturer). The late Irving Koch, a big Wichita refinery owner, was on the national council of the John Birch Society.

Wichita is also the scene of Kansas' worst race problems. Many of the whites who came in the '40s and '50s to man the aircraft factories were from the South, particularly adjacent Oklahoma and Arkansas. It may have been inevitable that they would clash with the blacks—who numbered 26,841 by 1970 and were confined, except for a minuscule minority, to a 100-block ghetto in the northeast sector. Few American cities suffer from more rigid residential segregation. The frustration of the black community led to black extremism in the late 1960s, a situation exacerbated by the tough tactics of then-sheriff Vern Miller. Often angry young blacks congregated on street corners, throwing bricks at Miller's squad cars; amazingly the disturbances did not fan into full-scale rioting. The situation was cooled significantly by A. Price Woodard, an outstanding Negro city commissioner who became mayor for a year (on the city's rotation system) in 1970–71. School busing, an essential step to achieve school integration because of residential segregation, was delayed by court suits (still on appeal in early 1972) and the refusal of the Nixon administration to press for early action.

It would be unfair, of course, to depict Wichita as the only place in Kansas where race relations have been, or are, a serious problem. Only 25 years ago, there were still communities in Western Kansas where signs at the town limits announced that no colored persons would be allowed to remain there overnight. America's landmark school segregation cases will go down in history as Brown versus the Board of Education of Topeka, Kansas, because Kansas allowed first-class cities to set up and perpetuate racially segregated schools.

Wichita has tried to modernize itself, beautifying its main streets, constructing an expensive ($21 million) circular auditorium and a handsome contemporary-style library. Although the city has one of the country's highest numbers of automobiles, relative to population, it has laid imaginative plans for a 50-mile loop of picturesque trails along its rivers, through both country and downtown areas. The Wichita Symphony celebrated its silver anniversary in the late 1960s, and some local leaders (including a television station owner and Landon's son-in-law) have been working hard to spur development in the arts. Economically more significant are Wichita's many new motels, an evidence of the city's strategic location on U.S. 54 and the Kansas Turnpike.

Wichita's population grew by 46.4 percent in the 1940s and 51.4 percent in the 1950s but only 8.6 percent in the 1960s, the reduced growth rate of recent years due in part to a severe recession in the aircraft industry which sent unemployment soaring to 11 percent in 1970. The jobless rate was down to less than 7 percent by early 1972—in part, some thought, because many of the unemployed had fled the city. In the meantime, two major downtown hotels had been forced out of business.

One of the interesting state legislative battles of the 1960s turned on the proposal to create a third state university in Wichita. The industrial powers and other big property owners of Wichita launched a big campaign to have the municipal University of Wichita made into Wichita State University; this was done less out of educational zeal than a desire to reduce the large local ad valorem tax that financed the municipal university. Alumni of state universities fought tooth and nail to stop the move, which they said would dilute the resources of the state university system. But after a bloody fight the state takeover won a narrow victory in the legislature.

Kansas City, Kansas (population 168,213) is the state's second largest city; inevitably, it lives under the shadow of its big brother across the river, Kansas City, Missouri. Crossing the bridge from Missouri and going down the low-profiled main street on the Kansas side, one immediately has the feeling he has left the big city for the stretched out, low-slung, wide-streeted world of the Plains towns.

Kansas City, which used to live off the railroads and the packing houses, has maintained its strong industrial base, but not by accident. Years ago the city had the foresight to build the first industrial park in the West, and now it has many food-processing, electronics, and automobile assembly plants. New jobs have appeared to take up the slack from declining railroads and packing-house shutdowns at a rate of almost one a year.

The city fathers of Kansas City insist they've never countenanced the rackets and hoodlum-type operations that were rampant on the Missouri side, but the truth is that the Mafia was active in small gambling spots until late into the 1960s. A candid assessment heard locally: "We have no red light districts or the like, but there are some small crap games frequented by railroad men and blacks. I'm not saying you can't get a piece of tail or some marijuana."

Kansas City has had a constant Negro population of 17 to 20 percent since 1899 and is proud that the blacks on its police force actually number more—some 26 percent. Efforts have been made to give black leaders spots on city boards and commissions. Black home ownership is relatively high. Imaginative summer employment programs are run by the city for both black and white youth.

Kansas City's mayor until his defeat in 1971 was Joseph McDowell, a tall, iron gray-haired man with an earthy touch and blunt-spoken ways. He worked well with young blacks and even appointed an outstanding black chief of detectives, Boston Daniels, to be the city's police chief. McDowell was also the catalyst of a number of urban renewal projects, badly needed in decaying center-city sections which were described by John Gunther as "shipwrecked" a quarter of a century earlier. In a seven-by-three-block downtown area, the city constructed an indigenous mall with trees and flowers and architecture designed to match the natural themes of Kansas' landscape. But in 1971 McDowell was ousted from office—despite the overwhelmingly Democratic voting habits of the city—by a Republican, Richard Walsh, who argued that McDowell had been too cozy with the blacks and had concentrated on refurbishing downtown at the expense of municipal services for the suburbs. Under Walsh's housekeeping regime, Boston Daniels was eased out as police chief and the city began to catch its breath after the forward strides of the McDowell years.

Kansas City had the foresight, in the 1960s, to expand its limits by 50 percent, making an area large enough, in McDowell's words, "so that we can plan for the next half-century." The city also worked out, in conjunction with its Missouri namesake, a strong regional approach to government. The two cities began to cooperate with other counties in a metropolitan area planning commission (partly a device to get federal funding), formed an area transit authority under bistate authority, and filed together an urban renewal application for the stockyards area and for model cities money. They also set up "Operation Barrier" for their police departments, a device by which any or all of the five bridges crossing the river can be sealed off almost instantaneously to prevent flight of criminals. Similarly, the two cities and the area counties pool their law enforcement resources in a "Metro Squad" to combat major crime.

Kansas City is located in Wyandotte County, the leading Democratic county of Kansas. Next door is Johnson County, a Scarsdale-type suburban area which is among the highest in the U.S.A. in per capita income and, not surprisingly, the GOP's banner county in the state.

Topeka, Kansas' capital since statehood, is mainly a government town. Despite its population of 125,011—and a recent growth rate that tops all other Kansas cities—it has never lost its leisurely small-town flavor. Banks, holding a significant share of state deposits, are highly influential. Topeka has a big Goodyear plant, a DuPont cellophane factory, and other prospering industries. Within the city limits are 565 acres of Santa Fe Railroad shops and yards; a huge Santa Fe office building looms directly opposite the state capitol. Satellite shopping centers have diverted a lot of business from downtown, but the center city is striking back with a beautiful shopping mall, and the state government plans a large Capital Area Plaza for its facilities.

Kansan newsman Leroy Towns has written of Topeka, "It is a city—with suburbs and urban renewal . . . and wonder what happened to the dream of land and white picket fences. . . . A real city, in miniature, with eastside poverty, black tension and brown tension. Anger and frustration—a feeling that things are going sour." And still, Topeka remains a community of the Plains, open to the cruel vicissitudes of weather. In 1951 the Kansas River overflowed its banks, inundating large sections of the city. The millions of dollars since invested in levees and flood-control projects may help to prevent a recurrence, but some phenomena remain beyond man's control. In June 1966, a tornado streaked diagonally across Topeka. In its wake it left 17 persons dead, 500 injured, 1,600 homeless, and property damage of more than $100 million.

Kansas has a raft of smaller cities—Lawrence (45,698), Salina (37,714), and Hutchinson (36,885) the largest among them *—which are both manufacturing centers and agricultural marketing headquarters for surrounding farm counties.

Lawrence is also home of the University of Kansas, which now has an enrollment of 18,500 and is the key reason that Lawrence's population has soared 218 percent since 1940, with a growth of 12,840 in the 1960s alone. Plains States universities do not attract big-scale research and development plants like a Harvard or Berkeley, but they do provide major local employment and a plethora of motels, restaurants, and shops to service the student population. Traditionally the source of future Kansas leaders, the University of Kansas was convulsed in 1970 with firebombings (including over $1 million damage at the Student Union building), rock-throwing riots, curfews, and shooting that led to the death of two youths. Part of the trouble emanated from a dilapidated four-block area northeast of the campus known as "Hippie Haven" to the townspeople of Lawrence; another source was frustration and disorders among local high-school-age blacks, with whom the street people tended to identify; finally there was a radicalized segment of the student body, although the violence tended to come from nonstudents. Kansans were shocked not only by the burnings and casualties but by the emergence of such phenomena as communes in which young men and women students lived together, an epithet-laden underground press, and changes in dress and behavior that gave Lawrence the look of many radicalized East and West Coast University towns.

By 1971–72, however, a full-scale effort was underway to heal the wounds of the 1970 disorders. Lawrence's town leaders made a real effort to make the

* Excepting Overland Park (76,623), in the Kansas City suburbs.

students feel welcome and set up regular meetings with student leaders. A more peaceful era in town-gown relations seemed to be developing. Part of the better relationships was doubtless based on realization on both sides that violence could only be destructive to their mutual interests. But the town fathers were probably mindful of another fact: that with students eligible to vote at 18, under a residency requirement of only 30 days, a new and potent voting bloc had suddenly emerged in their midst.

Generally speaking, Kansas' cities of 10,000 or more have prospered in recent years (though both Salina and Hutchinson have lost population), while the smaller towns face the survival problems common to smaller trade centers throughout the Plains. Where a smaller city does grow, a variety of relatively artificial stimulants tend to be the reason. An example is Emporia, William Allen White's home town, which grew by 28.7 percent, to 23,327, between 1960 and 1970, even while the rural counties around it were declining in population. Emporia is even developing its own little suburbia now. More than two-thirds of the city's growth, according to a survey by William Chapman of the Washington *Post*, stemmed directly from increased enrollment at Kansas State Teachers College and a private institution, the College of Emporia. The city also attracted some new industries, including a plant of a fast-growing company, Iowa Beef Processors, accounting for 1,800 new jobs. But again, public money had a lot to do with the industrial growth: Iowa Beef selected Emporia not only because of its location in cattle country, at a key highway exchange with an interstate road, and because of relatively cheap labor, but because the city issued $4.5 million in tax exempt industrial revenue bonds to build the plant and buy the land and gave the company 10 years of real property tax exemptions.

The Amazing Menningers

With logic hard to question, many Kansans regard the Menninger Clinic in Topeka as their state's most important institution. The institution has been run with an amazingly practical and inventive bent by Drs. Karl and Will Menninger and their sons ever since its doors first opened in 1919.

Clinical care has always been and remains the focus of the Menningers' activity; since the original sanitarium was opened, close to 50,000 patients have been registered. The neuroses of a nation are reflected in the fact that at least 3,000 requests for help are made to the Menninger Clinic each year; some of those are referrals from other physicians but a surprisingly large majority from would-be patients themselves or their relatives. The Menninger Hospital can only handle about 200 patients a year, so that most care is on an out-patient basis. The Menninger Clinic—including the hospital, outpatient services, children's and neurological services—has 75 physicians, nearly all psychiatrists, on its staff. The Clinic has twice as many psychiatrists in training as any other medical campus in the country.

In addition to the wide area of clinical projects the Menningers conduct

—in one recent year, for instance, on subjects ranging from altered ego states to lobotomy to self-confrontation—the focus of the Menninger Foundation is on preventive psychiatry or, put in a broader context, fostering the mental health of the whole society. "We psychiatrists simply can't see all ill people ourselves," according to Dr. Herbert Modlin, head of the clinic's department of preventive psychology. "So we hope by counseling leaders in various fields, we can provide a multiplier effect." This work began in the 1950s with week-long seminars for business executives, simply training them in the understanding of people and trying to avert incipient mental health problems of employees. Later special programs for clergy were instituted.

> We organize our programs, [Modlin says] around the great social institutions which influence everyone's life: law, religion, education, industry, welfare, medicine. All these settings influence mental health and illness. . . . If we can work with these leaders and help them become more sensitive to the mental health aspects of their clients, parishioners, students, patients and workers, it may be possible to intervene early enough so that people may be helped before they start to decompensate and become depressed or become neurotic or withdraw into delusions and actually end up in the clutches of the police department, or the welfare worker, or the rescue mission, the lawyer's divorce office, or the Florence Crittenden Home for Unwed Girls.

The two most inventive community psychology programs in the United States in recent years may well have been the Menninger project in East Topeka and a similar undertaking in Chicago's Woodlawn community. Both are poor communities; in East Topeka the population mix is one-third black, one-third Mexican, one-third caucasian; in Woodlawn, 95 percent black. Now favored in this type of program are storefront clinics, preferably on a main traffic artery in low-income neighborhoods; thus the poor are not forced through the psychological barrier of going "uptown" to the hostile office building world where psychiatrists might normally be found. Modlin explains:

> We simply realized that most American psychiatry has been private, for middle-class people, assuming the patient will take his own initiative in coming, can participate in solving solely psychological problems, and that he is verbal and of good intelligence. The result is that large segments of the population are ignored. With the whole social ferment of recent times, we're becoming more aware of this and trying to see what kind of delivery system we can develop for the traditionally ignored—the poor, the aged, the mentally retarded, the alcoholic, the legal offender.

As Modlin describes the East Topeka experiment, it is one in which standard psychiatric diagnoses have been largely discarded. To tell someone he suffers from compulsive neurosis or a narcissistic character disorder is rather meaningless, Modlin points out, when the real problem is how to persuade a 15-year-old boy not to drop out of high school or what to do with a 14-year-old girl who's pregnant or how to get the old man to quit drinking up his paycheck on the weekend:

> We're trying to intervene with failing families, to determine if we mental health people have anything to offer. We receive referrals from the public welfare department, the juvenile parole officer, the school principal or public health nurse, all saying, in effect, "My God, I'm at my wit's end with this family." Then we try

to practice a client-oriented agency consultation, whether it be a breakdown in negotiations between a paranoid woman and the welfare worker, or where a school principal can't get a mother to come in to discuss a child with problems, or where two old sisters and their brother won't open the door to a public health nurse. So we go in and try to solve all the problems! Sometimes we wonder, "What is a psychiatrist doing here?"

But it's necessary, Modlin says, to help solve people's immediate and overwhelming problems before trust can develop. "Perhaps after three or four months," he adds, "you've solved their welfare problem or whatever, and then you can sit down at the dirty kitchen table with a woman over a sloppy cup of coffee and she'll start to tell you about her miserable childhood."

I asked Dr. Modlin if there had been an increase in the rate of mental illness in America since World War II.* His reply was that in terms of classic psychoses and neuroses, apparently not; the World Health Organization, for instance, finds a fairly uniform 1 percent of the population in all lands afflicted by schizophrenia, regardless of immediate environmental factors.

But there has been a dramatic rise in the indexes of American divorces, crime, juvenile delinquency, illegitimate births, and drug use. If these are to be defined as psychological disturbances, then the mental health of the United States has taken a severe turn for the worse. Clearly, preventive psychiatry programs like the Menningers' are likely to include almost every kind of social ill on the list that psychiatrists must concern themselves with. Dr. Karl Menninger, in fact, would add one we have not even mentioned yet—the open resort by protesters to violent street demonstrations and the destruction of property, balanced by the demand of some for ruthless counterviolence. One wonders if psychiatry has the depth to penetrate into such monumental societal problems, even with their obvious implications in the field of mental health. If anyone has the courage to attempt the task, it may well be the men of the Menninger Clinic, working from their unlikely vantage point near the center of the Great Plains.

* The Menningers recall two major revolutions in United States psychiatry since World War II. The first, in the immediate postwar era, was reorganization of Veterans Administration hospitals to provide advanced treatment with the use of drugs and milieu treatment. A new attitude emerged: that patients *could* be cured. Thus recovery rates in mental hospitals rose dramatically and the "Snake Pit" era of restraining cages, boards and chains, straitjackets, and metal grillwork window screens passed forever. Even in the 1950s, the Menningers themselves were building security rooms and facilities for violent patients into their hospital. But they have found no need for such facilities. Tranquilizers have played a major role, but also the simple discovery, as Dr. Modlin describes it, that "even though ill, patients see what's expected of them. If you expect a patient to be untidy, to defecate, to throw the radio across the room, he will. But if you put the most disturbed patient in a room with a rug on the floor and a lamp on the table, he won't destroy it."

The second psychiatric revolution came in development of community mental health centers throughout the nation. They were pushed forward in part because of officials' desperation at the unending, high cost of maintaining patients in big state mental hospitals that cannot attract sufficient physicians, nurses, or social workers, and where many patients develop "hospitalism"—a good adjustment to a regressed level of living. The community facilities, by contrast, can keep a patient living at home most of the time; he is in a context of maximal demand to make satisfactory readjustment to society.

OKLAHOMA!

OKLAHOMA is such a young state that men still live whose memory spans all the years since statehood came in 1907. A prime example is E. K. Gaylord, who arrived in Oklahoma City in 1902 and prospered for decades as publisher of the *Daily Oklahoman* and *Times*. (Still going strong and apparently in excellent health, Gaylord was looking forward to his 100th birthday in March 1973.)

Another man whose memory goes back almost to statehood is Otis Sullivant, a native son whose father had homesteaded in 1889, the year of the "run" that brought Oklahoma its first legal white settlement. Sullivant started covering politics for the *Oklahoman* in 1927 and kept busy at the job for 40 years, getting to know tens of thousands of Oklahomans in every hamlet of the state. His county-by-county election surveys were a detailed miracle of grass-roots pulse-taking (without benefit of professional sampling techniques); as far as I know, they have been fully matched by only two other political reporters in the U.S., George Mills of the Des Moines *Register* and John Corlett of the Boise (Idaho) *Statesman*.

When I planned some days of interviewing in Oklahoma, I wrote Otis, just retired from the newspaper, asking for suggestions about whom to see (besides himself). His reply covered a lot of what needs to be said about the Sooner State:

> Neal, Oklahoma is a great state. Its people have the heritage of the pioneers, Indians through the Five Civilized and many other tribes. It started as an agricul-

tural state, developed oil, went through the droughts and depressions, and now is trying to build and develop industry. It has a big welfare program, ranking at or near the top in per capita expenditures for welfare and percentage on the rolls. Like so many other states, Oklahoma seeks and sections of the state depend upon federal installations. It is sending far more students to college, and one of the constant wrangles is for sufficient money for common schools. . . .

Underneath, the Establishment runs the state. In the background is oil, with its powerful influence which now is directed largely to protect itself against added taxes or government interference. The metropolitan press, banks, utilities, agriculture, labor and other liberal elements figure in, but the power is with the conservative forces and the great wealth of the state is doing a good job protecting itself from taxation for state purposes. . . .

Oklahoma was agrarian, conservative, against federal bureaucracy, Democratic with a strong tincture of Populism at statehood. It is now tending toward a conservative side, but really just against the existing order of things. In a showdown on domestic issues the majority will be more liberal than conservative.

At statehood, the voter was independent, even ornery, and he didn't bow to authority or worship the man in high position. He was quick to be against, and the attitude was reflected in the near impeachment by the house of representatives of a governor in 1920, and the impeachment and ouster of two governors by the house and senate in 1923 and 1929.

Today, the voter is independent, doesn't hold too much to the line of conservative or liberal. . . .

The voters of Oklahoma are not too intelligent, are too quick to downgrade and to be against. They fail to inform themselves, are too prejudiced, and that is true as much in the country clubs as in the rural areas. [But] I think the voters of Oklahoma are as smart, or smarter than those in New York, New Jersey and many other states. They are influenced and prejudiced, but no one tells them how to vote.

I like to tell the story of one of my poll takers. We had covered the state. We had been in the beer parlors, beauty shops, stores, banks, stopped the farmers and loafers on the street. As we finished up and started home, I asked him: "You have been all over the state, now what do you think of the great unwashed?" He was a slow talker and I must have driven a mile before he answered: "Otis, I think they are getting about what they deserve."

Just what Oklahoma voters have turned out to "deserve" is a spicy assortment of politicians ranging from rambunctious old "Alfalfa Bill" Murray to that amiable pirate, Robert S. Kerr, and the diminutive, self-effacing man who is now Speaker of the U.S. House, Carl Albert. We will return to them shortly as we move through the story of this boisterous prairie state that has contributed Will Rogers, Pearl Mesta, Jim Thorpe, and Mickey Mantle to the world, fathered the illustrious University of Oklahoma football team, won fame as a great state of cowboys and Bible-belt fundamentalism, and been forever endeared to the country at large through Rodgers and Hammerstein's exuberant song in the musical of like name, *Oklahoma!*

Be all that as it may, it was the Indians who were there first. Even the name Oklahoma is Indian, from the Choctaw words *okla* (people) and *homma* (red). It was coined by Allen Wright, a Choctaw chief, in 1866. So it is the Indian story that deserves to be treated first.

"As Long as the Grass Grows and the Waters Run"

Less than a century ago, it was the announced policy of the U.S. Government that the land now Oklahoma be pure and simple "Indian Territory," free of white men altogether and for all time. As the historical chain of events goes, the first European intrusions occurred in 1541 when deSoto and Coronado both ventured through parts of what is now Oklahoma, finding no gold but rather great reaches of tall prairies grass and full rivers. Then, for over two centuries, the nomadic Plains Indians remained the only permanent occupants, disturbed only rarely by a few trappers or traders. In 1803 the land passed into U.S. control as part of the Louisiana Purchase from France. In the following decades, the old South—Tennessee, Alabama, Georgia, Mississippi—put increasing pressure on the federal government to relocate the "Five Civilized Tribes"—Cherokee, Seminole, Choctaw, Creek, and Chickasaw—who still disturbed the peace with occasional uprisings and occupied land the white men coveted. Oklahoma was a great and unknown no man's land, and the red men could be safely dispatched there. And so it was that the tribes were obliged to agree to their "removal" to what would be an inviolate "Indian Territory"—a land with a great invisible wall surrounding it, one the U.S. Government promised would be theirs and theirs alone "as long as the grass grows and the waters run."

The "Trail of Tears" by which the Five Tribes were herded westward from the Old South remains a dark blot in our history. When Army troops came in to round up the people for evacuation camps, many were totally unprepared; it is recorded that women left meals cooking over fireplaces, men dropped their plows, children forgot their toys as they were hurried away from their ancestral homes. Hunger, cold, tuberculosis, pneumonia all took a ferocious toll along the way, and of the Cherokees, 4,000 out of 15,000 perished before they reached Oklahoma.

The Five Civilized Tribes, already a largely literate and Christian group, soon reestablished themselves into quite successful communities in their newly ceded territory in Oklahoma. The territory for these nations was in the eastern part of the state; further out to the West the Plains Indians still roamed.

But the tide of white aggrandizement was not to be so easily satisfied. Stagelines, then railroads, and finally the Texas to Kansas Chisholm Trail of cattle began to criss-cross the territory. The nations found themselves involved in the Civil War, a conflict in which they suffered much and gained nothing. White settlers began to sift westward and squat on Indian lands. The railroads sent out professional white parties to destroy the buffalo, thus destroying the livelihood of the Plains Indians.* In response to violent disputes

*** According to one history, there was a pathetic legend, spread from tribe to tribe across the Plains, that the buffalo had gone underground. The earth had opened to receive the great beasts and had sheltered them. Somewhere below the earth the buffalo were grazing happily and peaceably again. The Indians believed that when the white man left the Plains, the buffalo would return. (Edward C. McReynolds *et al.*, *Oklahoma: The Story of Its Past and Present*—University of Oklahoma Press, Norman, 1967).**

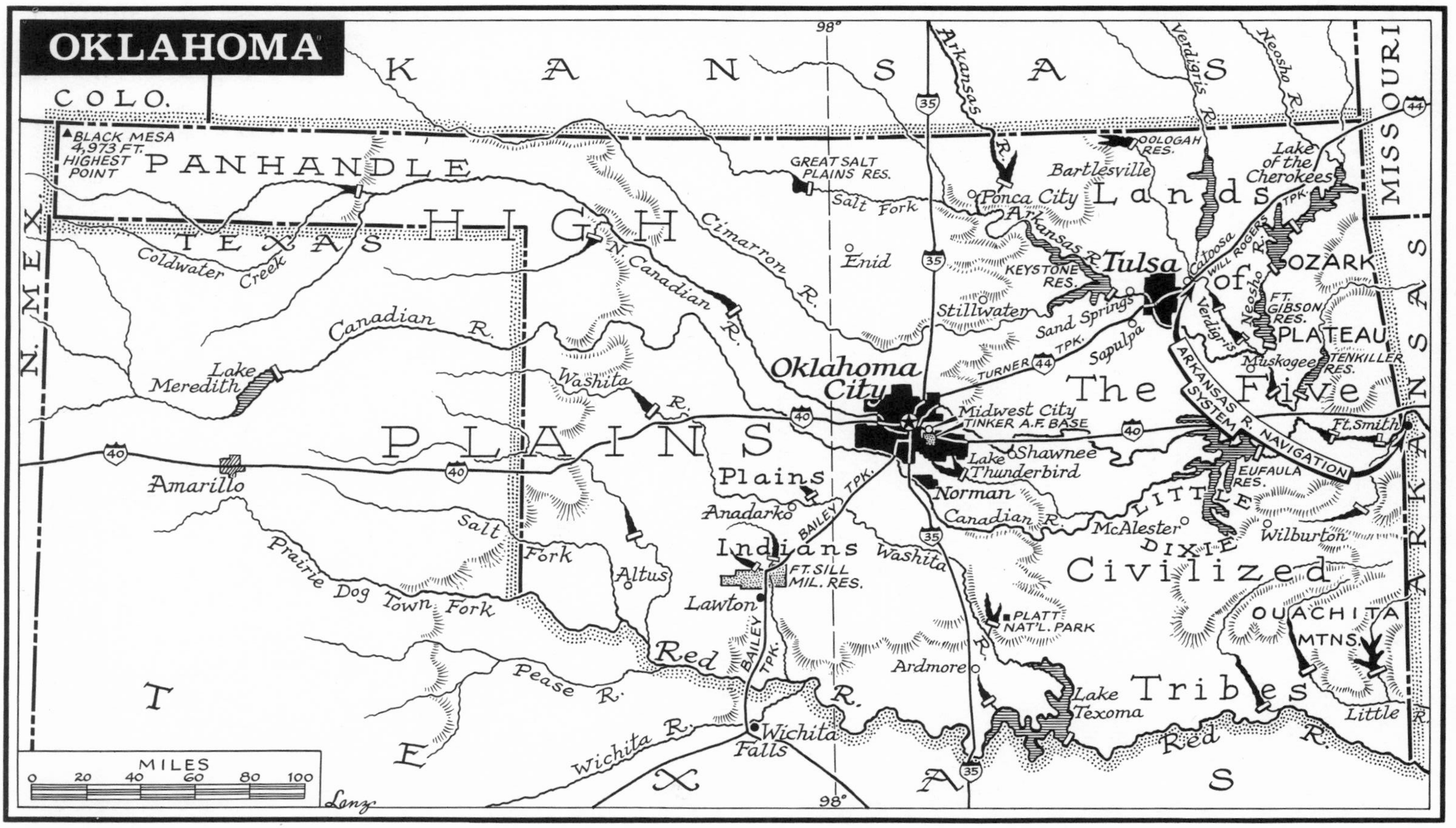
OKLAHOMA
KANSAS
COLO.
N. MEX.
MISSOURI
ARKANSAS
TEXAS
BLACK MESA 4,973 FT. HIGHEST POINT
PANHANDLE
HIGH PLAINS
Plains Indians
The Five Civilized Tribes
Lands of
OZARK PLATEAU
LITTLE DIXIE
OUACHITA MTNS.
ARKANSAS R. NAVIGATION SYSTEM
Oklahoma City
Tulsa
Midwest City
TINKER A.F. BASE
Lake Thunderbird
Shawnee
Norman
Enid
Stillwater
Ponca City
Bartlesville
Sand Springs
Sapulpa
Catoosa
Muskogee
Ft. Smith
McAlester
Wilburton
Anadarko
Lawton
FT. SILL MIL. RES.
Altus
Ardmore
PLATT NAT'L. PARK
Wichita Falls
Amarillo
Lake Meredith
Lake Texoma
Lake of the Cherokees
OOLOGAH RES.
KEYSTONE RES.
FT. GIBSON RES.
TENKILLER RES.
EUFAULA RES.
GREAT SALT PLAINS RES.
Arkansas R.
Verdigris R.
Neosho R.
Salt Fork
Cimarron R.
N. Canadian R.
Canadian R.
Washita R.
Salt Fork
Prairie Dog Town Fork
Red R.
Pease R.
Wichita R.
Little R.
Coldwater Creek
TURNER TPK.
WILL ROGERS TPK.
BAILEY TPK.
98°
MILES
0 20 40 60 80 100
Lenz

and sporadic raids by Indian hotheads, the U.S. Army in the 1860s and '70s carried on a bloody "pacification" campaign strikingly similar in some of its basic aspects to the Vietnam war a century later—including near massacres of entire villages where rebellious Indians were thought to be taking shelter among the more peaceable.

In their eastern Oklahoma lands, the Five Civilized Tribes perfected sophisticated nation-type governments, ran excellent schools with a number of white teachers, and published newspapers. When land-hungry whites suggested the Civilized Tribes were holding more land than they really occupied or needed, the Indians reacted with strong initial hostility—seeing, understandably, the first step down another Trail of Tears. Educators, churchmen, and other groups across the United States opposed any expropriation of surplus Indian lands in Oklahoma. But the pressure of white settlers for fresh land increased constantly, and by the 1880s large camps of "Boomers" were settling around the fringes of Oklahoma, waiting a chance to enter and homestead. Finally, the Creeks in 1889 offered to sell land they owned in central Oklahoma, and the federal government quickly agreed on a price. President Benjamin Harrison announced that on April 22 of that year, a big chunk of territory in central Oklahoma—the "Unassigned Lands"—would be opened for white settlement.

Oklahoma histories glow with excitement when they talk of that day. Thousands of hardy young settlers and their families surrounded the Unassigned Lands on every side. Federal troops formed a fence between the home-seekers and the land, and the rules were that any settlers who had ventured earlier, and thus illegally, onto these lands, thus acquainting themselves with the most select parcels of land, would be ineligible for homesteading. But proving that someone was a "Sooner"—and this is the origin of that word—was often difficult if not impossible, and hundreds may have been hidden in the woods and gullies that April 22. Most of the people, however, waited behind the lines, and then at noon a cannon boomed and the legal Boomers went rushing across the lines. On foot they came, or on race horses, or driving two-wheeled racing sulkies or farm wagons or high bicycles and jumping off the steps of a special, slow-moving Santa Fe Railway train. Quickly the flagged stakes, marking out homesteads or plots in the designated towns, formed their patterns. That morning the Unassigned Lands had an official population of zero; that night it was some 20,000. Among the cities that sprouted from the prairie in a single day were Oklahoma City, Guthrie, Norman, and Stillwater.

The 1889 Run broke the dike; soon the Indians found themselves obliged, by one means or another, to surrender more and more of the territory once held inviolate. Three more runs between 1889 and 1895 opened up an additional 10 million acres. The Indian nations struggled for several years to remain independent of the Oklahoma Territory, but gradually they lost virtually all of their land. Numbers had as much to do with it as anything else; by 1895, for instance, whites outnumbered Indians four to one in a population of 350,000. Congress in effect put the national governments of the Five Civilized Tribes under a death sentence by decreeing they would end their legal power in March 1906.

Then came the final glimpse of Camelot for the Indians—a meeting of representatives of the tribes in August 1905, where a constitution was adopted for a new Indian state of the Union, to be called "State of Sequoyah." Though Indians dominated, many whites or half-bloods participated—among them "Alfalfa Bill" Murray (who had married an Indian woman) and part-blood William Clem Rogers, father of the famous Will. Covering the eastern end of Oklahoma, the state of Sequoyah would have been almost equal to the white-dominated regular territory farther to the west. The constitution the Sequoyah assemblage wrote was approved by the people of the Indian Territory, 56,279 to 9,073. But the idea was killed in Congress, reportedly because Republicans feared the Sequoyahns would vote Democratic. One can only speculate about what it might have meant to the United States in the 20th century to have had in Congress a true Indian state, with the diversity of race, the freshness of viewpoint, and the feeling of solidarity with all American Indians that its representatives would certainly have evolved.

As it was, the bill authorizing a single state of the Oklahoma and Indian Territories sailed through Congress in 1906. The constitution written the next year in preparation for official statehood was an example in bad lawmaking, 10 times as long as the federal Constitution. But the people approved it, 180,333 to 73,059, and Oklahoma on November 16, 1907, became the 46th state of the Union. (The only four still younger are Arizona, New Mexico, Alaska, and Hawaii.)

Today Oklahoma's Five Civilized Tribes, stripped of most powers except ceremonial, continue with their own councils and chiefs and structures and cultures in eastern Oklahoma; out in the western reaches of Oklahoma, there are still many Plains Indians, including Cheyennes, Apaches, Arapahoes, and others. History was made in the 1960s when for the very first time there was a joint meeting of the chiefs, both of the Five Tribes and of the Plains Indians. In terms of living standards, the Civilized Tribes are said to be more fortunate. But this is only comparatively so. In rugged beautiful Adair County in eastern Oklahoma, a land of rocky hills and colorful scrub oaks, one finds the highest Indian contingent of any county in the state. Most of these are Cherokees. But 90 percent of the families are on welfare. In all America, in fact, there are only a handful of counties where the indexes of economic well-being are so low.

Oklahoma, according to the Census Bureau, now has more Indians than any other state. The 1970 figure was 98,468, an increase of 52 percent since a decade before. While the official Census Indian figure represents only 3.8 percent of Oklahoma's total population, I have heard estimates that there are really as many as 200,000 full-blooded or almost full-blooded Indians in the state. I have also heard it suggested that as many as 500,000 Oklahomans—a quarter of the total population—may have some drop of Indian blood in their veins. The degree of intermarriage is remarkable, unmatched in any other state, and those who do have Indian blood tend to be quite proud of it. Many of the state's prominent leaders, from its earliest days down to the present, have been part Indian—though very few, one notes with interest, full-blooded Indian.

An imaginative program for the state's Indians was launched in the mid-1960s by a group brought together by LaDonna Harris, a half-Comanche and wife of then-Senator Fred Harris. The organization, Oklahomans for Indian Opportunity, has been trying to help Indians with their problems of identity (with young people especially in mind), to set up day care centers, organize buying clubs for groceries and other purchases, and move toward work with the estimated quarter of all Oklahoma Indians who live in the big towns—Tulsa and Oklahoma City. Mrs. Iola Hayden, former director of OIO, told me a major part of the program was to give the traditionally shy and reticent Indians a chance to assert themselves, to build self-confidence and take a more aggressive attitude in school and work situations. That effort contributed, of course, to the wave of national Indian militancy in the early 1970s. OIO, in the meantime, began to concentrate more on Indian self-help economic projects.

To hear Mrs. Hayden, the common belief that discrimination against the Oklahoma Indians has ceased, and that they are free to enter the larger society, is simply false. She speaks of the high Indian school dropout rate, of school counselors telling Indian children they lack the intelligence to go on to college, and self-fulfilling prophecies that Indian children (some of whom enter school not even speaking English) will be quiet and withdrawn and ineffective in school. For Indians everywhere in the state, and especially in the west, she said, there is an alarming shortage of jobs. And living conditions can be frightful; she cites the instance of an aged woman in western Oklahoma living in a drafty old unpainted shack that is frigid in winter, filled with flies in summer, dampened by a leaky roof, and infested with scorpions and an occasional rat.

A world away from these conditions is Cherokee W. W. Keeler, who was president of Oklahoma's giant home-based oil company, Phillips Petroleum, until his 1973 retirement. Keeler is principal chief of the Cherokee Nation, a post to which he was first appointed by President Truman in 1948 and in which he has begun many programs to improve his people economically. Sometimes forgotten is the fact the Keeler is only one-sixteenth Indian by blood—but that kind of blood ratio is not untypical of many leading figures of the Civilized Nations. Both Presidents Eisenhower and Kennedy asked Keeler to be commissioner of Indian Affairs, a position he declined. But he has served on countless Presidential commissions, conveniently helping the red man's cause while the public image of Phillips Petroleum prospered happily at the same time. In 1971, when the Cherokees regained the right to select their own leaders, Phillips was elected to a four-year term as principal chief.

But men of Keeler's stature are few and far between, and the more typical Oklahoman image of the state's Indians was expressed in an interview with Jenkin Lloyd Jones, editor of the Tulsa *Tribune:*

> The ability of the Indian to assert himself in the white man's world is limited. Under his tribal system, the male was the hunter and warrior, the squaw the raiser of the children and keeper of the tepee. The squaw never lost her job. But when the buffalo disappeared and the sheriff wouldn't let him make war anymore, the male sat and vegetated. He was not willing to buy the white man's standard of values. A tragic thing results—the Indian is stubborn and won't do it the white man's way. But unfortunately, we're not going to evacuate Oklahoma and the buffalo are not going to come back.

And so the ancient quandary persists. A prevalent "myth" in Oklahoma, as I have heard it told, is that the Cherokee are becoming so rapidly assimilated that they will be "bred out" in another generation or two. Sociologists Albert L. Wahrhaftig and Robert K. Thomas did a study of that idea in the late 1960s and found it quite unfounded.* The Cherokees, they reported, are "a populous and lively community" who inhabit the rough "Ozark" country of the old Indian territory of northeastern Oklahoma, with thousands more in the towns and small cities. (The 1970 Census found a total of 27,197 Cherokees in Oklahoma.) In a process going back over more than a century to the time of the March of Tears, the Cherokees divided into two groups. One group, the still very identifiable hill people, maintain the pure blood line and speak the pure language. These are the Cherokees with a per capita income measured at only $500 in the 1960s, many living in conditions of "virtual peonage" because of job market discrimination—a group whose lot is as pitiable as that of any other minority group in America. On the other hand, the group of Cherokees most visible to the outside world, and the kind most Oklahomans think of when they suggest total assimilation, are the intermarrying kind, descendants of those who cooperated with the federal government from the time of the great removal to the West onwards. They are now, the sociologists report, "assimilated and functionally white Americans, though fiercely proud of their Cherokee blood." Even though the newfound militancy in Indian youth is disturbing the old patterns, it seems likely that the two big Cherokee groups, having gone their separate ways for 140 years and more, will do so a while longer.

Three Top Sooners: Alfalfa Bill, Bob Kerr, Carl Albert

Knowing three key Sooners tells a lot about what Oklahoma has been and may be becoming:

- William ("Alfalfa Bill") Murray, chairman of the convention that drew up the state constitution in 1907 (a task at which he wore out three gavels), later Oklahoma's depression-times governor. Murray was a successful courtroom attorney in his early years with sharp native intelligence that led to his suggestion that the farmers put nitrogen back into their cottonfields by

* "Renaissance and Repression: The Oklahoma Cherokee," in *Trans-action,* February 1969.

planting legumes—thus the "Alfalfa Bill" nickname. But in the hard-times year of 1930, Murray let alfalfa stand for hayseed. He ran for governor against a wealthy oilman by touring Oklahoma in his old car, abjuring political banquets for curbside cheese-and-cracker meals from paper bags, letting his long mustache go untrimmed and ragged and the trousers of his old brown suit bag at the knees—all ways of crystallizing the common-man image and recalling Oklahoma's pioneer beginnings. "I'm not an extremist. I believe firmly in our capitalistic plan—if capitalism can be forced to restrain its ungodly greed and serve the needs of humanity," Murray declared.

In office, Murray was in fact no radical and even opposed President Roosevelt's programs to create jobs through federal funds. But colorful he remained throughout. John Gunther recalled that an unsuspecting visitor to the gubernatorial offices, sitting in a chair carefully placed three feet from Murray's desk, might try to hitch himself closer—only to discover that the chair was nailed to the floor and hear Murray shout, "What the hell do you want?" He often went barefoot and kept his socks in his desk. One thing Murray did was to break the legislature of the impeachment habit it had developed in the 1920s. When a legislator suggested impeaching him, Murray said he had done nothing that the legislators hadn't done themselves—"except think." "If you have any impeachment ideas in your heads, hop to it," he said. "It'll be like a bunch of jackrabbits tryin' to get a wildcat out of a hole."

■ Robert S. Kerr, Oklahoma's first native-born governor, who made it from the log cabin where he was born in 1896 to become a multimillionaire oilman and—along with Lyndon B. Johnson—one of the two most effective power-brokers the U.S. Senate has seen in modern times. Kerr was a great bear of a man (six feet, three inches and between 220 and 275 pounds), jovial, exuberant, a formidable opponent in every sense. He never got a degree but passed bar examinations in 1922, cut his political teeth as state American Legion commander in 1926, made a great fortune in the oil business, served as governor in the mid-1940s, and then went on to the Senate, where he served for 14 years before his death in 1963. Kerr was a fervent Baptist and taught a Sunday School class any weekend he might be back in Oklahoma City. Dean A. McGee, his partner for many years in the highly successful Kerr-McGee Oil Industries, told me Kerr had been "a man of complete integrity, big-hearted, highly intellectual, a great doer, a real Christian gentleman who lived his religion."

Others have not been so charitable, suggesting that Kerr used his Senate position to defend and profit personally from the 27½ percent oil depletion allowance and many other bills of direct aid to Kerr-McGee with its far-flung interests in petroleum, natural gas, beryllium, boron, helium, potash, and uranium.* *Time*'s very responsible Capitol Hill correspondent, Neil

* Thanks to the depletion allowance, Kerr-McGee paid less than 13 percent income tax on total aggregate profits of $77 million in the seven years before Kerr died, according to records of the Securities and Exchange Commission. Kerr-McGee cornered about a quarter of all known uranium sources in the U.S., winning so many government contracts that competitors appealed to the Justice Department for an investigation of "political influence."

MacNeil, reported * some years after Kerr's death that he had been "one of the most ruthless politicians ever to enter the Senate:

Caustic and bruising in debate, utterly careless of his colleagues' sensibilities, Kerr had risen under the Senate's seniority system to a position of immense power, in effect controlling the decisions of both the Finance and Public Works Committees while he chaired the space committee. He exacted a price for every favor he gave, even from the President. "Bob Kerr never does anything for nothing," said one of Kennedy's aides. Kerr bragged that he was against "any combine I ain't in on," and once he threatened to take Senator Paul Douglas out into a Senate hallway and thrash him. In 1962, according to Bobby Baker's testimony at his trial for tax evasion, Kerr wrung $99,600 from officials of a California savings-and-loan association while the Senate was considering a tax bill they opposed.

Kerr, of course, was no longer around to defend himself against Baker's accusation. Kerr's personal finances remained a tangle for several years after his death, beacuse—incredibly—this man of so much wealth and influence had died without writing a will.

■ Carl A. Albert, who was elected in 1971 as Speaker of the House of Representatives, one of the two or three most powerful positions in the United States government. Albert was born 62 years earlier in a farmhouse at Big Tussle—a little hamlet near McAlester, in "Little Dixie," the poorest part of southeastern Oklahoma. He was the son of a tenant farmer and sometime coal miner, didn't live in a house with electricity or running water until he was 16, and wore bib overalls to school. Later Albert went on to the University of Oklahoma, and John Fischer of *Harper's Magazine*, a fellow student, recalls a first impression of the future Speaker: "He was five feet, four inches tall, with jug ears and the face of a startled prairie dog; and he wore the kind of clothes which were considered sharp in those days by the smalltown customers of Al's Cut Rate Toggery." But even then, Fischer records, Albert showed "charisma." The source of the ambition might have been the drive of so many short men to excel, but Fischer guesses "he was driven like most of us in those Depression days by a desperate eagerness to escape from poverty. . . . Anybody who tried to scratch a crop out of [southeastern Oklahoma's] red dust was doomed to a meager, anxious and scrabbling life."

Albert quickly proved himself, winning debating honors, chairmanship of the university student council, election to Phi Beta Kappa, and a Rhodes scholarship. He studied three years at Oxford and earned two law degrees. Along the way, the little man also excelled at wrestling and learned Spanish, which he still speaks fluently. In the Army in World War II, he rose from private to lieutenant colonel, seeing service in the South Pacific. Returning to McAlester in 1946, he saw a chance to run for Congress, took it, and won over four other candidates by just 359 votes.

Since then, Carl Albert has never had an even close election, and his whole life has been the U.S. House—except, of course, for the two times a month when he flies home, rents a car, and drives alone to talk with the home folks at every little rural crossroad. In Washington, Albert has suc-

* In his book *Dirksen: Portrait of a Public Man* (New York: World Publishing Co., 1970).

ceeded through unflagging attention to the personalities and needs of his fellow lawmakers. His approach is strictly low-keyed, using persuasion rather than high-pressure tactics to get the cooperation of others. Scarcely a soul can be found who does not like Albert, and he is respected for his scrupulous honesty. (He refuses big campaign contributions from anyone, including oil and labor interests.)

Albert's district is just across the Red River from the one in Texas that the late Sam Rayburn used to represent, and the two men became close friends in something akin to a father-son relationship. (They also shared an unusual attribute in the wheeler-dealer atmosphere of Texas and Oklahoma politics: unquestionable personal integrity and a refusal to obligate themselves financially to the special interests.) Rayburn gave Albert his start on the party ladder in 1954, by selecting him as whip, and from there on Albert had more than enough personal support to win the majority leadership when Rayburn died in 1961, and the Speakership succeeding John McCormack in 1971. Throughout his career, he has voted like many a Northern liberal, but his conservative appearance and local pride in his rise to leadership have been so great that few if any home-district problems have been posed. Albert's two greatest problems have been his 1966 heart attack (a severe blow from which he seemed to have recovered completely at the time he was elected Speaker) and the ill fate of being chosen permanent chairman of the 1968 Democratic National Convention in Chicago. Wittingly or not, Albert came across as the tool of high-handed managers determined to run that convention in a way that would suppress any real dissent among the delegates.

Albert's far greater task as he began his tenure as Speaker was to restore the U.S. House to its constitutionally envisioned role as a thoroughly democratic, responsive organ of the people's will—rather than the seniority-encrusted, privilege-preoccupied body which McCormack and even Rayburn had allowed it to become. Some said the "little giant from little Dixie" was too nice a guy to effect the deep-seated reform required; others claimed there was steel yet unknown in the man. The record, at the end of Albert's first two years as Speaker, was mixed. All too often, he yielded to the whims and opinions of his committee "barons" or moved much too late in the legislative process to curb them most effectively. President Nixon and his legislative tacticians seemed more adept at getting what they wanted out of the House than the Speaker. Ralph Nader's congressional study faulted Albert for having a press secretary and a public relations consultant but virtually no professional staff to research issues or ride herd on legislation coming before the House. On the other hand, Albert did push House Democrats to offer alternatives to several Nixon programs, especially in the economic field. He won approval of some reforms, like recorded votes on floor amendments (for the first time in history) and spreading subcommittee chairmanships to more junior members. As Congress opened in 1973, Albert promised new toughness and tightened his control over the important Rules Committee. But more pressure than ever would be on him to provide strong leadership and help right the modern imbalance of power in favor of the Executive Branch.

The Political Scoreboard

Sooners have packed more political feudin' and a-fussin' into the eight decades since the first Run than many states can account for in a century and a half of more placid existence. Many think of Oklahoma as a conservative state, but it has a radical streak from its Grange and Populist background; one reason the state constitution is so impossibly long is that it is chock-full of supposed safeguards against predatory corporation power, including a requirement that the governor at his inauguration swear not to accept a railroad pass. But, as editor Jenkin Lloyd Jones of the Tulsa *Tribune* counseled me, "this doesn't mean that corporations have had a bad time in Oklahoma. Far from it, they have the Corporation Commission in their pocket." (The Corporation Commission wields fantastic power, regulating all transportation companies, power companies, and the proration laws affecting oil companies.)

One thing was absolutely constant about Oklahoma politics, at least until the 1960s—the state's blind loyalty to the Democratic party. This was another of the "tantamount to election" states like the deepest South. The pattern was set in the first statewide election in 1907, when the Democrats elected a governor, two U.S. Senators, four of the five U.S. Representatives, and overwhelming majorities in both houses of the state legislature. Most of the county offices also went to the Democrats, laying the foundation for the rule by "county rings" which have used the one-party system to dominate from the county courthouses ever since.

What made and makes Oklahoma so Democratic? One reason is the surfeit of down-and-outers, James Oglethorpe's Georgia debtors on the second bounce and other dispossessed, who settled there. As far as such people could see, the Republican party was connected with (1) Reconstruction and pro-Negro politics, and (2) big Eastern business interests—both anathema to the hard-pressed Southern farmer. The early waves of settlement did include some Republicans from Kansas, Missouri, and the upper Mississippi and Ohio River Valleys, who tended to settle in northern and northeastern Oklahoma (including Tulsa) and add some Republican flavor. But it was the people from Texas, Arkansas, Georgia, Mississippi, and Alabama who occupied more populous southern and southeastern Oklahoma, including Oklahoma City. In "Little Dixie," the state's southeastern corner, they literally recreated the Old South in Oklahoma with a provincial, proud, dogmatic—and "brass collar" Democratic civilization. On a statewide map, it has been a rule of thumb that Democrats win south of the east-west running Rock Island Railroad Line, Republicans north of it. Actually, the political balance of power shifts north and south by one or two tiers of counties in each election. It has been a rare year when the Republicans have extended the line far enough south to win an election.

But there have been exceptions. Although no Republican won election as governor until Oklahoma was 55 years old, Republicans were sent to the U.S. Senate three times before the 1960s. The chaotic 1942 Senate election illustrates some of the difficulties Democrats sometimes made for themselves. Senator Josh Lee, a New Deal Democrat, was up for reelection. He had two formidable Democratic primary opponents, including a former governor. These opponents, or certainly their henchmen, persuaded two entirely unknown men named Josh Lee to file. The real Josh Lee survived the primary, only to be undercut by his Democratic enemies in the general election and lose to a Republican. Another familiar trick has been to split the vote against any prominent incumbent by entering against him a number of common citizens with illustrious names, likely to draw support away from any really serious opposition. Names like Oliver Cromwell, Mae West, Joe E. Brown, Brigham Young, and William Cullen Bryant have all appeared on Oklahoma ballots.

When the Republicans finally did manage to crack Oklahoma's encrusted Democratic habits by electing a governor in 1962, it was not only their excellent campaign organization in heavily Republican cities like Tulsa that did the job. Predictably, a Democrat helped—Raymond J. Gary, a conservative ex-governor of the 1950s, who tried again in the 1962 primary but lost. Gary's failure to support the Democratic nominee in 1962 was thought to have played an important role in permitting wheat farmer Henry L. Bellmon to win election as the first Republican governor in Oklahoma history.

Four years later, in 1966, Republicans elected another governor, Tulsa oilman Dewey F. Bartlett. This time, Democratic factionalism was not quite as rampant. Bartlett's election came as a surprise to many because he was a Roman Catholic and a Princeton graduate—hardly the right credentials in a hard-shell Baptist, distinctly non-Eastern state. Anti-Catholic sentiment was thought to have had a lot to do with the overwhelming Oklahoma defeats suffered by Al Smith in the 1928 Presidential election and John F. Kennedy in 1960. So heavy is Baptist influence in Oklahoma that it was not until 1959 that the voters finally agreed to do away with the prohibition clause written in their state constitution 52 years before.* Oklahoma's population is over 95 percent Protestant.

Under a new constitutional provision, Bartlett was the first Oklahoma governor eligible to run to succeed himself directly. Despite his conservatism and opposition to new taxes, the voters rejected Bartlett's bid for a second term in 1970, electing Democrat David Hall in his stead.

The partisan scorecard shows that in 246 elections to the U.S. House from Oklahoma, the Democrats have won 200 times, the Republicans 46 times. Henry Bellmon deserves the credit for building the first viable statewide organization the Republicans have ever had—one likely to continue growing as the state urbanizes. There is obviously latent Republicanism (or

* A newspaper report from Oklahoma City on Sept. 5, 1959, the day legal liquor returned to the state, contained these words of comfort for anyone concerned about how Sooners endured the drought: "Although the state has been constitutionally dry since statehood, nobody has suffered from a great thirst. Liquor has always been plentiful, with bootleggers doing a flourishing business throughout the state. Drinking Oklahomans have boasted that they have the finest service in the nation. It just took a telephone call to bring quick deliveries 24 hours a day and seven days a week."

at least conservatism) to draw on; since 1952, for instance, Oklahoma has voted Republican in every Presidential election except 1964. Bellmon himself won election to the U.S. Senate in 1968 by a substantial 50,462-vote margin over veteran Democratic Senator A. S. Mike Monroney, an Oklahoma fixture famed for his work in the fields of aviation and congressional reform. That same year, Nixon got 449,697 votes in Oklahoma, compared to only 301,-658 for Humphrey. Had it not been for George Wallace, who drew a significant 191,731 vote total, Nixon's win would have been all the more overwhelming. The 1972 elections seemed to prove the point, when Nixon swept the state with a plurality of 516, 934 votes (73.7 percent). On the same day, former Governor Bartlett took Oklahoma's other Senate seat for the GOP, beating a popular Democratic congressman, Ed Edmondson, by a margin of 38,722 votes (51.4 percent). But the Democrats actually picked up a long-time Republican House seat in the Tulsa area to control the new congressional delegation, five to one.

The greatest shift in Oklahoma politics, Otis Sullivant believes, is the "trend of thinking of young people away from the old Democratic line. They're still liberal but against the welfare state end of it. More and more are Republicans." But still, the GOP has a long way to go to effective local power. The state legislature elected in 1972 had a senate weighted 38–10 for the Democrats, a house with a 75–26 Democratic balance—the same almost hopeless outnumbering of the Republicans which had prevailed since statehood. The GOP is even worse off at the level of local government, where the courthouse rings are solidly Democratic except in a scattering of Republican beachheads.

Oklahoma Democrats have insulated themselves against adverse partisan trends by providing not a single straight ticket lever on voting machines, but three—one for national, one for state, one for local candidates. In paper ballot precincts, the voter actually gets three separate ballots.

The saga of Fred Harris demonstrates how dangerous it can be for an Oklahoma politician, regardless of his partisan label, to become known as a strong liberal. A promising young state senator generally regarded as a moderate Democrat, Harris first won election to the U.S. Senate in 1964. After a few years in office, however, Harris seemed to go too far to the left—on issues ranging from antiwar demonstrations and crime control to race relations—for Sooner tastes. Among other things, Harris played a key role on President Johnson's National Advisory Committee on Civil Disorders, which produced a report citing "white racism" and lack of concern as the underlying cause of urban riots. (However courageous, Harris's work for minorities was little appreciated in Oklahoma, a state where the themes of Old Dixie linger on. The minorities constituency in the state—the Indians, as well as the 171,892 blacks counted in the 1970 Census—lacks strong political organization.)

After comanaging Hubert Humphrey's 1968 Presidential campaign, Harris served a year as Democratic National Chairman. By 1971, at 40 years of age, he had moved so far from Oklahoma political orthodoxy that he announced he would not run again for the Senate in 1972 but would mount an "exploratory 'New Populist' campaign" for the Democratic nomination for President.

Harris' Presidential campaign lasted but a few months, ending abruptly in November 1971, when he announced he was "broke" and the campaign $40,000 in debt. His platform was apparently too far to the left, even for the big liberal contributors to Democratic causes.

If outspoken liberalism is unpopular in Oklahoma, so is any effort to win office just on the basis of glittering personality. The point was illustrated in 1964, when the Republicans ran for the U.S. Senate a man who was a literal Sooner State institution—Bud Wilkinson, former football coach at the University of Oklahoma. Wilkinson lost that year to Fred Harris, whose personal glamor could scarcely compare. The reason for Wilkinson's defeat long confused me, until I read a piece by managing editor John Carmody of *Potomac* magazine in the Washington *Post*. Here are a few paragraphs that also say a lot about the Oklahoman character (Carmody is talking about Wilkinson and "the picture we had drawn in our minds during the Fifties and early Sixties out in the Plains country"):

> One had to be out there then to understand the impact of this man [Wilkinson] on a whole state, a whole region, through his insistence on what now seem wonderfully simple disciplines and ingenious little marks of success.
>
> There was the unheard-of DC-6 belonging to OU, landing those always lean, always crewcut, always tied and jacketed, almost always white young Sooners at some windblown airport near Boulder or Lincoln on a gray, threatening fall Friday afternoon. . . .
>
> There was a hint of what he meant to the Southwest in the oddly touching parties that bubbled in hotel lobbies in some out-of-the-way place later those Saturday nights: the alumni in their gaudy Big Red jackets, the Oklahoma women in their print dresses, some overworked pianist hacking away on "Boomer Sooner." . . .
>
> And somehow it was all there, the job that Bud had done on the big oil money mentality and the Joads alike, restoring regional pride and taking the sting out of that lonely Saturday night feeling one can get over great stretches of the Southwest even today. . . .
>
> "Bud was always a lot more than just a whistle and a sweat shirt," says one old friend. "He changed the whole image of the state *and* his profession. He didn't jump his contract. His kids dressed the right way. His own graduates . . . went on to be in his image. Winners. He was low key." This same man recalls how, in 1964, when Bud Wilkinson changed his Democratic registration and ran as a Republican against Fred Harris he "didn't vote for Bud. I didn't want him mixed up in a business like politics, frankly. He was better than that and a lot of my friends thought the same way."

Why do Oklahomans take such a low view of "politics"? The answer may go back to the 1920s and the gutter fights over impeachment of governors. It may be the recollection of the era of cronyism, patronage in virtually all state government jobs, and highway and election scandals that lasted well into the postwar period. A general clean-up of government was effected by J. Howard Edmondson (the brother of Ed Edmondson), a controversial but courageous governor of the late '50s and early '60s. (Elected at 33, Edmondson arranged to have himself appointed to an interim term in the Senate just after Kerr's death, but Harris defeated him in the next Democratic primary.

He is still remembered, however, as the man who insisted on the merit system in state employment, put through a state central purchasing system, and led the successful drive to repeal prohibition. Many believed he erred in trying to do too much and in acquiring something of a playboy image—and thus terminating a promising political career at a very early age. He died in 1971.)

Yet another reason for Oklahomans' low view of politics may be the scandal that enveloped the Oklahoma Supreme Court in the mid-1960s, leading to the impeachment of one justice and the conviction of two others on charges that included bribery and criminal evasion of taxes. Probably the most shocking case of all for Oklahomans was the successful IRS prosecution of Justice Earl Welch, a respected jurist from Antlers, Oklahoma, a Cherokee and former chairman of the Judicial Council of the state.

State Government: Reforming, Cautiously

The story of what Oklahoma did to revamp its court system tells a lot about how far the state has come—and not come—in developing a clean and progressive system of government. Up to the 1960s, judges had always been elected on a partisan ticket. Earl Sneed, former dean of the University of Oklahoma Law School, then came forth with a proposal for selection of judges at both the trial and appellate court level on the model of the so-called "Missouri Plan," under which a commission of laymen and lawyers gives the governor three names whenever there is a vacancy. The governor selects one of the three, who serves until the next general election, when the public votes "yes" or "no" on retaining him for additional six-year terms. Secondly, Sneed proposed replacing a topsy-turvy court system that had grown to 13 separate tribunals since statehood, substituting the American Bar Association's "court of justice" concept in which a state supreme court controls all courts of appeals and district courts.

Sneed later told me that when he proposed all this, he didn't believe it had "a ghost of a chance" of passage, chiefly because it would erase the control the legislature had had over the court system ever since statehood and would disrupt local politics by such "radical" steps as abolishing the archaic local justice-of-the-peace system. But the far-reaching reform proposal caught the vision of many young attorneys, the League of Women Voters, and some of the state's major newspapers. Seeing no chance for approval of the reform by the legislature, they gathered 142,377 signatures to put the whole reform on the ballot as an initiative proposal for vote of the people. Opponents quickly challenged the petitions, but by the time they could be declared legal the legislature had gone ahead and enacted its own plan. It was a more limited reform, based on the Illinois system, which retained essential legislative control of the courts but which even Sneed and his followers considered much better than Oklahoma's old system. The legislature quickly submitted its plan to a vote of the people, who approved it. Starting in January 1969, Oklahoma had a whole new court system.

Meanwhile, back at the supreme court, the original Sneed plan petitions were suddenly found valid and submitted for a vote. After years of no chance for reform, the voters suddenly had a *choice*—to keep the more limited legislature-written reform plan they had already approved, or going an extra step to the Sneed plan. The Sneed plan was endorsed by the major newspapers of Oklahoma, but it encountered heavy opposition—both from the legislators, who said their own plan should be tried out in operation first, and from county officials who suddenly realized how much power they had already lost over courts under the legislature plan, and that the Sneed plan would diminish their influence over the judiciary almost completely. When the returns were in, only three of 77 counties had voted for the Sneed plan, and it lost 171,545 to 115,654. What had been demonstrated was the firm, enduring power of Oklahoma's county rings.

The issue of county power is one that escapes most American voters today in their preoccupation with cities and the much more visible state governments. Obviously the breaking up of Oklahoma into 77 administrative units of a day's horse-and-buggy ride makes little sense in the late 20th century. But ancient forms of county power hold on with amazing tenacity. Of state revenues distributed to localities, Oklahoma cities get only 2.3 percent, while over 30 percent goes to the counties. The local county commissioner is likely to exercise the ultimate political power in his bailiwick. Few are the state legislators who will want to cross him. And by a thousand favors, from tax concessions to clearing snow from private roads, county commissioners can entrench themselves with their local constituencies.

Knowledgeable Oklahomans tell one that the state constitution and the entire state government are badly in need of reorganization. Oklahoma has 137 state departments and agencies with overlapping and sometimes conflicting jurisdictions and countless impediments to the exercise of clear executive authority. Constitutional revision could shorten the state ballot, put more power in the hands of the governor, and effect major revision in school financing. Another problem that needs attention is existing law which permits gross inequalities in tax valuations and assessments across the state. Another candidate for change is a 1941-vintage budget-balancing amendment which prohibits the legislature from appropriating more money than it raised in taxes the year before. With inflation, this has meant that Oklahoma can appropriate less than it is actually getting in revenue, leaving much-needed money idle for a full year. The elected state treasurer has complete say over which banks will get idle state funds (usually about $240 million), and traditionally half the amount is in interest-free accounts while the other half earns only a nominal 2½ percent interest. Properly invested, the money could bring Oklahoma government an extra $6 million a year in income.

Institutions like the Oklahoma Academy for State Goals have called for thoroughgoing constitutional revision. But in 1970, when the voters were given the choice of two avenues to reform—calling of a state constitutional convention, or article-by-article revision—both proposals were beaten by margins of better than 7–3. Only two counties, both urban, were in favor. Again, it was rural county leaders who led the opposition. Two academicians had proposed consolidating the 77 counties into 20, and while the proposal was not even involved in the vote, the emotional issue of county power had been raised, only to thwart change once more.

The innate conservatism with which Oklahoma views the world was illustrated by two spectacular resignations of officials in 1970. First came corrections director Arnold Pontesso, a 30-year veteran of federal corrections work who had taken over the state post in 1967 with an eye to instituting far-ranging changes. "We cage people like animals in a zoo," Pontesso said. "But we not only pay our real zookeepers more than our people working in prisons, we provide bigger and better cages in real zoos."

As a way to prepare young offenders with a good chance for rehabilitation for life on the outside, Pontesso took $100,000 of a federal grant and leased two pleasant motels in Tulsa and Oklahoma City for the convicts to stay in for the 90 days prior to their release. They were to be allowed to go outside to scout for jobs and study. The Okie reaction was immediate and negative. Local property owners complained that the value of their property would be reduced, or that convicts might escape and harm them. Legislators suggested "mollycoddling" of criminals. To such objections, Pontesso replied it would be less dangerous than dropping the same men in the downtown section three months later with $25 each and no supervision. When he was summoned before a state legislature committee to explain his program, Pontesso opened his statement with a resignation, personally blistered the senate president pro tem, and denounced politics in general. (The state's chief penal facility is still the Oklahoma State Penitentiary at McAlester, which was built 60 years ago for 1,000 inmates but in 1972 had an all-time high of more than 2,300 convicts behind its walls. It has a recidivism rate of two-thirds, and Pontesso's successor has described it as a "horrible, run-down, dilapidated prison.")

The second resignation was submitted by the president of the University of Oklahoma, J. Herbert Hollomon, a distinguished metallurgist and assistant secretary of commerce under the Kennedy and Johnson administrations. Hollomon had been hired from out of state three years before in a conscious move to get a man who could enhance OU's national reputation. But an abrasive manner, impolitic steps to shake up and streamline the university administration, and a lenient attitude toward student protesters got Hollomon in hot water with everyone from entrenched faculty to Governor Dewey Bartlett. Oklahomans were not pleased by an Easterner's suggestions that their lack of financial support showed their provincialism, or that their heart was not in racial integration.* No little rage fell on Hollomon when he banned "Little Red," an Indian student in war paint and feathers, who had traditionally done a little dance out on the field when the Sooner football team scored a touchdown. This, said Hollomon, made "a mockery of the

* Hollomon had a point about Oklahoman attitudes on school desegregation. The Oklahoma constitution still provides for the "establishment and maintenance of separate schools for white and colored children." The schools, in accordance with U.S. Supreme Court directives, have in fact been largely integrated. But in 1970, a proposed constitutional amendment went on the state ballot outlawing "segregation of children in public schools in the state of Oklahoma on account of race, creed, color or national origin." The voters *rejected* the proposal.

Indians." Finally, after Hollomon stepped lightly in dealing with mild student antiwar protests, the wave of anger against him became unbearable. The regents voted to extend his contract for another year, but Hollomon quit with a blast at the governor and "the very real threat of tyranny we now face."

Taxes and education have been traditional points of contention in the Oklahoma legislature, but up to the early 1970s the state was clearly behind the national averages by practically every measure. At the start of the decade, for instance, direct personal taxes, as a percentage of income, ranked only 37th among the 50 states. "Saving factors" were the $50 million received annually from severance taxes (mostly on oil) and one of the highest levels of federal grants among the states. Oklahoma was spending proportionately more on public welfare than any other small or medium-sized state of the Union—$94.60 averaged out over every man, woman, and child in the state in 1969–70, for instance. Welfare expenditures were 30 percent more than the state was expending on all levels of education. Oklahoma had the country's highest percentage of children between five and 17 years enrolled in school, but this may have been part of its problem. Expenditures per pupil ranked 46th among the 50 states, and teacher salaries about 40th. In 1965, after the people voted down a sales tax increase designed to aid schools, sanctions were voted against Oklahoma by the National Education Association on the recommendation of the Oklahoma Education Association. ("Resentment against more pay for school teachers goes back to the days of the rural school when the farmer who realized little cash in a year was envious of pay for the slip of a girl teaching school and boarding with his family," Otis Sullivant has written.) One way Oklahoma could improve its education effort would be further school district consolidation; the number of school districts has gone down from over 6,000 to 705 in recent years, but the state could perfectly well get along with 100.

In gross dollar terms, Oklahoma makes a very respectable effort in higher education, and 65 percent of its high school graduates go on to college, compared to a national average of 55 percent. But the state supports 18 colleges and universities when it could provide better education with only a third that number. About 40 percent of the 80,000-odd college students attend the two leading institutions, the University of Oklahoma at Norman and Oklahoma State University at Stillwater.* A lack of attractive in-state job opportunities makes Oklahoma one of the states which in effect trains and then exports a surplus of university graduates. The state is just beginning to support a full junior college program, which could train more young people to a level commensurate with actual employment needs.

Under prodding from the state's freshman governor, David Hall, the legislature in 1971 enacted the first major tax increase in 35 years. Hall had campaigned the year before on a no-new-tax program, but he shook the state by

* The University of Oklahoma has an international reputation in the fields of geology, petroleum engineering, and publishing. The university press has been one of the nation's finest for many years, and publishes some of the very best books on the government and politics of states across the whole midsection of the U.S.A.

proposing, the first day he was in office, tax hikes totaling $83 million. Eventually the legislature approved less than half that amount—a $21 million increase in the gross production tax on oil and gas, and a $17 million income tax increase.* But the tax increases represented an historic turn for Oklahoma. With the new revenues, it was possible to make significant increases in state aid for the public schools and universities. Perhaps more importantly, a stunning defeat had been dealt the state's wealthy establishment, including the mighty petroleum industry and the conservative metropolitan dailies. A newspaper not part of the establishment camp, W. P. Bill Atkinson's *Oklahoma Journal*, editorialized: "David took on Goliath and beat him. . . . It was David Hall versus powerful interests who have held the whip hand in Oklahoma politics for half a century." And correspondent Jim Standard of the very establishmentarian *Daily Oklahoman* observed that Governor Hall had shown "immense political skills" in getting so much of his program through a skeptical legislature. The public school and higher education lobbies, hungry for new revenues, also helped Hall win his victory. (Hall's political touch seemed to be slipping in 1972, however, when the voters, by a thumping 3–1 margin, rejected a $250 million bond issue he had proposed.)

Geographic Oklahoma and the Waterway

Washington Irving, lucky enough in 1832 to be able to join a group of Army rangers in a tour over much of what is now Oklahoma, later wrote in his *Tour of the Prairies* that the region consisted of "hill and dale, brush and brake, tangled thicket and open prairie." The theme of geologic diversity still holds over this sprawling state—basically a big rectangle 305 miles from east to west, 210 miles from north to south, with an odd 165-mile-long panhandle protruding over Texas from its northwest corner. The state's shape has been likened to a butcher's cleaver, with the panhandle representing the handle and the line of the Red River, which defines the southern boundary, like an irregular cutting edge. The state is actually tilted eastward—from a low point 290 feet above sea level in the southeast to the high point, Black Mesa, a lava-capped mesa some 5,000 feet above sea level which is located in the Panhandle near the Colorado and New Mexico borders. (Along with the highest elevation, the Panhandle has the fewest people—only 26,779 in its 5,695 square miles.)

The 98th meridian, where the grassy lowlands of the Mississippi Valley fade into the high and dry Great Plains, slices down through the state a few miles west of Oklahoma City. Annual rainfall goes as high as 50–56 inches in the southeastern corner, where the visitor discovers bayous and huge water cypress trees like Louisiana's. All the way out to Oklahoma City,

* The income tax was made to conform to the federal, with elimination of loopholes that permitted using the federal tax as an exemption in computing the Oklahoma tax, plus a provision that had let corporate stockholders off from paying tax on dividends. The net result of the reforms was to make the affluent shoulder a much larger share of the tax burden. One reason that Oklahoma has had a quite regressive tax structure is the weakness of organized labor. Only 16.7 percent of the labor force is unionized, a lower share than in 40 other states. The unions have shown little political clout.

the moist winds blowing up from the Gulf of Mexico deposit enough rainfall for crops of cotton, soybeans, and grains. But in the westernmost reaches, only dry farming of winter wheat and cattle grazing are practicable. On the High Plains at the tip of the Panhandle, precipitation dips to an arid 16 inches a year. Here one finds the stretches of prairie plowed up for wheatlands in World War I, later the heart of the Dust Bowl in the 1930s, when farmers saw their crops shrivel back into the ground and many a soul called it quits and headed for California.*

Since Depression days, prosperity has returned to the High Plains. The reasons: more moist years, massive pumping of underground water, and soil conservation practices that include planting of millions of shelter belt trees, cross-wind plowing in open fields, and letting huge stretches return to pasture through planting of the wind- and erosion-resistant native grasses. A leading state educator told me that western Oklahoma today is the source of many fine, brilliant young people. "The families who couldn't take the Dust Bowl moved away, and by a survival-of-the-fittest we're left with a healthy breeding stock of handsome, sturdy, smart people," he said. But if the severe droughts of 1970 and 1971 are an omen, further tests may be in store for the hardy remnant left on the High Plains.

Southeastern Oklahoma went into deep recession in the 1920s and has never truly recovered. Today, a traveler through the region sees hundreds of dilapidated houses and islands of hillbilly poverty; I have heard that a major chunk of the population is on welfare. On many hilly farm sites, ranging from 40 to 100 acres, farmers' widows now live on relief, their children having long since departed. But there are some better-off farms, an amount of income from oil and recreation, and the hope of new industry symbolized by a $150 million Weyerhauser paper mill announced in 1969. Northeastern Oklahoma, by contrast, has the big and bustling city of Tulsa and an abundance of power-producing natural resources—natural gas, coal from the Arkansas River Valley, and hydroelectric power.

Geographically, eastern Oklahoma includes parts of two low-lying mountain systems—the Ozarks, overflowing from Missouri and Arkansas on the northeast, and the Ouachitas, also shared with Arkansas. Both are regions of natural beauty, especially the Ozarks with their hardwoods and flamboyant autumns. The pines of the Ouachitas support a healthy lumber business. But the really exciting story of eastern Oklahoma is water. Within little more than a generation, it has been transformed from marginal scrubland to an aquatic paradise. Some of the work was done by the state, most notably Lake O'The Cherokees, which has a shoreline of 1,300 miles. But mostly, the federal government is to thank for huge lakes and reservoirs like the Eufaula, Fort Gibson, Tenkiller Ferry, and Thunderbird. They provide hydroelectric power, flood control, irrigation and municipal water supplies, and of course

* The fearsome winds of Dust Bowl days created legends and tall tales aplenty. John Gunther recalled the one about the "crowbar hole." This was a hole in the wall of a house, through which one could check on the weather outside. If a crowbar, shoved out through the hole, were to bend, the wind velocity outside was normal; if the bar broke off, it was "better to stay in the house"

abundant new playgrounds for boaters and water-skiers and fishermen. With 679 square miles of water, this part of the state has a ratio of water to land higher than Minnesota's.

There have been times when Oklahoma had more water than it liked. Will Rogers once wrote: "When the Arkansas, Red River, Salt Fork, Verdigris, Caney, Cat Creek, Possum Creek, Dog Creek, and Skunk Branch all are up after a rain, we got more seacoast than Australia." It was the gruesome spectacle of flooding of the Arkansas that prompted the late Senator Kerr to undertake the battle for the Arkansas River navigation and flood-control project.

Less romanticized than other great American rivers like the Missouri, Ohio, Columbia, and Mississippi, the Arkansas is nonetheless one of the longest—1,450 miles from its headwaters near Leadville, 13,000 feet high in the Rockies, across Colorado, Kansas, and Oklahoma, and then into the Mississippi. The river had once been heavily traveled, with steamboats pushing as far as Muskogee. But the river's mud made boat boilers burn, and many sidewheelers sank after being ripped by snags or grounded on the sandbars of a waterway which boatmen grumbled had "a bottom too near its top." By 1910, the perils of the river bottom and competition from railroads had driven out the last steamboats.

But the idea of making the Arkansas again navigable died hard. Will Rogers once wrote to President Coolidge suggesting the idea—though Rogers is better remembered for having once cracked that it would cost less to pave the Arkansas than to make it navigable. Newt Graham, a Tulsa civic leader, kept up the campaign to develop the river over several decades. Finally, with Kerr's conversion to the cause and his rise to power as chairman of the Rivers and Harbors Subcommittee of the Senate Public Works Committee, he was in a position (starting in 1956) to get the massive appropriations necessary to start serious work on the project. Eventually the price rose to a staggering $1.2 billion, more than the Panama Canal and the St. Lawrence Seaway combined, the biggest single project ever tackled by the Army Corps of Engineers. For this fantastic outlay, the country got itself a navigable 446-mile channel, running all the way from the Arkansas' mouth on the Mississippi to Catoosa, a Tulsa suburb and old railhead on the Verdigris River (a tributary of the Arkansas) where cowboys used to end cattle drives and whoop it up on Saturday nights. The big ditch ranges from 150 to 300 feet in width, is at least nine feet deep, and includes 17 locks and dams to facilitate the movement of ships and barges over the 420-foot elevation differential. Instead of a dangerous, meandering stream, the Arkansas has been transformed into a series of placid lakes and canals. Ten of the dams—two in Arkansas, eight in Oklahoma—provide hydroelectric power (three billion kilowatt-hours of electricity per year). And seven upstream reservoirs (all in Oklahoma) provided the needed flood protection.

To landlocked Oklahomans, still struggling to shake off the last vestiges of the Depression, the waterway seemed like a promise of prosperity beyond their wildest dream. Kerr set the theme by writing in his book, *Land, Wood and Water,* that while agriculture and oil had played the major role in Oklahoma's first half century of development, "in the next 50 years water will become the dominant asset, the 'white gold' of our economy. The Arkansas Valley will rival the great industrial valleys of the world." What would create this new Ruhr? The central element is transportation cost—the simple mathematics that show it costs, on the average, 6.5 cents to ship a ton of freight one mile by truck, 1.4 cents by rail, and 0.4 cents by water. Coal reserves in eastern Oklahoma and western Arkansas are known to total three billion tons, and now they can be gotten out economically. The prices on shipping out the area's other resources—oil, limestone, timber, wheat, chemicals, soybeans, cement, stone, brick—all dropped sharply with opening of the waterway. Shippers are expected to save $40 million a year. Before the waterway opened, the first new factories were going up along its shores; eventually there will probably be $800 million in industrial construction, providing 20,000 new jobs. Tulsa and its port at Catoosa, some of the optimistic Sooners believe, will become great transshipment points and the center of a thriving industrial belt along the banks of the waterway, with immense benefits for Muskogee and Arkansas river cities as well.

There are cynics—men like John W. Barriger, retired president of the Missouri-Kansas-Texas Railroad, who calls the waterway "the greatest boondoggle since the building of the Tower of Babel," and those who recall that the St. Lawrence Seaway had been hailed as one of the great economic events of the century, only to end up in disrepair and almost obsolete a decade after its opening. The project profoundly alters the natural shoreline of the river and potentially the ecology of the whole region, but it will be years before the Engineers get around to filing an environmental impact statement. Sometimes forgotten is the fact that the waterway will permit cheap importation of heavy materials *into* Oklahoma, slowing down, for instance, the possible development of a local steel industry.

Overall, the Engineers stoutly insist, the waterway will bring $1.50 for every dollar invested by the taxpayers. The canny Oklahomans and Arkansans in Congress made sure the waterway would succeed, both by getting the huge federal outlay to build it and by stipulating (1) that the waterway would be toll-free (in sharp contrast to heavy fees on the St. Lawrence Seaway) and (2) that the federal government would bear the entire operating costs of $16 million to $18 million a year. Should a common taxpayer from some other region object, one can almost hear the ghost of Senator Kerr laughing off the impertinence. Every congressman, he once told a reporter, "represents one or more" of the country's basic economic elements. "That's what our representative government is supposed to be. The sum total of those pressures working through Congress is the catalyst that produces our laws. I'm not ashamed of it. I'm proud of it."

Outsiders may find it hard to appreciate what the taming of the Arkansas, including not only locks and dams but also channel rectification work to control the meandering course, means emotionally to Oklahomans. In 1970, when Lyndon Johnson went to Sallisaw to dedicate the Kerr Lock and Dam on the river,* publisher Wheeler Mayo of that city wrote:

> At the Kerr site my mind spanned a lot of years and I recalled back in the early 1930s I lost a brother in the shifting and treacherous quicksands of this once destructive, untamed stream. My brother, Dale Carnall Mayo, got trapped in the quicksand and drowned less than a quarter of a mile up the river from the site where former President Johnson spoke. . . .
>
> I had some strong feelings about the misery and despair the river caused thousands of people before the lock and dam and navigation program was put on its feet under the direction of the late Senator Kerr.

The Okie Economy

Oklahoma has always been a poor country cousin to bustling Texas and its northern Plains States neighbors but several degrees better off than the Deep South states to its east. Its weaknesses have centered on the decline of cotton, the vicissitudes of wheat, and until the very recent past, a paltry industrial base. Had it not been for oil and federal defense employment, Oklahoma could have been in almost as dire straits in the postwar era as it was during the grim Depression years. As one of the state's respected businessman-politicians told me (asking specifically that he *not* be quoted by name):

> We have a subsidized and exporting economy. Oklahoma has always exported its people, oil, timber, farm products. If you take away the federal subsidies for lead, zinc, petroleum, welfare, agriculture and defense, you have nothing left—take these things out of Oklahoma and you don't even have a corpse.

Getting more specific, the same man pointed out that Tinker Air Force Base has three times as large a payroll as any private employer in the state, that the FAA center in Oklahoma City is as large as any private employer, and that to those one could also add Fort Sill, the big Clinton-Sherman Air Force Base, and the Naval Ammunition Depot at McAllister. (According to government statistics, direct defense-generated civilian employment accounts for 4.3 percent of the labor force, overall federal civilian employment for 5.9 percent, both figures among the highest in the Union.)

Oklahoma's population figures reflect the shaky base. The 1970 Census found 2,559,253 people in the state, only 7 percent more than in 1930. In fact, 42 of the state's 77 counties have fewer people now than they did when Oklahoma joined the Union. (The population actually declined in the 1930s and 1940s by a total of 15 percent, then rose 4 percent in the 1950s and 10 percent in the 1960s.)† The per capita income in the state rose sharply in the postwar years, but by 1971 it was still only $3,506, or 15

* The entire system—officially named the McClellan-Kerr Arkansas River Navigation System—was officially dedicated by President Nixon at Catoosa in June 1971.

† If the Census count of Oklahoma in 1970 had been 235 people less, the state would have lost one of its six seats in the U.S. House under the national reapportionment plan for the 1970s.

percent below the national average. The average factory worker in Oklahoma earns substantially less than the average across the country.

There are compensating factors and some silver linings. The cost of living is less than in most areas of America. Sixty-two percent of the state's people live on the land, in small suburbs, or in cities of less than 30,000 people. Although half of Oklahoma's counties still lost population in the 1960s, the massive shift from farm and town to city (and often out of state altogether) was stemmed.* Hundreds of prosperous little factories have been induced to locate in rural towns, making use of state legislation which makes it possible for counties to sell general revenue bonds for the building of plants which may then be made available to industries on a lease-purchase agreement. The money can be used for land, buildings, and equipment, so that a manufacturer just has to bring in inventory and hire the people. Plants making furniture, clothing, carpets, and machine parts, and processing poultry and meats, have been most numerous. For example, Congoleum-Nairn put in a floor tiling plant at the small city of Wilburton, deep in the "Little Dixie" district of southeastern Oklahoma, creating jobs for 350. To build the $760,000 plant, new water and sewer lines were needed, which the U.S. Economic Development Administration financed at 70 percent of cost because of the area's "depressed" designation. The Ozarks Regional Commission supplemented with another 10 percent, and the county floated a bond issue to finance the remaining 20 percent. One can imagine the economic impact on a county whose total assessed valuation had been only $6 million.

Perhaps the most unusual story is that of Sequoyah Carpet Mills, started by Don Greve, a young Oklahoma dynamo who had grown up in rural poverty in a chicken house with a poured concrete floor. He started into business at 19, became a Methodist lay preacher, and seeing the plight of the Indians decided in 1962 to move into textiles with a carpet mill at rural Andarko in southwestern Oklahoma (a place which calls itself "Indian City USA"). Greve put together a financial package of $390,000 in federal funds, $60,000 from a local electrical co-op, $60,000 from a state industrial-loan agency, still another $60,000 from the merchants and townspeople of Andarko, and $200,000 from himself and four other investors. Of the first 55 hired—almost all Indians—only three had held jobs lasting from one year into another. Eventually, employment at Andarko rose to 700 employees—in a county without a single industry beforehand. By 1970, Greve had 10 rural plants, nine of them in Oklahoma.

The industrialization drive was picked up later in the 1960s by Republican Governor Dewey Bartlett, who launched his "Okie" program to draw industry to Oklahoma, especially its rural areas, through a variety of tax incentives and promises to tailor-make vocational courses for potential workers in specific industries. Bartlett hit on the "Okie" theme as a way to transform Oklahoma's decades-old image of a dusty, backward place, engraved on the

* Between 1940 and 1960, there was a net outmigration from Oklahoma of 622,000 people; by the 1960-to-1970 decade, however, the tide had reversed and there was a net inmigration of 13,000.

mind of anyone who ever read *Grapes of Wrath*. Okie was declared an acronym for "Oklahoma, Key to Industrial Expansion." Bartlett became what General Electric board chairman Gerald L. Phillippe called an "aggressive bearcat of a governor," leaving not a stone unturned in his search for new industries. And annual new investments in the state did more than double, and then triple, their previous levels. Big cities got some major plants, like $53.2 million invested by American Airlines in Tulsa or a $48 million investment by Dayton Tire & Rubber in Oklahoma City. But the small-town gains were even more significant for their localities: $2 million for a St. Joe Paper Co. plant at Sapulpa, $7 million invested by the Swan Rubber Company in Stillwater, a total investment of $3 million by National Zinc at Bartlesville, $5 million by Armco Steel at Sand Springs. Oklahoma's total employment rolls failed to expand faster than the national average, but the new jobs doubtless prevented more unemployment and encouraged often-complacent small localities to go ahead with better schools, libraries, hospitals, and municipal facilities.

The only serious criticism leveled against the Bartlett drive was that the state itself was being shortchanged by a "giveaway" gimmick of excusing new businesses from property taxes for 30 years. Democrat David Hall made some use of that issue in a 1970 campaign in which he narrowly defeated Bartlett. And no sooner had Hall become governor than "Okie" became a forbidden word at the State Capitol.

One must also report that all is not well with the industries in Oklahoma's small towns. In 1972 a subsidiary of American Metal Climax, Inc., announced it would close down its aging smelter in the little northern Oklahoma town of Blackwell (population 8,645). The reasons: unprofitability of the obsolete zinc smelter and an antipollution suit by several local farmers who objected to the low, thick cloud of acrid smoke from the plant. The shutdown meant that Blackwell would lose 800 jobs and an annual payroll of $5.5 million that had been the lifeblood of the community for many years.

Oil continues to play a big role in the Oklahoma economy; there are 80,000 oil and 8,000 natural gas wells operating in 72 of the state's 77 counties. But as Dean McGee (of Kerr-McGee) pointed out in an interview, "We're over the hump on oil and gas production." The number of exploratory rigs in Oklahoma has dropped by almost 50 percent in the last few years. In 1970 some 224 million barrels of oil and 1.5 billion cubic feet of natural gas were sent to market, bringing oil companies $964 million from their Oklahoma operations. Among the states, Oklahoma was fourth in oil (behind Texas, Louisiana, and California) and third in natural gas (behind Texas and Louisiana).

The history of Oklahoma's oil industry goes back to 1880, when the first "wildcatting" began, and 1897, when a well at Bartlesville began production. The big pools started coming in a decade later, and with them the problems of ruthless exploitation of a natural resource. For decades, no attempt was made at conservation, and the life of every important field was shortened by the wastage of millions of barrels of oil and billions of cubic feet of gas. The courts countenanced every evil practice, as this early court decision shows:

> . . . every landowner or his lessee may locate his wells wherever he pleases, regardless of the interest of others. He may distribute them over the whole farm, or locate them only on one part of it. He may crowd the adjoining farms so as to enable him to draw the oil and gas from them. What then can the neighbor do? . . . Nothing; only go and do likewise.

Many landowners profited handsomely from the sale of oil leases on their lands, and perhaps none so royally as the Osage Indians, who were made the richest race of people per capita in the world by oil leases in 1921.

Hard times came in the 1930s, when the opening of the East Texas oil fields in the midst of the general Depression drove the price of Oklahoma crude down to as low as 10 cents a barrel. Even though Governor Murray sent in the National Guard to close down the oil fields and enforce proration, there was a widespread traffic in "hot oil" smuggled out of the state. Since then, the Oklahoma Corporation Commission has administered an effective proration program. This program held down production in the early years, but recently the state's reserves have become so depleted that the oil companies have difficulty producing their allowables in any event. To bring in new fields, oilmen have been forced to turn to extremely high-cost drilling. In May 1972, the world's deepest oil well—30,050 feet—was drilled as a wildcat venture by the Lone Star Producing Company in Beckham County in western Oklahoma. Sixty percent of the state's oil is now taken by secondary recovery methods, especially by water flooding of subterranean cavities to force the previously untapped oil to the surface.

The decline of Oklahoma petroleum reserves has forced the state's two big homegrown oil companies—Phillips Petroleum and Kerr-McGee—to survey far and wide for additional fields and to move into new "energy" sources and markets. Phillips Petroleum, with headquarters in Bartlesville, has spread its oil exploration efforts to the North Sea, Africa, the Midwest, and Alaska's North Slope. The company also operates eight nuclear reactors for the Atomic Energy Commission.

Dean McGee happily recounts the success story of Kerr-McGee, begun as the Anderson-Kerr Drilling Company by the late Senator Kerr and a partner in 1929. The company furnished drilling holes for other promoters, then began to acquire its own leases, and in 1937 made what the oil world considered a masterful move by hiring McGee himself away from Phillips Petroleum. McGee was already recognized as one of the nation's top oil geologists. With his technical competence, Kerr-McGee was ready in the wake of World War II to begin seismic exploration work and drill far off the Louisiana coast, inventing a whole new technology for distant underwater drilling. The company also became expert in extracting liquids from natural gas, producing propanes and butanes and fuels used in the petrochemical business. When the U.S. Government mounted its program to discover uranium, Kerr-McGee took the lead and acquired valuable properties in New

Mexico and Wyoming; later it began to produce the enriched pellets that go into the cores of nuclear reactors, and still later went into the so-called nuclear fuel cycle, transforming uranium into a gas called uranium hexafloride which then goes to one of the government's gaseous diffusion plants for enrichment. Kerr-McGee also mines coal in Oklahoma, produces railroad crossties from 260,000 acres of timberland it got through mineral land acquisition, and in 1968 acquired the American Potash & Chemical Co. (producing potassium, boron, and sodium from California desert deposits). It has been deep into the fertilizer business since the mid-1950s. The company remains a major Oklahoma employer, but its out-of-state operations (based on annual sales of about $500 million) are just as great.

Neither Kerr-McGee nor Phillips Petroleum has ever been shy about exerting political influence for their own special ends. In the 1930s, they worked together on the campaign that led to the incredible decision that drilling for oil would be permitted in the residential areas of Oklahoma City and even on the grounds of the State Capitol itself. Phillips owned key leases, and Kerr got the drilling contracts and helped persuade the voters to approve the drilling in two successive referenda. Phillips had to spend a lot of money to win that battle, but the immense oil field under the city is still producing. One of the derricks, close to the front entrance of the Capitol, was given a coat of gold paint in honor of its special location.

Frank Phillips, founder of Phillips Petroleum, was a Nebraska-born barber who made his way to Bartlesville in 1904, telling a brother: "I think people are going to buy quite a passel of these gasoline buggies, and they need gasoline to make 'em go. It may be this thing has a future." When he died in 1950, Phillips Petroleum was worth $660 million and operating in more than half the states. Debs Myers tells the story of the reporter who once approached Phillips rather apologetically in a hotel lobby and asked, "Is it true, Mr. Phillips, that you used to be a barber?" Phillips replied: "You're damned right, and if you can latch onto a pair of shears and come up to my room, I'll give you a better haircut than you got right now." Mr. Phillips also had quite a touch for philanthropy; for one thing, he paid off the debt of every church in Bartlesville.

Phillips' successor, "Boots" Adams, was an ultraconservative Democrat but put a lot of money into Kerr's campaigns. Adams was succeeded, in turn, by W. W. Keeler, the Cherokee chief to whom I referred earlier in this chapter. Keeler is a liberal Republican and thus quite an anomaly in Bartlesville, a fantastically conservative town. But no matter who is in charge at the moment, Phillips Petroleum is somehow at the center of Oklahoma politics. "The company owns several members of each house of the legislature, but I can't prove it," one Oklahoma oldtimer told me. Apparently the lobbying operation is extremely effective, and the company has traditionally spent whatever money it feels it needs to in seeing that its friends are elected to office.*

* Phillips has been having some difficulties in recent years in getting enough crude oil to supply its national network of service stations plus plants producing fibers, plastics, and chemicals. But its 1971 sales of $2.4 billion earned it a very respectable place of 37 on *Fortune*'s list of the biggest U.S. industrial corporations.

The 1971 tax increases, which upped the gross production tax on oil and gas from 5 to 7 percent, came as a real shock to the industry. Phillips and the other big companies, never before defeated on a vital issue, had failed to invest the money and effort they customarily have in the 1970 elections—reaping the whirlwind of a governor not beholden to them and an unusually independent legislature. They could actually count themselves lucky that the legislature rejected Governor Hall's original plea for a brand new severance tax on natural gas, which would have cost them $39 million a year.

In addition to Phillips and Kerr-McGee, big oil companies like Texaco, Mobil, Humble, Atlantic-Sinclair, Sun-Sunray DX Division, and Amerada Petroleum (now merged with Hess Oil) maintain large operations in the state. The employment rolls of men working in oil and gas extraction, refining, marketing, and oil field machinery production totaled 51,500 in 1969, their paychecks feeding $344 million into the economy. The total number of oil and gas workers was actually less than it had been a decade earlier, however; to find the really dynamic elements of the economy, one had to look to manufacturing, trade, services, and—at least in terms of employment—government, which added 57,600 workers in the 1960s for a new total of 185,000, taking home paychecks of $1.1 billion a year.

Oklahoma farmers have been producing almost $1 billion worth of livestock and cash crops in recent years, and agriculture—especially when one takes into account food processing and other related "agribusiness"—is still the single largest element in the economy. Wheat overthrew cotton as the major crop a full generation ago, and now soybeans are crowding out whatever cotton is left. More than 70 percent of the farm dollar volume comes from the sale of beef cattle and other livestock.

The disastrous 1930s, when topsoil and black blizzards choked cattle and crops and some 350,000 farmers fled the state, will pass out of active memory and into history in not too many years now. But the farm exodus begun then continues; between 1940 and 1969, the number of farms dropped from 179,687 to 83,037, while their average size grew from 194 to 434 acres and the average value of land and buildings from $4,625 to $74,838.* *Time* magazine in 1970 interviewed Ross Labrier, a rancher from the Panhandle who now owns 23,000 acres valued at $2.3 million and has 400 cattle. Labrier recalls that when the Dust Bowl days came, "the small ranchers who had about 160 acres fled first. Those who didn't leave joined the WPA. We bought the repossessed lands from the bank." For the land, Labrier paid some $15 an acre. Thus it was that some of Oklahoma's present fortunes were made from the misfortunes of earlier Okies. (The 1970 Census found less than 8 percent of Oklahoma's people were still living on farms.)

By latest readings, Oklahoma trailed only Kansas and North Dakota in wheat production and rated fifth among the states in the number of cattle on its farms. Its income from cotton was just a third of what it earned from wheat and less than 5 percent of the national output. The planting patterns

* And even with the bigger, more prosperous farms, many a farmer feels obliged to hold a job in a nearby town to make ends meet.

—cotton in the southeast, wheat in the northwest—fitted what Senator Kerr's businessman son William told me in summarizing the Oklahoma economy. "Take per capita income, tax bases, valuations, or expenses for education," he said, "and you will find they go straight up from southeastern to northwestern Oklahoma."

Urban Oklahoma and the Press

Burgeoning Oklahoma City and Tulsa dominate urban Oklahoma and compete to see which can grow the fastest and bestest. So far Oklahoma City has the population edge—362,046 (metropolitan area 640,889 in 1970) compared to Tulsa's 327,183 (metro 476,945). Tulsa added population about twice as fast in the 1960s, but Oklahoma City got the edge in size by annexing huge chunks of surrounding land (to a total of 636 square miles, which for a period of time was the largest land area of any city in the U.S.). Tulsa is the self-proclaimed "Oil Capital of the World," with the headquarters of such giants as Skelly and Cities Service (though it recently lost Sinclair to Dallas). Oklahoma City, on the other hand, has added a long list of blue-chip industrial firms through an aggressive chamber of commerce factory recruiting job unequaled in the U.S., backed up with government-backed bonds to help attract new industries. Tulsa expects vast new industrial riches with the Arkansas River Navigation System terminating at its front door, but Oklahoma City—after long delays—has embarked on an exciting and ambitious downtown renewal program and can boast the splendid new $3 million Mummers Theater, a cultural gem in the nation's southwestern reaches, not to mention the very admirable National Cowboy Hall of Fame.

Oklahoma City is remembered as the city which popped up out of the prairie between noon and sunset on April 22, 1889. Before that, in the words of Oklahoma Historical Society president George H. Shirk (quoted in the *National Geographic*), the location "was just a dusty depot on the sun-scorched prairie. A stop for Santa Fe trains. No trees. The entire water supply came from a single well, about where Broadway and Main Street meet today." After the famous run, Oklahoma City became a big country cattle town and state capital, and prospered as a major city on the main line of the Santa Fe. It got in on the real big and fast money when oil hit in the 1930s. (In addition to the wells around the State Capitol, there are rigs on the lawn of the governor's mansion.)

A touch of the exploitive, get-rich-quick psychology the oil derricks represent still lingers in Oklahoma City. But there are some new, softer themes to life there. In 1971 the voters elected Mrs. Patience Sewell Latting as their mayor—the first woman to head an American city of more than 200,000 people. Mrs. Latting, 53 at the time of her election, had begun in politics through the Parent Teachers Association and the League of Women Voters. In 1966 she wrote the reapportionment plan approved by the Oklahoma legislature. Her principal efforts on the city council, before election as mayor, had been to get strict enforcement of housing and zoning codes and to secure for Negroes a bigger share in city government. (Blacks, indeed, formed part of her winning coalition.) A major plank of her platform was to purge "cronyism" from city government. Mrs. Latting's election over businessman Bill Bishop was not universally hailed; one male city councilman commented that "the citizens will soon find out they have been hornswoggled into making the biggest mistake they have ever made." * Mrs. Latting, as if in reply, depicted Oklahoma City as a "gangling teenager" and said she hoped her administration would bring more "maturity."

Oklahoma City's mass media were subjected in 1968 to a rare piece of scrutiny by a federal agency. Two minority members of the Federal Communications Commission reported that there were "essentially two classes of purveyors of information and entertainment for the people of Oklahoma City and, for that matter, of the entire state of Oklahoma. In the first class fall those which are owned and controlled by the Gaylord family. In the second class fall all the rest." The report went on to define the Gaylord empire: Oklahoma City's two largest newspapers, the *Daily Oklahoman* (morning) and *Oklahoma City Times* (afternoon); WKY-TV and WKY-AM, Oklahoma's biggest broadcasting stations; television stations in Fort Worth-Dallas, Houston, Milwaukee, and Tampa; the *Farmer-Stockman* (an agricultural monthly which reaches nearly half a million farmers in the Oklahoma-Texas-Kansas region); and RX *Golf and Travel* (a golf and travel magazine).

Centenarian Edward King Gaylord, undisputed ruler of this empire, has for decades been the most powerful man in Oklahoma City—for that matter, in all of Oklahoma. His victories go back to the successful campaign to get the state capital transferred from Guthrie to Oklahoma City. The *Oklahoman* has campaigned against labor, against government spending, against liquor and sin, for toll roads to get early Oklahoma out of the mud, for getting big military bases into Oklahoma, and, at least in recent years, for letting the Republicans in. When "Alfalfa Bill" Murray ran for governor in 1930, Gaylord called him a "wildman" and "unconscionable liar." He has not backed a Democratic Presidential candidate since 1932.

Over the years, every major political figure in Oklahoma has traipsed up to 4th and Broadway to visit Mr. Gaylord. The old saying is that "he may not be able to elect you but he sure can kill you." Democrats remember with some bitterness that Gaylord asked Senator Monroney to help get urban renewal funds for a multimillion-dollar convention center in downtown Oklahoma City. Monroney succeeded when most funds were drying up, but then a few months later the *Oklahoman* turned around, endorsed GOP candidate Bellmon for the Senate, and blasted Monroney for supporting the Great Society's giveaway programs.

William G. Kerr, son of the late Senator and a potential future governor or Senator himself, criticizes the *Oklahoman* for "repetitious inculcation of

* The politicians in he-man Oklahoma are not known for softness toward women. In 1972 the legislature turned down the proposed amendment to the U.S. Constitution guaranteeing equal rights for women.

conservatism—a status-quo negativism and opposition to public investment and capitalization." Gaylord, he points out, was born three years before Custer fought at the Big Horn, and was old enough to vote for President in 1896. He was president of the Oklahoma City Chamber of Commerce in 1917. "How," Kerr asks, "can he have a realistic view of the world today?"

FCC Commissioners Nicholas Johnson and Kenneth A. Cox, in a case study on Oklahoma broadcasting issued in 1968, sought to make a classic presentation, using Oklahoma as a sample state, of the need for the government to examine more closely the credentials and actual performance of broadcasters who receive "a grant of great power and wealth, 'a license to print money.' " The television industry, they noted, averages about 100 percent return on depreciated tangible investment and about 40 percent on gross revenues, figures that would be the envy of any other industry. Yet in Oklahoma broadcasting, Johnson and Cox said, "the concept of local service is largely a myth." Referring specifically to the Gaylord-owned WKY, the commissioners said it did provide somewhat more local programming than any other station in the state. "But its lead is not significant, and the level of its performance in this regard is so low that its superiority is not in itself a cause for great self-satisfaction or praise. . . . Because of the power and financial capacity of WKY and WKY-TV, and because of the great newsgathering resources of the parent organization, we think these stations could make a far greater contribution to community public needs and interests than they are presently providing."

Finally, the commissioners—members of a clear minority on the FCC—suggested that the commission "be wary of permitting so many mass communications outlets to accumulate in the hands of a single organization."

Tulsa made a start in 1879 as a post office on the pony mail route through Indian Territory and as late as 1905 was called Tulsey Town, an unkempt frontier settlement where—in the words of one settler—"we had to dodge roaming hogs, goats, and cows when crossing, and sometimes wild animals would venture into the middle of town." But in 1906 the big break came with the discovery of the Glenn Oil Pool nearby—the greatest high-grade petroleum strike up to that date. Tulsa's canny town fathers persuaded hundreds of oil companies to set up their headquarters in town. Prosperity came to Tulsa much earlier than to Oklahoma City. The city's per capita income is still several hundred dollars over the income of its big rival to the west, and by the same measure, its conservatism is much greater.

Tulsa is home base for one of America's most famed fundamentalist evangelists, the Rev. Oral Roberts, known in past years for his televised faith healings, more recently for Christmas and Easter television specials that may draw as many as 25 million viewers. About 1,400 students now attend Oral Roberts University, which occupies a $30 million, 500-acre campus (including a modernistic 200-foot "prayer tower" which has become Tulsa's biggest tourist attraction). Roberts, a country boy from Pontococ County, Oklahoma, who came to Tulsa a quarter century ago with $25 in his pocket and a slogan—"Expect a miracle"—can take justifiable pride in the fact that his university won full accreditation in less than six years. He has become a pillar of the Tulsa community, a bank and chamber of commerce director, and altogether welcome locally, where his various activities are thought to add $15 million to the economy. "Wholesomeness will be a way of life here," Roberts announced for his university. Church attendance for students is compulsory, they must wear shirts, ties, or dresses to all classes, and they are prohibited from "(a) profanity, (b) smoking, (c) gambling, (d) cheating, (e) drinking alcoholic beverages of any kind, and (f) immorality."

Tulsa is also the stamping ground for the paragon of right-wing religiosity, the Rev. Billy James Hargis, whose Christian Crusade and American Christian College have headquarters a few miles out of town. The Hargis operation fails to match Roberts' in either magnitude or respectability.

While I was visiting Tulsa, one of its most influential citizens told me his was "a square city—the last place you'll ever see a topless waitress." To test the theory, I dropped into the bar across from my hotel that evening. The waitress' first question: "Are you from the ABC Board or the vice squad?" A hard drink, though illegal, was quickly served, and the entertainment featured a sensational strip-tease act of a black-haired "beauty" who toted six-shooters and ended her act clad exclusively in a strategically held cowboy hat.

In Presidential politics, Tulsa may be the most conservative big city of the U.S.A. today. Tulsa County went overwhelmingly for Barry Goldwater in 1964, gave Nixon and Wallace a combined 77.0 percent of its vote in 1968, and Nixon alone 77.8 percent in 1972.

The conservative temper of Tulsa is fostered by two rightward-oriented newspapers, the Tulsa *Tribune* and Tulsa *World*. The former is edited by an urbane newsman and syndicated columnist, Jenkin Lloyd Jones, who served recently as president of the Chamber of Commerce of the United States. Jones takes pleasure in running a paper with no need "to pull punches"; among others, he had antagonized local Catholic priests by his editorials for birth control and Jews by criticizing the concept of Israel as a joint state and religious community. The papers are Republican in local politics, but the voters surprisingly independent; in fact, more Democrats than Republicans have been elected in the past two decades. Thomas Frasier, a local Democratic power, claims that Jones and *World* publisher Byron V. Boone consistently back candidates for mayor who will appoint them to the fair and airport authority boards, which "really run the town." The Democrats work from a coalition of minorities, including labor, Negroes, Roman Catholics, and city workers. Frasier likes to recall the election the Democrats won under his leadership in the mid-1950s. "The papers said we had no chance, but we beat 'em by about 10,000 votes, and by the next morning I was a machine boss and have remained so ever since."

Tulsa takes justifiable pride in its Philbrook Art Center, with an outstanding collection of Indian and Southwest art, and the Thomas Gilcrease Institute of American History and Art. Both museums were outright gifts of rich Tulsa oil families. Nor can Tulsa's young people be called Okie yokels:

in a recent year, two local high schools—Will Rogers and Tulsa Central—were among the select group of 38 schools in the entire United States with more than 20 National Merit Scholarship finalists.

There are still more contradictions. Tulsans will tell you they have better race relations than Oklahoma City. But this city witnessed one of the cruelest race riots of American history, in 1921. Blacks and whites seeking work as roustabouts in the oil fields began fights on the city streets. Then white vigilantes invaded a black district and laid it waste by fire. By the time the smoke had cleared, close to 40 people were dead.

Finally, a physical impression: With its gleaming high-rises and highly advanced airport, Tulsa gives an impression of order and modernity, of the possibility of creating the constructive new society out of a proper mix of steel and concrete and glass. But suddenly you notice streets running at wild angles into each other, out where everything should be perfectly plotted. It turns out that the main street was surveyed by a railroad engineer who ran his line at right angles to the tracks, thus causing the downtown district to be built "cattywampus," as the older-timers put it, while the rest of Tulsa is laid out according to the compass points.

Oklahoma's continuing small-city and rural complexion is underscored by the lack of large cities after Oklahoma City and Tulsa. Lawton, in southwestern Oklahoma, was the last of the state's cities to be born, overnight, out of the dust and clamor of an Indian reservation opening. That was in 1901; then in 1903 nearby Fort Sill became the U.S. Army's principal artillery school, and Lawton has lived and prospered under the shadow of that gigantic military reservation ever since. The 1970 population was 74,470.

Next in population is Norman (52,117 people in 1970), set close to Oklahoma City and home of the University of Oklahoma. Enid (population 44,008) is a big wheat and oil center in the northwestern part of the state.

Muskogee (population 37,331), in the heart of the onetime Indian Territory in eastern Oklahoma, is by Oklahoma standards an old town (1872); it now hopes for new prosperity because of its strategic location on the Arkansas River Waterway. A $4 million port has been built, and new industries are expected. Muskogee recently endured the tortures of one of the worst police scandals ever reported outside America's best cities. But these days, the town's image is set indelibly by Merle Haggard's top country music song of 1970, *Okie from Muskogee*. In Muskogee, we were reminded, such phenomena as burning draft cards, smoking pot, beads, and shaggy long hair are scarcely known; instead the big things are football, leather boots, and a healthy respect for the college dean:

> And I'm proud to be an Okie from Muskogee;
> A place where even squares can have a ball.
> We still wave Ol' Glory down at the Court House,
> White lightning's still the biggest thrill of all.
> In Muskogee, Oklahoma, U.S.A.*

*** From the song *Okie from Muskogee*, written by Merle Haggard and Roy Edward Burris. Copyright © 1969 Blue Book Music, Bakersfield, Calif. Used by permission. All rights reserved.**

TEXAS

LAND OF THE MONIED "ESTABLISHMENT"

Big, brawling Texas, always the braggart in the family of American states, has been obliged in recent years to take a long, hard look inward. Simultaneously, Texas' image to the world has been transformed. A change of character and complexion that would normally take generations seems to have occurred in a twinkling of time.

To appreciate the change, one needs only to think back to a decade ago. Remembering that we speak as much of image as reality, recall what Texas stood for. Its global image was of a vainglorious, blustering, illiberal kind of place where money was worshipped without shame. Its man in the Senate, Lyndon Baines Johnson, was the most consummate wielder of power that chamber had seen in years and years. Money and power—the two words seemed to add up to Texas. Non-Texans remembered perhaps a glimmering of the Alamo, of the tradition of fiercely independent Americans who had migrated to a huge land north of the Rio Grande and built themselves a "civilization." But Texans themselves permitted and abetted a distortion of the Texas tradition, a bigger-and-bestest-of-everything braggadocio that evinced sometimes wonder, sometimes scorn from afar.

Writes historian Joe B. Frantz, a Texan:

Whether you . . . thought that Texans were pleasant buffoons, a bit tiresome but still good for some extravagant yaks, or petted Texans the way you might a cavorting Eskimo husky; whether you were impressed with the private airplanes, Olympic-sized swimming pools, 40-foot fireplaces, or ranch females built with all the reassuring solidity of an Anheuser-Busch draft horse, or whether, like my thrifty Illinois father, you always felt a bit superior to those Scripture-quoting Texans who spouted waste-not, want-not slogans while cotton wore out their black land, rivers carried their farms to the Gulf, their farm machinery rusted and ruined for want of simple upkeep, their Negroes rusted and ruined on a diet of cornbread, syrup, and grease, their Mexicans' insides exploded on corn, hot chilis, and amoebic dysentery, and their bankers refused credit to rehabilitate acres that cried for comeback—regardless of how the non-Texan viewed the Texan, he gloried in some aspects to him, commercialized and exploited him where he could, and steadily built the myth. . . .

It is easy to say it all changed that sad November day in 1963 in Dallas, and that single event should not be underestimated. But there was more. There was the little pinprick of the Texas balloon the day that Alaska joined the Union, and suddenly Texas suffered the indignity of being but the *second* largest state. There was the important shift of national attitudes in the 1960s, when the United States began to wonder if values like biggest and richest counted for so much, and the country began to look to the deprived in its midst, and Texas' blacks and downtrodden Mexican-Americans were suddenly no longer mute about their own fate. Who, as the more sensitive value system of the 1960s began to take form, could still be impressed by the boasts of Dallas that it had the biggest churches anywhere in Protestantism, when government statistics showed the lowest per capita income anywhere in America in the counties along the Rio Grande? How could one remain open-mouthed in amazement over Houston's phenomenal economic growth, when the price for it (especially in petrochemicals) was some of the vilest air and water pollution anywhere in the world?

Finally, there was the Presidency of Lyndon Johnson. First he helped Texas regain its self-confidence after Dallas, when the state went through a time of sadness and perplexity such as Texans had never before experienced. But then Johnson, through his own excess of promise and unhappy ending as President, ruined the Texan image even more. Now, writes Texas novelist Larry McMurtry, "we aren't thought of as quaintly vulgar anymore. . . . The majority just find us boring. . . . Having yielded Mr. Johnson, it is hardly to be expected that the state will yield anything funny in the next few years, much less anything aesthetically interesting."

As for bragging, McMurtry aptly sums it up: "Texans have finally learned that bragging is a form of discourse they can no longer afford. The old, loud, vulgar, groin-scratching Texan is rapidly giving way to a quieter sort of citizen, one who knows how to live with his itch." Not all do, of course. In Dallas, I was regaled with the story of the Texan who went to New York and encountered a young lady of the town with whom he then went to bed. The next day a furtive little man accosted the Texan, showed him pictures of himself in various compromising positions from the night before, and said the photos would cost him $1,000 each. The Texan replied: "OK, I'll take three of those, four of these, six of these. . . ." There are still stoutly attested stories of wives who run up bills of over $200,000 at Neiman-Marcus, and of the rush of Texan males to buy their own ranches and run cattle as a proof of their place in the world.

Some of the richest Texans of all time—men like Sid Richardson of Fort Worth, Clint Murchison of Dallas, and H. L. Hunt of Dallas—never went the road of flamboyance. Billionaire Hunt, of course, has financed no end of right-wing propaganda activities, but the man himself has stayed somewhat in the background in his great mansion, a bigger-than-life reproduction of Mount Vernon. Most of the latest generation of Texas millionaires—bankers, petrochemical magnates, computer wizards, financiers, insurance men, with names like H. Ross Perot, John Mecom, Jr., Lamar Hunt, and Joe Albritton—have tended to be quieter and less eccentric men than the millionaires of the '30s and '40s. Perot has said he is willing to use half his vast fortune from the Dallas-based computer software company he founded to right social ills in America; among other projects, he has made highly publicized journeys to the Far East in chartered planes to try to get the release of American prisoners of war in Vietnam. In 1971, he was making headlines by coming to the financial rescue of the New York brokerage house of F. I. DuPont, Glore, Forgan, William R. Staats. This may be flamboyance, but of a kind Texas never knew before.*

Now almost forgotten in Texas is a man who was briefly a millionaire, fertilizer tycoon and swindler Billie Sol Estes. His multimillion-dollar empire was based on fraudulent credit, including fertilizer, grain elevators, and cotton allotments; for a while Estes was much admired as the Bible-quoting "boy wonder of West Texas agriculture," but it all came crashing down when he was arrested in 1962 and sent to federal prison for mail fraud and conspiracy. (In 1971, Estes was paroled to work on his brother's farm.)

And now there is a conscious effort on Texans' part to deflate some of the old swashbuckling image that surrounded the state's cattle barons and rich oilmen. Congressman Bob Eckhardt of Houston reminds a visitor of the rather unprepossessing surroundings of the ordinary Texas cattleman. His ranch house "may ramble all over the place," but it's one-story and very utilitarian. The only plantation houses in Texas, Eckhardt points out, were built in the river-bottom areas of East Texas by men rich through cane and cotton, not cattle. "The cattleman," he says, "tends to wear hat and boots worth in the aggregate about $100, and everything else in between about $11.50 at J. C. Penney. Fancy boots have developed only in the last few years. It's a lobbyist's flair and probably borrowed from the movies."

There is also the renewed suggestion that the Texas tradition belongs to many more than the privileged Wasp elite who occupy the heights of the

* Not everyone is enamored of the Perot record. *The Texas Observer,* drawing in part on a muckraking account in *Ramparts* magazine, charged that Perot's data processing firm, Electronic Data Systems, used federal money to develop a data processing system for 10 states' medicare-medicaid programs, "snookered" government bureaucrats into buying a "sweetheart contract," and then obliged government to pay dearly "for a process it paid to develop in the first place." The *Observer* jeeringly quoted Perot: "Any man born in the United States of America is twice-blessed. And he is thrice-blessed if born in Texas."

TEXAS
MILES
0
100
200
NEW MEXICO
OKLAHOMA
ARK.
LA.
MEXICO
Gulf of Mexico
HIGH PLAINS
CENTRAL PLAINS
TRANS-PECOS TEXAS
EAST TEXAS (PINEY WOODS)
BALCONES ESCARPMENT
BLACKLANDS
GULF COASTAL PLAIN
Amarillo
Lubbock
Midland
Odessa
Abilene
San Angelo
Wichita Falls
Fort Worth
Dallas
Texarkana
Tyler
Waco
Trinity R.
Johnson City
Fredericksburg
Austin
Beaumont
Port Arthur
Houston
Texas City
Galveston
San Antonio
Crystal City
DUVAL COUNTY
JIM WELLS COUNTY
Corpus Christi
King Ranch
PADRE ISLAND
Laredo
FALCON DAM
Brownsville
AMISTAD DAM
Rio Grande
BIG BEND NATIONAL PARK
8751 FT.
GUADALUPE MTN'S. NAT'L. PARK
El Paso
Ciudad Juarez
Lenz
0
10 MILES
UNIVERSITY PARK
HIGHLAND PARK
GREATER SOUTHWEST INTERNATIONAL AIRPORT
Irving
Trinity R.
Dallas
Oak Cliff
Arlington
Fort Worth
DALLAS—FORT WORTH TURNPIKE
HOUSTON INTERCONTINENTAL AIRPORT
0 2 4 6 8 10 MILES
BAYPORT INDUST. DIST.
Baytown
Houston
Buffalo Bayou
Ship Channel
Pasadena
ASTRODOME
Galveston Bay
Clear Lake City
NASA MANNED SPACECRAFT CENTER

Texas power structure and have monopolized attention for so many decades. The historic essence of Texas, Joe Frantz suggests, is not any narrow corral but "its universalism and its diversity." A lion's share of the early settlers came from the nearby Southern states, "for reasons of propinquity. But other participants came from Indiana, New York, Massachusetts, and from beyond —England, Ireland, Denmark, France, German states, and Africa. Truly they were a United Nations' force dedicated to building a social and political climate in which men could go their separate, non-conforming ways without fear." The real Texas tradition, in this view, runs from old Sam Houston bravely warning against joining the Confederacy (and being removed from the governorship for his apostasy) to Stanley Marcus urging modern-day Dallas to face up to its slums and discard its spirit of absolutism, to Mexican-American farm workers in a long, dusty march to demand a share of their birthright.

Are such events simply quixotic assaults on an entrenched establishment of wealth and power that is not about to be dislodged or even threatened? The weight of evidence is in that direction. With few exceptions, the essential power in Texas has remained in the hands of an immense oil-insurance-banking-construction axis so close to the ruling political circles that the two have seemed virtually indistinguishable.

But things have happened in Texas that make one wonder. In the 1960s, the Texas legislature passed the first minimum wage law in the state's history, and made it—wonder of wonders—apply to *farm workers* as well as those in industry. The state elected its first Mexican-American Congressmen, and in 1972 sent its first Negro to the U.S. House. Closed, conservative Dallas chose as mayor a man worth $100 million (no surprise) but then he launched perhaps the United States' most advanced program to involve ordinary citizens in long-term planning of their city (a fantastic surprise). Radical protest by young Chicanos about the feudal white control of Rio Grande counties, while outside the political mainstream, has contributed to new ferment among a long quiescent people and the probability of great change in the years to come.

So one can detect the stirrings of a new era. No one expects the citadels of wealth and power to topple. But there will be renewed competition for influence. As oil, the exploitive product, declines in relative importance, petrochemicals and other industries involving more unionized labor, and also a more independently minded management and technician class, will continue to rise. While Texas universities are scarcely hotbeds of radical thought, they do create a current of opinion to the left of establishmentarian thinking. Texas' dispossessed millions will increasingly demand a say about their lives and their society, and will be heard more. Within a few years there will be a state income tax and, with it, at least a partial redistribution of the wealth. The breakdown in old-line Democratic "regularity," triggered by conservative Republicans and new Democratic activists, has already stimulated a refreshing wave of citizen political participation. In short, the Lone Star State of the 1970s seems destined to have a more open society than at any time since the days of her infancy. Perhaps there will be a rounding of the circle, a return to the spirit of those early years when the early Anglos and indigenous Mexicans made successful common cause against the oppressors from Mexico City. In victory, it will be remembered, they established their own republic (1836–45), a boisterous experiment in frontier democracy without parallel in the settlement of the continent.

The Economy: Good Times Come to Texas

Forty years ago, Texas was drifting along as a rural, agrarian, poor state. Almost 60 percent of its 5.8 million people lived on farms or in little towns, making their living principally from cattle and cotton. Then, in the 1930s, the great East Texas oil field came in, to be followed a few years later by major discoveries on the West Texas plains. Thousands of Texans became proficient in the skills of exploration and drilling for oil, hundreds became millionaires in their own right, the great pools of petroleum generated equally great pools of risk capital, a gigantic petrochemical industry formed and Texas became one of the great manufacturing states of the Union in chemicals, electronics, aircraft, and metals. Military bases sprouted in World War II, and in the postwar years Texas became the country's second largest defense contractor (after California). Dallas and Houston, the big financial, legal, and headquarters cities, grew into great American metropolises, continuing their growth through the 1960s and into the 1970s at a stunning rate.

By 1970, 11,196,730 people lived in Texas. Only 20 percent of them lived on farms and in little villages, which had fallen from 3.4 million people in 1930 to 2.3 million in 1970. Virtually all the growth had occurred in 24 metropolitan areas (more than any other state), scattered from Texarkana in the northeast to El Paso in the west, from Amarillo in the north to Brownsville in the south. The aggregate metropolitan population was 8.2 million, about 74 percent of the total Texas population. At the same time, the per capita income of Texans rose from $478 in 1929 (then 68 percent of the national level) to $3,682 in 1971 (89 percent of the U.S. average). Texans have a long ways to go, however, before they can be complacent about poverty in their midst. A 1972 study by the Texas Office of Economic Opportunity showed that a fifth of the state's people were living in poverty; with 5 percent of the nation's population, Texas had 10 percent of the country's poor. The burden of poverty fell most heavily on the young and the old; the OEO study found that a fourth of Texas' children and fully 40 percent of its elderly were living in poverty.

Texas remains the preeminent oil and gas producing state of the nation. In 1970, more than a billion barrels of oil were produced at a value of over $4 billion; gas production of 8.5 billion cubic feet was valued at $1.2 billion. The petrochemical industry born during World War II continues to grow, up 25 percent even since 1960. It is centered in Houston, Beaumont, and along the whole Gulf Coast in a complex informally called the "spaghetti bowl"—a reference to the thousands of miles of pipelines running from one factory to the next. Led by chemicals, total manufacturing output has topped $12 billion a year.

Texas oil production is still increasing and seems sure to remain Texas' dominant industry through the end of this century. But the great boom period has ended, and no one expects any more major discoveries. There are now less than a fifth as many exploratory rigs in Texas as there were 15 years ago. Secondary recovery techniques (such as the pumping of water underground to force pockets of oil toward the wells) have actually doubled Texas' reserves, but even at that, some wells are no longer able to produce their "allowables" under state oil conservation regulations. M. A. Wright, chairman of the board of Humble Oil (the largest Texas producer) pointed out in an interview that U. S. petroleum demand is increasing at about four percent a year, "but our reserves are not developing that fast." (The situation is especially grave in respect to natural gas; respected scientists project a serious shortage by the later 1970s.) Thus Humble and the other majors are engaged in aggressive global searches for new oil and gas sources and are heavily involved in the Alaskan North Slope development. They are also looking down the road toward eventual conversion to synthetic crudes. Major sources are expected to be the oil shale fields of Colorado, Utah, and Wyoming, and U. S. coal deposits that can be converted to gas. On the latter score, Humble has invested about $20 million in coal lands in the Illinois Basin and Rocky Mountains, and practically all the majors now see themselves as total energy producing firms, not oil companies alone. Nevertheless, they are sure to go slow on development of synthetics until they have depleted their existing resources in regular crude oil.

The technology of oil development has made it impossible for most of the old-style "shirttail" operators and wildcatters to remain viable. The reasons are fairly simple—drilling and pumping costs have gone up faster than crude oil prices, and virgin territory for drilling is becoming rarer and rarer. Wildcat drilling has fallen off about 40 percent in the last 15 years, and the day of the high-rolling wheeler-dealer with his big tan Stetson and gleaming cream Cadillac is on its way into history. The "independents" who do prosper, and indeed still drill the holes to discover most new oil, work in close cooperation with the majors who do the advanced geophysical and analysis work.*

A brief review of federal-state oil policy is necessary because it lies at the heart of Texas' drive for national political influence. A conservative economist, Milton Friedman, has written: "Few industries sing the praises of free enterprise more loudly than the oil industry. Yet few industries rely so heavily on special government favors." The special privileges started back in 1926

* In Dallas, I hoped to interview Jake L. Hamon, an "independent" of the old school who has prospered just as well in the latter-day oil world. This is the reply I received to my letter of inquiry:

> Dear Mr. Peirce:
> I regret that I will be out of the country on the days you plan to be in Dallas.
> I am not leaving because you plan to be in Dallas; I had already planned to go.
> Yours very sincerely,
> /s/ Jake L. Hamon

with enactment of the oil depletion allowance, which exempted from taxation 27-½ percent of the gross income from oil wells. That figure held inviolate until 1969, when it was reduced to 22 percent on the crest of a taxpayer revolt. Even if all costs have been covered, the depletion allowance can be taken throughout the life of an oil well. State limits on production, begun in the name of conservation but continued (many believe) for the purpose of propping up prices, were begun in the 1930s. Allegedly to ward off heavy foreign oil imports that would discourage domestic oil exploration, a national oil import quota system was instituted in 1959 and is still in effect.

Critics claim that the oil import quotas result in $5 billion higher prices paid by U. S. consumers each year. The depletion allowance, they say, costs the federal government about $1.3 billion a year in taxes not paid. Major oil companies pay a laughably low percentage of federal tax on their net income. Some examples from 1971: Standard Oil of New Jersey paid 7.7 percent on $2.7 billion net income, Texaco 2.3 percent on $1.3 billion, Gulf 2.3 percent on $1.3 billion, Mobil 7.4 percent on $1.2 billion, Standard Oil of California 1.6 percent on $856 million, etc.

Oil companies reply that they pay billions of dollars each year in various other forms of taxes, including local levies. "The whole case for the . . . depletion allowance," according to Houston oilman J. R. Parten, "rests upon national security. We have fueled two world wars, largely out of our oil and gas resources, and in my opinion this would not have been possible without the tax incentives." The same rationale is used to justify oil import quotas. "If we took off the import controls," Humble's Wright says, prices would fall so far that "U. S. oil exploration would fall off rapidly and much of our oil —maybe half—would come from abroad.* Do we want the U.S. to be, like Europe, dependent on foreign sources of energy, to accommodate its needs?" In a national emergency, oilmen argue, the country would want to have ample domestic reserves. That argument is somewhat vitiated, however, by the fact that America generally has a 10-year reserve in already tapped wells from which it could draw, and there is some doubt that a national emergency would last that long. Also, new energy sources like oil shale could be exploited more rapidly in such a situation.

Whatever the merits, one indisputable fact is that Texans and their Southwestern neighbors have held crucial seats of national power which have enabled them to protect the industry's tax advantage and import quotas. For years, Lyndon Johnson of Texas was Senate Majority Leader and later President. His colleague, Speaker Sam Rayburn, was a zealous guardian of the gates to the tax-writing House Ways and Means Committee for two decades. Oklahoma's Senator Robert S. Kerr, a wealthy oilman himself, was the powerful number-two man on the Senate Finance Committee for several years;

* Since my interview with Wright, however, the cost differential between U. S. and foreign oil prices has shrunk substantially. By spring 1972, the demand for oil had grown so much that Texas wells had to be opened to 100 percent of their ability to produce—but still had difficulty meeting the needs of domestic refiners. The second Nixon administration, according to a late 1972 report by Richard Corrigan of the *National Journal,* was preparing programs to stimulate a rapid growth of domestic oil and gas production—even if that meant higher consumer costs and additional environmental hazards.

since 1966 the chairman of that committee has been Louisiana's Senator Russell Long, who is reported to have made $1.2 million on oil leases since 1964. Texas' Robert B. Anderson became Secretary of the Treasury in the Eisenhower Administration; another Texan, John B. Connally, was appointed to the same post by President Nixon.

Even today, Texas' power in Congress remains formidable. In addition to its Senators, the state has a hefty bloc of 24 House seats. Rep. George H. Mahon reigns over the House Appropriations Committee, the foremost holder of the national pursestrings. The chairman of the House Banking and Currency Committee, Rep. Wright Patman, is now in his late seventies but still a vigorous scourge of big banks, high interest rates, and the foundations (but no enemy of big oil). Rep. Olin E. Teague is both chairman of the Democratic Caucus in the House and of the Science and Astronautics Committee. Even liberal Senator Ralph Yarborough, before his 1970 defeat, defended the oil depletion allowance. An influential spokesman for the same cause in Republican circles is Senator John G. Tower, a staunch conservative, who has risen to high seniority on the Armed Services and Banking and Currency Committees.

The same congressional bloc makes it its business to defend Texas' big aerospace and defense industry, military and NASA installations, and also Texas farm interests. The state is the nation's No. 1 producer of cotton, an industry heavily dependent on federal farm subsidies, and in fact Rep. W. R. Poage of Texas is chairman of the House Agriculture Committee. Texas also grows some three million acres of wheat a year, another subsidy-dependent crop.

The other big Texas farm products are less tied to government largesse. Texas has traditionally been the nation's foremost breeder of cattle, shipping the animals to the Midwest for feeding and eventual slaughter ever since the days of the first great cattle drives. Today there are still more head of cattle being raised in Texas than any other state—over 12 million. But fewer cattle are being shipped away for fattening, and in 1971 the Agriculture Department found that Texas, for the first time in history, had surpassed Iowa in feedlot cattle counts. Most of the feedlots are in the Panhandle, an operation computerized and mechanized on a scale unparalleled in the Midwest. Slaughtering is increasingly done in-state, too. Together with Oklahoma, Texas in 1970 was marketing an estimated 3.2 million head of feed cattle in a year, compared with only 345,000 in 1955.

This is not to say that old style cattle raising has disappeared in Texas. Real cowboys still drive cattle in West Texas, and the huge cattle ranches still exist, each now complete with its own planes and airstrip.

Texas farm marketings have topped $3 billion in recent years, second only to California and Iowa. Livestock sales account for about 70 percent of the total. In addition to cattle, the state ranks first in the U.S. in sheep (three million to five million, depending on the year), and it is second in turkeys, eighth in chickens. Its rice, pecan, and peanut crops are among the country's largest, and it is first or nearly so in spinach, onions, carrots, cabbage, and watermelons. There are significant citrus crops in the Rio Grande Valley. The big growers there think they could make more money if they could produce more grapefruit, but there is simply not enough water to permit expansion of the industry. Even darker clouds over Texas agriculture are droughts and the prospect of exhaustion of the aquifers that have been tapped to irrigate great stretches of West Texas—a story to which we will return later.

The Establishment: Power Unparalleled

Up to now, Texas political life has been directed by a single monied establishment. In no other state has the control been so direct, so unambiguous, so commonly accepted. The establishment has its roots in the banks and law firms of Dallas and Houston and, to a lesser degree, those of Austin. Its untold billions of wealth are in oil, insurance, high finance, construction, broadcasting, real estate, electronics, and the manufacture of weaponry. Its spokesmen are the great metropolitan dailies of Texas—papers like the Dallas *Morning News*, the Houston *Chronicle*, and the Fort Worth *Star-Telegram*—and, in turn, the great bulk of the state's television stations. Lyndon Johnson was very much part of this establishment; John B. Connally is the epitome of it.

A strong argument can be made that the pivotal figures of postwar Texas history were not Johnson or Rayburn, but Allan Shivers (the conservative governor, in office from 1949 to 1957), and Connally. Connally's story, in particular, is quintessentially Texas. He grew up in a farm town near San Antonio, one of seven children of a dirt-poor butcher, farmer, and later bus driver. But no one would dream today that Connally came to town on a load of cobs; in all America, there are few politicians who can compete with him for cool, suave manners, good looks, and height, a man never ill at ease. San Antonio lawyer John Peace, who met Connally at the University of Texas (*de rigeur* training ground for aspiring Texas politicians), recalls even then a quality about the man that made others "want him to be chairman of the board," without resenting his position at all. Predictably, Connally was elected UT student body president and was on his way politically.

"Connally did more to make Johnson than anyone else in the U.S.," Peace insists, recalling that most of the Johnson forces were originally Connally people whose "first loyalty and tie was to Connally." The group included Jake Pickle and Frank Ikard (both of whom later became Congressmen, and Ikard later the chief oil lobbyist in Washington), John Singleton and Hal Woodward (now federal judges in Texas), and many others. "From the juices of youth and loyalty [to Connally] we helped, all the way back to LBJ's first race for Congress, then his Senate elections." LBJ, Peace admitted, would regard this interpretation "as heresy," and of course it would be foolish to discount the contributions made to Johnson's rise by men like Franklin Roosevelt and Sam Rayburn.

Finishing law school in 1938, Connally started almost immediately as an aide to freshman Congressman Johnson in Washington, and though he was to take countless other jobs in the succeeding years, he never really left Johnson. He served four and a half years in the Navy during the war, rising to the rank of lieutenant commander and winning decorations for combat duty on the carrier *Essex;* then he went back to Austin and used his mustering out pay to open a radio station. In 1948, he was the ramrod of the initial election of Lyndon Johnson for the U. S. Senate, operating in the thick of the events which led to the appearance of a miraculous uncounted vote box from Jim Wells County that suddenly turned a narrow Johnson loss into an 87-vote victory.

In 1951, Connally moved to Fort Worth to become an attorney for Sid Richardson, who had amassed a fortune of some $2 billion in oil, making him one of the richest men on earth. Now the skein of corporate directorships began to form as Connally served as director (or officer) of the Richardson Oil Co., Richardson Carbon Co., the Richardson Foundation, the New York Central Railroad, and four broadcasting companies. Testifying before a Senate committee in 1961 (during confirmation hearings for his appointment as Secretary of the Navy in the Kennedy Administration), Connally revealed a Texas-sized list of duties he had been assigned by his friend and employer Richardson, including "problems concerning the production of oil and gas, and the running of two radio stations, the running of a television station, and operating cattle ranches of approximately 4,000 head on 70,000 acres of land, running five drugstores in Fort Worth, various mining interests, housing development corporations, a carbon black plant, a gasoline extraction plant," etc., etc. In 1956 Connally had been sent to Washington to lobby for a "fair market price" natural gas bill that would have profited the gas industry between $2 billion and $12 billion over time; as it turned out, the bill passed, but President Eisenhower vetoed it because of the taint of scandal following the charge of Sen. Francis Case of South Dakota that an oil company lawyer (later identified as John M. Neff) had offered him an improper campaign contribution in exchange for his vote. Subsequently Neff and Elmer Patman of Austin, Texas, both attorneys for the Superior Oil Co., were indicted for failing to register as lobbyists and pleaded guilty. That same year, Johnson urged Connally to register as a lobbyist, but he refused to do so. Connally was never directly implicated in the offer to Senator Case, but he and Patman were called "the Gold Dust Twins" by other gas lobbyists.

When Connally went to work for Richardson, the old man had promised: "I'll pay you enough so Nellie and the kids won't go hungry, and I'll put you in the way to make some money." He kept his promise. Connally steadily built his fortune during the Fort Worth years, and in 1959, when Richardson died, he became one of the executors of his estate, work for which he eventually received compensation of $750,000. In 1965, he purchased the 14,500-acre Tortuga Ranch in South Texas for about $300,000. By 1970, he owned several other substantial pieces of property, and by his own admission it was all done with borrowed money.

Stephen D. Berkowitz, in a muckraking account of the Connally record in 1971, wrote:

> While much of the impetus behind his meteoric rise can be traced to the New Deal and its aftermath, like Johnson, Connally has been embraced by ultraconservative cattle barons, bankers and oil magnates as one of their own. . . .
>
> Connally's earliest ties were with the Austin-based grouping which grew up in the hothouse atmosphere of cost-plus contracting and political pork-barreling during and immediately after World War II. Spearheaded by political power in Congress—especially in the important House and Senate military appropriations committees—this grouping began to expand and develop strong interests in a number of areas; banking and land; large-scale construction; oil drilling and exploration; broadcasting; and insurance. Directly or indirectly each of these was dependent on federal largesse: *construction* on funds for building military bases, dams, and pipelines; *broadcasting* on federal licenses; and *oil drilling*, in many cases, on leases and direct subsidies. . . .

Throughout the Connally career, one hears of his business and political contacts growing wider, year by year. His work for Richardson brought him into contact with the Murchison clan, which has major interests in railroads, steel, insurance, and oil. Among his close contacts were Ed Clark, a lobbyist, bank executive, and later Ambassador to Australia; J. C. Kellam, a business executive with broad contacts, president of the LBJ Corporation and former chairman of the Texas State Colleges Board of Regents; Robert Phinney, destined to become director of the Internal Revenue Service; Willard Deason, who became a member of the Interstate Commerce Commission. . . . The list goes on and on. At the same time, Connally remained a chief political operative for Johnson, lining up financial backing among his oil industry friends, serving as LBJ liaison man with local Democratic leaders, and working for Johnson's unsuccessful bids for the Presidential nomination in 1956 and 1960.

As close as the LBJ-Connally relationship was over the years, it is worth noting that there were profound differences between the two men. Connally has never shown any discernible interest in the plight of minorities in America, while it was Lyndon Johnson who, as Senate Majority Leader and later as President, secured approval of the first and then the most monumental civil rights acts of the century. Nor was Johnson ever as close to the oil and gas community as Connally. Harry McPherson, a Senate aide to Johnson in the late 1950s, wrote later of that period:

> Johnson had no special love for the oil and gas industry in Texas; oil men had never been among his most ardent supporters in the days before he became Majority Leader and acquired such power over their fortunes. . . . Yet Johnson did his part. He helped to lead the fight for state control of the offshore oil lands and against federal regulation of gas prices at the wellhead. He was careful about assignments to the Finance Committee, where the depletion allowance lay like a ruby in a wall safe. . . .
>
> Having secured the benign indifference—if not the active support—of Texas' most powerful economic interest, Johnson was free to pursue other goals. His refusal in 1956 to sign the Southern Manifesto against the Supreme Court's ruling on school desegregation was possible not only because a substantial minority

of Texans were black or brown, but because he was sound on oil and gas. Conservatism on that issue allowed him to work for the Civil Rights Act of 1957 and 1960, for public housing and urban renewal, and for foreign aid; this at a time when Texas school boards were throwing out textbooks that even discussed the UN. . . .

Johnson had another string to his bow. He was The Leader—a great and famous public figure. Texans were rather proud that one of their own occupied such a position. They allowed him leeway on many issues of less than critical significance to them, and could even tolerate, without accepting, his progressive views on race.

When Johnson became Vice President, Connally was appointed Secretary of the Navy—not, Connally told one biographer, as a result of LBJ's intervention, but rather on the direct suggestion to President Kennedy of House Speaker Sam Rayburn. Connally was to stay with that job less than a year, however, before returning home to run for governor. The rather false issue used against Connally in that 1962 campaign was that he was running as "Lyndon's Boy." Actually, Johnson had always had a great disdain for state government and tried to dissuade Connally, telling him he already had a more important job in Washington (where, as LBJ saw it, the real action was). But there were strong reasons for Connally to run. He and some of his old political-business colleagues, then in their mid-40s, detected what they thought was drifting in the Texas economy, a failure to be really competitive with the East and California in education or business growth. They were determined to make Texas a Class A state, not to go, as one told me, "the route of Mississippi, Alabama, and Louisiana." The Connally group saw Price Daniel, then the governor, as a drifter and do-nothing figure, or even worse, a man developing dangerous populist ideas through his opposition to a business-backed sales tax. Finally, Connally and his friends were determined to prevent decisive change in Texas' one-party system, to freeze out the Republicans (who had won Johnson's old Senate seat in 1961) and keep out of the statehouse the left wing of the Democratic party (militant unionists, liberals, and minority group leaders).

So Connally came home, took the air-strip set away from Daniel, and ran well ahead in the first primary. But he failed to make 50 percent and was forced into a runoff with an aggressive young liberal named Don Yarborough (no relation to Senator Ralph Yarborough). The runoff vote was a perilously close 565,174 for Connally, 538,924 for Yarborough. As it was, Connally succeeded only through all-time record spending made possible by contributions of his oil industry friends and associates, plus the monolithic backing of the state press. According to writer Robert Sherrill, only one of the 114 daily newspapers of Texas endorsed Yarborough, who had "the entire financial and industrial community arrayed against him." A victory by Yarborough would probably have accelerated by a decade some of the liberalizing changes in state government now likely to take place in the 1970s; unlike many Texas liberals, Yarborough had a tough pragmatic streak and ability to deal effectively with a broad range of the political spectrum. (He ran again for governor in 1964 and 1968 and lost both times.)

Connally took office in January 1963, and in November of that year President Kennedy scheduled his ill-starred trip to the state to try and calm the fierce internecine war between the liberal wing, led by Senator Ralph Yarborough, and the conservative wing, already becoming known as the Connally wing. In the Presidential motorcade going into Dallas, Connally had a coveted seat in the Presidential limousine and was almost killed by a bullet; he has told friends his doctor said he survived only because he slumped forward and staunched the flow of blood from wounds in his chest.

After Dallas, Connally was politically invincible and coasted to easy second- and third-term victories in 1964 and 1966. He proved a master of articulation of Texas' long-term needs in fields ranging from constitutional revision to higher education, public school reform and water supply. (As Dallas newsman Jim Lehrer suggested to me, "he could see further than the next bridge on the Trinity River.") But Connally proved to be an aloof figure in Austin, lacking determination to follow through on many of his own proposals. Part of Connally's problem may have been his very conservative friends; when he appointed them to a constitutional revision commission, for instance, few of the needed structural reforms, including annual legislative sessions, better pay for legislators, or a cabinet system, emerged in the final product.

Labor and the minorities got the back of Connally's hand. He boasted of voluntary integration in Texas but opposed the Kennedy-Johnson Administration's public accommodations law as striking at "one of our most cherished freedoms—the right to own and manage private property." He showed contempt for Mexican-American farm workers marching to Austin and refused to support the state minimum wage law they asked for. This was balanced by more appointments for Mexicans—at least politically "acceptable" ones—than any prior governor had made. But the sales tax was doubled under Connally, without corresponding increases in taxes that affect the wealthy. Connally became a superhawk on the Vietnam war and assailed "peace" demonstrators as "bearded and unwashed prophets of doubt and despair" for whom, as he put it, "liberty is merely a license to preach and practice individual and ideological perversions of their responsibilities as free men." Connally specifically included the late Martin Luther King, Jr., in that group. At Chicago in 1968, he led the fight for a platform plank backing up the Administration on the war, and threatened Johnson's reentry into the Presidential race if his conditions were not met.*

By the time Connally left the governorship, a national image of Texas as an aggressive, space-age-oriented state was well established—a far cry from the Old South syndrome of a few years before. The Houston and Dallas areas were in the midst of spectacular booms. The gap between Texas and national per capita income (an area in which Texas has always lagged) had

* Connally was outraged with Hubert Humphrey for permitting the convention to drop the unit rule for delegate voting, a traditional source of power for the state's conservative Democratic establishment, and was also upset that Humphrey would not even consider him for the Vice Presidency.

been significantly narrowed. Almost 1,500 new plants were settled in Texas and 150,000 new industrial jobs were added; tourism doubled to about $1 billion a year, with 140,000 new jobs. Unemployment levels were among the lowest in the nation. Some of Connally's conservative friends might object to the increase in the state budget (up from $1.3 billion to $2.5 billion during the Connally years, much of the new money from expanded federal aid under LBJ), but there was little arguing about the general prosperity. A significant share of the budget increase went to higher education.

Texas also enjoyed a great military-industrial boom in the 1960s. During World War II and Korea, pressure from Johnson and other members of the congressional delegation had helped—along with the Texan climate—to make the state a center for military training and manufacturing. By the mid-1950s, there was scarcely a Texas city of significant size without one or more major military facilities nearby. In Congress in the 1950s, Johnson used his role as Senate majority leader to fight for higher military appropriations than the Eisenhower Administration wanted. But with Johnson installed as President and the Vietnam war build-up underway, the spigot could be turned on in deadly earnest. From a 1963 level of $1.2 billion in defense prime contract awards (representing just 4.3 percent of the national total), Texas' gross receipts climbed 242 percent to $4.1 billion in 1968 (10 percent of the national total). And these figures do not even include the NASA Manned Spacecraft Center, which was located at Houston as a result of Texas' political muscle under the Kennedy Administration.

When 1969 came, Lyndon Johnson retired to his ranch to nurse his investments and write his memoirs. John Connally, still a vigorous 52, did nothing of the sort. Instead, he moved his center of operations to Houston and became a partner in Vinson, Elkins, Weems and Searls—the biggest law firm in Texas, and one long regarded as the state's most powerful lobbying group. (Until his death in 1972, James Elkins, Sr., the firm's senior partner, was the most influential man in Texas in determining which candidate the establishment would bankroll in governorship campaigns.) Connally was also invited to sit on the board of directors of the huge First City National Bank of Houston, twice the size of its closest Houston competitor. The senior chairman of the board of First City National was James Elkins, Sr. Another member of the board was (and is) George Brown of the huge Texas construction firm, Brown & Root, which does about $1.5 billion business a year (second largest in the U. S.).* Brown & Root has played a powerful role in Texas politics over several decades, and George Brown's brother Herman was perhaps Johnson's first major financial backer. George Brown's participation in First City National links the company with oil drilling (Halliburton) and land companies, steel (Armco), pipelines (Texas Eastern Transmission), airlines

* Brown & Root was one of four companies that did a billion dollars' worth of business in Vietnam. It has operated since the late 1960s as a quasi-independent but wholly owned subsidiary of Halliburton Co., which provides oilfield services and owns a research subsidiary that makes explosives and pyrotechnic ordnance in Arlington, Texas. Connally became a member of the Halliburton board of directors in 1969.

(TWA) and a major conglomerate (ITT). Connally brought some of his own connections, since he sat on the boards of directors of the Gibraltar Savings Association (Houston) and the U. S. Trust Co. (New York).

Then, in 1970, the Texas political world was shocked by Connally's decision to become Secretary of the Treasury in the Nixon cabinet—a decision Lyndon Johnson learned of only after it had been made. With consummate skill, Connally convinced the President to abandon the failing old economic "game plan" and embrace a New Economic Policy—of which Connally himself was the chief architect—that included wage and price controls, devaluation of the dollar, and tax cuts (especially for business).* Soon the economy was recovering from its stagnation and inflationary drift. Then Connally began to operate in the international sphere, winning historic agreements to realign exchange rates in a way more favorable to the United States and to reform the world monetary system. (Critics, however, said that Connally's abrasive nationalism would undermine the traditional "partnership" within the North Atlantic community and accelerate the trend to protectionism and splitting of the free world into restrictive blocs.)

After a year and a half as the superstar of an otherwise dull cabinet, Connally tired of the Washington pressures and decided to return to private life. He rejoined his old Houston law firm, now renamed Vinsons, Elkins, Searls, Connally and Smith to reflect his name. The ties with Richard Nixon remained warm, however, as the President came to Texas twice in a few months for big barbecues at Connally's south Texas ranch. As columnist David Broder later reported the scene of the first evening, in April 1972:

> The flagstone ranch house was ablaze with light. The magnificent live oaks in the yard were hung with pots of orange mums, swaying in the evening breeze; more flowers floated in the pool, and the sweet scent of the prairie grass mingled with the odors of the steaming barbecue.
>
> The guests arrived Texas-style, setting their executive jets down on the Picosa Ranch airstrip, with the great red Santa Gertrudis cattle watching.

The guest list, Broder said, was a "directory" of the members of Texas' monied establishment. Among those present were former governor Allan Shivers, oil and banking mogul John D. Murchison, H. L. Hunt's son Nelson, Dallas billionaire H. Ross Perot, Houston millianairess Ima Hogg, former Dallas Mayor Erik Jonsson, George Brown, and one of Connally's early, wealthy backers—Perry Bass of Fort Worth. The guest list included lawyers, ranchers, land speculators, broadcasters, and publishers and editors known for their steadfast allegiance to the establishment.

After supper, the President spoke to the guests for an hour, warming their hearts by an assurance that America would never be defeated in Southeast Asia, that he would stand "against the trend toward permissiveness . . . and weakness" in American society, that more—rather than less—should be done to mold the tax laws to provide incentives for the oil industry, that people on

* Connally was also the chief salesman of the $250 million loan guarantee designed to save Lockheed Aircraft from bankruptcy.

welfare should go out and get jobs for themselves, and that busing for school integration ought to be opposed. The President, Broder noted, never hit a "false note" with his audience:

> He told them exactly what they wanted to hear. He praised their friend and host and hero John Connally, who saved the state government from a serious liberal challenge in 1962 and gave them six years more of freedom from corporate income taxes or real utility regulation; the President called Connally a man "capable of holding any job in the United States."

Mr. Nixon made another interesting comment that day at John Connally's ranch. "Now," he said, "I feel I've seen what Texas is supposed to be."

In the autumn of 1972, Connally took on the national chairmanship of Democrats for Nixon and hinted that if the McGovernites remained in control of the national Democratic party, he might consider leaving the party. Speculation continued that he might actually switch parties and seek the Presidency as a Republican in 1976. But Connally's friends in the Democratic establishment doubted if Connally would actually take that step. Although the prospect of the Presidency is "heady wine," one of them pointed out to me, several persons in Connally's immediate family had died of heart attacks in their mid-sixties. Connally, he said, knew that the same thing might happen to him in the late 1970s or early 1980s—and that he would be 59 years of age in 1976. "Why should Connally take the risk of all the additional burdens of a Presidential candidacy—especially in view of that potential health problem?" Connally's friend said. "Life is personally much pleasanter for him when he can spend the week doing business in Houston, and then fly down to the ranch and 'away-from-it-all' each weekend."

Connally in 1973 did switch his formal allegiance to the Republican party, serving briefly as a White House adviser to the Watergate-afflicted Nixon White House and then starting extensive national travels to build up support as a potential candidate for the Presidency in 1976. He was well received at Republican gatherings across the country, but his close ties with Nixon (who seriously considered nominating Connally for Vice President, after the forced resignation of Spiro Agnew), and more particularly his identification as a spokesman for big oil interests at the very time those corporations were coming under the most severe public attack, cast long shadows over his prospects. Also, many Republicans still seemed to regard Connally as a "Johnny-come-lately" to their party; among party conservatives, California's Ronald Reagan seemed the preferred candidate.

Finally, it was doubtful whether the members of the Democratic establishment—even under Connally's leadership—would move over to the GOP. Former Congressman Joe M. Kilgore noted: "Most business interests see that if they move into the Republican party, they will see their own influence in Texas diminished." Even having one of their own in the White House, it appeared, might not justify that risk.

The endless chains of inter- and intra-city, family and club, formal and informal relationships which characterize the Texas monied establishment would no doubt delight a man whom some regard as the godfather of it all—Jesse Jones, the great financier-builder of Houston and owner of a good chunk of other Texas cities as well. Jones topped off his career by going off to Washington to use his marvelous skills as head of the Reconstruction Finance Corporation and later as Secretary of Commerce. The foundation he left behind in Houston still exerts a major influence in the city. Among its holdings is its voice to the world, the Houston *Chronicle*. But in Jones's day, things were essentially simpler. The Texas of the 1930s was still a largely unformed place as the initial fortunes were just being made out of the East Texas oil fields. Today the monied structure is many times as large as it was, has expanded into highly innovative fields (universities, computer companies), and under Johnson and Connally has extended its power into the very heart of national decision making.

Texas' monied establishment has its Achilles heel—ethics. There is not even in theory a line between private interest and public responsibility, as the establishment sees it. For instance, if an establishment politician appears on the scene without prior wealth, steps are taken to see that he stays a poor boy no longer, apparently with little concern that his independence might be undermined in the process. A favorite way to do this is to sell a man stock in an up-and-coming local corporation. One of the establishment's banks is lined up to lend the man money to buy the stock, with the securities themselves the sole collateral.

Campaign contributions, as in so many states, are the primary vehicle for the transfer of private money to politicians. In 1970, reporter Morton Mintz of the Washington *Post* undertook a study of the identity of contributors to that year's election in Texas. (No Texas paper chose to do the same research). Mintz found that oilmen accounted for almost 46 percent of the individual contributors of $5,000 or more in his half-million dollar sampling, while bankers, mutual fund managers, and others in the financial world accounted for another 19 percent. Then there were major gifts from contractors, insurance men, realtors, and doctors. Liberal Senator Ralph Yarborough reported $247,652 in gifts that year, of which only a paltry $8,300 came from labor union sources.* Instead, Yarborough had a scattering of larger gifts from business and liberal leaders. "But," Mintz reported, "businessmen's contributions of $5,000 or more seemed to fall like confetti" into the coffers of Lloyd M. Bentsen, Jr., the banking, insurance, and mutual funds multimillionaire from Houston who defeated Yarborough in the primary, and Republican Representative George Bush, who lost the general election to Bentsen. Both Bentsen and Bush ended up receiving and spending about $1 million. Sen. John Tower reported spending more than $2.5 million in his successful 1972 reelection campaign—the most expensive campaign (except for President) of any candidate in any state that year. How men with that kind of support can defy the monied establishment, even if the notion should cross their minds, is hard to imagine.

One of Texas' emissaries to Washington, East Texas Congressman

* The low labor total for Yarborough is hard to believe, since his reelection was a prime goal of the Texas AFL-CIO. Certainly if political organizing services were counted, he received immense labor assistance.

John Dowdy, in 1971 won the distinction of being the first sitting Congressman to be convicted of a felony in more than 15 years. A man of pompous ways and conservative philosophy, Dowdy had risen to a position of power on the House District of Columbia Committee, a position from which he crusaded against alleged irregularities in urban renewal programs and the idea of letting any homosexuals work for the government. But a federal jury in Baltimore convicted Dowdy of receiving a $25,000 bribe to thwart a federal investigation of a shady home improvement company, and of conspiracy and perjury. A $21,000 defense fund raised in his behalf by the right-wing Liberty Lobby, plus the apparent willingness of some of his friends to perjure themselves on Dowdy's behalf, failed to save Dowdy. Despite Dowdy's failing health, the prosecutor in the case, Stephen H. Sachs, asked that Dowdy be given a substantial prison sentence to demonstrate to convicted persons and others alienated by American society "that the war against crime is not just the war of the powerful against the powerless." The judge sentenced Dowdy to 18 months behind bars and a $25,000 fine.

At the opposite extreme from Dowdy on the integrity scale is a young Republican conservative from the Houston area, Congressman William R. Archer. He has made a full disclosure of his financial interests, going well beyond legal requirements, and even took the unusual step of relinquishing his bank holdings and directorships when he was named to the House Banking and Currency Committee.

In 1971, a sordid scandal broke into the open with revelation that a single bill passed by the Texas legislature in September 1969 had profited several leading Texas politicians, including Gov. Preston Smith, speaker of the house Gus Mutscher, and state Democratic party chairman Elmer Baum, by a total of $359,150. The federal Securities and Exchange Commission began a full-scale investigation of what it called a multimillion-dollar case of stock fraud and influence peddling. The scandal also involved the collapse of a Houston bank and one of the largest FDIC payoffs of insured deposits in the national history of bank failures. At the center of the whole mess was an admitted swindler, Houston banker and real-estate promoter Frank W. Sharp. After the SEC built an impressive case against him on fraud charges, Sharp pleaded guilty and received a light $5,000 fine and a three-year probation sentence—part of a deal in which he then became a federal witness and proceeded to implicate many Texas political figures, especially Democrats. Mutscher resigned as speaker, and Baum as party chairman, and in Washington, no less a figure than Will R. Wilson, chief of the Justice Department's Criminal Division, was asked to resign. Wilson had once been Sharp's personal attorney.

Mutscher and two aides were subsequently indicted for conspiracy to accept a bribe. The state contended that they had accepted secured loans from Sharp to buy stock in Sharp's National Bankers Life Insurance Company, making a big profit when the stock went up because of manipulation. This, the prosecution contended, was a form of bribery to get the legislature to pass bills removing Sharp's Sharpstown State Bank from federal control and examination. The trial took place in the homely, cordial city of Abilene where a jury later described "quintessentially Abilenean"—the women in print house dresses from Sears, the jury foreman a 28-year-old freshman at McMurry College wearing a cowboy shirt and jeans—took little more than two hours in finding the defendants guilty. The life style of Gus Mutscher, the son of a farmer who married Miss America of 1964, had long before advanced to a much fancier level; perhaps the jurors sensed something of how the plain people of Texas had "been taken" by their elected leaders.

The prosecutor, in his summation, had told the jury they bore responsibility for the future of Texas. People are always complaining, he noted, "Why don't they do something about the mess in Austin? You," he told the jury, "are now 'They.' If you think what is going on in Austin is O.K., then you can put your Good Housekeeping seal of approval on it by saying 'not guilty' in this case. If you think this practice is O.K., then let's sanction it and get it out in the open. If we can't convict a high public official on the evidence we've got here, then we might as well turn our state capitol over to the money-changers."

Mutscher and his codefendants got five-year probated sentences, but as the *Texas Observer* noted, on the same day "a kid in Tyler got eight years in the penitentiary for possession of a joint of marijuana."

Unless a federal agency had intervened, the Sharp case would probably never have come to light in Texas—a state where manipulation of government for direct personal gain has been commonplace, and the press has generally been in league with the conservative establishment. Practically the only liberal opinion organ and consistent muckraker in the state has been the biweekly *Texas Observer*, published in Austin. It has probed into areas largely ignored by the establishment press, ranging from statehouse scandals and the plight of the minorities to the anatomy of the establishment itself. Ronnie Dugger, the *Observer*'s editor and later major contributor, molded the paper into a sheet of liberal thought read by opinion leaders of every stripe (though the circulation, in 1972, was still only 12,000). Some of the *Observer*'s oldest friends felt its quality had begun to decline, with a superficial "new left" orientation to much coverage, in the late '60s and early '70s. But associate editor Molly Ivins and her colleagues were catalysts in getting the rest of the press corps to respond to the Frank Sharp scandals.

After some delay, the major Texas dailies and news services—the Dallas *Morning News*, Dallas *Times-Herald*, Houston *Post*, Houston *Chronicle*, Associated Press, and the Austin-based Long News Service *—began to dig deeply into the Sharp affair and a bevy of unrelated scandals, big and small, in state government. As an example, the *Chronicle*'s Austin bureau, headed by Bo Byers, revealed how two state legislators were putting each other's children through college on each other's legislative expense accounts; the

* The Long News Service is perhaps the most sophisticated of its kind in a U.S. state capital. Stuart Long and his colleagues service some 18 newspapers and also have accumulated expertise in specific fields like insurance and water problems, which are the subject of individual newsletters the service publishes.

Long News Service followed up on the story and revealed such egregious payroll kickbacks by one of the legislators that he declined renomination and was indicted. The net impact of the muckraking and revelations was to make the public distrustful of almost anyone in office. In the 1972 primary, legislators, sheriffs, county commissioners, and even public weighers—most of whom had never even driven by the Sharpstown bank—went down to defeat.

Among the politicians on whom the voters vented their fury was Governor Smith, who received only 9 percent of the vote in his bid for a third term. The voters also dealt an apparent death blow to a political career many had considered one of the most promising in the entire United States: that of a brilliant young man named Ben Barnes.

Even now, the Barnes story is worth retelling. He was born in 1938 as the son of a hard-pressed Texas peanut farmer and spent his youth in the little hamlet of De Leon, where from the age of six or so everyone considered him a natural-born politician and leader. In 1960, at the age of 22, he ran for the legislature from his home area and won. No one took much notice of him, and his voting record was like an old mossback's except on civil rights. But Barnes came to the notice of the Connally crowd and was invited to a 1961 meeting of about a dozen men at a South Texas ranch to decide whether Connally should run for governor the next year. At about 3 o'clock in the morning, Connally's close friend Robert Strauss (later Democratic national chairman) took Connally aside and told him: "John, that dumb-looking red-headed boy was the astutest politician in this room."

Soon, good things started happening to Ben Barnes. In 1963, he became chief liaison man between Connally and the speaker of the Texas house. He also became a close friend of Austin attorney Frank Erwin, Jr., a Connally intimate and key member of the Texas establishment. In 1965 the house speakership suddenly became vacant. Barnes waged a blitz campaign and was elected speaker—at the tender age of 26.

Soon it became apparent that Barnes was getting some financial breaks that might not have come his way back on the peanut farm at De Leon. As Bo Byers, veteran Houston *Chronicle* capital correspondent, reported in 1969:

> For a man whose only jobs prior to election to the legislature in 1960 were relatively menial and whose legislative pay is $400 monthly, Barnes has done quite well financially. The combination of his rapid political rise and outward signs of affluence—expensive suits and shoes, quickness to pick up the tab for dinner parties and social outings, and heavy travel expense—has made Barnes the target of much inquiry.
>
> The common question is "how did Barnes happen to get where he is so fast?" There is no clearcut answer.

Soon afterwards, there were reports that with little personal financial risk, Barnes had acquired various degrees of interest in construction, broadcasting, apartment, hotel, and shopping center ventures. It also turned out that Barnes had a financial angel—a construction contractor from Brownwood, Texas, named Herman Bennett, who had been arranging rosy investment deals for Barnes since 1964 and had made a $100,000 interest-free loan to Barnes.

In 1968, Barnes ran for lieutenant governor and was elected. The lieutenant governor exercises almost dictatorial control over the Texas senate, just as the speaker does in the house. Barnes began to use his power more and more for liberal causes, and was the key figure in getting a minimum wage bill passed covering farm workers. If the states are to remain viable, he told me in a 1969 interview, "you have to be very liberal and progressive at the state level" or Congress will take over. Barnes also intimated that there would have to be much higher taxes because of the growing tide of problems—from pollution control to mass transit—in a state whose tax effort ranked only 44th among the 50 states. I concluded that if Barnes were elected, the establishment might find itself paying much higher taxes than it had ever reckoned with.

The apogee of Barnes' political career was a 1970 "Ben Barnes appreciation dinner" at Austin, at which Lyndon Johnson proclaimed: "Ben Barnes is the future. At 32 years of age, he's the youngest lieutenant governor Texas has ever produced." Johnson then pointed out that Presidents Jefferson, Jackson, Theodore and Franklin Roosevelt, and John Kennedy had all held important positions by the time they were 32. "Each of them wound up leading this country," Johnson said. "You and I know that Ben Barnes is going to lead it too."

A few months later, the Sharp scandal broke. Barnes' opponents made every effort to link him with it personally. They never proved a connection, though it did become known that Barnes had had a $60,000 loan with Dallas Bank and Trust, a Frank Sharp bank. As one newspaper noted, "Ben Barnes was investigated by every pertinent abbreviated agency from SEC to IRS to FBI to GOP. Out of it he escaped free of direct taint, but splattered with fallout." The fallout, in fact, was so great that in 1972, when he ran for governor, enjoying full financial support from the establishment, Barnes ran a poor third in the Democratic primary field.

One of the ironies of the 1972 election was that the man who won the Democratic nomination for governor, and subsequently the general election—multimillionaire Uvalde rancher-banker Dolph Briscoe—was the man at whose south Texas ranch John Connally had first told his associates of his intention to run for governor back in 1962, and Barnes had been singled out as "the astutest politician in this room." Briscoe's sole brush with elective office had been as a state representative in the 1950s, when he sponsored some relatively progressive bills. His chief attribute in 1972—aside from the posh campaign he could mount out of his own personal wealth—was that he had been away from the public trough in Austin so long. This permitted Briscoe to run as the candidate of reform, promising "honest" and "fair" government to the state. The outlook for the Briscoe governorship seemed to be a renewed sense of integrity in state government—but few if any of the fundamental social reforms needed to make Texas government truly responsive to needs of the people. The financial interests of the establishment, it appeared, would not be in jeopardy.

Politics, Texas Style

The Democratic party has been dominant in Texas since before the Civil War, its rule interrupted only briefly by a few years of Reconstruction in the 1860s and 1870s. There has not been a Republican governor since 1874. But a basic conservative-liberal split has existed and bobbed up periodically in Texas for the better part of a century. Farm depressions hit the state in the 1880s and 1890s, and Populists and Greenbacks exploited the discontent by turning the farmer's ire on the railroads which transported his crops, on the financial houses which held his mortgages, trusts which fixed prices on his supplies, and businesses and realtors who benefited from depressed farm values. In 1890, Texas elected an exceptional governor, James Stephen Hogg, who ran on a platform attacking business abuses and asking for trust and railroad regulation. In 1906, Governor Thomas Campbell, endorsed by Hogg, continued the fight by strengthening antitrust legislation, instituting control of lobbies, and setting a maximum-hour law for railroad workers. Interspersed between progressive governors of this type were men more pliable to the various special business interests.

Around the turn of the century, Texas' Republican party and other political splinters faded into insignificance. A poll tax law, adopted at this point, discouraged Negroes and old Populists from voting. Only the Democrats held a primary, and all the interest centered on it (Negroes were effectively excluded). Enough colorful personalities arose to entertain Texans for decades, while their state government largely marked time. The dominant figure from 1915, when he was first elected governor, until the 1930s, was James or "Farmer Jim" Ferguson, a stemwinder and self-professed champion of the rural voter. Ferguson opposed both Prohibition and the Ku Klux Klan, rather popular causes in those days. The state legislature caught Ferguson with his hand in the till, impeached him in 1917, and said he could never again run for office in Texas. Ferguson then hit on the strategem (then an original idea) of running his wife instead. The slogan was: "Two Governors for the Price of One." "Ma" Ferguson ran five times and was elected twice, in 1924 and 1932. (Then as now, Texas limited its governors to frustratingly short two-year terms, though they may run to succeed themselves). Generally speaking, the Fergusons were the liberals of their time.

A similar appeal to the rustics launched Wilbert Lee (or "Pappy") O'Daniel on his political career in 1938. O'Daniel had become known through his hillbilly band, which he directed on a daily radio program advertising "Hillbilly" flour and dispensing homilies to a statewide audience. Promising to give everyone over 65 a $30-a-month pension, abolish the poll tax, and defend the Ten Commandments, O'Daniel jumped into the 1938 gubernatorial primary and won without a runoff. He won again in 1940 and in 1941 ran for the U. S. Senate in a special election, defeating a young New Dealing Congressman, Lyndon Johnson, by only 1,311 votes. Sent back to Washington for a full term in 1942, O'Daniel continued to talk the language of the country people but voted like a Chicago *Tribune* Republican.

By 1948, it was clear enough to Pappy O'Daniel that his support had slipped, and he voluntarily retired. It was a crucial year: retirement of the last of the rustics, and the election of Lyndon Johnson to the Senate. It was also the last year that the Democrats would elect their Presidential ticket virtually by default in Texas.

The Republican party, long a hopeless minority with little interest save patronage, began to assert itself in these years. In 1952, many independents and former Democrats moved into the Texas Republican party and tried to get delegates favoring General Eisenhower elected to that year's GOP National Convention. It was the last thing that the party Old Guard, strongly in favor of Senator Robert A. Taft, wanted to see happen. (Texas Old Guard chieftain Henry Zweifel was quoted as saying, "I'd rather lose with Taft than win with Eisenhower.") The Eisenhower forces elected many delegates, but the party regulars succeeded in disqualifying many of them. This created a cause which the Eisenhower Republicans could use and publicize. National magazines helped dramatize the delegate "steal" issue, and the pro-Eisenhower delegates were seated at Chicago, giving "Ike" a psychological advantage that helped him win the nomination four days later.

The disillusionment of vast numbers of conservative Texas Democrats with their national party became nationally significant in 1952, when Governor Allan Shivers endorsed Eisenhower for President over Adlai Stevenson. With Shivers' help and the revitalized GOP effort, Eisenhower carried Texas that autumn and again in 1956. The form of present-day Democratic politics in Texas actually took shape in these years. On the right wing there is a group like Shivers who disagree so fundamentally with national party nominees that they frequently bolt to the Republicans in a Presidential election, although they remain officially Democrats and vote for conservatives in state and local primaries. To the left of these are the regular Democrats, who were led by Lyndon Johnson and Sam Rayburn in the 1950s and then came under John Connally's tutelage in the 1960s. The monied Texas establishment of which we have spoken embraces both the right-wing and the moderate Democrats. But it obviously excludes the left-wing of the Democratic party: organized labor, Negroes, Mexican-Americans, and assorted white liberal allies. The only statewide officeholder this group has ever elected was Senator Ralph Yarborough. He won in a special election in 1957, in 1958, and 1964—and lost to a conservative opponent in the 1970 primary.

The liberal Democrats continually hope, without quite succeeding, to become a majority force in their own party. In 1960, they tried to take over the state party convention, but Johnson and Rayburn easily beat them back. Often, they resort to the expedient of "going fishing" on election day, or actually voting Republican, when a very conservative Democrat has won their party's nomination. Eventually, they keep hoping, the conservative Democrats will be driven into the Republican party, at which point the liberals—or "real Democrats," as they put it—can take over the Democratic party.

The liberals first tried their strategy in 1961. The year before, Johnson had been elected Vice President on the ticket with Kennedy, carrying Texas by a narrow 46,257-vote plurality. Taking no chances, LBJ had also run for and been reelected to the Senate. When he resigned his seat, a conservative "brass-collar" Democrat, William Blakley, was appointed to fill it pending a special election. After an initial election eliminated other contenders, a runoff was held between Blakley and Republican John G. Tower. Members of the left-wing coalition decided Blakley would be worse than Tower. Tower won, becoming Texas' first Republican Senator of the century, with a bare 50.6 percent of the vote—thanks, no doubt, to the liberal coalition.

Again in 1966, liberal defections from the conservative Democratic nominee (Attorney General Waggoner Carr) led to the reelection of Tower, this time by an impressive majority. It seemed that the strategy was working, at least to the extent of driving some ideological right-wingers out of the Democratic party and into the Republican or, in years like 1968, into the Wallace movement. But the liberals continued to suffer from two imposing disabilities: lack of money and lack of a voice. In a statewide or Congressional campaign, they are simply incapable of raising funds anywhere comparable to what the business-oil establishment can and does make available to more conservative opponents. And with scarcely a major newspaper or major television station friendly to their cause, the liberals have great difficulty getting their message across.

The 1970 defeat of Senator Yarborough came as a bitter blow to the Texas liberals. A man of mercurial temperament, disdainful of the monied establishment, Yarborough has been the liberals' acknowledged leader and hero since 1952. Lyndon Johnson, an old enemy, arranged mediocre committee assignments for Yarborough in Washington, but he eventually shifted onto the Labor and Public Welfare Committee (of which he became chairman in 1969) and onto Appropriations. Yarborough was able to deliver on the kind of issues liberals believe in: achieving Senate passage of the broad minimum wage expansion bill of 1966, chief sponsorship of the landmark Occupational Safety and Health Act of 1970, passage of a GI Bill for post-Korea veterans, and federal funding for bilingual education programs to ease the transition into English of youngsters with alien mother tongues (a boon for Texas, where one child in six entering the first grade speaks Spanish). He also won approval of the new Padre Island National Seashore (on the Gulf Coast) and Guadalupe Mountain National Park (in West Texas).

Yarborough made an occasional bow to Texas regularity, like supporting the oil depletion allowance, but on almost every other issue he was against the establishment. He knew it and they knew it. The only question was when the opportune moment to defeat him would come; it arrived in the "law-and-order" atmosphere of 1970 and in the person of Lloyd Bentsen. Bentsen's previous public service was limited to six years in Congress from South Texas between 1949 and 1955, after which he returned home to concentrate on private business. But he had the advantages of ample finances, well connected campaign advisers like George Christian (former White House press secretary under President Johnson, who in 1972 would become a major national spokesman of Democrats for Nixon), and an advertising firm (Rives Dyke of Houston) with years of experience in political campaigns. Extensive polls were taken to gauge issues worrying the people—which turned out to be in the category of "youth rebellion," "social unrest," and "crime in the streets." A series of 30- and 60-second campaign films were then prepared to show that Yarborough was "ultraliberal" and out of touch with his people. After Yarborough's defeat, Maury Maverick, Jr., of San Antonio, a well known liberal leader, summed up his camp's reaction in words the *Texas Observer* chose to make into a headline: "It was anti-nigger, anti-Mexican, anti-youth, and sock-it-to-'em in Vietnam."

One reason Yarborough lost was a sharp decline in support for him among his natural allies, white working-class people. Many of them reacted positively to Bentsen's law and order appeal. Also, Yarborough suffered from a pitifully low turnout in Negro and Mexican-American areas, the product of overconfidence and poor organization of his campaign.

Undaunted by his defeat, Yarborough tried a comeback in the 1972 Democratic Senate primary—only to be defeated again, this time by a more centrist Democrat, Barefoot Sanders, who had been an assistant U.S. attorney general in the Johnson administration. Before the primary, the Texas Poll had shown that a majority of Texans still held Yarborough in esteem—but that few were anxious to see him return to office. Even a few liberals were relieved; one of them, quoted anonymously in the *Texas Observer*, said: "For years, whenever a liberal in this state considered a statewide race he naturally called Our Leader in Washington and asked for his advice. And Ralph's response was invariably, 'O, no, don't do that. That might hurt me.' And so none of us ever did. He has single-handedly prevented a new generation of liberal leadership from developing down here."

The 1972 primary season, however, did produce one colorful new liberal leader—Frances T. (Sissy) Farenthold of Corpus Christi, who ran for governor. The Vassar-educated daughter of an old Texas family, she had taken the leadership, in the 1971–72 legislature, of the so-called "Dirty Thirty" grouping of blacks, Chicanos, liberals, and a few Republicans who fought for a bicameral committee to investigate the Sharpstown bank scandal. Mrs. Farenthold bore many burdens as she entered the campaign. First, she was a woman in he-man Texas; second, she refused to trim her sails on stands like liberalization of the marijuana laws and curbing the Texas Rangers, thus winning the "liberal" tag in a state where "liberals" are expected to lose; and third, she suffered from meager financing and campaign organization. Some said her campaign was too shrill and strident, but her honesty and candor—and an outpouring of support from women, the minorities, some fellow socialites, and even some Wallaceites who liked her anti-establishment line—carried her farther than anyone might have expected. She placed second in the first primary, with 28 percent of the vote, and though she lost the runoff to Dolph Briscoe, she got a very respectable 45 percent of the statewide vote.

Having relinquished her legislature seat to run for governor, Mrs. Farenthold moved to Houston and told me she had no idea whether she would run for public office again. On the other hand, she was actually considered for Vice President on George McGovern's ticket in 1972, and her close supporters hope she can be a catalyst of a liberal revival in Texas in the next few years. Creekmore Fath, the veteran liberal organizer who managed her campaign, said, "If she runs again, we start with an organization in 150 counties. She's a real power, even out of office, and will remain so as long as she's a potential candidate." Billie Carr, chairman of the liberal Harris County Democrats, the state's most effective Democratic precinct-level organization, said Mrs. Farenthold "could be the spark, the enthusiaser for a real statewide grass-roots organizing effort" that could create a basis for future liberal Democratic primary victories.

The liberals' error of past years, Mrs. Carr said, had been to form state-level coordinating committees without substance or continuity. "My plan for organizing Texas would be to start at the bottom instead, just as I have with precinct work," she added. "I think that if we built from the bottom up, we could change this state, because I don't think Texas is a conservative state. It's just an uninformed and unorganized state." Effective organization, the liberals believe, would enable them to win more primaries because the minority bloc voters would not be so easily confused by the conservative press, or see their leaders bought off. As an example, they point to heavily Latin San Antonio, were liberal candidates often lose disputed primaries, even though the city usually goes Democratic, especially for liberal national candidates, in general elections.

Rather than turning to standard establishment types or full-blown liberals to lead its state government in the mid- and latter 1970s, Texas may instead choose to opt for moderate progressive Democrats similar in stamp to Reubin Askew of Florida, Dale Bumpers of Arkansas, or Jimmy Carter of Georgia. Ben Barnes, despite his establishment backing, might well have fitted this pattern if he had not been snagged on the ethics issue. But now attractive new faces are coming up among the Democrats. One of these is William Hobby, who ran on a reform platform to win the lieutenant governorship in 1972. Hobby is the son of a former Texas governor and of Mrs. Oveta Culp Hobby, who was Secretary of Health, Education and Welfare under President Eisenhower. He was executive editor of the Houston *Post* until his election, and actually got AFL-CIO endorsement when he faced and defeated state senator Wayne Connally, the brother of John Connally, in the Democratic runoff.

Another rising star among the Democrats is John Hill, a successful trial lawyer from Houston who ousted an entrenched establishment officeholder, Crawford Martin, in the 1972 primary for attorney general. Yet another is Robert Landis Armstrong of Austin, who was elected land commissioner in 1970 and again in 1972; to date he has been remarkably successful in getting such disparate groups as the environmentalists, big corporations, and organized labor to back him. Hobby, Hill, and Armstrong have all avoided the dreaded "liberal" tag, yet they seem to be men who would recommend sweeping changes in Texas government—if they think the political climate is right for change. (Mrs. Farenthold charges Hobby, Hill, and Armstrong with political expediency, saying that none of them were willing—as she was—to challenge Barnes. "The establishment will 'go' for them now," she said. "None of them represents a real break with the past.")

Organized labor has difficulty making a major impact on state politics, despite the politically attuned leadership of the state AFL-CIO. One reason is that Texas has about as many laws restricting unions as one can imagine, including right-to-work, anti-picketing, and prohibitions against collective bargaining by public agencies. Until 1969, Texas had the lowest rate of workmen's compensation of any state, and no minimum wage law at all. Of Texas' total work force of about 4 million, just over 10 percent are organized (one of the lowest unionization rates in the entire U. S.). Unions also have difficulty influencing their members in elections because the membership they do have is concentrated in eastern Texas, where racial antagonisms are the worst. Another problem has been schisms among the top leaders of the AFL-CIO, though this may be relieved by the 1971 retirement of president Hank Brown, a George Meany-style regular, and his replacement by his arch rival, Roy Evans, the first United Auto Worker to head a state AFL-CIO. In 1972, labor disappointed many Texas liberals when it chose to put all its money and organizational effort behind Yarborough's attempted return to the Senate, virtually ignoring Farenthold's more promising (and for Texas' own interests, more important) race for governor. That autumn, Texas labor chafed at the national AFL-CIO's prohibition against an endorsement in the Nixon-McGovern Presidential race. Evans organized an informal "Labor for All Democrats" organization, which backed McGovern, and found himself "called on the carpet" by national AFL-CIO leaders to explain his pro-McGovern activity. On election day, blue collar precincts were carried by Richard Nixon—though by 13 percentage points less than Texas as a whole.

Another group with reason to be discouraged, despite all brave hopes and efforts of recent years, are the Texas Republicans. In 1952, the party succeeded in shaking off the image of a back-room patronage operation, but the young professionals, oilmen, and assorted business types who moved in to man the party still had something of a country club image 18 years later. And they were hard put to outpromise the entrenched monied establishment on the Democratic side. Only a perfectly arranged disarray on the Democratic side—as Tower enjoyed in his three elections—permitted a Republican breakthrough. Otherwise, even exceptionally attractive candidates like George Bush of Houston and Paul Eggers of Wichita Falls went down to defeat (Bush for the Senate in 1964 and 1970, Eggers for governor in 1968 and 1970).

Under professional party leaders like state chairman and later national committeeman Peter O'Donnell of Dallas, the Republicans invested millions of dollars to build their position in Texas. But after Eisenhower's victories, they failed to carry Texas for a Republican Presidential candidate until President Nixon won the state with a massive million-vote plurality (67.0 percent) in 1972. (In 1968, Humphrey carried Texas with a plurality of 38,960 votes out of 3,079,216 cast. Wallace got a hefty vote—584,269—which might otherwise have gone predominantly Republican.) Except for Tower, the Republicans have not elected a single other statewide candidate. Foolishly, they climbed first and most enthusiastically on the Goldwater bandwagon in 1963–64, an exercise that almost obliterated the party in Texas. But eight years of rebuilding from that debacle yielded the Republicans only four of the 24 Texas seats in the U.S. House, 17 of the 150 seats in the Texas house, three of 29 seats in the U.S. senate, and so few county and municipal offices as to be laughable.

Every Texas analyst can give you a theory for the Republicans' failure. One is the very fact that Democrats so dominate local and state offices that all the real talent goes into that party's primary, leaving the Republicans empty-handed. (In 1972, voters in the Democratic primary outnumbered Republican primary voters by approximately two million to 100,000. Another theory is that the Texas Republicans' "me-tooism" in serving the monied establishment will cut little ice when the majority Democrats operate so effectively for Texas in Washington. (In 1968, the Republicans made much of their support for the 27½ percent oil depletion allowance, apparently to no avail. "Could it be," the San Antonio *Express/News* asked after the election, that "the average Texas voter suddenly realized he did not own an oil well?") Another criticism is that the GOP has been hostile to or at least indifferent to Latins and Negroes, in line with the Southern strategy born in the Goldwater days and carried on under the Nixon-Agnew Administration.* As long as the minorities represent about a third of the vote in Texas, and all their vote goes Democratic, the Republicans will have to win more than 75 percent of the remaining two-thirds to win elections. In a state packed still with brass-collar Democrats, many of them just as conservative as the Republicans, that task is extremely difficult.

The Republican bastions of modern Texas are Dallas and Houston, which are significantly also the centers of dynamic economic and population growth. Cities like Amarillo, Lubbock, Midland, Odessa, and sometimes Austin are also Republican, but San Antonio and El Paso are usually delivered to the Democratic column by virtue of their big Mexican-American vote. Fort Worth is classically a swing town. When one reaches the smaller cities and towns, Republican strength is submerged in a sea of brass-collar Democratic voters casting ballots like their fathers and grandfathers. One reason

* Both Bush and Eggers were quite friendly to blacks and Mexicans; Bush, for instance, had voted for the 1968 open housing law. But both men were so thoroughly identified with the Nixon-Agnew Administration that minority voters instinctively chose their Democratic opponents. Shortly before the election, columnists Rowland Evans and Robert Novak reported on Bush's visits to college campuses and Negro slums (something Bentsen would never have done) and observed: "Bush—young (46), handsome, a Connecticut Yankee turned Houston oilman—is a glittering exponent of the 'modern' school of Southern Republicans as contrasted with the 'primitives.' Like Gov. Linwood Holton of Virginia, Bush appeals to affluent suburbanites with economic conservatism while simultaneously wooing minority groups and labor. The 'primitives,' led by Sen. Strom Thurmond of South Carolina, concentrate on rural segregationist voters." There had even been a report that Bush, if elected, might have replaced Agnew on the 1972 Republican ballot for Vice President. But he lost by 155,334 votes (46.6 percent).

the Republicans lost in 1970, for instance, was an outpouring of country voters, mostly Democrats, intent on defeating a constitutional amendment to permit liquor by the drink (on a local option basis). A thirsty city vote defeated the rural types on this issue, but only narrowly, and a lot of politically disinterested Democrats had gotten to the polls as a result.

It should be noted that the big rural vote sometimes rears up to make decisions the monied establishment disapproves of. Preston Smith, the man who succeeded Connally as governor, was distinctly not Connally's choice. Smith's constituency was not big oil or chemicals but the trade associations and small businessmen—auto dealers, feed store operators, theatre owners—all over the state. He won election as governor by touring around to 225 counties acting as though he were running for county commissioner. Once elected, he turned out to be a routine seat-warmer, proposing few innovations in Texas government (though he had a good staff, and proved to be a master of grantsmanship). As noted earlier, his political career terminated abruptly after the voters learned of his personal involvement with Frank Sharp's stock manipulations.

Intraparty dissension also hampers the Texas Republicans, split between a dominant Dallas-based wing led by Peter O'Donnell and Republican National Committeeman Fred J. Agnich—both staunch conservatives—and an even more rightward-oriented faction guided by the fiery leader of the Houston Republicans, Mrs. Nancy Palm. Tower is closely allied with the Dallas group, and no favorite of Mrs. Palm, who told me in 1972 that Tower was responsible for the fact that the GOP failed to nominate candidates for nine of 13 statewide posts at stake, or 11 of the 24 U.S. House seats, or much more than half the state legislature seats. Tower and his allies purportedly held their punches so that the county Democratic machines would not be alarmed and Tower and President Nixon could slip to victory without full Democratic opposition. Tower's camp hotly denied the charge, but I found many Texas Democrats who agreed with Mrs. Palm's assertion that with President Nixon riding to a landslide victory in Texas, the Republicans had lost the opportunity of a generation to make themselves a strong statewide party. Mrs. Palm's own gubernatorial candidate, however, was partly at fault. He was Henry C. Grover, an archconservative party maverick who ran 682,000 votes and 21 percentage points behind President Nixon—but even at that, barely missed winning on the strength of Nixon's coattails. Fred Agnich, who in 1972 became the GOP's first floor leader of the century in the Texas house and would one day like to run for governor, told me that for the party to be taken seriously over the long haul, "you must elect a governor. He makes 3,000 appointments in two years. At that point you could begin to bust into the county courthouse power, making it worthwhile for people in the county governments to turn Republican."

Frances Farenthold said the Republicans had lost their best opportunity since Reconstruction in 1972. "It leaves a real question in my mind," she said, "how much they're committed to a genuine two-party system. With all their screaming about the one-party system, they seem pretty satisfied with the rule of the Democratic establishment." Another Texas Democrat put it even more succinctly: "When you get right down to it, the Republicans prefer it clubby."

They are becoming more and more influential on the national level, however. At the start of his second administration, President Nixon made Mrs. Anne Armstrong—former cochairman of the Republican National Committee and the wife of the big South Texas rancher—a counselor to the President with Cabinet rank. Mrs. Armstrong, who had made a strongly favorable impression with her keynote address to the 1972 Republican National Convention, was the first woman appointed as a counselor to Mr. Nixon. Another leading Texan in the Nixon administration was George Bush, first made U.S. Ambassador to the United Nations after his 1970 Senate defeat and, in 1973, chairman of the Republican National Committee. Senator Tower's substantial 1972 reelection victory was followed by his election as chairman of the Senate Republican Policy Committee. A strong defender of Texas military-aerospace-oil interests, Tower will likely be a leading backer of a staunch conservative for the next GOP Presidential nomination. (Acknowledging the Texas Republicans' problems with internal bickering, Tower's close associate Agnich noted that "nothing will unify us more than a confrontation with Eastern liberals.")

One startling change of recent Texas politics has been the expansion of the voting franchise. From the late 19th century until 1944, when the U.S. Supreme Court outlawed the white primary, scarcely any Negroes voted in Texas at all. The poll tax also acted as a depressant on voting. In 1920, only one in five adult Texans took the trouble to vote for President, in 1948 one in four. Then, with the Eisenhower races, interest quickened. By 1960, 41.4 percent voted. The 1960s brought two fundamental changes: the repeal of the poll tax in 1967 and, partly as a result of it, an increase in the number of voting age Negroes registered from the 1960 level of 33.7 percent to a 1972 level of 68.2 percent. But still, Texas has continued to rank among the bottom tenth of the states in the percentage of its voting-age people who turn out for elections. The 1972 turnout was a miserable 43 percent, even though the otherwise frustrated McGovernites had succeeded in pushing the registration rolls to an historic high of more than five million. (A high proportion of the new registrants were youth and minorities—who might make quite a difference in future Texas primaries.)

Up to 1972, the low turnout was attributable to some of the most restrictive and regressive election laws anywhere in America. Through 1970, Texas required all voters to reregister *annually*, by January 31 of the election year. No other state required annual reregistration, a deliberate device to hold down the size of the electorate and confine it to a controlled vote. (Among the strongest proponents of annual registration was John Connally.) Finally, a federal court in 1971 declared annual registration unconstitutional and a new law was passed making registration permanent as long as a person actually votes once every three years. Yet even then, the legislature was busy trying to hold down participation in elections by decreeing that the group newly enfranchised by constitutional amendment—the 18-through-20 age group—could only register to vote in the hometowns of the parents. Two North Texas State University students quickly challenged the law as unconstitutional, and the state attorney general and secretary of state ruled in their favor. Before that, the federal courts had stepped in to invalidate Texas' sky-high filing fees for office, a percent device to keep the poor and nonestablishment types off the ballot for many offices. So it is that official Texas, resisting to the last, is propelled toward levels of participatory democracy that might just set the older order on its head in our times.

A heady view of things to come was provided by the 7,782 delegates and alternates who attended the tumultuous 1972 Democratic state convention at San Antonio. In earlier years, Democratic conventions had been dominated by the white, middle-aged men of the ruling establishment, who were always able to parlay their majority in the state convention into a monolithic bloc under the unit rule at the national convention. But in 1972, the former leaders—Lyndon Johnson, John Connally, Preston Smith, Ben Barnes—were not even present. The establishment faction was in total disarray, the contingents of youth and women and blacks and Chicanos were vastly increased, and the forces backing George Wallace and George McGovern cooperated to the extent of seeing that each got its fair share of national convention votes. (A poll of the state convention delegates showed 33 percent for Wallace, 28 percent for McGovern, and the remainder for Humphrey or uncommitted—and precisely those percentages were applied to the 130-vote delegation sent to Miami Beach.)

One of the surprises was the delegates' rejection of Roy Orr, an establishment type who was Democratic state chairman, to be convention vice chairman. Instead, the McGovern faction nominated a black woman from Dallas, Mrs. Eddie Bernice Johnson, and in an uproarious two-hour ballot she was elected—with major support from the Wallaceites. Dolph Briscoe helped in the negotiations to get the balance of races and age groups required by national party rules on the delegation to the national convention. Maury Maverick, Jr., the San Antonio liberal and McGovern partisan, told me later that Briscoe had "run the fairest convention I've ever seen."

Government and Nongovernment

Texas fails to place well in any of the tests one might impose on government—breadth of services provided, innovative programming, tax effort and fairness, strong executive control, civil service, regulation of business and freedom from outside influence, and efficiency in the legislature.

As the 1970s began, Texas ranked this way in per capita government outlays for services, compared to the other states: 35th in welfare, 38th in health and hospitals, 26th in police protection, 35th in higher education, 37th in local schools. The state's tax effort (taxes paid in relation to personal income) was 49th among the 50 states.

With the exception of its excellent highway system, there are few areas of state legislation or programming where Texas may be considered a leader in the nation. "Nothing happens at the upper levels of our state government," a rather embittered liberal state legislator told me, "until we get sat on by the federal government." He named welfare administration, transportation control, and consumer protection as areas in which Texas government was especially weak. As an example, Texas offers splendid opportunities for rapid mass ground transit to serve its big cities; one can imagine a link connecting Dallas and Fort Worth, then a leg to Houston, spokes out to the Gulf Coast, and finally connection of San Antonio and Austin in a system serving a great megalopolitan region. But in 1970, rail transit in Texas was fast deteriorating, and the only subway in the state connected Leonard's Department store in Fort Worth with a parking lot a quarter mile away. No one in Austin was making further plans (though planning has begun for a possible rapid transit line connecting Dallas and Fort Worth and the new airport being constructed between them). Texans' love of the automobile seems to be second to none save Californians', and they think nothing of driving long distances, even through urban sprawl. ("Every time you drive to Houston, you get there 15 minutes earlier," goes a modern crack—referring not to improved highways, but uncontrolled growth out across the coastal plain.)

Texas' inactive state government is matched by a regressive tax structure. About 63 percent of government income is provided by sales, license, and property taxes which place the greatest burden on middle- and low-income persons. In 1970, one study showed that a Houston family in poverty at $3,500 a year paid 9.6 percent of its total income in state and local taxes. A family earning $25,000 in the same city paid 3.3 percent. At $50,000, the family paid a scarcely significant 2.5 percent. To a slightly lesser degree, the same type of discrepancies were apparent in other Texas cities. The better way to tap the growth in the state's economy would be an income tax, anathema in modern-day political debate in Texas. By 1973, no governor had ever proposed it, but its inevitability (in the face of grave budget deficiencies) was generally admitted. An ultimate establishment figure, Frank Erwin, made a speech late in 1970 saying that the legislature would have to pass either a sales tax on food (an especially regressive device) or a personal income tax. The alternative, Erwin said, would be to repeal salary increases for school teachers, turn 14,000 high school graduates away from state colleges and universities because there would be no room for them, tell the families of the mentally malfunctioning to keep them in back rooms at home, and inform the old, the blind, the fatherless children and indigent ill that the state won't help them any more. "I don't believe in this affluent society we're going to tell people we've got no way to take care of them because we don't want to pay taxes," Erwin said. (Instead of instituting an income tax or sales tax on food, however, the legislature simply upped the sales tax on all other items to 4 percent and added a passel of increased business franchise and "sin" taxes—on liquor, beer, cigarettes, and the like.)

A potential revolution in the financing of Texas government was triggered in 1971 by a suit brought in federal court by a 41-year-old San Antonio lawyer, Arthur Gochman. He became interested in the plight of Edgewood, an impoverished school district in the Mexican-American community of his city, discovering that the basic problem was not so much a lack of dedicated teachers and citizens as a frightening shortage of money to run a decent system. Research showed that Edgewood was taxing heavily for schools but, because of the poverty of the area, was producing only $21 per pupil in property taxes. The affluent community of Alamo Heights, by contrast, had a low tax rate but still produced $307 per pupil. And though the state government had a so-called "minimum foundation program" designed to equalize educational opportunity, Edgewood and Alamo Heights were receiving almost identical amounts of special help from outside.

Gochman took his case to federal court and won. In its decision, the court said that the existing structure of school financing "discriminates on the basis of wealth by permitting citizens of affluent districts to provide a higher quality education for their children, while paying lower taxes." The system, it was found, "tends to subsidize the rich at the expense of the poor, rather than the other way around," and thus violated the equal protection clause of the 14th Amendment.

The decision was appealed to the U.S. Supreme Court; if upheld, it would force Texas and other states to reexamine not only their school-financing methods but their entire state tax structures. Texas would be forced to increase its state taxes 100 percent—almost certainly adopting personal and corporate income taxes—to replace local school property taxes.

About 32 percent of Texas' tax dollar comes from various levies on business, most significantly the 4.6 percent tax placed on the value of oil at the wellhead. Congressman Bob Eckhardt of Houston served several years in the state legislature and made repeated efforts to increase taxes on oil and gas, all to no avail. He argues that Texas oil has been undertaxed because of the political power of the small producers and independents, who until recently were responsible for half the state's production. In Louisiana, by contrast, almost all the extraction is done by "majors" with headquarters outside the state, and "you can have a Huey Long fighting 'em like the devil and taxing the hell out of oil and gas." Eckhardt favors making the wellhead tax a graduated one, depending on the amount of production. This would increase the tax share of the 17 largest producers and bring the state an extra $25 million a year. He says it would relieve some competitive pressure on the small, marginal producer who is hard put to stay profitable in the face of oil imports and the monopolistic power of the international majors. There has also been pressure for some years to impose a natural gas longlines tax. Always lurking in the wings, if Texas gets really serious about new taxes, is a possible levy on corporate profits.

The regulatory bodies of Texas state government have never earned a reputation for toughness in dealing with private interests, nor have they received very strong mandates from the state legislature. Texas' industrial safety standards, for instance, are among the weakest in the country, and the same is true of its water pollution standards. An interesting special case, however, is that of the Texas Railroad Commission. In the 1930s, when the East Texas field was being depleted at a dangerous rate and the price of oil hit an all-time low, the Railroad Commission (which had been given the job of supervision since it had long regulated oil shipments by railroad tank cars) stepped in to set production "allowables." Martial law had to be imposed before the commission's quotas on production were obeyed, but ever since the commission has wisely conserved a natural resource by its orders. The simultaneous effect, of course, has been to profit the oilmen by keeping prices up through limited supply. Oddly enough, the railroad commissioners, like the members of the state board of education, are actually chosen in statewide popular elections.

As for the Texas judicial system, one might accept the judgment of retired Supreme Court Justice Tom C. Clark, a native Texan, who has depicted it as antiquated and designed to serve a bypassed agrarian society.

Efficient government in Texas is hampered by the 1876-vintage constitution, packed with provisions to limit the executive. Most of the actual governing is done by more than 200 boards with overlapping six-year terms. The governor gets to appoint 700 or 800 men to these commissions, but as a rule they are unpaid and simply turn administration over to the staffs they hire. Agencies become semi-independent satrapies, and their heads stay in year after year. Terms are rotating, so that a governor must be in office several years before he gets any kind of control. Even then, departments often function as if others simply didn't exist. The employment commission and welfare department, for instance, should work together closely, but they don't. Institution of any modern management techniques in such a structure is virtually impossible. Texas is completely lacking in a civil service system for state employees, but the fact of one-party control—inhibiting mass firings and hirings when administrations change—has made for relative stability.

The governor's powers are also extremely limited vis-à-vis the legislature. Ben Barnes stated that "the lieutenant governor's office in Texas is by far the most powerful. . . . Our chief executive definitely needs more power and our lieutenant governor's office [powers] need to be diluted." The lieutenant governor, who presides over the senate, and his counterpart, the speaker of the house, actually appoint all legislative committees and chairmen and assign all bills to them. Much important legislation ends up being written by conference committees with five members appointed by the lieutenant governor, five by the speaker. "They operate with a free hand, and it's really a very poor system," Barnes stated. Interestingly, he made his observations while serving as lieutenant governor, after four years as speaker. Some important reforms in the legislature, including a limited seniority system to curb the unfettered appointive powers of the lieutenant governor and speaker, and controls on conference committees, were adopted in the reform surge of 1972. And that fall, the voters approved a proposal to let the legislature write a new state constitution, which might effect even more fundamental reforms if it were eventually approved by the people. The most obvious reform, of course, would be a cabinet form of government.

Court-forced reapportionment brought many new urban legislators to the Texas house and senate during the 1960s, promising long-term change in those bodies. Among the early crop were some outstanding new legislators (including the first blacks in both houses). But the stand-outs tended to be the exception rather than the rule. Again to quote Barnes, "reapportionment has made the legislature more aware of city problems and progressive minded. But the city legislators have to spend so much money to get elected that it's been my experience that many of them are so indebted to special interest groups, bloc votes, and political bosses that they don't have enough time to spend on actually solving city problems." Rural legislators, he said, build up more seniority and effective leadership, and "many of them are stronger men."

Another point worth noting: conservative Democrats remain firmly in control of both houses of the legislature. Court-ordered subdistricting of the metropolitan counties is opening more seats for Chicanos, blacks, and Republicans. But no one expects a truly progressive Texas legislature to be elected in this decade—especially since the Republicans make even the conservative Democrats look liberal.

Which are the most effective pressure groups in Austin? I heard them identified as the Texas Chemical Council (which was especially powerful under Connally), the Texas Midcontinent Oil & Gas Association (the major oil front), the Texas Independent Producers & Royalty Owners, the Texas State Teachers' Association, the Texas Manufacturers' Association (important in labor legislation and pollution control), the Texas Medical Association, the Texas Motor Transport Association, and various insurance organizations. Most lobbies pick ex-legislators to represent them in Austin.

The Texas legislature has come in for some stiff criticism in recent times. A 1971 report by the Citizens Conference on State Legislatures ranked Texas only 38th among the 50 in an aggregate rating of its ability "to perform in a functional, accountable, informed, independent and representative manner." Among the major deficiencies of the legislature are lack of annual sessions, too many committees for efficient operation (45 in the house, 27 in the senate), lack of year-round staffing for major committees, and the lack of legislative independence created by the power placed in the hands of the presiding officers. All seem to be failures that a big and prospering state like Texas could easily correct.

What it might take to improve the moral tone in Austin is another question. In 1968, Mrs. Lee Clark, wife of a Dallas legislator, wrote of the legislature as "an ethical brothel" and recorded this incident:

> My husband was punching his voting button against an especially odious piece of legislation when he noted on the electronic board that a colleague seated close by was recorded for it. He turned to the man and asked how on God's earth he could vote for such a thing and still keep his dinner down. The legislator, stumpy and smoke-infested, walked over, hoisted his arm around my husband's shoulders, and affirmed with a certain pride: "I'm just a political whore, boy; that's what I am, a political whore."

He is definitely not alone. The Texas Trial Lawyers Association, fighting hard against "no fault" auto insurance that would compensate victims regardless of fault—and take away a lucrative business for many attorneys—is especially active in Texas, both in elections (where it takes credit for causing nomination of several state senators) and during legislative sessions. According to a former officer of the national trial lawyers' group, "an open bar and buffet lunch" is available at the Texas Association's Austin office every day the legislature is in session; each day 25 to 30 legislators stroll over to indebt themselves a bit further.

Vast differences of quality appear at the various levels of Texas government. For the most part, the state's cities are well administered, with an exceptionally high number of professional city managers. A promising "COG" (council of governments) movement is developing in Texas, as a way to tie together smaller governments over hundreds of square miles. (The most outstanding of these, the North Central Texas COG, is discussed in the Fort Worth subchapter below). "The COGs," Rep. James H. Clark, Jr., of Dallas told me, "will end up relating to the federal government while the state government sits here complaining about its loss of prerogatives."

When it comes to rural county government in Texas, the sands of time seem to have stopped running a few decades ago. County judges or commissioners are often heavy-handed papas who run their little domains with an iron hand. Voter registration records are often kept in a haphazard way, thus inviting irregularities, and the local powers have available to them a road and bridge fund to buy people off. Population is declining in a majority of these counties, and the low income levels create a demand for old-age assistance and welfare funds that is a major economic drain on the rest of the state. Yet in the late 1960s, even while studies were revealing shocking conditions of hunger and malnutrition in rural Texas, almost half the counties were refusing to participate in federal food programs for the needy. The stated reason: the cost of administration—30 cents per person per month—was more than they could afford to pay.

Geographic Texas: From the Gulf to the Pedernales

Alaska's unmatched size notwithstanding, Texas remains a huge and multisplendored state. It covers one-twelfth the land area of the coterminous U.S.A., a territory as large as New York, New Jersey, Pennsylvania, Ohio, Illinois, plus all of New England combined. East to west, Texas extends 773 miles, north to south an intimidating 801 miles. Just one of Texas' 254 counties (of course no other state has so many) is larger than the entire state of Connecticut. There are more miles of roads and highways in Texas (247,000 in 1967) than there are miles to the moon.

The Texan empire is so vast that Stephen F. Austin, the Virginia-born "Father of Texas" who started the first important colony in 1821, once called it "a wild, howling, interminable solitude." Even with the civilizing influence of 11 million people, getting one's bearings is still difficult.

The basic division the geologists talk about is the Balcones Escarpment, a fault line that splits Texas into basic eastern and western regions. The line runs generally north to south, dropping from the Oklahoma border to a point between Dallas and Fort Worth and then by Waco, Austin, and San Antonio; there it veers westerly for 150 miles until it meets the Rio Grande and the Mexican border.

East of the escarpment lies the Gulf Coastal Plain—hot, low country (the center of Texas' oil and chemical industries) which includes big cities like Houston and Corpus Christi, the "Piney Woods" section covering the whole northeastern corner of the state (north of Houston, east of Dallas), and the fertile lower Rio Grande Valley, known for its winter gardens and citrus fruit.

Two plains regions lie west of the escarpment, actually the southernmost extension of two broad continental divisions. First come the Central Plains, which in some physiographic maps are shown to range as far northward as the Great Lakes; in Texas they vary greatly in form, but are mostly rolling prairie between 1,000 and 2,500 feet in altitude, classic cattle, sheep, and goat country that was once the southernmost range of the buffalo. Farther west lie the arid, level High Plains, which form a clear-cut belt all the way to the Canadian border along the North Dakota and Montana lines. The entire Texas Panhandle lies within the High Plains region.

Finally, there is the desert-like triangle of westernmost Texas, which actually lies south of New Mexico. This is Trans-Pecos Texas, a land of gaunt scenery, high mountains (actually the southernmost extension of the Rockies), mesquite, cacti, and lonely distances. Here one finds the Big Bend National Park on the Rio Grande, the newer Guadalupe Mountains National Park on the border with New Mexico, and, at the state's westernmost extremity, the city of El Paso. At El Paso, the average annual rainfall is less than eight inches; a measure of the contrast of Texas places is that at Houston, a few hundred miles to the east, the figure is over 45 inches (with humidity to match).

With that capsulated geography in mind, we may retrace our steps at more leisure, taking in, along the way, a glimpse of those multitudinous Texas cities. We will leave only the three largest urban conglomerates—Houston, Dallas–Fort Worth, and San Antonio—for separate treatment later.

The Gulf Coast, with its 370-mile long window to the sea, is Texas' most cosmopolitan region, heavily peopled with Mexican-Americans toward the Rio Grande and mixtures of rural white Southerners, Negroes, and Cajuns up toward the Louisiana border. The shallow gulf has formed incredibly long sandbars, which form a series of long sand islands, protecting most of the shore from direct ocean weather. The most famous of these is the most southerly, 117-mile-long Padre Island, a creation of the winds, tides, and storms stretching from near the Mexican border to Corpus Christi and made officially into a national seashore by act of Congress in 1962. These same gulf shores hold scores of bird sanctuaries that shelter the millions of waterfowl who have made the coast their wintering ground. The coastal marshes and bayous are a strong magnet for fishermen and hunters, the beaches and lagoons for swimmers, beachcombers, and sailboat enthusiasts. Men have dredged 13 great deepwater ports out of the sand bars and shallow bays, their waters plied by commercial shrimp fisherman and bargeloads of oil, petrochemicals, cotton, wheat, and cattle.

The contrast of the Gulf with inland Texas is immense; as Texan writer Lewis C. Fay observed about Padre Island, "It's easy to forget the loneliness of the plains and the stark violence of the mountain canyons. For here is neither loneliness nor violence. Here are peace, and the swoop of seagulls, and the soft purples of twilight plunging into east-dark sky."

Some of Texas' most important oil fields lie in an arc just inland from the Gulf, as do the low, damp lands in which a major portion of the U. S. rice crop is produced. Not to be overlooked is the huge 118-year-old King Ranch, covering 865,000 acres, the equivalent of 1,350 square miles, traversed by more than 500 miles of paved road, the grazing land of some 45,000 head of cattle and more than 2,000 horses, including some of the nation's finest thoroughbred racing stock. There is simply no ranching operation in all America in any way comparable to the King Ranch, which has branched out in recent years to put the Santa Gertrudis breed of cattle—which it developed—into Australia, Brazil, Argentina, Venezuela, and Cuba. Robert Kleberg, now in his mid-seventies, has been president and chief executive of the King Ranch and the dominating force within the multibranched Kleberg family for more than half a cenutry now. Oil was discovered under King Ranch land in 1939, and by the late 1960s there were 504 oil and 138 gas wells, bringing the owning Kleberg family fantastic yearly earnings of $20 million—compared to livestock operations which *Fortune* in 1969 estimated probably did not exceed $5 million annually.*

A review of the major gulf area cities, moving northeasterly: Corpus Christi (1970 population 204,525, up from a mere 27,741 in 1930) booms with a magnificent yacht basin and marina in its downtown section, plus oil in its backlands. It refuses to be daunted by events like the 1970 hurricane which damaged 80 percent of its buildings. Up the coast, the history of Galveston (population 61,809) includes "The Storm" of 1900, a hurricane that demolished the city and left more than 6,000 dead. These days, Galveston is still staggering from a state crackdown in the late 1950s on its then notorious gambling, prostitution, and narcotics trade. Now the city has a cleaner sea-and-surf tourism but seems forever afflicted by environmental pollution, including raw sewage and petrochemical discharges into its bay. (The Washington-based Conservation Foundation in 1972 issued a report saying that Galveston Bay was "a severely damaged estuarine area" that within the next few years might become so clogged with silt and heavy with nutrients that "the marine life will suffocate, and what remains will be a stinking cesspool, issuing its putrefaction into the Gulf of Mexico.")

Beaumont (115,919) and Port Arthur (57,371), both parts of the Houston industrial triangle, were spared a purge of their illegal vices when

*** Readers interested in the fabulous story of the Klebergs and King Ranch, a true American classic, should see Charles J. V. Murphy's article "Treasures in Oil and Cattle," in *Fortune*, August 1969.**

the state government cracked down on Galveston. But the denouement, when it finally came in 1961, was a sensation. For three days, a state legislative investigating committee televised its hearings into gambling, prostitution, and liquor violations in the two cities. It is said that business and life in the whole county came to a virtual standstill as everyone watched, with fascination, as the lurid tale evolved on the screen. Now Beaumont and Port Arthur are "clean" like Galveston, but honesty does not always equal prosperity, and all three cities have lost population since 1960.

Politically, the Gulf Coast cities are the most liberally Democratic in Texas, a phenomenon explained by the high proportion of organized labor, a heavy black contingent, and many Roman Catholics. But along with Houston, the northeastern Gulf cities have many rural immigrants from the Deep South, and race tensions to match. Yet there is a positively Mediterranean atmosphere to a place like Port Arthur, where many Cajuns came in to work in the refineries; the telephone book is full of French names, and French dishes are popular in the local restaurants. Near Beaumont lies the inconspicuous mound of earth called Spindletop, where the first great oil strike of Texas history was made in January 1901. The 1,060-foot hole punctured in the earth by engineer Anthony F. Lucas, history records, hit a "salt dome" in which oil was under such pressure that it shot up in a great, black fountain that covered the surrounding countryside with 25,000 to 100,000 barrels in a day. Oilmen and promoters swarmed onto the Gulf Coast, great firms like Texaco and Gulf were born, and Texas became the center of the American petroleum industry.

As important as it was, Spindletop would be dwarfed in importance by the strike made 170 miles north, in the peanut and sweet potato patches of Rusk County, in 1930. A determined old "wildcatter," 71-year-old C. M. "Dad" Joiner, had sunk his last dollars into a makeshift drilling rig that finally hit oil at 3,600 feet, thus opening up the vast East Texas field—the greatest field ever located in the United States until, possibly, the North Slope Alaska strike of the 1960s.

The great oil strike never altered the character of East Texas. It remained—and remains—the "piney woods" it has always been, a touch of the Deep South, the most backward section of all Texas. The best explanation I have ever seen comes from a novel by an East Texan native, William Humphrey, *The Ordways* (published in 1965). The first settlers, from the South, he records, "came out of the canebrakes and the towering pines" to see a sight amazing—and frightening to them:

> Mountain men, woodsmen, swampers, hill farmers, they came out into the light, stood blinking at the flat and featureless immensity [of the open Texas prairie] spread before them, where there were no logs to build cabins or churches, no rails for fences, none of the game whose ways they knew, and cowered back into the familiar shade of the forest, from there to farm the margins of the prairie like a timid bather testing the water with his toe. . . .

What they chose to farm was principally cotton, and many ended up importing slaves, and thus was born the only old-style plantation civilization in all of Texas. Just in the past generation, the ruined old East Texas cottonfields have largely been converted, either to tree farms—the piney woods produce a billion board feet annually, nearly all of Texas' lumber production—or to grazing lands and feedlots to satisfy the immense appetite for beef of the millions in Dallas, Houston, and other cities of metropolitan Texas.

An interesting battle took shape in the early 1970s over the proposal to create a 100,000-acre Big Thicket National Park just north of Beaumont. David W. Hacker, in the *National Observer*, has characterized the Big Thicket as "one of the scruffiest pieces of real estate I have ever seen," yet also one of great primitive beauty and "the only spot where the flora and fauna of the evergreen Appalachia meet tropical life." On the negative side, he reports "swamps, mosquitoes, mud, moccasins (water), and thickets of yaupon, vines and palmettos so impenetrable that a hiker's eyes run the risk of puncture." But within a few miles of each other there are 2,000 species of plants, from orchids to sugar maple, palmetto to ferns, including live insecting-eating plants. And the wildlife is said to include everything from "coral snakes to blue racers, otters to armadillos, alligators to anteaters, ibis to the ivory-billed woodpecker." The most determined opponents of the national park idea are big national paper and publishing companies, who gather huge harvests there and then turn the land into farms of slash pine.* But there are others, without a direct economic interest, who feel the Big Thicket has already lost so much of its integrity that it should have some lesser designation, like national monument or recreation area. While Congress debates, some 50 acres a day are being cut off.

East Texas politics are both populist and racist. In 1968, Wallace got 35 percent of the vote here, his best showing in the state. Negroes represent 40 to 55 percent of the population in some counties but can, to date, count none of their number as elected officials; the baronial system of white county bosses still holds firm. Former state representative Curtis Graves, a Negro, told me: "Traditionally the people who are elected in East Texas are those who can hate the most. There are still killings by local sheriffs and the establishment. One young man was shot with handcuffs on, allegedly running away from a policeman. . . . He had front entrance wounds. You know that all Negroes run backward. Everyone knows that. I call it murder."

Starting just west of the piney woods, in a broad swatch coming down from Oklahoma and reaching almost to the gulf, is a strip of dark, rich prairie soil some call the Blacklands. Sorghum, soybeans, and corn, supporting a flourishing cattle industry, have gradually replaced cotton here.

Five major Texas cities—Dallas, Forth Worth, Waco, Austin, and San Antonio—lie astride the Blacklands. Surely the loveliest and most livable of these is Austin, possessed of the state capitol, the University of Texas campus, and in recent times an increasingly prosperous base in "light and clean" industry which helped to balloon the population from 132,459 in 1950 to 251,808 in 1970. Now the massive $18.6 million complex of the Lyndon Baines Johnson Library and School of Public Affairs, planned on a typically Johnsonian grandiose scale that dwarfs the libraries of previous Presidents,

* One major land owner is Time Inc. Dr. Peter Gunter, chairman of the Big Thicket Association, charges that not one of Time Inc.'s publications has taken a stand for the national park idea or even reported thoroughly on the conservation issues at stake.

crowds the already jam-packed campus of the University of Texas.*

The most outstanding achievement of the Connally administration may have been the effort to transform the University of Texas into one of the leading state universities of the country and create an academic establishment and training capability to draw aerospace-type industries. A major point of emphasis was improving the faculty and library resources at the mother campus in Austin. By 1970, UT had become one of the nation's outstanding teaching and research institutions and rated among the top 15 universities in the American Council on Education's report on graduate education. And it had become a truly statewide institution with branch campuses at Houston, El Paso, Arlington, Odessa, Dallas, and San Antonio, including several medical schools.†

Trouble was waiting, though, in the person of Frank Erwin, Jr., Connally's close personal and political friend, whom he appointed to the board of regents in 1963. Erwin's love for UT was hardly to be doubted, but his idea of a great university turned out to be one in which teachers teach but steer clear of politics, students study and never demonstrate, and the regents govern at his direction. Erwin was enraged by any student demonstrations (of which UT had relatively few) and became upset with professors and administrators who refused to crack down hard on any student insurgence.

By 1971, there was real question whether UT could retain its newly won academic eminence. In less than a year, Erwin had forced the dismissal or resignation of Chancellor Harry Ransom (a nationally renowned scholar), the vice chancellor for academic affairs, the president (Norman Hackerman) and vice president of the Austin campus, the dean of Austin's highly regarded college of arts and sciences (John R. Silber, now president of Boston University), and three of five teachers who had held the title of "university professor." Erwin stepped down as chairman of the regents in 1971 but would remain a board member until 1975 and was replaced by a man of the same ideological stripe.

Physically the UT campus at Austin still manages a pleasing ambience, the intrusion of new steel and concrete structures like the LBJ Library notwithstanding. The Spanish accent of the earlier architecture gives a strong flavor to the scene. It may all be in some danger, however, in a continued orgy of building. The campus will not soon forget the day in 1969 when Frank Erwin personally directed bulldozers in a run-in with students who opposed ripping out stately old oak and cypress trees to make way for expansion of the football stadium. The campus still has its 21-story tower, that illustrious landmark from which a deranged young gunman named Charles

* More than 3,000 national leaders of both parties attended the May 1971 dedication of LBJ's library, including a smiling President Nixon obviously hoping to charm Johnson and the Texas Establishment into neutrality if not some kind of support in 1972. The massive library is filled with Johnsonian artifacts, his sayings engraved on stone, and bigger-than-life photographs of him. It is all centered on a seven-story-high Great Hall where the 31 million Presidential documents (in red buckram boxes with the Presidential seal) soar up before one's eyes in Pyramid-like glory. But there was a problem neatly summed up by David Broder in the Washington *Post:* "Big as the Johnson library is, it is not as large a monument to his Presidency as the Vietnam war."

† In all, Texas has 124 institutions of higher education. Among the private universities, Rice (at Houston) and Southern Methodist University (at Dallas) are generally considered the most illustrious. UT was peaceably integrated in the mid-1950s but still has only a few hundred Negro enrollees. The major Negro universities are Texas Southern University at Houston and Prairie View A & M.

Whitman perpetrated a grisly set of 14 murders on a summer day of 1966.

Austin's other great landmark is the 308-foot-high capitol building, set in lovely tree-filled grounds and commanding a long view down Congress Avenue, the city's major thoroughfare. Of course the capitol building is the largest in any of the 50 states, and in likewise typical old-Texas style, one learns that it was paid for by deeding more than three million acres of public land to a Chicago syndicate in return for building it. But in other ways, Austin is so un-Texan. Austin is described quite accurately by Texas novelist Larry McMurtry as "a pretty, sunny town, the climate warm, the sky blue and unsmogged," where "the sun sets plangent and golden into the purple of the Austin hills at evening, and the moon, whiter than a breast, lights the Colorado River." I have visited there several times and found the beauty, indeed, to be present, and in the nearby Austin lakes too. Adding to the Austin spirit is the remembrance of two late and renowned literary figures: Walter Prescott Webb, scholar of the American frontier and incomparable chronicler of the Western plains and desert (whose insights underlie much of what is written of the Great Plains in this book), and J. Frank Dobie, a social historian and chronicler of Western folklore who is among the best-loved of Texas and Western writers. Both men were professors at the University of Texas.

Austin was one of the places in Texas to vote *against* secession at the start of the Civil War and has long been regarded as a rather liberal and enlightened place in Texas politics. In 1968 Wallace's vote there was only half his statewide average. But the late 1960s also saw open housing lose in a referendum, after which the three city councilmen who had been for it were all voted out of office. In 1971, however, there was a moderate-liberal comeback, supported by a coalition of white liberals, blacks, Chicanos, and the young—including, for the first time, a substantial vote by university students.

Our account returns later to the most metropolitan Blacklands cities (Dallas-Fort Worth, San Antonio), but a word might be said about Waco (population 95,326), midpoint between Austin and Dallas. Waco is filled with so many lavishly built Baptist churches that some have nicknamed it the Baptists' Rome. Baylor, the well known Southern Baptist university, is in town too. Waco survives off surrounding farmlands and big factories of General Tire & Rubber and Owens-Illinois Glass. Oddly enough, it is the home base of an extremely skillful and influential fund-raiser for liberal political contenders and the "peace" cause, insurance executive Bernard Rapoport.

West of Fort Worth, Austin, *et al.*, the Central Plains begin. The ride west from Austin is best known since it leads through the famed hill country to the LBJ Ranch. Anyone who has traveled this country will respond to Theodore White's vivid description in *The Making of the President—1964*:

> Hill country is poor country. You drive west toward the Texas horizon, and slowly that horizon begins to pucker into what the geologists call the Edwards Plateau. The best word for the panorama is stark—it begins to roll, and rolls on, and continues to roll on for 200 miles in harsh, low hills, none higher than 600 or 700 feet. . . . These hills are primeval, hard, unending. . . . Today it is bleak

land, with a beauty that comes only in spring when bluebonnets flower and the grass grows sap-green. But from the remaining clumps and wisps of bunch grass one can imagine the tufted landscape as it must have been when the grass reached saddle-high, . . . when the buffalo roamed as they did until the settling of the Johnson family and its neighbors. . . .

But the white man ruined it. He ruined it by overgrazing it with cattle that cropped the grass to the soil and let the soil erode; he ruined it by planting cotton and mining the soil of its nutrients, neglecting it. By the time Lyndon Baines Johnson was born it was worn and poor—the kind of country that bred agrarian radicals and Texas statesmen.

Johnson, one of those Texas statesmen himself, was responsible in large part for the outpouring of federal largesse that has begun to bring his beloved Hill Country back to life. The Pedernales Electric Cooperative (which Johnson personally persuaded President Roosevelt to approve), USDA-advised conservation and grass-planting programs, soil-bank payments, dams, federally subsidized highways, the Colorado River Authority whose dams harnessed and tamed waters that had ravaged the land—these and a host of other benefits can be traced directly to Johnson or to Democratic administrations, from FDR's to his own. Each program has been a little more generous for the Hill Country and Austin than other places (and one can only wonder at what the federal budget might have been if every locality in America had received equal treatment).

The luckiest place of all, perhaps, was little Johnson City (population 767), which was a decaying, unpaved cowtown when LBJ went to Washington and a thriving tourist mecca when he returned, prospering with a 50-unit, $650,000 housing development for its aged and poor, an $840,000 federal grant for a 30-bed hospital, and a small federal building to house the post office and local federal offices.

The heat has long been sapped out of the controversies about how it was that Lyndon Johnson, a poor man in his youth who spent almost all his adult years in public service, managed to acquire a fortune estimated at up to $20 million, centered in radio-television, banking, and land holdings within or near Austin. He was a man of magnetism and power; he had friends, like his close friend A. W. Moursund and others, who enjoyed making money with and for Johnson; when it came to FCC supervision of Johnson radio-TV holdings, or any other form of government licensing, it was no wonder that the benefit of the doubt in any decision would be in favor of the rising Congressman, then Senator, later Vice President and President of the United States, a man not lightly to be crossed. The complex and interlocking interests of Johnson and his friends, in everything from cable television to stock in major Austin and other Texas banks, was a wonder to behold, but not a single crusading journalist ever suggested a thread of illegality in what was done.

Johnson's return home from Washington raised no small fears in Texas that he might be planning a new, swashbuckling career in local politics, in banking, or on the UT campus at Austin. As it turned out, he played a muted role in Texas politics (advising, more frequently conciliating warring Democrats), and in fact he appeared none too often on the UT campus. The last years were peaceful ones for the suddenly quieted senior statesman, a low-keyed finale to a furiously active life. Death came in January 1973, four years and two days after Johnson had left the White House.

As a postscript to Lyndon Johnson the Texas politician, I might add a cogent observation made to me by George Reedy, LBJ's onetime press secretary. It was fortuitous for Johnson, Reedy points out, that he came from rather "neutral" political ground in Texas—not oil-dominated Dallas or Houston, or segregationist East Texas, or machine-run Mexican-American counties of south Texas—but rather the Hill Country (and Austin, which was in his congressional district). Relatively independent of the entrenched forces in the state, Johnson could play one off against the other, raising himself to the pinnacle of national power.

Just a few miles west of the LBJ Ranch is the little city of Fredericksburg, a reminder of the strong German heritage of many counties in this part of Texas. Fredericksburg was founded north of the Pedernales in 1846 by an expedition of 120 men, women, and children headed by Baron Ottfried Hans von Meusebach, a fearless man noted for his brilliant red hair and beard. Until a few years ago, German was still taught in the public schools, and Germanic landmarks and customs still abound: the quaint, octagonal Vereins Kirche that was originally set directly in the middle of Main Street, lovely Abendglocken (evening church bells), Sängerfeste (song festivals), and an annual summertime Schützenfest (target-shooting festival). The Germans who settled Fredericksburg and other towns like New Braunfels in the Hill Country were liberals and revolutionists who scorned slavery and the Southern decision to side with the Confederacy; for almost a century afterward, they continued to vote more Republican than other Texans.

Before we leave the Central Plains, three other cities require brief mention. Wichita Falls (population 97,564), near the Oklahoma border, is a dull-faced North Texas oil town. It also has a hefty payroll from nearby Sheppard Air Force Base, and culture intrudes in the form of Midwestern University, where Republican John G. Tower was a professor of political science before his forensic skills and good luck catapulted him into Lyndon Johnson's old Senate seat in 1961. Some 140 miles southwesterly is the fabled old cattle town of Abilene (population 89,653), living off an air force base, regional oil and agricultural activity, and miscellaneous manufacturing. A few more miles south is San Angelo (population 63,884), heart of one of the world's greatest sheep and goat-raising territories—and, oddly enough, now site of an aircraft plant in which some 100 Texans take orders from a team of Japanese executives from the factory owners, Mitsubishi Heavy Industries.

From the Panhandle to the Rio Grande

Now we move onto the High Plains. I still recall my first drive up from Wichita Falls toward Amarillo on the Panhandle, seeing the ground turn flat, so incredibly flat, and the fields of wheat stretching out endlessly across the prairie. We drove on for hours, and then the first structures jutted up on the horizon, and if I am not mistaken, we drove another full 20 miles until we actually came on them. They turned out to be huge grain elevators, outside Amarillo. Here Texas gets its only taste of the "continental climate": frigid winters, hot summers, and the wind blowing and blowing and blowing. In winter "blue northers" roar down the unbroken sweep of the Panhandle plains, and there is an old saying, "There's nothing between them and the North Pole but a barbed wire fence—and that's down most of the time." Up to 1870, the Panhandle was shunned by white men as uninhabitable, a place where "a man might wander aimlessly until the blistering sun and the windblown dust finally felled him." Then came the buffalo hunters and, after them, the first ranchers and settlers, battling the winds and intermittent droughts. World War I stimulated such a huge wheat demand that the number of farms on the Panhandle and related plains area below it increased 48 per cent in five years; then with the native buffalo grass plowed under, wind erosion took hold, production fell precipitously, and Texas took years to dig away the Dust Bowl wreckage and recultivate the earth. In the early 1950s, another cruel drought hit western Texas. And starting in late 1970, there was yet another. In an interstate area similar to that of the Dust Bowl of the '30s, rainfall dropped to minuscule levels. Great dust storms rose up with dust-laden winds covering hundreds of miles. The earth simply lacked moisture for nonirrigated crops of many types. (Later droughts also hit eastern Texas, not enough to parch crops but serious enough to raise worry about the water supplies of major cities.)

Except in drought times, the High Plains now support not only wheat but a thriving cattle industry and huge cotton harvests. There is even some protection from drought, since some 6 million acres are irrigated from underground wells, enabling farmers to grow sorghum grains in vast quantities and feed hundreds of thousands of head of cattle. (The country's biggest cattle auction takes place in Amarillo each year.) Ten percent of the cotton grown in the U.S. is harvested within 50 miles of Lubbock, which has long since replaced East Texas and the Blacklands as the cotton center of Texas.

The people of the plains tend to be tough, independent, politically conservative types—in some people's eyes, the purest examples of *Tejano erectus* to be found anywhere.

Three big cities thrive on the High Plains—Amarillo, Lubbock, and Midland-Odessa. The only one of the group most non-Texans have any image of is Amarillo (1970 population 127,010), the natural capital of a huge region extending over all the Panhandle and deep into Oklahoma and Kansas. Aside from its renowned attractions of high winds, oil, cattle, and wheat, the town actually has some civic attractions you might not expect on the prairies (even a zoo and several good art galleries). In recent years the city has been a citadel of right-wingism with one of the country's most powerful John Birch Society chapters. Lubbock (population 149,101) is not well known because as recently as 1940, the Census count was only a fifth of that. I can think of no other American city that has grown so fast in modern times on the basis of agriculture. The local economy is also boosted by Texas Technological University. There is lots of prosperity but also poverty, especially among Mexican-Americans. In the mid-1960s, a local newspaper identified one rural-urban slum, within a mile of the city limits, "featuring pig pens, outdoor privies and junked cars." In May 1970, 600 ramshackle wood houses of Lubbock's "Little Mexico" were virtually leveled by a vicious tornado, which killed 20 people. It was Texas' worst since 1953, when a twister reeled out of a thunderstorm at Waco and killed 114 persons.

Still farther to the south, on the harsh and desolate West Texas plain about on the level of the southern border of New Mexico, are Midland and Odessa, begun 90 years ago as sidings on the line of the Texas and Pacific Railway line from Fort Worth to El Paso. In the 1940s and 1950s, they became gold dust twins of the rapid oil and gas exploitation of the 90,000-square-mile Permian Basin. Midland, which had 5,484 people in 1930, boasted 62,625 in 1960; Odessa grew from 2,407 to 80,338. Then, in the 1960s, as the oil boom began to wind down, both cities lost a small percentage of their population. Midland has been a city of millionaire owners, of white-collar workers and executives, working in big high-rise office buildings incongruously set on the plains. Odessa, by contrast, is a hard-hat town, filled with roughnecks, roustabouts, maintenance men, and engineers.

Now our focus shifts 225 miles westward, over the ravished glories of Trans-Pecos Texas, and we are at the westernmost extremity of this gargantuan state, and the city of El Paso. Together with its sister city of Ciudad Juarez, directly across the Rio Grande, El Paso forms part of the largest bilingual metropolis on an international boundary anywhere in the world. Spurred on by military installations and new industries, El Paso more than doubled its population (from 130,485 to 276,687) between 1950 and 1960, and then added another 16 percent growth in the following decade for a 1970 total of 322,261. Juarez has about 438,000 people, and its recent rate of increase has been three times that of El Paso. The sister cities are physically imposing, with towering mountains impinging deep into their central districts. El Paso is visited by almost three million U.S. tourists each year, most of them planning to cross the wide-open border into Juarez, where diversions start with exotic shops and markets and bullfights with illustrious matadors and end with a spirited nightlife and wide-open prostitution—all strong drawing cards for the *turistas*.

El Paso's ingrained attitude of indifference toward the impoverished Mexican-Americans in its midst, especially those in the festering southside ghetto, began to loosen some in the late 1960s as civic leaders took an interest in programs to alleviate severe unemployment and the problems of youth, vandalism, and narcotics use. The city's population, in the 1970 Census, was 58 percent Mexican-American. Twenty-five percent of those families —and 61 percent of unrelated Mexican-Americans—were living in poverty. More than half the Chicano adults had never made it past grade school.

Even the El Paso Chicanos with steady jobs are likely to live close to the poverty line. The average hourly wage in manufacturing in 1972 was

$2.56 an hour—93 cents below the state average and the lowest of any Texas city. Some 18,000 to 20,000 are employed in the garment industry, of whom only a small fraction have been unionized. In 1972 a classic labor-organizing struggle, reminiscent of the violence-laden struggles in other parts of America in the 1930s, erupted as thousands of Chicano workers at the Farah Manufacturing Company, a $160-million-a-year maker of slacks and jeans, went on strike demanding union recognition. Farah's management, with support of the El Paso establishment, adamantly refused unionization and vowed never to relent. In retaliation, the Amalgamated Clothing Workers of America organized a nationwide boycott of Farah products. The national AFL-CIO endorsed the boycott, charging Farah with trying to break the strike with tactics "from the Dark Ages of American labor relations," including the use of "vicious attack dogs, court orders barring peaceful and legal picketing, arrests in the middle of the night, unlawful discharge of workers for union activities, and personal intimidation and coercion." The National Labor Relations Board issued a complaint backing up most of the union charges.

El Paso is the site of the U.S.A.'s largest electrolytic refinery (Phelps-Dodge) and also the largest custom smelter in the world (American Smelting and Refining Company). ASARCO in 1972 found itself the object of a suit by the city of El Paso and the Texas Air Control Board when tests showed that many children in the poor Mexican-American community of "Smeltertown" surrounding the plant had ingested abnormally high amounts of lead into their blood. (Lead can affect the brain and cause convulsions.) The company gave in, agreeing to pay fines, underwrite medical expenses of the injured children, and install $750,000 of new control equipment to reduce pollution from the huge smokestack that rises on El Paso's western skyline.

Perhaps the most important single factor in the El Paso economy is the $268 million annual payroll for military installations which include gigantic Fort Bliss (home of the U.S. Army Air Defense Center), William Beaumont General Hospital, and nearby White Sands Missile Range and Holloman Air Force Base. To round out the picture, we should mention a complement of lively cultural activities (symphony, theater, museums), and the University of Texas at El Paso, the new name for the old School of Mines and Metallurgy. By 1975, enrollment is expected to reach 20,000. All in all, the showing is not bad for what was a dusty border town of 736 souls when the Census first included it, 90 years ago.

Low-priced Mexican labor provides a stimulus for economic growth in border towns like El Paso, but it is also a strong depressant on wages for American nationals. The lowest per capita income rates in the U.S.—just above $1,500 a year—are found along the Rio Grande; conversely, the Mexican areas with the highest incomes are directly across the river. Writer Paul Horgan writes * of the Rio Grande as it divides Texas and Mexico:

> From El Paso southeastward, every United States town has its Mexican counterpart across the river. Commerce, appetite and corruption draw them to-

* In "Pages from a Rio Grande Notebook," part of his 1970 book, *The Heroic Triad* (New York: Holt, Rinehart and Winston).

gether. Language, national boundary and law keep them apart. The river itself is hardly an obstacle anywhere, for it can be waded for most of the year, whatever else its common uses may be. . . .

Along the way, the river passes through the most desolate desert-like country, in serpentine fashion around the mountains of the Big Bend, then onto flat terrain and into the semitropical climate of the Lower Rio Grande Valley where citrus and palm grow. The only major settlements, both far downstream, are Laredo (population 69,024—crossing point for the Pan-American Highway), and Brownsville (population 52,522). After Brownsville, the terrain turns to marshland, a haven of waterfowl. Here, Horgan writes:

> The wasted flood plain is running out with the continent. . . . Through a waste of sand, misty air and silence, in the presence of no human concern, having come more than 1,800 miles from mountains nearly three miles high (in the Colorado Rockies), the Rio Grande at last enters the Gulf of Mexico and the sea.

Water Notes

With good reason, Walter Prescott Webb classified all of Texas from San Antonio westward as "desert rim" territory. Each of the cities there has had to depend on rather precarious sources of water, often involving importation over long distances. Most of the territory was restricted to grazing or dry farming until the 1940s, when discoveries were made of enormous amounts of water in aquifers far below the bone-dry surface of the land. Thousands of artesian wells, many sunk thousands of feet, have made possible vast harvests of cotton and grain sorghum and maintenance of huge feedlots for cattle. In West Texas, where as late as the 1950s thousands of farmers fled before drought conditions, the impact has been almost beyond description. In fact, by the late 1960s it was estimated that 75 percent of the state of Texas' *total* water consumption was from underground sources.

But the underground water, built up over centuries, is not being replenished and in fact is dropping in many areas (especially the West) by two to three feet each year. By 1985, according to state officials, the huge Ogallala aquifer in West Texas will begin to decline as a source of supply. Then that area, which presently accounts for most of the irrigated farmland in Texas, will be forced to start a retrenchment to dryland farming with markedly adverse effects on Texas' farm output. By the year 2020, according to state estimates, remaining water sources will supply only 50 percent of Texas' total developed irrigated acres.

Thus it came about that Texans spawned the idea of the most fantastic water diversion scheme ever known to man. Some 12 to 13 million acre-feet of flood water would be taken from the Mississippi River each year at some point in Louisiana, imported to East Texas, and then conveyed hundreds of miles to West and South Texas in an open-air, cement-lined canal that would probably have to be 300 feet wide and 40 feet deep. A total of 18 dams and reservoirs would be constructed to hold the water until the times of year when it was needed—thus flooding a quarter of a million acres of land in East Texas. Critics said the canal system would alter the natural flow of every river and estuary in the state. The principal line would move 500 miles westward across East Texas to Lubbock on the High Plains, supplying Dallas, Fort Worth, Abilene, and San Angelo, and then, by pipeline, loop southwesterly to El Paso (with a possible extension to New Mexico). Another would stretch 418 miles down the Gulf Coast, bringing supplemental water to the big cities there and helping to meet municipal and irrigation water demands of the Lower Rio Grande Valley. The water for West Texas and New Mexico would have to be pumped at least 3,000 feet uphill; about seven million kilowatts of electricity would be required to do the job.

The cost of all this? The figure of $9 billion was used in the late 1960s, but by 1971 the estimate had escalated to $13.5 billion. That would be four times the cost of the stupendous, controversial California Water Plan, and close to six times the cost of the TVA in its first 30 years of existence. The federal government would be asked to pay about two-thirds of the cost (mostly in loans to water users)—apparently a not-impossible goal because the chairman of the U.S. House Appropriations Committee was Rep. George H. Mahon of Lubbock, Texas, where the irrigators are in most need of the new water supply. A total of $3.5 billion would have to be raised by Texas cities and water districts to acquire reservoirs and conveyance facilities so that they could tap into the federal system, and in 1969 Texas voters were asked to approve bonds in that amount. If there ever was an establishment-backed idea, this was it. A "Governor's Committee of 500" was formed to back the amendment, chaired by Gov. Preston Smith with three immediate past governors (including Connally) as cochairmen. Opposition was most apparent in Houston, which wondered if it would get its money's worth back, and the *Texas Observer* in Austin crusaded against a great "boondoggle." But there was general amazement when the voters, by a narrow 315,139–309,409 vote, actually said no.

Backers of the Texas water plan had said its approval would lead "to unprecedented economic growth and prosperity for the entire state," its defeat to "decline and stagnation caused by the lack of adequate water." Critics pointed out, however, that with interest, the actual cost to Texans of the 50-year bond program would be more than double the $3.5 billion face cost—"the state amount enriching two or three generations of investors." Some of the repayment would have to come out of Texas general revenue. The real gainers, critics said, would be big corporate farms of the western plains, with small taxpayers and average citizens bearing the greater part of the cost. Some saw a move by the power structure to fill its own coffers.

Finally, critics of the water plan said, it was doubtful that Louisiana would permit exportation of Mississippi River water in the first place. In his 1971 Sierra Club book, *The Water Hustlers,* John Graves quoted Louisiana's Senator Russell Long as saying: "Texas will get our water over my dead body."

The water plan is still being studied, and if federal agencies find it feasible, it will provide one of the most fascinating political fights of modern times, rife with implications about the importance of agriculture in the U.S. economy and the power of the Texas establishment to get approval, both in Washington and among Texans themselves, of this most grandiose of water schemes.

A big enough federal water project is already underway in Texas: the $1 billion Trinity River Waterway, involving construction of a navigation channel 370 miles long from the Gulf of Mexico to Dallas and Fort Worth. Proponents like Rep. Jim Wright of Fort Worth point out that the Fort Worth-Dallas area is the second largest population center of the world (after Mexico City) without connections to a major waterway. Everything from wheat to gravel to petroleum will presumably be carried by barge, at a fraction of present rail or truck costs, when the navigation channel is completed. In addition, it is expected to stimulate new industry along its banks and to have side benefits in flood and water quality control. The project was long advocated by Texans in Washington and finally authorized by Congress in 1965. Despite a tight budget policy against "new starts," President Johnson included it in his final budget, and money was approved by Congress in 1969.

Aside from giving Dallas-Fort Worth an opening to the sea, the Trinity River Waterway will also connect with the Gulf Intracoastal Canal which, when completed, will run all the way from Brownsville, Texas, on the Mexican border, to the west coast of Florida. But, like the Texas water plan, the Trinity River project has its critics. Elizabeth Drew, writing for the *Atlantic Monthly*, quoted an unnamed Texas politician as saying: "It's the wildest scheme I ever saw. They have to dig every foot of it. Then they have to put expensive locks in. You could put five railroads in for that price. I'm not carrying any brief for the railroads. You could put in a railroad and make the government pay for every inch of it and call it the United States Short Line and save a hell of a lot of money."

Even without the Texas water plan and the Trinity River project, Texas must be classified as one of the most dammed-up and reservoir-rich states of the Union. By the 1960s, it ranked fourth among the 50 states in its volume of inland water, covering nearly 4,400 square miles of lakes and streams. A huge portion of this was accounted for by man-made lakes and reservoirs, generally paid for by the federal government. Northwest of Austin, a series of reservoirs on the Colorado River (not to be confused with its far western namesake), originally planned for flood control, power, irrigation, and city and industrial use, had also created one of the most desirable recreation areas of the American interior. There were large multipurpose reservoirs on the Brazos River, above Waco, and on the Trinity River in the Fort Worth-Dallas area. On the Red River, forming the boundary with Oklahoma, there was huge Lake Texoma, and in extreme eastern Texas there was the Sam Rayburn Reservoir on the Angelina, with a normal capacity of 4.4 million acre-feet. Down on the Rio Grande, there were two massive joint U.S.-

Mexican projects—the Falcon and Amistad reservoirs.

Together with countless other reservoirs scattered across Texas, these facilities offered the state a flood defense it had never enjoyed before—even though there was danger that with time, silting might render some of the dams useless. For normal industrial and municipal use, assuming a moderate population growth, there was a good water supply to carry Texas well into the 21st century. Why then the Texas water plan and Trinity River project? A desire, it would seem, to accelerate population, industrial, and especially agribusiness growth to absolute conceivable maximums. Yet no one had ever really spelled out the desirability of such a course for Texas.

Houston: Boom Town on the Bayou

Houston, Texas, sixth largest city in the United States, having registered an impressive 31 percent population gain in the 1960s, is expected to double its population of 1,232,802 people in the 1970s. (Counting the metropolitan area, almost two million people already live there.) Among the 50 largest cities of America, there is only one growing as fast—Phoenix—and its population is less than half of Houston's today. *Fortune* has identified Houston's great new growth as a management boom, based on the decision of scores of great American corporations to move major operations, or even headquarters, to the city. Brash Houston promoters point out to industrialists in the problem-plagued Northeast that they can avoid congestion and high costs—in fact, even reduce their labor costs substantially—by a move to Houston. Thus having already established itself as the greatest commercial and population center of the Southwest, Houston shows its usual ebullience and vigor as it tries to fulfill the predictions of admirers who say it will be, by the year 2000, one of the great cities of the world.

The irony of it all is the location. Beset by fantastic heat and humidity, Houston was just a mosquito-infested, muddy tract of land near the sluggish Buffalo Bayou in 1836 when two New York real estate developers, the Allen brothers, paid a dollar an acre to buy it from the widow of the great Texan settler, John Austin. The late Marvin Hurley, executive vice president of the Houston Chamber of Commerce, cheerily observed that it was "the most inhospitable place to start a city that anyone could have found." Air conditioning takes the worst edge off that condition, and no one thinks of Houston as a sleepy bayou town anymore. Instead, Houston is spoken of as a remarkably open, young, informal, progressive city—and a place that revels in the conspicuous consumption of its new wealth. Other Gulf-area cities, like New Orleans and Galveston, might as easily have seized the place in the sun Houston has made its own, but they were encumbered by a clannishness and old-family culture.

It was old Jesse Jones, the renowned "Mr. Houston" of his time, who summed up Houston the best, shortly before he died in 1956: "I always said that someday Houston would be the Chicago of the South, and it is. Railroads built this town, the port made it big, cotton and cattle kept it rich, oil boomed it, and now we're the chemical capital of the world. Growing, growing, growing, that's Houston."

Amazingly, Houston was still growing at the start of the 1970s, and at an ever accelerating rate, precisely when most of the U.S. was cooling off from the "Soaring Sixties." *Fortune* declared in 1971 that Houston was in a great "management" boom, evidenced not by refineries or mills but rather by "curtain-wall skyscrapers, shopping arcades, and new suburban homes." Between 1959 and 1969, office space in the central business district rose from 10 million to 16.4 million square feet, but by the end of the 1970s the figure was confidently projected at 50 million. An interesting change in the type of new development was also occurring. During the 1960s, suburban office space rose from two to nine million square feet and there was a great concentration on low-level shopping centers, parks, apartment complexes and offices that gave the city a horizontal look. But around the start of the 1970s, developers and especially the big corporations decided the time had come to return to and humanize downtown with large but well proportioned developments, fountains, small shops, and living areas. The airy, multitiered Galleria shopping area on the city's outskirts was a splendid example of the quality that Houston—if it really wanted to—could achieve.

Anyone who has visited Houston in the last 20 years can appreciate the desirability of tasteful, big-scale corporate development in center city. Alone among the great cities of America, Houston has no zoning, and city planning has been at a minimum. While many great office buildings already stand there, the spaces between them are often a dreary no-man's land. For an interview with M. A. Wright, chairman of the board of Humble Oil, I went to Humble's handsomely designed white marble skyscraper, the way to Wright's office preceded by long, carpeted corridors with rich wood doorways. From his office, there was a stunning view over some distance to the south, the white Astrodome glistening in the morning sun. But directly below, all around the building, the view was of one- and two-story ramshackle retail outlets, endless parking lots, and empty spaces, the prototype of the city where the planners never had their day. (A local editor explained the lack of zoning to me this way: "Houston is populated with people from small towns and farms of the old, rural South. Their salient characteristic is fierce, don't-fence-me-in individualism—the psychology that 'If I want to have a pigpen in my backyard, by God I can!' ")

Zoning or not, a lot of impressive building had been done in Houston by the start of the 1970s. From a slight distance, where one couldn't see the blank spaces between, the vista was one of a spectacular skyline of shiny new squares and rectangles, topped by the oil company signs like those one normally sees lining the tawdry auto alley approaches to American cities. Closer examination of the city reveals some splendid embellishments, including the Houston Civic Center with a convention hall and the celebrated Alley

Theater. The theater is designed in free-flowing castle-like style of sand-blasted concrete with nine great turreted towers, a building its architect (Ulrich Franzen) said was intended to be "as ancient as stone and as modern as Houston.*

Houston's most grandiose construction undertaking of the 1970s is to be what the local press unabashedly calls "the boldest, biggest, and most imaginative downtown redevelopment project ever attempted"—the massive Houston Center. It will cover 75 acres immediately east of the principal Main Street thoroughfare, land which for decades has been a hodgepodge of filling stations, unsightly warehouses, parking lots, and cheap hotels. The sponsor is Texas Eastern Transmission Corp., a prosperous firm that never before ventured beyond its basic business of transporting and selling oil and gas products. The development will cost $1.5 *billion*, but it is only one of several developments in central Houston and its suburbs that rank in the several-hundred-million-dollar class, combining office buildings, apartments, enclosed shopping centers, gigantic parking facilities, and entertainment and cultural facilities. The largest "new town" in America, "the Woodlands," will be built in the next years 30 miles north of Houston on 17,000 acres of land assembled by Mitchell Energy and Development Corp. of Houston. It is expected to have a population of 150,000 by 1992.

Such are the Bayou City's incredibly ambitious plans. The question raised is—why Houston? Foremost, there is the momentum Jesse Jones began. Secondly, land, construction, and operating costs are substantially lower than in most other large cities (as an example, $30 to $35 a square foot construction costs, compared to as much as $45 in New York.) Building economies stem in part from the absence of zoning, since projects can be started without long and costly fights with a political bureaucracy. State taxes are low, and commercial property in Houston, according to Ralph Nader, is being assessed "at a rate approximately one-half that used for residential property." The reason is not hard to divine, since major industries in the city are actually allowed to evaluate *their own worth* for taxation purposes. The city assessor claims he has no appraiser on his staff qualified to place a tax valuation on industrial facilities, so "we just have to take their word for it." Yet another inducement tempting large corporations is that Houston's cost of living ranks among the lowest of major U. S. cities, meaning that labor can be paid less. Between 1967 and 1970, it was estimated that 5,000 executives and middle-echelon employees of major corporations had moved to Houston, including about half of Shell Oil's New York staff.

Any view of Houston's successes must be considered in the context of the city's remarkable strides throughout this century. First came the Houston Ship Channel, opened in 1914, which snakes through some 50 miles of bayou, river, and Galveston Bay shallows to the Gulf of Mexico. Thirty-six feet deep

* The illustrious Alley Theater owes its founding and existence to a remarkably inventive Houston woman, Mrs. Nina Vance, who fought for regional theater before the words were invented. The Ford Foundation gave $2.4 million and Houstonians, from schoolchildren to oilmen, gave $900,000 for the new building opened in 1968.

and 400 feet wide, the channel is big enough for large oceangoing ships. There had been commerce to Houston before 1914; in fact, flat-bottomed boats had worried their way up the bayou for decades, dodging mud shoals and alligators, their topsails often ripped by overhanging branches, all in the interest of bringing out that great product of the times—cotton. The new channel sliced shipping costs for cotton and other farm goods (still important cargoes) and made it possible for Houston to become the greatest oil port of the world.

In terms of total tonnage, the port of Houston ranks third in the U.S., behind New York and New Orleans. It is seventh or eighth in foreign trade, a factor that seems to contribute to Houston's very open economic and political atmosphere (especially in contrast to other Texas cities). Thirty-nine foreign countries have consulates in Houston, and close to $400 million worth of trade is done each year with Japan alone. The deepwater port gives Houston a stake in a national free trade policy and makes it much less parochial than inland cities like Dallas.

Spindletop made Houston a big oil center, and the visitor need only glance at the names on the skyscrapers of downtown Houston to see who's there now—Gulf, Shell, Texaco, Conoco, Humble, Tenneco, Texas Gulf Sulphur, Texas Eastern, Schlumberger Limited—in several instances, world headquarters of those gigantic firms. The location is a logical one; if one draws an arbitrary circle 600 miles from Houston, territory which would be well inside the area served by Houston with pipelines, rail, and truck, the daily oil production is 5.9 million barrels of oil—nearly three-quarters of the nation's total output. And annual gas production of 14 trillion cubic feet is nearly 90 percent of the nation's total.

Oil was a huge business before World War II, but then came the great petrochemical thrust that stemmed from disruption of the hitherto-dominant German chemical industry, combined with the need for synthetic rubber after the Japanese closed off U. S. raw rubber sources in the South Pacific. Some $325 million worth of petrochemical and synthetic rubber plants were constructed along the Ship Channel during the war, and since then the dramatically increased world demand for chemicals has resulted in about $3 billion in petrochemical investment in the Houston area. The industry has been based largely on the hydrocarbon from oil and natural gas, plus two other resources abundant in the Houston area—sulphur and salt. A whole range of plastics and synthetic materials have emerged, with Houston the national center of it all.

Unfortunately, the environmental impact of the industry is immense. The Ship Channel, with miles of refineries and almost all of Harris County's 150-odd chemical plants along its banks, is so high in bacteria counts that people are warned not to let it touch their skin. The channel has long since been devoid of any aquatic life, the bottom is lined with a pollution-bred putrid sludge, and the surface is frequently covered with floating grease, oil, debris, and colored chemicals. There is so little natural flushing action that, as one official has put it, "virtually everything that keeps the channel wet is industrial effluent." * Compounding this "ecological Armageddon," as some have called it, is the fact that the port of Houston is literally ready to explode. Seventy percent of the cargo which moves through the port is classified as dangerous, and with a lack of licensing requirements for river pilots, sometimes an inexperienced tugboat captain will be pushing three to six barges of highly explosive material around the multitudinous curves of the channel. What happens if a huge fire does erupt in the channel? Just one fireboat, 20 years old in 1970, and with a maximum speed of eight knots, would be on hand to fight it. (State legislation passed in 1971, enhancing the port authority's power in the safety area, may begin an improvement.)

The channel and its chemical plants also make Houston's air incredibly vile when the wind blows in an unfavorable direction. In 1969, one company at Houston was said to dump 48 tons of sulphur dioxide and sulphur trioxide into the air every 24 hours. Whether the stiffer new standards set by the Texas Air Pollution Control Board will correct the situation, it is still too early to say.

Despite the importance of oil and chemicals, Houston's economy is not of the single-track variety. Instead, it is what the economists call "vertically integrated." Oil and gas are at the base, topped by succeeding layers of petrochemicals, metal fabrication, and food processing. Not far from the port, U. S. Steel recently built one of the largest and most automated steel works in the nation, and total manufacturing payrolls are close to $1 billion annually. The status of the Houston area and the port as a great farm center is often forgotten; Harris County ranks second in all of Texas in its numbers of cattle, and the region provides nearly 30 percent of the national rice production. The port of Houston is the country's number one wheat exporter, and in fact more than half the port's export tonnage is in farm products.

To all of this, of course, one must add a rapidly growing service industry, a huge medical research center, a booming convention business, and the federal space program. But NASA notwithstanding, only a small fraction of the area economy is dependent on government contracts. Metropolitan Houston is relatively "depression-proof." It is no wonder that so many top managers of major U. S. corporations now live in Houston (often at New York's expense). And the economic power structure includes—and some say is even dominated by—the big law firms, which end up being the negotiators, arbiters, and processors of the million and one deals, from downtown building to oil leases and shipping deals, that keep Houston humming.

The 154-acre Texas Medical Center in Houston, which treats close to 150,000 patients in a year, is a wonder of the medical world with its 10 major hospitals and clinics, three medical schools, and three research institutes. Major news coverage has centered around the fancy medical services,

* A field investigation team of the federal Environmental Protection Agency found in 1971 that 315,000 tons of suspended solids were dumped into the ship channel each day, including 1,600 pounds of lead, 5,000 pounds of cadmium, 7,900 pounds of zinc, 300 pounds of chromium, 400 pounds of phenols, 1,000 pounds of cyanide, and 55,000 pounds of oil and grease—plus 215 million gallons a day of domestic waste. Congressman Eckhardt of Houston urged the federal government to limit the discharges, saying action was necessary to save Galveston Bay, and that if control were left to state officials, they would "study the problem to death."

including open-heart surgery, transplants, all sorts of cardiovascular work, gleaming machines, and wonder drugs. The two great and renowned heart surgeons, who have fallen into bitter feuding in recent years, are Drs. Michael DeBakey and Denton Cooley.

Few spots on the American continent have been so totally transformed as one 22 miles southeast of center Houston, on the flat, green carpet of the Coastal Plains near Clear Lake, a place where cattle roamed and bounty hunters tracked wolves until a very few years ago. This was the site of a 30,000-acre ranch, owned by one of those fabulous, eccentric Texas millionaires, J. M. (Silver Dollar) West.* Back in 1938, West had sold his ranchland to Humble Oil & Refining, and from this ownership it passed in the early 1960s to the U. S. government. The purpose: to construct the Manned Spacecraft Center of the National Aeronautics and Space Administration, the command post for man's flight to the moon. Eventually, some $312 million was spent on a vast complex of buildings and equipment. Most Americans were keenly aware of just one activity: actual control of manned missions in space, beginning in 1965 and culminating with the successful lunar landing in 1969 and subsequent Apollo trips to the moon. A lot else happened at this huge NASA facility, however, including testing of explosives and rocket thrusters, an antenna test range, space environment simulation and flight acceleration chamber, the testing of crew equipment, and finally the training of astronauts.

The manned space program contributed handsomely to the Houston economy. A peak of more than 4,000 personnel at Clear Lake produced an annual payroll of $100 million in the late 1960s, and some 10,000 other workers in nearby supporting industries earned $250 million a year. It was the kind of economic stimulus hundreds of American cities would have loved —and which Houston, among them, probably needed the least. But the selection was made in the days before anyone thought of population dispersal, and when rawboned, old-style Texas pressure politics were still in style in Washington. At the time Lyndon B. Johnson was Vice President and head of the National Aeronautics and Space Council. Sam Rayburn was still Speaker of the House. Houston's Congressman Albert Thomas was chairman of the House Appropriations subcommittee handling NASA's budget, and President Kennedy needed his help on several other funding bills. James E. Webb, then head of NASA, was a close friend of LBJ. Another figure seemed to play no little part: George Brown of Brown & Root, LBJ's close friend. Brown was also chairman of the board of trustees of Rice University, which was interested in seeing the center come to Houston. Brown was said to have played a central role in having Houston selected after one of the most spirited competitions for a federal installation the country had ever seen. The other contending areas perhaps never realized how strongly the odds were against them. Putting the manned spacecraft center at Hous-

* After West's death in 1957, eight tons of silver dollars were found in a secret cellar of his Houston home. He had loved to scatter them around town, tossing them to pedestrians out of the windows of one of his 41 Cadillacs.

ton instead of Cape Kennedy almost surely added hundreds of millions of unnecessary dollars to the nation's space budget—an egregious example of Texas' private profit at the national taxpayers' expense.

In December of 1972, the astronauts of Apollo 17 completed what would probably be Americans' last trip to the moon in the 20th century—thus casting a pall over the future of the Houston center. But even with the glamor and top payrolls gone, the center would still have a role in upcoming projects—the earth-orbiting Skylab, a joint docking mission with the Soviet Union, and a returnable space shuttle bus for the late 1970s. One thing seemed certain: Clear Lake and its environs would never be the same again. Satellite industries, hotels, shopping centers, and suburban subdivisions have sprouted up across the Texas plain, filling the empty spaces and crowding the oil refineries and tortured pipework of the chemical plants. The Clear Lake Basin area, including both the NASA facility and Ellington Air Force Base, had about 50,000 people in 1965. According to the optimistic projections of the Texas planners, there would be 280,000 by 1980.

Some miles northwest of Clear Lake, a ways south of central Houston, lies that most splendiferous of all modern Texan creations, Roy Mark Hofheinz's Astrodome. The Astrodome is the world's first and only all-purpose, air-conditioned domed stadium, 4½ times the diameter of Rome's Colosseum, a colossal amphitheater that cost $38 million. Within its vast cavity, rising 208 feet above the flat plains (and surrounded by a sea of 30,000 parking spaces), one finds the great field for football, baseball, soccer, boxing, motorcycle racing, polo, bloodless bullfights, curling, and Gaelic football, with 45,000 upholstered armchairs for the spectators. There is also a variety of glittering restaurants and bars (including, of course, the longest bar in Texas), the Astrodome Club with thick carpets and rich, tapestried walls for season ticket holders, and finally, in the ethereal blue upper reaches of the stadium, 53 very exclusive sky boxes that rich Texans can rent for $18,000 to $24,000 a season. Behind the sky boxes are posh and garish private salons for party giving, each equipped with closed-circuit television of the field, a Dow Jones monitor, a bar and kitchen.

Roy Hofheinz, the man who conceived, financed (through public bonds) and now directs Astrodome-Astroworld, is the prototype of the *echt*-Texan promoter, equipped with physical bulk, string ties, a huge cigar, and ego to match. His daughter was moved to write a book about him, in which she said he was "a dreamer, a big thinker, a doer, and, most of all—a finisher. He is both lovable and bold, crude and suave, profane and gentle, shy yet outspoken, flamboyant, dynamic and charming." It has also been said that Hofheinz has "a mind as quick as a cash register."

Inevitably, Astrodome has some critics, most articulate among them the novelist Larry McMurtry. After an early visit to the huge white dome poking "soothingly above the summer heat-haze like the working end of a gigantic rub-on deodorant," McMurtry suggested that "pallid though the argument may appear, it seemed a bit conscienceless for a city with leprous slums, an inadequate charity hospital, a mediocre public library, a needy symphony, and other cultural and humanitarian deficiencies," to sink tens of millions of dollars "into a ballpark."

Houston: The Human Element

Geographically, Houston is a sprawling city, covering 434 square miles, the fourth largest in area of the U.S. (after Jacksonville, Los Angeles, and Oklahoma City). Under state law, the city has extraterritorial rights that enable it to stop new incorporations over an area of some 2,000 square miles and regularly annex huge chunks of land, preventing the kind of white noose suburbia that plagues so many American cities. Heavy industry is generally confined to the area along the Ship Channel on the city's east and southeast, and most of the industrial workers live in that part of town. Huge middle-class, white-collar areas are north and south of the city, and out to the west are the poshest executive type communities like River Oaks and others around Memorial Park.

Negroes, who numbered 316,992 in 1970 (25.7 percent of the population), are scattered through many parts of Houston, much like the pattern in Atlanta, though the heaviest concentrations are in a Y-like shape with the convergence point at center city. Together with Mexican-Americans, who number about 140,000 in Houston, Negroes occupy the worst slum areas like Pear Harbor, Sunnyside, Third Ward, and Acres Homes; within such areas are found pockets of the classic Southern slum dwelling, the shotgun house.

Jobs are unquestionably the worst problem of blacks and Mexicans, a continuing problem despite an innovative annual city-sponsored Job Fair that has been quite successful in getting employment for young men just entering the job market. At 1970 hearings of the federal Equal Employment Opportunity Commission held in Houston, its chairman, William H. Brown, III, said Houston was a "very sick city" for not providing more jobs for minorities. Several major firms (with Gulf Oil and IBM singled out for special criticism) were found to have black and Latin employment far below the share of the population those groups represent.

Yet despite such discouragements, leading Houston blacks are willing to acknowledge that the job situation for blacks has indeed improved vastly over the past 10 to 15 years. There has even been a flickering of help from the kind of white business establishment least known for helping Negroes—the Rotary Club. The Houston Rotary, which claims to be the world's largest local Rotarian group, in 1969 began a tentative but promising program for its members to counsel with and assist up-and-coming black businessmen.

Houston's Mayor Louie Welch set up a human relations division in his administration that spearheaded a Job Fair (beginning in 1965) and unusually innovative police-community relations projects. The police agreed to set up an observer corps of black and Latin youngsters who were even allowed to ride around in patrol cars from time to time to see how the police function on the job. Despite this and other efforts, however, ugly incidents have occurred in Houston, including a 1970 shooting by police of several young blacks (one of whom was killed) near the headquarters of a black militant group allied with the Black Panthers. In 1971 Welch won reelection as mayor by strongly endorsing the city's tough law-and-order police chief, Herman Short, whom blacks had accused of responsibility for incidents of police brutality. Welch defeated 33-year-old Fred Hofheinz, son of Judge Roy Hofheinz. Hofheinz ran as a liberal. Welch ended up with 53 percent of the vote in the runoff and would probably have done much better if he had not been tainted by the story of a big loan he made from a bank controlled by the convicted stock manipulator, Frank W. Sharp.

Militant black activity in Texas is extremely limited compared to other metropolitan areas of the country. I have heard this explained on the grounds that Texas has been more "open" than other Southern states, and that blacks live better, even in the Houston and Dallas ghettos, than in the North. Houston blacks have made great political advances in recent years, sending members of their race to the state legislature and in 1971 electing their first member of the Houston city council.

I was surprised when I went to Austin to walk into the senate chamber and see the presiding officer wearing a yellow dress and black skin. It turned out to be Houston's Barbara Jordan, temporarily lent the gavel by Lt. Gov. Barnes. Many regard Miss Jordan, a calm liberal, as the single most influential black in Texas politics. She went to Boston University Law School, came back to Houston with a law degree and no clients, and decided to get into politics. In the 1960 campaign, she began licking stamps and sweeping floors at the Kennedy-Johnson campaign headquarters but soon advanced and in 1962 and 1964 made strong though losing races for the state legislature when elections were all at large in Harris County. Then came court-forced redistricting, and she found herself in a senate district that was 46 percent black. By winning 98.6 percent of the black vote and 37 percent of the white vote, she won election in 1966, the first Negro state senator since 1883. She turned out to be an able legislator, eventually got a major committee chairmanship (Labor and Management Relations), and was an important figure in passage of a law setting up Texas' first fair employment practices commission, as well as landmark workmen's compensation and minimum wage bills. In 1972 she became president pro tem of the senate and made history by becoming—for a day—the first black woman ever to serve as the acting governor of an American state. (The temporary elevation came when both the governor and lieutenant governor were out of the state.)

As time went on, Miss Jordan began to get support from some of Houston's business establishment and in 1972 she easily won election to Congress from a new Houston House district, about 50 percent black and 15 percent Mexican-American, which emerged from redistricting after the 1970 Census. She became the first black member of Congress from the South since 1901.

The longest tension between the races in Houston has revolved about the school system, sixth largest in the nation and largest in the South, extending far into the suburbs. For most of 20 years up to 1969, the school board was controlled by a coterie of right-wingers who furiously fought integration, banned books that hinted of internationalism, insisted on massive doses of Texas history, and hounded opponents on the board or in the school administration. But the right-wingers were not always conservative with the taxpayer's money. Just before they were finally voted out of office in 1969, they completed an opulent white marble administration building, complete with fountains, gardens, and ornamental staircases, that cost the taxpayers $6 million. At about the same time, the board decided to eliminate free kindergarten classes for 18,000 children, most of them poor blacks and Mexican-Americans. The reason given: lack of funds. One establishment-type figure in Houston, not normally given to strong language, described the board to me as "a dumb, backward looking, incompetent bunch of racists," which had hired "a school administration not much better."

Finally, a broad coalition formed to elect qualified board members. The group included Republicans, Democrats, liberals, conservatives, professors, priests, housewives, businessmen, real estate salesmen, college professors, Negroes, Anglos, and Mexican-Americans, united simply in the interest of better quality education. And in 1969, it won 4–3 control of the school board. One of the new members was a prominent local Negro, the Rev. D. Leon Everett, pastor of the Jerusalem Baptist Church. The new board recruited Dr. George Garver, an extremely skillful young educator of liberal leanings, to be superintendent of the 240,000-pupil district. Garver began to uncover and correct many financial irregularities in the system and to institute competent professional evaluation of personnel. Somehow he crossed Everett and was actually dismissed in 1971 when Everett suddenly sided with the conservatives on the board. But the public outcry against the firing was so great that the conservatives were all ousted in the following elections and the newly constituted board promptly reinstated Dr. Garver.

A coalition known as the Harris County Democrats has been active in Houston for years, combining labor, Negroes, Mexican-Americans, and liberal whites; in the 1950s, it often made headlines as it sought to liberalize not only the official party organization in Houston but also the state Democratic party. (Among the celebrated leaders of that era was Mrs. Frankie Randolph, who combined the attributes of scrappy liberalism and substantial wealth. For years, she personally bankrolled the *Texas Observer*. Another woman, Billie Carr, has been the chief of precinct organization for the Harris County Democrats and a leader for the liberals in the intraparty wars.) Victories have alternated between the liberal and old-line, conservative Democrats in Houston, with liberals gradually winning the upper hand. But the disputes have so immobilized the regular party organization that in 1968 the various camps couldn't even reach enough accord to open a party headquarters for the Presidential campaign. Even within the liberal camp, unity is elusive; the local AFL-CIO, for instance, has pulled out of the Harris County Democrats in a dispute with the white-collar reformers. Low voter turnout among the minorities has frequently plagued the liberals, though they have been working for years at building registration and political awareness in the black and Chicano ghettos.

At the same time, the Republicans have made important strides in the Houston area, their numbers swelled by the ever increasing numbers of middle-management conservatives moving into the area. They have also benefited from the professional guidance of their full-time volunteer county chairman, Mrs. Nancy Palm, a former conservative Democrat. In statewide and Presidential elections, the balance of Harris County has now moved to the Republican side.

Violence has played a special part in Houston's life for many years. The most recent and publicized episodes came in 1969–70 when right-wing elements, including members of the Ku Klux Klan, began what seemed like a systematic drive to rid the city of all forms of liberal thought. Twice in a five-month period, the transmitter of KPTF-FM, the listener-supported station of the Pacifica Foundation, was ripped by explosions that forced the station off the air for months. The office of a New Left tabloid, *Space City News,* was bombed and its employees subjected to threats, their autos burned and riddled with bullets. Hippie cafes went up in smoke, and many liberal opinion leaders were subjected to ominous threats. Through it all, the Houston police seemed singularly powerless. Outside of the beleagured left and liberals, no one seemed too concerned about the violence in the city. The Houston *Post* did condemn the Pacifica bombings as "a throwback to barbarism reminiscent of the book burning of Hitler's Germany," but regular press coverage did not make of the violence the *cause célèbre* one might have expected. Finally, after much pressuring from the National Association of Broadcasters and others, the FBI agreed to move into the Pacifica station investigation and aided the local police in the arrest of a suspect well known in the city all along—Jimmy Dale Hutto, leader of the local Ku Klux Klan. He was later convicted of conspiracy to destroy the transmitters.

When Jimmy Dale Hutto was arrested, he was found to have a loaded .45-caliber revolver with him. That in itself, however, is nothing unusual in Texas, where a pistol is about as easy to purchase as a bottle of cough medicine, where it is legal to carry a loaded rifle or shotgun down Main Street, and where the law allows a man to shoot his wife's lover if he discovers them in the act of sexual intercourse. Houston for several years led the nation in per capita murders. Just in a one-block stretch between the Houston courthouse and Main Street, there are three places where a man can buy a gun for under three dollars. Many of the killings take place in sleazy little Houston cafes where customers drink it up heavily on Saturday nights.

As far as Texas courts are concerned, a man is usually much better off to be convicted of murder than drug possession or child molesting. Things do not seem to have advanced far from the frontier psychology of a judge in the 1930s, who proclaimed, "In Texas the first question to be decided by a jury in a homicide case is, 'Should the deceased have departed?' " To this day, five-year suspended sentences are frequent in murder cases. But in 1968, Lee Otis Johnson, a young black Houston dissident identified with civil rights causes, was convicted of giving an undercover agent one marijuana cigarette. His sentence: 30 years in the state penitentiary.

Before we depart from Houston, we must mention its two powerful, separately owned and operated newspapers—the *Post* (A.M.) and *Chronicle* (P.M.). The *Chronicle,* as previously noted, is owned by Jesse Jones' legacy, the Houston Endowment Inc., which has substantial interests in some 100 corporations, including downtown office buildings, hotels, oil royalties, ranchland and blue chip stocks. *Chronicle* editors have learned not to buck those interests. The *Post* is the domain of that attractive and forceful woman, Oveta Culp Hobby, who served in the Eisenhower cabinet and had the remarkable foresight to select that promising young multimillionaire, Nelson A. Rockefeller, as her chief deputy. Her son, William P. Hobby, Jr., became executive editor of the *Post* and proved himself an able journalist before plunging into elective politics to win election as lieutenant governor in 1972.

Dallas: Tragedy and Growth

> On the 22nd of November, 1963, three shots rang out under a Texas sky—and the brightest light of our time was snuffed out by senseless evil. The voice which had always been calm even in the face of adversity was silenced. The heart which had always been kind even in the midst of emergency was stopped. And the laugh which had always been gay even in reply to abuse was heard no more in the land.

With those words, Theodore Sorensen, confidant and counselor of the fallen President, John F. Kennedy, described his death in Dallas. The trauma of the event still numbs the mind, for its unspeakable cruelty, for the dark tide of violence it set loose in our time. I sought many other ways to start this Dallas subchapter, but there was no avoiding that central event by which Dallas became known to all corners of the earth.

Yet, having said it, there is little to add to the millions and millions of words, wise and foolhardy alike, that have been written of the assassination, of the presumed murderer Lee Harvey Oswald and his murderer Jack Ruby, of troubled Marina Oswald and the exploitress Mother Marguerite, of the Secret Service, the Dallas police and the Warren Commission, and all the rest.

Today at crowded Dealey Plaza, that junction place of superhighways where it all took place, the Texas School Book Depository Building still stands, gaunt and ugly as ever, purchased in 1970 by a collector of Kennedy memorabilia from Nashville. At a site 200 yards from the assassination, was dedicated a 32-foot high cenotaph, or empty tomb, in 1970, the design of New York architect Philip Johnson. It is 50 feet square and roofless, and Kennedy's name appears in gold on a slab of black garnite. No member of the Kennedy family appeared for the dedication, which was a boosterish sort of affair at which County Judge W. L. Sterrett noted that the memorial was on one of 37 blocks "which have been cleared of flophouses, beer joints, and liquor stores" to bring new life to downtown Dallas. Gleaming new skyscrapers stand nearby, part of a dramatic renewal project financed by John and Clint Murchison, Jr., and Texas Bank Chairman W. W. Overtown. And the life of Dallas goes on.*

Oswald's politics, with their Cuban-Soviet tinge, were diametrically opposite to Dallas' prevailing conservatism. But it is extraordinary that the deed of violence was performed in a city where violent rhetoric had come into vogue, where Lyndon Johnson and his wife were subjected to shouting, shoving, and spitting in the 1960 campaign, and United Nations Ambassador Adlai Stevenson had to bear similar abuse in October 1963.

Why right-wing extremism in Dallas? One reason is the new money syndrome. Dallas has thousands who have come into new wealth of the kind their parents never knew. Unlike those who have been wealthy over many years, they harbor deep resentments against taxes and see the chief tax collector, the federal government, as a threat to their gains. Another factor is the strong—almost overwhelmingly—Protestant complexion of Dallas, stemming in major part from its Deep South roots. The First Baptist Church, with a membership of about 15,000 and annual budgets of about $2 million, is the biggest Southern Baptist Church in the U.S. The Highland Park Methodist Church has 9,000 members, the Lover's Lane Methodist (what a wonderful church name!) some 6,000. It is a city where sermon titles like "God's Business Is Big Business" are not considered offensive, and where the churches have steered deliberately clear of social action. In this milieu, bland Protestantism seems to give way to uninhibited superpatriotism. This is probably true less of regular church-goers than those who have taken the free-wheeling and judgmental side of Protestantism a step further into dogmatism and rude intolerance of dissent.

On the religious scene, the watershed event of more recent years was doubtless the gathering in Dallas of 80,000 young people from all over America (and some 60 foreign countries) for "Explo '72," the largest religious camp experience ever seen in America. The Rev. Billy Graham, a dominant figure in the gathering, called it a "religious Woodstock." Officially sponsored by the Campus Crusade for Christ International, an evangelical and theologically conservative group, "Explo '72" was designed to bring the public into contact with the burgeoning (and proselytizing) Jesus Movement of the early 1970s. The issues of the Vietnam war, poverty, and racism were scarcely mentioned; the emphasis was on personal salvation with Jesus as the "one way." Critics discerned strong patriotic and establishment overtones—perhaps a benign indifference to social problems but no hint of right-wing extremism.

But to return to the early '60s: the ultraconservative tide that peaked then was aided and abetted by the Dallas *Morning News*, which even permitted publication of a hateful advertisement against President Kennedy the

* So, we might add, does the love of firearms in the city where one killed a President. In 1971 the Dallas International Bank began giving away Browning automatic rifles as an inducement for new accounts.

day he was to appear in Dallas (though, to its credit, the paper had been curbing its editorial page vendetta against the national administration and printed a gracious editorial of welcome that day).

After the assassination, there was a tremendous backlash against right-wingism. The Dallas *Times-Herald*, which had been quite conservative, moderated its positions; the *News* became less strident. Stanley Marcus, president of Neiman-Marcus, placed a widely read New Year's Day advertisement in the papers in which he said: "The [absolutist] is the man who thinks that he alone possesses wisdom, patriotism, and virtue, who recognizes no obligation to support community decisions with which he disagrees; who . . . views the political process as a power struggle to impose conformity rather than [as] a means of reconciling differences."

To a degree, right-wingism went underground in the mid-1960s, even though Dallas remained a closed community to outsiders, one intensely aware of its own image and resentful of much of the outside world. Then came 1968, and the Wallace movement made it somewhat "respectable" again to rail against the old, suspected Eastern liberal establishment and to take semi-racist positions. A big fund-raising lunch was held for Wallace in Dallas with reports (unconfirmed) that $2 million was raised for his campaign.

Still, there was reason to believe that Dallas would not return to the extremism of the early 1960s. At City Hall, there were signs that the ancient resistance against accepting "tainted" federal money was breaking down. The *Times-Herald*, already moved to an essentially centrist position editorially, was purchased by the Los Angeles *Times* in 1969; in time this might mean a strong infusion of new thought and direction, along progressive lines, in step with the changing impact of the Los Angeles *Times* in Southern California in the last several years. The Dallas *Morning News*, while still the spirit of establishment conservatism on its editorial pages, had by the early 1970s established itself as Texas' best paper in the breadth of news coverage and begun to print more and more news of dissident points of view.

Finally, the Dallas news-reporting scene was enlivened when the city's aggressive public television outlet, KERA-TV, inaugurated a "Newsroom" on the model of the successful experiment pioneered by San Francisco's KQED during a newspaper strike in 1968. The idea is to go beyond the crime-sports-weather syndrome of local commercial television with a format in which reporters, grouped informally before the cameras, actually discuss, analyze, and even argue the news. KERA hired an illustrious local newsman, Jim Lehrer (author of *Viva Max*, from which a successful movie was made) as its "man in the slot" for Newsroom; Lehrer in turn assembled a young, socially conscious staff that began to report on local events—education, environment, politics, county government, welfare, and poverty—in a probing way Dallas had never seen before. The objections of the Dallas conservatives were immediate and predictable, especially as some blacks and longhairs got included in Lehrer's reporter panels. (Early in 1972, Lehrer left Dallas to assume the prestigious position of public affairs coordinator for the national Public Broadcasting Service.)

If the fine arts can be taken as a gauge of civility and diversity in culture, present-day Dallas is also making forward strides. In a city where "lasso artists" once dominated, a group of talented young painters and sculptors has emerged. In 1972 the Walker Art Center of Minneapolis initiated a kind of "home and home" exhibition exchange with the Dallas Museum of Fine Art featuring sophisticated new art coming out of centers at the geographic extremes of the Great Plains States. The renaissance in the visual arts in Texas has been underscored by the opening of splendid new museums in Houston (designed by Mies van der Rohe), Fort Worth (Louis Kahn), Amarillo (Edward Durell Stone and B. R. Cantrell), and Corpus Christi (Philip Johnson, with John Burgee).

While all this was transpiring, the suffocating hold on Dallas of its highly organized establishment power structure was beginning to loosen, ever so slightly. The organization which symbolizes, and in effect *is* the ultimate power in Dallas, is the Dallas Citizens' Council. Before we discuss the Council, however, let it be said that despite the conservatism of all but two or three of its members (including Stanley Marcus), it has never been associated with the militant right-wingism of Dallas. Instead, the Council's interests have been civic and philanthropic or, to put it more precisely, to do whatever is good for business growth in Dallas.

Membership qualifications for the Dallas Citizens' Council are fairly simple. You must be the president or chief executive officer of your company. You must have the ultimate authority in your company, to commit it to civic expenditures (for hospitals, United Fund, symphony drives, or whatever). And you must be invited to join the Council. Almost inevitably, you will be a millionaire—the leading force in one of the big Dallas insurance, banking, retailing, finance, real estate, contracting, oil, or savings and loan organizations, or the media.

The founder of the Council was the late R. L. ("Bob") Thornton, chairman of the Mercantile National Bank and four-term mayor of Dallas. Born in a dugout in the village of Hico, Thornton had little formal schooling and gleefully butchered the English language as he hailed the deeds of the "dydamic men of Dallas" and announced: "Ain't nobody built anything big enough in Dallas. As soon as it's built, it's outgrewed." All of this, Warren Leslie points out in his book, *Dallas Public and Private*, was simply an act, part of the unique personality of a man of enormous charm and humor and gift of phrase. Thornton for years headed the State Fair of Texas, which draws 2.5 million people to Dallas each year. He was willing to gather money for any cause important to the city, and even headed a funds campaign for the Dallas Symphony Orchestra although he had never attended a concert. ("Coldest snake I ever touched," Thornton said in the middle of that campaign.)

In his later years, Thornton was the man who got Dallas to go along with peaceful integration of schools, hotels, restaurants, stores, and public facilties. A member of the Citizens' Council later explained how it was done: "Thornton just came up before us and told us what had happened in other cities. He told us how much business had suffered in Birmingham, New Orleans, and the rest. He told us how much it would cost Dallas if we couldn't solve the problem quickly and peaceably. There was not a single piece of sentiment at the meeting. It was not an argument of whether Negroes should be integrated or not. It was simply a matter of dollars and cents." (Or, as state representative Zan Holmes, a Dallas Negro, told me, "They moved when they had to—a typical example of the power structure smart enough to move just in time, staying one step ahead. It's one major reason we avoided riots here.")

The Dallas Citizens' Council has some 200 members, which means a small inner coterie has to make most of the decisions. Erik Jonsson, a former head of DCC and mayor from 1964 to 1971, has long been of that group—indeed it was a decision of the DCC inner circle that made him mayor originally, with practically no one in Dallas objecting. While he served as mayor, a "Mutt and Jeff" pair of Councilites emerged as the two most powerful figures of Dallas—John M. Stemmons, a six-foot, six-inch executive in commercial investments and properties, and Robert Cullum, the diminutive chairman of the board of Tom Thumb Stores. Other powerful figures were C. A. Tatum, president of Texas Utilities and chief leader in Dallas' successful integration, and James Aston, chairman of the board of Republic National Bank. In 1967, the DCC spearheaded the successful drive for a $175 million bond issue, largest ever proposed for a Southwestern city. Stemmons and Cullum, especially, gave their time, speaking all over the city and persuading leaders of all political and racial groups to support the effort.

Under the Citizens' Council there is a larger group of aspirants known as the Dallas Assembly. The original idea was to involve younger men, presidents of companies, who were climbing the ladder to a Citizens' Council position. By 1969, the Assembly was beginning to age, and an even younger group of aspiring Dallas businessmen formed a group. All the branches, however, seem firmly committed to the same goals—expressed in words like "keeping Dallas clean," "getting good government," "avoiding ward politics." If any indiscretions in a man's personal life become known, he is immediately frozen out of the structure. Bucking the decisions of the powerful men at the top of the DCC would also be fatal. Actual political activity is taken care of by a DCC offshoot known as the Citizens Charter Association, which almost always dictates the choice of mayor of Dallas and other major city officeholders. The control of big business is further extended through its close alliance with the conservatively oriented Dallas *Morning News* and the television and radio stations.

A system which leaves so much power in the hands of so few is bound to evoke criticism. Warren Leslie noted that "in the end, government by private club is government by *junta*, whether benevolent or not." Richard Austin Smith wrote for *Fortune* in 1964 of a feeling on the part of DCC critics that the Council was doing too much for too many, that it was a "self-perpetuating oligarchy" that made major decisions molding the political, cultural, economic, and social life of the entire Dallas community despite the fact that it was "unreachable" by the majority of Dallasites. It was precisely that issue that in 1971 permitted an insurgent candidate, Wes Wise, a 42-year-old political neophyte and former television sportscaster, running on a shoestring budget of $15,000, to win election as mayor. It was the CCA's biggest defeat in several decades. Wise's message, in intense personal campaigning, was: "Too much is decided by too few. The little people must have a voice."

The wave of resentment against the CCA oligarchy would doubtless have risen earlier and stronger in Dallas if it had not been for the visionary program to involve Dallas citizens in planning for their own future which was undertaken in the mid-1960s by the Dallas establishment's own man, then-Mayor Erik Jonsson. I spent several hours with Jonsson, an engaging blue-eyed Swede, on a leisurely Saturday morning while he was still in office. I came away feeling I had met one of the most dedicated, able men to lead an American city in our times. The story is best told in his own words:

> I had been mayor for three months or so when "I discovered I wasn't farming as well as I knew how," as the old Arkansas saying goes. I was reacting to emergencies rather than trying to control the events before they became events—the universal problem of cities. I said to myself, "Old boy, you're not using all the things used in a lifetime in business and industry. It's time to get back to the fundamentals of good management principles and see if they can't be applied here."

Jonsson then recalled the success of his firm, Texas Instruments, in increasing its business 30 percent a year, compounded annually, and speculated that one reason for that performance was management's insistence on setting sound goals and reevaluating them constantly in the light of experience.

> But cities rarely do this. They live within one- and two-year budgets. Planning is usually limited to the expected lifetime of a few politicians in their jobs. Mayors and councilmen are often just two- and four-year people and their own career objectives are often outside city government. . . . Cities rarely look at the totality of their problems, unlike corporations which think five to 10 years ahead, the better ones 20 to 30 years ahead. In cities, the squeaky wheel gets the grease. The newspapers are full of headlines on the immediate problem; the politicians react.

So it was that in December 1965, Jonsson picked the downtown Rotary Club for a famed "Days of Decision" speech in which he asked: "Shall we deal adequately with the future or be run over by it?" Jonsson named a 27-member Goals Planning Committee for Dallas and then called on 12 local writers to draft 12 essays highlighting the city's problems. Six months later Jonsson expanded his first (and very establishment-oriented) group of 27 to 87, including 10 blacks, a number of college students, and 20 percent women. For three days, he took them to the little town of Salado, halfway to Austin, and told them to hammer out mutually agreeable goals.

> I went from group to group for those three days, and slept no more than three hours a night. And at the end of the conference, several people came to me and used similar words—"You know, when I came here I looked at my opposite numbers and here were far-left Democrats and far-right Republicans and here

were Negroes and Latins and whites, and here were Catholics, Protestants, and Jews, and here were well-educated people and the stockroom clerk and the transcontinental truck driver, and here were preachers, and educators and heads of corporations. And I said to myself, 'Nothing will ever come of this; we can't even talk to each other. We have nothing in common.' But I found when I got talking to these people that they weren't really so far at all from what I've been thinking." And then came the payoff phrase—"This has been almost a religious experience."

The consensus of Salado, together with the 12 original study essays, was published in a 300-page paperback of which 20,000 copies were distributed in the city. Late in 1966, 33 "town hall" type meetings were held all over Dallas, attended by some 6,380 people. The Salado 87 then reconvened, heard the major modifications requested, revised some 60 percent of their recommendations (but few fundamentally), and in 1967 another book came out with 114 goals outlined. The next problem was to blueprint means for achieving the goals, a task assigned to 12 task forces manned by 293 Dallas citizens.

By late 1970, work had started on three-quarters of the goals and some had already been achieved. Public school kindergartens, which Dallas had lacked, were begun. The ambitious Dallas-Fort Worth Regional Airport was under way, financed in part by the 1967 bond issue which had borrowed from the earliest findings of the goals program. Family planning services were being expanded; the city had a new pretrial release system; a community relations commission (originally opposed by Jonsson himself) was in operation. The proposals, which would take many years to complete—far beyond Jonsson's own retirement as mayor in 1971—would have a major physical and programmatic impact on Dallas, touching the lives of virtually all its citizens. Even those who felt the "committee system" had watered down many goals, acknowledged the immense benefit in involving such a broad cross-section of the people. (The only serious private grumblings were said to come from some members of the Dallas Citizens' Council, Jonsson's old alma mater.)

> The goals program [Jonsson said] has value because it comes from the people, not a few. The problems of our society must yield to systems approaches. But people have to be included: they must be willing to accept and tolerate the solutions. . . . We have to change the forces that generate among people living closely together from centrifugal to the centripetal—to make them pull together instead of flying apart. . . . There is no avoiding this task, because if the major cities go down the drain, my friend, the whole society goes with them.

One of Jonsson's chief concerns, he said, was getting young and highly trained personnel for city government:

> Most cities hold down on staff in order to save taxes. There are few young people in city government. They go where the glamor is, where the stock options are, the big, quick rise to money and fame. And the dedicated ones almost always go to the federal government—at least 95 percent of them—even to the Peace Corps with no money. After all, that bunch down at city hall, who wants to rub elbows with *them?*

Dallas, it might be noted, is the largest city in the world with a city manager–city council form of government; thus it has a fairly unique capacity to maintain programs over a continuum and to hire bright young executives and promise them a real career.

But to return to Jonsson for one last thought. Why, I asked him, did a man of his age (mid-sixties) and standing (he is personally worth about $100 million) choose to undergo the pressures of city government when comfortable retirement was open to him? His reply, in part:

> The Council asked me to serve in February 1964. It was in the wake of Kennedy's assassination, and the town needed to be pulled together. We were seen falsely, all over the world, as a city of hate—which is the last thing Dallas really was or is. . . .
>
> I've since weathered three elections. . . . I look at myself as just as draftable for a public purpose as a kid is to go to Vietnam. Why the hell shouldn't they draft me if I'm needed? I don't think a man can lay down his kit of tools as long as they are useful. My philosophy is you're in a society, and you owe a great deal to it. What good is a man? As I think of him, he has to fulfill the requirements that come out of saying, "The value of a man to his society is the sum total of all he puts in it in a lifetime, less the cost of sustaining any negative forces he's supplied to it in his time."
>
> I look back on some of my early years as years when I didn't do very well for my society. I didn't do what I could do. I'm accelerating as my life goes on. I'm trying to make up for what I should have done. It's that simple.

Dallas: A Wooden Spoon Turned to Gold

Dallas, I heard it said, was the city born with a wooden spoon in its mouth. Its location was remote, it had no port or access to the sea, the farmland about it was not particularly fertile, and anyway neighboring Fort Worth soon monopolized the western cattle trade. Nor have oil or gas ever been found beneath it.

But cotton buoyed the early economy after the railroads were bribed or forced to divert their tracks through the town. When the East Texas oil field came in four decades ago, Dallas quickly cashed in as banker for the operation. Hundreds of Dallasites became millionaires, and the huge capital reserves created were then available to finance more exploration for oil and also diversification into fields like insurance and electronics manufacture. Dallas also became a great gateway for the Southwestern trade, leading the region in banks, distribution, and even fashions.

Dallas' population has been soaring upward in the postwar era at a rate just a little behind Houston's. In 1940, there were 294,734 people in Dallas, in 1970 a total of 844,401; within that period, Dallas had risen from 31st largest city in the U.S. to eighth largest, while Houston rose from 21st place to sixth. If one adds in neighboring Fort Worth and the entire metropolitan area of the two cities, the 1970 total is 2,318,036, more than the Houston metro's 1,985,031. Between them, these two great centers, one dominating the Gulf Coast and other northern Texas, account for about 40 percent of the population and perhaps two-thirds of the economic activity of Texas.

By a dollar-and-cents measure, Dallas' wooden spoon has turned to gold. A 1969 study of the top 100 Texas-based companies showed that 38 had their headquarters in Dallas, compared to 31 in Houston. Dallas was also booming as regional headquarters for national firms, with offices of 311 of the 500 largest industrial corporations on *Fortune's* list. The city had Texas' largest bank (Republic National, with assets of more than $2 billion), the regional Federal Reserve Bank, and 200 insurance companies with assets of some $13 billion. The manufacturing economy was humming along with technologically advanced, "clean" high-growth companies. Early in the 1960s, Dallas was deliberately cut out of new federal employment through Democratic retaliation against the city's extremist right-wing Republican Congressman of the time, Bruce Alger. But Alger was beaten in 1964 and times changed; by 1970, there were 13,000 federal employees in Dallas and the number was continuing to grow as a result of President Nixon's designation of the city as the center for Southwest regional offices. The city was the nation's No. 4 cotton market and farm implement center and had more than 500 million-dollar-asset firms.

Old-fashioned entrepreneur daring had a lot to do with Dallas' postwar growth. Midas stories like that of Erik Jonsson, who built Texas Instruments from a $2 million-a-year business in 1946 to an $850 million giant, abound. In 1963, for instance, 29-year-old Sam Wyly, a self-described "small-town boy from Louisiana," took $1,000 worth of savings and started a company to solve problems by computer for nearby firms. Six years later, his University Computing Company had grown to an international computer network employing 5,000 people in 50 cities and doing more than $100 million in business. Even when UCC stock took a big tumble on the stock market, Wyly was working on plans for a company (Datran) to build a nationwide system of microwave transmitters to transmit data in direct competition with no less an adversary than American Telephone & Telegraph.

Another, even more famous story is that of James J. Ling, a one-time oil roustabout and self-taught financial wizard who succeeded in building Dallas' Ling-Temco-Vought from a small electrical contracting firm back in 1959 to the 14th largest industrial firm of the U.S., doing $3.75 billion worth of business, a decade later.* Much of that multibillion dollar volume, however, represented the business of a broad array of other firms, including Jones & Laughlin Steel, brought in by acquisition and merger in a heady process of conglomeration. But when the stock market soured and investors decided conglomerates like L-T-V were spread too thin, Ling suddenly faced crises in carrying the huge debt incurred through acquisitions. Government trustbusters sued to force L-T-V to divest itself of its Jones & Laughlin stock. With debts mounting rapidly, the L-T-V directors, including spokesmen for

* Aside from business acumen, politics had something to do with L-T-V's success. Seats on private company planes were regularly made available to Texas Congressmen commuting between their home state and Washington. After the 1970 election, the Associated Press reported L-T-V executives had given $100,000 in campaign gifts through a "Citizens for Good Government" front, including $2,000 to House Republican Leader Gerald R. Ford of Michigan. In violation of federal law, the committee made no public report to Congress.

Dallas banks carrying a major share of the company's indebtedness, forced Jim Ling to relinquish his executive control of the company. Short months after that crash landing, Ling was back in business again with a new conglomerate (Omega-Alpha, Inc.) that soon had annual sales of close to $400 million.

One Dallas firm, we might add, knew when to sell and is very happy for it. In 1968, when the sale of fabled Neiman-Marcus to the less fancy Broadway-Hale Stores was announced, it seemed as if a part of the soul of Dallas had been sold out. But president Stanley Marcus and his brothers were left in control in Dallas, and when the high-fashion business went sour in 1970–71, the Marcus family was left holding $20 million in relatively unscathed Broadway-Hale stock. "I'm still the happy bride," Marcus said in 1971. *Forbes* magazine added: "Nothing like a marriage in the nick of time."

Big-scale office-commercial-apartment buildings in Dallas is failing to keep pace with Houston's phenomenal levels, but the performance is impressive enough on its own. Gradually, Dallas has shifted away from single boxlike downtown office buildings that fill their site areas and create the gloomy downtown canyons sociologists complain about. The new, multi-building projects feature street-level stores, sunken plazas between buildings, fountains, and other amenities.

Dallas' answer to the massive Houston Center project is called Griffin Square, a $200 million project on 32 acres of old railroad and warehouse property. The land was assembled in 1970 in what the Dallas *News* termed "the largest downtown land transaction in Dallas since John Neely Bryan subdivided the prairie." The plans include a 913-foot-high cylindrical office-hotel tower to be the highest building west of the Mississippi. Dallas is also receiving a $21 million Federal Center and a daringly designed new City Hall, akin to Boston's in its unusual form and monumental size.

At the same time, big things have been happening in the suburbs where costs are lower, more architectural flexibility is often possible, and massive freeways (like a new $100 million roadway named after Lyndon B. Johnson) provide easy access. Several large projects have already gone up, and the biggest of them all, a $150 million, 131-acre multiple-use office center (Park Central) in North Dallas, was begun in 1970 by Dallas developer Trammel Crow. Excellence of design is assured by the participation of Atlanta's John C. Portman, Jr., designer of the Peachtree Center.

Writer Warren Leslie has defined five general socio-geographic areas of Dallas—"five cities in the middle of nowhere." There is, of course, downtown, packed with hundreds of thousands of busy workers in the day, left to conventioneers at night (Dallas is strictly a home entertainment, not a nightclub city). The inner city alternates between great skyscrapers and tawdry structures like a fifth-rate short-order and beer place across the street from Neiman-Marcus and a Gospel Mission that gathers up its human outcasts each night half a block down the street.

Out beyond Dealey Plaza on the west is the sprawling community of Oak Cliff with several hundred thousand people. As one goes from east to west in Oak Cliff, the houses and apartments progress from a seedy mediocrity to high quality. Some sections are enhanced by that Dallas rarity, hills and woods.

North Dallas is the fashionable part of town, where house prices rarely dip below $30,000 and frequently go well over $100,000. This is the home of the establishment and would-be establishment types. In the postwar era it has stretched farther and farther north with huge residential building projects on the flat prairie; Leslie quotes a prominent builder as saying, "I sometimes wonder how far north these nuts will go in order to be chic. I have a feeling it's St. Louis." Within North Dallas, there are two independent islands, the incorporated townships of Highland Park and University Park, surrounded entirely by city territory. The *median* value of a house in Highland Park is $49,700, in University Park $32,700. (The Dallas median value, by contrast, is $16,700 and the statewide figure is $12,300). The two communities have been depicted in the past as 100 percent white. This is not exactly true. Of the 5,231 owner-occupied homes in University Park, one is owned by a Negro; in Highland Park the figure is two out of 2,636. Actually the 1970 Census found just over 100 Negro families renting in the two communities, although these may be live-in servant families.

University Park is the home of Southern Methodist University, an institution best known for its football team though it does have a much commended new Fine Arts Center which complements the cultural contribution of the Dallas Symphony Orchestra (the city's pride and joy, recently in financial trouble), the Museum of Fine Arts, and various presentations at the Frank Lloyd Wright-designed Dallas Theater Center.

There is also an "apartment Dallas" which grew up after the war as an exception to the old rule of single-family homes. The first and most prestigious apartments were on Turtle Creek, between center city and Highland Park; then more and more sprang up all over Dallas. Like so many southwestern cities, Dallas also has a good share of young-singles type complexes.

Finally, there are the slums, clustered west and south of center city, almost in the shadow of the downtown skyscrapers. The community of West Dallas, close to Oak Park, was not even a part of the city until about a decade ago, and many Dallasites seemed willing to ignore the unpaved streets, the shacks, and the outdoor privies. To their credit, the newspapers supported the drive for annexation, which was eventually successful. Conditions in parts of South Dallas, where a high percentage of Dallas' 210,342 blacks live, have been just as scabrous, although as in so many Southern cities, one hears local blacks and whites alike insisting conditions are nothing to compare with big-city slums of the North. One reason conditions have improved has been enforcement of Dallas' housing code belatedly adopted in 1957. Code enforcement was one of the few areas in which Dallas was willing to accept federal aid, even while it continued to resist urban renewal and Model Cities assistance.

Fort Worth: Cowtown Gone Modern

Nothing in Texas seems so immutable as the fact that Dallas and Fort Worth are different. Though a mere 33 miles divide them, John Gunther wrote, there "is a chasm practically as definitive as the Continental Divide." Dallas was forever written of as the place where the East ends, Fort Worth as the place "where the West begins." Even geologically, there is some truth to this; Dallas' climate and topography belong to the Mississippi Valley, but it is just west of Fort Worth that the land slopes into the gently rolling prairies of the Central Plains. The split is a little like that between St. Louis and Kansas City, or between Tulsa and Oklahoma City—the eastern partner more cosmopolitan, more given to fineries like specialty clothing stores, to big finance and the arts, the western partner more masculine and down to earth, a place of cattle trade and cheap bars, of an open society and western cordiality. Gunther wrote of Dallas having "suave and glittering clothes that look like the pages of *Vogue*," while Fort Worth was a "cattle annex" with an atmosphere "almost that of Cheyenne during the rodeo."

A quarter century later, the economies of the two towns—especially Fort Worth—have been turned upside down. The ancient and bitter rivalry between the two has been greatly ameliorated. And those 33 miles are filling up so fast with factories and suburbia that it will all soon be a single metropolis. Yet somehow the fundamental difference in character remains. Dallas is still uptight, self-conscious, often intolerant. Fort Worth is relaxed, gentle, and courteous. Much of the flavor of the small town is still there, even though the population reached 393,476 in 1970. In Fort Worth, people rarely bother to lock their cars. Instead of sullen stares between people on the sidewalks, one sees nods and smiles. Political extremism is virtually unknown. The stranger is welcomed warmly.

Fort Worth, it can be reported conclusively and finally, is no longer "Cowtown, U.S.A." Swift & Co., the last big meat processor, closed down its Fort Worth plant in April 1971. Now, where a thousand carloads of livestock poured daily into 100 acres of stockyards for their last roundup, silence reigns. The great cattle industry had been born back in the 1870s, boomed through World War I and into the 1920s but then began a slow death with the great Depression. Good roads and trucks made cattle shippers less dependent on the railroads, cattle buyers began to go to cattle auctions directly in the ranchlands, and eventually local feedlot operations made it possible to fatten animals and then truck them directly to slaughter.

In place of cattle, Fort Worth turned to aerospace. Convair, bought out by General Dynamics, got in on some of the great defense contracts of the postwar era, including the highly controversial, multibillion dollar TFX (F-111) project. At one point General Dynamics hired 28,000 workers at Fort Worth, though the figure had sunk substantially by the start of the 1970s. The Bell Helicopter Company became another major aerospace manufacturer, with 85 percent of its output going to the military. Finally, the L-T-V aircraft production facilities at Arlington, east of the city, hired several thousand workers from Fort Worth. The aerospace giants had heavy parts and service needs, stimulating the growth of well over 1,000 subcontractors around Fort Worth, most specializing in electronics and tool manufacture. The aerospace business, however, was a perilous one. In 1970, the loss of the $1.8 billion B1 bomber contract to North American Rockwell stunned General Dynamics executives at Fort Worth, some of whom wept when the bad news came. The company said it would eventually have to lay off 14,000 workers. And Bell Helicopter's outlook after the end of the Vietnam war was not bright at all.

The 1960s brought a major revitalization of downtown Fort Worth, which at one point had 60 vacant stores and seemed to be dying. One major point of the revitalization is a striking convention center, its great round shape contrasting with the rectangular high-rise office buildings.

Proof that the old rivalry with Dallas has been tamed is the half-billion-dollar regional airport the two cities are building jointly at a point equidistant between them (precisely 17 miles from each city limit). It will be the largest commercial airport in the world—some 16,000 acres, equal in size to all of Manhattan Island. The airport has already touched off frenetic land speculation in the surrounding area and a $1 billion building boom. Symbolic of the boomtime psychology in the Dallas-Fort Worth corridor is the city of Arlington, a little hamlet with more prairie dogs than people two decades ago. Then, in 1951, a remarkable 25-year-old promoter named Tom Vandergriff, the son of a multimillionaire car dealer, became Arlington's mayor. In the succeeding years Vandergriff sparked these developments for Arlington: a General Motors assembly plant which grew to have 5,000 employees; construction of a 2,000-acre lake so that prospective businesses would not have to worry about water shortages in a drought-prone region; attaching the local junior college to the University of Texas system (UT-Arlington now has 15,000 students); engineering of the Dallas-Fort Worth Turnpike, which puts Arlington in easy commuting distance of both major cities; a gigantic private amusement park called Six Flags Over Texas; a 35-acre Seven Seas marine park (which comes complete, according to one account, "with two million gallons of salt water, killer whales and a covey of penguins that know how to roller skate"); and construction of a big stadium that made it possible to lure the Washington Senators baseball team from the nation's capital. (The team, of course, has dropped the "Senators" tag and is now known as the "Texas Rangers.") Vandergriff remains Arlington's mayor and guiding spirit to this day. The city's population rose from 7,692 to 90,643 between 1960 and 1970, and a figure close to 300,000 is predicted by 1980.*

* Arlington is not the only city in the corridor to have grown so spectacularly. The towns of Hurst, Euless, and Bedford, prairie way stations a few years ago, had no less than 56,580 people among them by 1970. And Irving, on Dallas' western border, rose from 2,621 in 1950 to 97,260 in 1970—up 2,700 percent! Texas' latest sports arena extravaganza was completed at Irving in 1971 for the use of the Dallas Cowboys, just in time for them to win that year's National Football League championship and the Super Bowl. Cowboys owner Clint Murchison financed the entire $25 million stadium out of his own funds, designing it exclusively for football. Thus it is a bit smaller than Houston's Astrodome but has many of the same appurtenances, including luxurious upper-level suites that sell for $50,000—undecorated.

A landmark in cooperation between Dallas and Fort Worth was the formation in 1966 of the North Central Texas Council of Governments, the first of what were to become many "COG" organizations in Texas. Within a few years, the North Central COG included 137 communities. The original impetus for COGs came from federal legislation like the 1962 Highway Act, which required urban transportation studies by metropolitan-wide agencies in order to qualify for more federal highway funds, and from urban planning grant funds which financed creation of COGs. But officials like William J. Pitstick, executive director of the North Central Texas COG, see far more long-term significance. Most city managers, Pitstick points out, are burdened with "day-to-day" problems that can range from garbage collection and catching dogs to answering complaints. A COG director, by contrast, can concentrate on long-range planning and effective coordination in areas like regional water supply and pollution control, sewage, criminal justice, highways, airports, and the like. Pitstick believes that "the evolution of the councils of governments movement is the second most significant achievement and noteworthy innovation in the 20th century—the first being the development of council-manager government," a step which indeed effected a fundamental reform of local government several decades ago. (Yet to be seen, of course, is whether COGs, without taxing powers, are really "toothless tigers," as some critics say, and whether mere delegation of various communities' elected officials to sit on COG boards can substitute for direct election of people's representatives. An early test of the North Central COG will be the extent to which it can control the development boom in the 20 cities and towns around the new airport. The choice there, as *Business Week* has observed, will be between "an efficient and pleasant new urban environment" and "the unsightly, congested jumble of houses, offices, stores, and plants that is typical of so many developed suburbs.")

Fort Worth has an establishment group informally referred to as "the Seventh Street crowd," a counterpart to the Dallas power structure. But the Seventh Streeters, when they venture into politics, seem to have lost as often as they have won in recent years. For decades, the late Amon G. Carter, publisher of the Fort Worth *Star-Telegram*, was *the* power in the city; in fact it was thought foolhardy to do anything in the city without his approval. In 1954 an aspiring young politician named Jim Wright decided to run for Congress and had the audacity to announce without going first to Mr. Carter for permission and blessing. Carter exploded with a page one editorial damning Wright, and Wright replied in kind by paying $974.40 for a three-quarter-page ad in the *Star-Telegram* with some thoughts never before heard in Fort Worth: "The people are tired of 'One-Man Rule' . . . You have at last met a man, Mr. Carter, who is not afraid of you . . . who will not bow his knee to you and come running like a simpering pup at your beck and call." Wright won the election and still serves in Congress, and the *Star-Telegram*'s candidates are often defeated in elections. (Ironically, the paper now backs Wright in his reelection campaigns.)

Wright has done yeoman service pressing for Fort Worth's big business interests on issues like the Trinity River waterway and the TFX, but his credentials in the eyes of the establishment were never quite good enough to get the financial backing for a U.S. Senate race. He had hoped to run in 1966, but when he went on television to ask 25,000 Texans to send in $10 each so he could run a campaign free of control of the special interests, the return (gifts from only 7,000) was not enough to justify the race. Candidates for office, Wright said, discover "that the first thing they must do is not talk publicly about what they would like to do for the country but to talk privately with certain people about why their election would best serve their narrow economic interests. They're not all slant hole well operators or loan sharks, but that's not the point. The real point is that [the] power structure which pays the piper and calls the tune is entirely too narrow for a really healthy democracy."

Fort Worth is a city free of most pollution, with clean streets and clear skies; the pockets of poverty (Mexican-Americans and Negroes) are scattered and light in population. Likewise, the posh areas of Fort Worth (most notably Westover Hills) are only a fraction of the size of those in Dallas. Preeminently, this is a middle-class, middle-income city, and one of moderation. Though Negroes represent only 20 percent of the population, for instance, one sits on the city council, another on the school board. Even labor and management, which used to suffer bitter splits in the city, are talking more amicably with each other these days.

This is not to suggest a millennium in Fort Worth. As I wrote this section, a *Texas Observer* arrived with an exposé of the Joe Louis Addition, an all-black section on the Trinity River bottoms in Fort Worth, where the people pay city taxes but there are no city water lines or sewer lines, the streets are not paved, the garbage is not collected, and the rats are not exterminated. When the city planning commission held a zoning hearing on the Joe Louis community, an elderly black resident, Harry Smith, rose with the aid of his thick, old cane and glared at the commissioners. "We don't live in America!" he declared. "People in America don't live the way we do down there! Why do they take our tax dollar and don't do nothin' about it?" No one answered.

San Antonio: 254 Years Old and Thriving

> *San Antonio . . . is of Texas, and yet it transcends Texas in some way, as San Francisco transcends California, as New Orleans transcends Louisiana. Houston and Dallas express Texas—San Antonio speaks for itself. . . .*
>
> *We have never really captured San Antonio, we Texans—somehow the Spanish have managed to hold it. We have attacked with freeways and hotels, shopping centers, and now . . . HemisFair, but happily the victory still eludes us. San Antonio has kept an ambiance that all the rest of our cities lack.*
>
> —*Larry McMurtry,* In a Narrow Grave: Essays on Texas

Even while the French were settling New Orleans, the Spanish advanced northward from Mexico and in 1718 founded San Antonio and made it the capital of their province of Texas. Franciscan friars came and erected a series of missions. Four of these—San José, Concepción, Capistrano, and Espada—still stand, and together with the Alamo and the Spanish Governor's Palace, their wonderfully distinctive style is a reminder of empire, a tie to the past that the rest of Texas scarcely knows.

In 1821 Spanish rule gave way to Mexican; then came 1836 and the war of Texan independence and the tragic heroism of the 187 men, Anglo and Latin alike, who died defending the Alamo. Nine years followed under the Republic of Texas, and in 1845 the United States flag—San Antonio's fourth—was raised.

Right after the Civil War, San Antonio became the first of the cowtowns of the legendary West, a base area for the cattle trails—Chisholm, Shawnee, Western—heading up to final destination points in Missouri, Kansas, and Nebraska. The railroad came in 1877, and the lusty business of the open range made San Antonio into a veritable cattle capital, filled with picturesque saloons and gaming tables where men whose herds ranged over millions of acres played recklessly for high stakes. Eventually the cattle trade began to share the scene with pedestrian breweries, cement factories, milling, and oil. San Antonio became one of the great military cities of the United States. But still, that Spanish admixture and Latin population remained, together with a strong dose of German immigration that leavened the urban mix and created an atmosphere unduplicated anywhere in America.

Through downtown San Antonio, on a meandering course once known as "A-Drunken-Old-Man-Going-Home-At-Night," runs the San Antonio River, America's most delightful city waterfront. It had once been little more than a neglected slough that periodically overflowed nearby districts. But in the 1930s an ingenious flood control program, carried out by the WPA, resulted in rock retaining walls, picturesque footbridges and walkways, and landscaped banks. Today this four-mile "Paseo Del Rio" is lined with restaurants and shops, an open-air theater, and nightclubs, a place of life and joy that draws one irresistibly. The River Walk was extended in 1964, and a special side channel replete with the same ferns and magnolias extends to a lagoon where San Antonio's new convention center and Theater of Performing Arts now stand. Gondolas run along these waterways, and if you stay in one of the hotels along the river, you can go to the theater or restaurant by boat.

On occasion, San Antonio will do something really boosterish, like the 1968 HemisFair staged to celebrate the city's 250th birthday. On 92 acres near center city that had long been due for urban renewal, 33 world nations erected striking pavilions. The city got a new landmark in the 622-foot Tower of the Americas with its revolving restaurant. Culturally, HemisFair will long be remembered; for instance, even Russia's Bolshoi Ballet journeyed deep into the heart of Texas to perform. Financially, the results were not so happy; the six million people who came were four million less than the city had hoped for and the final operating deficit was an immodest $7.4 million. Some of San Antonio's poor thought the fair was a wasteful boondoggle. But permanent good has come from HemisFair, too. In 1972, arrangments were made for the National University of Mexico to establish a permanent branch campus in San Antonio, using six foreign pavilions at HemisFair Plaza. The university branch was an outgrowth of extension courses taught by Mexican professors in San Antonio ever since 1943, focused on Mexican culture, historic and modern.

Razzle-dazzle, Texas-style promotions are strictly out of character for San Antonio, however. It is an essentially finished city, with a complement of old and powerful families who made their fortunes from ranching or industry generations ago. San Antonio is occasionally accused of provincialism and having a closed society, but at the same time it is an informal place in a Southwest sort of way, and not at all stodgy. As substantial wealth is gained by aggressive business leaders outside the old family circles, San Antonio may begin to show more business-civic aggressiveness.

A glance at San Antonio's skyline reveals its dowdy middle age. From the HemisFair tower, one sees scarcely any buildings of postwar vintage. The big office structures are all of the more conservative styles of the '20s and '30s. The exceptions are a new hotel and a few other more modern structures around the HemisFair site. Much of the inner city is occupied by parking lots. From the same tower vantage point, one looks west past center city to the heavily Latin areas, east to San Antonio's larger pockets of Negroes, north to the wealthier precincts of the old Anglos, and south to a mixed bag of neighborhoods, plus a lot of the military-industrial complex.

The 1970 Census found that 341,333 San Antonians—55.5 percent of the city total—were Mexican-Americans. The informal Jim Crow practices prevalent until the 1950s have disappeared, and now there are many Mexican-Americans of high professional standing who are silently but rapidly integrating the entire area.

Still, there is the great West Side barrio, one of the most striking slums of the continent. For block after block after block, the tiny shacks and hovels stretch on, many with outdoor privies and lacking water, the conditions not much better than those suffered by destitute blacks along the Mississippi Delta. But the Mexican-Americans add verve and color to San Antonio. Throughout the barrio, people are everywhere, on the sidewalks, in the streets, on porches, leaning out of windows, a moving, laughing, and yet sad mass of humanity.

Until the mid-1960s, goverment largely ignored the barrios. Since then, activity has been intense, including some $10 million of federal money spent annually by the city's community action agency, the Economic Opportunity Development Corporation. A Roman Catholic priest, the Rev. John Yanta, became head of the San Antonio Neighborhood Youth Organization, an important arm of the local war on poverty. Several energetic settlement house programs were sponsored by the Episcopal, Presbyterian, Catholic, Methodist, and Christian Churches. And, since the late 1960s, San Antonio has had a new bishop, the Most Rev. Patricio Flores, himself a Mexican-

American who is deeply interested in his own people's cause (though he defends the church from charges it is reactionary). Among other things, Flores has devised a Chicano mass in which the folk music of the people is used. Flores replaced Archbishop Robert E. Lucey, who for decades had governed the vast San Antonio diocese that reaches down to and along the Rio Grande. Lucey for most of his career was regarded as a progressive and courageous defender of the downtrodden, especially Mexicans and Negroes. But at the end he veered sharply to the right and was bitterly attacked by many of his own priests for his dictatorial ways. Fifty-one of them went so far as to dispatch a letter to the Pope demanding Lucey's removal. Finally, he retired voluntarily.

A 1972 survey of Spanish-speaking San Antonions found that about six out of 10 could be classified as urban poor, with another four in a more middle-class status. In comparison to Spanish-speaking peoples in Los Angeles, Chicago, and New York, those in San Antonio were much more likely to have been born in the United States (85 percent) and to have lived in their present homes for many years. They also placed more reliance on the self, one's family, and church, rather than government agencies in times of crisis. What they wanted most from government was not improvement in housing, or new schools, or drug control—but rather street repairs and better highways.

Since the 1950s, many of San Antonio's city elections (all nonpartisan) have been won by candidates of the Good Government League, a group of private citizens who started as a reform group but later became highly conservative. The long-time mayor, elected with League support, was Walter W. McAllister, 82 when he finally retired in 1971. His relations with the Mexican-Americans were disastrous, based on remarks like these: "Welfare is like feeding the birds in the summer. You don't want to give them too much or they won't go away in the winter and will starve." Or, on a nationally televised program in 1970: Mexican-Americans are "wonderful people who love music, dancing, and flowers but who just do not have as much ambition as Anglos." Albert Peña, then Bexar County Commissioner, said McAllister was mouthing "the same old gringo racist rhetoric."

San Antonio government gets a distinctly conservative input from the Good Government Leaguers, but enough other types are elected (including a few Mexican-American city councilmen) to keep the city, as a whole, off the extremist track. The San Antonio newspapers are essentially conservative on local politics and centrist on national politics. Business influence is strong in the city, but by general agreement not as overwhelming as in Houston or Dallas.

The most powerful single San Antonio politician of the last two decades has been Henry B. González, the liberal Democratic Congressman. Of him, we will have more to say (along with Albert Peña, the brown power militants and others) in the "Mextex" subchapter. One loss to modern San Antonio has been the decision of Maury Maverick, Jr., son of the courageous New Deal Congressman and an imaginative figure in his own right, to stay away from elective politics. He served in the state legislature in the 1950s, fighting things like the Texas Un-American Activities Committee, was beaten for the U.S. Senate in 1961, and since then has stuck to the practice of law, defending conscientious objector youngsters, much to his economic detriment. The elder Maverick, who stood for "Liberty and Groceries," was one of the first friends of the Mexicans in the West Side barrio and got Eleanor Roosevelt to visit San Antonio, starting the city's first public housing. He was also the key figure in getting the WPA to beautify the river. He made the mistake as mayor in the 1940s, however, of letting a local Communist speak at the civic auditorium. This touched off a rampaging riot that enabled Maverick's enemies to depict him as a Red sympathizer and defeat him at the polls. Whether one agreed with the Mavericks' liberal politics or not, they always cut a colorful swath and often turned out (like a Norman Thomas) to be thinking years ahead of their time—a rare commodity in Texas politics.

Even without the supercharged atmosphere of a Houston or Dallas, the San Antonio population has risen smartly in the postwar years. Counting surrounding Bexar County, the figure was 338,176 in 1940, 500,460 in 1950, and 830,460 in 1970; as for the city alone, it had 654,153 people in 1970, making it 15th largest in the U.S.A.

The military is definitely the biggest business in San Antonio, a city long nicknamed the "mother-in-law of the Army." The single largest employer of the area is Kelly Air Force Base, a massive repair and maintenance facility for aircraft that hires 24,000 persons locally.

The military hospitals, along with a number of civilian facilities, including the new University of Texas Medical School, are fast making San Antonio into a leading medical center of the U.S. The military bases and hospitals, of course, are an inducement to military personnel to retire in the San Antonio area. Many of the officers retire in their forties after 20 years of service and have been able to get attractive jobs in the local economy. Another inducement may be San Antonio's salubrious climate (hot but not too humid summers, winters with morning temperatures in the mid-30s rising to the 70s by later in the day). One mystery to me, however, is how San Antonio has been able to absorb so many military, including retirees, without getting the reservoir of archconservatives apparent in a city like San Diego. To the contrary, one hears that the constant change of population created by military assignments, plus the broad experiences of the military, have actually contributed to a harmonious community and the lack of narrow views.

Mextex

The 1970 Census found 2,059,671 Spanish-speaking Texans—virtually all of them of Mexican heritage. One finds them still in the quiet, sunbaked towns of Rio Grande Texas and near the Gulf, in the vast San

Antonio barrio, in Corpus Christi or El Paso or Brownsville, and now in ever increasing numbers in metropolitan areas like Houston and Dallas, and even around farming cities like Lubbock on the High Plains. Statistically, the Mexican-Americans of Texas are more and more in urbanized areas (65 percent, the 1970 Census said). But their most vivid existence is still centered on the land or in the smaller cities of the Valley.

The life story of these people was traditionally one of cruelest poverty: their income but a fraction of Anglos, education minuscule (with substantial illiteracy), all but the most menial jobs denied, and of course the barriers of language. Outright discrimination—in schools, public places, restaurants, theaters—was often as cruel as that practiced on Negroes. Only a small, small minority managed to earn an average or better-than-average income, to keep their children in school through high school, or to send them to college. Real change did not begin until World War II, the civil rights efforts of the 1950s and 1960s, and the development of the Mexican vote into an independent, not-for-sale commodity in the 1950s and 1960s. A key development, many now think, were the Viva Kennedy Clubs of 1960, of which a San Antonio Mexican leader (and now Congressman), Henry B. González, was national cochairman. Here was a fellow Roman Catholic running for President, and one who really seemed to care.

For generations, the Valley counties were under the unshakable hold of "heavies," or *patrons*, who were sheriffs and judges, frequently tied in with the Texas power structure of oil, gas, and banks. The *patron* would look after the well-being of his Mexican charges like a northern city ward leader and obligingly pay their poll taxes for them. In return, the Mexicans would simply wait for a signal on how they should vote, and scarcely a man or woman would deviate from the *patron's* instructions.

The most famous *patrons* have been the Parrs of Duval County in the dusty oil-cattle-sagebrush territory of South Texas. Archie Parr, the original *patron*, came on the scene as a red-necked cowhand around the turn of the century, slowly built economic and political power, served 20 years in the state senate, and died rich in lands and cattle. His son George expanded the usual benevolent ways of the patron by maintaining an army of some 200 gun-toting *pistoleros*, who masqueraded as deputy sheriffs and helped keep the electorate in line. Starting in the 1920s, individual state candidates blessed by the Parrs usually received close to 100 percent of the vote.

All of this received ample national attention in 1948, when Lyndon Johnson ran against former Governor Coke Stevenson for the Democratic Senate nomination. When the final statewide returns were in, it seemed that Stevenson had won by a margin of 112 out of nearly a million cast. Then, on the sixth day, Precinct 13, a Parr stronghold in neighboring Jim Wells County, sent in an amended return with 203 more votes—201 for Johnson, 2 for Stevenson. The new totals made LBJ Senator with a plurality of 87 votes and won him the nickname "Landslide Lyndon." In that same election, Duval County itself went 4,622 for Johnson, 40 for Stevenson. Nor was this an isolated instance. In 1944 Starr County, directly on the Rio

Grande a few miles south of Duval, cast 1,396 votes for Stevenson for governor and exactly two votes for eight other candidates on the ballot. In Starr, it was the Guerra family which provided the *patron* and the power.

Former Senator Ralph Yarborough tells a colorful story of his attempt to campaign for governor in 1954 in Laredo, largest city in Webb County, which had been boss controlled for decades:

> No candidate for governor had spoken in Laredo for 30 years. I was warned not to come through. I said I was coming through there with all the flags flying. That night, they fired off a Chinese bomb within 10 feet of the platform where we were speaking. It let off a tremendous roar but hurt no one. The crowd was 98 percent Latino; the local powers had hoped to scare them off. But I was making a special appeal to veterans, and they are not scared by explosives. Next thing, a huge fiery cross, doused with gasoline, was moved up and set afire right behind where I was speaking.

Webb County, Yarborough recalled, customarily went against him 10–1. The heavies of many Valley counties still supervise a controlled vote, in fact. One of the most efficient of these is still George Parr of Duval County. In 1972, Duval gave 84 percent of its vote to McGovern—compared to his meager 33 percent in Texas as a whole. In the 1970 Democratic Senate primary, Parr decided to back Yarborough over Lloyd Bentsen. The vote: 3,993 for Yarborough, 264 for Bentsen.

But political and economic progress, as it came, came slowly and presented new sets of problems. After the U. S. Commission on Civil Rights held open hearings in San Antonio in 1968, the findings were summarized this way:

> Outside forces predominate in the life of the Mexican-American. He is forced to migrate thousands of miles to other states for farm work; he is forced to move into hostile cities in the quest for a better life; he is forced to cut ties with the familiar way of life, in order to relocate where the opportunity is best; he is forced to send his children to schools where an alien language and tradition may abort aspiration; he is forced to accept the lowest paying jobs, menial labor, and often forsake hope for anything better.

Mexican-Americans from Texas constitute a huge proportion of America's migrant farm workers. Their preponderance is borne home if one looks at a map of the U. S. showing the travel patterns of the migrants. One flow (mostly Negroes or Puerto Ricans) goes up from Florida as far as New York State and New England in the East; then there is another Western division (largely Mexican), up from Southern California, through the Central Valley into the Pacific Northwest.

But there is one great central migrant system, and its massive roots blanket South Texas like those of a mighty tree. The great branches push up through the heart of the continent. One stops in just a few hundred miles, still within Texas, for cotton on the High Plains. Another moves across New Mexico and Arizona and then joins the stream of California Mexican migrants picking cotton and a multitude of fruits, from strawberries at Salinas to apples in Washington. One of the Texan branches heads northwesterly

Travel Patterns of Seasonal Migratory Agricultural Workers

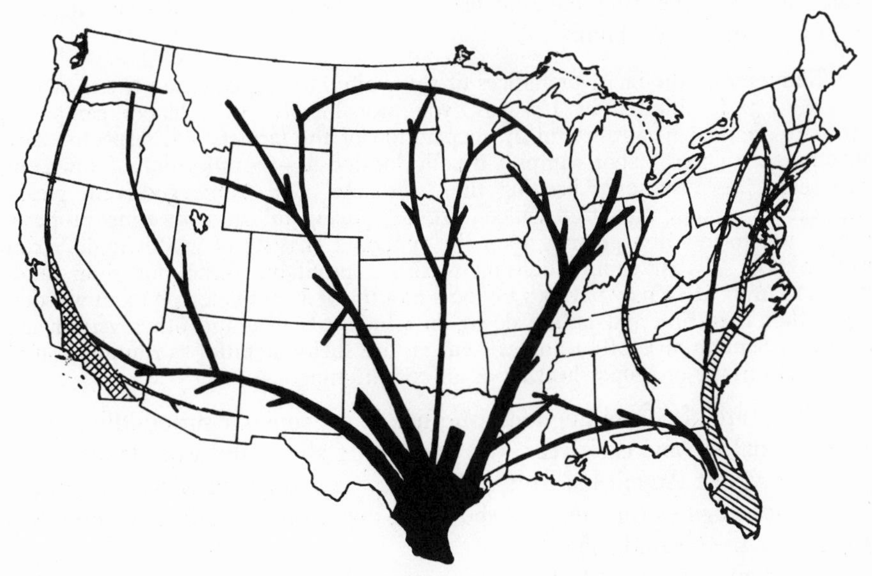

Source: U. S. Public Health Service.

to Colorado, Wyoming, and Montana, chiefly for sugar beet harvesting. Another group of migrants goes straight up through the Central Plains to help with grain harvesting as far north as the Dakotas, though mechanization is cutting back on the need here. Finally, one great migrant branch heads toward the Great Lakes to help harvest vegetables, tomatoes, apples, berries, peaches, nuts, and potatoes.

Year after year, the great waves of migration originate out of Texas in early spring, rise to cover the continent by autumn, and then subside again toward the ancestral homes on the Rio Grande. Writers Michael McCrery and Sixto Gómez have painted a touching picture of the life of Mexican-Americans who feel they have no real alternative to the life of following the crops and doing stoop labor:

> Shunned by the racist prejudices of the white farming communities in which you work and inhibited by low pay, you probably live in a "labor camp," a fifth-rate ghetto officially set up by cooperation of the farmers and respective city government. These "labor camps," usually located 20–30 miles out of town, in part serve the purpose of keeping the "wetbacks" (or "those goddamn greasy Mexicans," as they are often called) from "moving in" and lowering property values, not to mention preying upon the supposed chastity of white Anglo-Saxon womanhood. "Labor camp" housing is also a profitable racket for slum landlords. A family of 12 may pay $50 to $60 a month for a cramped, one-room wooden shack that is rotting and falling down, in which rats, lice and other vermin are rampant. Sanitation is often non-existent, as are such amenities as running water, toilets, electricity or proper heating or air conditioning. . . .

There are of course migrants who live in far superior surroundings, earn a substantial income each year, and have a life style (and expectancy) akin to that of most Americans. But such cases are a tiny minority. Agriculture Department figures for migrants showed a median income level of only $1,200 a year in the mid-1960s.

An irony—one might almost say a scandal—is that no one really knows how many migrant workers there are. Low estimates are around 200,000, high estimates close to 400,000. If one adds in the families and nonworkers who accompany the migrants, the total may run close to 800,000 to 1,000,000.

Despite the vast flow of migrants out of Texas, perhaps 75,000 to 100,000 stay entirely within the state, picking early crops in the Lower Rio Grande Valley and late crops on the High Plains. And despite all the federal job training and educational programs, the Mexican-Americans in Texas face a seemingly permanent, almost fatal type of competition: the hundreds of thousands of illegal immigrants from Mexico. No one knows just how many such entries there are, though the figure must surely run into the hundreds of thousands. Since the legal flow of temporary workers under the *bracero* program terminated in 1964 (to the dismay of the big growers who had profited from the exceedingly inexpensive labor), illegal entries have soared.* Along the entire Mexican border, 43,789 illegal immigrants were seized in 1964, but 348,172 in the year ending June 30, 1971.

*** The *bracero* program was inaugurated by Congress in 1942 when manpower was exceedingly short, and later continued at the insistence of the growers. Congress finally abolished the program in 1962.**

One major point of illegal entry is El Paso, where 43,640 were apprehended and sent back in 1970 alone. The bulk of the wetbacks at El Paso, I heard, enter the U.S. through huge underground sewage conduits that go into the river, much like the fabled sewers of Paris. The illegal immigrants simply go down to the riverbed and enter by one of the sewers, and thousands must succeed in escaping capture. There are highly professionalized smuggling services. A Mexican will pay the smugglers between $125 and $250 to be brought across the border under the most optimal conditions, and sometimes even be led far into Texas or up to the Midwest. Congressman Henry González told me that in summer of 1970, driving over a small ranch road north of Uvalde, some 70 miles from the Rio Grande, he suddenly came on a single file of men, knapsacks on their backs, scurrying through the bush—apparently wetbacks from a crossing point along that stretch of the river.

Each illegal immigrant is easy picking for unscrupulous employers who can pay disgracefully low wages, ignore all Social Security or other benefits, and in the process depress the wage scales for the great legal body of Mexican-Americans. González was the leading force in getting Congress to discontinue the *bracero* program, just a year after he entered Congress in 1962.

Even today, the U. S. Immigration Service refuses to crack down on Mexicans who hold resident alien cards but actually live in Mexico and commute over the border daily. David North, former assistant to Labor Secretary W. Willard Wirtz during dismemberment of the *bracero* program, writes: "The Immigration Service, with some justice, is regarded by its critics as the lackey of the Establishment, actively or passively greasing the way for the entry of tens of thousands of alien workers, who, poor souls, busily depress wage levels along the border, increase unemployment among U. S. residents, discourage union organization, and increase migrancy."

A movement like César Chávez's farm workers in California will never succeed in Texas, one concludes, until such conditions are corrected. Nevertheless, the effort is being made. Chávez has taken a lively interest in the Texas situation, visiting the state quite frequently to confer with farm and AFL-CIO union leaders. In 1966, during the first year of Chávez's grape strike in California, one of his lieutenants, Gene Nelson, showed up in Rio Grande City to investigate rumors of rebellion among the melon pickers of Starr County (average annual income $1,000, poorest county in Texas and 18th poorest in the U. S.). Under Nelson's leadership, some 1,300 Mexican-American farm workers soon joined the new union. Earning 65 cents an hour for a 10- to 18-hour day, it could have been argued they had little to lose. Predictably, the growers were adamant against recognizing the union, and a strike was called. The Texas Rangers were called in, ostensibly to keep peace—but in fact (as a three-judge federal court later affirmed) to side with the owners and intimidate the strikers. But while the strike failed, its byproducts would long be remembered in Texas.

The first was a great march, modeled after the Delano-to-Sacramento march in California. Out of Rio Grande City on the Fourth of July, 1966, they began, led by a Catholic priest and a Baptist minister, the marchers including some wonderful brown- and leathery-faced old men, veterans of thousands and thousands of days working the fields of the Valley, carrying with them a dignity and purpose as Texas had perhaps never expected to see in its *Mexicanos*. Allies were soon forthcoming. The state AFL-CIO raised $17,539 to support the costs of the march. Archbishop Robert E. Lucey of San Antonio, long interested in the plight of the poor in South Texas, held a mass for the marchers and said: "It is with a large measure of reluctance and regret that we endorse and approve your demand for an hourly wage of $1.25. No sane man would consider that a fair wage in these days. . . . $1.25 is ghastly recompense for exhausting labor under the burning sun of Texas."

As the march went along, others joined in—laborers in Corpus Christi and Houston, steelworkers from Port Lavaca, teachers, college students, even some government workers. On the final day at Austin, 40 Negroes, completing a 200-miles walk from Huntsville in East Texas, would merge with the group.

Perhaps the greatest surprise came a few days before the marchers were to enter Austin. Suddenly, autos holding Governor Connally, Attorney General Waggoner Carr (then running for the U. S. Senate), and Ben Barnes (then speaker of the Texas house) swooped down on the line of march some miles north of New Braunfels. Connally's message to the strikers was simple. He told them (1) he would not be in Austin to meet them, despite their invitation, (2) and that even if he planned to be in Austin, "I still would not have met with you . . . because I'm not unaware of the difficulties that have arisen out of marches throughout this nation [which] for various reasons have resulted in riots and bloodshed . . .", and (3) that they should be complimented on having a peaceful march—so far. (It would remain peaceful to the end. Connally, one of his critics said later, "thought he was still on the ranch; he thought he was still the Anglo foreman talking to those little Mexicans back on the ranch in Wilson County, telling the people to go on back home.") And after some minutes of talk, during which Connally refused to commit himself for a Texas minimum wage, his cavalcade of Lincolns swept away from the disappointed marchers.

Spirits soon buoyed, however, and on Labor Day, 64 days after their start, the line of marchers (now swollen to 6,500) streamed into Austin to be met by 4,000 supporters at the capitol steps and a round of brave, glad oratory. The *Texas Observer* welcomed the marchers with an editorial saying: "The Valley farm workers who are walking 490 miles from Rio Grande City to Austin have walked step by step from obscurity and exploitation into Texas history."

And so it was to be. In two and a half years, the minimum wage law indeed became law. There were reverses too—like the failure, in 1967, of the strike at Rio Grande City. Later, as we shall note, the Mexican-Americans of Texas began to divide into old-style "liberal" and new-style "militant" camps. The march and that Labor Day in Austin might be to Texas what the 1963 Civil Rights March in Washington became to America—an exultant day of unity when all seemed possible, to be followed by an ugly day of reckoning of division and violence. But still, one knew Texas could never regard its Mexican-Americans, and its farm workers, in quite the same light as before. Their cause, like Martin Luther King's in Washington, might be delayed, perhaps for many years. But each (and of course they are closely allied) would remain the creative and emergent force of its place in time and history.

The Mexican-Americans' quandary is what form their Texan "revolution" ought to take, and what type of leadership they ought to turn to. As a people, they have never been able to organize into strong political units, choose able leaders, and stick with them; many are the jokes, indeed, about the surfeit of would-be Mexican leaders and their inability to lead anyone but themselves. Right after World War I, there was the League of United Latin American Citizens, which still exists, most of its members now prospering in the professions or business, a Latino country club set. After World War II, Dr. Héctor García established the American G. I. Forum, a veterans group to aid Mexican-Americans. The Viva Kennedy movement of 1960 evolved into PASO (Political Association of Spanish-Speaking Organizations), which in turn was supplanted by two or three others including MAPA (Mexican-American Political Action organization), the Southwest Council on La Raza, and MAYO (Mexican-American Youth Organization)—the latter two more radical offshoots of modern times.

In like fashion, the Mexican-Americans are confused about what manner of man they should recognize as a leader. San Antonio's Congressman Henry González should perhaps be considered first, because he was in truth the first Mexican-American to win election to the Texas legislature in 110 years (by winning a senate seat in 1956) and later the first Mexican-American Congressman in the history of Texas—or for that matter, any other state—in 1961.

González's Mexican roots are as direct as can be. In 1911, five years before his birth, his father, then mayor of a town in Mexico, had barely escaped revolutionaries' bullets and brought his family across the Rio Grande to San Antonio where for 40 years he would edit a Spanish-language newspaper, always so Mexican in his thinking that he refused to become a naturalized U. S. citizen. Young Henry started part-time work when he was 10 years old, taking the taunts leveled at "greasers" in the San Antonio streets; years later, even after election to the San Antonio City Council, he would get another taste of discrimination when he and his family were ejected from a public park reserved for "white only." "When I ran for state senator from Bexar County (San Antonio) in 1956, that was considered as unachievable and as radical as if I were to tell you I was going to seek the Vice Presidency next year," González told me in 1971. He did win—by 309 votes out of 100,000 cast, after three recounts.

Big, loquacious "Henry B." soon made his mark in the state senate, fighting with a record-long filibuster a move which was then afoot to uphold and enforce ancient patterns of racial segregation in the state. Other legislators respected him, but to run-of-the-mill Texas conservatives the González name was anathema. The level of debate in those years was illustrated by a full-page ad taken out by González's 1960 state senate primary opponent. It accused González of being a former "union organizer" and thus, by implication, out "to destroy our 'Right-to-work' law in Texas" and a man sure to support that horror of horrors, "a state income tax!" González replied: "I never was a union organizer. If I had been this town would be organized—and it isn't."

In 1961, the San Antonio seat in the U. S. House opened up and González ran. Even more groups joined his coalition of Mexicans, teachers, policemen, firemen, and unionists. As González puts it, "my five years in the state senate had proven to some local oilmen, to some people who had been against me in previous elections, that I was honest, that I did work, and that I was fair." His enemies see it differently—that this may have been the moment when González "sold out" to the "Establishment." I have heard the process described as one in which the Establishment "picks off" Mexican or Negro leaders who might be dangerous to its interests, by a mortgage, or a loan, or social inducements (invitations to parties), or in the case of politicians, campaign contributions. In the case of Negroes, one then says the man "has been seen"; Mexicans call him a "coyote." Yet the charge, leveled at González, is highly dubious, because in subsequent years he voted a virtually 100 percent liberal line in the House, championed progressive legislation, and on occasion was known to rebuff efforts of special interests to compromise his position.

González insists he is a Congressman for all his constituents, not just the Mexican-Americans. "I don't want to be the Moses of the Mexican people. I don't pretend to be. I don't have that ambition," González insists. Instead, he turns out to be a superbly successful politician (reelected by overwhelming margins) who happens also to be a Mexican-American.

Good for Henry, yes—but how about the rest of Texas' Mexican-Americans? The radical and militant among them despise him, because they see him as the greatest obstacle in their road to revolution, a buffer between them and the Anglo community. And I heard only abuse for González from Bexar County Commissioner Albert Peña, a nationally prominent Mexican-American who accused González of "never helping any Mexican trying to confront the power structure," and of being an "Establishment liberal [who] expects always to get the Mexican-liberal vote [and] thinks the other side will aid him financially." González's comments about Peña were no more flattering, in a personal dispute that covered neither side with glory and underscored the popular image of Latin leaders always being at each other's throats. (In 1972 Peña was defeated for reelection as county commissioner by another Mexican-American who had previously been an administrative assistant to González. Peña's lackadaisical campaign, plus commercials on local Spanish-speaking radio stations accusing him of being a Communist, were important factors in his defeat. The Communist charge was patently false, because Peña attends Mass daily and is really an old-fashioned Catholic radical.)

Peña was a bridge to the ultramilitant young Mexican radicals who emerged in Texas in the late 1960s, quickly ruffling the feathers of establishments, Anglo and Latin alike. The first visible step was the formation in 1967 of MAYO (Mexican-American Youth Organization), the brainchild of five young Mexican-American college students who were depressed by the slow progress of their race in civil rights and disgusted with the policies of traditional leaders. After a number of staged confrontations with the local power structures, both in San Antonio and some of the smaller villages, the young Chicanos *—as they prefer to be called—switched their attention to the lower Rio Grande Valley in 1970, formed their own political party (La Raza Unida) and actually won several elections in areas where Mexican-Americans are a clear majority of the population.

One of the most remarkable interviews I have ever had was with the brilliant and charismatic leader of MAYO, José Ángel Gutiérrez, a native of Crystal City, Zavala County, in South Texas—some 125 miles south of San Antonio. Crystal City has a Mexican population of approximately 80 percent and will be remembered as the place that startled Texas when it elected five Mexican-Americans to its city council in 1963, an unheard-of event up to that time. Even though the Mexicans today control the mayor's job, the council, and the school board, some say the real power lies with the exclusively Anglo large landowners and major businessmen. For years, Crystal City has had a good thing going through the prosperous farm trade of the Winter Garden area in which the town (1970 population 8,104) is located. A statue of Popeye, that belligerent spinach-eating sailor of yore, adorns the town plaza, recalling Crystal City's claim to be the "spinach capital of the world." There is a well-to-do, overwhelmingly Anglo part of Crystal City, with neatly paved roadways passing middle-class homes and some high-priced ranch houses. Then there is the other side of the track, where the Chicanos inhabit a collection of wooden shacks on unpaved, muddy streets.

José Ángel Gutiérrez was born in Crystal City in 1944, just after John Gunther had passed through Texas making interviews for *Inside U.S.A.* "Because I was a doctor's son in Crystal City," Gutiérrez explains, "I was respected by the Anglo people—I call them gringos now—and I was accepted by the Mexican people because I was Mexican, and I lived in the neighborhood." But then, when he was 12, his father died, and "all the respectability was lost, because I was just another Mexican." Everything seemed to underscore the racial issue for Gutiérrez. "I started having an interest in girls, and at that time, my concept of pretty was white—you know, a blond chick with blue eyes, etc., something I couldn't have. And when I started messing around with them, I got burned."

Gutiérrez got elected president of the student body, and saw how the faculty "balanced" the tickets to give Anglo children more than their share of school positions and honors. Then came the 1963 political movement of the local Mexican-Americans, with which Gutiérrez became involved as a teenager, and his first inflammatory oratory that led to a scuffle with the Texas

* The term has been traced to the Indians of Mexico, who pronounced *Mexicano* "Meh-chee-cano" and then shortened it to "chicano." The term still has a long way to go before it is accepted by those to whom it is applied. A 1972 survey of Spanish-speaking people in San Antonio turned up these percentages for various descriptors: Chicano 13.5 percent, Spanish-speaking 15.5 percent, Mexican 14.2 percent, American 18.7 percent, American of Mexican descent 25.5 percent, Latin 6.5 percent, Boricua 6.1 percent.

Rangers, who "proceeded to beat the crap out of me." Gutiérrez's only thought was "about getting revenge," but while he would have liked to do it physically, he finally decided another way would be "to get into the [Mexican-American] movement and really raise some hell."

Gutiérrez has been raising hell ever since, using skills of political organization, infiltration, and agitation which come to only a handful of people in any generation. At each of the several colleges and universities he attended, he organized the Chicano students to force concessions from ruling "gringo" administrations that were forever, by Gutiérrez's account, discriminating against Mexican-American students in forms both subtle and gross. It was hard for Gutiérrez to forget that at Uvalde Junior College, where he started out, he was labeled as a communist and atheist when he presumed to run, as a Chicano, for student body president. He received 89 votes—the precise number of Mexican-American students enrolled in a student body of 400. His tactics thereafter were a classic of minority group agitation to control a majority: packing of meetings, carefully planned appeals to the consciences of "liberal" Anglos, rewriting of student body constitutions through no little subterfuge, taking control of a student body newspaper by abusing the Anglo editor, illegal use of ID cards to vote several times in student elections.

By 1967, Gutiérrez and a small coterie of other like-minded young Chicanos were ready to start a full-scale movement in Texas. The trouble with the existing Mexican organizations, they decided, was that their programs "were not geared for the barrios." As Gutiérrez puts it, "we felt we were victims of cultural genocide. Everything we stood for—mariachi music, speaking Spanish, frijoles [beans] and tortillas, or being a Catholic—was wrong in the eyes of the 'system' ". So MAYO was formed, and while Gutiérrez somehow found time to get married, have a child, make a start on his Ph.D. program, and serve in the Army for four and a half months, a brilliant approach to getting money was devised. "We said, it's amazing how all of these flunkies have sat around here and not even tapped foundation life." So the MAYO organizers set up a group they called the Mexican-American Unity Council, called on some of the professors and politicians, and said "now we need to have you guys be our funding agency." At the same time, reports came of similar movements in New Mexico, Arizona, and California. And in New York, the Ford Foundation was beginning to feel that Mexican-Americans were the most disorganized and fragmented minority in American life and needed national organizations to serve their social, economic, and political needs. As a result, a New Southwest Council for La Raza was set up in Phoenix with $630,000 in Ford money, involving some of the region's most prominent Mexican-American leaders (including Albert Peña of San Antonio). The Southwest Council, in turn, channeled $110,000 to the Unity Council in San Antonio. Just as importantly, Ford gave $2.2 million to a new Mexican-American Legal Defense and Educational Fund (MALDEF), with national headquarters in San Antonio. Ford's idea was that the Southwest Council would be like the NAACP, the MALDEF like the NAACP Legal Defense and Educational Fund.

Whatever New York thought, Gutiérrez and his friends had their own plans. "Ford didn't have much choice in the matter," Gutiérrez told me. "It was one of those situations that either you come across with money and be able to plug us into the system or we just tear the hell out of everything out here." Not content with the Ford money, with which they put most of their associates on payrolls of one type or another, the MAYO group also appealed for and got major assistance from the federal "war on poverty" programs, Model Cities, and church groups.

Of all the Ford-funded activities, the legal fund (MALDEF) developed as the least controversial. By April 1970, it claimed it was involved in 155 cases affecting 100,000 Chicanos from Texas to California—an historic legal breakthrough for a chronically unrepresented and discriminated-against people. But other MAYO activities, generally directed by Gutiérrez, ran into some trouble. There was an effort, at Peña's urging, to get involved in local elections, giving clandestine support to a Republican candidate against Henry González and trying to elect some of their own number to the city council. Both efforts failed, after arousing the predictable storm of protest.

Then, in spring 1969, Gutiérrez began to resort to some highly inflammatory oratory. The enemy of all Chicanos, he proclaimed, was the "gringo" —that brand of Anglo who "has a certain policy or program or attitude that reflects bigotry, racism, discord, prejudice, and violence." Usually Gutiérrez talked of fighting the gringo politically or economically, but he also said: "We have got to eliminate the gringo, and what I mean by that is if the worst comes to the worst, we have got to kill him."

The rough language was an invitation to counterattack, and Congressman González quickly grasped the opportunity. In a series of speeches on the House floor in Washington, González said the Ford Foundation was supporting a group of "Brown Bilbos" practicing a "new racism" in Texas.

González now claims that he blew the whistle on MAYO just in time. "The only reason you haven't read a headline—'Violent Revolution in San Antonio—Men Shot'—is that I staved them off."

Finally, in June 1969, Ford officials summoned Peña, Gutiérrez, Velázquez, and others involved in the La Raza operation to a meeting in the foundation's great glass house by the East River in New York. There was reportedly a stormy session in which Mitchell Sviridoff, Ford's national affairs director, bluntly announced no more Ford money would go to MAYO. Peña told Sviridoff what he could do with all $3 billion of the foundation's assets.

A mere reduction in foundation money, however, was not to silence José Ángel Gutiérrez, a supremely self-confident young man, reveling in his own powers of organization, leadership, oratory, agitation. (He is also an extremely pleasant person to talk with, and it seems hard to imagine him following through on his murderous threats. Despite the oratory, in fact, MAYO's activities had not led to violence up to 1971.)

Where would he like to see his whole movement in five years time, I asked Gutiérrez. "All over the Southwest," he replied. "And we're going to—that is, if I can stay alive."

As a first step, Gutiérrez returned to Crystal City and organized a massive student boycott at the local schools against mean and petty racial policies. Then, in 1970, Gutiérrez shifted his organizing skills to his new Chicano political party—La Raza Unida. For many Chicanos, the old love affair with the Democratic party was out of date. As one labor official put it, "When President Kennedy and Bob Kennedy died, the Democrat party died for the Mexican-Americans in Texas." A new party would provide a point of racial pride for Chicanos. It would be able (they hoped) to seize power in Mexican-majority counties and exercise a bargaining power in major statewide elections. The effort started well in spring 1970, when Raza Unida candidates indeed won control of the school boards in Crystal City—Gutiérrez himself becoming school board president—and in nearby Carrizo Springs and Cotulla.

By 1972, Raza Unida was able—by the petition route—to qualify itself for the statewide Texas ballot, nominating candidates for governor and four other posts. Ironically, the Chicanos who abstained from the spring Democratic primaries, so that they would be eligible to sign Raza Unida's petitions, were numerous enough to account for the defeat of several liberal Mexican-American leaders, including Peña and state senator Joe Bernal in San Antonio.

In the autumn election, the party's dynamic gubernatorial candidate, 29-year-old San Antonio lawyer Ramsey Muniz, got more than 200,000 votes (6 percent of the total). Muniz drew enough support to make Dolph Briscoe the first Texas governor in 78 years to be elected with less than a majority of the popular vote. Muniz predicted that Raza Unida would soon be up to 10 percent of the vote so that "we'll decide every governor's race from here on out."

In local elections, the party was electing a number of officeholders in overwhelming Chicano South Texas counties like Zavala and LaSalle. But even in the heaviest Latin areas of South Texas and the lower Rio Grande Valley, the vote for statewide offices showed Raza Unida trailing far behind the major parties.

In the meantime, the founding convention of a national-level La Raza Unida had been held in September 1972 in El Paso, with delegates present from 16 states. The raucous convention sessions were marked by a demand for complete Chicano community control and rhetoric against the "gringo" whom Gutiérrez said "has divided us, raped us, robbed us, and repressed us." The party refused to endorse any Presidential candidate; in fact Gutiérrez, elected La Raza's first national chairman, counseled Chicanos not to vote for President at all. Available evidence suggests that only a small percentage of Mexican-Americans followed that advice.

Thus La Raza Unida faces the same difficulties of all third parties and radical political movements—winning much publicity but few elections. Its second problem is that the number of counties which have actual Mexican-American majorities is limited. By rejecting membership in the dominant local political party (the Democratic), a Raza Unida contender forecloses his own possibility for election. And if past history is a guide, it may be impossible ever to form the Mexican-American vote into any kind of monolithic bloc. Texas Chicanos are by no means the unified, liberal group of voters which outsiders often assume them to be. Rather, they are members of a pluralistic and diverse culture, people whose roots may go back to the very early Southwest or to very recent migration from Mexico. They have always been split into myriad factions, a fact well illustrated by San Antonio, the biggest Mexican-American city of Texas, which for decades was the center of plots and counterplots by a heady variety of native Mexican factions ranging from Carranzistas and Óbregonistas to Villistas and Maderistas.

Traditionally, Texas Mexican-Americans have voted overwhelmingly Democratic in Presidential elections. But in 1972, the pattern shifted abruptly. In some strongly Latin counties of South Texas and in the Rio Grande Valley, the Nixon-Agnew ticket got as much as 65 percent of the vote. In the Texas cities, Mexican-Americans remained more Democratic, but there was a sharp split in the vote according to the economic status of Mexican-Americans. Low-income Chicano precincts went big for McGovern, but in middle- and upper-income areas, Nixon ran even, or even ahead. The Nixon administration had made a very active effort to woo the Spanish-speaking vote, appointing 51 Spanish-speaking persons to supergrade positions and pouring $20 million into projects for Mexican-American communities in Texas alone.

The ambivalence of the Latin vote is apparent in the Mexican-Americans sent to Congress from Texas. In San Antonio, the choice is a standard liberal like González. But the Mexican-American Congressman from the southernmost counties of the state, Eligio de la Garza, is an establishment man who votes a strongly conservative line in Washington—and has it accepted.

While a group like La Raza Unida may give Mexican-Americans a feeling of identity, the Latin politicians who hope to advance far must appeal beyond their own ethnic group. When González ran for the Democratic nomination for governor in 1958 and the U. S. Senate in 1961, he was apparently hurt by his name and ancestry, though he insists many non-Mexicans voted for him. Now he believes the day has come when a qualified Texas Mexican-American, with a moderate image and broad backing, could be elected statewide—especially if he ran as a team candidate with a gubernatorial candidate with the huge cash resources a contest requires.

The establishment politicians, of course, prefer a politician of González's complexion to the militants of La Raza Unida stripe. Lt. Gov. Ben Barnes told me: "Henry B. has done more for the Mexican-American than any other man in the United States. He was out on the floor of the (state) senate talking about these things 15 years ago while those kids were still in short pants. He'll come back to San Antonio . . . and he'll get 85 to 90 percent of the vote down there. A militant is never going to have any real political strength—I don't care whether he be black or white or Mexican-American."

The problem is that, down through history, the ideas and stimulation of militants have been necessary to make establishment politicians move. Without that kind of pressure, a suppressed people like the Mexican-Americans of Texas would stay down forever. And in political terms, one can now begin to foresee the issues around which Texan Chicanos will rally in the 1970s and beyond. There will be an increasingly sharp demand for an end to all forms of discrimination—in schools, in public and private employment, in contests for public office. Popular Mexican causes will also include higher minimum wage laws and stopping the flow of cheap labor from across the Rio Grande. No matter what measure one uses, the fruits of generations of deprivation abound in the Mexican-American community. According to the 1970 Census, Texas' Chicanos had only two-thirds the income of Texas Anglos, and proportionately two-and-a-half times as many lived in poverty. The average level of education was an appallingly low 7.3 years of school completed—substantially lower than Texas Negroes, and in fact the lowest level of any substantial population group in the entire United States.

Important strides are now being made in bilingual education, as more and more public schools offer Spanish from the first grade forward as a second language. A bilingual commission has been set up under the Texas Education Agency, partly funded by a federal grant and headed by a Chicano, Dr. Severo Gómez. Joe Frantz, a member of the commission, writes:

> I visited several primary grades in McAllen and Edinburg, both border towns, in which the children of migrants are being taught entirely in Spanish. A group of brighter kids you have seldom seen. An experiment was made in Brownsville of sending four kids from Anglo middle-class homes to schools on the Mexican side of the river to be instructed entirely in Spanish. These kids showed the same symptoms that have always plagued the young Latino in this country—disinterest, sullenness, trouble making, and so on.

The Mexican-Americans are likely to keep up their agitation for abolition of the 150-year-old Texas Ranger force, a group surrounded by mystique like few others in the world. The Rangers, Walter Prescott Webb once wrote, were men who "could ride straight up to death." But part of their historic work was to disperse Indians and Mexicans for the benefit of Anglo settlers, and critics maintain that the elite unit, now 83 men strong, remains in effect a private police force to protect the interest of the wealthy landholders and ranchers. Chicano politician Joe Bernal has labeled them "the Mexican-Americans' Ku Klux Klan." In 1970, the state advisory committee to the United States Commission on Civil Rights recommended the Rangers be disbanded because they had engendered "fear and bitterness" among Mexican-Americans. Capt. Clint Peoples, director of the Rangers, scoffed at the idea: "The people of Texas could never vote to abolish the Rangers and no legislature would stand for it," he said. "Abolish the Rangers? Why, that would be like tearing down the Alamo."

In social terms, it may be that the average Mexican-American is much closer to assimilation into the white culture than the militants' angry charges and demands would lead one to believe. With a decent income and ability to speak fluent English, Chicanos are at no overwhelming disadvantage in modern U.S.A., and can certainly exist like other minority groups which conform to most American norms while retaining traces of their distinctive cultural identity. "I resent the term 'brown power,' " says Dr. García, founder of the old GI Forum. "That sounds as if we were a different race. We're not. We're white. We should be Americans. But we should eat enchiladas and be proud of our names."

In 1970, *Newsweek* interviewed Peter Torres, Jr., a 36-year-old San Antonio politician who is close to the militants. Torres understands the stakes exceedingly well:

> Many Mexican-Americans believe you can't fight City Hall. You don't question the *patron*. You don't question police brutality. I grew up in a poor section of west San Antonio and I saw people beaten in the streets. If you were poor, you said, "*Que puede hacer uno?*"—What can one do? Well, the young people today aren't going to play patsy for the establishment. There's an awareness of something among the young people that is either going to make this country and take us on to greater glories—or destroy us.

ACKNOWLEDGMENTS

THESE BOOKS HAD TO BE, by their very character, a personal odyssey and personal task. But they would never have been possible without the kind assistance of hundreds of people. First there were those who encouraged me to go forward when the idea was first conceived: my wife Barbara (little imagining the long curtailments of family life that would ensue, and whose encouragement was vital throughout); my parents and other relatives; my editor, Evan W. Thomas, vice president and editor of W. W. Norton & Co.; John Gunther; my agent, Sterling Lord, and his assistant at that time, Jonathan Walton; Richard Kluger, Bernard Haldane, Roan Conrad, Joseph Foote, and William B. Dickinson; Thomas Schroth, then the editor, and Nelson Poynter, publisher of *Congressional Quarterly;* Richard M. Scammon, director of the Elections Research Center and coauthor of *The Real Majority;* and D. B. Hardeman, professor of political science and biographer of the late House Speaker Sam Rayburn. Later on, those who encouraged or helped me to keep the project moving included F. Randall Smith and Anthony C. Stout of the Government Research Company, publishers of the *National Journal.* A fellowship at the Woodrow Wilson International Center for Scholars provided intellectual and physical sustenance.

My very warmest thanks go to those who read the draft manuscript in its entirety: Evan W. Thomas; Russell L. Bradley; Jean Allaway; Frederick H. Sontag, public relations consultant of Montclair, N.J.; Kay Gauss Jackson, former critic for *Harper's Magazine;* Donald Kummerfeld of the First Boston Corporation; and copy editor Calvin Towle at W. W. Norton & Company. In addition, each of the state chapters was submitted to several persons living in, and having extensive knowledge of, the state in question. The returning corrections and amendments were immensely helpful. The names of those readers appear in the longer list of names below; I choose not to list them here lest someone hold them responsible for something said or unsaid in one of the chapters, and of course the full responsibility for that lies with me.

Various friends and associates helped with many of the details of research, and for that I am especially indebted to Oliver Cromwell, Monica Benderly, Barbara Hurlbutt, Richard Baker, Prentice and Alice Bowsher, Sarah Rohlfing, John Gibson, and DeMar and Claudia Teuscher. And without the cheery and efficient services of my typist, Merciel Dixon, the manuscript would never have seen the light of day at all. Rose Franco of W. W. Norton helped in innumerable ways; I am indebted to designer Marjorie Flock of the Norton organization; and credit goes to Russell Lenz, former chief cartographer of the *Christian Science Monitor,* for what I feel is the superb job he did on the state and city maps.

Across the country, people gave generously of their time to brief me on the developments of the past several years in their states and cities. I am listing those from the nine Great Plains States below, together with many people who helped with national and interstate themes. The names of some officials are included whom I had interviewed in the year or two prior to beginning work on this project, when the background from those interviews proved helpful with this book. To all, my sincerest thanks.

PERSONS INTERVIEWED

Affiliations of interviewees are as of time of author's interview with them.

AGNICH, Fred, J., Texas House Republican Leader and Republican National Committeeman, Dallas, Texas
ALLAWAY, Howard, National Aeronautics & Space Administration, Washington, D.C.
ANDERSON, John, Former Governor of Kansas and Chairman, Citizens Conference on State Legislatures, Kansas City, Mo.
ANDERSON, MERRILL, President, Iowa Farm Bureau, Des Moines, Iowa
ANDING, Thomas, Director, Upper Midwest Research & Development Council, Minneapolis, Minn.
ANGELIDES, John, City Hall Reporter, St. Louis *Globe-Democrat,* St. Louis, Mo.
ARMSTRONG, Robert Landis, Commissioner of General Land Office, State of Texas, Austin, Texas
BAGGETT, Bryce, State Senator, Oklahoma City, Okla.
BAILEY, Charles W., Editor, Minneapolis *Tribune,* Minneapolis, Minn.
BAIRD, Stuart G., Director, Information Services, Macalester College, St. Paul, Minn.
BALL, Edgar L., Legislative Representative, District 37, United Steelworkers of America, Houston, Texas
BARNES, Alan, Senior Research Associate, Texas Research League, Austin, Texas
BARNES, Ben, Lieutenant Governor, Austin, Texas
BARNETT, Robert, Legislative Assistant, Office of Governor Norbert Tiemann (Neb.)
BARABBA, Vincent, Chairman of the Board, Decision Making Information, Los Angeles, Calif.
BARRETT, James L., Attorney, Oklahoma City, Okla.
BARTLETT, Dewey F., Governor of Oklahoma
BEAN, Woodrow, Democratic Leader, El Paso, Texas
BENNETT, Charles L., Managing Editor, *Daily Oklahoman & Times,* Oklahoma City, Okla.
BERRA, Paul, City Treasurer and Democratic City Chairman, St. Louis, Mo.
BERRISFORD, Christopher, Headmaster, St. Mark's School, Dallas, Texas
BIGGS, William, Sr., Attorney, St. Louis, Mo.
BLATNIK, John A., U.S. Representative from Minnesota
BOLLING, Richard, U.S. Representative from Missouri
BORCHERT, John R., Professor of Geography, University of Minnesota, Minneapolis, Minn.
BOWEN, Richard L., President, University of South Dakota, Vermillion, S.D.
BOYD, William J. D., Assistant Director, National Municipal League, New York City
BRAUN, Rex, State Representative, Houston, Texas
BRODER, David S., Correspondent and Columnist, Washington *Post,* Washington, D.C.
BROWN, Richard, Texas Municipal League, Austin, Texas
BUDIG, Gene, Administrative Assistant to the Chancellor, University of Nebraska, Lincoln, Neb.
BURGER, Alvin A., Executive Director, Texas Research League, Austin, Texas
BUSBY, Horace, Former Presidential Assistant, Washington, D.C.
BYERS, Bo, Bureau Chief, Houston *Chronicle,* Austin, Texas
CAMP, John N. Happy, U.S. Representative from Oklahoma
CARR, Mrs. Billie, Chairman, Harris County Democrats, Houston, Texas
CASEMENT, Loren E., Assistant Professor, Department of Economics, University of Nebraska, Lincoln, Neb.
CASSELLA, William N., Jr., Executive Director, National Municipal League, New York City
CASTRO, Tony, Correspondent, Dallas *Morning News,* Dallas, Texas
CHOATE, Robert, National Institute of Public Affairs, Washington, D.C.
CHRISTIAN, George, Former Press Secretary to President Lyndon B. Johnson, Austin, Texas
CHRYSTAL, John, President, Iowa Savings Bank, Coon Rapids, Iowa
CLARK, James H., Jr., State Representative, Dallas, Texas
CLAY, William L., U.S. Representative from Missouri
CLEM, Alan, Professor of Government and Associate Director, Government Research Bureau, University of South Dakota, Vermillion, S.D.
COHN, Victor, Science and Medical Editor, The Washington *Post,* Washington, D.C.
CONRAD, Charles, *The Pioneer,* Bismarck, N.D.
CONRAD, Roan, Managing Editor, *The Pioneer,* Bismarck, N.D.
CONWAY, Jack, Director, Center for Community Change, Washington, D.C.
CORNELIUS, Samuel J., Director, Technical Assistance Agency, State of Nebraska, Lincoln, Neb.
COURSEN, Robert, Research Manager, Minneapolis *Star & Tribune,* Minneapolis, Minn.
COWAN, Howard, Vice President for Public Affairs, Public Service Company of Oklahoma, Tulsa, Okla.
CROSLEY, Carlton W., Crosley & Foster, Inc., Webster City, Iowa
CURRAN, Charles E., Kansas City Association of Trusts and Foundations, Kansas City, Mo.
DANIEL, John A., Attorney, San Antonio, Texas
DAVIS, Ilus W., Mayor, Kansas City, Mo.
DESSAUER, Phil, Associate Editor, Tulsa *World,* Tulsa, Okla.
DOBSON, Richard, Political Editor, Minot *Daily News,* Minot, N.D.
DODDS, William, Political Director, United Auto Workers, Washington, D.C.
DONNELLY, Owen, Administrative Assistant to Sen. George McGovern (S.D.)
DORNBUSH, Sturgis R., Vice President, E.C. Rhodes Co., Aberdeen, S.D.
DOUGHERTY, Bill, Democratic National Committeeman, Sioux Falls, S.D.
EAGLETON, Thomas F., U.S. Senator from Missouri
ECKER, Peder K., Attorney and Former Democratic State Chairman, Sioux Falls, S.D.
ECKHARDT, Bob, U.S. Representative from Texas

EISELE, Albert, Washington Correspondent, St. Paul *Pioneer Press & Dispatch*
EMMERICH, John, Editorial Page Editor, Houston *Chronicle*, Houston, Texas
EVANS, E. S., City Hall Reporter, St. Louis *Post-Dispatch*, St. Louis, Mo.
EXON, James, Governor of Nebraska
FARENTHOLD, Mrs. Frances, State Representative and Former Gubernatorial Candidate, Houston, Texas
FARR, George, Former Democratic State Chairman, Minneapolis, Minn.
FATH, Creekmore, Attorney and Democratic Campaign Leader, Austin, Texas
FELLMAN, Richard M., Attorney, Omaha, Neb.
FIKE, Stan, Administrative Assistant to Sen. Stuart Symington (Mo.)
FLACH, Jack, Political Editor, St. Louis *Globe-Democrat*, St. Louis, Mo.
FORSYTHE, Robert A., Attorney, Former Republican State Chairman, Minneapolis, Minn.
FRALEY, Frederick W. III, Attorney, Dallas, Texas
FRANTZ, Joe B., Director, Oral History Project, University of Texas, Austin, Texas
FRANZENBURG, Paul, Former Lieutenant Governor, West Des Moines, Iowa
FRASER, Donald, U.S. Representative from Minnesota
FRASIER, Thomas Dee, Attorney, Former Democratic City Chairman, Tulsa, Okla.
FREELAND, Roy, Secretary, Kansas Board of Agriculture, Topeka, Kan.
FREEMAN, David, Executive Director, Council on Foundations, New York City
FREEMAN, Orville, Secretary of Agriculture, Washington, D.C.
GARDNER, Bill, Bureau Chief, Houston *Post*, Austin, Texas
GARRIZON, Denzil, State Senator, Oklahoma City, Okla.
GARST, Roswell, Farmer, Coon Rapids, Iowa
GAUTHIER, Paul, Editor, Adams County *Free Press*, Corning, Iowa
GIBBONS, Harold, President, Missouri-Kansas Council of Teamsters, St. Louis, Mo.
GIBSON, D. Jack, Republican National Committeeman, Sioux Falls, S.D.
GONZÁLEZ, Henry B., U.S. Representative from Texas
GRAHAM, Evarts A., Managing Editor, St. Louis *Post-Dispatch*, St. Louis, Mo.
GREEN, J. Patrick, Attorney, Omaha, Neb.
GREVE, Don, President, Sequoya Mills, Oklahoma City, Okla.
GRIFFIN, John, Businessman and Republican Leader, Sioux Falls, S.D.
GUNTHER, John, Author, New York City (deceased)
GUNTHER, John, U.S. Conference of Mayors, Washington, D.C.
GUTIÉRREZ, Jose Angel, Mexican-American Youth Organization, San Antonio, and subsequently Founder and Chairman, La Raza Unida, Crystal City, Texas
GUY, William, Governor of North Dakota
HARDEMAN, D. B., Professor of Political Science and Former Research Assistant to House Speaker Sam Rayburn, Washington, D.C.
HARDING, Kenneth, Executive Director, House Democratic Congressional Committee, Washington, D.C.
HARRIS, Fred R., U.S. Senator from Oklahoma
HAYDEN, Mrs. Iola, Director, Oklahomans for Indian Opportunity, Norman, Okla.
HAYSBROOK, Robert, Senior Vice President, U.S. National Bank, Omaha, Neb.
HEARNES, Warren, Governor of Missouri
HELLER, Donna, Former President, Kansas League of Women Voters, Lawrence, Kan.
HELLER, Francis H., Vice Chancellor for Academic Affairs, University of Kansas, Lawrence, Kan.
HERMAN, Dick, Political Editor, Lincoln *Journal*, Lincoln, Neb.
HESS, Robert, Administrative Assistant, Office of Rep. Joseph Karth (Minn.), and Former Executive Vice President, Minnesota AFL-CIO
HILL, Peter, Artist, Faculty Member, University of Nebraska, Omaha, Neb.
HOBBY, William, Executive Editor, The Houston *Post*, and Lieutenant Governor-elect, Houston, Texas
HOFFMAN, Hattie Belle, Van Cronkhite & Maloy, Inc., Dallas, Texas
HOLMES, The Rev. Zan. W., State Representative, Dallas, Texas
HOWE, Woodson, City Editor, Omaha *World-Herald*, Omaha, Neb.
HUGHES, Harold E., U.S. Senator from Iowa
HURLEY, Marvin, Executive Vice President, Houston Chamber of Commerce, Houston, Texas (deceased)
IKARD, Frank, President, American Petroleum Institute, Washington, D.C.
JANUREK, Tony, Plant Guide, Morrell & Company, Sioux Falls, S.D.
JENSEN, Dwight, Press Secretary to Sen. Harold Hughes (Iowa)
JENSEN, Samuel, Attorney, Omaha, Neb.
JESSEE, Randall, Director, Division of Public Affairs, U.S. Environmental Protection Agency, Iowa-Kansas-Missouri Region, Kansas City, Mo.
JOHNSON, Nicholas, Commissioner, Federal Communications Commission, Washington, D.C.
JONES, Jenkin Lloyd, Sr., Editor, Tulsa *Tribune*, Tulsa, Okla.
JONSSON, J. Erik, Mayor of Dallas, Texas, and 1972 Chairman, Texas Committee for the Reelection of the President
JORDAN, Barbara, State Senator, Houston, Texas
JUSTICE, Blair, Head, Human Relations Division, Office of the Mayor, Houston, Texas
KANTOR, MacKinlay, Author, Sarasota, Fla., native of Webster City, Iowa
KARRIGAN, Ellsworth, Associate Editor, Aberdeen *American-News*, Aberdeen, S.D.
KELLY, Mike, Press Secretary to Sen Thomas Eagleton (Mo.)
KERR, William G., Business Executive, Oklahoma City, Okla.
KILGORE, Joe M., Former U.S. Representative, Austin, Texas
KINGMAN, Joseph R. III, Senior Vice President, First National Bank of Minneapolis, Minneapolis, Minn.
KIRKLAND, Lane, Secretary-Treasurer, AFL-CIO, Washington, D.C.
KOLDERIE, Ted, Executive Director, Citizens League, Minneapolis, Minn.
KRUPNICK, Samuel, Krupnick & Associates, St. Louis, Mo.
KUTAK, Robert J., Attorney, Omaha, Neb.
LANDON, Alf M., Former Governor and Presidential Candidate, Topeka, Kan.
LANIER, Robert, Democratic Fund Raiser and Officer, Main Bank & Trust Co., Houston, Texas
LATTING, William, Mid-Continent Oil & Gas Assn., Tulsa, Okla.
LEE, Ralph, Chief Etdiorial Writer, *Daily Oklahoman & Times*, Oklahoma City, Okla.
LEHRER, Jim, KERA-TV, Dallas, Texas
LINDECKE, Fred, Political Editor, St. Louis *Post-Dispatch*, St. Louis, Mo.

LONG, Stuart, Long News Service, Austin, Texas
MABRY, Drake, Assistant Managing Editor, Des Moines *Tribune,* Des Moines, Iowa
MacDONALD, Kenneth, Editor & Publisher, Des Moines *Register & Tribune,* Des Moines, Iowa
MARGOLIS, Larry, Executive Director, Citizens Conference on State Legislatures, Kansas City, Mo.
MacGREGOR, Clark, Counsel to the President for Congressional Relations, Former U.S. Representative from Minnesota
MATTHEWS, Steve, Executive Director, Texas Municipal League, Austin, Texas
MAVERICK, Maury, Jr., Attorney, San Antonio, Texas
McCARNEY, Robert, President, McCarney Ford, Bismarck, N.D.
McCUE, George, Art & Architecture Writer, St. Louis *Post-Dispatch,* St. Louis, Mo.
McDOWELL, Joseph H., Mayor, Kansas City, Kan.
McGANNITY, Dr. William, University of Texas Medical Branch, Galveston, Texas
McGEE, Dean A., Chairman of the Board, Kerr-McGee Corporation, Oklahoma City, Okla.
McNUTT, Gale, Correspondent, Houston *Chronicle,* Houston, Texas
McGONIGLE, George, Model Cities Director, Houston, Texas
McGREW, James W., Research Director, Texas Research League, Austin, Texas
McPHERSON, Harry C., Jr., Special Counsel to the President (Lyndon B. Johnson), Washington, D.C.
McQUAID, Joseph, Assistant City Editor, Minneapolis *Star & Tribune,* Minneapolis, Minn.
MERTENS, Ronald J., Nebraska Department of Economic Development, Lincoln, Neb.
MILLS, George, Political Writer, Des Moines *Tribune,* Des Moines, Iowa
MITAU, G. Theodore, Chancellor, Minnesota State College System, St. Paul, Minn.
MODLIN, Dr. Herbert, Director, Department of Preventive Psychology, The Menninger Foundation, Topeka, Kan.
MONDALE, Walter F., U.S. Senator from Minnesota
MONROE, Jim, Legislative Assistant to Sen. Fred R. Harris (Okla.)
MOORE, Joe G., Jr., Commissioner, Federal Water Pollution Control Administration, Department of the Interior, Washington, D.C.
MOORE, Stanley, Secretary-Treasurer, North Dakota Farmers Union, Jamestown, N.D.
MOOS, Malcolm, President, University of Minnesota, Minneapolis, Minn.
MOREHEAD, Richard, Austin Correspondent, Dallas *Morning News,* Austin, Texas
MORGAN, Ray, Kansas Political Writer, Kansas City *Star,* Kansas City, Mo.
MURRY, C. Emerson, Director, North Dakota Legislative Council, Bismarck, N.D.
NAFTALIN, Arthur, Former Mayor of Minneapolis, Professor of Public Affairs, University of Minnesota, Minneapolis, Minn.
NORDSTROM, Carl C., Assistant General Manager and Research Director, Kansas State Chamber of Commerce, Topeka, Kan.
O'BRIEN, Ed, Correspondent, Washington Bureau, St. Louis *Globe-Democrat*
OWENS, Edris, United Auto Workers, Des Moines, Iowa
PALM, Mrs. Nancy, Chairman, Harris County Republican Committee, Houston, Texas
PARKER, Lawrence K., Manager, Parade Homes, Kansas City, Mo.
PARKER, Paul L., Vice President, Employee and Public Relations, General Mills, Inc., Minneapolis, Minn.
PEACE, John, Attorney, Houston, Texas
PEARSON, James B., U.S. Senator from Kansas
PEIRCE, Frederic M., Chairman of the Board, General American Life Insurance Company, and Chairman, Federal Reserve Board, St. Louis, Mo.
PEÑA, Albert A., Jr., Commissioner, San Antonio, Texas
PETERSON, Wallace, Chairman, Department of Economics, University of Nebraska, Lincoln, Neb.
PFAUTCH, Roy, Civic Services Inc., St. Louis, Mo.
PITSTICK, William J., Executive Director, North Central Texas Council of Governments, Arlington, Texas
POHLENZ, Dean, Administrative Assistant to Sen. Roman L. Hruska (Neb.)
POTTER, Todd, Director, Bureau of Employment Security, Department of Labor, Washington, D.C.
PROCTOR, Alvin, Vice President for Academic Affairs, Kansas State College, Pittsburg, Kan.
QUIE, Albert H., U.S. Representative from Minnesota
QUINN, Donald, Director of Communications, Citizens Conference on State Legislatures, Kansas City, Mo.
RAMIREZ, Henry M. Chairman, Cabinet Committee on Opportunities for Spanish-Speaking Peoples, Washington, D.C.
RAPAPORT, Bernard, Democratic Fund Raiser and President, American Life Insurance Co., Waco, Texas
RAY, Robert, Governor of Iowa
REEDY, George, Former Press Secretary to President Lyndon B. Johnson, Washington, D.C.
RHODES, E. C., President, E. C. Rhodes Company, Aberdeen, S.D.
RHODES, Jack A., Director, State Legislative Council, Oklahoma City, Okla.
ROBINSON, Clark, Former President, North Dakota Farm Bureau, Cole Harbor, N.D.
ROOS, Lawrence K., Supervisor, St. Louis County, Clayton, Mo.
RUDDY, Robert, Legislative Assistant to Sen. Karl Mundt (S.D.)
SCAMMON, Richard M., Director, Elections Research Institute, and Former Director of the Census, Washington, D.C.
SCHAFER, Harold, President, Gold Seal Company, Bismarck, N.D.
SCHEMP, Clark, Superintendent of Schools, Leola, S.D.
SCHMITT, Henry J., Publisher, Aberdeen *American-News,* Aberdeen, S.D.
SCHNAIDT, Otto, Dentist, Leola, S.D.
SCHRADER, George R., Assistant City Manager, Dallas, Texas
SEARS, Hess T., Secretary, Equitable Life Insurance Co. of Iowa, Des Moines, Iowa
SHELLUM, Bernie, Correspondent, Minneapolis *Tribune,* Minneapolis, Minn.
SHOCKLEE, Father John, St. Bridgit's Church, St. Louis, Mo.
SIDEY, Edwin, Editor, Adair County *Free Press,* Greenfield, Iowa
SIGMAN, Robert, Missouri Political Writer, Kansas City *Star,* Kansas City, Mo.
SMITH, Ed W., President, North Dakota Farmers Union, Jamestown, N.D.
SMITH, Henry, Public Information Office, Bureau of the Census, Washington, D.C.
SNEED, Earl, Executive Vice President, Liberty National Bank & Trust Co., Oklahoma City, Okla.
SONTAG, Frederick H., Public Relations Consultant, Montclair, N.J.
SORENSON, A.V., Former Mayor, Omaha, Neb.

SPILHAUS, Athelstan, President, American Association for the Advancement of Technology; former Dean, Institute of Technology, University of Minnesota

STANDARD, Jim, Political Writer, *Daily Oklahoman & Times,* Oklahoma City, Okla.

STOCKTON, Dr. John, Texas Research League, Austin, Texas

STRASBAUGH, Paul, Executive Director, Oklahoma City Chamber of Commerce, Oklahoma City, Okla.

STRAUSS, Robert, Democratic National Committeeman, Dallas, Texas

SULLIVANT, Otis, Former Political Editor, *Daily Oklahoman & Times,* Oklahoma City, Okla.

TAYLOR, Monte, County Election Commissioner, Omaha, Neb.

TIEMANN, Norbert, Governor of Nebraska

TUCKER, Ray, Former Mayor, St. Louis, Mo. (deceased)

URBAN, Thomas N., Mayor, Des Moines, Iowa

VAN CRONKHITE, John, Van Cronkhite & Maloy, Inc., Dallas, Texas

VAN NOSTRAND, Morris, State Representative and Editorial Page Editor, *The Nonpareil,* Council Bluffs, Iowa

WADSWORTH, Homer C., President, Kansas City Assn. of Trusts & Foundations, Kansas City, Mo.

WALSH, Travis, Managing Editor, Tulsa *World,* Tulsa, Okla.

WHITE, John C. Commissioner of Agriculture, State of Texas, Austin, Texas

WHITNEY, Wheelock, Investment Banker, Minneapolis, Minn.

WIECK, Paul, Correspondent, Albuquerque *Journal,* Washington, D.C.

WILLIAMS, Joe B., Research Consultant, Elmwood, Neb.

WILSON, Larry, Political Editor, Omaha *World-Herald,* Omaha, Neb.

WOLFE, Kenneth, State Senator, St. Louis Park, Minn.

WRIGHT, Frank, Washington Correspondent, Minneapolis *Star & Tribune*

WRIGHT, Jim, U.S. Representative from Texas

WRIGHT, M.A., Chairman of the Board, Humble Oil & Refining Company, Houston, Texas

YARBOROUGH, Ralph, U.S. Senator from Texas

YOUNG, Douglas, Executive Director, Minnesota Environmental Controls Citizens Association, St. Paul, Minn.

YOUNG, Jim, Political Writer, Daily *Oklahoman & Times,* Oklahoma City, Okla.

YOUNGBLOOD, Richard, Business Editor, Minneapolis *Star & Tribune,* Minneapolis, Minn.

BIBLIOGRAPHY

DESPITE THE EXTENSIVE INTERVIEWS for these books, reference was also made to books and articles on the individual states and cities, their history and present-day condition. To the authors whose works I have drawn upon, my sincerest thanks.

NATIONAL BOOKS

Barone, Michael, Ujifusa, Grant, and Matthews, Douglas. *The Almanac of American Politics—1972.* Boston: Gambit Publishing Co., 1972.

Book of the States. The Council of State Governments. Published biennially, Lexington, Ky.

Brownson, Charles B. *Congressional Staff Directory.* Published annually, Washington, D.C.

1969 Census of Agriculture, Bureau of the Census, Washington, D.C.

1970 Census of Population, Bureau of the Census, Washington, D.C.

Citizens Conference on State Legislatures. Various studies including *The Sometime Governments: A Critical Study of the 50 American Legislatures,* by John Burns. New York: Bantam Books, 1971.

Congress and the Nation, 1945–64, and Vol. II, *1965–68.* Congressional Quarterly Service, Washington, D.C., 1967 and 1969.

David, Paul T., *Party Strength in the United States,* 1872–1970 (Charlottesville: University Press of Virginia, 1972).

Editor and Publisher International Year Book. New York: Editor and Publisher. Published annually.

Employment and Earnings—States and Areas, 1939–69. U.S. Department of Labor, Bureau of Labor Statistics, Washington, D.C., 1970.

Encyclopedia Americana. Annual editions. New York: Americana Corporation. (Includes excellent state and city review articles.)

Farb, Peter. *Face of North America—The Natural History of a Continent.* New York: Harper & Row, 1963.

Fodor-Shell Travel Guides U.S.A. Fodor's Modern Guides, Inc., Litchfield, Conn. (In several regional editions, the best of the travel guides.)

From Sea to Shining Sea—A Report on the American Environment—Our Natural Heritage. President's Council on Recreation and Natural Beauty, Washington, D.C., 1968.

Gunther, John. *Inside U.S.A.* New York: Harper & Row, 1947 and 1951.

Life Pictorial Atlas of the World. Editors of *Life* and Rand McNally. New York: Time, Inc., 1961.

McPherson, Harry. *A Political Education.* Boston: Little Brown, 1972.

The National Atlas of the United States of America. Geological Survey, U.S. Department of the Interior, Washington, D.C., 1970.

Pearson, Drew, and Anderson, Jack. *The Case Against Congress.* New York: Simon & Schuster, 1968.

Phillips, Kevin H. *The Emerging Republican Majority.* New Rochelle, N.Y.: Arlington House, 1969.

Rankings of the States. Published annually by the Research Division, National Education Assn., Washington, D.C.

Ridgeway, James. *The Closed Corporation—American Universities in Crisis.* New York: Random House, 1968.

Saloma, John S. III, and Sontag, Frederick H. *Parties: The Real Opportunity for Effective Citizen Politics.* New York: Knopf, 1972.

Sanford, Terry. *Storm Over the States.* New York: McGraw-Hill, 1967.

Scammon, Richard M., ed. *America Votes—A Handbook of Contemporary American Election Statistics.* Published biennially by the Governmental Affairs Institute, through Congressional Quarterly, Washington, D.C.

Scammon, Richard M., and Wattenberg, Ben J. *The Real Majority—An Extraordinary Examination of the American Electorate.* New York: Coward-McCann, 1970.

State and Local Finances. Published periodically by the Advisory Commission on Intergovernmental Relations, Washington, D.C.

State Government Finances. Published annually by the U.S. Department of Commerce, Bureau of the Census, Washington, D.C.

Statistical Abstract of the United States. Published annually by the U.S. Department of Commerce, Bureau of the Census, Washington, D.C.

Steinbeck, John. *Travels With Charley—In Search of America.* New York: Viking, 1961.

Steiner, Stan. *La Raza—The Mexican-Americans.* New York: Harper & Row, 1969.

Survey of Current Business. U.S. Department of Commerce, Office of Business Economics, Washington, D.C., monthly. August editions contain full reports on geographic trends in personal income and per capita income.

Thayer, George. *The Farther Shores of Politics.* New York: Simon & Schuster, 1967.

These United States—Our Nation's Geography, History and People. Reader's Digest Assn., Pleasantville, N.Y., 1968.

Tour Books. Published annually by the American Automobile Assn., Washington, D.C.

Uniform Crime Reports for the United States. Published annually by the U.S. Department of Justice, Federal Bureau of Investigation, Washington, D.C.

Whyte, William H. *The Last Landscape.* Garden City, N.Y.: Doubleday, 1968.

Williams, Joe B. *U.S. Statistical Atlas.* Published biennially at Elmwood, Neb.

The World Almanac and Book of Facts. Published annually by Newspaper Enterprise Assn., Inc., New York and Cleveland.

REGIONAL BOOKS AND SOURCES

Walter Prescott Webb's *The Great Plains* (Boston: Ginn, 1931), is still the classic work on this region of the country. An excellent modern review of many aspects of the region's life appears in *The Plains States* by Evan Jones and others (New York: Time-Life Library of America, 1968); this volume includes William Inge's sensitive introduction on the character of these states and their people.

Other sources referred to include "Grass," by William Cotter Murray, *American Heritage,* April 1968; "Quiet Falls Across the Plains," by Dale Wittner, *Life,* June 25, 1971; "The Dust Bowl in the 1970s," by John R. Borchert, *Annals of the Association of American Geographers,* March 1971; "Farm Education: The Obsolete Dream Machine," by Lauren Soth, *The Nation,* May 31, 1971; "Revolutionary Change in the Nation's Largest Business," by Nick Kotz, Washington *Post,* Nov. 29, 1971; "Clinging to Way of Life, A Farm Family Fights for Economic Survival," by Susan B. Miller, *Wall Street Journal,* Dec. 28, 1971; "That Dammed Missouri River," by Gordon Young, *National Geographic,* September 1971; "A Storm Roils the Mississippi," by David W. Hacker, *National Observer,* Dec. 28, 1970; "Plain Talk from Kansas" and "New Plain Talk from Kansas," by Alf M. Landon, New York *Times,* Nov. 30, 1970, and Feb. 1, 1971.

MISSOURI

Irving Dilliard's perceptive analysis of Missouri and its personality is from *I'm From Missouri: Where Man and Mule Shaped the Heart of a Nation* (New York: Hastings House, 1952), with photographs by Allyson Painter and text by Dilliard. A very informal treatment of the state's character is MacKinlay Kantor's *Missouri Bittersweet* (Garden City, N.Y.: Doubleday, 1969). The best work I found on the state's politics is the Missouri chapter of *Politics in the Border States* by John H. Fenton (New Orleans: The Hauser Press, 1957). An excellent summary of the state's regions and their politics, "Missouri Presidential Elections, 1916–60," by Clyde Burch, was inserted in the *Congressional Record,* page A825, on Feb. 2, 1962.

Missouri's three major newspapers—the St. Louis *Post-Dispatch,* St. Louis *Globe-Democrat,* and Kansas City *Star*—all provide ongoing coverage of state and city affairs heavily relied upon in this chapter. In addition, the following articles provided important background and quotes:

HISTORY, GEOGRAPHY, ECONOMY "Missouri—A National Composite," *Fortune,* July 1945; "A Little of Everything—Missouri," New York *Times,* Oct. 4, 1956; "Where the Trails Began," by Gayle P.W. Jackson, "1,160 Civil War Encounters in Missouri," by Jacob H. Wolfe, "Rivers Gave Missouri Early Economic Boost," by L. Brewster Jackson, "Backroads Customs Go Back to Frontier," "Economic Potential Not Being Realized," by William H. Kester, "Springfield Is Gateway to Lake Resort Areas," "Industry Diversified in Joplin," "Past Is Present in St. Charles," and "The Family Farm Remains, but with New Technology," by Wayne Leeman, all articles in the St. Louis *Post-Dispatch,* Aug. 8, 1971; "How They See It in Hannibal, Mo.," by Harold B. Meyers, *Fortune,* December 1969.

GOVERNMENT, POLITICS "School Funds Hiked at Expense of Welfare, Health," "State Colleges In A Fiscal Bind," and "State Hopes for U.S. Aid to Avert Tax Hikes," by Fred W. Lindecke, St. Louis *Post-Dispatch,* Jan. 23, 24, and 25, 1972; "Campus Vexed at Plan to Split Missouri U.," by Dana L. Spitzer, St. Louis *Post-Dispatch,* Dec. 19, 1971; "Missouri's Freedom of Information Center," by M.L. Stein, *Saturday Review,* March 13, 1971; "Fight To Depose State as Billboard King," by Donald Tapperson, St. Louis *Post-Dispatch,* Jan. 30, 1972; "Broad Support from Young People," interview with Christopher S. ("Kit") Bond, *U.S. News & World Report,* Nov. 20, 1972; "New Face," by Alan L. Otten, *Wall Street Journal,* September 1972.

"The Dawn of Danforth," by Peter Benchley of *Newsweek* in Seattle *Post-Intelligencer,* April 4, 1969; "Young Lawyer-Priest Battles Symington," by James M. Perry, *National Observer,* Sept. 21, 1970; "Senator Benton Was a Political Giant," St. Louis *Post-Dispatch,* Aug. 8, 1971; "Stu Symington: The Path of a High-Level 'Defector,'" by Ward Just, Washington *Post,* April 7, 1969; "The Education of a Senator," by Flora Lewis, *Atlantic Monthly,* December 1971; "Rep. Hungate Quits D.C. Panel in Protest," by David R. Boldt, Washington *Post,* Dec. 11, 1971.

ST. LOUIS "St. Louis," by Robert Paul Jordan, *National Geographic,* November 1965; "Total City, U.S.A.," *Newsweek,* Feb. 26, 1968; "St. Louis: Can the Decay Be Stopped?" by Monroe W. Karmin, *Wall Street Journal,* March 2, 1972; "Prestigious University Club Moving to County," by Olivia Skinner, St. Louis *Post-Dispatch,* Feb. 23, 1972; "St. Louis Riverfront Coming Back to Life," by Sue Ann Wood, St. Louis *Globe-Democrat,* April 20–21, 1968; "St. Louis Board Approves Laclede's Landing Renewal," *Preservation News,* June 1969; "Mod Plan for Dowager Depot," by Robert E. Hannon, *St. Louis*

Commerce, October 1971; "St. Louis Pruitt-Igoe Called 'National Disgrace,'" *Human Events,* June 8, 1968 (based on coverage by Larry Fields in the St. Louis *Globe-Democrat*); "Public Housing: 'It Makes Animals Out of People,'" by Robert C. Maynard, Washington *Post,* Dec. 16, 1969; "The Case History of a Housing Failure," by John Herbers, New York *Times,* Nov. 2, 1970; "Arson for Profit Held Spur to Cities' Decline," by Andrew Wilson, Washington *Post,* Nov. 22, 1971; "Trouble with the Rubble" and "St. Louis Votes End to All Public Housing," by Andrew Wilson, Washington *Post,* Oct. 5 and Nov. 12, 1972.

"St. Louis: Transportation Gateway to the World," *St. Louis Commerce,* December 1971; "Now: Traffic Jams on U.S. Rivers," *U.S. News & World Report,* Sept. 20, 1971; "St. Louis Makes the World Move," by Al Foster, *St. Louis Commerce,* October 1971; "Competing Like Tigers in a Troubled Company" (about Monsanto), *Fortune,* November 1971; "Shoe Worker Trapped in Import Disaster Area," by Eugene A. Kelly, *AFL-CIO News,* July 3, 1971; "Rapid Transit Said to Offer Jobs, Money," St. Louis *Post-Dispatch,* Feb. 24, 1972.

"Bleak Picture of a City with Financial Woes," by John Angelides, St. Louis *Globe-Democrat,* Jan. 8, 1969; "The Mob—It Racks Up Overtime on a Government Payroll," and "A Two-Faced Crime Fight in St. Louis," by Denny Walsh, *Life,* Feb. 14, 1969, and May 29, 1970; "Shenker Quits Crime Panel," by Karen Van Meter, St. Louis *Post-Dispatch,* Jan. 28, 1972; "New Approaches to the Chronic Drunkenness Offenders," by David J. Pittman, *State Government,* Summer 1968.

"Harold J. Gibbons—Teamster Boss," by Sally Bixby Defty, St. Louis *Post-Dispatch,* May 11–14, 1969; "'Stripling' Deals Defeat to Long, St. Louis Union," by Charles Edmundson, Memphis *Commercial-Appeal,* Aug. 11, 1968; "New Steamfitter Boss Found Shot to Death," St. Louis *Post-Dispatch,* Feb. 25, 1972.

"Racial Division Problem Stays in Spotlight Here," by Robert Adams, St. Louis *Post-Dispatch,* March 23, 1969; "A New Way to Build with Blocks," by John G. Rogers, *Parade,* Dec. 14, 1969; "William Clay: A Militant with a Knack for Wins," *Ebony,* February 1969.

"St. Louis County Reform Clicks," by James M. Naughton, Cleveland *Plain Dealer,* Aug. 11, 1969; "Clayton: The Spectacular Growth of a Regional Center," by Shirley Althoff, St. Louis *Globe-Democrat,* Sept. 6, 1970; "Fail to Prevent Racial Discrimination in Suburbs of St. Louis," by Seth S. King, New York *Times,* Jan. 18, 1970; "Job, Housing Bias Found in St. Louis," by Robert C. Maynard, Washington *Post,* Jan. 25, 1970; "The Battle of the Suburbs," *Newsweek,* Nov. 15, 1971; "Bulldozers Turn Up Soil and Ill Will in a Suburb of St. Louis," by B. Drummond Ayers, Jr., New York *Times,* Jan. 18, 1971.

KANSAS CITY *The Pendergast Machine,* by Lyle W. Dorsett (New York: Oxford University Press, 1968); "Kansas City Has Its Chin Up," by Stanley High, *National Municipal Review,* October 1941; "Pendergast Front Caves In," by Dwight Pennington, *Christian Science Monitor,* Aug. 8, 1952; "Kansas City: Innovative, Friendly," St. Louis *Post-Dispatch,* Aug. 8, 1971; "Hallmark 'Cares Enough' to Help Redevelop Heart of Kansas City," Louisville *Courier-Journal and Times,* May 11, 1969; "U.S. Journal: Kansas City," by Calvin Trillin, *New Yorker,* May 11, 1968; "Kansas City Hurt by 196-Day Strike," New York *Times,* Oct. 18, 1970; "Downtown Hotel Era Fading," by B. Drummond Ayres, New York *Times,* Feb. 23, 1972; "Kansas City International—A New Era Dawns," by Richard Nenneman, *Christian Science Monitor,* Nov. 7, 1972; "Airport to Lift Economy Hopes," AP dispatch in Atlanta *Journal and Constitution,* Oct. 15, 1972.

IOWA

Numerous feature articles and regular coverage of the Des Moines *Register* provided invaluable background for the chapter, including a series by George Mills, "Iowa's Amazing Past," appearing between Sept. 14 and Nov. 9, 1969. Other articles providing useful information:

ECONOMY AND ENVIRONMENT "The Farmer's Lot," *Forbes,* Nov. 1, 1969; "Pipeline to Corn Belt," by Merelice K. England, *Christian Science Monitor,* May 15, 1971; "Now It's Beef and Mutton," *Newsweek,* Nov. 8, 1971; "Ask Action on Feedlot at Oakland," by Jerry Szumski, Des Moines *Register,* Sept. 7, 1969; "Iowa Balks at River Pollution Cleanup" and "Iowa Refuses U.S. Prescription for Curing Waterway Pollution," by Gladwin Hill, New York *Times,* April 7 and 21, 1969; "U.S. Orders Iowa: Clean Up the Rivers," by George Anthan, *National Observer,* Nov. 3, 1969; "You Won't Find Many Dying from Hunger but Malnutrition Is Very Large Even in Bountiful Iowa," by Mark Arnold, *National Observer,* Aug. 7, 1967. Various publications of the Iowa Development Commission provided numerous facts and figures.

GOVERNMENT, POLITICS "Iowa Reforms School Aid, Requires Conservation," *State Government News,* August 1971; "Iowa: Intra-Party Battle," *Ripon Forum,* September 1971; "Iowa General Assembly Completes Shortest Session," by Russell M. Roos, *National Civic Review,* May 1972.

"Harold E. Hughes: Evangelist from the Prairies," by Larry L. King, *Harper's Magazine,* March 1969; "Senator Hughes Urges Drug Law Overhaul," Washington *Post,* August 1969; "Sen. Hughes in the Slow Process of a Decision to Run," by David S. Broder, Washington *Post,* March 4, 1971; "Messiah from the Midwest?" by Nick Kotz and James Risser, *Washington Monthly,* May 1970; "For God and Country," by Paul R. Wieck, *New Republic,* May 15, 1971; "Hughes Quits as Presidential Aspirant," by R.W. Apple, Jr., New York *Times,* July 16, 1971.

"Iowa's Mr. Gross Wins Fame by Viewing Life with Jaundiced Eye," by Norman C. Miller, *Wall Street Journal,* 1969; "H.R. Gross: The Conscience of Uncle Sucker," by Jacques Leslie, *Washington Monthly,* August 1971; "Frustration of a Rural Republican," *Time,* Nov. 22, 1971.

OTHER "The Beautiful Land," New York *Times,* Sept. 30, 1956; "Starving in Iowa—for Affection," by Veryl Sanderson, Des Moines *Register,* Oct. 19, 1969; "Iowa's Dutch More Dutch than Dutch?" by Lillian T. Drake, *Christian Science Monitor,* May 25, 1971; "In Iowa City, Good Writing Thrives like Hybrid Corn," by B. Drummond Ayres, Jr., New York *Times,* Feb. 4, 1971; "Ames, Ia.," *U.S. News & World Report,* May 11, 1972; "Striking It Rich in Forest City," *Forbes,* June 1, 1972.

MINNESOTA

Minnesota is fortunate to have an excellent modern analysis of its political structure, *Politics in Minnesota,* by G. Theodore Mitau (University of Minnesota Press, 1960, 1970). A comprehensive but unexciting review of the state's past is *History of Minnesota* by Dean Blegen (University of Minnesota Press, 1963). A lively account of the 1966 DFL bloodletting, together with a good short political history of the DFL, appears in *The 21st Ballot,* by David Lebedoff (University of Minnesota Press, 1969). Another superior analysis of the state's politics appears in the Minnesota chapter of *Midwest Politics,* by John H. Fenton (New York: Holt, Rinehart & Winston, 1966). The small-city syndrome (St. Cloud in particular) is examined in *Micropolis In Transition: A Study of a Small City,* ed. Edward L. Henry (Collegeville, Minn.: Center for Study of Local Government, St. John's University, 1971); The Humphrey-McCarthy story is best told in *Almost to the Presidency: A Biography of Two American Politicians,* by Albert Eisele (Blue Earth, Minn.: The Piper Co., 1972).

The chapter relies heavily on regular coverage by the Minneapolis *Star* and *Tribune,* including the Minnesota Poll published therein and a short history of the *Tribune, Sunlight on Your Doorstep,* by Bradley L. Morison (Minneapolis: Ross & Haines, Inc., 1966). Also of use were various publications of the Citizens League, the Upper Midwest Research & Development Council, the Minnesota Department of Economic Development, and the Advisory Committee on Intergovernmental Relations (especially the 13th Annual Report, *Federalism in 1971: The Crisis Continues,* published in Washington, February 1972). Other sources consulted included:

GENERAL *The Minnesota Republican Neighbor-to-Neighbor Drive: Successful Small Gift Solicitation,* by Thomas L. Pahl (Princeton, N.J.: Citizens' Research Foundation, 1971); "Computing Democratic Winners in '72," by Alan L. Otten, *Wall Street Journal,* Dec. 11, 1970; "A 'Re-Baptism' for Gene McCarthy," by Austin C. Wehrwein, Washington *Post,* Jan. 9, 1972 (reprinted from Minneapolis *Star*); "Lindstrom Plans to Attack Conservative Business Ties," "Conservatives' Use of Funds Is Revealed," and "Report Warned of Lobbyist Ties to Conservatives," by Bernie Shellum, Minneapolis *Tribune,* April 16, 19, and 23, 1972; "Minnesota Launches a Press Council," by Alfred Balk, *Columbia Journalism Review,* November/December 1971; "Minnesota Press Forms a Council," by Seth S. King, New York *Times,* Jan. 30, 1972; "St. Cloud, Minn.: A Small City Faces Special Problems of Growth in the U.S.," by Seth S. King, New York *Times,* Nov. 25, 1971; "A Different Type of College: It Comes to the Student," *U.S. News & World Report,* Oct. 4, 1971; "Minnesota College with No Campus, Classrooms or Grades Opens," by Andrew M. Malcolm, New York *Times,* Feb. 4, 1972; "Mondale Seen as Presidential Prospect," by David S. Broder, Washington *Post,* Oct. 30, 1972.

ENVIRONMENT "Lake Pollution Minnesota Issue," by Seth S. King, New York *Times,* Feb. 15, 1970; "A Housewife Battles the Giants to Save a Great Lake's Beauty," by David W. Hacker, *National Observer,* Dec. 18, 1971; "EPA Chief Bucks GOP Donors," by Rowland Evans and Robert Novak, Washington *Post,* Dec. 30, 1971; "Snowmobile Transforms Once Quiet Rural Winter," by Andrew H. Malcolm, New York *Times,* Feb. 11, 1972; "Boon or Bane?", *Newsweek,* Jan. 24, 1972; "Public Fights A-Power," by Victor Cohn, Washington *Post,* Oct. 19, 1969.

TWIN CITIES "Strategies—Having Started with Sewers, the Twin Cities Council Goes After Tougher Regional Problems," and "Twin Cities—A Strong Sense of Regional Unity . . . ," by Ted Kolderie, *City,* August 1969 and January-February 1971; "Minnesota's Metropolitan Tax Pool," by Paul A. Gilje, *City,* Fall, 1971; " 'Metro' Government, Twin Cities-style," by Edmund Faltermayer, *Life,* Jan. 21, 1972; series on the "Minneapolis Decision Makers" and "St. Paul Decision Makers." by David Nimmer, Minneapolis *Star,* Dec. 2–12, 1968, and June 9–20, 1969.

"System Beats Genius Mayor," by William C. Barnard, Cleveland *Plain Dealer,* Feb. 5, 1969; "More Mayors Bow Out," and "Worries of the Blue-Collar Urban Voter," by Monroe W. Karmin, *Wall Street Journal,* April 21 and July 8, 1969; "In Politics, It's the New Populism," *Newsweek,* Oct. 6, 1969; "Minneapolis: Life Under Stenvig," *Newsweek,* June 4, 1971; "Minneapolis Re-elects Stenvig; Margin Is Better than 2½ to 1," by Seth S. King, New York *Times,* June 9, 1971; "What Finally Crippled the Cowles Empire," *Business Week,* Sept. 25, 1971; "The Last Look," *Time,* Sept. 27, 1971; "Jobs: Bringing the Plant to the Slums," by Timothy D. Schellhardt, *Wall Street Journal,* Oct. 22, 1969.

"St. Paul and the American Condition," by Midge Decter, *Harper's Magazine,* June 1969; "Booked for Travel: Going Home," by David Butwin, *Saturday Review,* Feb. 5, 1972; "3M: Little Drops of Water, Little Grains of Sand," *Forbes,* Sept. 1, 1969.

NORTH DAKOTA

North Dakota is fortunate to have an exceptionally perceptive modern history, *History of North Dakota* (Lincoln: University of Nebraska Press, 1966), by Elwyn B. Robinson, professor at the University of North Dakota. Robinson's book supplied a number of facts and quotes (such as those from Eric Sevareid) and suggested several lines of analysis of the state's character.

Other published sources of North Dakota background consulted: regular coverage of the Fargo *Forum,* Minot *Daily News* and *Morning Pioneer* (Mandan); several articles on North Dakota's state-owned enterprises and tourist potential by Dick Youngblood in the Minneapolis *Tribune,* Sept. 28 and Oct. 5, 1969; "An Englishman in North Dakota: Size Breeds Attitude," by Brian Goodey of the University of North Dakota, Fargo *Forum,* Nov. 10, 1968; "Thousands Flee the Towns of America's Lonely Plains," by Douglas E. Kneeland, New York *Times,* Feb. 14, 1971; "Idea of Taking 'North' Out of North Dakota Reaches Serious Stage," Fargo *Forum,* May 27, 1970; "Coal Men Rush to Bountiful Western Fields," by Thomas Lindley Enrich, *Wall Street Journal,* Nov.

11, 1970; Chapter 3 (about the Fort Berthold Indians) in *Dams and other Disasters,* by Arthur E. Morgan (Boston: Porter Sargent, 1971).

"North Dakota: No Registration Required," *National Journal,* Sept. 18, 1971; "NPL Crosses Fence in North Dakota Politics," by Robert C. Albrook, Washington *Post,* 1956; "TV Blitz on the Prairies," by George Lardner, Jr., Washington *Post,* Oct. 28, 1970; "North Dakota Exposed to a Heavy Barrage," by Nick Kotz, Washington *Post,* Nov. 22, 1970.

"More Educators Endorse Informal Classrooms," by Richard Martin, *Wall Street Journal,* Dec. 1, 1970; "North Dakota Moves to Make Elementary Education Less Rigid," by William K. Stevens, New York *Times,* Oct. 11, 1970; "Experimental School in North Dakota Trains Teachers to Transform Classrooms," by Vito Perrone, New York *Times,* Jan. 11, 1971; "Promise of Change in North Dakota," by Henry S. Resnik, *Saturday Review,* April 17, 1971.

SOUTH DAKOTA

Prairie State Politics (Washington: Public Affairs Press, 1967), by Alan L. Clem, is not only the best book on South Dakota's politics but also has excellent insights into the state's character. Somewhat more recent data appeared in the *South Dakota Political Almanac,* also by Clem (Vermillion: The Dakota Press, University of South Dakota, 1969). Reference was also made to Herbert S. Schell, *History of South Dakota* (Lincoln: University of Nebraska Press, 1961).

Other sources included regular coverage of the Sioux Falls *Argus-Leader* and Aberdeen *American-News* and the following articles:

"The 1968 Election in South Dakota" and "The 1970 Election in South Dakota," by Alan L. Clem, *Public Affairs* (Government Research Bureau, University of South Dakota), February 1969 and February 1971; "McGovern in South Dakota," by Peter Schrag, *Atlantic Monthly,* October 1971; "I Have Earned the Nomination," interview with George McGovern, by Richard Meryman, *Life,* July 7, 1972; "Man from Mitchell," by James M. Perry, *National Observer,* May 13, 1972; "The Long Journey to Disaster," *Time,* Nov. 20, 1972; "George McGovern: The Apostle of Truthfulness Pays Dearly," by William Greider, Washington *Post,* Nov. 8, 1972.

"Gold Means Dead Water in Deadwood," by David W. Hacker, *National Observer,* March 22, 1971; "The Mountain Versus Korczak Ziolkowski," by Roy Bongartz, *Esquire,* March 1971; "Crazy Horse Sculptor Works on Big Scale," by B. Drummond Ayres, Jr., New York *Times,* June 9, 1970; "Wall Drug," by Bob Livingston, Minneapolis *Tribune Magazine,* Sept. 21, 1969; "Lodi, Calif.: A Home for Ex-Dakotans, Without the Snow," by Douglas E. Kneeland, New York *Times,* Feb. 19, 1971; "Nightmare in Rapid City," *Newsweek,* June 19, 1972; "Frontier Heritage Lives," by Sid Moody, AP dispatch in *Atlanta Journal and Constitution,* Sept. 10, 1972.

"Wounded Knee Still Festers," by William Greider, Washington *Post,* Feb. 23, 1969; "A Glimmer of Hope for Rosebud's Sioux," chapter of *The Plains States,* by Evan Jones (New York: Time-Life Library of America, 1968); "The Culture of Bureaucracy: Washington's Other Crime Problem," by John H. Rothchild, *Washington Monthly,* August 1970; "U.S. Funds Are Changing World of Sioux," by B. Drummond Ayres, Jr., New York *Times,* June 5, 1970.

NEBRASKA

Nebraska's politics and unique institutions are well described in a series of "Depth Reports" prepared by students at the School of Journalism at the University of Nebraska; those relied on most extensively for this book included *Public Power in Nebraska* (March 1963) and *Prairie Paradox—Nebraska, Its Politics* (September 1966). The best state history is James C. Olson's *History of Nebraska* (Lincoln: University of Nebraska Press, 1966). Reference was also made to the Nebraska chapter of *States in Crisis,* ed. James Reichley, (Chapel Hill: University of North Carolina Press, 1964); *Nebraska's Constitution—Tired Blood or Hallucinogenic,* undated paper by Hale McCown, Justice of the Nebraska Supreme Court; and *The Nebraska Economy—A Brief Overview,* an undated paper by James Maynard of Wayne State College, Wayne, Nebraska. An outdated but still fascinating view may be found in *Nebraska—A Guide to the Cornhusker State,* compiled by writers of the Writers' Program of the WPA (New York: Viking Press, American Guide Series, 1939).

Regular coverage of state activities and editorials in the Omaha *World-Herald* and Lincoln *Journal* provided much background; other articles consulted included: "The Nebraska Unicameral," by Richard D. Marvel, *State Government,* Summer 1969; "Lobbying in the Nonpartisan Environment: The Case of Nebraska," by Bernard D. Kolasa, *Western Political Quarterly,* March 1971; "Twenty Top Omaha's Power Structure," by Paul Williams, *Benson Sun,* April 7, 1966; "Nebraska's Wide Open Spaces Pose Problems for Candidates", by Richard Witkin, New York *Times,* May 12, 1968; "The Healthiest Spot in North America," by Joan Younger Dickinson, *Holiday,* May 1969; "Going Rural: Nebraska Typifies Industrial Migration in Midwest," by Seth S. King, New York *Times,* Dec. 20, 1970; "Go, You Big Red," *Life,* Nov. 26, 1971.

"Nebraskans Chafe Under Tax They Thought Was Buried," by D.J.R. Bruckner, Washington *Post,* Feb. 21, 1968; "In Midwest, the Media Must 'Make Sense,'" by James T. Wooten, New York *Times,* Dec. 6, 1969; "War at Iowa Beef," *Newsweek,* Nov. 17, 1969; "Struck Beef Company Sets Up Armed Camp," *AFL-CIO News,* Dec. 6, 1969; "Winners and Losers" (about Iowa Beef Processors Strike), *Forbes,* April 1, 1970; "Nebraskans Spell Governor, T-i-e-m-a-n-n," by Fred Kiewit, Kansas City *Star,* May 30, 1967; "Onetime Mayor of Small Town Now Is Governor of Nebraska," by Robert Pearman, Kansas City *Times,* Dec. 9, 1966; "Tiemann Faces Stiff Challenge," by B. Drummond Ayres, Jr., New York *Times,* May 11, 1970; "Nebraska: A Matter of Money," *Newsweek,* May 11, 1970; "Nebraska Passes Emergency Bill to Avert U.S. Welfare Aid Cutoff," New York *Times,* April 1, 1971; "Death of Indian Sparks Protest," Associated Press dispatch in New York *Times,* March 8, 1972; "Turning Point in Indian Protest," by Richard La Course, *Race Relations Reporter,* May 1972; "Increased Nebraska School Aid Vetoed," *State Government News,* June 1972.

KANSAS

No single book captures both the history of Kansas and its modern development, though there is an adequate single-volume history, *Kansas: A History of the Jayhawk State* (Norman: University of Oklahoma Press, 1957). A perceptive study of William Allen White in relation to Kansas' development, from which considerable material for the chapter was drawn, is *William Allen White's America* by Walter Johnson (New York: Holt, 1947). Alf Landon's career is covered well in *Landon of Kansas* by Donald R. McCoy (Lincoln: University of Nebraska Press, 1966). Dated but still useful is *People of Kansas* by Carroll D. Clark and Roy L. Roberts (Kansas State Planning Board, 1936); the book has an excellent introduction by White.

Continuing political coverage of Kansas by the Kansas City *Star* was useful in preparation of the chapter. Data on Kansas' farm economy was obtained from the 1969 Census of Agriculture, state agriculture bulletins, and three excellent articles: "A Smell of Success Covers the Dust Bowl," by John Morton (a native Kansan) in the *National Observer*, Sept. 22, 1969; "Kansas Beef Income Is Double Its Wheat Revenue," in the New York *Times*, Nov. 16, 1969; and "Troubles in the Farm Belt Pose 1972 Peril to Nixon," by B. Drummond Ayres, Jr., New York *Times*, May 7, 1971.

An excellent discussion of the modern Kansan temperament appeared in "What's the Matter with Kansas?", by Kenneth S. Davis, New York *Times Magazine*, June 27, 1954.

Other useful articles: "The 1964 General Election," by Professor Marvin Harder, *Wichita State University Alumni Magazine*, 1965; "Docking's '72 Plans—Kansas Guessing Game," by Ray Morgan, Kansas City *Star*, Oct. 17, 1971; "GOP Governor Race Considered," by Roger Myers, Topeka *Capital-Journal*, July 4, 1971; "Sen. Dole, Pro-Administration Maverick," by Robert L. Bartley, *Wall Street Journal*, Jan. 15, 1971; "Demos Covet Two Republican Senate Seats," by Roger Myers, Topeka *Capital Journal*, Aug. 29, 1971.

"State Economic Development Project Is Progressing," by Lynne Holt, Wichita *Eagle and Beacon*, May 11, 1969; "Small-City Boom Deceptive," by William Chapman, Washington *Post*, March 15, 1971; "Census Data Kept at Kansas 'Bank,' " by Seth S. King, New York *Times*, Feb. 14, 1971; "The Three Forests of Kansas," by John K. Strickler, *Kansas!*, third issue, 1971; "How to Discover the Real America—The Flint Hills of Kansas," by Michael Frome, *Changing Times*, June 1968; "Wichita, Kans.," *Time*, April 6, 1970; "Hike/Bikeways," *Kansas!*, first issue, 1972; "Topeka, Kansas," by William H. Cape, *Metro-Urban Newsletter*, March 1972 (published by Institute of Public and Urban Affairs, San Diego State College); "Kansas City's Top Cop," by Lacy J. Banks, *Ebony*, October 1970; "Professor Landon Lectures," by Ray Morgan, Washington *Post*, Dec. 15, 1968.

"Campus Unrest Shakes the Old Certainties in Kansas," by Haynes Johnson, Washington *Post*, May 3, 1970; "Burning Kansas," *Newsweek*, May 4, 1970; "Death in Lawrence," *Newsweek*, Aug. 3, 1970; "Kansas Inmates Protest by Self-Mutilation," by John Kifner, New York *Times*, Dec. 4, 1969; "Marijuana: Random Harvest in the U.S.," by John Kifner, New York *Times*, Nov. 7, 1969; "The Magic of Menninger," *Medical World News*, March 27, 1964.

OKLAHOMA

Sources of general usefulness on Oklahoma's development include *Oklahoma: A History of the Sooner State*, by Edwin C. McReynolds (Norman: University of Oklahoma Press, 1954); *Oklahoma: The Story of Its Past and Present*, rev. ed., by Edwin C. McReynolds, Alice Marriott, and Estelle Faulconer (Norman: University of Oklahoma Press, 1967); *Oklahoma: A Guide to the Sooner State*, compiled by writers of the Writers' Program of the WPA (Norman: University of Oklahoma Press, American Guide Series, 1941); "Oklahoma," by Debs Myers, chapter of *American Panorama* (Garden City, N.Y.: Doubleday, 1960); *Natural Resources of Oklahoma* (Washington: Department of the Interior, 1969); "Oklahoma, the Adventurous One," by Robert Paul Jordan, *National Geographic*, August 1971; "Oklahoma 1970: The Dust Bowl of the '30s Revisited," *Time*, Jan. 26, 1970; review articles on Oklahoma history, politics, and government, by Otis Sullivant, appearing in the *Sunday Oklahoman*, spring and summer 1968.

Other Sources: General coverage of the *Daily Oklahoman*, the Tulsa *Tribune*, and other state newspapers, plus the specific articles named below:

GOVERNMENT AND GENERAL "Tax Revenue," by J.L. Robinson, *Oklahoma Business Bulletin*, March 1970; "Oklahoma Off the Wagon," New York *Times*, Sept. 6, 1959; "Constitutional Reforms Proposed," by Jim Young, *Sunday Oklahoman*, Dec. 29, 1968; "Shake-up at Oklahoma," *Newsweek*, Aug. 10, 1970; "Motel Lodging For Prisoners Brings An Outcry," by Ralph Marsh, *National Observer*, June 29, 1970; "Oklahomans Reject Three Amendments," *National Civic Review*, May 1970; "Prisons Change Little in 47 Years," by Robert B. Allen, *Daily Oklahoman*, Jan. 30, 1972; "State Legislative Session's End Leaves Tally up to Voters," by Jim Standard, *Sunday Oklahoman*, June 13, 1971; "David Did in Goliath Again," editorial in *The Oklahoma Journal*, May 6, 1971.

POLITICS AND PERSONALITIES "Democrat Dominance Gone in Oklahoma," by Charles Whiteford, Baltimore *Sun*, Oct. 14, 1968; "You Can't Take the Football Out of Wilkinson," by John Carmody, Washington *Post Potomac Magazine*, Oct. 25, 1970; "Blatant Bob Kerr: 'Hell, I'm in Everything!'," chapter of *The Case of Congress*, by Drew Pearson and Jack Anderson (New York: Simon & Schuster, 1968); "Oil and Politics," by Ronnie Dugger, *Atlantic*, September 1969; "Albert: 'Little Giant from Little Dixie'," by Richard L. Lyons, Washington *Post*, May 24, 1970; "Speaker Carl Albert: The Little Giant Everybody Loves," *Parade*, Jan. 31, 1971; "The Coming Upheaval in Congress," by John Fischer, *Harper's Magazine*, October 1970; "The Custodian of the House," by Richard L. Lyons, Washington *Post*, Dec. 6, 1971; "What Makes Fred Harris Run?", by Thomas J. Foley, *Washingtonian*, December 1969; "Oklahoma's Salesman-Governor," *Business Week*, Oct. 11, 1969; "Bartlett Holds Edge in Okla.; He Kept

Campaign Promises," by Eve Edstrom, Washington *Post*, Nov. 1, 1970.

ECONOMY AND WATERWAY Various publications of Oklahoma Industrial Development and Park Department; "Oklahoma Has Ranked High as Oil Producer Since 1901," by Guy A. Doodine, Dallas *Morning News*, Sept. 1, 1970; "My Time Is Running Out," (regarding Keeler of Phillips Petroleum), *Forbes*, July 1, 1970; "The Proud Demonstration at Anadarko," *Reader's Digest*, April 1966; "Black Day in Blackwell: A Community Already Bitter Over a Pollution Suit Learns the Smelter that Pollutes Is Closing Down," by Danforth W. Austin, *Wall Street Journal*, May 18, 1972; "Seaports for an Inland Empire," *U.S. News & World Report*, May 25, 1970; "Rivers: Unlocking the Arkansas," *Time*, Oct. 11, 1968; "Tulsa Expects to Become an Ocean Harbor as Arkansas-Oklahoma Channel Is Finished," by James C. Tanner, *Wall Street Journal*, Nov. 27, 1970; "The Waterway that Couldn't Be Done," *Business Week*, Sept. 12, 1970; "Dedication of Locks, Dams, Along Arkansas Fulfill Part of Kerr's Dream," by Wheeler Mayo, *Sunday Oklahoman*, Oct. 25, 1970; *Arkansas River and Tributaries—Multi-Purpose Plan Arkansas and Oklahoma*, publication of U.S. Army Engineer District, Little Rock, Ark., and Tulsa, Okla., 1968; "Goodbye to Landlocked Economy," by Ed Montgomery, *Oklahoma's Orbit* magazine with *Sunday Oklahoman*, Jan. 19, 1969; " 'Seaports' for Oklahoma," *U.S. News & World Report*, Feb. 11, 1963; "Project Making Arkansas River Navigable, Once Scorned, Now Wins Increasing Support," by John Lubell, New York *Times*, June 6, 1971; "New Waterway: Monument or Tombstone?" by Peter C. Stuart, *Christian Science Monitor*, Aug. 14, 1971.

INDIANS "Renaissance and Repression: The Oklahoma Cherokee," by Albert L. Wahrhaftig and Robert K. Thomas, *Trans-action*, February 1969; "The Theft of a Nation: Apologies to the Cherokees," *Ramparts*, September 1970; "LaDonna Harris Is a Senate Wife with More on Her Mind than Mid-afternoon Teas," by Dan Blackburn, Washington *Post Potomac Magazine*, May 24, 1970; "Cherokees Fight Poverty, Illiteracy," by Frye Gaillard, *Race Relations Reporter*, Nov. 16, 1970.

CITIES "Oklahoma City," by Milton MacKaye, *Saturday Evening Post*, June 5, 1948; "Oklahoma City Uses Cluster Plan," by Katherine Hatch, *Race Relations Reporter*, Oct. 1, 1970; "Oklahoma Acquires a Theater," New York *Times*, Dec. 4, 1970; "Publishers: Survival of the Fittest," *Time*, May 3, 1968; *Broadcasting in America and the FCC's License Renewal Process: An Oklahoma Case Study* (statement by Commissioners Kenneth A. Cox and Nicholas Johnson on the occasion of FCC's renewal of licenses of Oklahoma broadcasters, Washington, 1968); "From P.T.A. to Mayor: Mrs. Patience Sewell Latting," by Martin Waldron, New York *Times*, April 14, 1971.

Various reports of the Public Service Co. of Oklahoma, Tulsa; "In Affluent, Conservative Tulsa, Revivalist Religion Is a Big Business," by John Lubell, New York *Times*, Nov. 22, 1970; "Oral's Progress," *Time*, Feb. 7, 1972; "Miracle U," *Newsweek*, Feb. 7, 1972; "Two Giants Rising in the Southwest," *U.S. News & World Report*, Feb. 11, 1963; "Muskogee, Okla., Model City in Country Music Song, Is Torn by a Police Rift," by Martin Waldron, New York *Times*, Jan. 10, 1971.

TEXAS

These books provided generally helpful background and, on occasion, some good quotes: *In A Narrow Grave—Essays on Texas*, by Larry McMurtry (Austin: Encino Press, 1968); *Texas After Spindletop*, by Seth S. McKay and Odie B. Faulk (Austin: Steck-Vaughn Co., 1965); "Texas, A Politics of Economics," chapter of *Southern Politics In State and Nation*, by V. O. Key (New York: Random House, 1949); "Texas: Land of Conservative Expansiveness," by O. Douglas Weeks, chapter of *The Changing Politics of the South*, ed. William C. Havard (Baton Rouge: Louisiana State University Press, 1972); *The South Central States*, by Lawrence Goodwyn (New York: Time-Life Library of America, 1967); *Texas: A Guide to the Lone Star State*, (Hastings House, New York: American Guide Series, revised edition, 1969); *Metropolitan Texas: A Workable Approach to its Problems*, report of the Texas Research League (Austin, 1967); *Texas Almanac* (Dallas *Morning News*, annual). A stimulating (but error-ridden) account of the Sharpstown Bank scandal is included in *Shadow on the Alamo: New Heroes Fight Old Corruption in Texas*, by Harvey Katz (Garden City, N.Y.: Doubleday, 1972). The same theme is treated more responsibly in *Texas under a Cloud*, by Sam Kinch, Jr., and Dr. Pen Proctor (Austin: Jenkins Publishing Co., 1972). For a colorful view of Texas civilization a generation ago, the reader is referred to Jaime H. Plenn's *Saddle in the Sky: The Lone Star State*, (Indianapolis: Bobbs Merrill, 1940).

Other sources: The most probing coverage of the Texas statewide scene has for years been provided by the *Texas Observer*, a liberal biweekly published in Austin, and materials from its past issues were widely drawn on in preparing the chapter. Also consulted was ongoing coverage of major Texas dailies including the Dallas *Morning News*, Houston *Chronicle*, Houston *Post*, as well as the specific articles cited:

GENERAL "The Fabulous State of Texas," by Stanley Walker, *National Geographic*, February 1961; "The Tin Star State," by Gary Cartwright, *Esquire*, February 1971; "The Texan Myth and Tradition," by Joe B. Frantz, *Texas Observer*, May 1, 1964; "The Guns of Texas," by Eric Morgenthaler, *Wall Street Journal*, Nov. 20, 1969; "The Phenomenal Custom," by Gary Cartwright, *Texas Observer*, Dec. 19, 1969; " 'Pot' Giver Gets 30-Yr. Taste of Texas Justice," by Molly Ivins, Washington *Post*, Nov. 29, 1970; "Texas: Land of Wealth and Fear," by Theodore H. White, *The Reporter*, May 25, 1954.

"ESTABLISHMENT," CONNALLY, SCANDALS "Texas Establishment Is Alive and Well—Somewhere," by Lee Jones, *Houston Chronicle*, May 1, 1969; "Everyone Eager to Help in the Texas Campaign," by Morton Mintz, Washington *Post*, Nov. 22, 1970; "Texas Records Show Businessmen Are Biggest Political Givers," by Morton Mintz, Washington *Post*, Dec. 6, 1970; "Can a Rich Guy Lose in Texas?," by William W. Hamilton, Jr., *The Nation*, Sept. 28, 1970; "John Connally and SMIC," by Stephen D. Berkowitz, *Ripon Forum*, February 1971; "The Connally Years," *Texas Observer*, Oct. 4, 1968; "Connally and the Issue," *Texas Observer*, Aug. 9, 1963; "Connally and the Richardson Estate," *Texas Observer*, May 1, 1964; "Juan John's Fortune," *Texas Observer*, Jan. 8, 1971; "A Matter of Sides," *Time*, July 27, 1970; "New Texan on the Potomac," *Time*, Dec. 28, 1970; "John Connally's Other Careers," *Newsweek*, Dec. 28, 1970; "Deep in the Heart of Texas: A Barbecue Spiced with Politics," by David S. Broder, Washington *Post*, May 2, 1972; "The Republocrats," *Time*, May 15, 1972; "Connally's Record Gets Mixed Reviews," by H. Erich Heinemann, New York *Times*, May 17, 1972; "Mr. Connally Resigns," editorial in New York *Times*, May 17, 1972.

"The Heir Apparent," by Dennis Farney, *Wall Street Journal*, May 14, 1969; "Ben Barnes: Young, Smart and Possibly Another LBJ," by Bo Byers, Houston *Chronicle*, Jan. 5, 1969; "The Barnes Dinner," *Texas Observer*, Sept. 4, 1970; "Barnes and the Senate Liberals," *Texas Observer*, May 9, 1969; "How Good Ol' Boys Seek Glory in Texas," by Wesley Pruden, Jr., *National Observer*, Feb. 15, 1971; "Barnes: Another Super-Texan in Johnson-Connally Mold?" by Jack Waugh, *Christian Science Monitor*, Feb. 8, 1972; "Money and Ben Barnes," *Texas Observer*, March 3, 1972; "The Trial of the Abilene Three," *Texas Observer*, March 31, 1972; "The Texas Banker Who Bought Politicians," by A. James Reichley, *Fortune*, December 1971; "Texas House Speaker Convicted of Bribery Plot," New York *Times*, March 16, 1972; "Dowdy Convicted in Bribe Case," by John Hanrahan, Washington *Post*, Dec. 31, 1971.

JOHNSON "Unpredictable LBJ—Seems Like Old Times on the Pedernales," *U.S. News and World Report*, Sept. 7, 1970; "Return of the Native," *Time*, Nov. 8, 1968; "A Financial Empire Is Awaiting Johnson," by Saul Friedman, *Charlotte Observer*, Nov. 17, 1968; "LBJ In Retirement—Still A Busy Man," *U.S. News and World Report*, Sept. 29, 1969; "Back Home Again in Johnson City," by Bill Porterfield, New York *Times Magazine*, March 2, 1969; "Nixon-Johnson Axis," by David S. Broder, Washington *Post*, May 25, 1971.

POLITICS "Results Show Texas Still One-Party State," by Felton West, Houston *Post*, Nov. 5, 1970; "Texas Primary Candidate Fee Ruled Illegal," Washington *Evening Star*, Dec. 20, 1970; "Election Law Changes Needed," Houston *Chronicle*, Jan. 21, 1969; "Committee Calls for Permanent Voter Registration," by Mary Rice Brogan, Houston *Chronicle*, Jan. 16, 1969; "GOP in Texas Shattered by Loss at Polls," Los Angeles *Times*, Nov. 22, 1970; "The GOP's Southern Star," by Rowland Evans and Robert Novak, Washington *Post*, Nov. 1, 1970; "How Texas Became a No-Party State," by Paul B. Holcomb, *State Observer*, Oct. 19, 1953; "A Texas Size Political Battle," by David S. Broder, Washington *Post*, March 8, 1971; "The Winnahs," *Texas Observer*, Nov. 13, 1970; "Opportunity Without Parallel," by Michael S. Lottman, *Ripon Forum*, July-August 1970; "Texas Democrats Seek to Avoid 1970 Primary Fights for Top Offices," by Neal R. Peirce, *National Journal*, Dec. 6, 1969; "Oil, Defense Firm Political Funds Didn't Report Gifts," Associated Press dispatch in Washington *Post*, April 11, 1971; "Young Voter Residency Killed," *Texas AFL-CIO News*, September 1971; "Labor Witty-Gritty," *Texas Observer*, Aug. 22, 1971; "Microcosm in Texas: An Achilles Heel for a Liberal Coalition," by E. Larry Dickens, *New South*, Summer 1971; "Sissy Farenthold of Texas: She Just Might Be Governor," by Ann Waldron and Robert Sherrill, *The Nation*, April 24, 1972; "Texas Reformers Beat Ben Barnes, Gov. Smith," by Bo Byers, Washington *Post*, May 7, 1972; "Rank and File Seize Convention in Texas," by Martin Waldron, New York *Times*, June 15, 1972.

"Yarborough's Record," by Ronnie Dugger, *Texas Observer*, April 3, 1970; "Yarborough's Safety Bill Becomes Law," *Texas AFL-CIO News*, January 1971; "Yarborough Named Panel Chairman," by Sam Kinch, Jr., Dallas *Morning News*, Jan. 11, 1969; "Yarborough's Final Record," by Pete and Elizabeth Gunter, *Texas Observer*, Dec. 25, 1970; "Hot Time In Texas for a Flaming Liberal," by R. W. Apple, Jr., New York *Times*, April 26, 1970; "Politics, Politics! or Whither Texas Liberals?" by Molly Ivins, *Texas Observer*, Dec. 31, 1971; "Nixon Leads by Country Mile in Texas but State Politics Stay Much the Same," by Neal R. Peirce, *National Journal*, Oct. 21, 1972.

STATE GOVERNMENT "Texas Taxes Texas Taxes," by Ronnie Dugger, *Texas Observer*, Jan. 29, 1971; "May the Lobby Hold You in the Palm of Its Hand," by Lee Clark, *Texas Observer*, May 24, 1968; "Lawyers' Plan to Beat No-Fault Aired on Hill," by Morton Mintz, Washington *Post*, May 7, 1971; "The Emperor of U.T.," *Time*, Aug. 10, 1970; "Hooking Horns at U.T.," *Newsweek*, Feb. 1, 1971; "Higher Education in Texas," *Texas Observer*, Dec. 13, 1968; "Equalization Rule on School Spending Pressed by Texans," by John P. MacKenzie, Washington *Post*, May 4, 1972; "Revolution in School Financing," by Burt Solomon, *Texas Observer*, March 31, 1972; "Courts in Texas Outdated, Former Justice Clark Says," by Jay Dorman, Houston *Post*, Sept. 13, 1972.

ECONOMY "Cattle: Marketing Improves," by James J. Nagle, New York *Times*, Nov. 15, 1970; "Texas Now Rates No. 1 in the Fattening of Cattle," by Martin Waldron, New York *Times*, Sept. 21, 1971; "The Oil Lobby Is Not Depleted," by Erwin Knoll, New York *Times Magazine*, March 8, 1970; "Oil and Politics," by Ronnie Dugger, *Atlantic Monthly*, September 1969; "Flashy Texas Millionaires a Dying Breed," by Nicholas C. Chriss, Los Angeles *Times*, Nov. 29, 1970; "Super-Rich Texan Fights Social Ills," by Jon Nordheimer, New York *Times*, Nov. 28, 1969; "H. Ross Perot Pays His Dues," by Fred Powledge, New York *Times Magazine*, Feb. 28, 1971; "Texas Facts" (compiled and published by the Texas Highway Department); "Wildcatting for Oil Becomes a Game of Percentage," by B. Drummond Ayres, Jr., New York *Times*, March 26, 1971.

WATER "Texas Project Upsets Arkansas, 2 Neighbors," *Arkansas Gazette*, Dec. 20, 1968; "Dam Outrage," by Elizabeth Drew, *Atlantic Monthly*, April 1970; "The Texas Water Plan—Biggest Boondoggle in History?," by Mary Beth S. Rogers, *Texas Observer*, Aug. 1, 1969; "Texas Water News," advertisement in Dallas *Morning News*, Aug. 3, 1969; "The Billion Dollar Boondoggle," *Texas Observer*, Dec. 17, 1971; *The Water Hustlers*, by John Graves (New York: Sierra Club, 1971; "Weather: Dust Bowl 1971," *Newsweek*, April 26, 1971; "Drought and Dust Storms Ravaging Much of Texas," by Martin Waldron, New York *Times*, April 12, 1971.

HOUSTON—ECONOMY *Decisive Years for Houston*, by Marvin Hurley (Houston Magazine, 1966); *Houston, The Bayou City*, by David G. McComb (Austin: University of Texas Press, 1969); "Houston: Oil at Bottom of Texas-Sized Boom," by Nicholas C. Chriss, Los Angeles *Times*, June 21, 1970; "'Don't-Zone-Me-In' Houston Is Fastest-Growing U.S. City," by George H. Favre, *Christian Science Monitor*, Jan. 3, 1969; "Houston May Be No. 2 by 1972," by Tommy Thompson, Houston *Chronicle*, Jan. 18, 1970; "This Is Houston," supplement to Houston *Chronicle*, March 9, 1969; "Greater Houston: Its First Million People—And Why," *Newsweek*, July 5, 1954; "Houston Is Where They're Moving," *Fortune*, February 1971; "Houston: Boom in the Heart of Texas," *Business Week*, May 23, 1970; "City of Tomorrow Planned Here," by Charlie

Evans, Houston *Chronicle,* Oct. 11, 1970; "Forward-Thinking Texans Have Their City Booming," by Frank Schneider, New Orleans *Times-Picayune,* May 11, 1969; "Shell Oil Plans Real Estate Development on 526 Acres in Houston Near Astrodome," *Wall Street Journal,* June 10, 1970; "Houston Seeks the Refugees," *Time,* June 8, 1970; "Midtown Building Boom Will Add More Skyscrapers on Houston Skyline," by Charlie Evans, Houston *Chronicle,* Sept. 5, 1970; "The Playhouse Is the Thing," *Time,* Dec. 6, 1968; "Alley Theater in Houston Opens Its Home," New York *Times,* Nov. 27, 1968; "The Texas Tornado," by Thomas Thompson, *Life,* April 10, 1970.

"Space Age Transformed Ranch Into Megalopolis," by Nicholas C. Chriss, Los Angeles *Times,* July 23, 1969; "An Ecological Armageddon," by Kaye Northcott, *Texas Observer,* Feb. 6, 1970; "Pollution Checks Grow," by Harold Scarlett, Houston *Post,* Nov. 2, 1970; "Houston Port Volatile," by Jim Barlow, Dallas *News,* Feb. 22, 1970; "Channel a Cesspool," by Susan Kent Caudill, Houston *Post,* Oct. 11, 1970; "Water Pollution in Texas Studied," by Martin Waldron, New York *Times,* June 8, 1971.

HOUSTON—RACES "Boom in Houston No Boon to Blacks," by Paul Delaney, New York *Times,* June 8, 1970; "Rights Aide Criticizes Houston as Federal Job Hearing Opens," by Paul Delaney, New York *Times,* June 3, 1970; "Rights Aide in Houston Charges Threats to Victims of Job Bias," by Paul Delaney, New York *Times,* June 4, 1970; "Houston Companies and Unions Face Charges of Discrimination," by Paul Delaney, New York *Times,* June 5, 1970; "Putting Together a Coalition in Houston," by Harold A. Nelson, *New South,* Fall 1970; "Psychotherapy for Houston Police," by L. Deckle McLean, *Ebony,* October 1968; "Black Capitalism: A Rotary Takes the Plunge," by Paul Bernish, *Wall Street Journal,* Aug. 27, 1969; "Houston School Board—an Ideological Camp," by Nicholas C. Chriss, Los Angeles *Times,* Dec. 25, 1969; "Desegregation Moves in Houston Made Amidst Clamor of Protest," by Martin Waldron, New York *Times,* March 1, 1970; "Turnabout in Houston?" and "Back in the Saddle," *Newsweek,* Sept. 13, 1971, and Jan. 24, 1972.

HOUSTON—POLITICS "Liberal Demos Ask New Blood Reorganization," by Fred Bonavita, Houston *Post,* Dec. 9, 1968; "Houston Postmortem," by Tony Proffitt and Hawkins Menefee, *Texas Observer,* Dec. 19, 1969; "Police a Key Issue in Houston Race," by Martin Waldron, New York *Times,* Nov. 14, 1971; "A Texas Battleground" (interviews with several Houston political leaders), by David S. Broder and Haynes Johnson, Washington *Post,* Dec. 26, 1971.

DALLAS—GENERAL *Dallas Public and Private,* by Warren Leslie (New York: Grossman Publishers, 1964); "Dallas-Fort Worth," chapter of *Cities of America,* by George Sessions Perry (Freeport, N.Y.: Books for Libraries Press, 1970); "Dallas in City-Planning Forefront," and "Dallas Spells Out Goals in Paperback Series," by Jack Waugh, *Christian Science Monitor,* Nov. 24, 1970; "Dallas Code No Cure-All, But It Helps," by Dave Beckwith, Houston *Chronicle,* March 3, 1969; "How Business Failed Dallas," by Richard Austin Smith, *Fortune,* July 1964; "Up the Establishment," *Newsweek,* May 3, 1971.

"Dallas Memorial Dedicated to Kennedy 200 Yards From Site of Slaying," by Martin Waldron, New York *Times,* June 25, 1970; "Dealey Plaza," by Liz Smith, *Holiday,* November 1969; "A 'Religious Woodstock' Draws 75,000," by Edward B. Fiske, New York *Times,* June 16, 1972; "Spreading the Gospel of Explo '72," by Michael Kernan, Washington *Post,* July 4, 1972.

"Where God's Business Is Big Business," *Time,* Nov. 8, 1968; "Los Angeles Times Seeks Dallas Paper for $91.5-Million Stock," by Henry Raymont, New York *Times,* Sept. 15, 1969; "KERA's Newsroom," by Jack Canson, *Texas Observer,* Sept. 18, 1970; "Why Dallas' Public Television Station Is Emerging as a Major Communications Force," by Carolyn Barta, *Dallas,* August, 1970; "Big D" and "Bonanza for Art," *Newsweek,* Aug. 7 and Oct. 16, 1972.

DALLAS—ECONOMY "Dallas Boasts Big Share of Texas Top 100 Firms," by Al Altwegg, Dallas *News,* July 13, 1969; "Dallas First as Texas Business Hub," New York *Times,* July 20, 1969; "Federal Employee Growth Continues in Dallas," by Earl Golz, Dallas *News,* Oct. 4, 1970; "Dallas Boom Adds 228,380 Jobs," by Al Altwegg, Dallas *News,* Jan. 26, 1969; "Room For Rent," by John Davis, *Dallas,* November 1969; "Going Up: Some Major Structures," by Doug Domeier, Dallas *News,* May 11, 1969; "In Dallas: A Skyline in Change," New York *Times,* August 9, 1970; "Big Griffin Square Deal Closed," by Dorothie Erwin, Dallas *News,* Feb. 3, 1970; "Wesley Goyer Jr. And His Golden Acres," by John Davis, *Dallas,* June 1970; "How a Good Idea Can Be Turned Into Riches," *U.S. News and World Report,* Dec. 15, 1969; "Loss Leader," *Newsweek,* June 1, 1970; "Ling Tries Old Tricks at a New Stand," *Business Week,* Oct. 30, 1971; "Happy Bride," *Forbes,* March 1, 1971; "Hard Bargain?" *Forbes,* Feb. 1, 1972.

FORT WORTH, "CORRIDOR" "Happy Triumph of a City that Once Seemed a Place to Run Away From," by Thomas Thompson, *Life,* Oct. 2, 1970; "Air Power Propels Fort Worth's Upward Economic Spiral," by Guy Halverson, *Christian Science Monitor,* March 28, 1969; "Hitting the Skids," by W. Stewart Pinkerton, Jr., *Wall Street Journal,* Aug. 24, 1970; "The Joe Louis Addition," *Texas Observer,* Dec. 25, 1970; "Fort Worth: Cowtown May Become Nowtown," New York *Times,* Jan. 3, 1971; "Texans' Failure to Back Rep. Wright with $10 Bills Dooms Senate Dreams," by Richard L. Lyons, Washington *Post,* Jan. 12, 1966.

"Vast Effect Seen From Dallas Airport," New York *Times,* Feb. 15, 1970; "The Land Boom at a Texas Airport," *Business Week,* March 11, 1972; "Carnival in Texas" (about Arlington), *Newsweek,* Dec. 31, 1971; "Bait that Caught the Texas Rangers," *Business Week,* April 1, 1972; "Texas Stadium: Football's Newest Theater," *Dallas* (magazine) *Visitor's Guide,* Spring 1972.

SAN ANTONIO "The Part of San Antonio Tourists Do Not See Is Mexican-American and Poor," by Weldon Wallace, Baltimore *Sun,* Nov. 15, 1970; "Checking HemisFair's Figures," *Texas Observer,* March 28, 1969; "Fair Enough," *Newsweek,* Sept. 30, 1968; "Booked for Travel," by Horace Sutton, *Saturday Review,* May 9, 1970; "Western Hemisfair," by Richard Spong, *Editorial Research Reports,* March 29, 1968; "The Priests' Rebellion," *Newsweek,* Nov. 11, 1968; "Review of Maverick Book," by Ronnie Dugger, *Texas Observer,* Dec. 25, 1970; "National University of Mexico Agrees to Set up Branch Campus in Texas," by Kemper Diehl, *National Observer,* March 18, 1972.

OTHER CITIES AND PLACES "Austin Is Bustling as Johnson Labors to Set the Record Straight," by Henry Raymont, New York *Times,* Nov. 9, 1969; "Austin's New Politics," by Dean Rindy, *Texas Observer,* May 21, 1971; "Austin Snares U.S. Jobs," Dallas *News,* Aug. 20, 1969; "Amarillo: The Show Goes On," by Buck Ramsey, *Texas Observer,* May 23, 1969; "Lubbock Left a Dead City by Tornado," Washington *Post,* May 13, 1970; "Rio Grande: Odyssey from a Wintry Birth," by Paul Horgan, Washington *Post,* Aug. 9, 1970; "El Paso: Profile of a City," *Moni-*

tor (magazine of Mountain States Telephone Co., Nov. 2, 1968); "Classic Labor-Organizing Drive Splits El Paso," by Homer Bigart, New York *Times*, Sept. 11, 1972; "A Classic Labor Organizing Struggle," by Tony Castro, Washington *Post*, Sept. 28, 1972.

"El Paso," by James Conaway, *Atlantic Monthly*, March 1972; "Polluted Town Doesn't Want to Move," by Robert A. Wright, New York *Times*, May 17, 1972; "Cultural *Shokku* in Texas," *Time*, Nov. 22, 1971; "Big Thicket Blues," by Pete Gunter, *Texas Observer*, Oct. 22, 1971; "Creepy and Scruffy? Yes—But Beautiful," by David W. Hacker, *National Observer*, April 22, 1972; *The Story of Fredericksburg*, ed. Walter F. Edwards, (Fredericksburg Chamber of Commerce, 1969); " 'A Stinking Cesspool' " (about Galveston Bay), *Texas Observer*, Sept. 8, 1972.

MEXICAN-AMERICANS "Tío Taco *Is* Dead," *Newsweek*, June 29, 1970; "Latins in U.S. Trail in Income," by William Chapman, Washington *Post*, March 3, 1971; "The Mexican American," *Civil Rights Digest*, Winter 1969; "The Misery of Our Mexican Americans," by Michael McCrery and Sixto Gómez, *Ripon Forum*, April 1969; "The Chicanos Want In," by Leroy F. Aarons, Washington *Post*, Jan. 11, 1970; "Chicanos Troubled," by John Geddie, Dallas *News*, Sept. 20 1970; "Chicanos in Texas Bid for Key Political Role," by Martin Waldron, New York *Times*, Aug. 2, 1970; "Tyranny in Texas," by Harold H. Martin, *Saturday Evening Post*, June 26, 1954; "Mexican-American Drive Makes Gringos the Target," by Carlos Conde, Houston *Chronicle*, April 6, 1969; "Labor Day in Austin," by Greg Olds, *Texas Observer*, Nov. 13, 1966; "Texas Unionists Win School Bias Lawsuit," *Texas AFL-CIO News*, June 6, 1970; "Schools in Texas Face Rights Fight," by Martin Waldron, New York *Times*, Aug. 30, 1970; "Chicano Power," by Stan Steiner, *New Republic*, June 20, 1970; "MAYO Members Most Active of Activist Chicanos," by Leo Cardenas, San Antonio *Express*, April 16, 1969; "Brown Power Victories May Spur a New Push," by Richard Beene, Houston *Chronicle*, April 19, 1970; "Walkout in Crystal City," *Texas Observer*, Jan. 2, 1970; " 'Brown Bilbos' Scored," by Kemper Diehl, San Antonio *News*, April 15, 1969.

"Ford Foundation: Its Works Spark a Backlash," by Laurence Stern and Richard Harwood, Washington *Post*, Nov. 2, 1969; "Liberal Hits Ford Foundation," by Victor Lasky, *Human Events*, May 10, 1969; "Texas Rangers Dodge Critics as Ranks Swell," Atlanta *Journal and Constitution*, Sept. 21, 1969; "Texas Rangers Not a Hero to All," by John Kifner, New York *Times*, March 23, 1970; "The Texas Ranger . . . His Heritage, His Modern Role and His Critics," by Stan Redding, Houston *Chronicle*, Feb. 9, 1969; "La Raza Convenes," by Tony Castro, *Texas Observer*, Sept. 22, 1972; " 'Mextex' in '72," *National Journal*, Oct. 21, 1972; "Texas Chicanos Voted GOP; New La Raza Unida Got 6%," by Tony Castro, Washington *Post*, Nov. 13, 1972.

INDEX

Page references in **boldface** type indicate inclusive or major entries.

Scale of Miles
0 100 200 300 400 500
CAN
WASH.
Seattle
Olympia
Spokane
MONT.
N.D.
Helena
Butte
Portland
Salem
ORE.
Eugene
Bismarck
Billings
IDAHO
S.D.
Aberdeen
YELLOWSTONE NATIONAL PARK
Boise
Pierre
WYO.
CALIF.
NEV.
Pocatello
Casper
Great Salt Lake
NEB.
Ogden
Oakland
Reno
Cheyenne
Salt Lake City
UTAH
Carson City
Sacramento
COLO.
San Francisco
YOSEMITE NAT'L. PARK
Denver
Colorado Springs
Mt. Whitney
GRAND CANYON NAT'L. PARK
Las Vegas
Santa Barbara
Farmington
Santa Fe
ARIZ.
Amarillo
Los Angeles
Albuquerque
San Diego
Phoenix
Pacific Ocean
N.M.
Wichita Falls
Lubbock
Tucson
Fort Worth
El Paso
TEXAS
Austin
U. S. S. R.
Kotzebue
ALASKA
Nome
Fairbanks
CANADA
U.S.S.R.
U.S.
Anchorage
Juneau
MEXICO
Bering Sea
MILES
0 200 400 600

THE GREAT PLAINS STATES

Author's Travels

MINN.
Duluth
Lake Superior
Sault Ste. Marie
WIS.
St. Paul
L. Michigan
L. Huron
MICH.
Lansing
Detroit
Madison
Milwaukee
IOWA
Chicago
Gary
Des Moines
ILL.
IND.
Indianapolis
OHIO
Columbus
Springfield
MO.
Kansas City
E. St. Louis
St. Louis
Cincinnati
KY.
Louisville
Frankfort
Charleston
W. VA.
Cairo
TENN.
Nashville
Knoxville
Chattanooga
ARK.
Memphis
Little Rock
Huntsville
MISS.
ALA.
Birmingham
Jackson
Selma
Montgomery
LA.
New Orleans
Houston
Dallas
Gulf of Mexico
Tallahassee
FLA.
Atlanta
GA.
Savannah
Jacksonville
Cape Kennedy
Tampa
Miami
S.C.
Columbia
Charleston
Charlotte
N.C.
Raleigh
Richmond
VA.
Norfolk
Washington
MD.
DEL.
Dover
Atlantic City
Philadelphia
N.J.
New York
PA.
Scranton
Pittsburgh
Harrisburg
Cleveland
L. Erie
Buffalo
Rochester
L. Ontario
Albany
N.Y.
Burlington
VT.
Montpelier
N.H.
Concord
MAINE
Augusta
Portland
Boston
MASS.
R.I.
CONN.
Atlantic Ocean

A.-Annapolis
B.-Baltimore
W.-Wilmington
T.-Trenton
N.-Newark
N.H.-New Haven
H.-Hartford
S.-Springfield
P.-Providence

KAUAI
NIIHAU
OAHU
Honolulu
MOLOKAI
MAUI
HAWAII
Hilo
Pacific Ocean
MILES
0 50 100 200